Architecture
and
Interior Design

View of the Peloponnesus, Greece, as seen from Agamemnon's citadel Mycenae, built between ca. 1550 and 1150 B.C. From here in the Argolid western culture will descend down through the centuries. (Photo Researchers, Fritz Henle, photographer.)

ARCHITECTURE AND INTERIOR DESIGN

A Basic History
Through the Seventeenth Century

VICTORIA KLOSS BALL

A Wiley-Interscience Publication
JOHN WILEY & SONS
New York • Chichester • Brisbane • Toronto

Library of Congress Cataloging in Publication Data

Ball, Victoria Kloss.
   Architecture and interior design.

   "A Wiley-Interscience publication."
   Includes bibliographical references and index.
    1. Architecture—History. 2. Interior decoration—
History. I. Title.

NA200.B15   720'.9   79-21371
ISBN 0-471-05162-4
ISBN 0-471-08719-X pbk.

Printed in the United States of America

10 9 8 7 6 5 4 3 2 1

To the memory of
my husband

GEORGE COLBURN BALL

Consultants

Dr. Anna Brightman, Professor of Interior Design
  the University of Texas at Austin

Dorothy G. Shepherd, Curator of Textiles
  the Cleveland Museum of Art
  Adjunct Professor of Near Eastern Art
  Case Western Reserve University

Dr. Mary L. Shipley, Professor of Interior Design
  the University of Arizona at Tempe

Dr. Marion E. Siney, the Hiram Haydn Professor of History
  Case Western Reserve University, Cleveland, Ohio

Dr. Charles W. York, Professor of Interior Design
  the University of Texas at Austin

Preface

These paragraphs are an attempt to explain the what, why, how, and perhaps the whereto of these volumes. They have been written to refute the seemingly prevalent idea that architecture and interior design are autonomous arts. Rather they are skills that are joined in purpose and should have similar basic preparation. Possibly then they might be more aptly executed by different persons with differing talents.

Architecture is far more than empty frames and spaces: it deals with a structure and habitable volume. Architecture is great art only when its forms, setting, and contents make a whole as seen within its culture. In the present books we are concerned with buildings and their furnishings which involve all those heterogeneous artifacts, utilitarian as well as ornamental, that contribute to satisfactory interiors. How much of our valuable museum space is devoted to them!

To limit the compass further our focus is on the aesthetic concepts that bind the architectural complex. Construction and purpose are treated as they contribute to them. Architecture and its components are viewed in the light of their ability to create an interesting unity of space, color, and texture that will serve a mutual purpose. The intention—the *why*—of this work is to provide a coordinated history of those arts that have contributed toward such total architecture.

The organization—the *how*—is chronological. The usual division of art periods is followed for convenience. The subject matter emphasizes western civilizations. Other cultures, however, have been touched on whenever they have been influential or have become important ancillaries.

Each chapter is introduced by excerpts from contemporary thought because the writing of an age is one important index to its character. These quotations are followed by a brief summary of the salient facts of concurrent civilization. From there the course lies with architecture and the principal decorative arts. Here again the aesthetics of the total art form is held to be the determining principle. In this regard, as the leading style centers move west along the Mediterranean and then north across the Alps and over the Atlantic, it is both interesting and important to note the role played by regional genius.

The division into two books has been made for several reasons. In addition to the practical ones concerned with ease of handling and accommodation of production, ideational logic favors the separation. Book 1 explores the transition from an early Asiatic culture to an emerging European. This period is germinated in the crucible of Greece and Rome and develops through the seventeenth century. Then, despite the roots and the maturation that had taken place, a new coupling of elements occurs. Book 2 deals with changes since this time. It describes a culture that was bred from a New World view. America may have been the catalyst, but, as Greece led to Europe, so America stands at the gateway to horizons far more extensive. Both books may be purchased and read independently. Together it is hoped that they will throw some light on the reasons for the past and the expectancies for the future—in the arts with which they deal.

I chose my illustrations from the many possible ones because I felt that they were both significant and representative. Only concretely, by means of buildings and their interiors, can the story come alive. Other historians may prefer other choices: herein lies a challenge to further and deeper study.

We can reenter past cultures in the buildings that remain and the belongings placed therein. When carefully documented and examined, they give proof that the purpose of art (a purpose that is peculiar to art) is to bridge the islands of experience on an intuitive level. Works of architectural art convey an ineffable spirit of time and space. If these volumes serve to illustrate this truth, then the picture of sources, of roots, and of future directions will begin to emerge.

*   *   *

It has been my privilege to have known and worked with many who have understood the arts. I should somehow like to thank them all for the enrichment they have given my life. Among these friends some have put their shoulders to the wheel and have given these pages a shape that they never would have had but for such help. First there are those invaluable critics who have donated their time and their special knowledge. They have contributed suggestions for reorganization; they have corrected statements; they have spotted obscurities of expression. Although my work may fall far short of the critic's expectations, nevertheless what virtues it has are in no small degree due to the following scholars, from each of whom I have received thought-provoking criticism and excellent counsel: Dr. Anna Brightman, Professor of Interior Design, the University of Texas at Austin; Dorothy G. Shepherd, Curator of Textiles, the Cleveland Museum of Art, and Adjunct Professor of Near Eastern Art, Case Western Reserve University; Dr. Mary L. Shipley, Professor of Interior Design, the University of Arizona at Tempe; Dr. Marion E. Siney, the Hiram Haydn Professor of History, Case Western Reserve University, Cleveland; and Dr. Charles W. York, Professor of Interior Design, the University of Texas at Austin.

The kind help and encouragement of the following friends is also gratefully acknowledged: James S. Ackerman, Pietro Belluschi, Arthur H. Benade, Rita Blumentals, Lindsay O. J. Boynton, Ruth E. Bowman, Mrs. William P. Cordes, George E. Danforth, William B. Denny, Frances K. Dolley, Hope L. Foote, E. Blanche Harvey, Mr. and Mrs. Herbert Kemp, Mr. and Mrs. Donald Mac-Closkey, Nanno Marinatos, Frederick A. Miller, Thomas Munro, C. W. Eliot Paine, Ernst Payer, William Priestley, Richard A. Rankin, Bertha Schaefer, Mrs. Albert Schug, G. E. Kidder Smith, Martha Thomas, and Dorothy Turobinski.

I wish to acknowledge with special appreciation those friends who helped with funds in furthering the travel and research required for this work: A. Leroy Caldwell, Grace P. Neal, and John C. Pearson.

Recognition and gratitude should go to Gordana Ukmar, who organized the figures and executed many of them, and to Robert Lloyd, who helped with the photographic reproduction work. The remaining figures were drawn by Harriet and Allen Raphael. My gratitude and admiration is extended to Virginia Benade for her skilled and untiring effort in putting the text into presentable form and in pursuing the acquisition of the illustrations. Without her the book never could have achieved publication.

To my Wiley editor, Wm. Dudley Hunt, Jr., I am indebted for his belief in this sort of manuscript and for his guidance of it and me through the complexities of the publication process.

Obviously many museums, libraries, and historical foundations have assisted with data and with photographs. To them I wish to say thank you. The generous cooperation of the Cleveland Museum of Art, with whose collections I have long been in contact, was accorded to me by its director, Dr. Sherman E. Lee, and its excellent curatorial staff.

I want to express my appreciation for the assistance of my husband George Colburn Ball. He spent many hours on documentation and used his photographic skill in taking many of the illustrations.

VICTORIA KLOSS BALL

Chagrin Falls, Ohio
April 1980

Contents

Architecture
and
Interior Design

What Are We Talking About?

The thing that is important is the thing that is not seen. . . .
Yes, I know . . .
All men have the stars, he answered, but they are not the same things for
different people. For some, who are travelers, the stars are guides. For others
they are no more than the little lights in the sky. For others, who are scholars,
they are problems. For my businessman they are wealth. But all these stars
are silent. You—you alone—will have the stars as no one else has them.

Antoine de Saint Exupéry, *The Little Prince*
New York: Harcourt, Brace & World, 1943, p. 103

HISTORY

History is the record of the passage of time, the story of changes in nature and in the human experience. It is the mind of man that has interpreted this chronicle and so in a sense each of us makes his own version of the past.

The historian tells us how nature impressed the transient eons in the erupted mountains, in the crustaceans solidified in rock strata, and in the ossified imprint of reptilian feet on the quarry bed. He clarifies the relation between a flint arrowhead and its cultural milieu. He explains how the facts of history are interconnected.

From such recording one thing stands out crystal clear—history foretells as it retells, and if we are sensitive to its nuances we can see the future written in the past. In no field is this so true as in art, where creation springs from the ability to dig below the immediate rationale to a deep well of accrued instinct and stored wisdom.

There is no art that so closely touches humanity as the art that has created its material environment. We are about to consider its phases. The story discloses much about human practicality, rationality, emotions, and ingenuity.

ARCHITECTURE

Building is one of the creative activities of mankind and architecture is defined as the art or science of building. Certainly both build___
architecture are principa___
mental art. But what is ___
the two terms? Surely th___
more fundamental than i___
of a long period of specia___
or in apprenticeship. His___
swer to our question.

Primitive societies, wh___
learned to build, but they ___ ___ markedly develop the science, and especially not the art, of architecture. The reason is obvious. Three interrelated considerations are germane to architecture and these three develop slowly in a culture or indeed in an individual. Planning comes first. By this we mean the judging of spaces and their interrelations with respect to intended uses. Then

appropriate construction techniques must be considered. And, while working on these problems, the aesthete will try to visualize the building in order to make it a delight to the senses.

A Roman architect, Vitruvius, during the first century A.D., named these three requirements: *convenience, durability,* and *beauty*—terms that have rung down the centuries as architectural standards. When Vitruvius elaborated the idea of convenience, he had something more in mind than the concept of suitability to overt purpose. For him an edifice needed to incorporate the idea of its purpose. A temple should induce a feeling of reverence; a palace should look as though it were a dwelling of importance. An architectural complex should not only be practically functional (suited to use and durable) it should be expressively so.

INTERIOR DESIGN

The unique business of interior design is to implement architecture by qualifying the spaces for occupancy in the manner intended by a preordained program. For this reason it is not only an anomaly to separate interior design from architecture; it is by definition impossible to do so. Therefore Vitruvius's mandates apply to building design, both inside and out. Materials, structure, spaces, colors, and textures may be slightly different but concepts must mesh. Because of the ___egrity of architecture, we frequently make no ___ical distinction in description between the ex___or and the interior of buildings. At other times ___ ___ay seem better to discuss them separately ___ly because at various historical periods the ___on between the two was not close.

___terior design is part of architectural design ___ it specifically handles interior furnishings.

___e Lindbergh, in *Locked Rooms and Open Doors,* speaks of her acquisitions, observing that ". . . beautiful possessions like silver, pictures, furniture, were tangible expressions of spiritual values you believed in. In a sense, then, they are creation too."[1] This statement definitely and accurately suggests an expressive value that resides in things quite independent of and beyond their intrinsic worth—a value that Mrs. Lindbergh with her special sensitivity would be the first to recognize. This meaningful factor need not have a high price tag, although history tells us that precious materials and talented artistry and craftsmanship are not cheap. Nor, on reversing the coin, can money guarantee intangible values. In short, furnishings are so integral a part of a larger, more comprehensive architectural setting that in order to ensure a well-tuned, smooth-running piece of environmental machinery all manner of correlations must mesh.

THE DECORATIVE ARTS AND DECORATION

Design, of course, whether one is speaking of it in relation to architecture or to interiors, is not the same thing as decoration, although it may include the latter as an instrument toward effectiveness. Decoration implies something added to an object for the ostensible purpose of augmenting its aesthetic quality. This definition is not meant as condemnation nor as any judgment of the inherent value of ornamentation. One of the most interesting lessons of history is the revelation of how early and in what manner mankind sought to embellish and enrich through decoration. Decoration, however, always remains an addition to something else. Design, on the other hand, is inherent in the relations between parts of a whole. Thus, when the designing sense is focused on creations intended for overt function, it must right-

fully include thought for use. In other words, decoration both in architecture and interiors must consider service.

PEOPLE

There is no way to evade the issue—design in the arts related to our surroundings must consider people and their needs, both obvious and hidden. Therefore the architect or the designer must try to understand man in his current state of culture. This is a tremendous commitment, yet it is amazing how well the leaders have often succeeded in suiting, as it were, the pattern to the cloth. This relationship between a culture and its buildings we shall be talking about. History may tell about buildings and artifacts, but the inferences drawn from them are what concern us. And inferences are about people.

YOU

Each person sees with his own eyes and understands with his own mind. Therefore any talk about people, decoration, interior design, architecture, or history must in the final analysis relate to personal interpretation, which, of course, will be different for every individual. May each of us augment the following pages by means of an ever-enlarging experience and an ever-enriched understanding and judgment.

Figure 1.1 (G. C. Ball)

CHAPTER ONE

Prehistory: European Focus

O pine-tree standing
At the side of the stone house,
When I look at you,
It is like seeing face to face
The men of old time.

The Priest Hakutsu (Japan, 704)
Translated by Arthur Waley

BEGINNINGS

Paleolithic Culture

Who does not wonder about his forebears? We reach back long ago to many kin, to far places, and perhaps to lost lands since demolished by rifts and seas. Nevertheless, modern western culture, around which our plot centers, springs predominantly from Europe and tangent soils.

Archaeology searches tirelessly to learn the facts about the human span which covers, by last count, close to three million years—a mere thousandth of the life of our planet. Nearly a million years ago a drop in the earth's temperature inaugurated cycles of extreme cold when glaciers covered most of the European continent. These fluctuated, after prolonged intervals, with undue heat. During the latter periods the human species, one branch of which can be traced to Africa, pushed north with the tropical animals—the elephant and the mammoth—sharing with them the wide valleys and hunting them for food.

In the swath cut by the third ice age, which began its relentless journey south about 240,000 years ago, human remains have been found on European soil among the bones of northern animals like the reindeer, the woolly rhinoceros, and the bear. This is a certain sign that on this occasion man did not turn back to the tropics with the onslaught of the cold but remained in the north to inhabit its wasteland. He had not persevered too soon, because during the last glacial recession waterways flooded the land bridges to Africa with the result that Europe, which had long been somewhat isolated by those earth convolutions that created the great mountain ranges of Anatolia and the Caucasus, became finally a separate continent.

The First European Artists

Many of the inhabitants of Europe have in their veins the blood of paleolithic old stone man (named for the cruder character of his flint weapons), for he was not annihilated when later immigrants arrived. Paleolithic man was our first known artist. He made engravings on pieces of rock or bone; he carved stone figurines and low-relief friezes, found near the entrance to caves; and he painted murals of powerful bison, lithesome deer, and the fleet horse, murals that are seen deep in the recesses of such caverns as La Madeleine, Lascaux, and Altamira in France and Spain. Anthropologists identify several subtypes of art as significant of particular paleolithic civilizations that belong to a complex of approximately 25,000 years.

This art represents an advance in the ability of man to create, to be human. It may be that this quality alone raised our ancestors to supremacy. Humans were now able to isolate an imagined world from the actual and to regard the former as material for contemplation. Here we see the beginning of conjectural thinking: "What could happen if . . . ?"

Influential Developments in the Near East

As the ice receded the peoples responsible for this first art dispersed and seem to have disappeared as definite cultural identities. In the Near East a new concept of civilization was developing. In the fertile valleys of the great rivers—the twin Tigris-Euphrates and the Nile—people did not rely exclusively on the kill for sustenance. They had learned to cultivate the grain grasses. They lived in communities that were stable because that mode of life was required by their new technique. Jarmo, one of the earliest Mesopotamian agricultural villages, has a conjectural date of the mid-seventh millennium. Long before written history Jarmo's inhabitants sowed, reaped, ground, and parched grain. They domesticated many animals and raised them as stock. They left a store of bone and stone jewelry and unbaked clay as well as stone figurines that indicate an appreciation for the aesthetic as well as the utilitarian. The term neolithic (literally "new stone") has been used for this cultural level because it is accompanied by an improved technique of chipping and polishing stone weapons and tools.

Neolithic Culture in Europe

Neolithic culture appeared in Europe about 3000 B.C. Evidence forces the conclusion that agriculture was a transplant from the Near East and Egypt onto the continent we are considering. As food became available and livelihood more certain the younger members of old agricultural villages were emboldened to start out in search of new farmlands. By repetition of this process the farmers eventually traveled far. They are known to have intruded into the rich valley of the Danube from Mesopotamia and to have infiltrated into the west by way of northern Africa and the southern Levant, fanning out until the vanguards of the immigrants met in Germany and eastern France.

The First Indo-European Migration

The first large-scale migration of nomad hunters and herdsmen from the Eurasian plains likewise entered Europe at a time roughly contemporary with the spreading of the husbandmen. Characteristic interments, which always included prized battle axes, are found as far northwest as England and southeast into Anatolia. These tribesmen brought the Indo-European language which in some derived form is spoken by most Europeans.

The First Cultural Plateau

Europe by 2000 B.C. possessed a broad and relatively homogeneous culture compounded of the mores of hunters, farmers, and herdsmen, each group having contributed according to time and location. Such an equilibrium has been precarious throughout history and has never lasted long.

America, No Cultural Laggard

America was probably settled in a manner similar to Europe. It is believed that the original inhabit-

ants were immigrants from Asia. The hunters had arrived by 10,000 B.C., having traveled north in the Orient until stopped by the Chukchi Sea, whence they crossed the Bering Straits to the Pacific coast. By accurate dating it is known that they had reached the Straits of Magellan by 7600 B.C. Agriculturalists may have been in America before they appeared in Europe: primitive maize had appeared in the Arizona bat caves by 4000 B.C.

ARCHITECTURE

Types of Primitive Building

The concept of spirit life and existence after death probably antedates domesticity. Sepulchres as homes for the dead and temples as sacred places in which to worship took precedence over houses for the living. Throughout Europe tombs, known in one form as *dolmens,* consisted of a chamber of upright stones and capstones and may date to mesolithic times (between paleolithic and neolithic). Stonehenge (Figure 1.2), thought to be a temple erected to the worship of the sun or possibly to the marking of time by the same source, took form when the native hunters of Britain came into contact with the newly arrived agriculturalists (ca. 2000 to 1500 B.C.). No temples in Europe are associated exclusively with hunting civilizations.

Only when the hunter turned farmer did he begin to build dwellings to provide for himself

Figure 1.2 Stonehenge. Salisbury Plain, Wiltshire, ca. 2000–1500 B.C. Diameter, 97 ft. (British Crown Copyright; reproduced with permission of the Controller of Her Britannic Majesty's Stationery Office.)

Figure 1.3 An interior of one of the seven cottages of the Stone Age settlement at Skara Brae, built by a far-northern European colony of pastoralists, ca. 2000–1500 B.C. Excavated by Gordon Childe in 1927–1930. The Orkney Islands, Scotland. (British Crown Copyright; reproduced with permission of the Controller of Her Britannic Majesty's Stationery Office and by permission of the Department of the Environment.)

and his chattel (Figure 1.3). The herdsman, whose prime possessions were on the hoof, geared his folds for movement, so that some form of tent, such as the *tepi* of the American Plains Indian or the ingenious *yurt* of the Eurasian tribesman, resulted.

Civic patterns came later—walls arrived with the need for protection and municipal buildings came with government and civic pride. On the Aegean islands of Lesbos and Lemnos there are remains of neolithic towns which show a scheme of tightly locked cell houses with common party walls. No one building seems grander than another. They centered around an open area, a market place or civic center, which descended to Greek and Roman cities as *agora* and *forum*, respectively.

Primitive Structural Systems and Forms

Despite the engineering skills shown in megalithic monuments, the structure of prehistoric European buildings was simple. The hovels of neolithic farmers were small cells made of local materials—stone, mud brick, reeds, timber, rammed earth, and their various combinations. In northern Europe, where forests provided suitable wood, the basic rectangular shape can be seen in the buildings of the excavated village of Barkaer in Jutland (ca. 2500 B.C.). When the available building material was more flexible, the right angle, the mark of the engineer and the mathematician, was used. At Orchomenos, a small town in central Greece in which the last excavated levels show rectangular buildings dating from about 1500 B.C., the earlier layers disclose round, elliptical, apsidal, and finally rectangular forms in sequential order.

Europe's First Formal Architecture

Architectural evidence in and adjacent to Greece suggests a formal architecture as early as the third millennium at a time when the country was in other cultural aspects far behind her Asiatic neighbors. Whenever an affluent society appeared on the Greek archipelago, its principal domestic complex incorporated a central building known as a *megaron*. The megaron is characterized as a separate unit with a threefold division of pillared portico, narrow vestibule, and a main room that contained a central hearth surrounded by columns to provide roof support. Other more private rooms might be appended or found as cell types off an adjacent courtyard.

In the mountain-girt plains of Thessaly lie the acropolises of Dimini and Sesklo (Figure 1.4). The megaron form found on these sites is quite complete. Megarons synchronous with the Thessalian have been unearthed near the Isthmus of Corinth and in the Aegean. Farther south in the Cyclades, however, no plans approaching the formality of the Greek isolated dwelling have been discovered so early.

Developed megarons that date several hundred years later than Dimini have been excavated on the first and second building sites at Troy as well as eastward in Anatolia. This indicates that the plan was more than a sport in the locality.

Farther afield in the territory which is now Romania a neolithic culture evolved from which offshoots are thought to have been projected into the Balkans and northern Greece. Near Bucharest, at a level contemporary with Troy I, megarons were built on hillocks of earth.

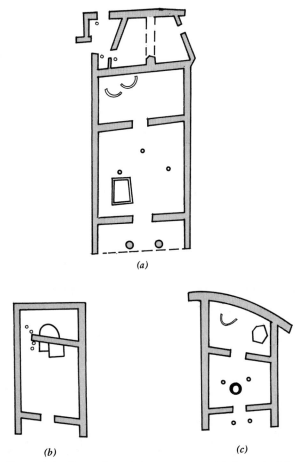

(a)

(b)   (c)

Figure 1.4 Examples of the megaron: (a) from Sesklo; (b) and (c) from Dimini. Thessaly, 3000–2000 B.C. (Adapted from Bertha Carr Rider, *Ancient Greek Houses*, Argonaut, 1964.)

Here, then, we begin to encounter the entangling question of the origin of influences. The answer may be allied to the story of folk wanderings, but of this we can never be sure.

Italy

As we move westward to Italy we must descend later in time to find comparable societies. Many neolithic farming villages have been located in the district of Loggia, in the heel of the peninsula. Their houses are typical *wattle and daub* (branches and clay) huts with central hearth and smoke hole, probably the archetype of the Italian *atrium* tradition (see Chapter 4).

There is evidence that a new people armed with bronze weapons crossed the Alps from the northeast during the second millennium. They are the folk called *terremare* from the particular kind of earth found in the Po Valley (*terra marna,* organic composts). Their hut houses were no more advanced than those of the south, but they introduced the lake dwelling, known as the *lacustrine.* Inland lakes all over Europe have yielded remains of these ingenious causeway houses built on piles over water by prehistoric people who fished as well as sowed and reaped.

INTERIOR DESIGN

Interior design, like architecture, scarcely reaches any formative state in Europe in the years we are discussing. If there is no evidence of overall planning in interiors, the era is nonetheless marked by the beginnings of the useful and decorative crafts that accompany civilization.

TEXTILES

Origins of Textile Technology

One technical advance suggests another. About the time that the herding of flocks and the growing of seed were understood the discovery was made that the wool of sheep and the bast fiber of flax could be strengthened by combining several strands and giving them a twist. This process is called *spinning.* In the most common primitive method of spinning a mass of carefully adjusted fibers is placed onto a *distaff* which is held in one hand while the other pulls out several strands and attaches them to a *spindle* or stick. This is thrown downward with a twisting motion, regulated in its momentum by a *whorl* or round bead of ceramic or other material. Once the yarn has been properly twisted it is wound onto the spindle and the process is renewed. Later this procedure was made continuous and the twirling was made easier by the propulsion given by a wheel. Spindle whorls are as numerous as pottery shards in most prehistoric excavations and their presence indicates the beginnings of textile technology.

Earlier textiles were made by simple means,

generally without special tools (e.g., felting, knotting, and braiding). More advanced technique required the use of a mechanism known as a loom which holds one set of threads in a fixed position so that a second set can be interlaced at right angles with them. This process is known as weaving.

Near the middle of the last century a season of severe drought called the attention of archaeologists to several lacustrine villages exposed along the shores of Swiss lakes. Many artifacts were found, including flint and bronze implements that had been preserved because of their immersion in water. The culture of the inhabitants was in the transitional stage between the ages of stone and bronze and has been dated as early as 3000 B.C. Well-preserved pieces of matting and basketry indicated the use of natural fibers even before the spinning of thread. In addition, weaving weights and spindles turned up and, even more important, skeins of threads, plaited belts, woven cloth, and even pile matting appeared. Thus we know that an agricultural civilization developed quite early in Europe and was not laggard in practicing some of its representative arts.

CERAMICS

Ceramic Technology

Ceramics, which seem the most fragile of creations, nevertheless are of a most enduring material. The making of pottery coincides with the agricultural developments of neolithic man. Like a child creating mud pies, the ceramist was so delighted with his ingenuity and made so many pieces that it has been impossible to lose them all.

Actually the first European pottery antedates a settled abode. It was made by groups of late paleolithic fishermen-hunters of the Baltic coast, who left records of their camps in the form of mounds of oyster shells and kitchen debris—called *kitchen middens*—which date as early as 5000 B.C. In these are found shards (broken fragments) of crude wares that were made before the advent of farming in Europe.

The *composition* of ceramics is clay or fine-grained earth that will absorb water to become plastic and will relinquish it on firing to harden. This sounds like play, but it is really a compli-

cated matter. Most local clays consist of a mineral mixture in a finely dispersed condition called a colloidal solution. It is akin to the mixture of butter fats and protein materials found in milk. The clay minerals are crystalline. On proper heating they become dehydrated and oxidize to form new crystals of other minerals which are held together by interlocking or by being surrounded by noncrystalline glass made from certain of the components.

Primitive man was at first not too knowledgeable or selective about this process. It required much time to accumulate the experience that taught him how to mix and refine his clays and to regulate his fires to obtain desired qualities. Intrinsic ceramic values consist in impermeability to liquids and a refractory character, coupled with beautiful structural shape and decoration. It is easy to appraise the first two qualities; the last relate to personal opinion. Many times during the long history of earthenware (the comprehensive type name, a synonym of ceramics but often implying a coarse ware) the pieces have been technically high standard but artistically poor. The reverse has likewise occurred.

Variations in body and style have made pottery a source for the interpretation of prehistory. Potsherds are like open books which may disclose native aptitudes and aesthetic potential. As in art in general, however, students are baffled by similarities in the work of peoples continents apart and whether to credit a common center of influence or a common level of culture is a moot question.

The *method of forming* a pot may differ somewhat in the following chronological sequence. It can be shaped directly by hand manipulation or ropes of clay may be coiled on themselves to fashion a bowl or jar. The pottery wheel was not in evidence until the third millennium in lower Mesopotamia at Ur. This wheel can be made to rotate swiftly by pulleys. The artisans of Ur possessed the fast wheel. On it a pattern form is placed to facilitate the shaping of a piece by manipulation known as *throwing*.

One unwritten aesthetic criterion relevant to pottery is that its appearance should relate to its *medium* (materials and processes). Accordingly, wheel-turned pottery is best adapted to and early assumed a rounded shape (Figure 1.5). Some ce-

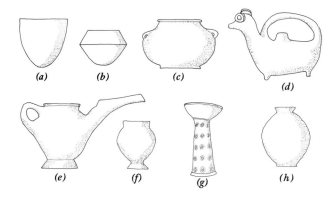

Figure 1.5 Basic early pottery shapes: (a) continuous or rounded; (b) carinated; (c) complex, with small lug handles; (d) anthropomorphic; (e) with spout; (f) with base; (g) fruit stand; (h) with pronounced rim.

ramists even insist that the finished piece should show the marks of rotation. The opposite of this principle of continuity is called *carination,* or the breaking of contours, usually by a horizontal ridge. It is sometimes argued that this indicates a more careful analysis of divisional functions. Carination appeared early in Egypt and was subsequently seen on the continent. Wares from Asia Minor introduced complex shapes and spouts and handles as well as stands appeared. Animal forms were pressed into service as utilitarian pots.

The *type of firing* in relation to the basic ingredients of a clay influences the color and body of a ceramic. High-temperature firing with plenty of oxygen causes more complete vitrification and the pieces emerge buff or red, depending on the initial color of the clay. When there is insufficient air, carbon monoxide rather than dioxide forms in the kiln. Under such circumstances, known as *reduction firing,* the body will turn black by carbon smutting. Such carbonaceous wares are characteristic of ceramics from the Danube valley and from Anatolia, the mountainous territory of northern Asia Minor. The rims and often the interiors of Egyptian pots are frequently burnished black. Controlled reduction firing is a technique carefully used by later Chinese ceramists to obtain unique color effects.

Ceramic Decoration

Random knops or lumps of clay stuck onto a vessel are early examples of the exercise of a decora-

tive sense. Likewise, simple incised decoration is noted. In the kitchen middens not only was the ceramic composition poor and the body thick but ornament was limited to crude scratchings near the rim, which might have been done with a tined instrument, thus inducing *combed patterning.* The imprint of basketry or coarse cloth pressed against the surface of a piece created a pleasing texture.

As the techniques of making and applying pigments were slowly evolved more complex patterns were possible. Various hypotheses have attempted to account for the character of such ornament as it appears on prehistoric types. One explanation deals with the relation between *natural, stylized,* and *abstract* (nonrepresentational) design. According to this theory, a representational form, like that of cave art, is thought to be the work of a society that has just learned how to create imagery. At that important moment of discovery conception was focused on an approximation of nature. Later, as nomadic man joined extensive migrations, he found less time for artistic indulgence and a succinct stylized pattern resulted. When agriculture finally forced a sedentary existence, ceramic designs may have been influenced by the geometry of textiles.

The early development of ceramics in Europe can best be followed in the Mediterranean lands, where we are faced with maritime enterprises that burgeoned during the third millennium. Among the many Aegean islands that participated in this trade *Crete* was one of the few that was large enough to have sustained a neolithic agricultural civilization. The curtain of prehistory likewise rises on neolithic agricultural *Greece.* Like Crete, its southern shores were early affected by the mercantilism of the Near East and Egypt.

The first neolithic pottery of this entire region is scarcely distinctive or significant—it is of principal interest to the cultural anthropologist. Its body was well potted but, because of irregular firing, most pieces had a gray cast. In one handling a dark paint was used to produce a pattern, the forerunner of Cretan dark-on-light wares (e.g., the octopus vase, Chapter 2). Again white paint was placed on a burnished dark ground, similar to the light-on-dark of later times. Likewise the southeastern European archipelago was marketing a cruder mottled and burnished slip-covered pottery variously known as *Vasiliki* (from Crete) and *Urfirnis* (from Greece), which became the principal commodity of the Cycladic trader. It is found as far east as the Crimea and west to Spain.

Patterns on localized eastern Mediterranean pottery were ingenuous neolithic zags. With the passage of time torsional effects, curvilinear designs, and spirals grew in importance. None of this artistry was tectonic in the sense of relating to the shape of the piece. It is often noticeable, however, that the simple lines seem to have a uniquely propulsive nature as though they were bent on going somewhere. They seem at times like moving contrails of a future jet age.

North of the Black Sea, in the trans-Carpathian lowlands equivalent now to the Russian territory of Moldavia and a portion of the Ukraine, a culture known as the *Tripolje* flourished before 3000 B.C. We have already remarked about the novel megaron-type house found near Bucharest in borderland territory. This district produced one of the most amazing ceramic products of the prehistoric world, known only as the *black earth pottery* and seen now in the Hermitage Museum in Leningrad (Figure 1.6). Oddly, this ware has a fine, thinly potted, and well-fired red or buff body, burnished to a gleaming bronzelike sheen. The pots were often ornamented with black paint or

the pattern, covered with white, was reserved in the base color.

It is the embellishment imposed on this pottery that is unique and fascinating. It consists almost exclusively of some variations of the S spiral which at first is spotted, like the Mediterranean spirals, rather freely over the jar. The decorative curves then begin to encompass the entire surface, and later the sensitivity of the artist led him to create a pattern from the background as well as the foreground. A spatially complex design finally evolved in which interest fluctuated back and forth in a movement akin to that induced by an Arp painting or a Henry Moore sculpture.

The *Danubian* civilization, itself made up of a number of subcultures, is one of the most enduring and best-known neolithic civilizations in Europe. It grew on the central European loess lands north of the Serbian Danube and extended far to the east and west and north to the edge of the glacial moraines of Poland, Germany, and the Netherlands. Ethnologically this culture is interesting because it probably represents a combine of peoples that started with the primitive hunters and expanded to include neolithic farmers and herdsmen from the south and east and possibly the west. Culturally it is important because its arms fold Europe in its earliest civilized arc.

We find Danubian pottery of interest now because its style of decoration exhibits two tendencies, both important to later European art. In one the imposed curvilinear trace seems almost to possess a kinetic life of its own. This is the kind of force that appears in the figures of later Celtic and Scandinavian decoration, a much more vigorous development than found in the simple early flails on Greek pottery.

The other important Danubian development—a tendency to be more tectonic—is seen most frequently southward into the Balkans (Figure 1.7). The spirals, often interspersed with straight lines and knops, are placed to conform to and strengthen the structural shape. This becomes one of the outstanding marks of later Greek design, as it had been of the Persian.

In a period around 1800 B.C. in *Western Europe* many graves yielded an unusual receptacle known as a *bell beaker* because of its characteristic bell shape with rounded bottom, concave

Figure 1.6 Pottery from the Tripolje Culture, ca. 3000 B.C. The Hermitage Museum, Leningrad. (Courtesy of the Hermitage Museum.)

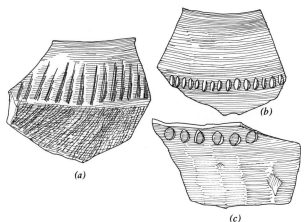

Figure 1.7 Tectonic design on prehistoric Danubian pottery from archaeological site of Butmir: (a) and (b) ribbed; (c) knopped. (Adapted from H. Frankfort, *Studies in Early Pottery of the Near East,* Royal Anthropological Institute, 1927.)

neck curve, and pouring lip. Bell beakers have been found west to Ireland and north to Denmark, and a few have turned up in Hungary to the east. The body and decoration are advanced. They were made of refined clay which turned red or black on firing and were covered with slip and burnished. The added designs were incised and consist of tectonically placed straight lines that suggest textile inspiration.

The center from which came this spate of jars seems to have been Spain in the neighborhood of Carmona near Seville. It is generally agreed that their production was in the hands of newly arrived neolithic groups who migrated from North Africa near the beginning of the third millennium. Almost simultaneously traders came in search of western metals. As Spain is rich in both copper and tin, the unusual bronze civilization that developed there would spread far, carrying ceramics in exchange for needed commodities from the north.

STONES, METALS, IVORIES

When a tribe accumulates wealth, whether by the sword or trade, the economic social division that begins is evidenced by the way a chieftain is buried with a grandeur beyond the reach of the peasant. Precious stones, metal artifacts, and ivories are tangible signs of material value because of their rarity and relative imperishability. Such wealth is priceless when embellished with the skill of the craftsman and artist.

This category presents great organizational difficulties for the historian who deals with the classification of the material aspects of a culture (e.g., divisions into paleolithic, neolithic, copper, bronze, and iron) while at the same time correlating social factors (e.g., hunting versus farming; prehistoric versus historical). For example, metallurgy had its main cultural development in the Near East and we must turn there to examine its beginnings and growth (see Chapter 2). European civilization, at a later date, however, learned new technologies from its Asiatic neighbors and developed them with relative rapidity (the Bronze Age began before 3000 B.C. in Egypt and the Near East but did not reach England, as a distant outpost, until ca. 1650 B.C.).

Coastal inhabitants built seafaring ships for the purpose of reaching out to countries rich in ore. Soon many European shores were feeling the quickened pace of commerce. Traders who needed Cornwall tin and Baltic amber introduced metal-working skills to the north almost on the heels of agricultural neolithic technology. The world of the European farmer was rapidly shrinking. This sort of advancement telescoped a long period of development in the east into a comparatively short one in the west.

Mercantile commerce was responsible for bringing wealth to neolithic civilizations, which wealth in turn soon created those social strata that are noted in the treasures of the grave finds. Likewise the attendant improvements in the vehicles of commerce enabled a prehistoric people to transport precious raw materials to their craftsmen (e.g., the gold of British artifacts that came from Ireland and Scotland, the amber that came from Jutland). Thus the world broadens as it quickens and the destiny of Europe as a technological leader can be predicted.

CHAPTER TWO

Prehistoric and Early Historic Periods

THE NEAR EAST, EGYPT, CRETE, AND GREECE TO ca. 500 B.C.

I made an end of war,
I promoted the welfare of the land,
I made the peoples rest in friendly dwellings,
I did not allow trouble makers in their midst.
The great gods called me,
And I was the beneficent shepherd of righteous sceptre,
And benign my shadow spread over my city.
I took to my bosom the peoples of Sumer and Akkad,
And they prospered under my protection.

from the Epilogue of Hammurabi's Code
James Bennett Pritchard, Editor,
Ancient Near Eastern Texts Relating to the Old Testament, 2nd ed.
Princeton: Princeton University Press, 1955, p. 178.

BEGINNINGS OF HISTORY

The preceding quotation may sound like political braggadocio. Historically, the important fact is that it could be written and that it became possible to produce biographical data at a time when kings, and more precisely emperors, appeared on the horizon.

It is difficult to pinpoint the date when the period of unwritten history closed and that of the written book opened. About 5000 years ago writing was developed in the great river valleys of the Nile and the Tigris-Euphrates. It occurred first in the form of pictograms, which then evolved into syllabic symbols. Mesopotamian writing is called *cuneiform* because of the wedge (Latin *cuneus*) shape of its characters. Egyptian writing, which had a somewhat parallel development in the same millennium, is known as *hieroglyphic,* from the Greek words *hieros,* meaning sacred, and *gylphein,* to carve.

Although written recording was an invention that expedited other developments by the storage and transferal of knowledge, nevertheless literacy is but another example of the specialization and attendant wealth that enabled a people to afford a learned group of priests, scribes, and accountants.

What we call civilization is the result of an eternal struggle by man to survive in a natural world that more often than not has been hostile to his needs. To gain the upper hand the human species not only produced a superior technology (i.e., agriculture, husbandry, metallurgy) but it devised new forms of social, political, legal, and economic structure in answer to the need for ethical coexistence. The created environment responded—cities, kingdoms, and empires grew to replace and augment small agricultural villages.

The Near East

Southern Mesopotamia was formed by alluvial deposits of the two rivers—the Tigris and the Euphrates—which drain its plains. It was first inhabited when settlers from the upper river basin drifted down to the land created from the waters. This was the delta that was buried and reborn after the mythological deluge which is now historically equated with the flood celebrated in biblical legend. Before this event a people known as the Sumerians had come from some conjectural source and joined the native population. It was their superior culture that seems most in evidence, postflood.

In the late third millennium lower Mesopotamia was conquered by the Semitic Akkadians (2450–2270 B.C.) from farther up the rivers. In the next move the Akkadians lost their supremacy to newly emerging southern nations that now welded Mesopotamia into a larger political complex known as the *Babylonian Empire*. It was destined for a time to rule the entire twin-river valley. Hammurabi, its sixth king, is famous for his great library and his codification of the laws into a form unsurpassed before the Romans.

In upper Mesopotamia, meanwhile, the Assyrians, a preponderantly Semitic folk, had assumed the hegemony of a group of loosely knit states and were successful in warding off neighbors who cast a covetous eye on their territories. Later, forced to fight for autonomy, they whetted their war machine and by availing themselves of a new technology of iron weapons eventually created one of the most extensive eastern empires over which they ruled from Egypt to the Iranian plateau. About the same time there developed the small principalities of the Hittites of the Anatolian plateau and the Mitanni of northern Syria. Here they imposed themselves as ruling aristocracies. Their territory provided a battleground for Egyptian and Mesopotamian disputes and their culture became a melting cauldron for aesthetic character.

Egypt had been made relatively self-sufficient by her agricultural economy in a fertile alluvial plain. She was likewise more protected from the eastern states and from the semibarbaric invasions of southern tribes by two seas, a narrow isthmus, and a desert. After the kingdoms of the upper and lower Nile were united under Menes, as the first pharaoh of the Old Kingdom, Egypt did not enter into major wars of conquest until the second millennium. Nor was she signally successful in them until the time of the Empire and the reign of Tuthmosis III. Then her boundaries were extended eastward until she came into contact with the fully developed power of the Assyrian empire.

Although Egypt, possibly due to her isolation,

remained a cultural entity, the early first millennium B.C. witnessed inroads of eastern philosophy under Akhenaten, invasion at the hands of the Assyrians, and final domination in 525 B.C. by the Persians.

Who were the Persians? One general definition would be that they were the peoples who inhabited the mountainous and triangular-shaped plateau land lying east of the Mesopotamian plain, between the Caspian sea on the north and the Persian Gulf to the south. Although primarily an agricultural and stock-breeding country, the territory possessed wealth in minerals and today we recognize its riches in oil reserves. The country's strategic position as the hub of the great lines of communication between East and West renders it as important in today's international economy as it was in its prehistory, which archaeology dates at least to the mid-eighth millennium B.C.

Around the beginning of the first millennium B.C. intruders from the north pressed across the adjacent borders of many of the more advanced civilizations to the south. These new immigrants were warriors, nomads, and possibly herdsmen, pressed on by unknown pressures and hungers. Besides invading Persia, they entered Asia Minor and Greece, countries in which their presence affects our story.

One group of kindred Iranian tribes settled in the north of the Persian plateau as Medes and farther south as Persians. Eventually these recent migrants became the strongest strain in the population and, after years of adaptation, effected consolidations that resulted in a dynasty known as the Persian *Achaemenid*. Under a succession of enterprising leaders—Cyrus II, Darius, and Xerxes—this house established the first empire to rule all the Near East and to battle Europeans on their own soil.

Such a great state, of course, did not spring into being all at once. One of the first nations to have been conquered was the Assyrian. To accomplish this the Persians made allies of the Babylonians, who had come under Assyrian suzerainty. As so often happens in such cases, Babylon then emerged in a brief ascendancy as an autonomous kingdom known as Neo-Babylonia but eventually succumbed to her more powerful neighbor and in 538 B.C. became a Persian satellite.

We have called attention to the advanced technology and superior organizational skill of the Near Eastern peoples which enabled them to rule large sections of the civilized world. Likewise we must acknowledge in their psychological make-up a mystical and philosophical cast of mind that fostered some of the world's great religions and ethical systems. Zoroastrianism, monotheism, Judaism, Christianity, and Islam, with their concepts of right and wrong, all originated in this part of the world. The intellectuality that conceived such ideology had an important effect on the future of Europe.

In considering the development of Greece during the last years of the second millennium, we must reckon with the certainty that a new wave of men, part of the broader spectrum of the folk hegiras at this time, descended from the Balkans in the north. They penetrated into Thessaly and ultimately the northern Peloponnesus. These were the Achaean Greeks, who built such citadels as Tiryns, Mycenae, Arne, and Argos. It was their language, the Greek, that survived. Some believe them to have been the Minoan overlords of the Mediterranean island of Crete and masters of the palaces of Knossos and Phaestos. At present the matter of origins has not been satisfactorily settled. Crete and Greece remained small maritime kingdoms throughout the second millennium, owing their riches to the fact that they were packhorses for the orient. Otherwise theirs was an agrarian economy.

A linear script in a form called *B* was found in the Achaean cities of Mycenae and Pylos and likewise at Knossos in Crete. This writing occurs on administrative tablets concerned with the stewardship of goods. It indicates communication between the islands and the mainland and is evidence of the earliest literacy known in Europe.

ARCHITECTURE AND INTERIORS

Prehistoric Structural Systems

The early builder in a land that used small building blocks or pliable material such as mud or reed began by constructing a monopode product—a wall sufficiently thick, narrowing toward the top—an entirety that was capable of support-

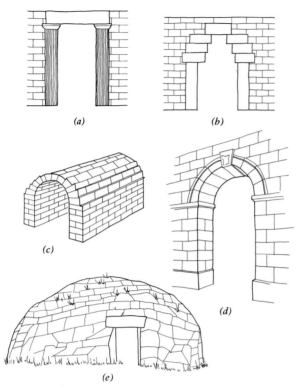

Figure 2.1 Structural systems: (a) trabeated (post and beam); (b) corbel arch; (c) vault (d) voussoir arch; (e) dome.

ing a superimposed load but, of course, enclosed little space.

Advancing on this technique, forms of the trabeated and arcuated structural systems were the basic developments (Figure 2.1). Both began early in Mesopotamia.

The *trabeated* building system (from the Latin *trabs,* meaning beam), which creates the rectangular form, might more cogently be termed the *post and beam* system because upright posts bear the weight of superimposed beams. Because the purpose of any architectural alignment is to enclose space and to resist those forces that seek to demolish walls and roof, it is apparent that trabeation works best when large, strong building members such as hard timber or stone are available. In southern Mesopotamia they were not, and, except for the reeds used in domestic architecture and some date-tree wood, the material used was sun-dried brick. After about 2300 B.C., during the Akkadian dynasty, the kiln-dried product was often substituted.

Ancient architects early devised a more advanced method of building known as the *arcuated system,* which incorporates some form of the arch, vault, or dome. A structural system is more advanced whenever it is more economical of its building material in relation to interior capacity.

A *true and semicircular arch* is constructed from two concentric circles with a common center. The larger one forms the outer surface or *extrados* and the smaller, the *intrados.* The point from which the arch begins to curve is known as the *spring.* If any vertical blocks are added below the spring, they are called *stilting.* The arch with its stilting rises from the wall *pier* (section of a wall acting as a load-bearing member) or column.

All the forces that play on an arch are those of compression. They are weights that seek to crush or compress the material of which the arch is formed. In a true arch resistance is accomplished by the interlocking of triangular wedge-shaped pieces known as *voussoirs.* Voussoirs are finally held in position by a *keystone* fitted into the top of the arch. Once in place, all compression forces simply serve to hold the arch more tightly and to spread its stresses downward to the walls. Obviously these walls must be thick enough to resist any tendency toward an outward thrust. Another solution is to buttress them for that purpose. An arch is never rigid until its capstone is in position. Therefore formwork known as *centering* is required until that occurs.

Vaults are passages roofed over by a continuum of arches and, when semicircular, are called *barrel vaults.* A series of arches that may be imagined as rotating around the center of the first arch constitutes a *dome.* A passage borne on arches and having a vaulted or beamed ceiling is an *arcade.*

The Near East

The principal architectural developments and the earliest in the Near East took place in Mesopotamia, which provides our focus here for the architectural development of the entire region. Both trabeated and arcuated building systems began early in Mesopotamia and were possibly conceived from one building type, the home of the marsh Arab. One can see it in the delta today, constructed from bound bundles of tall reeds placed upright for supports, bent to join over the top for a roof, and all lined with interconnected matting—a handsome testimony to man's ingenuity in the face of a paucity of resources.

The principal architectural form in Mesopotamia remained the trabeated. The materials were sun-dried brick and beams of date palm or imported cedar. Vaults were limited to tombs and drains; the only arches supported the doors. The dome seems to have been used in Mesopotamia briefly in the very early Halaf period for the *tholos* (Greek word for the dome of a circular building) houses, which were soon replaced by structures of rectangular plan.

Lower Mesopotamia, a rich agricultural land that consisted politically of myriad independent city states, maintained its surplus—wool, dates, and figs—by a communal effort spent on irrigation. With only specialized food to spare, it was forced of necessity into trading for other commodities. Such a diverse economy distributed wealth fairly evenly, and the early political structure tended toward a social theocracy. The first rulers were priests, deputies of both church and state rather than a totalitarian power that could command fabulous means for expansive building. Public building in southern Mesopotamia thus concentrated on temples. The many unearthed in such settlements as Eridu, Uruk, Kish, and Khafaje, which date before the well-publicized destruction of Ur (ca. 1800 B.C. at the hands of Hammurabi, no less!) indicate that the Sumerian was a highly skilled builder.

These early sanctuaries were built on platforms, called ziggurats or temple towers, that were considered to be sacred mountains. Actually their religious purpose was to magnify the importance of the temple and to project it closer to heaven and thus to the god worshiped therein. Because the Sumerians, according to one theory, are believed to have come from Persia, these ziggurats may have been planned to substitute, in a low-lying flat country, for the natural prominences on which the Persian Zoroastrian worshipers built their fire altars. The religious significance of the mountain loomed large in Near Eastern ideology. It was thought of essentially as the home of and the source from which emanated all cosmic powers.

These platforms were built on receding blocks of sun-dried bricks which assumed the shape of a truncated pyramid. Over the course of time stepped terraces, which conjecturally supported verdure, were let into the sloping sides, and burnt brick was substituted for some of the lower courses, proof of developing aesthetic sensitivity and improved technology.

On top of the platform was the holy building, with its adjacent dwellings for the priesthood and probably the offices of a necessary ruling bureaucracy, which possibly included in later additions the palace or home of the king himself.

In studying the lower Mesopotamian temples certain facts of extreme importance to any study of architecture are to be noted. The Sumerian not only knew all the advanced structural architectural principles but he refined the design of his forms and decorated them. Evidence of this advancement relates to their external appearance. Realizing that a massive building on top of a staged incline might create the illusion of top-heaviness, the architect planned what is later known in Greek building as *entasis,* in which subtle curves in the slopes of the planes establish the visual stability that a straight-line silhouette would have denied. In addition to this design refinement, it should be mentioned that instead of having the shape of a simple box, as their materials might have dictated, these temples borrowed from the reed construction of the Arab's house the repetitive visual units created by the supportive bundles of tall reeds and translated them into spaced external buttresses and eventually semiattached columns. These units had no structural necessity, but they broke a monotonous surface to create interesting shadow effects as the building mounted high under a tropical sun. Similar abutments, which later served practical as well as aesthetic purposes, reoccur frequently down through the European centuries.

In addition to these formal nuances, the Sumerian left a legacy of unusual architectural decoration. Even the earliest reed houses seem to have been covered with mud or gypsum plaster and the walls were often whitewashed. When this technique was transferred to temple architecture, the mud walls were sometimes enlivened with myriad chromatic ceramic cones, their broad bases painted in blue, yellow, and red hues, fixed

Figure 2.2 Copper relief portraying the benevolent eagle god Im-dugud above two stags. From the temple at al-Ubaid, ca. 3100–2500 B.C. Height, 107 m, width, 2.37 m. Columns enriched with cone mosaics of red and black stone and mother-of-pearl. Frieze of sacred cattle of limestone on copper. In foreground cases: copper protomes of lions. British Museum, London. (Reproduced by Courtesy of the Trustees of the British Museum.)

in geometric patterns in the clay matrix. Such embellishment occurred as early as 3000 B.C. in the temple at Uruk and an elaboration of this technique is found (Figure 2.2) in the little temple at al-Ubaid. This building had a porch in front, the columns of which were encased with copper, and copper lion protomes flanked its doorway. Other columns were enriched by cone mosaics, embellished further with semiprecious stones and mother-of-pearl. Above the porch columns, and conjecturally supported by them, was a large copper relief 42 in. high, which portrayed the benevolent, eagle-winged lion, Im-dugud, the rain god, above two stags. A copper-sheathed row of sacred oxen stood on the outer edge of the platform itself, behind which the wall was further decorated with colored clay cones in

floral patterns, again in conjunction with stones. Still higher were two copper reliefs similarly elaborated with limestone and white shell. Remnants of interior walls indicate flat color with geometric designs. Flat color, low relief, and mosaic have remained typically eastern forms of wall enrichment.

Only as the sword forged small states into kingdoms and empires were there omnipotent overlords who could build large palace complexes. Although vestiges of several from lower Mesopotamia remain (e.g., Kish, ca. 2500 B.C., and Eshnunna [Tell Asmar], ca. 2000 B.C.), it is in upper Mesopotamia in the city of Mari (now in Syria) that we find our first well-preserved and important royal compound (ca. 1750 B.C.). The home of King Zimrilan, a contemporary of Hammurabi, contained multiple courtyards and surrounding chambers which accommodated the sovereign, his household, and a bureaucracy of public officials, servants, and priests. Some of the palace chambers were sanctuaries, which is a decided change from the earlier Sumerian schema in which the temple itself was the important building and chambers for the monarch might be adjacent. The assemblage included kitchens and baths and was in plan as elaborate as the palaces of Egypt and Crete which are better known to us (discussed later in this chapter) and which date almost a half millennium later.

Not only are furnishings preserved from Mari but painted murals (Plate 1) from the palace, really the first in a preserved state, are displayed at the Louvre. The style of the paintings combines some of the abstract and prescribed patterning of the east with a breath of the naturalism that blows across the heights of the north and west, lovely legacies from a very old crucible.

Still farther west on the shores of the Orontes river in the enclosure of King Yarim-Lim at Alalakh a unique type of formal building was called, from its local name recorded in Assyrian texts, a *bit hilani*. It was the central throne building of a palace complex and was found later in many of the Neo-Hittite or Syro-Hittite city states that were established in the district in the early first millennium B.C.

Bit hilani are typically approached by an imposing flight of stairs like those that have per-

Figure 2.3 Basalt lion's head from the base of the statue of the god Atarluhas. Royal Gateway, Carchemish, ca. 900 B.C. Height, 40 cm. British Museum, London. The complete restored statue is in the Archaeological Museum, Ankara. (Reproduced by Courtesy of the Trustees of the British Museum.)

sisted down through the ages as tokens of monumental architecture. One passes through an end-walled but pillared portico (somewhat like the later Greek temple *in antis*) to reach a throne room parallel to the facade. Behind it was a private suite of rooms. The *bit hilani* had two stories, the upper reached by a flight of stairs off the verandah.

We are especially interested in the finish of these throne buildings. The palace of Yarim-Lim provides the prototype. Its structure was basically half-timbered with mud brick filling. This type of construction is common farther north beyond the Taurus mountains in Anatolia (e.g., at Kültepe, ca. 2200–2000 B.C., an early Assyrian commercial outpost), where lower courses were of rubble and where for the first time we meet the half-timbered, load-bearing construction of northern Europe.

The lower courses of a *bit hilani* were faced with orthostats, which at Alalakh were a little over a meter in height. Here they were plain and

polished, intended probably as a utilitarian as well as a decorative feature. The carving on later Syro-Hittite revetments progressed from a flat, largely two-dimensional treatment toward a higher relief which in this respect points to the friezes of classical Greece. Above the orthostats the wall might have been whitewashed or faced with glazed polychromed bricks. These north Syrian orthostats were evidently also the source of inspiration for the similar Assyrian usage.

At the entrances to such palaces or as part of the gateway to a walled town we see what is probably the archetype of the guardian bulls of the later Assyrian palace at Khorsabad. Colossal watchdogs assume shapes that vary from unrecognizable monsters to borrowed sphinxes to handsome lions (Figure 2.3)—the last destined to travel far to the gates of Mycenae and to Trafalgar Square.

The columns in Syro-Hittite structures are some relation to those of contemporary Egypt in that they were elaborated from the undeviatingly round shaft of wood or brick to incorporate details such as animal bases or rounded moldings for purely decorative enrichment. In Yarim-Lim's palace the columns were similar to the mushroom-capped pillars of the Minoans at Knossos and are wider at the top than at the bottom, a form prescient of the work of Frank Lloyd Wright at the Johnson Wax Company's administration building in Racine, Wisconsin, built in 1949.

Although wall painting has been a decorative technique practiced since the earliest Sumerian times (e.g., Uqar, 3500 B.C.) and wall paintings are of continuing importance right down to Mari, Yarim-Lim's palace is the first example in the Near East of *fresco* used for this purpose. It is doubtful, however, that the technique was unique to Alalakh. Real fresco, which was raised to its greatest height in the murals of the Aegean, can probably be claimed as a skill endemic to the coastal regions of Asia Minor and doubtless other examples will be found there.

Fresco painting is an art that differs from painting on dry walls. It is done by mixing the paint with sections of wet lime plaster. In another variation of the technique, called *secco*, the design is painted on plaster that has been moistened to bond better with the coloring matter. Some pig-

21

ments react adversely to lime; therefore a knowledge of suitable media is the first requisite of the fresco artist. The virtue of the method is, among other advantages (see under Cretan frescoes), that of greater permanency.

The palaces of northern Syria thus have contributed in their construction, planning, and decoration some refinements and innovations that later affected Assyria, Persia, and Crete.

Moving back to central Mesopotamia and forward in time, our attention is commanded by the culture of the Assyrian empire. Because the palace of Sargon II (742–705 B.C.) is the most completely preserved, it may serve as an illustration of Assyrian regal architecture (Figure 2.4). On a 25-acre site, Khorsabad, near modern Mosul, was built against the limestone hills that form an extension of the Zagros foothills to the northeast. The rear palace wall was coextensive with the city's ramparts, somewhat like the arrangement in rectangular castles, such as Warwick in England. The river, which flowed not many yards from Khorsabad's door, was the source of its water as well as the terminus of its drains.

Assyrian palaces were built on platforms, here for purposes of security and for their ability to impress. It is thought that Khorsabad was approached laterally by ramps wide enough to accommodate horse-drawn vehicles. The main gate was guarded by Anatolian-inspired gypsum colossi, winged human-headed bulls called *lamassu* (Figure 2.5). Because these creatures were designed to be seen from the front or the flank, they had five legs, only two or four of which were visible from either of these positions. This

Figure 2.4 Palace of Sargon II, Khorsabad, eighth century. B.C.: (a) entrance court; (b) state or governmental center; (c) business and service center; (d) harem court (e) temple; (f) ziggurat. (Adapted from Sir Banister Fletcher, *A History of Architecture*, eighteenth edition, New York: Scribner's; London: Athlone Press, 1975.)

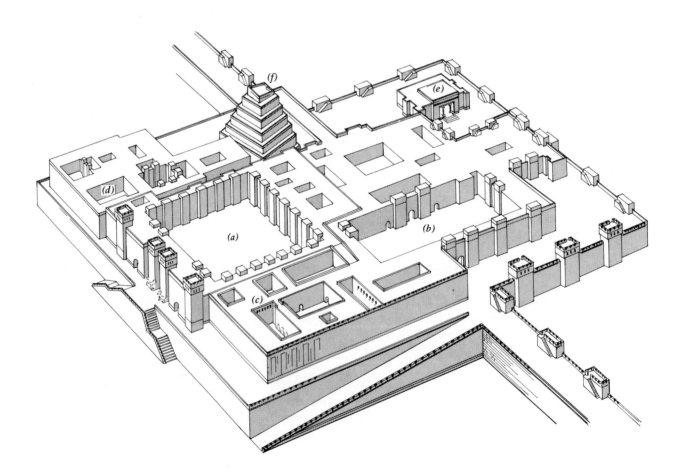

Figure 2.5 Winged human-headed bull (*lamassu*). Khorsabad. Reign of Sargon II (722–705 B.C.). Limestone. Height, ca. 14 ft. Louvre, Paris. (Musée du Louvre, Cliché des Musées Nationaux—Paris.)

is a curious anticipation of aspects of Picasso's painting which insist that the eye must be able to see all that the mind conceives—visual experience implementing the intellectual.

The structural walls of Assyrian palaces were sun-dried brick with *battlements* on the outer ramparts. Large defensive towers and regularly spaced buttresses gave to the whole the appearance of a fortress, which indeed it was. Later, from Byzantium, the crusaders carried this type of defense back to the grim fortifications of medieval Europe.

The functional spaces within Sargon's palace were irregularly grouped around three large courts. One was the state or governmental center, the second, the business and work area, and the last contained the king's private quarters. This tripartite division is characteristic of important eastern dwellings. They likewise differed from western homes because of the greater amount of seclusion accorded this last division. Because of the king's religious functions, several temples and a many-platformed ziggurat were included in the palace complex at Khorsabad.

The palaces of Assyrian kings turned their highly decorated sides inward—not for common eyes to see. The lower walls in the principal courts and assembly halls were lined with soft limestone ("Mosul marble") orthostats some 9 or 10 ft high and probably influenced by the architecture of northern Syria. The special significance here lay in their relief carving, which, because of its abundance and the aesthetic quality of its superior examples, should not be overlooked. Subject matter was largely narrative, centering around the exploits of the king, whether in battle or in the prowess of the hunt. Here the animals, the horses, lions, and gazelles, are drawn with close observation, if not sympathy, for the creatures of the stables and open spaces (Figure 2.6). In later Assyrian royal buildings the subject matter becomes more stereotyped—a mere recital of the homage paid to the empire by long processions of tribute bearers.

Above the stone the wall might be painted or given a frieze of glazed brick. In the late Babylonian period facing bricks were sculptured and enameled. These bricks composed the bull figures of the Ishtar gates (ca. 570 B.C.) in Babylon (Plate 2), which, incidentally, had returned to the four-legged variety. The Assyrians likewise used decorative ceramic tile for interior ornamentation. This practice was subsequently brought to a high state of development by such Anatolian folk as the Phrygians. It was the precursor of the colorful splendor of the Islamic mosques.

Figure 2.6 Limestone relief sculpture from King Assurbanipal's palace, Nineveh, ca. 650 B.C.: Hunting scene: wild asses pursued by mastiffs; a mare turns to heed her foal. Height, ca. 5 ft. British Museum, London. (Reproduced by Courtesy of the Trustees of the British Museum.)

23

Figure 2.7 Staircase to the Royal Audience Hall—the *Apadana*—with the Palace of Darius in the center left background. Persepolis, 521–486 B.C. (Courtesy of the Oriental Institute, University of Chicago.)

In consideration of developments to be recounted in the architecture of more western peoples it is significant that in Khorsabad there is no indication of windows, although ceramic pipes and open wells furnished fresh air and light, respectively.

With the conquest of Assyria and Babylonia by the Persians under Cyrus the Great in 538 B.C., the focus on Near Eastern architecture moves to Iran. Because the Iranians worshiped at altars in the open air, they built no temples. The most important buildings of the Persian Achaemenid dynasty were palaces, parts of which, being stone and glazed brick, are still to be seen. As works of art they are a synthesis of the styles of many subject nations given a formalizing stamp by the Iranian. As historical documents they represent the most eastern seat of power with which Greece and Rome had to contend.

Persepolis, which was destroyed by Alexander the Great in 323 B.C., is the most completely preserved complex of the Achaemenians (Figure 2.7). Persepolis was built near the modern city of Shiraz on a large stone platform inspired, perhaps, by those in Mesopotamia. Partly hewn from limestone cliffs, it had a natural means of defense. From the extant stone framework of columns and door and window jambs it is possible to reconstruct its architecture. Xerxes, in the full height of power, built the *propylaeum* or gateway. The names of Darius and Xerxes are associated with the great hypostyle audience hall known as the *apadana,* and Xerxes raised the magnificent building which is called the *Hall of the Hundred Columns.* The grouping of these buildings was not formally planned.

The Persepolis main structural system is trabeated, with walls of unbaked brick and stone columns that once supported the cedar roof. The roof timbers are gone, but many of the columns remain. They are attenuated in proportions. Their capitals bear an affiliation with the Greek Ionic through the Aeolic of Asia Minor. Above them is the unique Iranian contribution, the great impost block fashioned of paired protomes of the favorite Achaemenid symbols—lions, bulls, and griffins.

Wall ornament consisted of carved limestone revetments and sculptured glazed brick. The depiction of tributaries bearing gifts to the god-appointed king of kings, the sculptured repeti-

24

tions of the Persian Immortals (the group of noble soldiers who in the presence of intrigue following intrigue had remained loyal to the imperial throne)—all are highly stylized, yet show strong influence of Hellenic realism. It is known that Greek captives worked here and on the palace at Susa.

Little evidence of the interior details has survived, but Darius's foundation inscriptions from Susa tell us much. He speaks of the materials used and of the various people who took part:

> . . . Teakwood was brought from Gandara and from Carmania. The gold which was used here was brought from Sardis and from Bactria. The stone—lapis lazuli and carnelian—was brought from Sogdiana. The turquoise was brought from Chorasmia. The silver and copper were brought from Egypt. The ornamentation with which the wall was adorned was brought from Ionia. The ivory was brought from Ethiopa, from India, and from Arachosia. The stone pillars were brought from a place named Abiradush in Elam. The artisans who dressed the stone were Ionians and Sardians. The goldsmiths who wrought the gold were Medes and Egyptians. Those who worked the inlays were Sardians and Egyptians. Those who worked the baked brick (with figures) were Babylonians. The men who adorned the wall were Medes and Egyptians. At Susa here a splendid work was ordered; very splendid did it turn out. Me may Ahura-mazda protect, and Hystaspes who is my father, and my land.[1]

However we see it, the Persian buildings must have been dazzling. Their height (ceilings of the *apadana* were 65 ft) and the stylization of their decorative treatment would guarantee a distinctive elegance. In spite of some borrowing it bore the Persian stamp harnessed for the purpose of portraying regal power.

Egypt

Egypt comes early within the sphere of developed architecture and interior design. Egypt, the land, is essentially a one-way tract, easy to imagine as representing the human course from birth to death and readily associated with the pharaoh, the carnate god who had conquered all of the territory and people known to men of the Old Kingdom. Thus it was natural to imagine for him an everlasting life, and indeed a belief in immortality was part of Egyptian religion, at first postulated only for the pharaoh but later extending to the common people. Hence the legitimate effort to build regal and religious structures—the imposing flat-topped rectangular tomb houses or mastabas of nobles, the pointed pyramids of kings, and the later temples and rock-hewn ossuaries.

The sepulchres had a threefold purpose: the incarcerated body was to be so deeply hidden that theft would be defied (a vain hope, for the tomb of Tutankhamun was the only one ever found intact); the chambers were to be furnished with all the material necessities for the long journey through eternity; and last the building itself should perpetuate and endow with significance the hieratic concept of society. For these purposes who ever executed a more effective architectural pile than the everlasting homes of the rulers of the Nile? Imhotep, the royal architect of Zoser, the most important ruler of the third dynasty, is indeed the first name to come down through the ages as a designer as well as an engineer of buildings.

The duality of god in man led to a close connection between tomb, temple, and palace in Egyptian architecture. In fact, at times they formed one building complex. Forms were borrowed one from the other. A pictograph of an early palace of lower Egypt suggests a construction in which small pieces of wood were joined to provide upright supports similar to those of the reed hut. This style was later transferred to mortuary wood architecture (Figure 2.8). Called a *serekh* building [because the design of a palace is an element of the pharaoh's *serekh* (insignia)], it used long and narrow strips of wood with permanent wooden doors or mat-woven screens to fill the spaces between the uprights. When opened, they allowed the wind to sweep in. The appearance of this early structure was later duplicated in reticulated walls or by attached pillars. The prototype of buttressing is again evident. Thus Egypt invented one ideal form for softwood.

Egyptian architecture, however, owes its importance to stone—the world's first great trabe-

25

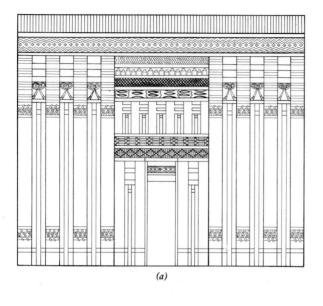

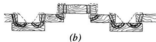

(a)

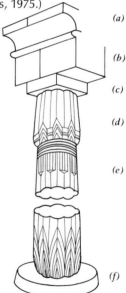

(b)

Figure 2.8 *Serekh* building system (conjectured): (a) central segment of stone sarcophagus of Fefi, made in imitation of a building; (b) plan of coffin construction detail using wood and lacings—a technique presumably used also for the walls of buildings. (Adapted from E. Baldwin Smith, *Egyptian Architecture as Cultural Expression,* Appleton-Century, 1938.)

ated architecture in that medium. Stone abounded in the highlands of Anatolia, but the people were not organized to handle it. In the Nile basin material and manpower met.

In the cliffs back from the silt bed of the river there is an abundance of building stone. Limestone is found in the north, softer sandstone south of Edfu, and granite occurs above the first cataract at Aswan. Specialized varieties such as the hard diorite, the soft alabaster, and basalt were quarried nearby. Although the land supported few trees other than the soft date palm and the acacia, the river banks yielded an excellent clay for bricks, the latter so good that the Egyptian could rely on sun baking and rarely resorted to kiln drying. Some building materials such as the tall cedar timbers from the Levant were imported—another handwriting on the wall of trade or war.

The remarkable contribution that Egypt made

to trabeated architecture was not so much in scale—although that could at times be terrifying—but in the inflection given to the building members. In the arcuated and pyramidal style the aesthetic appeal rests with the silhouette of circle and triangle against the sky; in trabeated architecture the ordered relation of pillar, post, beam, and superstructure must be counted on for any sensuous pleasure.

The pillar in Egypt was composed of three parts: the round *base,* the shaft or *column,* and the *capital* or ornamental heading. The purpose of the capital was to make a more functional and pleasing transition from the vertical shaft to the horizontal *lintel* or beam. An intermediary block, known as the *abacus,* was superimposed to strengthen the weight shift. (The base, of course, served a similar compressional purpose.) These soon became customary parts of an *order* or total arrangement of architectural components (Figure 2.9). A lintel is called an *architrave* when it becomes a facing member. Derivation is from the classical root *arch,* meaning principal, and *trabs,*

Figure 2.9 An architectural order—column with bud capital: (a) Egyptian gorge or cavetto cornice and roll molding; (b) architrave, beam, or lintel; (c) abacus; (d) capital; (e) shaft or column; (f) base. (Adapted from a model of the Temple of Amen-Re, Karnak, shown in Sir Banister Fletcher, *A History of Architecture,* eighteenth edition, New York: Scribner's; London: Athlone Press, 1975.)

26

meaning beam. The architrave is often left plain to emphasize the capital.

The *cornice,* which provided visual niceties of height and overhang, was the next superimposed member. The most familiar Egyptian cornice is the *cavetto* or *gorge,* the concave side of one-fourth of a circle planned to meet a vertical straight-line section. The *cavetto cornice* is one that, in its full curve in relation to column and architrave, enabled Egyptian architecture to paint boldly with sun and shadow.

Molding is a broadly interpreted word that refers to any additional pieces used in the modulation of a surface to give it various profiles. Throughout the centuries architecture has combined different moldings for this purpose. The Egyptian builder had few, the *roll molding* that simulated the horizontal reed bundles used as binders in early construction being the most prominent. The *hollow molding,* which was the crowning member of the cavetto cornice, was another.

The Egyptian was the first to experiment with the shape of the orders and particularly of the capital. In this member he eventually fashioned stone to resemble the flora of the river banks—the conventionalized closed bud or open flower (known as the *campaniform* motif) of the papyrus reed, sacred to the northern or lower kingdom, and of the lotus plant, revered in the south or upper kingdom (Figure 2.10). Again his inspiration came from the fronds of the ubiquitous palm. When the purpose of these members was remembered and adhered to, the Egyptian was on the way to creating architecture, for he modulated his imagery and still considered functionalism. Unfortunately he frequently used flat wall or pillar surfaces to register symbolic prescribed representation and the concept of total architecture thus escaped his grasp.

Nor did the Egyptian develop that careful deviation of measure within parts and relation of section to section that could have provided the visual satisfaction to be found later in the classic Greek temple. Some Egyptian columns did taper toward the top and bottom, but only because they were planned to imitate the natural diminution observed in plant forms rather than designed according to any abstract optical principle.

Post and beam, in Egyptian architecture, were reserved for interior load bearing and for the framing of openings. Small spaces were sometimes vaulted. The arch was well understood but trabeation took precedence. In early buildings, such as the two near Zoser's pyramid, the outline of the arch was traced in brick on the walls in a graceful but unstructural manner, possibly in perpetuation of the forms of canopies over sacred kiosks. Walls were solidly built of stone or brick. One of their outstanding characteristics was their slight *batter* or slope toward the exterior base. The purpose of this is conjectural but it may bear some relation to the observed pyramidal form of the pharaonic tombs.

The plans of Egyptian temples were ordered and generally bisymmetrical with respect to their major disposition of spaces. Ancillary to these, however, were many auxiliary rooms, intended no doubt for priestly functions, which were irregularly located and approached by devious corridors. Usually they were not lighted in any man-

Figure 2.10 Motifs frequently used on Egyptian capitals: (a) papyrus; (b) papyrus bud; (c) papyrus flower; (d) lotus; (e) lotus flower; (f) lotus bud. (After Borchardt.)

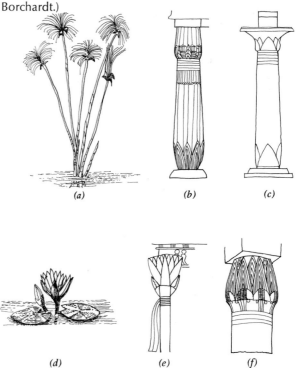

ner and their use must remain hypothetical. Bisymmetry nevertheless is a noteworthy feature in Egyptian architecture. It suggests that preplanning, that consciousness of the two halves to the whole, so essential to any large-scaled unity. It likewise indicates a rigidity of thought that could conceive only of a left- and right-handed total.

The temple complex was surrounded by a girdle wall, possibly intended for defense purposes but certainly needed to demark the area. The enclosure was approached from the river by a processional road and was pierced by a towering gateway. The ceremonial avenue was lined with the usual sculptures—sphinxes with human, lion, or ram heads—as tokens of regal power and flanked by tall, slender, granite obelisks, monumental monolithic pillars that further dignified the entrance. These shafts were square in plan and tapered to a pyramidal summit capped with metal. The largest obelisk in the world, which came from the Temple of the Sun at Heliopolis, is now in the piazza of S. John Lateran in Rome.

The facade of an Egyptian building or of the enclosing wall was broken by two towers shaped like truncated pyramids, called *pylons,* the Greek word for gateway. It is conjectured that the pylon itself or flagstaffs near the pylon might have supported banners that bore royal or religious significance. Thus descends the pylon that acts as a marker for present-day race courses.

Egyptian temples exhibited some but not undeviating similarities of plan. There was a pillared entrance court or portico that led to a large hypostyle (meaning *under the pillar*) hall. The most impressive hypostyle hall is in the Temple of Amon (Amen-Re) at Karnak near Thebes (Figure 2.11). Its overt purpose was to secure a large interior space. Beams, especially those of stone, can span a relatively short distance, and many supporting columns are required for a large one. To our eyes, accustomed to large spans made possible by modern engineering methods, a forest of masonry rather than a field of space seems to characterize the hypostyle hall. To the Egyptian interested in time and eternity rather than in space and extension this may not have been undesirable. It is interesting that Sumerian architecture also used the many pillared hall to gain interior space.

Ceremonial Egyptian religion as ritualized in

Figure 2.11 Hypostyle Hall of the Temple of Amen-Re at Karnak, showing clerestory windows. Egypt, nineteenth dynasty. Drawing after a model in the collection of the Metropolitan Museum of Art, New York.)

the temples, except on rare festival days, was not intended for the populace. The temple functioned more as a private oratory for the ruler and the priests, and no others were permitted beyond the hypostyle hall and into the inner sanctuary. In some temple complexes various pharaohs added their own contingent of buildings that resulted in a multiplicity of courts, halls, and sanctuaries within one walled enclosure.

In a hypostyle hall the inner pillars may be taller than the outer in order to clear wall space for grilled windows. This level which rises above its flanks is known as a *clerestory* and its windows are *clerestory windows.* Because of this system of fenestration the central mass of an Egyptian hall may tower over the lower courts and rooms to create a hierarchic form and allow for interior lighting.

If the royal tomb and the temple were of stone, the dwelling—even the imperial palace—was of mud brick. One was a house for eternity, naturally more important than a shelter for this transient life. Pillars in domestic work were wood or brick bathed in plaster. Flat roofs created outdoor living spaces. Surmounted by a *mulgaf* which allowed windward breezes to enter through one vent as hot air escaped leeward, the roof served to cool the house.

Most Egyptian dwellings have perished, as have countless civic structures concerned with the everyday business of a thriving civilization. Although excavations report towns and estates of every date, the fame of Egyptian domestic architecture rests with the city of Amenhotep IV because of the investigations by W. M. Flinders Petrie that disclosed its structures in the 1890s. Few travelers today ride out in the sands to see the bare outlines, which are little more than the ghost ramparts of a town. Yet these ruins have yielded valuable information about the plans, the building, and the decorative arts of their period.

Akhenaten (Amenhotep) the only monotheist in the long line of pharaohs, worshiped solely Aten, the sun god whose symbol was the disk (a god who did not exist in the form of a graven image) as his paternalistic version of omnipotence. In so doing he separated himself from the powerful group of priests of Amen-Re, of the Theban cult of sun worshipers, and thought to revivify a religion that had grown diverse, all-usurping, and nonsensically ritualistic. Changing his name to Akhenaten, he took up a new life in a new abode. His capital, Akhetaten or *Tell-el-Amarna*, is on the east bank of the Nile about 250 miles north of Thebes.

The city, a corridor barely two miles wide, is laid out on one of the earliest rectilinear plans, irregularly executed. Four main palaces lie along its axis. The best-preserved is located in the northern precinct. In describing it as a royal residence, the layout of temple architecture is somewhat duplicated because the basic type of planning for the two is the same.

Although the smaller Egyptian homes, like those of the Tell-el-Amarna nobles and the workmen on the project, were seldom bisymmetrical in plan, the north palace was rigidly so (Figure 2.12), duplicating in essence the type of planning that made the temple. Many town houses, such as the Theban home of one Thutnufer depicted on the walls of his tomb, were of several stories.

Inside the north Amarna palace the visitor is faced with a forecourt, adjacent offices, and a sanctuary. Hence three doors open onto a major court which contained a pool and verdure. The court was flanked on one side by quarters for the royal pets and on the other for state dignitaries, an odd but revealing juxtaposition.

The last division at this Amarna royal residence, the most sacred and private quarters, was entered through double doors that led off a columned portico or dais. We see this in pictographs of the public appearances of the ruler and his beautiful wife Nefertiti. Its function corresponded to that of the *window of appearances* in the temple.

The first room in the innermost sanctum was the hypostyle hall, thought possibly to be a general assembly room or dining hall for the court, behind which in this particular palace a transverse passage terminated in a flight of stairs at each end. One led to a window looking onto the harem court, the other overlooked the men's.

Because of the preservation of tomb interiors and later of the distinctive features of temple and domestic interiors, it is possible to recreate with a fair degree of accuracy the Egyptian manner of handling interior space. Egyptian interiors not only possessed the objects necessary to expedite their purpose (see section labeled Furniture) but likewise surfaces were interestingly embellished.

For consecrated areas walls were traditionally covered in stone low relief in which the background was laboriously cut away and the figures modeled against it. When, during the reign of Akhenaten, the tremendous task of building a complete city in a short span of time and with an army of comparatively new workmen called for speedier techniques, a process called sunken relief was practiced. In this only the outline of the figures was chiseled deeply and any modeling was done with a thin coat of plaster and paint. The process alone accounted for some of the freer and more dramatic aspects given to art at this time. On domestic buildings the only stone fittings were found in windows, doorways, and lustration slabs or in stone stelae of the royal family. Temples and offices of the great central palace at Tell-el-Amarna, however, were built almost entirely of stone.

Mural painting, a less expensive and quicker medium, was customary in domestic work. As time passed it invaded religious interiors as well. Walls were first given a coat of mud or gypsum plaster. When done on mud, these paintings are often erroneously called frescoes. Strictly speaking, this is not correct because the work was not done on lime plaster in accepted fresco technique.

The colors used were the primaries plus green, white, and black. Yellow from the ubiquitous ochre was likewise found in more saturated form

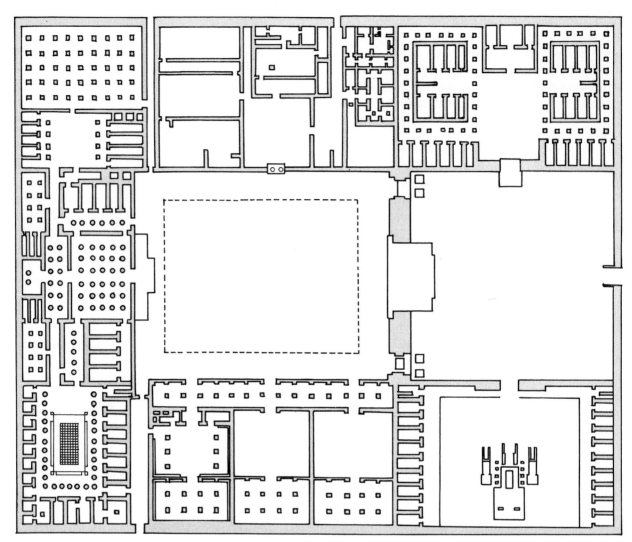

Figure 2.12   Plan of North Palace at *Tell-el-Amarna,* late second millennium B.C. (Adapted from E. Baldwin Smith, *Egyptian Architecture as Cultural Expression,* Appleton-Century, 1938. Courtesy of the Egypt Exploration Society.)

as the pigment orpiment. Red was dull, a mixture of iron oxide clay and haemetite ore. Blue calls for comment. It has been found as powdered azurite, a basic carbonate of copper. It is likewise celebrated in precious work as the much discussed Egyptian frit, a double silicate of calcium and copper heated to a degree not high enough for complete fusion and then pulverized. If this firing was at a less than 840 degree temperature, a bluish green resulted. The only other source of the Egyptian blue-green must have been mala-

chite, another form of the copper carbonate already mentioned for blue. Gypsum was used for white and black was derived from carbon.[2] To a large extent these colorants from clays and minerals have been the substances enlisted to turn the chalky world of black and white to accord with the hues of nature. From time to time new pigments (or dyes) would be added, but only after the colorants were synthesized in the nineteenth century were there any appreciable number.

Color usage in Egyptian art was frequently dictated by symbol. Wood and male skin were brown-red. Women's flesh was yellow. The god Amen in human form had blue coloring, and hair was often blue, a favorite color.

In mortuaries, if stone did not line the entire interior it was used as revetment with mural painting above. In any case, the intent of the pictures—to provide the deceased with a life in mime—prescribed the covering of all possible surfaces with replicas of this world's goods. The mural reliefs or paintings were usually arranged in bands or registers, of which there are customarily four.

Painted domestic interiors were less completely covered with pictorial elements. The lower part of the wall, the *dado* (derived from the Italian name for the section of a column base between upper and lower moldings), was white, black, or very dark blue.

Above the dado patterning begins. Whereas tomb painting might be on a dull yellow background, palace walls were frequently white. At Amarna large rosettes were painted on some surfaces and medallioned glazed tiles were used ornamentally in a manner akin to floral wallpaper today.

A deep and geometric frieze lay close to the ceiling. Its motifs were abstractions from nature and symbolism. Frequent was the block pattern interspersed with stripes, a formalization of the reed bundles known as the *dedu,* the early symbol of the god Osiris. When a diagonal is added, the thongs that attached rolled matting are indicated. The frieze may be surmounted by a capping design, frequently in the form of a *khecker frieze,* which simulates the knots of reeds tied above the flat roof tops in primitive shelters. Thus many functional components become stereotyped down the centuries to form well-known decorative motifs.

Small wall niches, conjectured from the plaster remnants at Amarna, may have harbored statuettes of deities, and there is some indication of a pharaoh cult in which images of the royal family were worshiped in this manner.

The wood beams as well as the plaster ceilings were covered with a regular pattern. Clay or brick floors were whitewashed and sometimes painted. Religious buildings were more likely to have granite flooring, adorned with all manner of costly inlays.

Windows were finished with wooden grilles, and tall cedar doors were double-hung in impor-tant locations. The *aedicule* (the complete architectural frame of an opening) was composed of broad supporting members and a lintel which might be corniced.

The content of Egyptian wall depiction is of great interest. In the temples and tombs the intention was, as has been said, to substantiate the belief that the future life was but a material extension of the present. To that end the pharaoh was shown in contemplation of all the activity that confronted him here—fowling, harvesting, fishing, and hunting. At this the native artist, when given full rein, could create a lively verisimilitude. He also perpetrated some of the earliest landscapes in existence. Generally his vignettes on pillar and wall were prescribed to carry a message, repetitious eyeballing of everyday life. For the most part they came off lamely in aesthetic appeal.

Egyptian representation throughout its long career remains flat, two-dimensional art. No attempt was made to create perspective through modeling, foreshortening, linear recession, or shadows. Grouping was dictated by similarity of ideas, and scale was a means of designating importance. The artist customarily drew the figure with head and legs in profile, whereas the upper torso and eyes were frontal (Figure 2.13). His was an intellectual rather than a visual approach. That this was true is likewise confirmed by the scale of the drawing in relation to the surface on which it was placed. Although the artist's hand was sure and the line work well done, nevertheless the size relation between the figures and the column or wall on which they were placed is so disparate that it precludes any feeling of scale or rhythmic progression.

The art style seen in Akhenaten's city differed from the symbolic conceptual art of Egyptian tradition. Following the death of the heretical monarch, the priest cult of Amen-Re quickly advocated a return of the capital to Thebes and gradually the desert took over the sand buildings as despoilers carried off the stones of Amarna. Fortunately some beautiful relics of the art of Akhenaten's reign were found in the ruins, including fragments of wall murals, like the one from the garden room off the harem court of the north palace and several from the painted floors

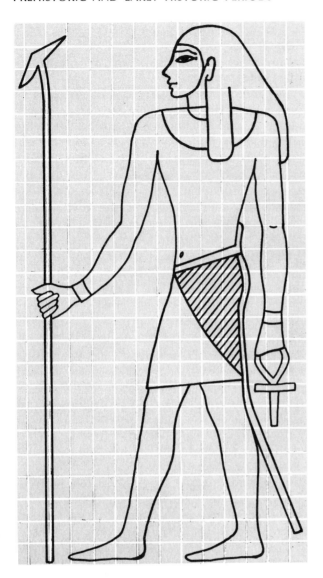

Figure 2.13 Egyptian representation of the human figure. (Illustration redrawn from *Meaning in the Visual Arts:* Papers in and on Art History by Erwin Panofsky. Copyright © 1955 by Erwin Panofsky. Reprinted by permission of Doubleday & Company, Inc.)

of the central palace. Likewise sections of both walls and floors were obtained from the pleasure palace of Maruaten, the pharaoh's daughter, which was in the south precinct.

The manner of painting indicates that a wave of naturalism had inundated Egyptian art, which, if it destroyed some of its formalism, made it more intimate, more interested in individualized characterization of the subject, more spontane-ous, and indeed more feminine. In the northern-palace frieze (Figure 2.14) we see both drooping and upright papyrus plants with every tendril outlined in delicate profusion. We are greeted by the lotus—full, half-opened, and closed—doves, kingfishers, and shrikes—all delicately poised on the stillness of the river banks and in the silent depths of the painted pool. The frieze ran con-tinuously around the room, in itself an innova-tion to Egypt where scenes were customarily compartmentalized.

In trying to understand the apparently sudden appearance of this impressionistic art, one re-members Gerzean predynastic pictures and the facility of the painters when not at the command of an authoritarian hierarchy. Indeed there is much in Tell-el-Amarna art, such as the close as-sociation of the pharaoh with the godhead, that seems to be a reversion to more primitive aspects of social life, before the era of the all-conquering, great warrior monarchs. Akhenaten might like-wise have been influenced toward grace by the exceptional women of his household, his lovely wife Nefertiti, his daughters, and his mother Thiy. His immediate predecessors had brought Egypt into contact with the world to the east, one source of his interest in the profound and com-plex metaphysical ideas of eastern philosophy and religion and probably in nonprovincial styles of art.

Such a man was not the strong administrator required to rule the affluent dynastic empire he had inherited. This is not to belittle his accom-plishments. His reign has left us a small but re-markable heritage of decoration that can rank with the achievements of all time.

Following Akhenaten, Nilitic temples and tombs strove to excel in aggrandisement—enor-mous without being majestic, commanding with-out granting satisfaction—until at last the Nile flowed into the Mediterranean and Egypt became enmeshed by European cultures that faced its northern shores. Her art had stood still too long.

Crete

By the mid-second millennium the advanced cul-tures of Mesopotamia and Egypt were not only affecting each other, they were facing the neces-

Figure 2.14 Detail of mural in the Green Room of the North Palace at Tell-el-Amarna. Pigeons and shrike among papyrus and lotus plants. Reproduction painting by Nina de Garis Davies for *The Mural Painting of El Amarnah*, H. Frankfort, Ed. (The Egypt Exploration Society.)

sity of coming to terms with the western societies of Europe and the Mediterranean. The excavations carried on by Sir Arthur Evans in Crete more than seventy-five years ago disclosed an advanced civilization contemporaneous with the empires we have been considering. And Crete is only a sail away from Greece (although Ulysses found the journey lengthy!)

Dates of Cretan history are flexible, but in general they are correlated with those of the Achaean Greek cultures. The Cretan names were assigned by Evans on the supposition that the most important king of Cretan palace building was the legendary Minos who exacted periodic tribute from Greek Athens in the form of the sacrifice of Athenian youths to the Cretan fabled half-bull, half-man creature known as the Minotaur.

Although the people who created the unique civilization that we call Minoan have not been definitely pinioned ethnologically, we have learned much about them from the remains of their largest palaces, those of Knossos and Mallia on the north central coast and of Phaestos and Hagia Triada on the south. Whoever they were, their geographical advantage on a large island with deep bays strategically placed between Asia, Egypt, and the European mainland put them in the direct line of trade and economic progress. Knossos was advantageously marked for a principal settlement. Located on a slight promontory between two harbors, it possessed just the vantage that was necessary to ward off piracy and to protect shipping.

There may have been a small palace here in the Early Minoan period when the principal economy of the island was located in the east in towns like Palaikastro and Vasiliki. Apparently this building was leveled about 2000 B.C., either by intention or by some natural catastrophe. Crete subsequently seems to have been united under a strong central government which could command resources. The Knossos palace then erected (which is called Palace I) is the first of which significant remains exist.

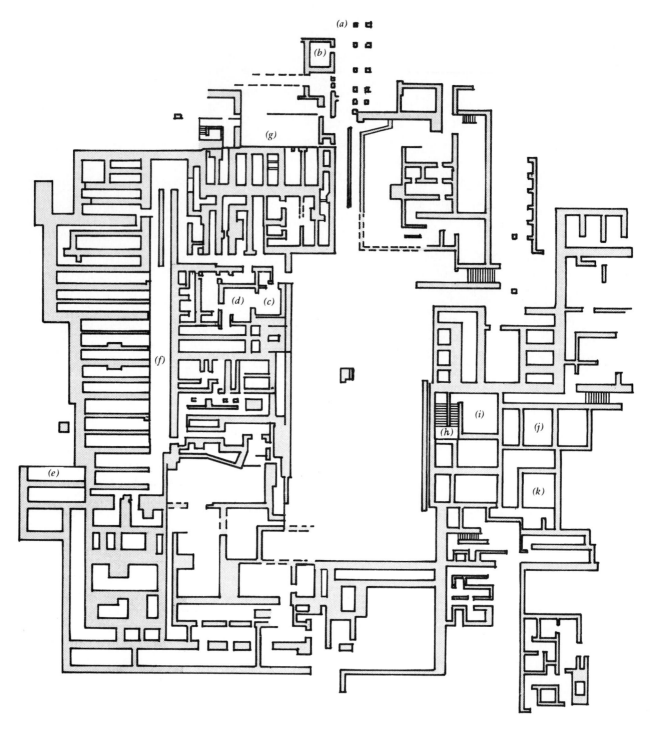

Figure 2.15   Plan of the Palace of King Minos at Knossos (Palace II): (a) north entrance; (b) guard house (c) anteroom to throne room; (d) throne room; (e) west portico; (f) long gallery with magazines; (g) northern bath; (h) great staircase; (i) hall of the colonnades; (j) hall of the Double Axes; (k) queen's megaron. Crete, ca. 1850–1700 B.C. (Adapted from Sir Banister Fletcher, *A History of Architecture,* eighteenth edition, New York: Scribner's; London: Athlone Press, 1975.)

34

The Cretan had not yet arrived at the point at which he could foreplan a large complex building. Knossos is indeed labyrinthal, an accumulation of small-chambered rooms centering around, but not necessarily connected with, a large open assembly court. The disposition more or less follows the eastern tripartite planning, and indeed how can you better it—work, social, and private? At the time of the second round of building (Palace II, 1850–1700 B.C.) the entire irregular jumble was conjoined by interconnecting passages and, although its maze character could not be altered, it was converted into a more highly articulated whole (Figure 2.15).

At least two cataclysmic earthquakes were responsible for subsequent demolitions and reconstructions on more prepossessing lines. Both (or were they somewhat continuous?) have been associated with the tremors that originated on the Aegean island of Santorini (Thera), now verified by seismology and fabled in classical writing as the quake that submerged Plato's famed island of Atlantis. The palace at Knossos owes its final form to reconstruction after these events. Its companion at Phaestos was deserted after the debacle and a new one was built at Hagia Triada. Archaeology continues to document additional palatial buildings of this amazing civilization which flourished on the island for what was in reality only a very brief period of time.

The last glory of Knossos was short-lived. In the fifteenth century B.C., near the end of the Late Minoan period, the palace was suddenly deserted. Its destruction may have been by fire, possibly by arson at the hands of a northern invader or probably, as Evans maintained, by another quake. It was never officially reopened.

Knossos, the largest of the Cretan buildings, may be taken as their prototype. It was north-south oriented contrary to the usual custom in the ancient world. The route into Cretan palaces was circuitous and narrow, thus implementing the protection factor. Isolated by the sea, the Cretan buildings were not otherwise unduly fortified.

Knossos was on three levels to the east where the household quarters were located. Many Aegean houses are so built, a necessity on the island hills. The requisite large stairways, at Knossos

five flights, were open to the sky, as were most of the inner courts. The whole complex gave the impression of belonging to a culture that enjoyed outdoor living. In the Queen's apartments in the private section we find the *Hall of the Colonnade* and that of the *Double Axes,* to be described in relation to the palace frescoes.

The public division to the west contained the magazines or storage rooms. Here large jars filled with grain were left as the stewards fled during the final hours. To the northeast were the artisan's quarters where *pithoe* or provision jars were in the process of being wheel-turned. The north entrance was narrow and more direct than the southern. It led to the central court and passed a room that has been designated a throne room. This chamber contained lustral areas and an imposing ceremonial seat.

Construction, known as cyclopean, was with large blocks of gypsum (limestone at the gateways) so carefully cut that no mortar was required for their laying. Inner space was generally spanned by wooden beams and wood was likewise used for the squat columns, tapered toward the bottom (Figure 2.16). They have not survived and their restoration must be predicated from the wall frescoes. Wherever several stories had to be supported the ceilings and the rectangular piers were stone. Much of the construction in small rooms was of load-bearing rubble, strengthened with wood and covered with plaster.

If Knossos was not outstanding with respect to formal planning or marked for advance construction, why is it important to art history? The essence of its worth is a spirit, compounded of many facets, which suddenly seems contemporary and European. Practical evidence is the sanitation system that was built during its last renovation. A circuitous drain, gypsum-lined baths, and provision for carrying off waste served the domestic quarters. Latrines could be flushed, and terra cotta pipes supplied clean drinking water. The kind of engineering skill required for these facilities bespeaks an intelligent, practical, comfort-loving people, the like of which would today raise a modern Hilton on a neighboring island.

Mechanical conveniences are, however, only minor contributions of the Cretan civilization. Their art, principally represented by the frescoes

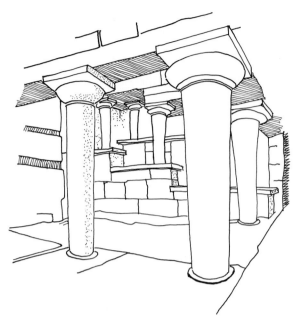

Figure 2.16 Columns in the grand staircase in the Palace at Knossos. (Adapted from John Gloag, *Guide to Western Architecture*, George Allen & Unwin Ltd., 1958.)

on the walls of their palaces and the objects that adorned their homes, tells their story clearly. Frescoes were not a major wall decoration at Phaestos and the work at Mallia was largely dry painting. But at Knossos the full glory of the fresco painter's art emerges. It is said that the lime plaster of the island is particularly hard and well-suited to fine work. In the large late frescoes the designs present strong tonal contrast that provides a maplike precision well-suited to an art that must be executed in sections. Only an area that can be finished while the plaster is wet is handled at one time. Beveled edges of plaster are best placed to coincide with a clear figure outline.

The Cretans likewise developed a modeled fresco technique (late Middle Minoan), just as the Mesopotamian advanced from flat to sculptured bricks. One outstanding relief fresco is the splendid figure of the bull on the North Porch. Although superlative frescoes (Plate 3) have been unearthed at Thera (also known as Santorini), the first of the mainland Greek examples are dated about 1400 B.C. and presumably must have derived from contact of the Aegean Greeks with the islands.

Life in all its forms constitutes the subject matter of these paintings. Early Knossos frescoes which showed the human figure were done to small scale. The fragment known as the *Saffron Gatherer* may be the earliest. It was found in the north keep near the throne room.

Among the later full-sized frescoes the *Toreador Fresco* is well known (Figure 2.17). Although only fragments remain, it has been restored with some assurance because apparently it served as a model for others found at Tiryns on the mainland. This piece pictures an event that possibly took place in the theater area to the northwest of the palace of a very skillful, surely ritual, performance in which both men and maidens engage a bull (suggesting the ancient myth of the Minotaur) and nimbly vault over his back as the horns are released for the next participant. It is portrayed in a realistic although somewhat conventionalized manner; for example, as in Egypt, women's skins are light, the men's are red. We see the small-waisted, lithe type of Cretan physique, probably significant of an active life and vaguely reminiscent of eastern rather than western figures.

Another synchronous fresco is the *Procession*, found in the *Corridor of the Procession* (west porch) as well as in the south *Propylaeum* (an architectural entrance similar in purpose to the Egyptian pylon). It depicts men and women, only a portion of their figures remaining, bearing offerings. The best preserved of the group has been called the *Cup Bearer*, an athletic youth with a restrained coiffure of wavy hair, who carries a tall ceremonial cup in a proud manner. The prescription for representing the figure resembles the Egyptian, with similar use of mixed viewpoints, some overlapping of forms to suggest recession, and, in the procession figures, the definite use of the base line. At other times the Cretan used the same impressionistic technique of floating figures in space that we have seen in Amarna art.

The procession scene is accompanied by border friezes, often bearing the Nilitic stripe-and-medallion motifs. More common is the overlapping circle and the northern favorite, the spiral. Occasionally, as in the throne room, an attempt was made to imitate marble with paint. In similar

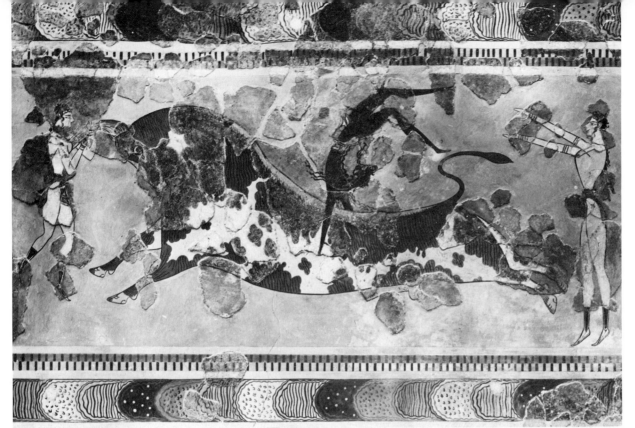

Figure 2.17 The Toreador Fresco. The Palace at Knossos, ca. 1500 B.C. Height, ca. 32 in. Restored. Archaeological Museum, Herakleion. (Photo Researchers.)

manner the Egyptian simulated granite. These are among the earliest examples of *trompe l'oeil* (deceive the eye) in decorative art, which is pure fakery, to be sure, and as such is always questionable, but it has introduced many delightful fancies to interiors.

In addition to the human subjects of Cretan frescoes, there are figures of symbolic interest. The zoomorphic griffins, half lion, half eagle, are hybrid monsters that appear prominently. Aeschylus called them the hounds of Zeus who never bark and are supposed to be the natural guardians of gold. Again they were associated with fire. A strain of logic runs through all of this, although the griffins end ignominiously on the furniture of Robert Adam and ludicrously in *Alice in Wonderland*.

This seeking for meaning behind the symbol has extended to the ornaments in the Hall of the Colonnade and the Hall of the Double Axes. In the first, restored through similarity with Tiryns frescoes, are the *figure-eight shields,* the counterpart of those used by the Achaean Greeks. Bor-

rowing certainly, but by whom? Likewise the double-headed axe is the Cretan variant of the ceremonial battle axes that have been associated with the inroads of the battle-axe peoples. A strange current theory identifies these axes with masons' marks. Take your choice!

It is in the portrayal of the local flora and fauna that the Cretan artist excelled. Here is an accomplishment that can be compared with no art except that which is at once young, alive, and exceedingly sensitive. One of the best examples of this talent is demonstrated in the fresco of the stalking cat (Figure 2.18) which came from Hagia Triada (ca. 1600 B.C.) and is now in the Herakleion Museum in Crete. The feline anatomy is all wrong but the very character of the animal with his plans for the pheasant is delightfully evil. Others of the frescoes like the one on the floor of the little shrine room of the palace that depicts *octopi and fishes* and another frieze from Knossos that portrays the *harpie and hoopoe* carry on this sort of impressionistic naturalness.

We know little of the Cretan's religion and science. His gods and goddesses find analogues in most primitive religions—the mother goddess, the lady who hunts, the master of animals, the "horns of consecration" (possibly the virility sym-

Figure 2.18 Fresco of a cat stalking a pheasant. Hagia Triada, Crete, ca. 1600 B.C. Archaeological Museum, Herakleion. (Marburg/Prothmann.)

bol of the bull), the benevolent snake (the good earth).

But in the larger scheme of things one cannot say that Cretan philosophy or art was narrowly hedonistic or sensual. Strangely, and with the ingenuousness of a young society in a safe and prosperous world, the islander has left a legacy in his creations that strikes to the core of all reli-

gion, to that change and growth which is the basis for all things worshipped.

The real worth of the Cretan artist relates to the spirit that animates his best examples. Not so accurately realistic nor yet so symbolically concrete or abstract as his Egyptian neighbor—who likewise painted people, cats, birds, fowl, and weeds—the Cretan artist provides a visual epithet of the movement inherent in his subject and of the quality that makes him alive. He gives substance to the manner in which flowers withstand the elements, in which nature preys and resists in order to live. The Cretan picture is of something happening, of transformation. Therefore it is the opposition of bird to the wind, the priming of youth for the leap, and the unfurling of tendrils with energy. Nothing is static. This is life itself—physical. Never before and seldom after has it been shown so well that we sense its union with all creation.

The Cretan's chief artifact, the dwelling, has been restored by the archaeologist to demonstrate in a Williamsburg way an ancient civilization. His palaces are the first of which we possess substantial remains. The Cretan built less formally and with even less appreciation for aesthetic nuances than his southern and eastern neighbors. His life was in the open court rather than in the cloister and hall. He embellished his home, inside and out, with brilliancy. He gave us indoor-outdoor architecture of considerable potential. And through his art he projects a sense of active life.

Greece

At this point, and for the first time with respect to any well-defined culture, our attention shifts to mainland Greece. From the middle of the third millennium and growing in importance for almost 1500 years, the Peloponnesus, that portion of the peninsula below the Isthmus of Corinth, appears to have been controlled by an association of small city states which formed an aristocratic, patriarchal, feudal society, although not at all of the political significance of the empires to the east and south.

Ethnically these Helladic Greeks were probably a mixture of a small percentage of paleolithic stock, plus the neolithic (Pelasgic peoples) and bronze-age infiltrations from the east, and the bronze bearers from the northeast, the Achaean Greeks. Reviewing the golden masks of their warriors as seen at Mycenae, we recognize a stocky, broad-headed type, very different from the dolichocephalic heads in the frescoes of Crete.

Extensive excavations at several Greek sites, including those of Mycenae and its neighbor, Tiryns, as well as of Pylos, where the linear script B, the earliest European writing, was located, indicate little that is at variance with the epic Homer

wrote, about the exploits of the Achaean heroes. One must guard against taking the tales of the great bard as being necessarily a true picture of conditions that antedated his life by about 500 years. Homer's society was not that of the men whose tale he told, and what he narrates must inevitably have been colored by his own times (as was Shakespeare's writing about King Lear). Therefore, although the agreement between these tales and the archaeological data is rewarding, it is interesting to note differences.

Both in Crete and in mainland Greece archaeology has disclosed treasure troves. On the mainland they are associated with grave circles, chamber tombs, and more than eighty tholos (round-domed) sepulchres. They embrace about 500 years following 1600 B.C. In addition to their contents, the tholos tombs are famous because of their corbeled arch construction. The corbeled arch is not a true arch; it is one in which projecting beams or stones support superimposed loads by continuing extension until the final gap is closed (Figure 2.1). These tombs are frequently called beehive tombs, among which the Treasury of Atreus is famous and that at Dendra is the only one whose contents have remained unscathed.

With respect to palaces, archaeology indicates that those of early Greece were highly fortified and that they were built as lofty citadels for purposes of defense (see frontispiece). A community of smaller unfortified buildings clustered nearby. At Mycenae the largest walls (Late Helladic, 1550–1150 B.C.) with the famous Lion Gates were extended to include some of them. In the Odyssey, which tells of the journey of an Achaean warrior returning after the siege of Troy to his home on an island off the west coast of Greece, Homer describes the abode of the swineherd who has acted as caretaker for his lord during the latter's absence. It shows the type of complex within which the Greeks, of whatever social level, lived.

. . . Odysseus fared forth from the haven by the north track, up the wooded country and through the heights, where Athene had showed him he would find the goodly swineherd, who cared most for his substance of all the thralls [slaves] that goodly Odysseus had gotten. Now

39

he found him sitting at the vestibule of his house, where his courtyard was builded high, in the place of wide prospect; a great court it was and fair, with a free range around it. This the swineherd had builded for himself, and his mistress and the old man Laertes knew not of it. With stones from the quarry had he builded it and coped it with a fence of white-thorn, and he had split an oak to the dark core, and without he had driven staves the whole length on either side set thick and close; and within he had made twelve styes hard by one another to be beds for the swine. . . .[3]

Here we see a slave population living in modest independence somewhere outside the domain of the master in a building similar in concept to the royal palace—an enclosed court, with a separate stone dwelling and cubicles along a wall.

In relation to the dwelling of the swineherd a socioartistic fact is demonstrated. In a feudal society of small landholdings, as represented by the hegemony of the Achaean Greeks, there is not the extreme separation of the classes that occurs in large imperial countries. This parity in earlier cultures is evident in their building arts in which, except in the matter of size, the homes of the rich and the poor do not greatly differ. As social divisions are magnified, a building form, which was held in common during more democratic days, may be abandoned by the aristocracy, yet remain with a humbler class and possibly put to a different use: the round hut of the chieftain is preserved in the granary of the peasant; the fortuitous and pragmatic planning of the early palace remains in the later cottage; the native construction with indigenous materials is seen in the provinces long after the regal city is dressed in marble and perhaps in foreign styles. Thus often the loveliest and most unaffected of a country's native architecture is passed by unheralded. This is the price that history pays for innovation, which is costly in materials and skills. Occasionally a culture, like that at the time of the English Tudors, could lift a homespun style into the realm of the architectural great merely because a wealthy English gentry maintained that closeness to the soil from which vernacular building had sprung.

To return to Greece, the *Palace at Tiryns*, excavated by the German archaeologist Kurt Müller, was reputedly the home of the fictional hero Heracles (Figure 2.19). Its plan is merely a variant on the typical. It was approached by a gate and passage that lay along the city's walls. Two large, open courtyards, entered through propylaea, led to the megaron proper. In Achaean practice the megaron preserves its ancient identity as a family or living hall, the nucleus of the northern European home. It stands separate and is not incorporated by common party walls with other sections of the complex. Although formal in its own plan, the megaron is not necessarily located on a central property axis.

The megaron is approached through a two-columned portico, the *prodomos*. Two pillars (called when so arranged *in antis*) stand against the side walls, which project as far as the front of the portico. There is no indication as yet that any visual refinements of the trabeated architecture were attempted. The prodomos leads by three doorways to a vestibule, from the rear of which one central door opens to the inner reception room, in the center of which is a hearth which is always surrounded by four columns. This is often spoken of as the place where the mistress sat with her handmaidens. A side door leads from the vestibule to the bath. At Tiryns the floor in this bathroom was one block of limestone with dimensions of 10 by 13 ft.

During the eighties of the last century the Greek archaeologist Chrestos Tsountas excavated the fictional home of Agamemnon at Mycenae. Here the plan is less complicated but similar to Tiryns. The inner hall measures 28 by 42 ft.

When the Helladic palace had two courts, the first was more generally used for foregatherings, sports, and business. The important second court was the *aule*, and in it was the altar to Zeus on which all ceremonial sacrifices were made. Off the aule are numerous rooms or *thalamoi* which opened onto a pillared walkway, known only in the late Greek (Hellenistic) times as a *peristyle* or many-columned space. It is thought on evidence from the Homeric poems that these shelters were the private rooms for the household. The thalamos for the lord and lady may have been in a more secluded spot. The aule was certainly the place where guests slept, quite out in the open, with bedding supplied from the host's stores.

The structure of these Achaean buildings was

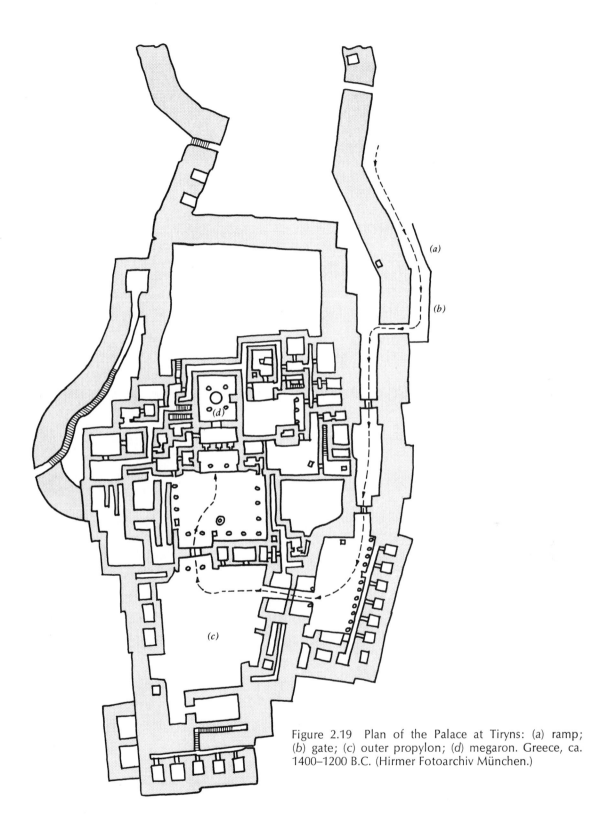

Figure 2.19 Plan of the Palace at Tiryns: (a) ramp; (b) gate; (c) outer propylon; (d) megaron. Greece, ca. 1400–1200 B.C. (Hirmer Fotoarchiv München.)

cyclopean stone in the lower courses and mud brick above. There is some evidence at Tiryns of wooden reinforcement, as in Anatolia. Thresholds were likewise lithic, despite the constant Homeric allusion to them as "ashen." The doors, if made of wood, were embossed with metal. They were double opening, rotating on pin hinges within frames that are still in upright position. Roofs are thought to have been flat and the interiors were lighted either by light wells or clerestory windows.

That the interiors of these mainland palaces were similar to those of Crete is a fairly accurate guess. Frescoes and painted floors offer such familiar scenes as bull leaping, dolphins, octopi, and processionals. At Tiryns alabaster slabs suggest that the inner propylaeum was adorned with a frieze done in the late Cretan style with borders of elongated rosettes interspersed with vertical stripes.

These Greek citadels somehow make a strong impression on all of us, although this may be due to the arduous climb necessary to reach their portals and it is certainly enriched by the "wide prospect" of Homer's tale. From this vantage point it is possible to look far, to imagine the race of hardy warriors as members of a direct, uncomplicated civilization not yet psychoanalyzed by such classical writers as Aeschylus, Sophocles, and Euripides—to visualize them enjoying a gracious manner of existence (by Homer's count) and possessing an incipient reasoned sense of justice and right, however primitive it may appear to us. From these heights we can see the first real conflict with more ancient eastern cultures projected. Western life will descend from here in the Argolid, down through the centuries, until, reaching a broader sea, it creates a less provincial world.

FURNITURE

Types

Except for Egyptian tomb furniture, which has been preserved because of the dry climate, our knowledge of ancient work must come from secondary sources, such as fragments, statues, models, seals, reliefs, paintings on walls and pottery, and written inventories. Although few furniture types are indicated, all were carefully developed, with some small evidence of change over an extensive period.

Construction

Our knowledge of early furniture techniques comes almost exclusively from Egypt; therefore we begin there. The major material used in Egyptian furniture was wood, which was often embossed or encased in precious metal. Frequently this coating is all that remains intact and occasionally it has been so well preserved that, on discovery, it could be refilled with plastic wood to reproduce the original shape. Ivory likewise served not only for plaques inset with precious stones or faience, but also as complete furniture pieces.

Wood veneering with its partner skill, inlay, was much in favor. Veneers as we know them from Egypt might be $1/4$ in. thick and were at first attached with pegs but later adhered by glue. One of the Tutankhamun chests contained 33,000 pieces of wood glued together as veneer.[4]

Excellent craftsmanship in wood joinery appears early and nearly all the standard methods were known. The difficult *mortise and tenon joint*, in which a projection in one piece fits tightly into a concavity in the next, was in use by the second millennium. It was sometimes aided by clever manipulation of leather thonging.

Finishes are not so easily identified because of deterioration and ambiguity of nomenclature in relation to composition. Much furniture through the ages was undoubtedly left in its natural state. We do not know to what extent oils, gums, resins, and waxes were used, but varnish is verified in Egyptian work by the eighteenth dynasty.

Paint was applied as a means of simulating materials, adding color, and depicting scenes. It was tempera over a coat of gesso. Gold leaf was also used.

Carving was widely practiced. Whether the turning lathe was known is a matter of dispute. Bending of wood is another process of debatable origin, but certain shapes suggest this method.

Both turning and bending were common by classical times. Indeed, by any count we must acknowledge the expertise of the craftsman at so distant a date.

Egyptian Furniture

It is a pleasure to study Egyptian furniture because of the numerous extant examples, because of the clear illustrations that have descended through tomb painting and models, because of its incorporation in seated statues, for its symbolism, and for its resemblance to counterparts today. Archaeology in Egypt has unearthed the remains of the world's oldest known wooden furniture, which are dated at the beginning of the third millennium B.C. Even at so early a time the extant fragments are well crafted.

The furniture of the Old Kingdom (2686–2181 B.C.) is represented by the grave finds of Queen Hetepheres in the Great Pyramid at Giza (Figure 2.20). The crypt that contained her belongings was discovered in 1925 by Dr. Reisner on an expedition from Harvard University and the Boston Museum of Fine Arts; hence replicas are in the latter institution and Egypt retains the originals. The Queen's furniture, restorable because of its thick coating of gold, consists of one armchair—the oldest chair in existence—a carrying chair, a bed canopy, and a demountable bed with headrest, together with the aforementioned box with bed curtains. These pieces from so early a tomb are representative of similar ones constructed over the next thousand years.

Tutankhamun, of the New Kingdom Eighteenth Dynasty, was the young son-in-law of Akhenaten and was not yet of age when laid to rest with all his grave equipment in 1352 B.C. In 1922 his tomb in the Valley of the Kings near Thebes was discovered by the English Carnavon expedition under Howard Carter. Along with fabulous articles of jewelry and household artifacts, more than twenty major furniture pieces were recovered, including the famous throne of the pharaoh (Figure 2.21). Most are now in the Cairo Museum. As would be expected, the Tutankhamun furniture exhibits a high standard of elaboration and its ornamentation shows the mark of the naturalism of the Akhenaten art revolution.

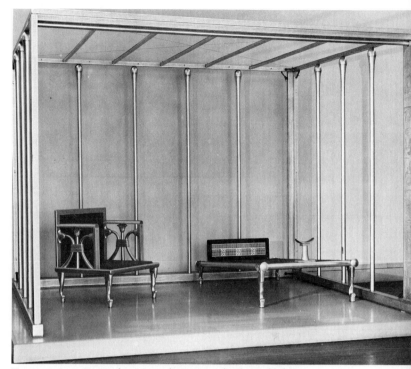

Figure 2.20 Reproduction of canopy, bed, and chair of Queen Hetepheres I. [Slope is toward the footboard], fourth dynasty, ca. 2500 B.C. Museum of Fine Arts, Boston. Originals are in Egypt in the Cairo Museum. (Courtesy, Museum of Fine Arts, Boston.)

Egyptian chairs and beds are low slung, possibly because of the short stature of the ancient people. Furniture legs often terminate in animal feet, raised on what is known as a *beaded cylinder*. Early chairs show a preference for the bull's hoof and later ones, for a feline foot. In Egypt it was customary to orient the animal's legs in the direction in which the beast would walk. This sort of representation undoubtedly has a symbolic connotation, harking back to the time when animal spirits inhabited the trees or when anthropomorphic gods were worshiped. It is noteworthy, however, that in bed furniture this orientation of the animal legs is toward the slightly higher head of the piece rather than toward the foot.

Finials on the protruding sides of the seats frequently terminate in lions' heads or the head of Hathor (the cow goddess) or Thoeris (the deity with hippopotamus features). Stretchers encase an interesting variety of symbolic material, often

43

Figure 2.21 Chair back rest, Golden Throne of Tutankhamun, from his tomb in Thebes, Valley of the Kings, eighteenth dynasty, ca. 1350 B.C. The scene illustrated shows the sun-disk shining on the anointing of the young king by his wife. Wood base inlaid with faience and lapus lazuli against a background of sheet gold. Cairo Museum, Egypt. (The Metropolitan Museum of Art, Photograph by Harry Burton.)

executed in ivory. We see the falcon of the god Horus, the misshapen little god Bes, patron deity of birth, the vulture deity Nekhbet, and the sacred cobra, the *uraei*. The sun disk, of course, appears on Akhenaten's furniture as it did later on that of Louis XIV of France. The design of the intertwined plant represents the alliance of northern and southern Egypt joined in the center by the symbol for "union." The sign for "life," the *ankh*, and the emblem for "dominion," the *was*, sur-

mounting the *neb*, meaning "all," appear on the handsome little toilet chest in the Tutankhamun find (see Figure 2.23).

Whereas early chairs had an uncompromisingly straight back it was later changed to one that, supported by back struts, was canted toward a curved seat. The back itself becomes rounded by the time of the New Kingdom. This progress toward standards of comfort is fairly universal in the history of furniture design.

Stools, the little brothers of chairs, antedate the chair with back and arms in early cultures. At first, both in Egypt and Sumeria, they have a square box shape and supporting struts that may be lattices of rush or reed or small upright pieces of wood. Egyptian U-shaped underpinnings may indicate wood bending. The saltires, or folding stools, had one interesting version in which ducks' beaks grasp the runners firmly in position. Another late form has concave curved legs like those the Greeks perfected in their klismos chair. This suave curve was favored in Egypt and may be indicative of a national tranquil disposition. Stool legs often joined the seat rail in a graceful transitional line.

Small tables surmounted with torus or round molding and cavetto cornices exhibit the same bracketing as stools (Figure 2.22). A small three-legged table may possess splayed legs of rounded

Figure 2.22 Wooden table from Thebes, seventeenth to eighteenth dynasty. Height, 32.3 cm, length, 63.5 cm, width, 31 cm. Metropolitan Museum of Art, New York. (The Metropolitan Museum of Art, Gift of Lord Carnarvon, 1914.)

shape. Large tables were not used in ancient cultures because the custom was to serve on small individual ones. Small stands for holding vessels are frequently seen.

The bed and canopy of Hetepheres were engineered to collapse for travel (Figure 2.20). The frame surrounding the pallet was ingeniously constructed with mortise and tenon joints lined with copper for easy dismounting. Copper curtain hooks appear on the inner frame, and the legs were attached with leather thongs for untying. Decoration was a colorful incised pattern. Some New Kingdom beds were extendable and collapsible.

The wealthy Egyptian slept with a hard headrest of ivory or encrusted wood. There was no headboard and the paneled piece that took its place was in reality a footboard.

Mention should also be made of the funerary couches of animal design depicted in tomb paintings and found in actuality in Tutankhamun's tomb. Noted by artists who accompanied the Napoleonic Egyptian campaigns, they had strong influence on early nineteenth-century furniture design.

Chests of various sizes were among the equipment of tomb and household (Figure 2.23). They were flat, rounded, and gable-topped. Frequently an analogy with the curved roof of the symbol for the sacred kiosk suggests significant contents.

Upholstery of loose cushions is illustrated on much ancient Egyptian furniture. Reeding and rush seats are an alternative.

Near East Furniture

There is no early furniture extant from Mesopotamia. In seals and reliefs, however, we gain a fairly accurate picture of the character of the most ancient Near Eastern work, which likewise had a history reaching back to the beginning of the third millennium B.C.

As in Egypt, the stool with boxlike proportions comes first and appears to have strengthening supports that may be variously interpreted as reed or wood.

Chairs with rudimentary backs appear by ca. 2500 B.C., and the curved back and roll-over top (the latter a typically eastern feature) appear by

Figure 2.23 Chest from tomb of Tutankhamun, Thebes, Valley of the Kings. Interior divided into sixteen compartments, eighteenth dynasty. Wood, partly gilded, partly ivory veneered; shod with silver. Height, 42 cm, length, 48 cm, width, 44.5 cm. Cairo Museum, Egypt. (The Metropolitan Museum of Art, Photograph by Harry Burton.)

the time of Sargon I (2370 B.C.). The *cabriole* or animal leg is seen in furniture shown on the ivories found in the royal tombs at Ur (2600 B.C.). In the Near East the predominant foot is the cloven one of the bull (note that the front and rear legs often proceed in opposite directions), although the claw foot is also present.

Later furniture exhibits greater elaboration. Even bronze, which is found in late Near Eastern furniture, has a semblance of lathe-turning, suggesting that wood was so treated. One notable style of foot is a replica of an inverted pine cone, a common emblem in eastern iconography. A leaf border simulates a ruffle and undoubtedly is the origin of *gadrooning* in later European development. Carving in the form of volutes, stylized florals, and animals is found. One specialized example of double volutes becomes in later Greek furniture a pattern in which the mass of the leg is carved away at the inner section, thereby minimizing its bulk. This kind of patterning is related to the double-C scrolls on European Baroque pieces and indicates a similar busy, energetic culture. Rams' heads as finials of chair side rails are uniquely Near Eastern.

Figure 2.24 Stone relief carving from palace at Nineveh. Assurbanipal and his queen at feast, showing couch, throne chair, tables, and footstool, ca. 650 B.C. British Museum, London. (Reproduced by Courtesy of the Trustees of the British Museum.)

The only extant examples of Mesopotamian furniture (entire pieces or parts) are confined to the period of Assyrian ascendancy. These owe their survival to the fact that they are bronze. Assyrian types are illustrated as well by stone carvings such as the one depicting King Assurbanipal (668–626 B.C.) and his queen at dinner, which validates the oriental custom of reclining while eating (Figure 2.24). Her majesty nevertheless is seated quite properly in an armchair.

Near Eastern furniture, with the possible excep-

tion of some found on Akkadian reliefs, shows a much greater rigidity of form than the corresponding Egyptian. Even in, or perhaps one should say especially in, Assyrian times this stiffness remains a notable feature. Likewise, although Near Eastern tables and beds were low by our standards, the seating furniture and accompanying tables often appear to be elevated on a platform designed possibly to give additional importance to the sitter. Some chairs have their accompanying footstools. The ingratiating curves of Egyptian work are not to be seen.

Cretan and Greek Furniture

Recent excavations reveal a few extant pieces of Cretan and Helladic furniture, but evidence is largely from terra cottas, miniature bronzes, and glyptics. The Linear B tablets describe some pieces largely for the purpose of mercantile inventory. Homer, of course, is profuse in detail. On the basis of the limited evidence it is not easy to see any connective trend between Helladic and classic Greek furniture, although a suave outline and, on the other hand, the use of deep turning are suggestions of two major persistent tendencies.

The intact stone throne chair from Knossos is, however, an exceptional and phenomenal piece (Figure 2.25). Its back is high, its edges are undulating curves that are typically Cretan, its legs form a smooth-pointed arch, and its straight, uncompromising overall rigidity is notable; all of

Figure 2.25 The Throne Room in the Palace of Knossos, Crete, ca. 1700–1500 B.C. (Hirmer Fotoarchiv München.)

this says clearly—early, luxuriant, and aristocratic. Just a little sharpening of contours, breaking of cymas, and cant to the back, and the France of Versailles is upon us.

TEXTILES

Near East

We know little about the early textiles of the areas and times covered by this chapter. In the royal cemetery at Ur, where the graves of the earliest rulers of Sumeria were discovered, Queen Shubad and her attendants had been interred in long-sleeved gowns, a fact that was deduced from the imprint of woven goods around their wrists. The preserved matting in which the bodies were wrapped is testimony to the fact that, before spinning, natural fibers were interlaced to produce a cloth of sorts. Representations of dress on very early Mesopotamian statuettes indicate an advanced textile vocabulary.

Figure 2.26 Vertical loom as depicted on the wall of the tomb of Khnumhotep at Beni Hasan: (a) warp beam; (b) weft threads; (c) warp threads; (d) heddle; (e) weft rod; (f) beater; (g) finished cloth; (h) breast beam. Egypt, twelfth dynasty, ca. 2000 B.C. (Drawing of a wall painting in the collection of the Metropolitan Museum of Art. Adapted from Ethel Lewis, *The Romance of Textiles,* Copyright 1937 by Macmillan Publishing Co., Inc., Renewed 1965 by Ralph Hammond.)

Representations of woven textiles also appear on the Near Eastern reliefs, not only as clothing but as upholstery, which often shows fringed edging and occasionally what appears to be embroidery. In the mural decoration at the palace at Mari (eighteenth century B.C.) a fringed and patterned textile is displayed as a wall hanging. There is just the possibility that this might illustrate one of the earliest tapestries (a weave in which the integral colored weft creates pattern—further described in Chapter 5). A fourteenth-century B.C. Egyptian textile has a narrow ornament of hieroglyphics that is tapestry woven.

The Egyptian was highly proficient in textile arts. In one predynastic tomb at El-Gebelein, near Thebes, a painted textile was discovered, a remarkable example, in its description of a hippopotamus hunt, of the ability of the early Egyptian to portray natural objects.

In Egypt the dry climate is kind to preservation. In the tomb of Queen Hetepheres boxes of the finest linen intended for bed canopy and curtains were located near her demountable bedstead. The looms on which they were woven were evidently still of primitive form but a vertical loom, with weights to hold down the warp, soon evolved, followed by another of horizontal design with two fixed warp rods. A vertical loom is depicted in an Egyptian tomb at Beni Hasan (ca. 2000 B.C., Figure 2.26). No other improve-

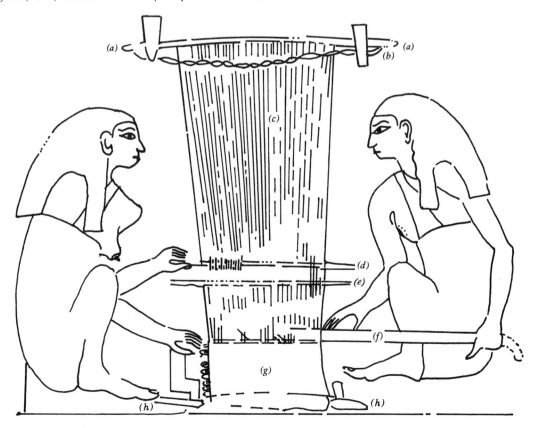

Figure 2.27 Pazyryk carpet. South Siberia. Time of the Persian Achaemenid Dynasty, 600–300 B.C. Width, 183 cm, length, 198 cm. Wool. Hermitage Museum, Leningrad. (Courtesy of the Hermitage Museum.)

ment except that of the *leash stick* inserted between the even-numbered warps and individual *heddles* to operate the odd warps occurred for many years.

In 1947 the first elaborate fabrics of the ancient Near East were discovered in a cache in a Scythian chieftain's grave high on the south Si-

berian steppes near *Pazyryk*. On stylistic evidence they are dated back to the time of the Persian Achaemenids. In one chamber an embroidered felt 12 ft long and a silk horsecloth that may have been Chinese were found. There were saddles and saddle trappings, all of which had been preserved for 2400 years in the ice.

Two small fragments of woven tapestry were most significant not only because they are early examples of tapestry technique but because the lions that are woven into the cloth are exact counterparts of others on a frieze in Darius's palace at Persepolis.

One article in the treasure was a wool carpet measuring 6 ft wide by 6½ long, which is now in the Hermitage Museum in Leningrad (Figure 2.27). The central field contains *quatrefoils* in Assyrian style, edged by a line of griffins and surrounded by a border of grazing stags, followed by a row of horsemen on plumed steeds with braided manes. The saddles are Achaemenid, the riders, dressed in the snug breeches of the Medes. Undoubtedly the nomad leader and chief had traveled far from Persia over the northern route into China. The Leningrad carpet is the oldest pile carpet in the world; in fact, about 2000 years older than any other.

CERAMICS

Near East

Credit for the earliest Near Eastern ceramics of any considerable importance must go to those found in Hassuna, a community in upper Meso-

Figure 2.28   Tell Halaf pottery. North Mesopotamian site in Khabur valley. Middle of the fourth millennium, B.C. Depth, ca. 8 in. British Museum, London. (Reproduced by Courtesy of the Trustees of the British Museum.)

Figure 2.29   Al-Ubaid pottery. Southern Mesopotamia. Sumeria, middle of the fourth millennium B.C. British Museum, London. (Reproduced by Courtesy of the Trustees of the British Museum.)

potamia (ca. 5600–5200 B.C.). Here pottery vessels with painted and engraved ornamentation were found. For our purposes we travel up the Euphrates River valley and down almost two millennia to view the pottery of *Tell Halaf,* which is especially notable for its painted decoration (Figure 2.28). The Halaf body is high-fired in good kilns. Halaf ware is painted, at first monochrome but later polychrome, in designs seemingly inspired by textile figures. Placed in bands or on a crosshatched field, the patterns possess a clarity and precision that approaches not only an elegant but a dainty and almost feminine character. V. Gordon Childe, the distinguished archaeologist of European civilization, speaks of the primitive potter as decorating "her products."[5] Halaf pottery would suggest that this was true.

The pottery of lower Mesopotamia achieved superior quality after the arrival of the Sumerians. One of the most noteworthy varieties is known as al-Ubaid (ca. 2600 B.C.) ware (Figure 2.29). (It must be realized that the names assigned to a certain classification of products are generally quite recent and often due to the fact that examples have been found in archaeological excavations on a site of that name. The ware itself may be found in a wider territory.) In ornamentation the al-Ubaid bowls in the British Museum exhibit geometrics of the usual prehistoric stamp.

Figure 2.30 Beaker from Susa. Iran, fourth millennium B.C. Painted fired pottery. Height, 28.5 cm. Louvre, Paris. (Musée du Louvre, Cliché des Musées Nationaux—Paris.)

A talent for handling animal life in a stylized and decorative way is evident. Here are remarkable examples of the native fauna, the long-horned ibexes, the deer, the goat, the swift saluki, and water birds, with very occasionally the introduction of the human figure. Here the ability to represent with quick, sure, straight, or full-curved strokes the outstanding qualities of a particular animal—the strength of cattle, the speed of the bird, and the compelling directional sense of the dog—is noted. These patterns also correlate with the vessel's shape. Persian art will reenter the orbit of European decorative arts at several later periods. The Susan bowls illustrate its best qualities. Here we have an elegant, restrained, formal appeal that has not lost vigor to an overly refined decorative sense.

We return again to Sumeria and the painted decoration on al-Ubaid ware. The patterns are not tectonically compatible with the vessel, like Susa ware, nor textural like the Halafian. Indeed they show a curious cross of the two as the mark of a prosperous and activist society.

During the bronze age, which largely corresponds to the early historic periods, the beautiful painted wares of the prehistoric potter were abandoned, their place having been taken by vessels of metal. Rough terra cotta and plain burnished wares were the rule for the utensils of daily life. The variety of forms was greatly increased. Grave goods included an astounding variety of vessels in theomorphic forms, evidently ritualistic.

A most significant development was the use of glaze, which is one of the most important contributions of the Near East to ceramic art. Its beginnings, however, belong to the history of ceramic art in Egypt (which follows immediately in this chapter). Its most important phase develops on later pottery of the Near East and on the porcelain of the Orient. Therefore we must postpone much of the story of glazes until later chapters.

However, the patterns often contain the exuberant curved line and are not tightly intermeshed like those of upper Mesopotamia.

To understand this Mesopotamian pottery it may be profitable to retrace our steps to Iran and specifically to Susa in its western territory. One of the world's finest painted potteries is found in those unbelievable vases from the deepest excavations at Susa of the fourth millennium (Figure 2.30). Even in these protohistoric times we note how the complex heritage of Iran affected the genius of a people. Iran stands at a prominent gate between nomadic life on the steppes of Asia to the north and agriculture on the plateaus to the south. This geographic position is indelibly impressed on the painted wares.

Egypt

The south door to Europe is Africa, particularly the land of the Nile. Predating Egyptian dynastic history, this area had a protohistoric time that is defined by the archeologists as extending from the fifth to the third millennium. Although the earliest handmade pottery of Egypt dates back to what is called the Tasian culture before 4000 B.C. and is well and truly potted, shape development and decoration (painted and/or incised) await at least the later Badarian culture of the mid-fifth millennium B.C. (names of prehistoric cultures derive from archaeological sites). The Egyptian frequently blackened the inner rim of his pots, possibly for aesthetic reasons or because of an inadequate knowledge of firing. He was slow to learn to use the potter's wheel, which did not appear in Egypt until the second dynasty, ca. 2980 B.C. In Mesopotamia, however, it is found several hundred years earlier.

The forms of this pottery progress in complexity as they did in that of the Near East. Carination appears early and rippled effects may occur at contour breaks. Handles of the lug variety appear, but the Egyptian rarely favored the elaborate shapes, the spouted ewers, and the vessels on pottery rings of the later Eastern wares.

The painted ceramics of this prehistoric era—generally white on red or purple on buff clay, according to the character of the river clay—deserve particular notice (Figure 2.31). They indicate that at his freest and best the Egyptian could depict motifs abstracted from both sea and land with a childlike appreciation for rhythmic repetition. But he did not yet integrate decorative design with the structural shape of the vessel. Painting, however, like elaboration in shape, was not characteristic of the long history of Egyptian pottery, most of which was undecorated. As in the Near East, with the advent of wealth and the availability of metals, ceramics were relegated to common utility and precious metals were favored by the rich. Only during the eighteenth dynasty, on the wares of Tell-el-Amarna (on jars covered with light blue coloring with details picked out in red and black) do designs, mostly floral patterns, reappear.

Glazing

The glazing of ceramics is a tale that introduces the study of glass. To prehistoric Egyptian Badarian civilization must go the credit for the

Figure 2.31 Painted protohistoric pottery vessel. Egypt, Gerzean culture, 4000–3200 B.C. The interpretation of such a typical design is conjectural. The wavy lines are probably water, the boat is clear, but the significance of its plumed tree is not. Nor do we understand the significance of the long-legged birds. British Museum, London. (Reproduced by Courtesy of the Trustees of the British Museum.)

introduction of *glazing*. Unrefined clays are porous and need a covering to make them watertight. For this purpose—glaze.

Glaze is a form of glass. True glass is made from sand (the silicon content) plus an alkali added for flux (usually sodium or potassium). In fine glasses other ingredients are included to add such qualities as hardness, clarity, color. The mixture can be melted and annealed (gradually cooled) to a clear amorphous plastic which has those properties of light reflection and refraction that we associate with glass.

Glaze, as distinct from glass, is used over some other material for the overt purpose above stated and for the additional aesthetic rewards that derive from its nature. Because it is used in conjunction with a base, glazing presents unique problems; for instance, it must fire with the body to prevent blistering, crawling, or crazing.

Egyptian glass and glaze both have a relatively high sodium content which enabled them to be fused at the low temperatures of the early pottery fires. A glaze of this composition, however, will adhere only to a body that in turn is highly silicious. Thus the first glazes were applied to semiprecious stones, such as steatite or quartz, which fulfilled the necessary conditions. This is the nature of the small Egyptian beads, the color of which is so frequently the beautiful blue-green that results from the firing of the copper salt malachite which is present.

During the next prehistoric epoch, called the Amratian, the Egyptian invented a silicious ceramic body about whose chemical nature there has been some conjecture. It is thought to have been a mixture of ground quartz (silicon) and soda. To this the Egyptian glaze would adhere. Glaze and body constituted the small amulets of the period. Egyptian glaze is known as *alkaline glaze* because of the relatively high percentage of alkali in comparison with the acidic silicate that is present in the glaze and body. It could not be used, as could the later Mesopotamian *lead glaze,* on an object of ordinary pottery clay, which would be fired at a higher temperature. In several rooms in the Saqqara pyramid complex of the third Egyptian dynasty, the walls are lined with lovely blue-green tiles. Glaze and body are presumably of the Egyptian formula.

Small Egyptian glazed pieces are commonly known as *faience,* taking this name from the town of Faenza in Italy, where glazed ware was produced much later. To our eyes the twelfth dynasty faience hippopotamus with painted floral designs covering his lumbersome carcass indicates a native sense of humor, but to the craftsman the patterns may only have represented shadows falling on a huge receptive surface.

Lead glazing was used from an early time in the Near East seen in the lead glazing that is found on Achaemenid brick reliefs at Babylon, Susa, Khorsabad, and Persepolis, and, indeed, excavations at prehistoric sites in Elam, which is in the western plains of Persia, indicate that lead glazing was used as far back as the late second millennium. Lead glaze is the type of glaze most characteristic of Near Eastern work. Lead glaze (like the alkaline Egyptian glaze) is a type of glass, in which the amount of lead is increased and the percentage of soda decreased to form a coating that can be fired at the temperature required for

ordinary pottery clays. It does not require a highly silicious substance for its base. The addition of oxide of tin to a lead base renders it white and opaque. It can then be used to cover unsightly clays.

Cretan Ceramics

Minoan ceramics present the most advanced art of the Aegean bronze-age potter. Before considering their significance, mention should be made of the fact that at Knossos from the Middle Minoan period and thereafter there was a factory that made Egyptian faience or alkaline-glaze frit ware. Vestiges of the industry were discovered in the artisans' quarters of the palace. (Here was found a famous faience piece known as the *town mosaic* because on it were pictures of town houses that confirmed the idea that they were made of brick, were multiple-storied, and had doors and windows, flat roofs, and penthouses. Inasmuch as the mosaic was contemporary with early New Kingdom work in Egypt, it is evident that city architecture was similar in both countries.)

Two famous faience figurines, probably representing a snake goddess and a votive priestess, respectively, were located in a depository in the Knossos palace. A similar figure in gold and ivory is in the Boston Museum of Fine Arts.

Faience, however, was an imported and isolated technique in Crete. The indigenous Early Minoan wares were a continuation of the neolithic buff-bodied pottery which had simple designs in red or brown luster paint—the *dark-on-light* goods.

In the Middle Minoan period Cretan potters began their *light-on-dark* style. Technically this was accomplished by placing patterns in light tones, with frequent use of white, on an even coat of black paint, possibly similar to the liquid clay used by the Greeks (see Chapter 3). The color range progressed to a polychrome yellow, orange, and red. Patterns changed from early geometrics to spirals and more natural forms. Near the slope of Mount Ida, close by the palace of Phaestos, a large cave tomb was found, which has lent its name, *Kamares,* to the best of this polychrome pottery. Much is thin-walled and comes close to vitrification. Some pieces, cup-shaped, are known as the *eggshell cups.*

Toward the end of the Middle Minoan and continuing into Late Minoan design tends to be exclusively white. Ornament develops that freedom which creates a surface spiral, such as we see on the lovely Knossan lily vase. In the Cretan middle-class settlement of Gournia, of all unexpected places, there was found one of the classics of ceramic design, the *octopus jar* (Figure 2.32). This used black paint on a buff ground in the older tradition. It is a freely conceived pattern such as no one but a natural artist could have executed, with swift curves epitomizing the organisms of the sea.

Near the end of palace culture designs become more formal and stereotyped, probably in response to Achaean influence. Many esteem these later forms (often named the *Palace Style*) because they are more tectonic and possibly more Grecian. But this was not the genius of the Cretan. The flora becomes foreign to his observation. Life has left the creation and it is ordinary.

Figure 2.32 The Octopus Jar. Gournia, Crete, ca. 1600 B.C. Height, ca. 8 in. Archaeological Museum, Herakleion, Crete. (Hirmer Fotoarchiv München.)

Greek Ceramics

Although a good gray-bodied pottery (named by archaeologists *Minyan ware*) with shapes that forecast later Greek classics seems to have spread over Greece with the coming of the Achaeans, the later, more highly decorated pottery vases found in Mycenae are stylistically allied to Crete. One is decorated with horizontal bands and border representing geese and embracing a pattern of light and dark swirling over the surface. There are other finds, not so easily pigeonholed, such as the *warrior vase.* Here a band of soldiers carrying the unique Achaean *figure-eight shields* are marching off to battle, leaving a weeping woman behind. These bearded, pointed-nose men seem more like Asia Minor types than Greek, but their formal arrangement in procession heralds the earliest Greek pieces of the next epoch.

GLASS

We have discussed the origin of glass when it was in reality merely an alkaline type of glaze used on the proper compositional body, preeminently an Egyptian development. Undoubtedly the Egyptian craftsman experimented with his medium until he arrived at the point where, because of the more complex nature of his material or the more imaginative use of his talents, he was able to produce objects that were vitric throughout. Calcium may have been added for hardness, boron to regulate viscosity. The Egyptian did not strive particularly for translucency because in his mind he was trying to imitate precious stones, not appreciating that the new material possessed unique values. This mistake of attempting to create something foreign to the nature of the material has been made over and over again in the artistic world.

Egyptian glass, of which we have extant examples from the eighteenth dynasty, was likely to be opaque and was colored to resemble turquoise, carnelian, jade, amethyst, and gold. It could be used only for making small objects because it was shaped by dipping a sandy core into the molten *metal* (the name commonly used

Figure 2.33 Glass amphorista. Egypt. New Kingdom, 1570–1085 B.C. Blue glass with yellow and white insets. Height, 8.3 cm. Metropolitan Museum of Art, New York. (The Metropolitan Museum of Art, Gift of Henry G. Marquand, 1881.)

Figure 2.34 Gold vessels from the Royal Cemetery at Ur. Southern Mesopotamia. ca. 3500–3200 B.C. University Museum, University of Pennsylvania, Philadelphia. (Reproduced by permission of the University Museum, University of Pennsylvania.)

for glass in the flux state) or by winding glass rods (glass that has annealed to a taffylike consistency) around a sandy core. In the latter method one practice was to use threads of variously colored glass on a soft vitric ground. While still pliable the form was elongated by pulling. This created the looped designs of the vessels known as *amphoristas* (Figure 2.33), similar in shape to but smaller in size than the *amphora,* the ancient storage jar. The Egyptians engraved and, more rarely, cut glass. These are the arts of incising a pattern by cutting with a wheel of copper or stone, respectively, after the metal is cold. They later made sheet glass, a technique practiced by the Romans and described in Chapter 4.

STONES, METALS, IVORIES

Many museums show lovely carved stone bowls of alabaster, steatite, and breccia taken from archaeological digs. Alabaster was brought from up-river and sculptured in low relief in southern Mesopotamia.

Early craftsmen possessed surprising expertise in the processing of precious metals—gold (Figure 2.34), silver (Figure 2.35), and sometimes *electrum,* an alloy of gold and silver. They knew how to *cast* their medium; how to do *repoussé,* in which hammering raises a design from below; *chasing,* in which a pattern is pounded on the surface with blunted instruments; *cloissoné,* in which thin metal wires form a pattern; *filigree,* in which openwork is made with wires; and *granulation,* in which a surface is encrusted with metal nodules.

Figure 2.35 Vase of the priest-king Entemena of La-gash. Southern Mesopotamia, ca. 2500 B.C. Silver with bronze base. Height, 35 cm. Louvre, Paris. (Musée du Louvre, cliché des Musées Nationaux—Paris.)

All of the techniques known to advanced work, with the exception of spinning metal plates, were practiced. Among them was the *cire perdue* or lost wax process, in which a model is first made in beeswax; this is covered with clay and heated to allow the melted wax to run out, after which the metal is poured into the cast and cooled. For hollow casting the wax mold is made around a sand core.

Precious metals were often combined with other materials, sometimes running the danger of appearing gauche to modern taste. The goat figures from the Ur necropolis in the British Museum and in the Museum of the University of Pennsylvania are intricate *tours de force* of gold,

silver, lapis lazuli, shell, and sandstone. They evidently served as supports, probably for offering tables.

More important than the precious metals is *copper,* which began to play its role in the advance of civilization around the beginning of the sixth millennium B.C., when it first appeared at Sialk on the Iranian plateau. The earliest copper objects found in Egypt date from the Badarian period of the mid-fifth millennium B.C.

Metallurgy, the refining of metals from their basic ores and the combining of metals by smelting as alloys to obtain desirable qualities, possibly began in a vague center somewhere northeast of the Caspian Sea, where ores abounded. Copper possesses properties of malleability, ductility, and toughness, which made it suitable for many purposes: for household vessels, for covering wooden beams, and as cores for less strong and more expensive materials.

It was not long before prehistoric metallurgists learned to smelt copper from its ores, to refine it, and eventually to combine it with tin and some zinc to form an alloy known as bronze. This possessed greater hardness plus the potential of being formed from the molten state, which ensured its desirability for superior weapons of any shape. In addition, it was possible to cast works of art. (The cast bronze statue of Queen Napirasu from Elam of the fourteenth century B.C., now at the Louvre, is of the incredible height of 1.29 m.) Economic advantage followed close on the heels of metallurgy.

The *age of bronze* is considered to have begun before 3000 B.C. in the Near East and Egypt and to have reached Europe by 2600 B.C. The period when both copper and stones were used for tools represents a transitional development between the neolithic and bronze ages. It is called the *chalcolithic* phase, a name that derives from the Greek word *chalkos*, meaning copper.

From an aesthetic standpoint the most important contribution to bronze art was made by the great kings of the Assyrian nation. This statement takes into consideration the volume of work done for them, the finesse of its execution, and its advanced character in terms of refinement and complexity of design. Bronze was used to enrich a luxurious mode of life—as furniture, as covering for doors, and as table utensils.

55

Fgiure 2.36 Ivory plaque, possibly part of a stool. Nimrud, central Mesopotamia. Ivory inlaid with lapus lazuli and carnelian, partly gilded and partly plated with gold. Height, 10.5 cm. British Museum, London. (Reproduced by Courtesy of the Trustees of the British Museum.)

The use of bronze did not, of course, exclude the use of precious metals, ivories, and stones, either in Egypt or the Near East. Furniture is encased in gold, mounts are of ivory (Figure 2.36) or alabaster, often set with jewels, and precious metals are raised to table plate. Exquisite small objects such as carved ivories, objects saved from the category of knick-knacks by their artistry, objects serving no overt function except to delight made their appearance. The treasures found in King Tutankhamun's tomb in Egypt are undoubtedly the most outstanding collection extant of artifacts made in precious media.

Among all this wealth of materials, however, bronze holds a unique and early place in Mesopotamia that was never quite equaled in Egypt. Bronze, in the early days of its alloyage and near the regions in which it first made its appearance, seems at times to have been more prized than gold or silver. In this category of outstanding bronze pieces the superb bronze bowls (and ivories) found at the Assyrian site at Nimrud must be placed (Figure 2.37). This is the real wealth of the Assyrian court. It is indeed surprising how much of it escaped the vandal, as in Egypt it did the grave and temple robber.

This imperial Mesopotamian art is sophisticated, some of the best ever done. It occurs at the confluence of courses: the forges of the ore country, the chisels of the Phoenician Levant, the imagery and stylizing talents of the steppes, the wealth of empires.

Who created these pieces? A mercantile school of craftsmen such as the ivory workers of Phoenicia or the metallurgists of Urartu? Palace schools whose craftsmen gravitated to the center of demand? Imported laborers whose presence may have been more urgently requested? Sargon II did not boast idly:

> I besieged and conquered the cities of Asdod, Gath, Asdudimmu [Syro-Palestinian towns]: I declared as booty his gods, his wife, his children, all the possessions and treasures of his palace, and also the inhabitants of his land.[6]

Devious are the ways of cross-pollinating art, and by the time of the late bronze age most of them had been practiced.

Persia has been no laggard in the sumptuous quality of its court treasures. Gold vessels in repoussé technique from northern cultures at Hissar and Marlik of the third and second millennia are outstanding. From the Achaemenids we have a magnificent gold cup in the form of a gazelle's head, a fine piece of Persian stylistic art. Gold bowls derived from floral sources also illustrate the Persian genius, and silver articles in the form of animal-shaped handles are prevalent. Many Achaemenid pieces (e.g., bronze horses) show Greek influence.

Popular interest today has been captured by

Figure 2.37 Bronze bowl from Nimrud. Central Mesopotamia, ca. 850 B.C. Depth, ca. 8 in. British Museum, London. (Reproduced by Courtesy of the Trustees of the British Museum.)

Figure 2.38 Scytho-Persian (Luristan) bridle bit with linked mouthpiece, ca. 200 B.C. Bronze. Museum of Fine Arts, Boston. (Courtesy, Museum of Fine Arts, Boston, Maria A. Evans Fund.)

crossed into the Mesopotamian highlands and onto the Anatolian plateau during the third millennium. These tablelands are rich in metals. The Alaca Höyük tombs of this district (2200 B.C.) yielded treasures similar to those of Ur which indicate by their heterogeneous nature that the natives were tradesfolk as well as skilled craftsmen. Recent studies have revealed the importance of the once little-known people of these upland tribes—the Hatti and later the Hurri, Mitanni, and Urarti—as interpolators between the economies of east and west.

In respect to style, the Anatolian kept closely to his Asiatic origins and used the animal motif in many ways. The drinking vessel called a *rhyton*, shaped like the protome (forequarters) of a beast, with a pouring spout at its base, originated (according to Wooley[7]) in Anatolia (Figure 2.39). In the early first millennium some remarkable tall bronze cauldrons and bronze buckets, known as *situla* and using animal-shaped supports, were located within the Gordium tombs. They were made by a people known as the Urarti, late conquerors of a section of the Hittite territory.

Crete and Greece

On the island of Lemnos, situated to the west of Troy and reputedly the home of the lame forge

the Luristan bronzes (Figure 2.38). These pieces, diversified in type, include daggers, axes, symbolic horse trappings, and animal statuettes. They came to light in the mountains of western Iran in Luristan largely as the result of unscientific archaeological excavations. Unfortunately it is difficult for this reason to authenticate them according to precise provenance, to time, and indeed in some cases to validity. A sufficient amount of scholarly work has been done, however, to warrant the statement that at least some of the objects are the creation of the Luristan mountaineers of the Zagros chain. These mountain people were skilled native metallurgists who came in contact with and worked for recent immigrants, the Indo-Iranians, who had descended about the year 1000 B.C. in a new wave from the Eurasian hinterland. These nomad warriors, whose life was on the horse and who thought of wealth in terms of the animals they tamed, herded, and hunted, wanted them perpetuated in effigy, much as the sailor likes pictures of the sea. Many of these pieces have the rhythmic vitality often given to an art near its fountainhead.

The districts of eastern Anatolia associated with such names as Alaca Höyük, Horoztepe, and Kayapinar Höyük are likewise important in any history of Near Eastern metal work. It is likely that trans-Caucasian tribes of metal workers

Figure 2.39 Syro-Hittite rhyton, ca. seventh century B.C. Height, silver section 22.9 cm; gold section, 10.2 cm. Funnel, silver; forepart of bull, gold. British Museum, London. (Reproduced by Courtesy of the Trustees of the British Museum, London.)

Figure 2.40 The Harvester Vase. Found in the Late Minoan tomb at Hagia Triada. Crete, ca. 1500 B.C. Carved steatite. Lower part is restored. Archaeological Museum, Herakleion. (Photo Researchers.)

god Hephaestus, a bronze civilization antedates Troy I (2600 B.C.). The Cyclades and Crete entered early into a bronze technology and by the year 2000 B.C. the mainland citadels showed articles of the new alloy. At that time, however, the treasures of these areas consisted of articles made largely from precious metals. Bronze was favored for the gear of the warrior—shields, swords, and helmets—which were often gold-encrusted and embellished with ivory and agate.

In the specific artifacts that were found during the Achaean era we gain a factual glimpse of the Greeks. Many are the articles of gold in a country not rich in gold ore. Here are rhytons in the form of a lion's head where the lion was not a native beast. Vessels in the shape of stags of the north and bulls of the Argolid appear. One sees the cups, small caskets, and bowls that constitute the amenities of living. Homer enjoys telling of them, narrating how Menelaus gave his guests

> . . . of the gifts, such are treasures stored in my house, I will give the goodliest and greatest of price. I will give the mixing bowl beautifully

wrought; it is all silver, and the lips thereof are finished with gold, the work of Hephaestus.

Again, Nestor gave to Athene the "chalice of gold" described as a two-handled cup. These and many similar objects have suddenly blossomed into reality.

The provenance of these articles may be debatable. In Crete famous pieces bear analogies to those of the mainland; for instance, look at the vessel known as the *Harvester Vase* (Figure 2.40), found in a Late Minoan tomb at Hagia Triada. It is carved from steatite and, although only the upper part remains intact, it can be restored to a shape that tapers at the bottom and has a low solid base. It shows a procession of men enjoying what appears to be a thanksgiving festival. The continuity of the scene is typical of Mycenaean pictorial narrative as opposed to Egyptian, where it occurs in the sole context of Amarna painting. The participants are engaged in boisterous celebration, high spirits, and fun—possibly in a less restrained manner but similar to that which Homer describes in the convivial entertainment of the Achaeans.

In gold the Cretan-Mycenaean did best with the repoussé technique. Repoussé may stem from the newly awakened interest in relief mod-

Figure 3.41 Vaphio cup. One of a pair. Scene of snaring a bull, ca. 1500 B.C. Found at Vaphio, near Sparta, Greece. Made of two plates of gold fastened together, the inner one plain and smooth, the outer with repoussé design. Riveted handles. National Archaeological Museum, Athens. (National Archaeological Museum, Athens.)

eling and anatomical correctness. It can best be observed in the twin *Vaphio Cups* found at Vaphio near Sparta (Figure 2.41). The workmanship is thought to have been Cretan; the spirit is Greek.

The subject matter of the Vaphio pieces is a pastoral concern for grazing cattle and for the capture of wild bulls. The scene is far removed from the sportive bull leaping of the Cretan frescoes. On the contrary, the snaring of the angry animals represents a utilitarian enterprise fraught with much danger and with brutal results. This is astonishing art, a combination of technical skill, a portrayal that is realistic, yet pulsing with rhythmic motion, intended for kings, yet close to the earth of animals and ordinary men. This is the dichotomy at the beginning of our European civilization, when classes still spoke to and understood one another but specialization was forcing separation.

Many of the Greek cups are not pictorial in the manner of the Vaphio masterpieces and are assumed to be ordinary tableware. The interesting fact is that, although handcrafted by the goldsmith's hammer, they show the development of only a few major shapes (Figure 2.42). It is almost as though the Achaean queen had ordered her plate in sets. The earliest cups have only one handle which is raised from a tongue of the metal. Later changes made the vessel taller and slimmer with the handle riveted to the body through horizontal plates. These come closest to the Vaphio types. Although the Greek goldsmith knew his soldering technique, he does not seem to have trusted it as his Asia Minor colleague did.

The second development is seen in the stemmed and footed goblet, similar to those found in Anatolia, some of which are inlaid with *niello* (an alloy of sulfur that acquires a rich black color), again suggesting eastern origins. A third shape is a very shallow bowl with one handle. Of the fourth type only one Mycenaean example is extant. It has two handles raised high above the body from a single sheet of gold. It is sharply carinated below the center; the lower part is convex, with a small base ring, the upper is concave. This lovely *kantharos* shape may be Nestor's two-handled cup, although a more or-

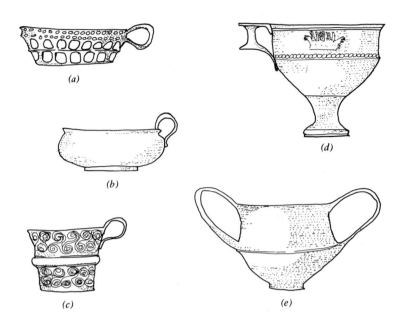

Figure 2.42 Greek cup shapes in gold and silver from shaft graves at Mycenae: (a) flat-bottom low beaker with handle; (b) cup with low base ring, handle may be riveted to cup; (c) cup decorated in two zones separated by roll molding; (d) stemmed and footed goblet; (e) *kantharos* (concave, convex with riveted handles). (Adapted from D. E. Strong, *Greek and Roman Gold and Silver Plate*, London: Methuen & Co. Ltd., 1966. Drawing by Clive Metcalfe.)

nate cup in the Athens National Museum is customarily accorded that honor.

In all Greek finds we see dining utensils, some plainly enough formed—embellished only with fluting or gadrooning—to belong to everyday living and numerous enough to suggest an affluent life. They are buried with their families as wealth and are given to guests as gifts according to the traditions of a tribal society. They may have been made in palace workshops and by craftsmen imported from some distance—indicative of mercantile ventures. Although the structural shapes are repetitive, the pictorial style is in the manner of Greek realism, yet it is not divorced from Cretan movement. In the handling of the subjects they introduce us to the mingling of cultures which was noticeable on the mainland at that time.

CHAPTER THREE

Ancient Greece

1100 B.C. TO A.D. 146

The vanquished withdrew, but no small number of them were hard pressed so that they missed the road and got into some private estate which happened to be surrounded by a deep ditch with no way out. When they saw this the Athenians held them back by confronting them with their hoplights. Then they stationed the light armed troops in a circle around them and stoned to death all who had gone inside. And that was a very sad thing for Corinth, but the main body of the retreating army reached home.

Thucydides, The Pentecontaetia, 1–106,
in *Ancient Greece: Sources in Western Civilization,*
edited by Truesdell S. Brown
New York: The Free Press; London: Collier-Macmillan Limited, 1966, p. 110.

O passer-by, tell the Lacedaemonians that we lie here in obedience to their laws.

Epitaph memorializing the Lacedaemonians
who fell at Thermopylae.

Solon, Solon, you Greeks are always children and aged Greek there is none.

Plato, The Timaeus,
in *The Works of Plato,*
George Burges, translator
London: Henry G. Bohn, MDCCCLIV, vol. II, p. 325.

Love is the hunger of the human soul for divine beauty.

Socrates, as quoted in Henry Thomas and Dana Lee Thomas,
Living Biographies of Great Philosophers
New York: Garden City Publishing Co., 1941, p. 4.

Now this is to march . . . to the affairs of Love . . . ; beginning from the things of beauty, to keep ascending, for the sake of the beautiful itself, by making use as it were of steps, from one beautiful object to two, and from two to all; and from the beauty of bodies (to the beauty of the soul) to that of pursuits, to that of doctrines; until he arrives at length from the beauty of doctrines (generally) to that single one related to nothing else than beauty in the abstract (and he knows at last what is beautiful itself).

Plato, The Banquet,
op. cit., vol. III, p. 553.

This shows that it is both natural and advantageous for the body to be governed by the soul, and for the emotional part to be governed by the mind or reasoning part; the opposite arrangement or even their being on equal terms would be harmful to all parts.

Aristotle, *Politics in Ancient Greece: Sources in Western Civilization,*
edited by Truesdell S. Brown
New York: The Free Press; London: Collier-Macmillan Limited, 1966, p. 129.

We all see that scientific knowledge is of things that are never other than they are; for as to things that do admit of variation we cannot, if they are outside the field of our observation, discover whether they exist or not. . . .

Take architecture. It is an art, that is a rational faculty exercised in making something. In fact there is no art which cannot be so described, nor is there any faculty of the kind which is not art.

Aristotle, *The Ethics of Aristotle,*
translated by J. A. K. Thomson
Baltimore: The Penguin Classics, 1959, book 6, pp. 174, 175.

Conditions on the Greek peninsula were unsettled for several hundred years after the Mycenaean era of the Achaean Greeks immortalized by Homer. A backward group from Epirus in the north, known as the Dorians and bearing iron weapons, began a southern trek that disrupted established societies as far south as Crete. A final shakedown left the Dorians making their most significant settlement in the Peloponnesus, the southernmost projection of the mainland, in which the principal city was Sparta (ca. 1100 B.C.). The Ionians of Attica, which had Athens as its metropolis, together with the inhabitants of Euboea farther north, were able to maintain control of the seaward arm of central Greece.

Because of the mountainous terrain of the country and the isolation of its harbors, the inhabitants were never united except as a federation. It remains one of the revealing surprises of history that their military forces were able to act with the necessary unity at the time of the Persian wars (500–479 B.C.). From the time of the Achaean monarchies Sparta remained one of the few city states to be ruled somewhat continuously by a king. Athens, by contrast, passed through a period of aristocratic rule by an oligarchy, followed by despotic reigns often holding favor with the eastern powers. She emerged finally as a nominal democracy, although governing privileges were extended only to a portion of the population.

The Persians came into conflict with the Greeks because of the alliances that the latter had made with sister Hellenic colonies in Asia Minor and which were inimical to the westward push of the Achaemenids during the fifth century B.C. Final and united stands taken by the Europeans and their allies forced the easterners to retreat. The victories at Marathon, Plataea, and Salamis were of momentous consequence for the future of Europe. Thereafter for many years east and west would develop their unique cultures, although each would continue to be influenced by and at times to wage war against the other.

Following the Greek victory over the Persians at the time when Pericles was the political leader of Athens, Greek art and architecture, literature, and philosophy blossomed in a manner that left an indelible stamp on the west. The quality inherent in this spurt of creativity is no more remarkable than the fact that it occurred during so short a span, scarcely a half century of time.

Then, divided against itself in the Peloponnesian wars, the entire country fell under the control of the two strong Macedonians, Philip and his more famous son, the young Alexander. By the military exploits of the latter many aspects of Hellenic culture penetrated the east as far as the Indus, where the armies turned back. Finally, during a period known as the Hellenistic, Greek art and culture flourished, particularly in the Greek colonies of Asia Minor, Africa, southern Italy, and Sicily, altogether known as *Magna Graecia*.

The livelihood of the Achaeans had come from herding and argiculture and from some cartage and piracy on the sea. The economy was helped by slave labor at home and warfare abroad. After the Dorian invasion there is every indication that conditions changed. The eighth-century poet Hesiod tells of toil as a way of life, for freemen as well as for serfs. Wealth, which may have accrued to noble families by the sagacious use of iron weapons, was likewise attainable by manufacture and trade. The rocky seacoast proffered wine and table oil in return for agricultural products. Silver was mined extensively in the vicinity of Laurion in Attica, and the ceramics of this district became staple articles of Mediterranean commerce. Coinage was introduced. Thus a commercial culture intruded. Greek cities grew at the expense of open areas and Greek settlements abroad fed the economy in turn.

The years that bracketed the middle of the fifth century B.C. were normative ones for the Greek genius. Then its image was brightest; then it displayed its unique character most clearly. This character often appears paradoxical. Actually its opposed facets may account for that uniquely valuable civilization that was classical Greece.

Greece was a relatively new power suddenly feeling its might. It had proved itself against a great empire whose culture had inherited and assimilated and developed all that was advanced in the civilization of the Near East. Plato, nevertheless, referred to the Greeks of this, their heyday, as children whose outlook, with its joy of life, athletics, and play, must have seemed like

63

the abandon of youth to anyone steeped in the cares of the older East.

Childishly, the Greek was an egocentric realist and saw in everything a reflection of his own image. He projected his own condition even on his imagination. Although a scratch beneath the surface would have shown the usual primitive worship of the forces of nature, nevertheless the Greeks soon provide human form for their pantheon and surprise us by endowing their deities with human attributes, vices as well as virtues.

Although these gods were frequently capricious, nevertheless, if properly wooed, they could be counted on for a great deal of magical help. Moreover, this everyday religion was a man-to-god affair, unencumbered by the intercession of a worldly ruler. This point of view produced a comparatively self-reliant people, confident of being able to shape their own freedom. As the Thermopylae epitaph suggests, they gloried in liberty even though it might provide death, for it did so in obedience to self-made laws.

In thinking of Greece many of us remember Greek art and Greek philosophy, both of which seem to belie any designation of childishness. The Greek scholar Edith Hamilton says, ". . . the Greeks were intellectualists, they had a passion for using their minds."[1] How true this statement is in relation to the entire population we have no way of knowing, but it is certain that they bequeathed a body of philosophical literature that the world treasures. Most of that which has been preserved came from the years following the Golden Age, when the course for the nation was not running so smoothly. When the Greeks used their minds, it is clear that their talent lay neither in the experimental scientific areas of the eastern astronomer-mathematician nor in the visionary outlook of the eastern religious prophets. They combined the two points of view. It was inquiry on a philosophical level that interested these young-old Greeks; and through it they perfected the discipline of logic. This means that theirs was the clarity of thought that could translate the mundane and concrete into the abstract and transcendental. They indeed had laser-beam rational minds which, when directed toward the learning of the East, introduced conceptions and a manner of thinking never again totally lost to western man. Their vision focused sharply on both fact and fancy; neither was considered valid unless it took into account the other. Their culture struck a rationalized balance between the two. Europe as distinct from Asia had come into being.

ARCHITECTURE

The Classic Tradition

An understanding of the details and organization of Greek and Roman architecture—known as *classic*—is important because it has been esteemed as a standard for at least half the years since its inception.

But what does the word *classic*, spelled with capitals, mean? The classic conception has two components, namely the elements of the architecture of Greece and Rome and their arrangement. Many of us when thinking about classicism address ourselves only to the first. It is the pillared portico, the pilastered wall, the triangular pediment over the porch that convey the symbol. However, in the Renaissance palazzo, the Georgian house, or even in some of the most satisfactory of contemporary buildings, it may be the clarity of form, the felt relation between parts—in short, the organizational factors—that are of the greatest significance in conveying a feeling of classicism.

Another meaning that may be given to the word *classic* is its reference to the developed phase of any art style when it seems to have attained its most characteristic expression. We speak then of its classic period. In the next two chapters we use the term to refer to the art of classic antiquity and to imply both its words (elements) and its grammar (organization).

Greek architecture is largely of simple trabeation and, perhaps because of this, is ideal for showing carefully contrived visual relations. Even to the casual eye the most famous Greek building—the Parthenon (Plate 4), a temple dedicated to the Athenian goddess Pallas Athene—embraces the pattern of visual distinctness from its major material of cleanly cut Pentelic marble (quarried from nearby Mt. Pentelicus) to its clearly articulated structural system, its bisymmetrical form, the repetitive rhythm of its external colonnades, and its sculptured tectonic ornament. It stands at the pinnacle of a development in which internal relations are so integrated that each part is closely knit into a corporate whole.

Greek Proportions

To comprehend not only how this was done but, more importantly, why, it is necessary to take a look at the Greek concept of proportion. You may then discard the entire system if you wish, but hopefully not before understanding that, to the Greek, proportion was tied in with religion and that the fundamental concepts of proportion, broadly interpreted, have some validity.

In Plato's dialogue, the *Timaeus*, the principal speaker is a disciple of Pythagoras, the late-sixth-century philosopher and mathematician. This is, of course, tantamount to saying that Socrates, spokesman for the propositions, was himself a believer and student of Pythagorean principles. Pythagoras was born on the Ionian isle of Samos but migrated to the Greek colonies of southern Italy because of tyranny at home. The Pythagorean theory, with its attempt to explain the universe by a mystical series of numbers, reveals eastern antecedents. Indeed, much Ionian metaphysics derives from the east.

Pythagoras assumed that the soul is governed by or is in tune with an abstract entity, the godhead, and proposed a number as the essence of each. (Is this far different from Einstein?) The god-created universe is similarly involved in this numerical order and responds to the mathematical control known as the *harmony of the spheres*.

Plato goes on to explain that auditory tonality is based on the well-established physical fact that the spatial measure of two vibrating strings of equal thickness controls their pitch. From this it is but a step to claim, however spurious in its connotations, that the physical world and the sensuous were mathematically united.

Perfection, Pythagoras-Socrates-Plato continues, is static. It is the *is*, the eternal, exemplified by sameness. (This idea does not seem so strange today, falling on ears tuned to entropy and the second law of thermodynamics.) It is di-

vine unity expressed by equality and undiversification. Here he illustrates with figures, the circle or sphere, the square or cube, and the equilateral triangle or pyramid.

But man and nature are *becoming*, they are growing toward the ideal. If there were no linkage through similarity of parts in this process, then no unified result, no approach to perfection, could be expected; hence the time-worn rule of *unity with variety*, but carefully planned variety, as the recipe for beauty.

Plato then describes ways in which numbers can explain this linkage, ways that he calls the *harmonic ratio*, the *arithmetic ratio*, and the *geometric ratio*. From our point of view Plato's description is an interesting intellectual feat of little practical value—just another example of the Greek tendency to hypothesize. The work of the famous Greek Alexandrian mathematician Euclid possessed more utility for the designer (Figure 3.1). Euclid demonstrated the geometric ratios in a series of figures produced by triangle and T-square, thus suited directly to work on the drawing board. One set of diagrams includes a number of square-root figures derived from the square and its diagonal, another from the rectilinear proportions growing from the diagonal of half a square. The latter are known as the proportions of the *golden mean*.

One more claim made by Plato helps us to understand the authority that his proportional system exercised. Plato tied it to religion, not only in speaking of the music of the spheres but in his statement that it was related to the measures of the human body. The gods were perfect, symbolized by the square and the circle. Just below them came man whose metrics took on the "progressive" or "becoming perfect" rhythms induced by interrelated geometric proportions. On the assumption that these proportions incorporate movement and growth—a specific sort of ordered change and variety within a circumscribed framework—Plato indeed proposed a fairly good recipe for art as well as for the "divine plan."

An unquestionable criterion for variety and change is not only that they should provide movement and growth but in doing so they must overcome and resolve tension. The Greek "becoming" proportions do this in a subtle way. Ex-

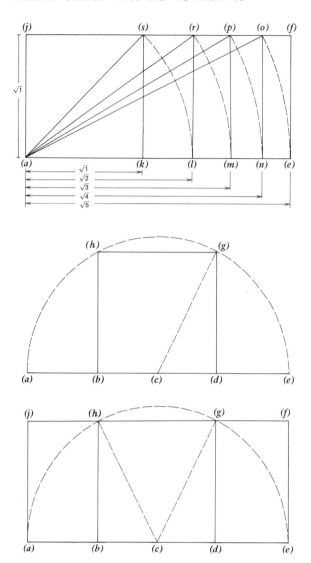

Figure 3.1 Method of constructing some of Euclid's key geometric figures. *Top diagram:* construction of root rectangles from the square. *Lower two diagrams:* construction of the *golden rectangle*—extreme/mean proportion (ADGJ and BEFH) from the square. AEFJ is a root-5 rectangle.

amined with a sensitive eye, it can be seen that the system grows from the alleged perfection of a module which expansion occurs and to which it always strives to return. This attempt to move two ways at once provides the inherent tensions and interest in good art.

Although when viewed as a system of psychophysics Pythagorean theories are wonderful examples of how rationality can become unreason-

able, they do provide a modular method of integrating shapes while at the same time forcing the eye into moving rhythms and introducing those variations that make for dynamics. It must not be forgotten that in a total design the visual force of shapes can be modified by contrasts in color and texture. Greek art owed its powerful clarity to clear-cut shapes and this may be one important reason that a mathematical theory of proportion originated in Hellas.

To what extent a Greek architect, such as Ictinus, used any of the proportional systems is a matter of conjecture. Nineteenth-century aestheticians drew up elaborate schema to show how Greek art might have fitted into a mathematical framework, but that could be a matter of forcing the figure into a girdle. The man who provided the original statement concerned with Greek architecture in relation to proportional systems was the official architect of the Roman Emperor Augustus (31 B.C.–A.D. 14). He wrote a series of ten architectural books commissioned as texts for the guidance of provincial builders in the far-flung reaches of the empire. The author's name was Pollio Marcus Vitruvius, who first codified the canons of classic Greek building. Knowledge of Vitruvius becomes extremely important to us, not because we necessarily plan our architecture exactly according to his precepts but because, from Roman times on, his books about Greek architecture became gospels to architects. Even during the unclassical Middle Ages they preserved an interesting life of their own.

Three facts should be kept clearly in mind with respect to Vitruvius. In the first place he was a Latin (with a Roman's love of prescribed order) who lived a full 500 years after the most important Greek buildings had been completed; he had in all probability never set foot on the *Golden Isles;* and, in addition to a desire to appear erudite, he had been assigned the job of instructing Roman architects by regimentation.

Actually, the books of Vitruvius are not difficult reading and he never hesitates to slide from believable recipes about architecture to the addition of some pseudoscientific gibberish of his own which can become intensely entertaining as a blueprint for the state of knowledge in his day.

Despite this somewhat cavalier account, it is

well to remind ourselves that Vitruvius was no superficial architect concerned only with the acceptable image of a building. As mentioned earlier, he gave as an ideal to his profession the time-honored trilogy of strength (durability), convenience, and beauty,[2] which we may construe as effective structure, suitability to use, and good design.

Vitruvius not only recommended Pythagorean proportions, he also described the classic orders in terms that have been copied and used in all eras that emulated the classic.[3] An *order* in architecture is the sum of the principal structural members handled according to one of the accepted modes (Figure 3.2). Within current memory the language of the orders was taught to all architectural students. Almost overnight this was swept away and it is rare today to see chiaroscuro on Greek pillars gracing a drawing board. The new approach to designing is all to the good if

some of the basic visual values inherent in Greek architecture are preserved.

The Greek Temple

Turning from the theoretical to the material, we look at the Greek temple in an attempt to understand its architectural worth and in it the character of Greek aesthetic attainment. The Greek temple was created as a building in which to house the image of the particular god to whom it was consecrated. It was thus by extension that the home of the divinity and its form were derived quite logically from the Greek formal edifice, the megaron. The general plan of a shrine, with its external colonnade, included an inner compartment (*cella* or *naos*) preceded by a porch (*pronaos*) and separated from a rear *opisthodomos* or semienclosed space. As the cult image was not intended for the use of a congregation, the *naos* was not large. Much of Greek religious as well as civic life took place in the open air. Therefore Greek architecture is not notable for interior space planning but rather for external effects.

The Parthenon (Figure 3.3 and Plate 4), prob-

Figure 3.2 Comparative proportions of the orders after Sir William Chambers eighteenth-century English architect: (a) Greek Doric; (b) Tuscan; (c) Roman Doric; (d) Ionic; (e) Corinthian; (f) composite. (Adapted from Sir Banister Fletcher, *A History of Architecture*, eighteenth edition, New York: Scribner's; London: Athlone Press, 1975.)

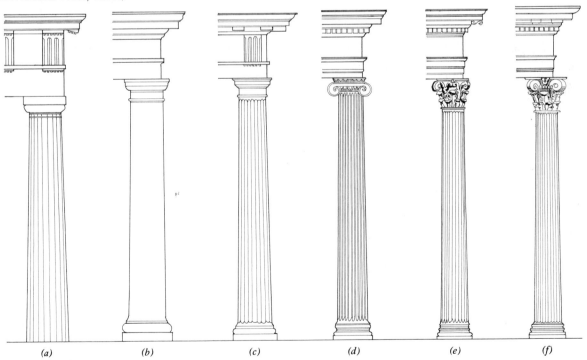

(a)   (b)   (c)   (d)   (e)   (f)

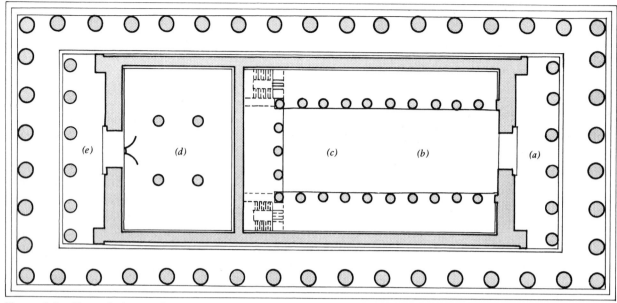

Figure 3.3 Plan of the Parthenon. Ictinis and Calli-crates, architects; Phidias, master sculptor. Athens. (a) pronaos; (b) naos; (c) statue; (d) *parthenon* (the room of Athena the Virgin); (e) opisthodomos. (Adapted from Sir Banister Fletcher, *A History of Architecture,* eighteenth edition, New York: Scribner's; London: Athlone Press, 1975.)

ably the most famous Greek temple, stands along the south side of the huge limestone platform known as the *Acropolis,* which forms an isolated hill in Athens. (*Polis,* which means *the city* re-ferred originally to the enclosure of the inner cit-adel by ramparts during Mycenaean times.) The high elevation of the building lends an incom-parable grandeur to the silhouette of this master-piece by the architects Ictinus and Callicrates, which almost in defiance of its craggy setting pro-jects its lucid perfection to view.

Often a temple did not stand in isolation but was part of a group of sacred buildings that in-cluded possibly several temples, religious store-houses for public offerings, known as treasuries, votive monuments, and gateways (*Propylaea*). The propylaion to the Acropolis was approached by a winding path that provided a pleasant as-cent for religious processions as they wound up-ward to the heights with their sacrificial offerings.

As trabeated architecture, the formal organiza-tion of a Greek temple was relatively simple. Over the years three characteristic Greek and two Roman developments of the orders took place, although the proportionate schema of each possessed infinite variety. The earliest and most severe of the Greek orders is the *Doric* (Figure 3.2), which reached perfection during the age of Pericles and in the building of the Parthe-non. (An earlier temple, also called the Parthe-non, existed on the Acropolis, but it was de-stroyed by fire, presumably during the Persian wars.)

The column, which in the other orders is a complex of base, shaft, and capital, is in the Doric devoid of a base and thus rests directly on the *stylobate* (the platform on which the colonnade was erected). Taking the Parthenon as a norm, the height of the columns was approximately 5.48 modules (here taken as the diameter of a column at its base). Along its shaft were shallow grooves known as channels or flutes. In the Doric order these are twenty in number and a sharp *ar-ris* or ridge occurs between them.

The Doric capital is approximately one-half module high. It consists of several shallow grooves called *annulets* and a rounded crown known as the *echinus,* above which is the *abacus* of width equal to the echinus. The Doric abacus is a broad square block.

The entablature, the three-part division of the elevation above the column, consists of *archi-trave, frieze,* and *cornice*—the horizontal load.

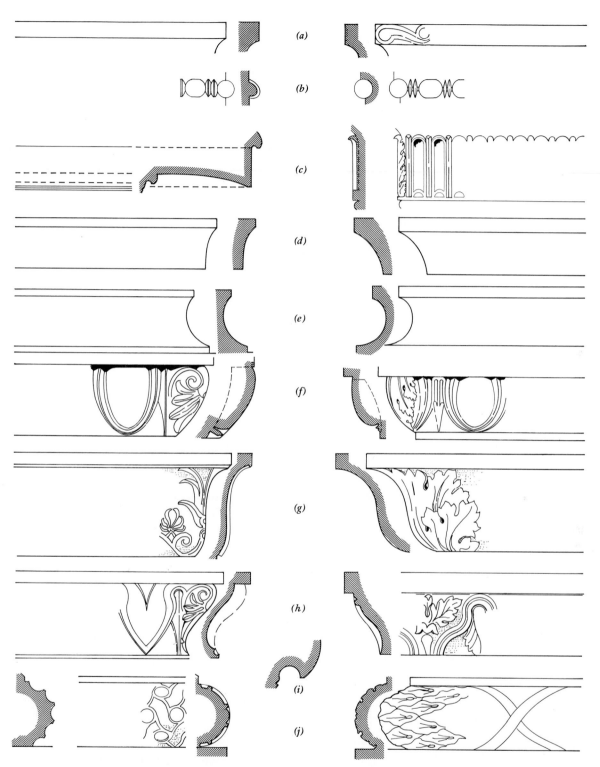

Figure 3.4 Greek and Roman moldings: (a) fillet; (b) astragal (bead and reel); (c) corona; (d) cavetto; (e) scotia; (f) ovolo (egg and tongue enrichment); (g) cyma recta (anthemion enrichment); (h) cyma reversa (ogee—leaf and tongue enrichment); (i) bird's beak; (j) torus. (From Sir Banister Fletcher, *A History of Architecture*, eighteenth edition, New York: Scribner's; London: Athlone Press, 1975.)

The Doric architrave, which is about one-half module high, has a plain surface topped with a *fillet* (Figure 3.4) or small band of molding called here a *tenia*. At the base of the tenia are bands of *regulae*, each with triangular pendant drops or *guttae*, presumably relics of an earlier wood construction and intended originally to secure the tenia with smaller boards and pegs.

The Doric frieze, which is about three-fourths of a module high, is composed of triglyphs or blocks carved to simulate a threefold division. In early wooden structures the triglyphs were the exposed ends of beams placed above each column to bear the superimposed load. Recessed between the triglyphs are thin slabs known as *metopes*. Originally they were squarish screen walls on which it later became customary to display painting or sculpture. Traces of brilliant color have been found on much Greek architectural detail, although apparently only certain parts were colored. The background of the frieze and cornice was red or blue. This might also have been true of the metopes. The mutules, triglyphs, and regulae were blue and the sculpture, varicolored. The soffit of the cornice, the top border of the metope, and the tenia at the top of the architrave were generally red.

The Doric cornice may be one-fourth of a module high with an extension of about one-third module. The lowest molding of the cornice is a corona molding which has a soffit or lower horizontal face extended from the building to prevent drip falling on it. The *mutules* are another series of blocks appended to the lower face of the corona. They are ornamented with vestigial pegs again known as guttae. Above the corona

are other moldings selected for the purpose of throwing interesting shadows.

The pediment is the triangular member above the entablature that forms the face of the double-pitched roof. Its moldings correspond to the cornice moldings. Its *tympanum* is the triangular enclosure within the moldings, often ornamented with sculpture (Figure 3.5).

The *Ionic* order, which bears a resemblance to the earlier *Aeolic* of Asia Minor, was first used in the Ionian colonies, where it is well illustrated in the Temple of Athena Polias at Priene of the late fourth century B.C. It appeared during the closing years of the fifth century in the north porch of the Erectheum on the Acropolis at Athens—the temple built opposite the Parthenon, a shrine to both Athena and Erectheus, the mythical king of Athens and foster child of the goddess Athene. This is the temple on whose south porch stand the six columns in the form of *caryatids* or female figures which serve as columns. The small marble temple to Athena Nike (the goddess of victory), also on the Acropolis on its southwest corner, was an Ionic temple.

The Greek column types vary in several ways. The Ionic rests on a base of several tiers and was usually about nine modules high. The grooves along its shaft are twenty-four in number and the arris is slightly less sharp, often moderately convex. They are separated by narrow flat bands. The Ionic capital, slightly higher than the Doric, consists of two volutes that run parallel to the architrave on the long side. Later Roman capitals frequently placed the volutes at the diagonal corners with respect to the axis of the architrave. The Ionic abacus is a low rectangle with a narrow cylindrical *bead* or an *egg and dart* molding. The Ionic frieze varies with the height of the column but is proportionally less high than the Doric. It consists of three *fascia* or vertical faces that pro-

Figure 3.5 Sculpture from east pediment of the Parthenon: *The Birth of Athena.* Designer-sculptor, Phidias. Athens. ca. 438–431 B.C. British Museum, London. (Courtesy of A. H. Benade.)

ject beyond one another, each growing broader than its lower neighbor. It is finished with a row of dentils or with a continuous sculptured band. The entire effect is one of graceful and attenuated proportioning.

The *Corinthian order,* the most efflorescent in form, was seen in Greece during the classical epoch but was not extensively used until a century later. One example at that time is the Coragic Monument of Lysicrates, erected at Athens to display the prize won by a *choregus,* or director of a chorus, in one of the dramatic contests in that city.

The Corinthian column frequently duplicated many of the characteristics of the Ionic, but the capital is higher than either of its Greek predecessors. It consists of two rows of alternating

acanthus leaves and stocks. There are volutes at the corners and smaller intermediary ones on the sides. The abacus is a concave block with a greater projection than the Doric or Ionic. At its center a small flower springs from the capital volutes. The Corinthian entablature is similar to the Ionic but is more elaborate.

Italy adopted the Greek orders, although the Italians altered the Doric by adding a base. They also added two orders, the earlier of which is known as the *Tuscan,* derived from the culture of Etruria in central Italy. Completing the quintet of what are generally known as the classic orders of architecture is the *composite order,* as defined in Renaissance literature by the architect Leon Battista Alberti and used in ancient Rome. It possessed characteristics of the Ionic and Corinthian.

According to Vitruvius, the proportional systems of the Greek buildings involved all possible interrelations of parts, such as the spacing between columns relative to their height and volume dimensions. As examples of intercolumniation he cites classes of temple: the *pynostyle,* with columns close together; the *systyle,* with wider intercolumniation; the *diastyle;* the *araeostyle,* whose spacing he considers too wide; and the favored *eustyle.* Here the intervals are two

Figure 3.6 Intercolumniation. The eustyle temple according to Vitruvius. Intervals are $2^{1}/_{4}$ modules. (a) plan; (b) front elevation. (Adapted from Vitruvius, *The Ten Books on Architecture,* translated by Morris Hicky Morgan. Copyright Harvard University Press, 1914. Reprinted by permission.)

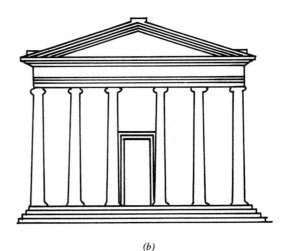

(a)

(b)

and a quarter modules, with slightly wider spaces toward the central intercolumniation (Figure 3.6). He speaks of the ideal number of columns in the front in relation to the sides of a Doric temple as six to thirteen, although the Parthenon carries eight to seventeen. The number of columns and their interspacing give the building its particular type of visual rhythm, which closely resembles musical cadences. The eustyle, for instance, has been compared to an "easy dignified walk . . . I would suggest for *Eustyle* 'andante.' "[4]

It is important to note here, as we did in the spiral designs on the Black Earth pottery, that the element called *shape* can apply to the actual physical *mass* or to the *space* between masses, which likewise has a shape. Mass and space are interrelated and both are important to the total design.

Whether or not the Greeks systematized their architecture to the extent suggested by architectural theorists, it is certain that they possessed the artist's eye and that their goal was visual perfection. To this end they introduced all manner of niceties for the purpose of making the appearance seem right from whatever angle viewed. The column shaft was given a gradual and slight widening at midheight, introduced for optical illusion, to prevent it from seeming to taper toward the top. This visual correction is known as *entasis.* For the purpose of appearing both tall and straight, the column did actually grow slimmer as it ascended. With the intention of altering an awkward appearance stylobates and architraves were curved slightly upward toward their centers and columns were tilted ever so little in various directions along an axis. It was the Greek way to hone a form until it was flawless. Frozen music it has been called, and although some critics may think it too glacial we can see in their architecture—the art that always requires the use of the ruler, the T-square, and the level—an added sensitivity that created perfection with clarity.

The cella of a Greek temple was generally oriented toward the east and was illuminated only by a large door at the end. Interior columns in a single row in the longitudinal center or more often in two rows that formed side aisles and a nave were frequently needed to uphold its flat roof. These columns were sometimes, as in the Parthenon, in two tiers (Figure 3.3) and were equipped with a gallery for viewing. The ceiling was of wood, although that of the colonnade might be ornamented with marble coffers.

The cult image of Athena in the Parthenon, in gold and ivory over a wooden core (a combination known as *chryselephantine: chrysos,* gold and *elephantinos,* of ivory), about 40 ft high, was the work of the sculptor Phidias, as was the colossal bronze statue of the goddess erected on the Acropolis and the frieze sculpture of the Parthenon. The bronze statue survives only in representations on Roman coins and in part of its base. The Temple Athena statue is preserved in several marble copies.

The *opisthodomos* of the Parthenon, known as the Virgin's Chamber (Athena was the virgin goddess) was apparently used as the hieratic treasury. It was protected by thick outer walls, and, around the inner columned nave of this chamber and the cella, lofty metal grilles that extended from floor to ceiling between the columns protected the contents. The columns of the Parthenon treasury were Ionic rather than the Doric of the external colonnade.

The Greek House

When the bronze-age civilization of Greece fell to the iron-age invaders, the palaces of the Argolid were no more, and it was at least half a millennium—a period longer in span than the years that separated Romulus Augustus, the last of the Roman emperors of the West, from Charlemagne—before the old standard of living was retrieved. Only in the more stable Asia Minor do excavations indicate that the earlier pattern had not entirely disappeared. British-Turkish diggings in the oldest section of the colonial Ionian town of Smyrna disclose megaron-type houses that date from the midninth until the late seventh century B.C.

Slightly farther north in Lydia, during the sixth and fifth centuries, the megaron-type house with its pillared portico on the narrow end and the *hilani* type with rooms ranged along a portico on the longer axis were in use. Often, as on the island of Cyprus, archaeology shows that dwellings changed from Asiatic to Greek planning systems during the preclassical centuries. This was easily accomplished because certain features, notably the open court with surrounding cubicles as part of the total domestic complex, were common to Mediterranean civilizations.

On the Greek mainland few remains of houses of the first millennium B.C. have been documented. The French archaeologist Bournouf in 1875 found fragmentary ruins of Athenian domiciles of the fifth and fourth centuries. These mean buildings, huddled together with common party walls, presented a blank aspect to the street. William Dörpfeld, who had originally worked with Schliemann at Troy, discovered sixth- and fifth-century houses in the outlying suburbs of Athens. These too proved to be of modest character. In several larger examples the important features of the Achaean palaces begin to reappear: the indirect route to the main court, the functioning of one large room as an *andron,* or men's quarters, with smaller rooms appended, and, in the town, a closed facade to the street.

Such evidence added to reports from literary sources has led Bertha Carr Rider[5] to reconstruct a composite of the classical Greek house (Figure 3.7). It was basically a series of rooms around an open court; the altar to Zeus was still at its center; toward the rear of the court was an important alcove or verandah (*pastas*) which may have substituted for the earlier andron; an adjacent entrance led to the *andronitis* used by the owner and his wife; opposite was the thalamos for the unmarried daughters. Another door led to a rear vestibule off which, and sometimes on a second story, was the *gynaikonitis* or quarters specifically for the women.

Following the classical period knowledge of the Greek house is more extensive. During the late twenties and thirties of this century a Johns Hopkins team of archaeologists, headed by D. M. Robinson, studied the relics of about 100 homes in the Macedonian city of Olynthus, which Philip of Macedon leveled to the ground and thus preserved in plan for posterity. These houses were arranged in regular blocks about 20 yd square of five houses each. Two blocks, back to back, formed a grid of streets. Although there is considerable diversity in the number and size as well as in the disposition of rooms, they are asymmetrically arranged around their frequently cobbled courts.

Most of the inner courts possessed a peristyle or a verandah supported by wooden posts on stone bases. The altar to Zeus was located in many enclosures, although this was no longer a universal custom and the sanctuary soon disappeared completely or was relegated to a minor position in an alcove.

Because no upper stories remain intact, their existence and character are conjectural. The shape of the openings must be surmised from excavated vase paintings on which they are tall and narrow.

Construction used in Olynthus was the time-old Greek formula of sun-dried brick above stone (in this case rubble). In at least one example there is evidence of burnt brick at the base of a column, the first known on the continent. Roofs were generally tiled.

Baths with terra cotta tubs and basins were

Figure 3.7 Reconstruction of plan of imaginary classical Greek house of the fifth century B.C.: (a) gateway; (b) door to court; (c) *court;* (d) altar; (e) sleeping rooms, storerooms, etc.; (f) *andronitis* (owner's family suite); (g) *gynaikonitis* (women's quarters); (h) door; (k) door; (m) *pastas* (verandah). (Adapted from Bertha Carr Rider, *Ancient Greek Houses,* Argonaut, 1964.)

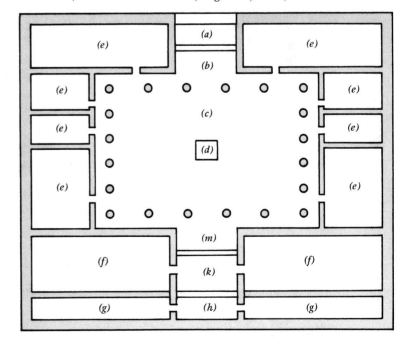

found, and drains to the street were placed in the walls or floors. Auxiliary pipes may have extended from the andron floor to carry off the refuse thrown there after meals. Although the Greeks luxuriated in bathing, their system of latrine sanitation seems to have been retarded, and the deep shafts for this purpose that occurred earlier in the homes of the eastern colonists did not appear on the mainland for several centuries.

Interior embellishment at Olynthus was done with stucco and paint. Occasional use was made of bands of Greek stylized patterns, but more often the decorating was done in the usual tiers of flat color. Ancient palettes were now augmented by several artificial colorants such as red lead (lead monoxide and peroxide) and verdigris (hydrated copper acetate). The range of hues is broadened from Hellenistic dates because of the acquired knowledge of pigment mixture.

Most floors were baked earth except in important rooms where mosaics of uncut pebbles were found. These mosaics at Olynthus, the earliest known in Greece, suggest a development of many centuries.

The third and second hundreds preserved several important houses for posterity. Although the extensive complex that remains at Palatitza in Macedonia is obviously a palace, those found at Priene in Asia Minor and at Delos in the Aegean apparently belonged to an affluent middle class. This is particularly true at Delos where a community of businessmen were engaged in the Asiatic-Roman trade.

Figure 3.8 Conventional plan of the Homeric Greek house: (a) altar; (b) courtyard; (c) prodomos; (d) portico; (e) ashen threshold; (f) megaron; (g) hearth; (h) stone threshold; (k) women's quarters; (m) chambers; (p) chamber of Odysseus; (r) "the innermost part." (Adapted from Bertha Carr Rider, *Ancient Greek Houses,* Argonaut, 1964.)

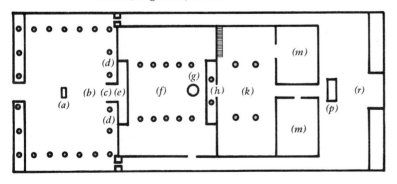

Vitruvius undoubtedly had such late buildings in mind when he described the Greek house. He speaks of it as containing two principal courts.[6] In reality only one house that answers this description has been found at Priene and it suggests a renovation in which two houses were joined for purposes of enlargement. Two-court houses are part of the late Roman scene when the Greek peristyle court was appended to the Roman atrium, as, for instance, at Pompeii.

Hellenistic houses at Priene and Delos were several stories high and in every detail suggest a return to the affluent manner of building in the Achaean tradition. Outer walls and stairs are stone; occasional columns are marble, and mosaics, now of cut stone, are common. Modeled stucco decoration and simulated stone dados are frequent. By inference from some small remnants mural design was often pictorial. Sanitary provisions have improved and latrines are common. So much can possibly be claimed for contact with the engineering genius of Rome.

At this point we turn to literature for data. The classic muse has richly endowed us with accounts of living conditions from the era of Homer (ninth century) until the coming of the Romans. We note that the Homeric house (Figure 3.8) furnishes a pattern that in major ways began a long tradition. Conventionally, the enclosure is bisymmetrical. It is entered by a gate (prothuron) to the columned courtyard (aule), wherein is the sacred altar. The megaron on the long south-north axis of this court is approached through a portico (aithousa) and an entrance space known as the prodomos. The door into the megaron is referred to as the ashen threshold (meilinos oudos). There is a hearth (eshara) at the far end of the megaron, beyond which and on the main axis is the stone threshold (lainos oudos) and door to the women's quarters (gynaikonitis). Farther to the rear are chambers (tholamoi), one of which Homer describes as the apartment of Odysseus. The existence of a room for women through which Odysseus must have passed is at variance with archaeological finds of an Achaean palace.

Actually Homer's account is true to the social conditions introduced during the almost half millennium of Doric occupancy. The eastern custom of a more cloistered existence for women had made inroads. During the classical period of the late fifth century the Greek wife did not participate in the social life of her husband. In vase scenes the only women present at banquets are obviously professional entertainers. This is corroborated by literature. A quotation from Menander (342–290 B.C.) reads:

Thou art going beyond the bounds assigned to a married woman, lady: for the door of the house that leads into the court is the customary limit beyond which a free woman may not go.[7]

The changes that occurred in the Greek house over the years of the first millennium are those that might be expected from the passage of time and a changed social order—smaller sizes, more congested surroundings, meaner skills, but withal a new class of fairly opulent landlords, a more luxuriant and eastern manner of fashionable life that eventually supported a return to artistic amenities and demanded the conveniences of sanitary engineering. Style, after all, is a response to history.

Civic Architectural Types

By classical times Greek society had moved to a city-state concentration. Greek architecture was for the *civis*. The tall hall was no longer large enough for male gatherings. In its place we find the *agora* (the market place), the magnificent *stoai* (colonnades attached to the sanctuaries or markets), and the *leschai* (gathering halls somewhat resembling our modern clubs). Gymnasiums served the men for active sport participation.

The town women could meet in the fountain houses where they went to draw water from the wells. Many representations of this scene are to be found on vases but whether this was a menial task allowed only to slaves is not clear.

It was in Hellenistic time with its need for rebuilding colonial cities that we find the first trials in city planning when the checkerboard grid patterns of Alexandria, Pergamum, Miletus, Priene, and Ephesus appear. These were elaborately ordered, with civic buildings, harbors, and access roads carefully planned. In contrast during the days of classical Athens the way of the Panatheniac procession toward the Parthenon was narrow and circuitous. Demosthenes (384–322) says:

In public then they completed for us edifices and ornaments of such beauty and magnitude in temples and dedications set up in them, that none of their posterity has the means of surpassing them, while in private they were so modest and so constant to the principles of the constitution that those of you who knew the kind of house that Aristeides inhabited and the other illustrious men of that time, realize that it was no more elaborate than the houses of their neighbors.[8]

In the open spaces of the stoas and temples of Greek civic life, even as in the courtyard and pastas of the house, are found the pleasant aspects of classical Greek living. A friend of mine, a young architect and a native of Mycinos, speaks of island homes built with a native stone plastered and painted with sand and asbestos to create a textured surface. Wood beams and doors are left in the natural state. Limestones are used for covering the flat part of the roof which extends over the living quarters and red tiles cover the pitched portions. Living is as much outdoors as in. Thus is combined today the stone and timber, flat and pitched roofs, indoor and outdoor rooms of Asia Minor and Greece. Le Corbusier also found this scenery beautiful. It is just probable that this loveliness brushed off in the concepts of the Greeks.

GREEK FURNITURE

Sources of Knowledge

We possess only fragments of Greek furniture because Greece had no dry sands or burial rites to preserve its perishables for posterity. Ample evidence of the nature of Greek furniture, however, exists in the literature and in the visual arts: the terra cottas, vase paintings, grave stelae, sculpture, stone amphitheater seats, and lead models.

Furniture of the Heroic Age

We must rely on literature for descriptions of furniture of the heroic age and assume, as we did with architecture, that the writer was describing objects of his own time with which his readers were familiar. Homer, in the simple direct tongue of Greece, pictures many pieces. From the Odyssey[9]:

> . . . and he led the goddess and seated her on a goodly carven chair, and spread a linen cloth thereunder, and beneath was a footstool for the feet.

Thus there were *chairs,* at least for goddesses, and carved wood was the usual material of fabrication. Likewise of Penelope we read this passage so succinct in its impression:

> . . . and on her fell a cloud of consuming grief; so that she might no more endure to seat her on a chair, whereof there were many in the house, but there she crouched on the threshold of her well-builded chamber.

Other seats were for the lesser:

> So Emmaeus looked about and took a settle that lay by him . . . this seat he carried and set by the table of Telemachus . . . and there sat down himself.

There were *tables:*

> . . . and drew to their side a polished table [note the finishing process].

Possibly some frames were collapsible:

> . . . and the maids cleared away the furniture of the feast.

Speaking of a *chest:*

> . . . whereupon Odysseus straightway fitted on the lid and quickly cast a cord upon it—a cunning knot which queenly Circe had once taught him. [The knot is an allusion to a manner of fastening around two knobs, also seen in Egyptian models.]

Although guests might sleep in the courtyard on bedding, there were *bedsteads:*

> So spake they, and it seemed to him that rest was wondrous good, the steadfast goodly Odysseus, on the jointed bedstead [meaning the car-

pentry jointing of two pieces of wood] beneath the echoing gallery. But Alcinous laid him down in the innermost chamber of the high house, and by him the lady his wife arrayed bedstead and bedding.

The manner of fashioning these articles may be surmised from the description of the making of a raft:

> Meanwhile Calypso, the fair goddess, brought him augurs, so he bored each piece and jointed them together, and then made all fast with trenails and dowels.

Here is the ever-rewarding story of man's relation to his human situation as it is revealed at the dawn of European literature. It is not trivial to note his respect for craftsmanship and his pleasure in the amenities of living.

Later Furniture

The Greeks of archaic and classical periods were never lavish in the amount of their furniture or in unnecessary proliferation of types. Storage furniture in the form of chests, a few seats, tables, and beds were the total. Some shelves are noted later and with them candelabra as lighting fixtures.

Chests come early to all civilizations, and the Greek progression is similar to the Egyptian. In Greece they change from simple rectangular boxes with panelled sides, the corner posts forming the legs, to later designs with gabled or arched lids. The method of securing them seems to have remained that of the cord knot around wooden pegs. As clothes were flat they could be folded and stored. The storage pieces that stood on the floor and might be designated as cupboards do not appear until the Hellenistic era. Before the advent of libraries and multiple small possessions there was little need for them. The Olynthus reports mention separate small compartments found in some of the houses. They may have served as built-in cabinets.

In any class-conscious society *seating furniture* possesses a hierarchy of subdivisions. In Greece, except for the *thronos* (Figure 3.9) which is for gods, heroes, or honored persons, there is no social significance intended by the forms. Some

Figure 3.9 Attic amphora, the *Birth of Athena,* mid-sixth century B.C. Zeus is seated on a throne, the back of which ends in a lion's head. Note legs with cut-out incisions. Black-figured pottery. Museum of Fine Arts, Boston. (Courtesy, Museum of Fine Arts, Boston, H. L. Pierce Fund.)

types answer the demands of convenience. Stools, for instance, were called *dipthroi,* readily transported and are often shown being carried. The folding stool was a *dipthros okladias.* Their heights varied, certain of them being low and serving as footstools. Benches, referred to as *bathroi,* were long stools designed to seat several persons. Some had solid ends but in general their legs copied chair styles.

The most beloved of the Greek chairs is the *klismos* or stool with a back (Figure 3.10). The root of the word is related to the reclining couch or to a back against which to rest. Its graceful curves have been reincarnated whenever and

wherever a revival of Greek influence is felt. Some of the klismos backs are shown attached at an oblique angle that signifies their use, in affirmation of their name, as a reclining chair. For us they answer the description of an *occasional* chair. This implies a seat that is pleasant to use, somewhat less formal than a throne, yet more comfortable than a stool.

The klismos at its best is pure solid geometry. It is one of the first pieces of furniture to be designed with the emphasis on volumetric space which it confines within its concave back and sweeping legs. Only its front presents a straight line, and later, as in the Egyptian chair, the central back brace. There is considerable evidence that the curves of this chair were formed by steaming and bending the wood, although with no examples extant proof is denied. When carved from the block, as the nineteenth-century examples were, the grain tends to split along its length, thereby weakening the structure. The back stiles and rear legs were made in one piece, and the rails were mortised into the rear and front legs, the latter ending flush or rising above the seat. Often front, and occasionally rear, legs terminate in a pointed projection at the seat rail, certainly an aesthetic rather than a functional dictation. Earlier forms of klismoi are likely to have animal feet and straighter legs. Abstract forms appear later. The tomb stele of the fifth-century matron Hegeso, which is now in the National Museum at Athens, is possibly the best known classical example of this genus.

A *kline* is obviously a *bed* for reclining (Figure 3.11). In later Greece, when the oriental custom of reclining at meals was adopted, the kline served for this purpose as well. From this convention the Latin name for the *triclinium* or dining alcove designed to hold three couches was derived.

Greek beds, like the Egyptian, were jointed rectangular pallets laced across to support the body. This thonging or plaiting of leather, rush, or fiber cord became the foundation of the seats in many chairs on which pillows and fabric coverings were thrown. Cushions or mattresses were stuffed with feathers or with coarser straw. Sheets are seldom referred to: in regard to such niceties the Egyptians were years ahead of the younger

Figure 3.10 Marble gravestone of Hegeso. Klismos. Athens, ca. 400 B.C. National Archaeological Museum, Athens. (National Archaeological Museum, Athens.)

nation. Even the Persians were disposed to consider the Greeks as a culturally backward people, and Plutarch (A.D. 50–120) relates that when Artaxerxes gave a couch to Timagoras he accompanied his gift with a deputy to demonstrate its proper making.[10]

Greek beds are equipped with headboards and some with footboards. The head of the bed might be slightly elevated above the foot, as in Egypt. The detached hard headrest of the latter country disappeared.

Low *tables* are common articles and in Greek vase painting are often shown being carried to a feast by a guest. Couch and table may be strapped

78

Figure 3.11 Greek pottery kylix illustrating couches and tables as used at a symposium. British Museum, London. (Reproduced by Courtesy of the Trustees of the British Museum.)

together and borne on the back of a servant. Later in history we note that guests are expected to bring their own dining "silver." Only today does a household furnish all the accoutrements for a party. Greek wives of classical periods, if present at table, sat in front of it on chairs, as in the East, and it is clear that they were never present when men, other than members of the family, were dining. Bear in mind that these customs were not those of the heroic age in which Homer wrote:

There the steadfast goodly Odysseus stood and gazed. But when he had gazed at all and wondered, he passed quickly over the threshold within the house. [Going to the mistress, he said,] "Arete . . . after many toils am I come to thy husband and these guests, and may the gods vouchsafe them a happy life." [He begs hospital-ity and safety home and then the ancient lord Echenus spake among them:] ". . . nor is it fitting that the stranger should sit upon the ground in the ashes by the hearth. Nay come, bid the stranger rise and set him on a chair inlaid with silver." . . . The mighty king Alcinous . . . took Odysseus by the hand . . . and set him on a shining chair. . . . And a handmaid bare water for the hands in a goodly golden ewer, and poured it forth over a silver basin to wash withal, and drew to his side a polished table.[11]

There are the guests, the family, the chairs, and the table, and luxurious appointments. Table heights in Homer's time are conjectural. When later they were placed in front of dining couches they were low.

The generic name for table in Greek is *trapeza* (Figure 3.11). The four-legged trapeza is the *tetrapous*. A three-legged variety is the *tripous* and was often designed as a footstool or pedestal. Little figures of dancing girls frequently adorn the tripous. On one vase painting Penelope's suitors are shown trying to escape their fate by holding up low tripoi as shields. Here, again, as in art throughout the centuries we have ancient tales garbed in modern dress.

One Hellenistic table, seen also in Egypt, is the round central pedestal table, often with three terminal supports. This table was taller and undoubtedly intended for holding some art object. Bric-a-brac arrives with affluence. One almost complete piece of Greek furniture was found at Luxor—a round tripous, the legs of which are animal-footed and swan-necked. It is now in Brussels. Fragments have been located at Olympia and one wooden table leg from south Russia is now in the British Museum. It is a remarkably close approximation to a French rococo cabriole. Bronze table legs have been located in Greek Sicily and at Delphi.

Except for the klismos, which in turn seems to derive from the thronos with solid legs and back and to be a typically Greek form, most Greek furniture indicates a stylistic derivation from Egypt and occasionally from Mesopotamia. In the first place there is the matter of legs. An early and persistent genre is the leg of animal form. The Greek version departs quite soon from the Egyptian natural rendering and presents a more stylized version with the feet going in opposite directions, sometimes directed outward and sometimes inward. This type of leg is at first comparatively straight, but in later examples the organic curve is apparent and we come closer to the true cabriole.

Originally all carved legs derived from the straight block, from which came several styles. One has the center of gravity high, like an inverted teardrop. It rises above the seat rail which is tenoned into it. Again we see the Assyrian pattern of a leg that resembles an Aeolian spiral cut through the fabric. This retains only what is necessary for strength in wood and thus veers again toward lightening the bulk of the piece.

Although, as previously mentioned, the actual date of the origin of the turning lathe is conjectural, it was much used after the seventh century B.C. Thence many of the rectangular forms become rounded and turned knobs, trumpet shapes, and vase designs are frequent (Figure 3.12).

The finials on many Greek chairs, in addition to the customary terminal volutes, often use the *anthemion,* the swan's neck and head, the ram's head, and the horse's forequarters. The horse, a comparatively new arrival on the peninsula, was duly loved.

Diminutive figures of all sorts, human, animal, and zoomorphic, handled as fill-ins between the braces of the furniture, can often be interesting parts of the piece and frequently give it symbolic language.

The finishing of wooden furniture was similar in Greece and Egypt. Natural oils, waxes, and resins formed the base of coatings. Painting, at first used to cover inferior and to simulate the graining of superior wood was used. This deception became fashionable in later Roman-Hellenistic communities and is much deplored by such Roman aristocratic writers as Pliny.

In these later affluent societies some of the most expensive enrichment was lavished on furniture and especially on tables that became, as it were, the show pieces. Although wood, such as maple, beech, and oak, was the common material in most work, elaborate inlays and veneers of precious woods, ivory, and tortoise shell were used. Plating with metals, gold, silver, and bronze were luxury fabrications. Solid bronze and marble were fashions derived from Rome.

TEXTILES

Legendary weaving in Greece was a family and gentlewoman's craft. This we note on vase paintings as late as the fifth century. The loom illustrated is a vertical one, warp-weighted and possessing only one operational cross beam. The warps are tied in bundles below the shed and attached to weights that hold them taut. In this loom the fabric is started at the top and the cloth is beaten upward. This is a primitive sort of apparatus, its only advantage being the flexibility it provides to operate the warps in hand patterning, possibly in tapestry technique. As Greek textiles are known to have been articles of trade, it is fairly certain that there was a thriving textile industry engaged in by men and probably using more advanced methods. Too little is known of this early product which is proclaimed in literature and visualized in art.

Some of the earliest Greek textiles of which we

Figure 3.12   Marble gravestone of Demetria and Pamphile. Athens, ca. 325 B.C. Kerameikos Museum, Athens. (Deutsches Archäologisches Institut, Athens.)

Figure 3.13   Woven fabric from a Greek colony in the Crimea, ca. fourth century B.C. Hermitage Museum, Leningrad. (Courtesy of the Hermitage Museum.)

have any positive knowledge were located during the latter part of the last century in sepulchres unearthed in the Crimea near the town of Kerch (the former Panticapaeum), which was a seaport of Greek colonization along the shores of the Black Sea. The excavations were conducted under the direction of the Hermitage Museum at Leningrad and the Russian Archaeological Commission. The textile finds, now at the Hermitage, provide a fairly representative illustration of the textile art of ancient Greece.

The Hermitage examples from Kerch number seven: six of wool fiber and one, probably a Chinese import, of silk. Two of the Crimean pieces are embroidered in gold. The Victoria and Albert Museum has another ancient Grecian textile of linen that incorporates silver foil.

The weaves used were the plain, the twill, and the satin and were further patterned by tapestry insertions, painting, and embroidery—the first extant illustrations of European textiles of such advanced techniques.

One of the most interesting of the woolen fabrics in the Kerch finds was part of a man's hat, which dates from the fourth century B.C. Its pattern, appearing, on both sides was characterized as a rep weave by Ludof Stepni, who first published an account of the finds in German. This design undoubtedly involves tapestry technique. It represents rows of ducks facing in opposed directions and is done in natural, well-preserved shades of brown (Figure 3.13). In this kind of weaving it is remarkable how well the artist contrives to proceed from one tone to another by subtle gradations, with fine taste shown in their selection and composition—still another example of the finesse with which the Greek endowed his work. The particular design here suggests patterns seen on costumes in Greek vase decoration. Some observers relate it to Egypto-Greek inspiration. The duck motif is an emblem belonging to the Goddess Aphrodite and her son Eros in Greek mythology and is thus appropriate to women's attire. In a smaller section of the same piece the duck rows alternate with rows of stags' heads. The stag was the symbol of longevity.

Also among these Crimean fabrics are painted textiles, one of which is made in a manner similar to that used much later in making cashmere shawls. It is composed of narrow bands of cloth sewn together and, in this Crimean example, overpainted. This fabric was a sarcophagus covering at a warrior's burial in the fourth century B.C. Six of the painted bands represent subjects from Greek legends, alternated with bands of floral design.

There are several embroidered fabrics in the Hermitage collection from the Crimean tombs, one of which most interestingly shows the figure of an Amazon dressed in a short Greek chiton with a yellow and green border. She is wearing high shoes and is mounted on a spirited horse. Among the embroidered fabrics are three done with gold from the third century B.C.

Hellenistic textiles were also found at Noin Ula in 1924–1925 by the Koslov Expedition to northern Mongolia. Although the precise provenance of these textiles has not been established, certainly the designs on a number of them relate to the Hellenistic world. One of their most interesting facets is their treatment with purple dye. Colors became more numerous and brilliant as the availability of colorants filled the maw of demand. In the Iliad Helen was weaving ". . . many battles of the horse-taming Trojans and the brazen-coated Achaeans on a purple cloth."[12] A purple dye called *purpura juice* was extracted from the shellfish of that name. Because it was very expensive, the phrase "born to the purple" gains meaning. Although the Phoenicians had the first monopoly of purpura production, the Greeks at Corinth and Hermione in the Argolid manufactured and marketed the dye. Vegetable colorings—saffron for yellow, oak bark and other tannics for brown, and the expensive indigo for blue—were sources of Greek revenue.

The Victoria and Albert has a fifth-century B.C.

linen embroidery from Attica (Koropi). It is a gauze-textured piece of pale green tabby (i.e., plain weave) with a brocaded design worked with silver foil. The pattern is a geometric réseau and each compartment contains a small lion passant.

A careful examination of the garments shown on Greek vase painting will give an idea of the magnificence of the Greek textiles. On the François vase, for instance, note the borders on the clothing of Hera and Zeus. Woolen cloth, falling in such beautiful folds when draped over the shoulder or belted at the waist, never made costumes that were lovelier.

CERAMICS

Prevalence of Industry

In Greece the production of ceramics was a flourishing industry and a major source of income. Export pottery consisted first of utilitarian articles such as the wine containers that have been found in many centers of ancient Mediterranean trade. In Alexandria, a late Greek city in Egypt, nearly 90,000 of these Greek storage casks, known as *amphora,* have been located. In addition, archaeological sites, particularly in the Athenian agora, yield shards of pottery vessels used by the ordinary family for cooking and eating. We read in Aristophanes's comedy, *Wealth,* that a certain impoverished citizen who suddenly comes into good fortune, exclaims:

> The cruet, tiny casserole, and cooking pot
> Have turned to bronze!
> These wretched plates
> For fish, well, they are silver, if you care to look.[13]

Not all Greek ceramic vessels were intended for lowly use. Some were surely ceremonial pieces or tomb and votive offerings. The late fifth century produced the Panathenaic vases, intended to celebrate certain feats of athletic prowess. (The Cretans presumably, the Greeks certainly, were the first to love to play.) Many vases were undoubtedly owned simply as household ornaments. To these purposes we owe great museum collections of Greek pottery, lovely for their shapes, their coloring, and painted decoration. Indeed Greek painting art is recorded in its ceramics, for most of its mural painting has been lost.

Shape Types

With respect to structural forms the Greeks were restrictive, preferring to develop a few to classic perfection (Figure 3.14). These forms have become, like the Greek idioms of architecture and furniture, the legacy of every age that has been influenced by Greek art. The *amphora* was used for wine storage. Although local potteries had their individual variations on the type, all were

Figure 3.14 Shapes of Greek pottery, 600–500 B.C.: (a) pelike—storage; (b) bell krater; (c) hydria—water jar; (d) amphora—wine storage; (e) psykter—for cooling wine; (f) volute krater; (g) kylix—for mixing wine and water; (h) lekythos—oil jar; (i) kantharos—drinking cup; (j) skyphos—drinking cup; (k) lebes—wine storage; (l) pyxis—toiletries; (m) oinochoe—pitcher. (Adapted from G. M. A. Richter, *A Handbook of Greek Art,* Phaidon Press, 1965.)

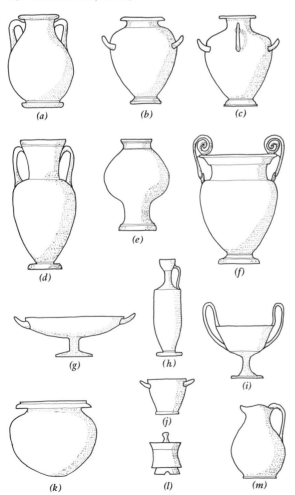

recognizable by their similarities—a high center of gravity, a narrow mouth, two handles, and a pointed bottom with a small knob affixed, intended as a leverage point for grasping or as a finial onto which to attach a base. The *pelike* and *stamnos* were likewise storage vessels.

The *hydria* with three handles on its upper rim was used for water. The *krater,* large and widemouthed, was intended for mixing wine and water for drinking, as was the Greek custom. Pouring was done from the *oinoche,* which resembled our pitcher. Drinking cups could be of the *skyphos* variety which were deep and had two horizontal handles, or of the *kylix,* a graceful shallow cup on a footed stem, correspondingly equipped. A *kantharos* was similar but had enormous pinions reaching from its base to high above its body, which must have impaired its function although they contributed to its grace. Quite the opposite was the *psykter,* an oddly shaped jar, fat in its center, used for cooling wine and fitting within a krater. A wine vessel called a *lebes,* in form a squatter amphora, the *pyxis,* with concave sides, for toilet articles, and the tall, narrow *lekythos* for precious oil were other familiar varieties. Again much later aestheticians demonstrated how the Greek ceramic shapes could be consistent with the Greek proportional system.[14] Whether true or not, they exemplify many of the same design principles that are valued in Greek architecture.

Composition and Technique

Greek ware is pottery, opaque and porous in its naked state. It is made from a good potter's clay which when well levigated fires to a light terra cotta color and has a slight gloss. With the exception of the largest vases, the pieces were thrown and turned on the wheel. Such details as spouts and handles were fashioned by hand and added later.

Authorities have entered into discussions concerning the nature of the black medium with which articles are figure painted or coated, with the design reserved. Should it be called a glaze or a variety of slip? According to Gisela M. A. Richter of the Metropolitan Museum of Art,[15] whose first-hand erudition is beyond cavil, it is not a glaze, strictly speaking, "for it contains insufficient alkali to render it fusible at a definite temperature. It is rather a liquid clay," which contains fine pieces of iron that change color from red, to black, to brown, according to firing conditions. With this reservation it may be called a glaze, for it assumes a high, hard gloss.

Chronologically, the first decorated pottery is known as *black-figured ware*. It was made on an unfired but slightly hardened body over which a thin clay wash was applied to provide a slight sheen when fired. Black glaze paint was used for the design, occasionally augmented by small amounts of red and white. In *red-figured ware,* which began about 530 B.C., the black clay glaze made the background against which red patterns were reserved. Black was added to the figures for contours and details. The design was originally made with a blunt instrument and some further use of the incision technique is found.

Firing these vases is a unique three-step process: first with full oxidation, then with a reduction fire in which too little air for complete oxidation is allowed, followed by another total oxidation. The reduction process turned the piece black, as in the cruder unglazed Danubian carbonaceous pottery long before. In the third kiln, although the dense glaze could not return to its original color, the more porous uncovered portions could admit air and return to normalcy. Further control of the glaze dilutions and the fact that white slip did not lose its color made subtle gradations possible. The almost certain addition of red ochre in spots after the firings served to intensify some areas.

A third category of techniques, synchronous with the red-figured ware, was one in which the vase was covered with a white slip and then decorated in black or mat color. To the *white pieces* other colors might subsequently be applied in tempera. These major techniques are frequently supplemented by variations.

Styles in Painted Decoration

Greek pottery is essentially painted pottery. It ranks high because of the artistic quality of its decoration as well as its body character. Painted decoration, however, changes its style in a man-

ner not observed in material or shape. The various distinctions bear an obvious relation to the historical background of Greece and in terms of broad strokes are not hard to follow.

Mycenaean pottery from southern Greece (the vase decorated with geese, late Minoan, and the octopus kylix, 1350–1100 B.C., both in the Metropolitan Museum) illustrates the free-flowing representational design of the Cretans but exhibits as well a more highly developed sense of the relation of applied pattern to the pot, of stylization, and of the ability to terminate a rambling impulse in the interest of greater formalism.

Then came the Dorians and possibly with them a reversion to abstract geometrics (the *Geometric Period,* about 1000–700 B.C.) reminiscent of

Figure 3.15 Geometric vase with *prothesis* theme (lying-in-state of the dead), eighth century B.C. A large vase often served as a tombstone. National Archaeological Museum, Athens. (National Archaeological Museum, Athens.)

prehistoric spirals. These patterns evolve into straight-line ornaments, wave patterns, and finally a style termed full-fledged geometric (Figure 3.15). Here all motifs are arranged in bands. The give and take, which we first noted in black-earth pottery, is recurrent. The presence of human and animal forms is again admitted and will become the theme of all later Greek painting.

The thread that runs through the development of pictoral illustration is the striving for more realistic portrayal of the human scene. In geometric ceramics the human figure is shown in silhouette or sometimes in outline with inner contours. All is in what the architectural draftsman would call an elevation view with no attempt at three-quarter turns or foreshortening. The surface is treated as a two-dimensional canvas divided into horizontal compartments. The rhythmic repetition of

straight-line elements, as exhibited in the large contemporary funeral procession vases, has a strong emotional impact. Because of the intended elegiac destiny of these ceremonial pieces, their beauty is one of restrained dignity rather than of contrapuntal vigor.

Following the Geometric Period is an interlude in the development of ceramic decoration which must be regarded as side-stepping Greek tradition. Known as the *Orientalizing Period* (about 720–550 B.C.), it takes to its heart the insignia of the East (Figure 3.16): the sphinx, the bull, the wild goat, and the birds, freely interspersed with the rosettes and palmettes that Greece finally claimed as its own. The painter makes more than his usual bow to the graceful sinuous Persian curves. Although Corinth and Athens were the principal cities engaged in this manufacture and

Figure 3.16 Oinochoi, the decoration of which shows eastern influence. Rhodes, late seventh century B.C. British Museum, London. (Reproduced by Courtesy of the Trustees of the British Museum.)

Figure 3.17 Black-figured Amphora with sphinx, Athens, late seventh century B.C. Agora Museum, Athens. (American School of Classical Studies at Athens.)

trade, the phenomenon was widespread. Euboea, on the mainland, and various of the Aegean islands, especially Rhodes, were important centers.

The pottery of these later sources, possibly because nearer the fountainhead of inspiration, seems more truly eastern in spirit. The Persian genius is unmistakably decorative. It may not be coincidence that many of the Greek and particularly the Corinthian pieces in the orientalizing style are small articles such as toilet jars, perfume bottles, or little figures in the round like the sage little owl at the Louvre. Miniature painting, however, was not confined to this early period. In Athens during the sixth century this small-scale work is represented by the *little master cups,* which are decorated with chaste taste.

Athens, at the same time that some of her wares were influenced by oriental fashions, manufactured pottery in which the growth of the Greek tradition can be traced. This accords with her reputation of insularity; she was the one city that had held off the Dorians. One of the indigenous characteristics of this Attic pottery of the late seventh century was its large size, both of the vessels themselves and the principal figures. Examples are to be seen in a number of black-figured pieces such as the amphora that bears the large sphinx which is now in the Agora Museum in Athens (Figure 3.17). This anthropomorphic creature, not architectonically treated, is a stern and not particularly pleasant reality. She is, however, a personage, and not just a sentimental and frequently insipid figment of the imagination.

Another of the large Attic vases in the National Museum in Athens tells the story of Heracles killing Nessos. (Nessos was a lecherous centaur whose involvement with the wife of the Hero Heracles, or Hercules, cost him his life.) This vessel illustrates another characteristic of Greek art—its story-telling propensity. The Greeks were much interested in sagas, the epic account of their history. Both the sphinx and this Heracles vase have been attributed to the same hand, that of the Nessos painter. Within the larger style complex the individuality of the artist begins to emerge.

In addition to their size, narrative character, and individualized presentation, these Attic jars possess a vigor that sets them apart; for instance, a spotted deer is the theme on an amphora at the Metropolitan Museum. The covering of the body of animals with a decorative pattern is an eastern mark. This particular deer is being attacked by a lion almost in the same stance as that of the lion that is killing the Ethiopian in one of the Nimrud ivories. In the broad border of the vase we again see Heracles and Nessos. Heracles has a distinct eastern profile and eastern rosettes and wave patterns appear. Despite these condescensions to the prevailing oriental fashion the amphora is unmistakably Greek in the inner tension of the action. The deer is suddenly surprised. The opposing move of the beast is clear. The horses, though stylized, display life and force. The leap into actuality is pregnant in any Greek presentation and is totally independent of its imitation of natural subject. This is the Greek genius dawning in pictorial art—the power of expression that derives from its organization. We saw it in Crete; it has become more emphatic and complex with the years. Realists as well as idealists which the Greeks were, they managed to imbue art with a large dose of tension, of a struggle whereof the outcome is in some doubt, before equilibrium is again established.

The *Classic Age* of Athenian pottery begins near the middle of the sixth century when that city dominated the Mediterranean trade in this commodity. Numerous skills in depiction were then utilized. As red-figured ware became more usual the painter was given more opportunity for free sketching and for the inclusion of inner linear detail. Corresponding to advances in sculpture and presumably in mural painting, skill in handling the human figure developed. Three-quarter views and foreshortening were achieved and greater adeptness in handling anatomy was attained. The body is suggested beneath the folds and is placed in more active postures. An attempt was made to locate scenes in space, with conventions of ground lines, atmospheric perspective (recession through bluer, greyer hues and less tonal contrast), and linear perspective (recession through lines converging to vanishing points). Bands of abstract ornament are placed where they will provide structural emphasis and separate the story-telling features.

As previously mentioned, the Greek ranks high as a weaver of stories. The painted vase was at

Figure 3.18   Detail of Greek volute krater on which is depicted the combat between Achilles and Hector, by the *Berlin painter,* ca. 500–480 B.C. British Museum, London. (Reproduced by Courtesy of the Trustees of the British Museum.)

once his book, his picture, and his scenario. That it should likewise be an object intended for overt use did not appear to be illogical. Greek pottery, first covered with scenes from the Trojan war, then from Hellenic mythology, and finally from daily life, tells tales that remained familiar to western civilization until the present generation has all but lost the golden thread. The Greek narrated with grandeur and gusto, in simple language but with a spirit kindred to that which inspired the classical theater from Sophocles to Aristophanes. The krater in the British Museum, which represents the fatal combat between Achilles and Hector (ca. 500–480 by the *Berlin painter*), partakes of the former (Figure 3.18) and many scenes on late Boetian vases represent the broad comedy of the latter.

At the precise time of the building of the Parthenon, during the golden age of Pericles, Greek vase painting grew freer. Individualized expression at times veered toward licence. Experiment

with spatial compositions with consequent loss of tectonic artistry availed itself of background scenery such as hills and clouds or of oversize figures. On one side the comic spirit became buffoonery. On the other topics were handled in stereotyped fashion as so many cult images.

In the fourth and third centuries the classical decorating techniques were superseded by the use of tempera-colored white slip. Three-dimensional modeling was frequent. Some products of this late period, such as the small terra cotta figurines known as *Tanagra or Myrina figures* (made in ancient Grecian Boetia at Tanagra or in Asia Minor at Myrina) are homely objects often handled in an ingratiating manner (Figure 3.19). They are among the first examples of art calculated to sell and to please the general public. The increasing use of naturalism without regard for design in these late works spells the end of any importance in Greek ceramic art.

Men, Inscriptions, and Signatures

Inscriptions occur on Greek pottery as early as the middle of the eighth century and signatures frequently in the sixth and after. Both add much to its interest for us. Even though little is known of the identity of the artist, one can easily trace the man through his style and thus gain a feeling for the *zeitgeist*.

In the Museo Archaeologico in Florence is one of the earliest of the documented pieces, the *François krater,* which is named for the man who found it in an Etruscan tomb near Vulci (Figure

Figure 3.19 Terra-cotta figurine from Myrina; two women gossiping, probably second century B.C. British Museum, London. (Reproduced by Courtesy of the Trustees of the British Museum.)

3.20). It is a large vase, 26 in. high, that contains on its body four rows of mythological figures, on its neck, details of a boar hunt, and on its foot, the recital of the battle between the pygmies and cranes. Additional pictorial panels are found on the handles. It was made between 575 and 550 B.C. and signed by *Kleitias* as painter and *Ergotimos* as potter, a pleasing custom that gave credit to the two skills involved.

Exekias, about a quarter-century later, acted as his own potter. Working in black-figured technique, he painted panels, moderate in size, that

Figure 3.20 (above) The François Krater. Made by Ergotimos and painted by Kleitas. *Top band,* the Kalydonian boar hunt; *second band,* chariot race; *third band,* the arrival of deities; *fourth band,* the pursuit of Troilus by Achilles; *fifth band,* animals and monsters; *sixth band,* battle of pygmies and cranes. Archaeological Museum, Florence. (Soprintendenza alle Antichità d'Etruria—Firenze.)

possess a restrained formal elegance. *Amasis,* working likewise with black figures, incorporates the same restraint in a more mannered movement.

During the last thirty years of the sixth century we recognize in *Epiktetos* one of the acknowledged master painters of the classic style (Figure 3.21). He, too, was his own potter, signing himself *epoiesen,* potter, and *agraphsen,* painter. This combination of skills contributed to a close liaison between shape and pattern in the finished piece. Epiktetos, who possessed a precise sure hand, arrived at results with an economy of strokes. He used the red-figured technique.

Euphronios, who was at times both potter and painter, represents the zenith of classic development. In his work we find an emotional artistry that was never excelled. It expressed the thoughts and ideals of a people. Using the term classic art in a normative sense, time seems frozen and the

Figure 3.21 (below) Youth with a horse. Plate made and painted by Epiktetos. Greece, ca. 510 B.C. British Museum, London. (Reproduced by Courtesy of the Trustees of the British Museum.)

epitome of a culture is made visual. With Euphronios one can speak rightly of an aristocratic ideal if the word is used to suggest that balance of thought and feeling to be associated with the elegance of true aristocracy in the Aristotelian sense. The Munich Museum kylix painted by this master on an unusual coral background, against which a young chlamyx-cloaked rider is shown, is a model for this ideal.

A red-figured kylix painted by *Douris,* who was active from 500 to 470 B.C., is an indication of the skill that the Greek artist attained in spatial composition. In the exterior scene of dancing maenads and satyrs and the interior one showing a prancing satyr there is the earlier use of the ground line coupled with the later drawing in three-quarter view. Overlapping figures indicate recession in space. Douris is noted for the crisp linear quality of his pattern.

Among those painters who preferred the white ground mention should be made of the *Achilles painter* who was so called because of the amphora attributed to him which showed the Greek warrior saddened by the enforced return to her father of Briseis, his favorite trophy of victory. In the work of this painter we sense something of the detachment that the artist must likewise have from life even when absorbed in intensely human dilemmas. Here the conception is achieved by the elongation of static forms and the addition of subtle sympathetic coloring.

The Excellence of Greek Ceramic Art

Is Greek ceramic art vaunted too highly? I do not think so. And, in addition to the praise it is accorded, we have come to realize that its characteristics are just those that constitute the exceptional contribution of the Greeks to art in general.

The Greeks succeeded in impregnating art with human appeal at the same time that they endowed it with ideal form. The balance they struck was nothing short of phenomenal.

The structural and functional form, as well as the tectonic adornment of Greek pottery, we have already discussed. In summary it can be said that the interweaving of these three factors is so well done that it places Greek ceramics on a plane with Greek architecture to give concrete

testimony to Vitruvius's trilogy of standards for the latter.

STONES, METALS, IVORIES

Art histories rightfully devote much space to a discussion of what is known as substantive (i.e., life-size and larger) Greek sculpture, produced from the mid-seventh century B.C. Not only was this one of the outstanding forms of Greek art, it was also one that illustrates the progressive changes in the ability of the Greek artist to understand and portray the human form, to set it into architectural compositions, and eventually to make it a vehicle for human emotion. Although many materials—metals, terra cotta, wood, ivory, and gold—were used, the limestone and marble pieces (all originally at least partly painted) have been the principal survivals, often only as Roman copies.

From an early archaic period of stylization through a classic development in the fifth century B.C., exemplified by such artists as Myron (the bronze *Poseidon* statue), Phidias (the Parthenon figures), and Polykleitos (the *Doryphoros,* a youth with a lance), to the later Praxiteles (*Hermes with the Infant Dionysos*), Skopas (*the Fight between the Greeks and the Amazons* from the mausoleum of Halikarnassos), to the late Hellenistic portrait sculpture we trace the mastery of naturalism in sculptural art through its successive stages. Our interest in Greek sculpture must center around its adaptation to building, and thus we find the work on such structures as the Temple to Zeus at Olympia and to Athene at Athens as the outstanding examples.

The Greeks likewise fashioned many small objects, both utilitarian and decorative, in metal and stone, quite a few of which are extant, dated through all of the styles of the first millennium B.C. Their survival is in part due to their less-than-monumental size. Too small to reach the melting pot or to attract the conqueror's avarice, they have lived to grace private as well as museum collections.

Among the most appealing are the bronze statuettes of animals, especially those of the horse,

Figure 3.22 Bronze statuette of a horse. Hellenistic, ca. 480 B.C. Height, 40.2 cm. Metropolitan Museum of Art, New York. (The Metropolitan Museum of Art, Fletcher Fund, 1923.)

Later ones, without handles, were often covered with cases modeled in low relief.

A few small statues of wood, often covered with gilded gesso, and some ivory, limestone, and alabaster sculpture, intended for personal adornment or as votive offerings, are counted among the minor treasures of Greece.

Greek vessels were likewise made of metal, the large ones usually of bronze. Some of these artifacts have traveled far. One noteworthy bronze is the enormous krater, more than 5 ft tall and 4 ft in diameter, found at Vix, south of Paris (Figure 3.23). It dates around 500 B.C. and is now in the Musée Archëologique at Chatillon, but whether it is of Greek or southern Italian craftsmanship has not been determined. It is of cast bronze, ornamented around its neck with a warrior frieze, above which is a tier of decorations comprised of a band of wave patterns with convex-concave flutings, motifs that were repeated on the base. The handles show a masterful ability to evolve stylized forms from such disparate ones as the lion, the snake, and the human.

Certainly the precious metals, gold and silver, represented in the Mycenaean treasure and recounted by Homer, would not have been absent from archaic Greece. It is only in the eighth century, however, and by contact with the affluence of Asia Minor that the luxury arts again appear. The sources of Greek gold were then principally in the coastal regions of Thrace and Macedonia and in a few of the Aegean islands. In 426 the Thracian mines came into Athenian possession and later passed to Philip II of Macedon, a source of revenue for each owner. The classical Athenians owned the extensive silver mines at Laurion at the base of the Piraeus. Recall that Xenophon, the Athenian military leader of the early fourth century, suggested that the Athenian economy might live on the labor of a vast horde of slaves mining at Laurion.[16]

Only a small number of early silver objects have survived. One vessel, made in bronze and gold as well as silver, has the form of a shallow, flat-bottomed bowl or *phiale* with a central boss or *omphalos* punched up on the inside. The *phiale mesomphalos* was a type derived from the Near East (Figure 3.24). It was intended for libations and the boss was used for a finger-grip in lieu of

which were principally the work of the fifth-century bronzesmiths (Figure 3.22). They may have been intended as votive offerings in the spirit of sacrifice of those things nearest and most dear. Although stylized, these Greek steeds possess a sturdiness and strength that is absent from their Italian counterparts such as the large terra cotta relief of winged horses in the Tarquinia museum.

Bronze statuettes of women, probably representing Aphrodite, the Greek Venus, are joined by small winged genii to mirrors to serve as handles. Ancient mirrors were circular bronze disks.

Figure 3.23   Bronze krater found at Vix, France, ca. 500 B.C. Greece or Southern Italy.
Height, 5+ ft, depth, 4+ ft. Musée Municipal de Châtillon/Seine. (Giraudon.)

a handle. Because so many examples have been found in treasury sanctuaries, undoubtedly some religious significance may be indicated. Most of the rare surviving silver pieces come from the Greek world of Asia Minor. A silver kantharos, now at the Louvre, was found at Rhodes and is dated in the first quarter of the sixth century B.C. This piece is overlaid with gold in thick foil, a quite usual practice in Greece.[17] Olympia on the Greek mainland has yielded small gilded silver counterparts.

The classical Greeks had the same problem as their ancestors of placating the barbarians to the north. Therefore it is not surprising that some of the finest examples of Greek silver have been located in the graves of people living along the fringes of civilized territory. These pieces are engraved as well as embossed. Often the articles exhibit a strange mixture of Achaemenid, Greek, and Scythian (or other barbarian) devices like those on a large amphora from Chertomlyk, Russia, now at the Hermitage Museum in Leningrad.

93

Figure 3.24 Silver *phiale mesomphalos*. Found at Èze in the Maritime Alps, late fifth century B.C. Depth, 20.6 cm. British Museum, London. (Reproduced by Courtesy of the Trustees of the British Museum.)

Dated about 350 B.C., its shape is Greek, its decoration, partly in repoussé and engraving, is of Greek inspiration, but the ornament on the neck is in high relief and represents a horse-breaking episode that features Scythian warriors. Beakers found in Bulgaria indicate local design but may possibly have been the work of Greek craftsmen.

By the end of the classical period it was more common to find gold and silver in the hands of private families. Most of the objects were duplicates of pottery shapes done in metal to indicate the affluence of the owner. Contact with Persia at the time of Alexander enlarged the repertoire of designs, such as the *phiale Achaemenid* with cyma-curved contours and fluted body or the popular deep bowl planned on similar lines but taller and narrower. Moreover, the eastern rhyton was common in Hellenistic Greece.

Table silver appeared for the first time as ladles, strainers, and drinking cups. The word for "spoon" exists in both Greek and Latin, although no Greek examples antedate the Christian centuries. Some plain oval dishes existed but there appears to be no receptacle that corresponded to our individual plates.

Therefore, although much of Greek production in gold and silver, bronze, and stone has been lost, we can deduce from the treasures that have been found that the Greek worked with artistry and skill in these media. Bronze was cast and silver began to be so treated.[18] although hammering was basic to most silver shaping. Chasing, embossing, and engraving were practiced. And in these treasured articles Greece began to share inspiration from the north.

DESCRIPTIVE SUMMARY

We have now arrived at a considerable plateau in any discussion of architecture or interior design. Much of Greek form came from the Near East. Greece likewise transmitted basic concepts, some of which were original contributions, to the west. By summarizing the Greek achievement we should gain a clearer idea of its magnitude.

Greek architecture, using a simple trabeated system as its means, surpasses any similar architecture that preceded. It did not appear as a mushroom growth but, through centuries of adaptation of foreign and indigenous forms, it became great. Visually this is true because its repetitive and sequential rhythms respond to the pulse of life.

Greek architecture was an architecture for exterior viewing. It was an architecture of the inner cloister and the open court. Therefore we cannot truly speak of its interior design—which at best was undoubtedly fortuitous.

Belongings are a different matter. Although they probably were not numerous by today's standards, those that have been preserved possessed an excellence of quality. Structural shapes in furniture, ceramics, and precious metalwork exhibit the same proportional expertise that we note in the foremost buildings.

Decoration on Greek shapes, from architecture

to tableware, surprises by its tectonic quality. Greek decoration ranks high not so much because it portrayed the human predicament—which it did—but because it did so with designs that, in addition to their use of rhythm and balance, exhibited the greatest of tensions in the manipulation of the design components. They illustrated a quiet superimposed on the contest of life. In this they far surpassed the Egyptians, who favored repose, or the Cretans, who introduced an invigorating motion. The Greeks did both, but took the action out into the battleground of storms and there resolved it in a balanced harmony.

As a youthful nation, making an initial exploration of the metaphysical world, it is not surprising that much of their decorative art is anthropological and representational. Astonishing is the deceptively simple union of this depiction with abstract design. Whence came the genius that could so interweave reality and particularity with abstraction so that neither suffered? How fortunate that the first real stronghold of civilization on the European continent should have presented such a poised picture. The Greeks designed so well that the danger lies in accepting their answers for all time. This they could not be.

CHAPTER FOUR

Ancient Rome

1000 B.C. TO A.D. 476

It is contrary to divine law that the Roman people should be enslaved, for the immortal gods have willed that Rome should have dominion over all nations.

Cicero. *Philippica*, VI, vii, 19.

In the whole moral sphere of which we are speaking there is nothing more glorious nor of wider range than the solidarity of mankind . . . and that actual affection which exists between man and man, which coming into existence immediately upon our birth . . . gradually spreads its influence beyond the home, first by blood relationships . . . and lastly by embracing the whole of the human race. This sentiment, assigning each to his own . . . is termed justice.

Cicero. *De Finibus*, V, xxiii, 65.

What pleasure can it give a cultivated man to watch some poor fellow being torn to pieces by a powerful beast or a superb beast being pierced with a hunting spear? . . . This last day was devoted to the elephants. The vulgar populace was enthusiastic, but there was no pleasure in it, indeed the show provoked some of compassion, a feeling that there is some kind of kinship between the great beast and humankind.

Cicero. *Epistulae ad Familiares*, VII, 1, 3.

O pitiable minds of men, O blind intelligences! In what gloom of life, in how great perils is spent all your poor span of time.

Lucretius. *De Rerum Natura*, I, 14.

HISTORY OF ITALIAN PEOPLES

The popular advice to do in Rome as the Romans do would be difficult to follow because the Roman state was comprised of many kinds of people and Roman civilization embraced many strata of society. In the years that encompassed the rise and fall of this nation Rome grew from little to large, poor to rich, humble to ostentatious. Her attainments were great. She bequeathed a legacy of brilliant literature, an ethical legal system, and an architecture of a high order of complexity. Supported by an efficient political organization (and army), she pushed her civilization far into barbaric lands. For her attainments she paid the piper. All of the vices were in her portfolio, including the fatal one of self-destruction.

It is difficult for any later age to understand the glory that was Rome. Like Greece she was a youthful nation closely associated with the practical affairs of life in which she demonstrated outstanding skills. She was less given to philosophy, to the art of inquiry. She was more remote from the influence of the East. Even her empire was in response to the "how" rather than the "why" of coexistence.

As time demonstrated the iniquities of the Roman government, as the state tottered to weaknesses within and strength without, written annals show that the simple faith of the nation's childhood was gone, with nothing found to take its place. Fortunately another culture, which renewed an ingenuous trust, engaged the Middle Ages. Our present concern, however, is for Rome and how she built.

The Villanovans

When the iron age began in Italy, somewhere around the year 1000 B.C., the culture of the bronze-making *Terremare* people in the north of the peninsula had been superseded by that of iron-knowledgeable tribes known as *Villanovans* (because relics of their civilization have been located at a village site of that name in the valley of the Po). It has never been established that the Villanovans were descendants of the Terremare. About all that is certain is that both were Indo-Europeans with cremation burial customs and that they lived north and west of Rome.

The Latins

The Latins or Latiums lived farther south. Their antecedents are not precisely known except in the negative sense that the district in which they lived was too highly volcanic to have harbored a paleolithic race. To the east and southeast of Rome were, respectively, the Sabines and Samnites. The Umbrians and the Oscans, closer to the spine of the Appenines, are thought to have been related to the Villanovans. As paralleled in Greece, Italy was inhabited by neolithic settlers from various sources who were pushed about but not completely devastated by the iron weapon bearers, the Villanovans, who in turn retained their own identity in sections of the peninsula.

The Greeks and Etruscans

About 800 B.C. Italy experienced two relatively peaceful invasions, the one by colonizing Greeks in the south and the other by the Etruscans in the north, a people whose origins are likewise in dispute. It is generally thought that they came from the Aegean, settled in central Italy, north and west of the Tiber, and, building on preceding cultures, created a unique synthesis of traits, the importance of which in the development of Rome has only recently been appreciated. By 500 B.C. the Etruscan star was descending, the economic prosperity of their league of cities having been challenged by the expansion of the Romans and by military defeats at the hands of the covetous Greeks.

Rome

Certainly the city that was to become Rome had its legendary beginnings in a fusion of peoples who saw in the location of the river Tiber, its surrounding hills, and low-lying Campagna the requisites for a satisfactory settlement. Archaeology supports the myth of seven early kings, the last three of whom were probably Etruscan overlords.

History begins with Rome as a republic. Military service, which had in the course of time become the draft, provides the clue to the social and political changes that resulted in this form of administration. During the almost 400 years of republican rule the city on the Tiber not only governed Latium but also enlarged its domain to include all Italy, form a cordon around the Mediterranean, possess Mesopotamia, and extend from the Rhine and the Danube westward through Britain. Corruption which gradually leaked into the state paved the way for a government by the few: first the triumvirate of Julius Caesar, Marcus Crassus, and Gnasus Pompey, then by Caesar alone, and finally, on Caesar's assassination, by the emperor Octavius Caesar, the August One.

The ensuing story is one that has been repeated throughout history. During the forty-four year reign of Octavius Rome began to put on its marble face and to write the literature that has earned for the period the sobriquet, "the golden age of Rome." Although the succeeding centuries represent the height of imperial grandeur, they indicate the time when the empire was beginning to feel the pressure of the barbarians at its boundaries. Rome had disclosed her glories to too many eyes. By the second century men of provincial origin became emperors. Trajan, a Spaniard, pushed the state borders beyond the Danube and erected a famous column to celebrate his victories.

By the third century the emperors were chosen by the army. A cloak of oriental splendor was given to the court. Diocletian shared his administration with a coemperor and thus prepared the way for the ultimate cleavage of the eastern from the western portions of the government. Constantine had made it possible for Christianity to become the state religion. Theodosius made a final attempt to rule simultaneously from Constantinople and the new western capital of Ravenna. The western area, however, soon fell to the Visigoths, the Germanic tribes from the north. In 476 the western emperor capitulated and returned the insignia of office to the eastern ruler. Politically the Roman state was broken.

ARCHITECTURE

The Romans were architectural borrowers of architectural dressing from Greece, of structure from the East. This statement is less than half true. They were imaginative and daring developers of classical forms and great engineers.

Materials and Structure

Italy's raw building materials were varied enough to whet the ingenuity of the artisan. Although wood framing with wattle-and-daub fill was undoubtedly used for the earliest huts; brick, both sun-dried and burnt, became a favorite. Natural volcanic stones, such as *tufa*, were abundant. Limestone and its marble form *travertine*, found in the eastern hills near Tivoli, were quarried. In addition there was the finest sand of a variety known as *pozzolana* (named for Pozzuoli, near Naples), which when mixed with lime and water makes excellent cement and concrete. This material enabled the engineer to build quickly, inexpensively, with strength, and in novel shapes.

Once masonry became general, Roman building, which in its earliest and simplest form was trabeated, became essentially that of load-bearing walls reduced to piers with the advent of arches and vaults. The first wall construction used rectangular stone piled in place with and without the use of cementing material. This is known as *opus quadratum* and can be seen in the lower courses of the walls at Pompeii, which for certainty date back to the sixth century B.C. The upper strata are rubble, or small volcanic stone units, to which the Romans assigned the name *cappellaccio*.

Evidence now seems to substantiate a date as early as the third century B.C. for the use of concrete in Roman construction. It was used alone or "dressed up" with brick or marble facings. The simplest, the earliest, and probably the strongest type of revetment was known as *opus incertum* (Figure 4-1). This consists of studding small, irregularly shaped stones into the concrete core to give the whole the appearance of rubble. The next development was called *opus reticulatum*. Here pyramidal shaped bricks were inserted into the background mortar in a lozenge pattern thought to resemble the meshes of a net, *reticulum*. Vitruvius warns against its lack of strength. *Opus testaceum*, the third method of concrete wall construction, used narrow bricks about $1\frac{1}{2}$ in. thick, today known as *Roman bricks*.

Another form, *opus mixtum*, involved the introduction of bands of tufa at intervals in the brick facing. Vitruvius insists that the walls were strengthened by it. Each of these styles may be seen at Pompeii and at the villa of Hadrian at

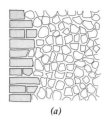 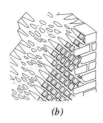 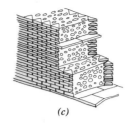 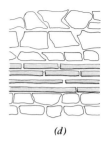

Figure 4.1 Roman brick revetments: (a) opus incertum; (b) opus reticulatum; (c) opus testaceum; (d) opus mixtum.

Tivoli. They add much visual and historic interest to a trip over the grounds.

With the phenomenal growth of Rome, the congestion of city life demanded spaces of greater magnitude. Vertical extension of piled up small apartments was required for dwellings, lateral as well as vertical for civic buildings. This need, however, can scarcely have become acute until the time of the empire, when, under Marcus Aurelius in the second century, the space enclosed within Rome's walls was magnified more than three times that encompassed by the Servian ramparts (traditionally named for the Etruscan King Servius Tullius, 578–534 B.C.—begun during his reign on still earlier defenses and completed in the early Republic, 378 B.C.). In this time Rome's population grew proportionately to a number possibly well over a million.

Whereas Roman building of the early Republic had relied largely on trabeated construction for its means, the architecture of the later Republic

and the Empire was predicated on the use of concrete as a material and vaulting as its structural principle. It has been documented that the Servian wall, with its arched casements, had been built by workmen imported from Sicily, where the arch and vault had arrived with the eastern colonists. The Romans were quick to recognize arcuated construction as the answer to their utilitarian needs. Over the years they perfected its geometric form and refined its appearance in such a manner that many of its possibilities were exploited.

The stupendous architectural feats represented by the Imperial Baths (the central hall of the extinct Pennsylvania Station in New York, which measured 340 × 210 × 100 ft high, was only slightly larger in area than the Baths of Caracalla, 211 A.D., which was its prototype) would have been unfeasible without precise skill in the manner of crossing one vault with another. The development of the *groin vault,* in which two semicircular tunnel vaults of equal span bridge a square crossing, was a particular Roman achievement (Figure 4.2). Developments in this type of vaulting are considered later with reference to Romanesque and Gothic work. For the present it is important to appreciate that the diagonal intersections in a groin vault, known as the *groins,* are the strongest areas through which physical

Figure 4.2 Roman vaulting systems: (a) barrel vault; (b) cross barrel vault seen from above; (c) cross barrel (groin) vault seen from below. (Reproduced by permission from the publisher from Helen Gardner's *Art Through the Ages,* Fifth Edition, revised by Horst de la Croix and Richard G. Tansey, © 1970 by Harcourt Brace Jovanovich, Inc.)

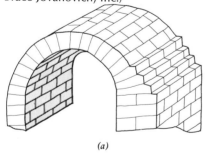 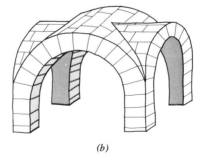 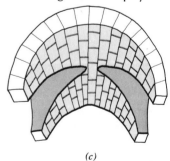

(a) (b) (c)

stresses are transmitted.[1] The groins and the piers that support them are therefore the principal load-bearing members and the intervening spaces may be regarded as shells that can have lighter construction.

Importance of Interior Space and its Treatment

Roman vaulting was an engineering accomplishment born of necessity. Nevertheless, it introduced its own aesthetics with a new conception of the importance of interior space and its artistic handling. This may best be illustrated in buildings of magnitude from the *Golden House of Nero* (54–68), the Colosseum (70–82), the Pantheon (120–202), to the Imperial Baths (211–305). It is evident also in the shops, warehouses, and tenements that lined the city's streets. Even the modest *domus* reflects a new-found consideration for the interior of a building.

Interior design, as we begin to use the phrase, now may be regarded as an entity, but not as one divorced from architecture.

To create design of this nature its is first obligatory to try to understand the interior space planned for the architecture in question. Roman architects not only placed emphasis on interior space, turned the building outside-in, so to speak, but also created space with an entirely new character. With the introduction of concrete vaulting, space could be set free from rectilinearity and smaller size and opened to curvilinearity and vastness. It could boast a comprehensible unity because the units demarked by the bay of a groin vault could easily be seen as subdivisions of the total space in a manner that spaces set off by many columns or walls could not. By a simple method of multiplication the knowledge of the whole comes from an acceptance of the integral quality of the part.

With this mental calculation of piers, groins, and bays, pronounced rhythm begins in interiors. This cadence might have proved sufficient in our eyes to project a naked beauty. To the Roman however, who had Etruscan and Greek prototypes available, plainness must have smacked of the prosaically utilitarian. Aesthetic qualities and that prestige which is so understandably linked to our own sense of beauty could result only from the use of columns, entablatures, and all the paraphernalia of classic vocabularies. It was in the solution to the problem of combining the arcuated and the trabeated systems into a unified design that the Roman genius forged a totally new architectural language (see Figure 4.7).

Historical Sequence

The primitive dwelling or building of the early iron age transmitted little except its spirit to succeeding life. From the ninth to the sixth century B.C. various nomad tribes seem to have taken up residence on the desirable sites on the seven hills that later constituted Rome. (These hills are the Quirinal, the Esquiline, the Caelius, the Aventine, the Capitoline, the Janiculum, and the Palatine.) The Palatine, always the most favored, became the nucleus of the "Eternal City." It remained the section where the Roman elite lived—from Republican nabobs to emperors.

It is of historical note that at least two centers of habitation have been excavated on the Palatine, which in their lower levels show traces of early iron-age dwellings. Likewise a necropolis was unearthed on the northeast side of the Forum near the base of the hill, which by its several artifacts can be dated to a period preceding the draining of the swampy Forum area in 575 B.C. Numerous crematory urns in the form of huts were found there. It is interesting that the cemetery contained both cremation and inhumation graves, as though it had been shared by groups with different burial customs. The history of the Palatine and Forum excavations can be reviewed in the respective Antiquariums of these areas.

The iron-age dwellings disclosed little that is unique. They were essentially of notched post-and-beam construction, round or rectangular in shape. Filling was wattle and daub, even over the high-pitched roof. Although smoke holes were provided, all cooking and heating was done, as it continued to be in Roman apartment houses of imperial days, on portable cooking stands, some of which were found *in situ* and others in graves. There are indications of porches with slanting roofs over wide doorways. The incinerary urns suggest incised decoration on the clay house coverings (our first pargeting) as well as carving on the porch columns. These simple wood cabins are certainly no cultural match for the dwellings of Homer's time with which they are synchronous nor indeed for the Achaean citadels that antedate them. No pretentions to architectural form are yet evident.

The picture changes when, about 800 B.C., Italy came within the orbit of Eastern influence. Whereas the art of the colonists and traders in the south was essentially Greek with oriental overtones, that of *Etruria,* the territory lying roughly between the Tiber and the Arno, possessed a unique character that was not entirely derivative. During its heyday the sphere of its practice extended to the Po in the north and into Latium in the south, thereby encompassing Rome. This civilization antedated the Roman by several centuries and grew to maturity while Rome was still a coalition of tribes.

Our study leads us to the Etruscan tombs, which because of their locations, affirm the existence of such cities as Cerveteri (ancient Caere), Tarquinia (extinct), Veii, Orvieto (ancient Volsinii), Perugia (now largely disappeared except for its tombs), Chiusi (ancient Clusium), and Volterra (ancient Velathri). Most were located in southwestern Tuscany where the concentration of iron mines to which Etruria owed its prosperity are found.

The Etruscans, depending on their stage of historical development, buried their dead according to various customs. The small graves of the Villanovans were followed by domed tombs when inhumation became a general practice. Later the burials, under earth tumuli, were in large chambers that simulated the interiors of the houses of the living. Sarcophagi as well as incinerary urns are present. Attic influence is contemporary with this late stage.

The *Tomba della Cornice* at Cerveteri is one of several that might be taken as a probable representative of the interior of an Etruscan house. This domical sixth-century tomb, partly rock-hewn, opened to a large inner space, to the rear of which were three chambers, the center one, the largest, flanked symmetrically by the other two. This is one of the first formal, bisymmetrical and, in particular, hierarchical treatments of interior space in western architecture. The Italian

archaeologist Amedeo Maiuri[2] sees in it a parallel or precursor of the plan of an old Italian type like the *House of the Surgeon* at Pompeii (to be described later; see Figure 4.4). One theory posits the ultimate origin of this Tuscan-Italian, three-room plan as Indo-European with counterparts in early Iranian dwellings.[3] This illustrates again how history is writ in artifacts of which none is more revealing than architecture.

In addition to the tombs, the Etruscans left to posterity the stone foundation courses of wooden temples and their terra cotta models (Figure 4.3). Vitruvius, writing from imperial Rome, devotes a chapter in Book IV of his *Ten Books on Architecture* to an account of the Tuscan (i.e., Etruscan) temple. Undoubtedly he was codifying and justifying the ancient temple of the Capitoline Jupiter which was dedicated in 509 B.C. and was probably the work of artisans from Etruria and especially of the man known as Vulca from Veii.

A composite description of this building approximates its general appearance. The temple was a gable-roofed trabeated structure with obvious antecedents in Attic Greece. There were differences. It stood on a high base or *podium* and was approached by a deep porch or *pronaos* of two rows of columns. Lateral columns were semiattached and thus the entire building was unidirectional and not intended to be viewed, as was the Greek temple, along the walkways of its colonnades. The columns were of the Tuscan order, similar to the Doric but with an unfluted shaft, and with a base, a simple capital, and an entablature without triglyphs or metopes, resting on exposed wooden beams. Its tile roof with wide overhanging eaves was ornamented with terra cotta *acroteria* (plinths with superimposed ornaments that stood on top of the angles of a pediment) and *antefixes* (ornamental blocks to conceal the edges of the roof tiles). The doors to the inner chambers and inner spaces themselves duplicate the Etruscan domestic three-room arrangement.

The general appearance of this building was thus severe and somewhat top-heavy. It was nevertheless powerful in its effect, for it carried the eye principally along one path, up the stair flight to the inner chambers. Its austerity can be seen in the studies made by Inigo Jones centuries later in

London (i.e., Queen's Chapel at St. James and St. Paul, Covent Garden).

Returning to the *city of the seven hills* at the time of the legendary kings, likewise seven in number, additional excavations in the Forum indicate that only with the reigns of the last three, those conceded to have been of Etruscan lineage, was there any considerable degree of change in the manner and style of building. With a date usually set at 575, the village life of Rome came to an end and she began to take on the aspect of an organized city. The Forum became a civic center as the Capitoline hill to the west began to serve as the seat of government. Fortifications incorporated in the Servian wall may have been begun.

The Etruscans were not slated to rule long in Rome. Near the end of the sixth century they suffered widespread defeats at the hands of the Greeks. The Roman Republic then began its era of expansion, carrying with its legions a firm administrative rule and a period of peace that promoted prosperity and the consequent growth of cities. It is at this time that the two provincial towns, Pompeii and Herculaneum, first come to

our attention. There we can see the first extant house of Roman antiquity.

These two municipalities, because of their advantageous placement, Pompeii above a river on a ridge of exceedingly high land and Herculaneum commanding a good habor south of Naples, were embroiled with various alien intruders, at first the native Oscans, then in turn the Etruscans, the Greeks (Cumae, 474 B.C.), the Samnites, and, after 80 B.C., the Romans. Following a warning quake of Mt. Vesuvius in 62 and the catastrophic eruption in 79, both Pompeii and Herculaneum lay where they fell, buried for eighteen centuries under lava and volcanic ash, respectively. Thus the character of these cities was preserved exactly as they had functioned on this fatal day. First unearthed during the eighteen hundreds and scientifically excavated since the late nineteenth century, the ruins are a monument to and a document of the civilization that perished there.

The plan of Pompeii, following its enlargement to the north and east after the Samnite invasion, was a regular grid of streets, the earliest documented occurrence of this sort in an Italian town.[4] In Italian towns the main street was called the

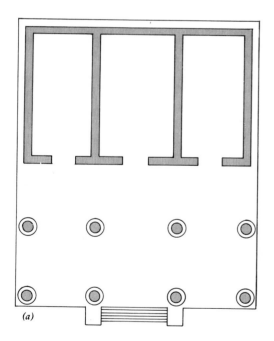

(a)

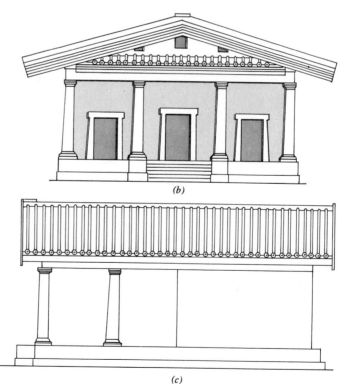

(b)

(c)

Figure 4.3 The Etruscan temple: (a) plan; (b) front elevation; (c) side elevation. (After Vitruvius.)

decumanus; the secondary ones at right angles were the cardines. The decumanus in Pompeii is the Via Dell'Abbondanza, leading from the Forum slightly northeast toward Vesuvius to the Sarno gate. The main cardus was the Via di Stabia, and off this in the most northwesterly corner of the new walled town was the oldest residential section, in which is located the House of the Surgeon (so called because of a case of surgical instruments found on the site). It dates from the fourth or third century B.C. and is illustrative of the Tuscan house type. It became the model of the dwellings of Roman patricians of Republican days, the Italian domus, before Greek influence in the Hellenistic period introduced the more luxurious style found in imperial Rome. Domus is the generic name of the city house of an affluent Roman family.

The surgeon's house (Figure 4.4) is made of large limestone blocks in the manner typical of early construction. The front is formidable in aspect, a stark wall pierced by only one opening, the tall door on pivot hinges. Entrance is by way of a vestibulum, an open doorstep, to which

Figure 4.4   House of the Surgeon. Pompeii, Italy, before 200 B.C. (a) vestibulum; (b) atrium; (c) impluvium; (d) alae (e) tablinum; (f) tabernae opened to street, (g) oecus. (Adapted from Bertha Carr Rider, Ancient Greek Houses, Argonaut, 1964.)

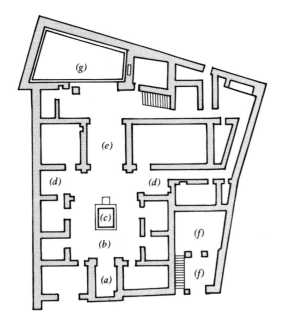

the household clients (in older Rome these were the free retainers) could come for the purpose of petitioning the master for their daily dole or where the populace might present petitions. The vestibulum is preserved as a public area throughout Italian building. Until quite recently one often saw a wedding party escorted from the church to the family's home by any and all, who came that far for their share of the festivities. It is named after Vesta, the Italian guardian of the hearth.

Beyond the vestibulum was a closed door, known as the ostium, which often gave its name to the passage, at the side of which is the doorkeeper's room. The ostium leads to the atrium proper. A vellum or curtain might be the only closing between the corridor and the main room or court.

The roof, gabled and covered with terra cotta tiles, was supported by wooden beams and rafters. Onto the former crossbeams or joists were affixed to produce a coffered ceiling, sometimes painted and ornamented. In a large atrium, where additional support was required, pillars were added in the center. This form was known as the atrium tetrastylon, if four pillars were used, or the atrium Corinthian, if more were needed. The atrium Tuscanicus was astylar or without pillars. An atrium tetrastylon can be seen at Pompeii in the House of the Silver Wedding named (somewhat anachronistically) for the silver wedding of the Italian sovereigns in 1893, when it was discovered.

These styles were all related to the roof problem and to drainage. It was customary to place the roof beams to allow for a square compluvium, or center hole, through which the rain water would fall into a basin known as the impluvium. In large houses, where the downpour might be excessive, the roof actually sloped toward the outer walls, and the major part of the water was carried off by the gutters. The fall of water into the central court must have been similar in effect to the beautifully conceived Mexican rain pillar displayed in the Archaeological Museum in Mexico City, a wonderful idea for a southern climate.

There were many rooms off the atrium and in time they were reserved for special uses. Three were against the rear wall in the early form of the house. The obvious inference is that these three

Figure 4.5 The House of the Faun, Pompeii, interior view of the atrium and the tablinum. Hellenistic Roman, second century B.C. (Photo Researchers.)

are to be associated with the three cella of Tuscan buildings, the broadest of which was usually in the center and was known as the *tablinum*. This room belonged to the head of the family and was used as a reception room or office where he might keep his tablets of accounts, hence the name. The other two were called the *alae*. These

Figure 4.6 House of the Pansa. Pompeii, Italy, second century B.C. (*a*) atrium; (*b*) impluvium; (*c*) peristyle; (*d*) oecus; (*e*) tablinum; (*f*) outer garden; (*g*) triclinium. Shops, service quarters, and rented quarters occupy additional areas. (Adapted from Sir Banister Fletcher, *A History of Architecture*, eighteenth edition, New York: Scribner's; London: Athlone Press, 1975.)

amounted to small niches or shrines in which the family records and the wax effigies of the family ancestors might be cared for.

Most Pompeian houses were more sumptuous than the House of the Surgeon. They indicate Hellenizing influences which beginning in the second century B.C., cropped up in Roman customs. The Pompeian *House of the Faun*, named after the little bronze statue of the dancing sprite found in its impluvium and now in the Archaeological Museum in Naples (with a copy replacing it at Pompeii), is one of the later type which has a *peristylium* or columned courtyard attached to the atrium (Figure 4.5). The atrium here is large, measuring 58 × 33 × 28 ft in width, depth, and

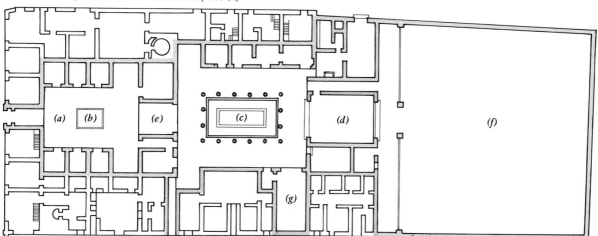

height, respectively. The ground dimensions of the atrium at the House of the Surgeon are 25 × 30. The peristylium of the *House of the Pansa,* a grandiose dwelling of the Samnite era, measures 60 ft long by 50 wide (Figure 4.6).

Because the annexation of a peristylium represented the height of fashion and affluence, some rearrangement of the atrium space was required to create a vista by which the second court might show off to advantage. The rear of the central tablinum was opened, although it could be closed by folding doors as the occasion warranted. The alae were pushed to side walls, and the narrow space they had occupied was converted to *fauces* or passageways, guarded by velli.

Although the peristylium became the family living quarters and the atrium took on the character of a forecourt, the latter was always venerated as the center of the home. Here the symbols of family identity were preserved. Livy tells in "Lucretia" that the spinning instruments were traditionally kept in the atrium where the Roman matron and her handmaidens had once sat. The symbolic marriage couch was preserved opposite the ostium, whence it derived its name, *lectus adversus.* The marriage table, likewise located in the atrium, was called the *cartibulum.*

The hearth, however, which had originally been in the atrium, was removed to a position near the kitchen or *culina* in a far corner of the peristylium. The household shrine dedicated to the *Lares and Penates* (i.e., the first, the gods who signified the family continuity, the second, the guardians of the well being of the house itself) was generally located near the culina. Occasionally it was situated in the dining room to facilitate the placing of a food offering before it. The Penates were two and their representations frequently stand adjacent to the *Lar* or lord of the household. Curiously the Lar might be the effigy of a boy holding a bowl in one hand and a drinking horn upraised in the other, whereas the Penates, or guardian spirits, usually two youths, could be supplemented by a beneficent serpent which received the offering. Such a shrine we see in the House of the Vettii at Pompeii, a house built by two prosperous brothers shortly before the fateful eruption.

The late Greek style of dining room with three couches, called the *triclinium,* was taken over by the Hellenized Romans. Pretentious homes might have several triclinia to make use of various orientations according to weather conditions. In late Greek triclinia the couches were placed on low platforms to facilitate drainage to the street.

In Rome sanitary facilities were close to the kitchen in order to economize on water carriage. In Pompeii, in addition to the street-corner wells, water was piped into private homes. In a city like Rome only the wealthy domi had such a supply. The aqueduct water was reserved for civic needs, for the baths, for semiprivate latrines, for the emperor's palace, and for the rich. The average tenement was without water.

The *cubicula* were sleeping rooms, off the peristylium or frequently on an upper story. Remnants of stairs are found at Pompeii. As homes grew more luxurious, specialized areas were multiplied. *Bibliothecae* or libraries attest to cultural pursuits and *cellae* to the presence of slaves who resided in the household. Another reception room or *oecus* might be in the rear with a *xystus* or garden adjoining.

Vitruvius gave prescribed proportions for most of the components of the Roman house. They were more the ideal than the actual. The incommensurate ratio of the square and its hypotenuse (the *root two* proportion because the short side of the rectangle is to the long as one is to the square root of two—an incommensurate ratio) is used to delineate the respective sizes of one type of atrium. His suggestion served as a guide to later architects in relation to the use of this proportion in principal rooms.

Admittedly a house in a provincial city would not represent the most advanced architectural principles of a period. It is nevertheless surprising to find that although the Etruscans had used the masonry arch in many of their utilitarian structures, such as city gates and aqueducts, Roman builders remained faithful to trabeation in many of their important buildings even as late as the reign of Octavius Augustus Caesar. The great temple known as the *Maison Carée* at Nimes, built during the first century B.C., may be taken as an example. This building is a combination of the Etruscan podium-type temple, built of large masonry blocks in the Greek manner and using the Corinthian column. Similar combinations of Greek and Etruscan trabeated architecture constitute the rationale of early building in the Roman fora.

Need has a way of changing things fast. An immediate necessity for more housing accommodations on limited space jettisoned the Romans into originating a type of architecture that is not found in the Hellenized civilization to the east. This was the high-rise apartment house or *insula* built in the capital, especially in the time of the Flavian emperors and later. It has been calculated that the *domi* in the imperial city numbered 1797; the *insulae*, 46,602.

Whereas the domus belonged to the affluent patrician, the *insula* or tenement belonged to the proletariat—the independent craftsman, the small tradesman, and even such semiprofessionals as schoolmasters, astrologers, and those who plied less savory occupations. It was the tradition of individually owned enterprise coupled with the sudden population explosion that created the unique Roman building complex. The knowledge that the Roman engineer had of Etruscan arcuated construction provided the means.

The usual insula unit had a wide opening to the street which could be securely barred at night. Here the shopkeeper might display his wares in space that was cavernous and cool at the rear and open to ventilation in front. A counter separated private from public quarters, but one only has to travel the circuitous thoroughfares of a central district today to realize that Domitian must have had his troubles in trying to enforce an edict that prohibited the display of merchandise in the street.

The artisan of the shop or *taberna*, as it was called, lived in a garret above his work. This was approached by stairs or ladder in the rear of the ground-floor quarters. The loft looked out through a small window and in more affluent conditions possessed a small balcony.

As the city grew and attracted vast armies of men to the service industries and to imperial officialdom, there was need for dwellings not connected with any shop. For the use of these occupants the insula rose in height. Livy mentions that a house with three stories existed in 218 B.C.[5] Vitruvius deals explicitly with the prob-

lems of safety involved with taller structures. The Roman answer was to build the ground floor with barrel or groin vaulting. This method of construction not only made possible the necessary broad openings for first-floor shopkeepers but also provided added strength for superimposed tiers of ordinary living accommodations. Access was supplied by a straight, steep flight of stairs that opened from a space between the shops. Who has not seen their descendants in Rome nineteen centuries later?

At first these new buildings were constructed of unsatisfactory, unsafe materials—wood, half timber, and shingles. Many collapsed from structural weaknesses; others burned. After a great fire in the reign of Nero—which is chiefly remembered because of the doubtful tale that the emperor fiddled while the town went up in smoke —a new city rose. Its structural material was concrete, used for the ground-story vaults which were then covered with tufa laid in reticulated pattern with the upper courses of baked tile brick. Later the buildings used brick alone for facing, and next to Augustus's official city of marble another proletariat version arose. Concrete was used for stairs and often for floors, although the loft floors and those of insulae without tabernae were still wooden.

The emperors Augustus, Nero, and Trajan each decreed a limit to the height of tenements, the most liberal standard being 60 ft. Laws were also made to restrict the width of balconies; but laws were often broken when private interests were at stake.

The somewhat standardized plans of insulae progressed from a single row of tabernae with dwelling spaces above to the more complex arrangements in which the insulae surrounded a court shared by its inhabitants. Their exterior architecture may have adopted the classical vocabulary of arches and pilasters and a central doorway leading through a vestibule to the inner yard, as in the *Casa di Diana* in Ostia, the seaport of Rome. Wealthy landowners combined the inner-oriented and often two-court domus with outer facade rental apartments of the insula variety which provided a source of revenue and a baffle against the noise of the street. This multiple-class dwelling, combined with accommoda-

107

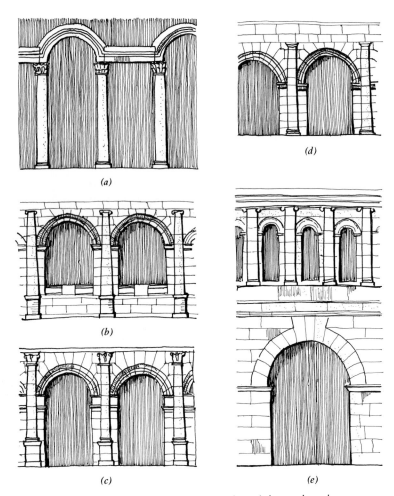

Figure 4.7 Various examples of the *arch order* as seen in Roman architecture: (*a*) arch supported by column; (*b*) arch raised in height by insertion of stilting to reach height of columns; (*c*) columns raised in height by insertion of pedestal; (*d*) arch raised in height by elongated voussoirs; (*e*) wall bearing part or all of load.

tions for small individually owned enterprises, was uniquely suited to a preindustrial era.

In Rome civic architecture kept pace with the domestic. The emperors were quick to see the need for public entertainment felt by a boxed-in population. They inaugurated the rich social institutions of the municipal theaters, the public baths, and even the spectacles of the arena. The temples and public buildings inspired civic pride by their magnificence.

Many buildings simply grew large, multicol-

umned, and monotonously uninteresting. In its early unpretentious form, seen in the "Temple of Fortuna Virilis" in Rome in the late second century B.C. we view the Roman temple at its best, a complex of Etruscan-Greek character but with a single large interior space that was used for displaying civic trophies as well as for housing the cult image. Again the early Romans built small temples in the round, possibly following a remembrance of their ancient round hut dwellings. These were likewise of trabeated construction with Greek peristyle dressing, as in the "Temple of Sibyl" at Tivoli.

Soon, however, the necessity for large and imposing interiors turned the attention of the Roman civic builder to the arch principle and to concrete as building material. Having perhaps a bit of an inferiority complex in relation to the superiority of Greek and Etruscan styles in art, he sought to aggrandize his buildings with the orders of architecture. This use of the arch for structural reasons, framed with paraphernalia from the trabeated columnar systems, has come to be known as the *arch order*, with Rome as its real creator (Figure 4.7). Notice how it was used in the triumphal arches which in imperial days were erected along the paths of victorious rulers (Figure 4.8).

Because Vitruvius prescribed the canons for the columns and their superstructures, geometry prescribed the height of the vault, and functional considerations somewhat dictated the overall size of space, one can see that the architect needed to juggle his possibilities with care.

To look at his manner of combining trabeation with arcuation let us first observe the *Pantheon* (Figure 4.9 and Plate 5), temple to the gods of the imperial Julian family. The Rotunda was built during the years of Hadrian's reign (A.D. 120–124), and the Portico in its present form was erected in 202 as a reconstruction and adaptation from one belonging to an earlier temple on the site. Here we have one of the most restful, majestic, inwardly oriented spaces ever created by man. Only the small *oculus*, or round opening 27 ft in diameter in the dome, gives any hint of the world beyond its doors. Externally the temple front seems appended to a totally unrelated round building with load-bearing walls, yet the

Figure 4.8 (above) The Arch of Constantine. Rome, 312 A.D. (Alinari/Editorial Photocolor Archives.)

Figure 4.9 (below) The Pantheon. Rome, A.D. 118–125 (rotunda. Dome: Depth, 144 ft, height from floor, 144 ft. (Alinari/Editorial Photocolor Archives.)

proportions between the major masses provide a rhythmic poise. The curved interior faces of the walls are punctuated and brought forward with classic *aediculae* and are recessed in column-supported niches, the whole repeating a similar undulating movement in the coffered dome.

In the *Colosseum* of the years 70 to 83 arch and pier visually lighten the structure of four superstories. The builder half-embedded his orders in the wall (*semiengaged*) Doric on the lowest level, then Ionic, and last Corinthian thus framing the arches and relieving the apparent mass as the amphitheater rose. The semidemolished present state of the building offers an excellent chance for judging how successful the attached ornament was in making a better visual design of the whole, creating from it something more human in scale even though its expression belied the grim acts in its interior.

Among all the Roman achievements the imperial baths and basilicas (law courts) show the greatest daring in the use of cross vaults to achieve large, integrated, interesting, and imposing spaces. Here the column usually substitutes for the pier to raise the groins to stupendous heights. (The *tepidarium* in the Baths of Caracalla was 108 ft high.) By crossing vast halls with still higher spaces a comprehensible organic unity was attained in interior architecture on a scale never before achieved.

In his handling of his problems, made more complex by insistence on complicating the bare engineering facts with what some might call superfluous decoration, the Roman exercised ingenuity (Figure 4.7). At times he rested his arcade on his column, as in the hemicycle arcade of the large pool known as the *Canopus* in Hadrian's villa. He could increase the height of the arch in relation to its width by inserting a *stilting* or vertical section between the *impost block* (the molding of a pier at the springing of its arch) and the spring. He could raise his columns onto pedestals; he might variously space his columns with respect to his arch. In his best building the Roman architect used his arch order with consummate skill.

No picture of Roman life would be complete without an understanding of its *villas* and *palaces,* two building types that have figured im-portantly in Italian culture. The Latin derivation of the word *villa* has the same root as *village*. It implied a country seat or farm. On the other hand, *palace* derives its meaning from the Palatine Hill, which since the rule of Augustus had been the location of the homes of the rulers of the empire. Hence the connotation is that of a royal dwelling and by extension any metropolitan residence of magnificence.

Originally the villa, land and supportive buildings, was associated with active farming, hence was divorced from the *urbs* in which congestion was the rule. By the time of the late Republic the capital's wealthy class was able to afford large country estates and enjoyed them as a respite from the bluster of the city.

Although these properties were comparatively self-sufficient, they were by no means economically lucrative. The younger Pliny (62–114), nephew and adopted son of the elder scientist and writer (who sacrificed his life by attempting to aid the victims of the Pompeian tragedy), wrote to his friend Gallus about his villa in Laurentium near the seaport of Ostia:

> The woods provide us with firewood and everything else we get from the city of Ostia. Indeed in a pinch we could find everything in the village which lies just beyond the next estate. In this village there are three very decent bathing establishments, quite satisfactory in case you arrive at the villa unexpectedly and are unwilling to wait while our baths are heating.[6]

As suburban living became more general, a distinction in terminology was made. The *villa rustica* remained the name of the ancient agricultural settlement, as described by Cato (234–149) in his *De Re Rustica*. The *villa urbana* was the name of the urban establishment transported to the country.

The emperor's home in Rome may have combined the essentials of both types of villa. Augustus was the first to build on the Palatine. His dwelling, named for his wife, is known as the *House of Livia*. (Another *domus Livia*, from which the well-known fresco was taken, was located at the Prima Porta near Ostia.) The first emperor's domicile was a relatively simple Greek-Roman house; that is, the Greek peristyle court had been added to the Roman atrium. Here Augustus is reputed to have lived in comparative austerity.

Among the remains of later palaces which lie buried on the Palatine the most famous is the *Golden House of Nero,* whose name referred to the gilding on its facade as well as to the connotations of its grandeur. Located in the center of the urbs on land preempted for the use of the ruler, it united country living and city architecture. It was a pretentious symmetrical building in the midst of an estate that featured agricultural conceits as later practiced at Versailles. Putting aside any legend of Nero's pastimes, here is evidence of an exotic mode of life made possible by untoward wealth.

Hadrian later built the Colosseum on a portion of the site that had been occupied by the golden palace, and other buildings that destroyed much of its substance soon followed. Its remains were unearthed during the Renaissance and were the object of archaeological investigation by the painter Raphael (1483–1520), who was then in charge of the Department of Antiquities for the state, an office that in itself was indicative of the reawakening of interest in the classical past. More accurate research has been done since a German archaeological team worked there during the early years of this century.

One room in the palace helps us to comprehend the extent of eastern influence on late Roman civilization. This enclosure, now thought to have been the dining room, was an octagonal space with a revolving ceiling with an oculus at its peak, the exact nature and purpose of which is conjectural. Scholars suggest that this architectural concept was influenced by the Near Eastern supposition of a "Cosmic Dome," an idea evidently brought to the West after Alexander's conquests.[7] The western mind was not only attracted by Oriental sumptuousness but likewise there was intercommunication in pure and applied science.

The principal import of Roman villa and palace architecture lies in its quite advanced treatment of architectural space. A typical domus as well as a Roman civic building was inwardly oriented and formally ordered. Even wthen the imperial fora took on a formal pattern in the disposition of its structures, the centripetal focus was evident in the arrangement of the total space of the area, and, when a garden was part of a villa estate, it began in a bisymmetrical and formal way.

Something beyond this, however, creeps into the situation. We note an appreciation of the irregular vista and the wilder scenery that extends beyond the proximate enclosure. Notice how this look at the far horizon, and at the heavens, begins at the time of Pliny and how it develops and is more fully understood at the time of Hadrian.

A look at Pliny's Laurentium villa. He first assures us in his letters that it is by no means palatial,[8] yet we know that he owned five hundred slaves and that his income of 20,000 sesterces ($80,000) was not meager.[9] He says:

> The first room we come to on entering the house is the atrium, small but not unpleasing; the next room is composed of two colonnades coming together to form the letter D enclosing a space which is small but pleasant and forming an excellent retreat in case of storm by reason of the protection offered by the windows and the overhanging roof. Farther on is an attractive anteroom and a very nice dining room which runs out towards the shore and is washed by the waves whenever the south wind ruffles the sea. It has folding doors and windows as large on each side and so you have three different views of the sea from the front and the sides, while from the rear you look back at the part we have just come through: the anteroom, the colonnades, the atrium, the woods, and far off in the distance, the mountains.[10]

Beyond the house he describes the garden. After calling attention to the small plants like the rosemary, the fragrant violets, and the laurel, he alludes to the trees, the evergreen shrubs, the plane trees, the black-shadowed cypress that contrasted with patches of sunlit lawn, the mulberry and figs in multitude, then the fountains and marble pools of water, the kitchen garden, and the vineyards. The present generation would enjoy "some shady paths for walking barefoot, soft, and yielding."[11] This, he says, "is all enclosed by a wall which is concealed by box trees rising in steps so as to hide it completely."[12]

111

He adds:

> Then comes a meadow the natural beauty of which is as great as the artificial beauty just described, then fields, and stretching off into the far distance, more meadows planted with trees.[13]

Pliny escorts us from a path traveled within the house proper to a formal garden that is the inheritance of all Romans, to the far away of the meadow, mountains, and sea. His spaces expand and contract, yet no part can be omitted from the whole if the totality of enjoyment is to be experienced.

From Pliny we move over a half-century to the more magnificent villa of the Emperor Hadrian near Tivoli. Its ruins provide visible evidence of a more complex spatial conception that integrated interior, exterior, and the land in a totally new way. Hadrian was a Spaniard by birth, one of the foreign rulers of Rome, vigorous traveler, sensitive student of Greek philosophy, restless melancholiac, artist, and amateur architect. He created his home in the Tivoli hills, a palace that looks to Rome in its vast vaulted spaces, to Greece in its paraphernalia of colonnades, statues, and works of art, but possibly derives its overall sense of moving design from the blood of Iberia and its mixed Celtic-Iberian mainstream. Seneca, Martial, Lucan, and many Roman writers of the first century, the time of Hadrian's predecessor Trajan, were, like the two emperors, born in Spain.

The Villa Adriana is uniquely built on an asymmetrical axis. Such order and unity as it possesses is attained by connecting buildings, intermediate gardens, water courses, and pillared walkways. It is a landscape you must traverse because new vistas are disclosed with every turn of the road.

In the *Serapaeum,* a large building probably planned as a dining hall, a circular apse 54 ft in diameter rises to a vaulted mosaic-encrusted semidome. Here the upward glance is offset by a course of fountains and falling waters. This arrangement is frequently known as a *nymphaeum* or shrine to the lovely divinities of nature known as nymphs—a pretty conceit. It expresses that love for water in motion that is to be seen in the stepped water runnels in Pompeian houses and which since the days of the seventeenth-century sculptor Bernini we forever associate with the

eternal city. Hadrian glorified curved spaces elsewhere on his 600 acres of total architecture. Every visitor should stand under the groins of the domed baths and again in the vestibule to the summer palace on the grounds. These so thrilled the arch-romantic Piranesi in the eighteenth century that he sketched them many times and left to posterity an enhanced feeling for the sky-bound spaces of the Roman mind.

In the colonnade surrounding the *Canopus* (Hadrian had a penchant for giving foreign place names to his creations—here one from a sanctuary on the Nile), the emperor created a graceful essay in space interpenetration by using both Greek trabeated and Latin arch forms. The arches rest directly on their column supports and alternate with a horizontal architrave to form an open series that bounds the circular end of the largest pool on the estate. This peristyle was studded with marble statues, copies of the work of such foremost Greek sculptors as Phidias, Polycleitus, and Praxiteles. Some are now in the Capitoline and Vatican Museums whereas all *in situ* are copies of the Hadrian copies.

In the late villas we note that towers become a part of the architecture. Even Pliny alludes to a "tower three stories high" from which he can view the landscape.[14] Later when Rome became unsafe they were included for protection.

About 150 years after the reign of Hadrian the Emperor Diocletian built his palace at Spalato, the modern town of Split. Its outer fortress walls now shelter centuries of semiattached conglomerate buildings which nestle in their protective shade. In the third century these ramparts enclosed an entire royal city with ample space for imperial mansions and outer chariot courses. Its ruins provided a source of neoclassic design produced by the eighteenth-century architect Robert Adam. The enceinte, however, is testimony to the fact that the Rome of peaceful vistas and daring construction, vast spaces, and ordered Greek proportions, could not survive the barbarian hordes.

INTERIOR DESIGN

Interior design, no matter who performs its services, involves more than the selection and arrangement of furnishings. Indeed, equipment may be meager in some interiors, as, for instance, in civic halls. The arrangement of the fittings must be a matter of conjecture until much later than the days of Rome when some sort of pictorial record can be trusted.

The treatment of interior surfaces qualifies architecture in all the ways suggested by Vitruvius. We have learned about it, through archaeological finds, from the very earliest times. Now, however, with Rome, the treatment of interior surfaces becomes historically interesting. In the Vitruvian trilogy the aesthetic purpose begins to loom large. If the others are not forgotten, this cannot be entirely decried.

Interior Details and Surfaces

Rome relied on statuary for much of its architectural enrichment. In important building this was often the stone plaque or frieze, as seen in the various commemorative arches and columns that dot the Roman landscape. Sculpture in the round was designed to fill the important interior niches, which, as in the Pantheon, were often treated to an aedicule of an arch order.

The Romans of the later empire also embellished their walls and ceilings with stucco reliefs. This was a means of decoration equally well suited to flat and curved surfaces because the motifs did not have to be large and modeling could be adapted to changing areas. Relief shapes acted as liaison between large vaults and floriated capitals. Most of the stucco patterns were low relief and use was made of some of the same details found in Roman wall painting.

The Romans elaborated the art of mosaics, using stone for floor patterns and often glass for murals. Being like gems, the glass tesserae were frequently used to line niches in which fountains and/or statuary were placed.

In the vestibule of the *House of the Tragic Poet* at Pompeii everyone is familiar with the mosaic-floor watchdog that bears the inscription "Cave Canem"—beware the dog—an early example of sympathetic magic or wishful thinking.

In the *House of the Faun,* again in the unearthed city, one of the most interesting Roman mosaics, the *Battle of Issus,* was found. This was the Cilician battle of 333 B.C. in which Alexander

the Great met and finally subdued the forces of the Persian king Darius. This mosaic is thought to be a Roman copy of a Greek painting, a fact that enhances its importance, for, despite the differences necessarily dictated by the technique, the Issus mosaic is a link to the lost paintings that are assumed to have been made in Greece in Hellenistic years. The Alexander mosaic is a complicated pictorial piece that shows figures in balanced tension—more reminiscent of Greek than of Roman style. It is now in the Archaeological Museum at Naples.

In far-off Britain Roman mosaics were excavated, some as deep as 19 ft, some exposed by bombings of World War II. A particularly lovely lunette which showed Venus rising from the sea is in the British Museum (Figure 4.10). It was found as far afield as Hemsworth in Dorset and seems particularly appropriate to its island home.

Surfaces on the smallest and least complicated of Roman buildings, the *domus,* were flat and comparatively large because the structural system was trabeation and the plan was inward-oriented. An affluent owner could afford embellishment and, to the Italian, this frequently suggested color. Historians have divided Pompeian wall painting into successive styles. The phenomenon of styles generally means the separation of social strata, for styles represent change, which is expensive. There is something based on the desire for social aggrandizement in the invocation of a new style. This motivation can easily result in a mere passing fashion, and there is some evidence that the wall murals of Pompeii exhibit a little of this arbitrariness in their nature.

The paintings on Roman walls have been divided into four distinct groups, although their stylistic barriers tend to become clouded. Before any of the four operated we recognize an instance of faking in what is called the *austere* or *inlay style* in which plaster-coated masonry walls are ruled in regular fashion to give the appearance of blocks of marble. This is the character of the walls in the *House of the Surgeon.*

In examples in all the styles of painting we find simulated wall divisions—horizontal bands and vertical panels—which suggest architectural orders. When the space is high, it is topped by an *attic story* that can be observed in the commem-

Figure 4.10 *The Birth of Venus*. Roman mosaic found in Britain at Hemsworth, Dorset. British Museum. (Reproduced by Courtesy of the Trustees of the British Museum.)

orative arches throughout the capital. Thus the decorative element would be located within easy reach of the eye.

A variety of colors can be found in these murals. A dark gray or black, representative of marble or of the earth, was often used for the upper portion of a room or for the section corresponding to the architectural stylobate. A vermilion or saffron yellow might push a background forward. A crisp green obtained from malachite (basic carbonate of copper) is seen in some areas.

The technique of the later murals is open to question. Was it secco on dry plaster or was it painting into the last wet coat, as Vitruvius advises?[15] Richter claims the latter and outlines the method.[16]

The first Pompeian style, often called *incrustation* (200–60 B.C.),[17] used the panels as a base for color treatment without placing any representation on them.

This flat treatment did not hold interest for Roman painters. Once introduced to the now-lost examples of Hellenistic murals, they began to simulate three-dimensional space and carried it beyond what we assume to have been the limits of Greek achievement. The second manner

114

of Pompeian painting (60–20 B.C.) makes use of this skill. It is called the *architectural style,* in which architectural elements, such as columns and arches, were used to frame the panels within which the painter would attempt to show an architectural scene rendered in linear perspective. This style can be seen best in the panorama painted on the wall of a cubiculum in the *Boscoreale,* a small villa near Pompeii (Figure 4.11). This decoration is now owned by the Metropolitan Museum of Art. Because the Roman had no clear idea of the geometry of such drawing, the rendering is done as if seen from many viewpoints with the eye scanning a wide area and shifting its focus as needed. One-point vision was not clearly understood until Renaissance scientist-artists studied its nature.

In the Boscoreale scene, however, we have a fairly convincing presentation, isolated in its architectural paneled frame, of a view of distant objects. Here is the breaking of the flat plane of the wall to allow the mind to escape outward into space. Although this may seem indefensible to those who subscribe to the idea that the flat surface should not be punctured by illusions, it does represent the pictorial analogue of the villa space concepts, the inside-outside and into-the-distance percept.

Within the architectural-style framework the Romans likewise developed the special category of landscape painting. Where the Greeks were seldom able to subordinate man to his surroundings, the Roman was a lover of the land for its own sake. This he expressed somewhat in the manner of the later Sung Dynasty painters of China, in a type of aerial perspective. This mode, often called *Hellenistic Impressionism,* had antecedents in Near Eastern art and may have come to Rome by way of Egypt and Alexandria, now so close under Roman rule. In the Latin examples two notes, merely hinted at previously, are strikingly dominant. The first is the opening of a vista into receding space and the second is the use of atmospheric color and light to gain this spatial quality.

Several examples may be cited to illustrate this most charming phase of Roman wall painting. There is the fresco now in the Villa Albani Galleries in Rome; the Odyssey scenes (Plate 6) taken from a domus on the Esquiline Hill, which

are now in the Vatican Museum; and the lovely frieze in the domus Livia at Prima Porta, now to be seen in the Museo delle Terme. The last is reminiscent of the garden at Akhenaten's palace. It achieves the ideal of bringing nature indoors, whereas the Boscoreale mural takes the eyes outside. The Livia painting tells its story in the continuous running manner typical of Greek books in which the scene becomes a picture-book scroll. This, we recall, was a unique feature of the Tell-el-Amarna painting. In Rome the single panel story was more general, although not universal.

The Romans likewise developed a realistic sculpturesque type of figure depiction at this time and used it in the confines of the architectural style. Some crossing over of the personages from one panel to the next occurs as the scene of action takes place in front of an architectural backdrop. This type of painting is to be seen in the *Villa of the Mysteries* outside Pompeii, with its murals of intimate scenes from the mystery rites of one of the esoteric religions that had filtered into Rome from the Orient. We note that these oversize figures convey a new experience of proximate flesh and blood quite removed from the more detached idealistic character of Hellenic human representation.

The third and fourth styles of mural painting need not be regarded as completely distinct from each other. Vitruvius[18] condemns them wholeheartedly as representative of the "bad taste" of his day. One man's meat is another's poison; the eighteenth-century neoclassicists enjoyed this Italian theatrical fantasia.

In the third style, often called the *ornate style* and sometimes the *actual wall style* (20 B.C. to A.D. 60), the panel surround is composed of pseudoarchitectural elements executed in flat tones. The supporting features, undoubtedly intended as mere wall dividers, are imaginatively conceived as vines sprouting tendrils, lifting candelabra, or enclosing vignettes. They contain a number of different paintings, fulfilling a function similar to that of the framed pictures on our walls.

The fourth wall treatment is known as the *intricate style* (Figure 4.12)—intricate in that it incorporates much that has preceded in one last gigantic heterogeneous effort. This final type of

Figure 4.11 The cubiculum of the Villa Boscoreale, near Pompeii, first century B.C. Second or architectural style of wall painting. Metropolitan Museum of Art, New York. (The Metropolitan Museum of Art, Rogers Fund, 1903.)

treatment became the norm for the empire and lasted throughout its existence. In the triclinium of the *House of the Vettii* at Pompeii there is a depiction of the infant Hercules destroying the serpent. An example in the fourth style, it illustrates through the emergence of light from the rear the new principle regarding light as an active element that serves to emphasize and orient im-

portant objects in space. The fact that this light was often somewhat arbitrarily and inconsistently used (e.g., the back-lighting of the columns changes to the front lighting of Hercules) does not detract from its aesthetic usefulness.

Indeed, if one has been trained to depict, hence to see, only in accordance with the laws of optics, then one might condemn Roman painting because in many ways it does not conform. In others—atmospheric recession, form through shading, particularized depiction, sensitive and sensuous use of color, and the presence of light —it does. The Romans—if the men who created these works were from Italy—were fine artists. And, with respect to multiple viewpoints, we feel differently about this since Picasso.

In addition to walls, ceilings, and floors, we must often consider the inner surfaces of windows and doors, for they have faces that can mar or make an effect. Doors in Rome, as noted in Egypt, were comparatively high and narrow; those in the *House of the Faun,* for instance, rose 12 ft.[19] At Herculaneum, because the inundation was by lava flow, some doors have been preserved almost intact. They are mortised to a hardwood cylinder, rotating outward in sockets placed in thresholds and lintel. The aedicule was often embellished with a classical order surround. In the Boscoreale painting an elaborate one of this sort can be seen. Squared pilasters and an entablature consisting of architrave, frieze, and cornice are indicated. This would be termed the full classical treatment.

The simplest openings had a broad wooden or stone lintel and side posts or possibly a molding enframement, seen in the *House of the Black Drawing Room* and in the *House of the Mosaic Atrium* at Herculaneum. Often a lintel extended laterally beyond the jambs of an opening. This is familiarly known as the *aedicule with ears,* a form immensely popular throughout the Renaissance.

We hear much of the fact that the Romans manufactured window glass and that their buildings had windows. This must not be interpreted in the modern sense—there were no large sheets of insulated glass, and except for the arched opening to a first-floor shop, unprotected by a complete closing, apertures were uncommon on the street side of buildings. Small ones are to be

116

found on the upper floors of insulae and some domi, the latter opening onto commonly owned peristyle courts.

Private windows and inner doors were sheltered by portieres (*velli*) hung from wooden rings, quite a few of which were unearthed at Pompeii. Grilles, finely meshed, provided some protection. Better homes probably used glass panes leaded in place and these may have been the type that Pliny describes. Shattered glass and lead strips have been found among the Pompeian ruins. Vellum and a substance called *lapis specularis,* similar to thin sheets of mica, were occasionally used.

The Roman, as seen in the details and surface treatments of the interiors of his buildings, was a man who thought in terms of reaching out to

immensity. Cicero's words in the beginning quotation of this chapter seem to indicate that what the Roman engineering genius made possible in architecture and what his tactical talent accomplished as a conquerer his decorative sense insisted on in his mural art. Walls are broken by coffers, niches, and projecting aediculae. Painted flat surfaces come close to being true perspective. Wall treatments maneuver to look out to vistas or to bring an idyllic illusion of natural scenery within. Mosaics with their colorful and scintillating shading belie any notion of confined surfaces. Yet the dressing is basically in terms of Greek forms: the orders and the ornamental vocabulary. It is almost as though the Roman needed to bolster his far-reaching ego with support from a preceding culture. That he combined the two eras with such skill is in itself an achievement not to be belittled.

Figure 4.12   Ixion Room, House of the Vettii. Pompeii, A.D. first century. Fourth or intricate style of wall painting. (Alinari/Editorial Photocolor Archives.)

ROMAN FURNITURE

Collections

In addition to the usual secondary sources of information such as literature, wall painting, and funerary monuments, we are fortunate in possessing numerous stone and metal examples of Roman furniture. These relics may be seen at Pompeii, Herculaneum, and the Archaeological Museum in Naples, in the Etruscan tombs and the Archaeological Museum in Florence, at the Vatican Museum, the Villa Giulia Museum, and the Torlonia Museum in Rome, and in other major collections throughout the world.

Materials and Techniques

Not only did the Romans use more furniture than the Classical Greeks but their examples were also more elaborate in material, technique, and form. Exotic woods were prized, the most costly of which was probably the wood of the citrus tree, which provided boards as large as 4 ft in breadth. Cicero may have said, "The Romans hate private luxury but love public magnificance,"[20] but he reputedly paid $20,000 in today's coin for a round table, the top of which was citrus.

Decoration of Roman furniture was likewise costly. Veneering with expensive woods and inlay with tortoise shell was favored, as was mounting with iron, bronze, silver, and gold. If Cicero spoke for the late Republic, he was certainly not a truthful commentator on the taste of the Empire.

Types and Forms

The basic character of Roman furniture indicated its descent from Greek styles. Certain types, however, were so favored or developed in the West that they merited the statement that they were Etruscan or Roman.

The important Greek chair, the *thronos*, becomes the Roman *solium*. One model, which was perfected in Etruria to the extent that it is usually labeled an Etruscan contribution, had a rounded back extending to form arms and solid sides (Figure 4.13). The Romans preferred a form with a

Figure 4.13 Roman *solium*. Replica of red marble throne in the Louvre, Paris. The Vatican Museum. (Alinari/Editorial Photocolor Archives.)

solid base terminating in the front in large scrolls or in similar oversized decorative features such as animal legs or human torsos.

Examples of the *klismos* chair are less frequent. In Rome it is called the *cathedra*. It often appears on wall paintings where it seems to be used largely by women. The cathedra gave its name to the bishop's seat in early Christian observance, hence to the cathedral, or seat of the bishopric (whence the phrase *ex cathedra*, to speak with authority).

Lower in the hierarchy of seats was the stool or *sella*, the Greek *dipthros*. Its forms were taken from more important pieces of furniture. The Metropolitan Museum of Art possesses an exceptionally lovely sella which is carved from marble, replete with cherubs, playful animals, and overflowing cornucopias, all sobered by partnership with borders of inlaid geometrics. Marble appointments were customary atrium or peristyle

Figure 4.14 Fulcrum to a Roman bed. Bronze with inlay of silver. Conservatory Museo, Rome. (Courtesy of the Musei Capitolini.)

ally possess both head and foot boards and sometimes the addition of a back, thus approaching the shape of some contemporary pieces. The fulcra, or end boards, of Roman couches were lavish, often executed in bronze, ivory, or silver. Their graceful cyma curves terminate in the head of an animal, such as the horse, a bird such as the swan, or occasionally the human torso. One intricate fulcrum (Figure 4.14) is in the palace of the town council, the *Palazzo dei Conservatori* on Rome's Capitol Hill. In addition to its spirited bronze top, which represents a long-eared, curly-maned mule necked with a halter of grape leaves, the panel proper is inlaid with silver and shows satyrs and maenads in a series of vintage scenes. A larger bust of a maenad nestles at its base.

Besides the customary low dining table (*mensa*), the Romans used higher ones for display purposes. The late Greek unipod was well represented in this group and the large rectangular form with solid ornamental ends was so favored that it became essentially a Roman piece (Figure 4.15). The *cartibulum* or ceremonial marriage table was in this category.

Much of the Pompeian furniture is considered to be of Greek craftsmanship. Certainly the lovely little flower stand in the Archaeological Museum at Naples, with its tripod legs surmounted by sphinxes, its garlanded swags, and its spiral braces, indicates that peculiarly Greek quality of stylized representation of the human form that lifts it above the vulgar.

accoutrements. The *curule* or folding stool (or chair) was common, possibly because of close ties with Egypt. Its very name derives from the fact that it became the customary seat for the Roman curules, or city magistrates.

The Roman bed or *lectus* was a valued piece of furniture. It has been mentioned that the ceremonial marriage couch was placed in the atrium on the marriage night and remained a symbol of connubial fidelity. During the empire the dining couches in the triclinia were for the women as well as the men of the family. Roman beds usu-

Many Roman tables had shelves for precious belongings. Indeed, cabinets for display purposes (known as *armaria*) may be said to have begun their prolific existence with the treasure-loving Romans (Figure 4.16). Even the sideboard or small rimmed table (*abacus*) for show of plate belongs to Hellenistic and especially late Roman times.

Figure 4.15 Marble table support with satyrs and griffins. Roman. The Vatican Museums. (Photograph by the Vatican Museums.)

Figure 4.16 Detail, Frieze of Cupids, House of the Vettii, Pompeii. Note the *armarium* or open-shelf cupboard. (G. C. Ball.)

Lighting devices are necessary paraphernalia and should be designed for beauty as well as for utility. The first artificial light came from wicks floating in oil. A safety device, seen in empire lamps, covered the vessel and allowed the wick to protrude through one hole while a smaller opening admitted the necessary air.

Roman lamps were planned as decorative objects. Among those found at Pompeii were many equipped with handles for carrying, others to be suspended from the ceiling by chains, and small boat-shaped table lamps. They were made of clay, iron, stone, and bronze and often had their own stands which ranged in height from 2½ to 5 ft. Some pedestals had a central shaft supported by a tripod base. Supporting a round vessel, they resembled our present-day table lamps.

Candles (*candelae*) with wick immersed in tallow were also used. Our name for the tall lamp stand, *candelabra,* designates the candle holder.

TEXTILES

Evidence of Roman textiles must be inferred from illustrations and the literature. Loose coverings on furniture, pillows, and hangings are clearly apparent in mosaics, wall paintings, and bas reliefs. Attached upholstery had not yet made its appearance, although the depictions indicate by the occasional absence of folds that fitting to the article was usual.

Wool and linen, supplemented by skins and rushes, were still the raw materials. The Romans practiced scientific sheep breeding and raising. The famous Tarentine sheep were developed and crossbred with the native white sheep of Spain to create the Merino brand. This was the work of Junius Coluella, a Roman living in Spain and Caesar's expert in husbandry.

Cotton awnings are said to have made their appearance during the late Republic. Obviously Rome was aware of the potentialities of this new fiber, for Pliny refers to the growing of cotton in Egypt.

Silk was still a more-than-luxury fiber. Introduced after the Parthian wars, it arrived in Rome via Persia. Waltzing[21] lists *serarii,* or manipulators of silk, among the trades of imperial Rome.

CERAMICS

The earliest important Italian pottery was the black or brownish reduction-fired ware of Etruria. Polished to resemble iron vessels, it was known as *Bucchero pottery.*

The Etruscans were skilled ceramists. Their terra cotta tiles became the customary roofing material of the peninsula. For pure technical skill some of their molded terra cotta statuettes are phenomenal. From such large pieces to the small

Figure 4.17 Arretine pottery bowl. Italian-Tuscan, ca. 200 B.C.–A.D. 100. British Museum, London. (Reproduced by Courtesy of the Trustees of the British Museum.)

canopic Villanovan jars in human form the vigor in their designs is a far cry from the prettiness to which later potters were often addicted. Many of these masterpieces were mold-formed and incised decoration was added.

This facility in mold work was transmitted to the Romans and used in their modeling and molding of stucco reliefs, wall plaques, and ceiling embellishments.

Arretine pottery, named from the town near Florence (Arezzo) where it was first found, dates from about 200 B.C. to 100 A.D. and is another example of molding technique (Figure 4.17). This ware had a red or occasionally black body, embossed and alkaline glazed.[22] Its generic name was *terra sigillata,* so called from the *sigilla* or incised stamps applied to the mold which then came out as embossing. Arretine ware was the common household pottery of the Roman world.

The theater-loving Romans produced another embossed ware called *Gnathian* for a location in Apulia, in the heel of Italy (Figure 4.18). Its glazed black body was decorated with a white and polychrome slip and embellished with theater masks and other stage paraphernalia.

Pottery that rather closely simulated Attic styles was manufactured in southern Italy and Etruria. Although painting on these pieces followed Greek precedence, the organizing sense of the Western artist was less highly developed. There is a tendency toward over elaboration of detail and always a provincialism that bespeaks the artist working in a foreign manner. As in Greece, names were associated with these pieces. From the fifth century B.C. we learn of the *Pisticci* and *Amykos* painters and, among others, of *Sisyphus, Darius,* and finally the *Taporley* group. The distinctions to be seen in the works of these painters constitute an interesting field for study.

Figure 4.18 Gnathian-ware vase. Southern Italy, early third century. B.C. Height, 46.2 cm. Cleveland Museum of Art. (The Cleveland Museum of Art, Purchase, John L. Severance Fund.)

GLASS

Pliny wrote:

> The highest value is placed upon glass which is entirely colorless and transparent as possible, resembling crystal. For drinking vessels, glass has quite superseded the use of gold and silver.[23]

There you have the Roman achievement in a nutshell. It must be remembered that this was the same Pliny (23 B.C.–79 A.D., the elder) who is responsible for the tale of the invention of glass by Phoenician merchants who, coming ashore with a cargo of natron, happened to place a cooking pot on a block of the material. The combination of sand, natron, and fire supposedly made the flux that annealed to glass.

Glass Blowing

Pliny's interest in glass was timely, for about the middle of the first century B.C. it was discovered, possibly in Syria, that glass could be formed by blowing. This facilitated the manufacture of many diverse shapes, opened avenues to the manufacture of glass of better quality, and led to other new methods of production and decoration.

Nearly everyone has witnessed the interesting feat on the part of a glass blower of *gathering* his metal from the *glory hole* or furnace. This operation is performed on the end of a long hollow rod known as the *pontil*. With lungs strained from long practice and fingers twirling the mass with magic dexterity, he produces from the inert globule any manner of fanciful shapes in the speediest of times. Pliny described this method as a wonderful new technique.

Because the blowpipe was hollow, it was less heavy than the solid copper rod it superseded. It could therefore be much longer. This enabled the operator to stand farther from the furnace, to handle his *gob* at a higher temperature, and to fuse its ingredients better. Without any change in composition this resulted in a clearer glass, although by our standards the Romans still "saw through a glass darkly," for no means of extracting the iron impurities that colored the batch had yet been found.

Syrian-Roman Glass

Roman glass really means glass of the Roman empire and should rightly include the contemporary glass of the Roman provinces to the east, south, and north. This includes glass from Syria, of which more is said in Chapter 5. Syrian blown glass, though relatively simple in shape, is frequently embossed in designs imitative of silver work. It is sometimes further embellished by cutting. Naturally of a soft yellow or delicate green color, gold powder was occasionally strewn on the glass gather and rolled into its hot surface. A glass known as *semé d'or* resulted.

Egyptian-Roman Glass

The Egyptians had always admired colored glass and soon began to produce glasses of many hues; for example, they made *millefiore* or thousand-flower bowls in which myriad colored ends of glass were inserted into a mold and fused. Precise or variegated patterns were the result, depending on the amount of reheating that was done.

Having engraved glass long since, it is not surprising that they should have perfected *cameo glass*. Here, a bowl of blue glass might be given an overlay of white. The outer covering was then cut away to reveal a blue background with a white pattern in relief.

The Portland Vase

The Roman vessel known as the *Portland Vase* (Figure 4.19) was of cameo glass and had been a funerary urn of the amphora shape. Excavated from a tomb in the seventh century, it came into the possession of the Barberini family. More than 100 years later it was purchased by the Duchess of Portland, whose husband lent the vase to Josiah Wedgwood, the potter, for copying. Wedgwood issued twenty-six copies in black jasperware. The original vase was placed in the British Museum where a crazed man subsequently shattered it. Pieced together, it is on display, like the Raphael tapestries in the Vatican whose exciting history will be recounted, somewhat the worse for wear!

Figure 4.19 Cameo glass funerary urn known as the Portland Vase. Roman. Height, 11 in. British Museum, London. (Reproduced by Courtesy of the Trustees of the British Museum.)

Window Glass

Window glass, as previously mentioned, appears with the empire. This glass was formed by placing a glob on a smooth surface and pounding it into flatness with a wooden mallet. This process could scarcely have made the windows at Versailles but it was a beginning, albeit one that had to walk backward during the ensuing centuries, when glass that let in light did not provide protection from the marauder.

Glassmen became wealthy as the demand for their product spread with the legions. Emperor Severus soon found taxation of glass houses profitable to the crown and his heavy toll spelled their doom, but by this time neither tax collector nor glassmen were to benefit long.

METALS

Although the Villanovans introduced the use of iron to Italy, only tools and weapons were made from this metal. The earlier Italian bronze culture was not displaced and indeed remained coextensive with the civilized world. The Etruscan people were both wealthy and luxury loving. Fine examples of bronze furniture, utensils, and statues were found in the tombs of their lordly class like the one named for its nineteenth-century discoverers Regolini-Galassi at Cerveteri. Likewise precious metals—gold and silver—were fashioned with a high order of skill. During and following the seventh century some of these metal objects may have come from Greece or may have been made by Greek artisans in Italy. The return of Greek prosperity after the recession caused by the Doric invasions may be accounted for by just such trade and intercourse.

The Romans of the late Republic and Empire, equally skilled as metal workers, formed objects that in technique and in design followed Greek precedents. By Hellenistic times the Greek supplies were loot for Roman conquerors and a route other than by commerce is indicated for Greek inspiration in Roman art. Many a Roman author speaks of the expensive craze for antique silver vessels among the rich. Martial in an epigram addresses Charinus as follows:

> You alone collected every kind of silver plate and you alone possess Myron's antique works of art, you alone an embossed product by Phidias, you alone the results of Mentor's toil.[24]

Collections

In times of peril treasures are victims to the plunderer and to the melting pot to ensure money for arms. Caches are likely to be quickly abandoned. To this last exigency we owe hoards of Pompeian silver. In 1895 a treasure was uncovered in a wine vat below a villa at Boscoreale. It is now at the Louvre. In Pompeii in 1930 at the *Casa del Menandro* a wooden chest with 118 pieces of family silver was unearthed. Much of a similar nature was discovered in the municipal gymnasium to which the unfortunate inhabitants fled for hoped-for security. The Museum at Pompeii and the Archaeological Museum at Naples should be visited to view these finds.

Other treasures have been located farther north. *The Hildesheim Treasure* (northwest Germany) with articles from the Augustan age represents Roman silver perhaps belonging to a Roman general or possibly looted by the barbarians and hidden for safekeeping. It was relocated in the Berlin Museum. Another assemblage of pieces which came to light near Bernay, France, undoubtedly belonged to the Temple of Mercury at Berthouville nearby.

English finds are being unearthed, as archaeological work goes on apace, chief among which is the *Mildenhall Treasure* of the fifth and fourth centuries found during the Second World War in Mildenhall, England, and now at the British Museum.

Types and Characteristics

The articles contained in these stores were the usual cups, dishes, sacrificial bowls, toilet pieces, and even some domestic furniture, such as tripod tables and candelabra. There were saltcellars and containers for pepper, sauce boats, platters, and many receptacles for special uses and with specialized names, much as an inventory of the nineteenth century would read. But for all of this the Romans are thought to have eaten with their fingers, inasmuch as the spoon seems to have been the only table tool commonly found. One type with a pointed end and a round bowl (the *cochleare*) was used for extracting shellfish. The other, known as the *ligula*, was ovoid in the bowl and about the size of a dessert spoon.[25]

The Romans favored high embossing on silver. This style of ornamentation is somewhat foreign to northern tastes, except as the seventeenth-century German and Dutch mannerist goldsmiths practiced it.

The Cleveland Museum of Art[26] has one very interesting beaker of Roman Empire silversmith-ing. It was found in 1862 among articles of silver and numerous coins at Vicarello, slightly north of Rome. Here sulfur springs associated with the worship of Apollo were located, into which such good-luck offerings had been tossed. The vessel under discussion had apparently been placed there for that reason. The method of fabrication demonstrated in this cup is the typical Roman double-wall technique in which the outer wall was hammered up in repoussé and enriched by chasing, the lining (added for strength) was shaped with the mallet, and the foot probably cast and joined to the rest.

The subject matter is likewise indicative of Rome of the day. First we see a shrine to the god Priapus (Figure 4.20), a lesser Roman deity thought to have originated in Asia Minor and propitiated as god of the fruitfulness of the fields and herds. He is seen as a rather serious-minded herm standing beside a pillar on which is mounted a disk of unknown significance. Such herms, often of painted wood, were frequently found in the Roman garden. In this case the divine image is being caressed by one maenad who sits quietly at his side as another (Figure 4.21) dances around him in frenzied motion. A satyr joins in the excuse for celebration.

An adjacent table carries receptacles for gifts of Greek pottery. Their representation is not done in consistent perspective, for the horizon height shifts often. Although roundness of form is suggested throughout, space is shallow and a flat backdrop forbids the spectator to enter at depth. Nevertheless the embossed table projects beyond the plane of the other reliefs—an illusionist device often seen in Roman work. The entire composition is securely anchored on a base line.

In this metal receptacle of the Augustan age we can read Roman interest in a derived cult, the emergence of new space treatments, and significant contrasts between quiet restrained treatment of subject matter and vigorous movement. The Archaeological Museum in Bologna owns a bronze Etruscan *lebes* handle (Figure 4.22). Its bisymmetrical sculpturesque forms, its conventional antefixes, and its Aeolian scrolls take us back 400 years to the day when Italian art inherited the equanimity of ancient Greece as well as a dramatic and austere counterpoint. The

Figure 4.20 Vicarello Goblet: The Shrine of Priapus. Vicarello, Italy, late first century B.C. to A.D. early first century. Silver. Height, 11 cm. Cleveland Museum of Art. (The Cleveland Museum of Art, Purchase from the J. H. Wade Fund.)

Figure 4.21 Vicarello Goblet: Dancing Maenad. Vicarello, Italy, late first century B.C. to A.D. early first century. Silver. Height, 11 cm. Cleveland Museum of Art. (The Cleveland Museum of Art, Purchase from the J. H. Wade Fund.)

Vicarello cup indicates how poise can be translated into passivity and vigor into abandoned motion. Art has split into dramatic contrasts that all but destroy unity of conception. The door is opened for the performance of the next act, when synthesis will create a new completeness as seen in the medieval complex.

DESCRIPTIVE SUMMARY

Roman building was more complex than the Greek. Using both trabeated and arcuated construction, it frequently annexed the structural components of Greek architecture—the column

and its load—as pure surface decoration. This borrowed finery, placed judiciously on the vast Roman forms, resulted in a unique expression of magnificence wedded to power. It was so right for the circumstance of the Roman state.

Thus Roman architecture became decorated architecture almost from its very beginning. The only exception occurred in the bald engineering feats of purely utilitarian structures such as the aqueducts. The really significant fact is not that the Roman felt the need for decoration but that, in its creation, he strengthened the sense of movement and space in his design. Breaks in the surfaces, whether real or illusory, opened up enclosures in favor of far horizons.

Figure 4.22 Handle of a *lebes* (kettle or cauldron). Etruscan, ca. 450–400 B.C. Bronze. Height, 14 cm. width, 24 cm. Museo Civico Archaeologico, Bologna. (Photo, Courtesy of the Cleveland Museum of Art.)

The Roman not only thought expansively, he thought exuberantly. His decorative forms, as well as his feeling for the necessity for their existence, indicate that his was not the taste for chaste simplicity. The tendency was toward profuseness of ornament. Subdivisions are connected by realistic bridges such as wreaths, cornucopias, and candelabra. Prominent motifs were the intertwined ribbons, the garlands, vases of flowers, baskets filled with earth's largesse, and fat little amorini lightly poised in space. There are so many of these pleasant depictions and all are certainly Rome's unique contribution to the decorative vocabulary of design. Balance them against the symbols of imperial pomp—the fasces, the imperial masques of the emperors—and the result is a picture of Rome.

As mentioned earlier, Roman art is one of contrasts and contradictions. It works with a phenomenal sense of bigness. It is, however, tightly regimented. This appears in its respect for bisymmetry, its regard for the classical canons, and its willingness to paint within the confines of the frame and to sculpture within the restrictions of forms such as the herm and column.

Roman legions covered much of Europe, but their allegiance was to the small walled city of the Tiber. Cicero writes of great fondness for his country home and its extensive acres; but Cicero fled back to his beloved Rome with every proffered opportunity for civic duty.

Contrasts mixed with passion can be counted on to create excitement in art. For better or for worse Italy will often be its fountainhead.

ORIENTAL INTERLUDE

The first reasonably direct contact of the West with the Orient occurred during the ascendancy of the classical world. This is the time of the great silk routes and, although Romans did not get to China nor Chinese to the West, their wares were exchanged. Thus for the first time it becomes

126

important to discuss here the decorative arts of the far East and especially of China.

Following the almost legendary Shangs, the Chou Dynasty ruled in Central China from 1027 to 256 B.C. In reality a feudal conclave, they held together the neolithic cultures of the central plains, maintaining a stability that formed the nucleus of the later empire of the Hans.

During the ascendancy of the Chou Dynasty China produced two great religious leaders. The first was Lao-tzu (born 604 B.C.), who taught a mystic version of the ancient animistic creeds. Confucius (K'ung Ch'iu, born 551 B.C.) was by comparison a social and ethical leader whose doctrine is strongly impregnated with excerpts dealing with problems of expedience in a feudal society. Thus he contributed to the permanence of the Chinese civilization during these formative years.

In the last years of the Chou rulers a family known as the Ch'ins gained control and in a short time forged an empire that was essentially coextensive with the present Chinese state. The Han Dynasty succeeded the Ch'in and ruled from 220 B.C. to A.D. 25. Theirs was a rigorous centralized government. They established the trade routes across both north and south China over which the Oriental silks were carried to Rome and Buddhist missionaries first entered the country. This event, although traditionally associated with the latter part of the A.D. first century did not gain national significance until the rule of the Tartar, or Wei, Dynasty (386–535).

Oriental Ceramics

Sometime during the late Chou Dynasty the Chinese learned how to make high-fired stoneware[27] (i.e., composed of ordinary clay fired at a temperature so high that its body becomes hard and nonporous). Perhaps *learned* is not the appropriate word. The deposits of *kaolin*, or china clay, capable of withstanding kiln temperatures necessary to create porcelain and the accompanying *petuntse*, or china stone, both requisite to the manufacture of *china* or *porcelain*, were close at hand, probably making the creation of porcelaneous wares an inevitable later happening. Porcelain was that vitrified,

often translucent, clear bell-like intoning material that was the gift of the orient to the arts of life. In the process of its manufacture the kaolin provides the body and the petuntse, the flux.

In the late Chou Dynasty glass was imported from the Near East. The inventive Chinese, however, soon developed it independently. At this time its importance lay in the impetus given to glazing as a ceramic technique. Some early Chinese pottery vessels have a glaze only on the upper surface; hence it is probable that this covering was fused from the feldspathic elements in the soil. Feldspar is a natural quartz rock, therefore similar to glass in composition. Although lead-glazed wares were imported into China from the Near East, lead glazing was also developed by the Chinese at that time.

Chinese ceramics are a story for Chapter 5. Certain persistent types, however, had their inception during the reign of the late Chous and Hans. *Yüeh ware* and *white slip-covered wares* were the most important. The former was a stoneware covered with an olive-colored iron oxide glaze and the ancestor of all of the later pieces known as the *celadons*. White slip covering forecast the precious Chinese white wares, the *blanc de chine*, in French parlance.

Burial figurines, substituted for the barbarous interments of the living with the dead, appear with the late Shang and early Chou Dynasties. Many were figures of horses. These burial statuettes reached the height of their excellence during the later T'ang Dynasty (Figure 4.23). Their bodies vary from a soft pottery to a hard porcelaneous stoneware, glazed in yellow, green amber, and bluish violet.

Although the painted pottery of the Shang Dynasty found at An-Yan and dating from about 1350 B.C. is remarkable for its fluidity of style, molded and incised decoration is usual to the ceramics of this early period.

Oriental Metalwork

During the Shang and early Chou periods the Chinese did some superb bronze work. Their skill is best seen in the ritual pieces used for sacrificial offerings. Technical efficiency never surpassed the heights reached in these vessels.

Figure 4.23   Camel. Amber lead-glazed earthenware. Grave offering. China. T'ang Dynasty, ca. late seventh to eighth century. Cleveland Museum of Art. (The Cleveland Museum of Art, John L. Severance Fund.)

Designs, however, although varying from standardized shapes, run a gamut of minor changes. From austere forms to those of tremendous plastic vitality, they descend to a less ornate and heavier style, with squatter proportions and realism substituted for stylization. Quite late pieces return to elegant but more playful concepts with inlays added to the all-bronze of former years.

The shapes of Chinese ceremonial bronzes have influenced those of Chinese ceramics. They differ from the shapes of Greek classical pottery; in general it may be said that their center of gravity is lower and that their upper flanges assume a calyx curve.

Oriental Textiles

Quantities of silk from the time of the Han Dynasty have been found in excavated sites as far west as Palmyra in Syria, which indicates that this luxury material was baggage for the caravan routes.

Some of these silks are in complex weaves, often termed in museum language "warp-faced compound weaves," although they are not technically the same as the Western compound weaves, which we consider later in greater detail. The motifs, sometimes geometric, consist of lozenges and rectangles, often with animal, bird, and flower inclusions. Motifs known as cloud bands weave in and out of other motifs, separating and binding them at the same time. The enclosed flora and fauna likewise developed along lines of greater animation and expressive movement.

There were also some fabulous and beautiful embroidered hangings and carpets found at Noin Ula in upper Mongolia which were the household and burial furnishings of the tribes who lived there. Here likewise were remnants of silks, some of them in full bolts. The Hermitage Museum has them.

Lacquers

The Oriental art of lacquer painting on wood, to be discussed later, owes its origin to artists of the late Chou Dynasty.

129

CHAPTER FIVE

The Middle Ages

300 TO 1550

THE OFFERING OF THE HEART

(Tapestry from Arras, XV Century)

Against a somber background, blue as midnight,
More blank and dark than cloud, as black as storm,
The almost moving leaves are almost golden,
The light is almost warm.

Seated a lady, wearing a cloak with ermine,
Holds in her hand, correctly gloved and bent,
A falcon, without feathered hood or jesses;
Her gaze is most intent

On what her hound, good little dog, is doing
Around her ankles, left front paw in air,
Regardless of the three white careless rabbits—
He does not see them there

Or turn as does the falcon, toward the gallant,
The gentleman, more elegant than smart,
Who comes, in crimson cloak with ermine lining,
And offers her a heart,

Holding it, chastely, between thumb and finger,
Whose "U" it does not fill, a plum in size,
A somewhat faded strawberry in color.
She does not raise her eyes.

How can a heart be beating in the bosom,
And yet held up so tiny in the hand?
Innocence, mystery; an Age of Science
Would hardly understand.

CULTURAL SPAN

More than 1000 years intervened between the creation of Constantinople as the eastern capital of the Roman Empire and the deaths in 1547 of Francis I of France and Henry VIII of England, monarchs so alike, yet so different. At the beginning of the epoch Roman civilization was sparring for a renaissance in the east; at the end East and West were separate and the seat of Western power had traveled north of the Alps.

Recent historical emphasis indicates that the Roman civilization had never completely died; it merely came under the influence of external forces and yielded to them in varying degrees.

Three major foreign elements intruded. The civilization of the East encroached through Byzantium and the trade routes. The crusaders were likewise responsible for the introduction of many innovations which an older civilization could offer to the newer fabric of the West.

Christianity imposed a new ideology on pagan classicism. Itself the heir of Hellenistic philosophy and eastern mysticism, it was preordained to provide the unstable and emerging cultures of Europe with the authority and faith that could mold them into a new world. Christianity was the all-pervasive cohesive force of medieval Europe.

The third characteristic which entered the bloodstream of life in the Middle Ages was that of barbaric virility. Originally somewhat tamed within the confines of Roman jurisdiction, it flamed into action as fresh hordes of nomads made inroads from beyond the Baltic, the Rhine, the Danube, and from the southern shores of the Mediterranean. Germanic tribes in the third century, the Huns in the fifth, the Moslems in the eighth, Norsemen and Slavs in the ninth—all squeezed former Roman territory until entrance was effected. In the process the eastern storehouse was again tapped, Graeco-Roman civilization was extended, Christianity was disseminated, and new energy was infused.

The domain of the old Roman Empire retained some vestige of cultural integrity during the first millennium of the Christian calendar. Only with the latter medieval period, often dated from the thirteenth century, were regional lines drawn as they are known today. Art historians, who are given to classification, distinguish certain subdivisions that prove helpful in understanding the entire Middle Ages.

Byzantium and Byzantine Art: 300–1453

It was the Byzantine East that was able to preserve the semblance of Roman law and order and while so doing formed a unique body of art that impressed many of its characteristics on the medieval creation of the West. This secondary influence is important to our story, but to understand it one must view Byzantine work at its source. Byzantine art is art as it developed around Byzantium (Constantinople) from the time that city was made the capital of the Roman Empire in the East until it fell to the armies of the Ottoman Turks under Mohammed II in 1453. Its beginning under Constantine, continued through the brilliant reign of the Emperor Theodosius in the fourth century, may be considered Roman (Latin) art reconverted to Christian necessities and influenced by Hellenistic and Near Eastern stylistic traditions.

By the time of the reign of the Emperor Justinian in the sixth century Constantinople had become not only the center of the classical sphere but also the richest, the most powerful, and the most glorified city in Christendom. Its art was a fusion of eastern, Hellenistic, Latin, and Christian character, properly termed Byzantine.

This art did not cease growing with the death of Justinian. From the ninth to the thirteenth century, following a lull due to the iconoclast movement of the eighth when all art was suspect, Byzantium witnessed its second golden age. A time of prosperity, it was a period of luxurious palace building and one from which the most opulent materials—textiles, ivories, mosaics, metalwork, and enamels—have survived to grace our museums.

After the fall of Byzantium to the crusading armies in 1204 and until its capitulation to the Turks in 1453 the empire declined in size and power. With the latter date, the trade routes through the Bosporus were closed to European traffic and although Byzantine art influence continued among minority groups (a phenomenon currently of interest to art historians) its effect on the European scene was minimal.

133

Western Europe: Late Antique and Early Christian Art: 410–800

From the time (410) that Rome was sacked by the Visigoths—a Germanic people from the north —until Charlemagne, king of the Franks, was recognized by the Pope as the secular ruler of a recreated Roman Empire (800), which included much of western Europe, this territory had known no political cohesion. These years may be viewed as a time of disintegration caused by earlier overexpansion when the Romans extended their boundaries to embrace peoples whose interests could be coidentified only nominally.

This gave rise to a series of barbarian kingdoms, especially after 476 when the last emperor of the west was deposed. The civic consolidation of towns was largely replaced by an agrarian society in which leading families and the church played conspicuous roles in providing oases of order.

Spain's story during the entire Middle Ages is unique. Moslems, followers of the prophet Mohammed (likewise known as people of Islam and again as Saracens), entered Spain from North Africa in 710. The intruders were called Moors, a folk of mixed Arab and Berber descent, who lived in northwestern Africa. In a few short years they had wrested control of the Iberian peninsula from the Visigoths, its latest conquerors. The Moslems were unable to penetrate France (Battle of Tours, 732), but for a period of 800 years, until Spain was welded into a monarchy under the Christian rulers Ferdinand and Isabella (1475), they remained and mixed the Saracenic and native Spanish cultures. This union represented a civilization—judged by its social, political, and economic institutions as well as by its learning— far in advance of its neighbors. It became a secondary source for the infiltration of eastern culture.

Spanish art, influenced by Islamic concepts, is called *Hispano-Islamic*. *Mudejar art* signifies a style created by the Christianized Moor, whereas *Mozarabic* is the term for the art of Christian Spain under Moorish rule.

In art parlance the period between 300 and 800 in Christianized Europe is known as the *Late Antique*, which merged into the *Early Christian*. To those who choose a dim view these years are often regarded as the *Dark Ages*, but to the art student, the ethnologist, and political scientist they trace not so much a stream that flowed uninterrupted from Mesopotamia and the Aegean westward to the modern world but rather the more complex records of buried and reentrant veins of occidental folkways that appeared in a fault of rock destined to produce the bed on which the medieval civilization was built.

Among various peoples, the Franks, west of the Rhine, established the first and most enduring order. From the Merovingian Frankish house, whence Clovis was traditionally converted to Christianity (496), to the Carolingian Dynasty descended from Charles Martel who repulsed the Moslems at Tours, the tactical alliance of church and state became a necessity that strengthened the hand of each. Charlemagne's ancestor Pippin was the first Germanic ruler to be anointed by the Pope in accordance with the ancient Jewish custom, thus giving the initial impetus to the belief in the divine right of kings upheld later by rulers of France and England.

Charlemagne and Carolingian Art: 750–987[1]

Charlemagne extended this sanction to include the reinstitution by the Pope of the nominal entity of the Roman Empire in the West, under which the aspiration to unite all Germanic peoples was legitimatized. During Charlemagne's reign his military prowess, statesmanship, and fidelity to the church were instrumental in reconstituting a degree of order in western Europe which had not existed for as many as five centuries. No less remarkable was Charlemagne's reverence for learning and classical culture which he may have viewed as a cementing influence on heterogeneous groups of subjects. It is not idle talk to speak of a *Carolingian classical renaissance*, as the art of the period demonstrates.

In France the descendents of Charlemagne lost control over the vast territory he had ruled. They retained direct command over only a small portion of modern France, named *Ile-de-France*, which had its capital in Paris. Much of the medieval history of this area consists of the attempts of the French kings, so ensconced, to gain control over their vassals.

In the reapportioning that occurred after Charlemagne's death one branch of his family eventually fell heir to central European territory (including Italy) and to the title of *Holy Roman Emperor.* Inefficient administration placed the empire in danger of collapse until the imperial ambitions were reinstated by Saxon kings from the southern Rhine, one of whom, Otto I, was crowned emperor by the Pope in 962. It is customary today to consider the art period that centered around his reign as *Ottonian.* German culture was then preeminent on the continent. From this time we notice the emergence of certain characteristics now associated with German art in general.

Romanesque Art: 1000–1200; Gothic Art: 1200–1550

The two names, *Romanesque* and *Gothic,* illustrate the difficulty of assigning dates to styles in art. In some areas the Gothic had not begun when the Romanesque declined elsewhere. In others the Gothic tarried as the early Renaissance flowered. Romanesque, which is bracketed 1000–1200, is the art of western Europe as it developed from local cultures. Thus it includes several subdivisions: for instance, *Norman art,* a section of Romanesque, is the art of England under its Norman kings. *Gothic* is the name assigned to European art during the period marked by the architectural development of the pointed arch from the round (1200–1550).

Although neither term is exactly accurate as description or chronology, both are useful in describing styles that can and should be kept distinct. The determinants of these modes involve an understanding of the changes that transpired in European society during the time span under discussion.

Feudalism

On the collapse of Charlemagne's empire and at a time related to the marauding invasions of the Norsemen, a politico-social arrangement known as feudalism evolved. Feudalism had its European inception in France in the late years of the Merovingians, when the necessity for protection gave a certain power and authority to local rulers, descendants of the "prominent" families who continued to live on their estates or *manors* during the unsettled centuries.

Medieval feudalism provided a degree of security and well-being. The strongest men (*lords*) gained the allegiance of others (*vassals*) on promises of protection. The feudal nobility were the political rulers of the land, although they were a numerical minority. The economic arrangement on which feudalism was based resulted from the pledged labor of the *serf* (*villein* or *peasant*) on the domains of the overlord. He might live on and farm certain sections of land in return for a portion of his labor. If the land changed ownership he went with it, nor could he leave one man's land for that of another. This aspect of feudalism had been inherited from the late Roman Empire when it was decreed that all workers were fixed on their jobs, a law made in an attempt to stem the tide of desertion which was the laborer's only refuge from intolerable conditions.

Contrary to the static condition of the serf, feudal lords often changed allegiance for some fancied advantage. The system of vassalage therefore eventually became a complicated network of affiliations which frequently led to civil war and economic uncertainty. There had always been a small group of *freemen,* artisans, merchants, and retainers, not bound to the soil. This group grew numerically as wars and plagues decimated European manpower. England, Italy, and France were the first to recognize these conditions and to declare certain men free. Elsewhere in Europe the final emancipation of the serf did not occur until centuries later.

Growth of Towns

Towns, like coinage, persisted throughout medieval Europe. Some, such as Carcassonne (now a restoration by the nineteenth-century French architect Viollet-le-Duc), which lay along the central route of the seasonal fairs, had survived since

Roman days. Along the trade routes of England, on which merchants congregated to exchange their wares and to ensure contracts, most of the towns were of Anglo-Saxon heritage, the *boroughs* and *burys* that dot the landscape. New market centers on the continent, known as *bourse* or *bourg* and clustered near the feudal strongholds, were often granted a charter by the king or central overlord as a checkmate of feudal power. The nucleus of a free town thus formed.

Some towns, for example, Bremen, grew from a bishopric established by Charlemagne. The port town of Aigues-Mortes in Provence was established by the French King (Saint) Louis IX in the thirteenth century as a royal settlement to induce trade. For a variety of reasons, then, freemen found it more to their advantage to live in a town rather than to remain in the country.

Thus many factors served to change the loose-knit agrarian civilization of the early Middle Ages into the feudal system that followed, then to a monetary civic economy of the twelfth to the sixteenth centuries. Politically, these changes strengthened the hand of a central monarchical rule which was the basic condition of western Europe during the seventeen and eighteen hundreds.

Medieval Thought

The thought of the medieval period, which superficially might be considered to have been preempted by the church, in reality exhibited many currents. A liberal creed, allowed in the formative years of Christianity, veered toward Neoplatonism, as a blend of mysticism and idealism set forth by the Egyptian philosopher Plotinus (205?–270).

Monasticism and the monastic orders had been the instruments for preserving what could be salvaged of ancient learning since the time when Cassiodorus (480–575) considered this conservation an important function of the *Benedictine order*. Gradually, with more settled conditions and the growth of urban life, cathedral schools and lay universities came into existence.

The rediscovery of the authentic texts of Aristotle and a concomitant infiltration of eastern ideas introduced by Arab and Jewish scholars, men who had kept alive the Greek tradition of

knowledge through reason, gave impetus to scientific procedure. Persons like Roger Bacon (ca. 1292) indicated an awakened interest in scientific thinking, whereas Dante (1265–1321), Petrarch (1304–1374), and Erasmus (1467?–1536) affirmed a humanist approach.

The counterpart on the emotional side was the cult of chivalry and romance that entertained the not-so-intellectual nobility during precisely those years when feudalism, as a useful institution, was spent.

It should be remarked that all this occurred well within the hegemony of the church which tended to grow centrally regimented in parallel fashion to the tightening of the bonds on the political level.

Within this framework we find the reasons for Medieval art.

ARCHITECTURE AND INTERIORS

Architecture in a somewhat comparable fashion to history underwent changes during the Middle Ages. Major building was ecclesiastic, with secondary emphasis on fortified dwellings. Only from the late medieval have civic buildings and unfortified houses been preserved. Interior design, therefore, is largely known through church architecture, and its objects were generally for religious enhancement. Not until such lavish courts as those of Burgundy of the fourteenth century are we retintroduced to secular furnishings of magnificence.

Byzantine Architecture and Interiors

In the early years of Christian church design the architectural requirements of East and West were similar, although both differed from the pagan Greek and Roman. The Christian church had to accommodate laity and clergy; the pagan temple housed only the cult image. The glorification of a Greek temple was therefore on the exterior; in a Christian sanctuary it progressed to the interior and then to a cooperative interior-exterior relationship.

As the ceremonies of the eastern church developed, the rites were conducted exclusively by the clergy and a central focus became essential. Aisles or additional areas could be ancillary and were kept somewhat separate. The Greek cross plan or a variant thereof was well adapted to this requirement. As the altar is in the central position, the need for glorifying this location both in structure and decoration led to the domed church and to the centering on the representation of the *Pantocrator,* or Christ depicted as ruler of the universe.

The natural desire to raise their churches to an imposing height and breadth was accomplished by one of two means of erecting a dome over a square, namely the dome on *pendentives* or on *squinches* (Figure 5.1). These forms were perfected by Byzantine architects advancing on Aegean and Syrian prototypes. *Squinches* are walls that truncate the corner of a square to effect a transition from rectangle to circle. *Pendentives* are triangular segments of a sphere made to fit into a gap left when a circular dome rests on the arches raised above the sides of a square. The thrust is assumed by the four piers at the corners of the square by transmission along the pendentives.

Byzantine architecture borrowed Roman groin vaulting for its subsidiary spaces. The building material was predominantly thin brick set into thick beds of quick-setting mortar. Later the Islamic builder fashioned much of his architecture with mortar and brick to form arch and dome embellished with patterned stucco and tile.

Once the principle of bridging large interior spaces was understood, it was exploited in Byzantium almost beyond structural limits (the first dome at Hagia Sophia collapsed in twenty-one years). *Hagia Sophia* (literally Holy Wisdom) at Constantinople (Figure 5.2) is one of the most complex and significant interior spaces in Christendom. It is not readily comprehensible except as studied from the plan (Figure 5.3). A central square is part of a slightly elongated rectangle. The corner piers of the square support the large arches on which rest the ribbed dome on pendentives in customary fashion. The central space, in turn, is elongated by two semidomes which serve as additional buttresses. The interior is further elaborated by an eastern apse countered on the west by an arched entrance. Four corner conches increase the support and the complexity. Independent of this inner structure, the outer rectangle houses the usual appointments of a basilican church.

The interior space of Hagia Sophia seems to move centripetally to the central dome where it picks up the rhythms of the curved volumes both at the ends and overhead. It also holds to its longitudinal axis through vertical planes open to arcades. This is not the quiet space of the Pantheon, restful in its vast circular enclosure. Here are spaces enmeshed in a fugue. It would almost seem that the half millennium separating the two structures had replaced too soon the quiescence of the East with the restless quality of the North and West. Then we recall that the West, as characterized by the Pantheon, was approaching the swan song of classicism. Hagia Sophia was premature in its vision of things to come (Figure 5.4).

Architectural spaces are not our only evidence. This great building with its myriad candles of light flickering through its many small windows and its reflections from glass mosaics and resplendent metals anticipated designing through light, which may have its philosophic parallel in the *leitmotif* of both Neoplatonism and Christianity.

Figure 5.1   The erection of a dome over a square: (a) by means of pendentives; b) by means of squinches. (Reproduced by permission of the publisher from Helen Gardner's *Art Through the Ages,* Fourth Edition edited by Sumner McK. Crosby, © 1959 by Harcourt Brace Jovanovich, Inc.)

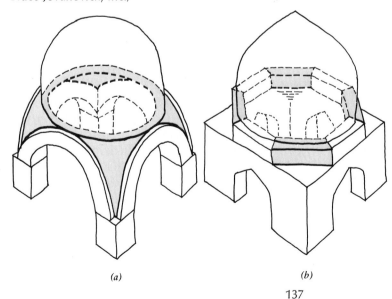

(a)   *(b)*

Figure 5.2   Church of the Hagia Sophia, Istanbul, 532–537. (Photograph by G. E. Kidder Smith.)

The medieval architect found himself confronted with difficulties in handling the columnar supports for larger arches and vaults. Not only were the canonical proportions forgotten—the slender shafts and small crowns and abaci they would have dictated were both physically and visually inadequate to bridge the transition between support and load.

The Byzantine builder solved his problem in two ways. He not only multiplied his columns at loading points, he broadened the base of support by means of the *block capital*. This device, which resembled an inverted and truncated pyramid, was used both single and double. Abaci were enlarged, in effect becoming *impost blocks* (a block on which the arch rests).

The incising of the capitals of these Byzantine columns was frequently done with a drill rather than a chisel. Begun earliest in Syria, where the use of a soft, soapy marble permitted this technique, the result was a sharply cut profile. Ornament so created makes the darkest of shadows, throwing them against the sides of the crisply relieved design. It is claimed that this undercutting actually disperses light and creates chromatic color. At least one must concede that a lighter, scintillating, textured fabric results.

On the domestic scene houses of the fifth and sixth centuries (which resemble late Hellenistic models like those we examined at Olynthus, Priene, and Delos) have been located in the East. In Byzantium itself no private dwellings of the first millennium survive. The most important complex of royal palaces has been the object of excava-

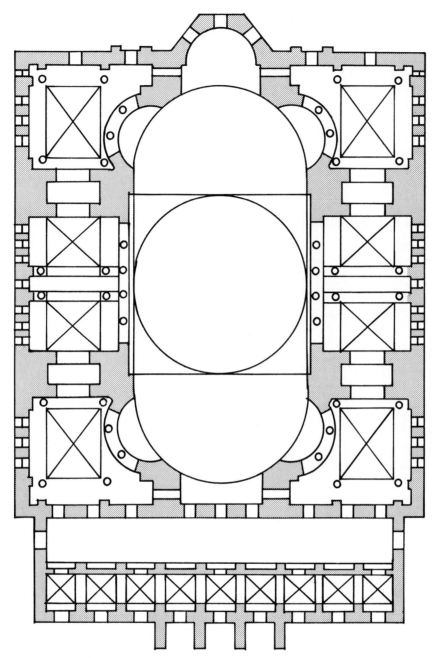

Figure 5.3 Plan of Hagia Sophia (showing only the principal area of the original church). Istanbul, 532–537. Anthemius of Tralles and Isidorus of Miletus, architects. (Adapted from Sir Banister Fletcher, *A History of Architecture,* eighteenth edition, New York: Scribner's; London: Athlone Press, 1975.)

tions by the Walker Trust of the University of St. Andrew since 1935. This grouping is located on a hill overlooking the Sea of Marmora where it meets the Golden Horn. As was true of Roman edifices on the Palatine, a succession of buildings has been conjecturally identified with imperial dwellings, in this case from *Justinian's House* (527–569) to Constantine VII's palace (the Em-

139

Figure 5.4 Church of the Hagia Sophia, interior, Istanbul, 532–537. (Hirmer Fotoarchiv München.)

peror Porphrogenitus, 912–958).[2] If they can be considered fairly representative, then a pattern seems to emerge. Their plan and style combine characteristics derived from imperial Rome (functionary apsed halls), from Greece (peristyled courts), and from the Orient (many isolated pavilions). The materials of these buildings lend themselves to the caprices of brick patterning on the exterior and to wall coverings of marble, mosaic, fresco, and stucco relief on the interior.

Late Antique and Early Christian Architecture and Interiors

Europe and the East had been a far more open road before the separation of the eastern and western churches, before the enmities that resulted from the clashes of the crusades, and before Slavish, Arab, Turkish, and Mongolian invasions closed portions of the Near East to the West. These historical happenings set up progressive barriers to the free mingling of ideas that had marked the early Christian centuries.

The Constantinian churches of Rome and the early ones of Milan and Ravenna (onetime capitals of the Western Roman Empire) illustrate the period of eastern and western fusion. In the mausoleum built in Rome for the Emperor's daughter (Sta. Costanza—350) we find within a simple exterior a circular-domed hall rising from a columned arcade (Figure 5.5). Light floods in from clerestory windows. The surviving mosaics of the ambulatory vault introduce the coloristic principle. Large narrative glass mosaics of Christian subjects are seen in the west for the first time in churches such as Sta. Maria Maggiore (ca. 430—Rome).

Ravenna maintained the closest contact with Byzantium. The mausoleum of Galla Placidia (424), half-sister of the Emperor Honorius, with

Figure 5.5 Plan of Sta. Costanza, an early Christian round church. The central dome structure is lighted by clerestory windows and the ring-shaped ambulatory is covered with a barrel vault. The church was originally attached to a Roman church. Adapted from Sir Banister Fletcher, *A History of Architecture,* eighteenth edition, New York: Scribner's; London: Athlone Press, 1975.)

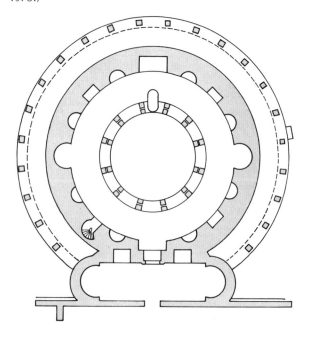

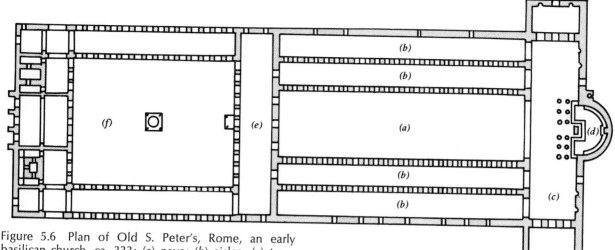

Figure 5.6 Plan of Old S. Peter's, Rome, an early basilican church, ca. 333: (*a*) nave; (*b*) aisles; (*c*) transept; (*d*) apse; (*e*) narthex; (*f*) atrium. (Adapted from Sir Banister Fletcher, *A History of Architecture,* eighteenth edition, New York: Scribner's; London: Athlone Press, 1975.)

its eastern dome on pendentives and its brilliant blue and gold glass mosaics, recreates a celestial fairyland. Everyone who loves color should journey to this somewhat out-of-the-way city on the Adriatic to visit the churches of the reigns of Theodoric and Justinian. The brilliant biblical scenes of the upper ranks of mosaics in S. Apollinare Nuova (490) were ordered by Theodoric, the Ostrogoth chieftain turned Roman exarch. Color must have appealed more to his primitive heritage than did the correct proportions of any classical orders.

The procession of saints seen in the lowest row of mosaics in S. Apollinare Nuova are a replacement made, ca. 549, after Theodoric's death because of the belief that the earlier group had not been orthodox. About the same date are the apse mosaics of S. Apollinare in Classe (535–549), which illustrate the Transfiguration (Plate 7).

S. Vitale (526–547) is remarkable in its space conception, in the decoration that includes the dome mosaic of Christ enthroned, and in the panel mosaics that bear the portraits of Justinian and his queen Theodora. The stylized frontal view of the figures—with their dark-colored and deep-set eyes and the repetitive rhythms of their draped forms—all indicate a change from the natural portrayal of classical art to a rendition that shows greater concern for the transcendental message of Christianity.

The usual conventions of location are respected in these murals. It was customary to decorate the triforium (i.e., the interior wall space between the roof of the aisles and that of the main building) with a pictorial history of the church. The task of conveying the meaning of the Christian religion was assigned to the hierarchical position of the apse. The apse spandrels were filled with the tall figures of the apostles.

These buildings of Ravenna, with the exception of the two churches dedicated to S. Apollinare, approach the eastern circular plan. The exceptions used the form of the Roman basilica which was basic to churches in the West. Its prototype was one of the classical meeting halls among which the law courts are the most familiar.

Neither in plan nor in structure were the early Christian basilicas exceptional (Figure 5.6). They were characterized by a *nave,* or central aisle, which extended from the principal entrance to the *chancel,* that part of the church surrounding the altar which was reserved for the use of the clergy and choir. The latter occupied the arms (*transepts, bema*) that reached laterally from the chancel to form a Latin cross. The essential separation between priests and laity was marked by internal screens. In the eastern church the screen that divides the nave from the chancel is called the *iconostasis,* literally the stationery support on which the sacred *icons,* or images, are placed. In

141

western churches it is known as the *choir screen.* When supporting the large cross, or *rood* (rod), it was known as the *rood screen.*

The high altar within the chancel, in the crossings of transept and nave, is the most sacred area. The eastern custom encloses the altar with curtains and parapets. In the West it is customarily surrounded by a *canopy* raised on columns, known as the *baldachino* or *ciborium.* It was granted the supreme effort of the designer's art. The *reredos* was the screen rising behind the altar. In addition to these fixed appurtenances, there were choir stalls and liturgical vessels and garments on which attention was lavished.

The nave was customarily flanked by two aisles from which it was isolated by colonnades supporting architraves. The substance of these members was often purloined from abandoned Roman stockpiles and thus strict classical proportions between corresponding parts were of necessity abrogated.

The entrance, which in the original Roman basilica had been in the center of the long flank, was placed on the narrow end, which soon became oriented toward the west. A *narthex,* or vestibule, was added to the nave, which then opened into an *atrium,* or enclosed courtyard. Each of these architectural subdivisions fulfilled a purpose in the ceremony, in which the separation of the initiated in the nave, the *catechumen,* or unbaptised, in the aisles, and the general public in the narthex and the atrium was the accepted rule.

In later developments there might be an enlargement to include several aisles, galleries above them, and often a *crypt,* or subterranean chamber, near the apse. The *apse* was the niche that faced the nave and extended from the rear of the chancel. It was originally the location of the elevated seat or *cathedra* for the bishop of the diocese.

These simplest of basilicas were equally uncomplicated in structure. Load-bearing walls, supplemented by post-and-lintel colonnades for the support of the galleries and with wooden trussing to hold up the gabled roofs, exploited no principle unknown to the Roman builder. Indeed, until arcades supplanted the trabeation of the earliest aisle divisions—and vaults, the aisle roofs—

the buildings did not exhaust the full Roman potential.

Domestic architecture of the *late antique and early Christian period* does not present so clear a picture. We are really in the dark ages of knowledge in regard to secular buildings between the time of the Roman debacle and the reign of Charlemagne. Our first clue is to be found not in intact edifices but rather in deductions that may be drawn from the mosaic floors of a dozen or more recently investigated villas strewn from southern France through Spain and across northern Africa. Undoubtedly the most exciting and famous is the "imperial villa" at Piazza Armerina in central Sicily (Figure 5.7), which is considered to have been the home of the Emperor Maximianus, coruler with Diocletian, and to have been built by him as his answer to the same necessity that forced the building of Spalato—namely the threat of the barbarians. Indeed, all of these villas must have been the homes of an enormously wealthy aristocracy which took up residence just as far as possible from the advancing hoards.

The ground plan of these houses is one of the major features to be discerned from their floor mosaics (Figure 5.8). In particular, it is noticed that the dining room or triclinium of Roman date has changed to become part of one large and important rectangular hall to which are appended semicircular apses. The latter may have provided the actual dining facilities for which the hall became a reception area. It is a form that indicates the late Roman and eastern predilection for circular space and may presage circular church apsidioles.

In addition to ground plans, the mosaics of these Roman ruins are important because of their representational character. Thought possibly to have been the work of a school of craftsmen from northern Africa, we see in some of the most pretentious southern examples another example of the mingling of cultures in the Roman area. In addition to the most advertised "bikini" mosaics at Armerina, we find the favorite eastern hunting scenes with animals foreign to Italy but common to such genre in eastern tabloids. In this context we are aware of a totally unoriental sense of excitement and movement and a dynamic cadence in flat patterning. The frontal view of the faces,

Figure 5.7 Mosaic pavement from Roman villa at Piazza Armerina, Sicily, ca. 300. (Alinari/Editorial Photocolor Archives.)

used in compositions predominantly profile, involves the spectator in an intimate sense of participation. How unclassical all of this is.

As times grew turbulent during the early fifth century it became customary to close the lower stories of the portico villas, transfer their pillared galleries to the second floor, and fortify the corner conning towers. These changes are likewise illustrated in contemporary mosaics and ivory reliefs. Boëthius suggests that similar reconstruction can be noted in town houses and that insulae replaced open shops with closures.[3]

During this troubled epoch town and country, and capital and provinces, tended to become more isolated from one another. Only a few Roman towns, often encouraged by their counts (the civic rulers appointed by the German provincial kings) to fortify their enclaves, remained to become important civic nuclei when later the peoples of the barbarian states ceased their wanderlust and settled down to a culturally more mature existence.

Carolingian and Romanesque Architecture and Interiors

Carolingian Church Architecture. In the year 800 King Charlemagne of the Franks journeyed to Rome, where Pope Leo III placed the imperial crown upon his head. This signified a religious sanction of a hoped-for rebirth of the Roman

143

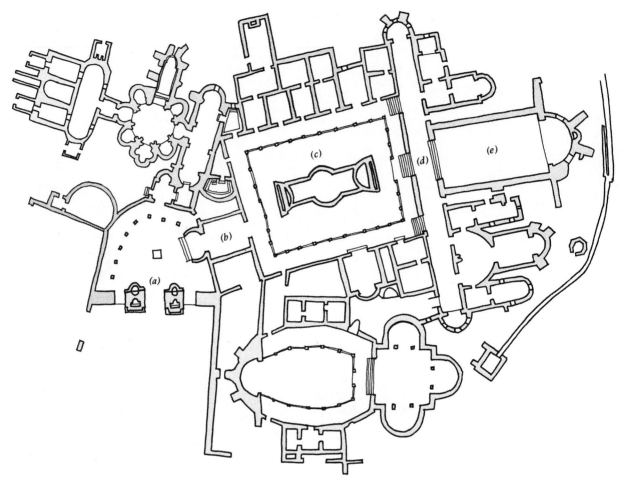

Figure 5.8 Plan of the Roman villa at Piazza Armerina, Sicily, ca. 300; (a) entrance; (b) vestibule; (c) peristyle court; (d) portico; (e) triclinium. (Simplified and adapted from Irving Lavin, "The House of the Lord. Aspects of the Role of Palace Triclinia in the Architecture of Late Antiquity and the Early Middle Ages." *Art Bulletin,* March 1962.)

secular domain now made in alliance with the sovereignty of the Christian church. Charlemagne was an exceptional man, possessed of that characteristic so essential to those whose fate it is to inaugurate a new world from the patchwork of the old—of being able to recognize and desire cultural quality. Illiterate himself, he sought the ambience of civilization for his reign.

A fearless soldier, he had conquered Lombardy in 774. This northern province of Italy, bounded by the Alps and the valley of the river Po, had become the center for the diffusion of skill in ma-

sonry by the offices of the *magistri comacini*. These were master masons allied in some sort of guild that provided training and professional ethical principles. Although a certain *Odo of Metz* was one of Charlemagne's masters of architectural works whose name has become associated with some of the innovations in Carolingian building, nevertheless the constructional methods that began to travel north of the mountains owed much to the skills of the Lombard guild.

We have already acknowledged the Byzantine character of the architecture of Ravenna. Charlemagne, who is known to have been well aware of the prestige of the eastern empire, is thought to have suggested the capital on the Adriatic as a research field for his architects. In its octagonal plan, its annular vaulted aisles, in use of mosaics, and in some of the rich fittings, the palace chapel of the Frankish king, *Aix-la-Chapelle,* borrows from this foreign source.

Some Carolingian buildings, such as the monastery church at Fulda in central Germany, used the basilican plan, in this case patterned after the old S. Peter's in Rome. This sort of Italian inspiration as evidenced in much Carolingian work earned for its architecture the name *Classical Carolingian Renaissance.*

But when the coin is turned we note that these late eighth- and early ninth-century structures of France and Germany speak a new language of the north. The fine Gallic masonry with clean-cut rectangular stone facing, wide mortar joints, round multiple towers, more elaborate western entrance complexes, asymmetrical groupings—all of these as they unite in a synthesis with the old—belong to the *proto-Romanesque.*

In much early Christian architecture flat interior walls and the absence of a skilled craft reservoir necessitated the discarding of wall mosaics for plaster and paint. Even fresco was used when means and skill permitted.

Romanesque Church Architecture. Following Charlemagne's reign, the widespread destruction of buildings at the hands of the Norse and Slavic firebrands posed the problem of restoration in a more durable manner. Masonry and vaulted roofs were thus the first characteristics of important Romanesque church architecture. A pleasant variation occurred in the patterned brickwork of the localities where clay was abundant and the brick tradition was strongest because stone was scarce. Hence it is to be seen in Lombardy. Eastern influence accounts in part for the brick building in certain churches of northern Spain. Spanish and Italian walls may be enriched with colorful marbles, sometimes, as at Pisa, striped in a mode known as *zebra work.*

The everyday skill in vault construction possessed by the Romans was relearned so that it was again possible to roof wide church naves with groin vaults. A further development was the *rib vault* in which the framework of diagonally arched ribs is independently constructed. This has the advantage of economy of centering during construction, of lighter cell structure, hence greater space potential, and of the possibility of opening a window area because the rib skeleton is largely load bearing and the walls as supporting members can be partially eliminated. Early rib vaulting can be seen in S. Ambrogio (begun ca. 1077) in Milan, the home base of the comacini. It was likewise used in Durham cathedral (begun in 1093), one of the first great Norman churches in England.

Anyone who thoughtfully considers these innovations which were the work of eleventh-century engineer-masons appreciates that here a structural principle was evolving to a degree that could merit a new name. If the lines of stress, carried along the groins, or later along the ribs, are countered by buttressing at strategic points, then the system becomes like a living organism, whose forces oppose one another and the connecting membrane decreases in importance in its effect on stability. The term *organic,* with its suggested analogy to living organisms, is appropriate because in an organic body the thrusts and counterthrusts with their accompanying tensions operate quite independently of the inert flesh that covers the skeleton. In respect to its structure this normative Romanesque architecture is a direct antecedent of the Gothic and both are heralds of much that is built today.

As compared with western architecture of the earlier "dark ages," the Romanesque was more complex and venturesome in plan, even as it had been in structure (Figure 5.9). The church nave was lengthened as well as broadened. Heights increased. The nave of Speyer Cathedral on the upper Rhine has a span of 45 ft, a length of approximately 235, and the height of the vault is 107 ft, almost that of Caracalla's baths. The heights at the crossing is half again as great!

The growing practice of sanctification, coupled with an increase in the number of masses read by the monks, led to the creation of numerous small chapels (*apsidioles*) which were placed adjacent to the apse or to the eastern transepts. These areas created the opportunity for the richest of adornment which was often given to commemorate some influential donor, much in the manner that a hospital wing is honored today.

Aisles were widened to keep pace with the nave and frequently multiplied, a necessary concomitant to the principle of division into bays brought about by the groin vaulting. It was diffi-

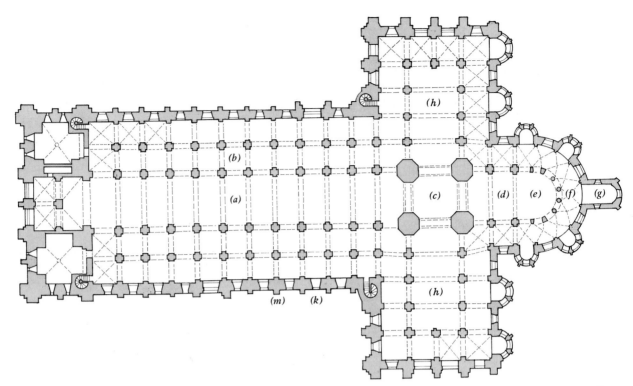

Figure 5.9   Plan of Romanesque church of St. Sernin, Toulouse, France, ca. 1096–1130: (a) nave; (b) side aisle; (c) crossing; (d) choir; (e) apse; (f) ambulatory; (g) chapels (apsidioles); (h) transept; (k) bay; (m) buttress. (After Viollet-le-Duc.)

cult to arch over the oblong compartment formed when a one-aisled church had circular vaults over the aisles that equated with the square ones raised over the nave bay. Thus the size of the nave determined not only the repetitive rhythm but also the width and number of the aisles. Hence the Romanesque architectural proportional system is modular and additive and the result of the necessities of the structure.

It must not be thought, however, that the systematizing of proportions by the medieval designer was as simple as the foregoing paragraph would indicate. The medieval mind was both pragmatic and mystical. If the interrelations of interior spaces were ultimately determined by practical considerations, their initial sizes, and indeed many factors related to the ultimate breakup of areas, were the result of reverence for certain mystical numbers and the use of the regular fig-

ures of Euclidean geometry to incorporate them into workable schemes. Neoplatonism, which was at the hard core of much medieval thinking, thus can be seen to derive from Plato's alliance of ideal configurations with the perfection of the universe.[4]

Ambulatories or walkways around the apse were likewise created to take care of the large numbers of pilgrims who visited the shrines of the saints represented in the apse chapels. *Chevet* is the French word for the apse with its ambulatory and chapels at the east end of the church.

Another innovation in the plans of some Romanesque churches consists in the doubling of the transepts, generally on the east end of the building but occasionally with one located on the west end. Galleries, too, are proliferated. *Galleries* are the upper stories built over the aisle ceiling and aisle roof and when open are used for overflow audiences. When closed toward the nave, the level was finished in early churches with a blind arcade called the *triforium*. The word is said to derive its meaning from the Norman arcades at Canterbury cathedral which had triple openings toward the nave. It is now frequently

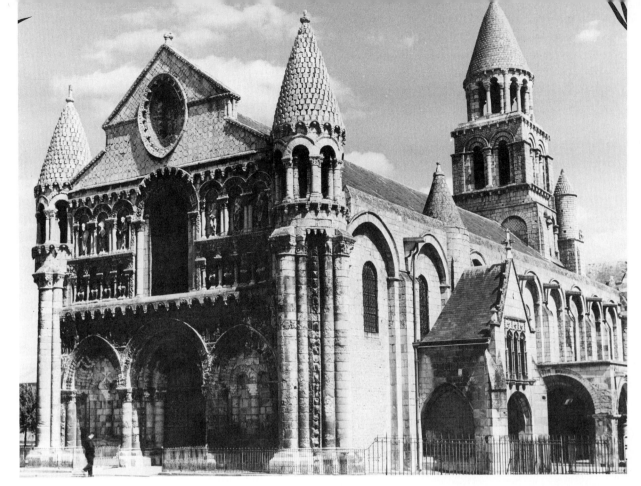

Figure 5.10   Notre-Dame-la-Grande, Poitiers, ca. 1130–1145. (Larrier-Rapho.)

used to describe an open or closed gallery in this position.[5]

The *tribune* gallery across the west end of the church took its name from the raised platform on which the tribune or Roman magistrate sat while presiding over the court. Here the Christian bishop would administer services and auxiliary masses might be conducted in a chapel contained in the gallery. Charlemagne, unlike the emperors of the East, firmly believed in the twin powers of church and state. Therefore he steadfastly refused to appear in the chancel as one who embraced in his person ecclesiastical and secular dominion. His appearances were in the tribunal at the west front.

A most striking feature in Romanesque churches is the proliferation of towers. The two on the west front house the stairs leading to the gallery. A large bell or lantern tower is often placed over the crossing. In Italy the heavy bells are in a separate building, the *campanile,* the most famous certainly being the leaning tower at Pisa (1053–

1272) and the one adjacent to the Duomo in Florence (1334) designed by the Gothic artist Giotto. These asymmetrically placed adjuncts illustrate how far northern Italy had strayed from stict classical bisymmetry.

The west end of the Romanesque church became a recognizably designed feature (Figure 5.10). It is noteworthy visually that many exterior details announce the distribution of interior spaces. Thus three doorways clearly mark nave and aisles. Pilaster strips on some of the Lombard and German churches suggest interior compartments. Over the central portal a circular window, known as the *wheel window,* discloses the position of the tribunal.

The Romanesque doorway recedes in a series of frontally oriented setbacks (known oddly enough as the *orders*) by which one is made conscious of the immense thickness of the wall. From this a low-lying horizontal thrust proceeds by a route of clearly defined divisions from atrium to chancel (Figure 5.11). All portions of the inner architecture assist in this empathetic illusion. Columns, for instance, are arranged with square or

Figure 5.11 Notre-Dame-la-Grande, interior, Poitiers, ca. 1130–1145. Polychromy is a later addition. (Courtesy of Dorothy G. Shepherd.)

Late Romanesque architecture, which gained in size and complexity, lost the clear-cut rectilinearity of space and strong directional thrust that characterized the earlier. Two new vectors enter to forecast the Gothic. The first, in point of time, is the diagonal that appears with the groin vault and becomes pronounced with the visual insistence caused by the ribs. The second is the vertical. The eye not only travels diagonally across a bay because of the vault it also travels upward to the crossing of groins or ribs. This double movement is pronounced at Speyer (1031–), with tall columnar shafts extending like so many organ pipes to the springing of the arches.

It is easy to see Byzantine influence in Romanesque architecture, especially in those aspects that might be termed decorative. The characteristics of columns are first to be noted. Western builders often used heavier and shorter shafts to carry the load, although clusters were also in demand. The latter are frequent in the colonnades of cloisters and are seen in the illuminated manuscripts of the era. Although they were united under a single architrave or impost, the design of the component members might be mutually different.

Northern Romanesque designers working in softer stone deep-cut their columnar capitals in a manner similar to the Byzantine. This occurred as early as the pre-Carolingian Celtic. It was carried as a stylistic tradition into many much later motifs, in which the Gothic pointed ivy and oak of French or German origin have a sharp definition quite different from some of the rounded forms of the Italian. Much Romanesque pattern bears relation to the interlaced and diagonal geometrics of the east. Provincial Romanesque ornament is on occasion relatively simple and sturdy in character and frequently exhibits that primordial fancy forever lurking in the medieval mind for the most capricious and imaginative of representations.

Monumental figure sculpture reappears as embellishment on Romanesque churches. Although such carving, executed in stone or occasionally in stucco, had continued sporadically since Roman times, its devotion to ecclesiastic themes and its frequent appearance remain as phenomena of the post-tenth centuries. Occurring first in the

equivocally round bases. A successsion of piers can serve the same purpose. Arches provide the bridges.

The famous St. Michael in Hildesheim (Germany, 1001—entirely rebuilt, ca. 1186), with its sheer triforium wall, flat ceiling, heavy rectangular posts and round columns, and its dominant high archway that demarks the chancel, is an excellent illustration. St. Michael, it will be remembered, was the patron saint of the church militant. It is difficult, when standing in such a building, to escape from the emotional dream of hearing the nave echo to the tread of crusading armies as they advanced for dedication. Hildesheim is a short distance to the north of Regensburg, whence the Emperor Frederick Barbarossa led his well-disciplined German contingent during the third crusade (1189–1192).

Figure 5.12 Ste.-Madeleine. Tympanum of interior portal of narthex. Vézelay, France, ca. 1120. (Photographie Bulloz.)

churches of Spain, majestic statuary finds its most striking form in those of southern France such as St. Sernin (Toulouse, ca. 1077), Moissac (Languedoc, ca. 1115), and Vézelay (Burgundy, 1096–1120; Figure 5.12). Although the outstanding position for such sculpture is in the tympanum (in medieval architecture this term refers to the space between arch and lintel) over the west portal—columns, plaques, and even capitals were transformed into representational decoration in the round. These are powerful medicine. Byzantine frontality involves the spectator in Christ's judgments; exaggerated linear contortion, elongated proportion, and concentrated sideward glance produce an insistent message, and the most horrifying images tell their emotional tale of that side of medieval existence from which there was no merciful release. Both in statues of rigid stance,

like those in St. Trôphime (Arles, ca. 1170–1180) and those of rhythmic movement at Autun Cathedral (Burgundy, 1120–), the sculpture is constructed as though bound to the architecture, to whose grim materials it offers adequate surface modulation and to the rough texture of which it offers appropriate relief.

Carolingian and Romanesque Secular Architecture. We turn to secular architecture from ca. 800 to 1200, naming it Carolingian and Romanesque for convenience in correlating with the usual art categories.

Although taking a secondary place in art histories, secular architecture begins to return to its former importance. People lived, defended their homes, and ruled their domains in a manner considerably removed from barbarism or nomadism, and they glorified their secular buildings in relation to their means and values.

The history of monasticism, which had its heyday from the tenth to the first of the twelfth century, suggests a prime reason for a considerable amount of building activity. Quite apart from the abbey churches that had to accommodate the local order as well as a visiting congregation (in all but Cistercian churches, which made no provision for the public), the monastic complex required all of the adjuncts of a self-sufficient community.

Monastic buildings are classified as abbeys or priories—religious establishments governed, respectively, by an abbot or abbess or a prior or prioress. The architectural format originates with the mother house, many times ruined, of the Benedictine order (S. Benedict, 480–544), begun in 529 at Monte Cassino between Rome and Naples. It was continued with the work of the Irish monks (conversion of Ireland by St. Patrick, ca. 389–461), whose missionary zeal created monastic centers in England, especially in Northumbria. It was from the cathedral school at York that Charlemagne summoned Alcuin (781) to take charge of his palace school, an act that signals the Carolingian renaissance in learning.

These early colonies were followed by a succession of monasteries, the most noteworthy of which was the work of the Cluniac and Cistercian monks, both reformed Benedictine orders dating from the tenth century. The plan of the mother house of the Cluniacs in southern Burgundy is interesting because it became normative. It was developed along lines set down in the famous sketch of a monastic complex (820) located in the library of St. Gall, Switzerland, where there was an institution belonging to an Irish order.

The plans of all monasteries thereafter were similar (Figure 5.13). The church and adjacent enclosed courtyard or *cloisters* were their nuclei. The monks led a secluded life and the monastery was preeminently for their use. The entrance for any admissible public was at the west end. The main farm buildings and service quarters were south. The most isolated quarters were located to the east and included the dormitory and separate living quarters for the abbot. Kitchen, refectory, and sanitary facilities were placed on the south side to take advantage of the terrain to permit water to flow from the first two to the last. Hospitals and a public hostelry were included, inasmuch as the monastery fulfilled these community needs. A monastery graveyard was adjacent to the private infirmary.

Many monastery buildings can be visited today, although unfortunately they are often in ruins. The Cistercian parent houses at Citeaux (1098) and Clairvaux (1115), likewise in Burgundy, were founded by the famous abbots Robert and Berwald, respectively. The abbey churches of this monastic order in England, such as Waverley (1128), Tintern (1131), Fountains (1135–1150), and Fontenay (1139–1147), France, tend toward the simplicity of plan and sound construction for which the Cistercian buildings were noted.

With the advent of the mendicant and preaching orders—the Dominicans, Friars, and others—of the thirteenth century, large houses were unnecessary. The Franciscan monastery in Umbria with its world-famous frescoes by Cimabue (1240?–1302?) and Giotto (1276?–1337) grew almost against the wishes of the humble St. Francis.

Monastery buildings were dignified with architectural character similar to that of the church proper. Thus they often suggest an idea of the transformation of the Romanesque style into a comfortable domestic environment. It should also be mentioned that the monasteries, especially those that enjoyed royal favor, housed the workshops from which the principal art production emanated. Manuscripts, ivories, objects of gold, and gems, which were in demand for church and court, were produced by monks or lay brethren in their employ.

Churches and their treasures may have been preserved, but the palaces of the mighty have for the most part been destroyed. Two of Charlemagne's, at Ingelheim (near Mainz) and at Aachen, are, except for Aachen's chapel, largely known through excavations and sketches. Both were built into a complex that included, as became customary, the palace church. Episcopal (meaning the connection with the bishopric) palaces are likewise so grouped.

In a later sense the word *palace* designates an important house of regal pretensions, which usually belonged to the nobility or to an officiating civic dignitary. The latter meaning is applicable in Venice, which had a representative type of government from very early days. Because the

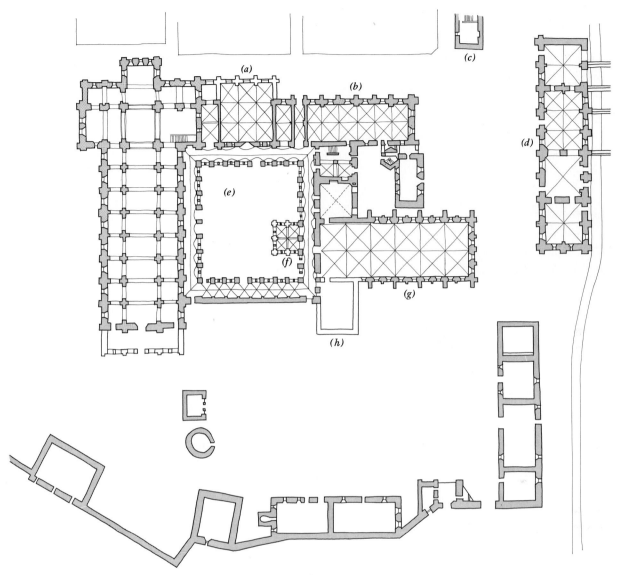

Figure 5.13 Plan of Fontenay Abbey (Cistercian), France, 1139–1147, with later additions and reconstructions: (a) chapter house; (b) monks' hall; (c) infirmary; (d) mill; (e) cloister; (f) *lavabo;* (g) refectory; (h) kitchen. (After Bégule.)

citizens depended on their island position for safety, their Medieval palaces did not assume the air of fortresses. The Ducal Palace, begun, according to tradition, as early as 814 for the first Doge of Venice, has been rebuilt after disastrous fires and owes its present Gothic form largely to a reconstruction in the fourteenth century.

In the far south in Sicily, under Norman rule, we find the most luxurious flowering of Romanesque domestic architecture. In a culture compounded of ancient Greek, Roman, Islamic, and Norman influences the pavilions are a resplendent motley of East and West. La Zisa (Palace of Delights), begun by the Norman, William I, is the principal document of the Norman rule in Sicilian domestic architecture. Here the exterior, somewhat fortresslike in appearance, is of later date. The interior, however, and that of its successor El Kubbah (the Cuba), built by the second

151

Figure 5.14 Court of the Lions, the Alhambra, Granada, 1309–1354. Length, 155 ft. width, 66 ft. (Courtesy of Dorothy G. Shepherd.)

William, belong to the same tradition as the Islamic domestic architecture of Spain.

A favorite example of this style is found in the Palace of the Alhambra at Granada, which was the home of the western caliph Abd-el-Walid. The word *Alhambra* means red in Arabic, and the Spanish palace has thick red brick walls. The Alhambra, and especially the companion summer palace known as the *Generalife,* belong in a later (thirteenth–fourteenth century) context. Because these Spanish and Sicilian palaces represent the last major wedding in the families of East and West, certain similarities and differences may be noted. Although formidable on the exterior, they are oriented within toward a succession of courts, surrounded by arched colonnades off which are inner rooms, white-plastered save for carved stucco or wooden decoration and tiled floors. The delights of water held in pools, fountains, and channels and the intricate, gilded stalactite stucco ceilings of major interior spaces make them true marvels of Aladdin's lamp. Washington Irving describes the *Court of the Lions* (named for the alabaster basin supports in the form of primitive-looking beasts purportedly carved by a Christian captive) at Granada (Figure 5.14):

. . . like that in most parts of the interior of the palace . . . characterized by elegance rather than grandeur, bespeaking a delicate and graceful taste, and a disposition to indolent enjoyment.

These buildings are the finale of components too disproportionate to be continued. Even the half-Norman emperor Frederick II, when he built in Apulia, constructed a fortified tower from rough stone, the aedicule of which was columned and pedimented in heavy scale in the Roman classical manner.

Farther north the fortified dwelling was a necessity. In Italy it is called the *castel;* in Spain, *alcazar;* in France, *chateau;* in Germany, *schloss;* in England, *castle*. Most were built in the years that bridged the Romanesque and the Gothic styles in architecture (1000–1500).

Italy was studded with *castels,* placed wherever valuable property needed to be guarded. Many, like the towers along the Amalfi, are only forts, which were often erected as a refuge from pirates. Others, near ancient cities, are more elaborate, such as the Castel dell'Ovo, seen by all visitors to Naples. This was the fortress of Frederick II, Hohenstaufen (1211–1250), used for the safekeeping of his treasure. Likewise in Naples is the Castel Nuovo, built by the French Angevin ruler Charles I (1279–1282) and reconstructed by the Spanish Aragons in the fifteenth century. The Castel Volterra, along the walls of the Tuscan town of that name, was erected against pillaging by the Florentines.

The history of Florence is typical of those northern Italian communities whose dependency on the neighboring hill towns and whose income from trade were jealously guarded. This was the cause for intramural as well as foreign rivalries. In Florence such buildings as the Palazzo Vecchio and the P. del Podesta (residence of the chief magistrate, now the Bargello and a national museum) are thick-walled masonry forts with their full document of battlements and a tall tower, said to be significant of a family's position and certainly useful as a watch turret. In Siena there is the P. Pubblico; in Milan, the fortress homes of the Visconti and Sforza. Every location presents its example.

We first noted defensive implementation atop

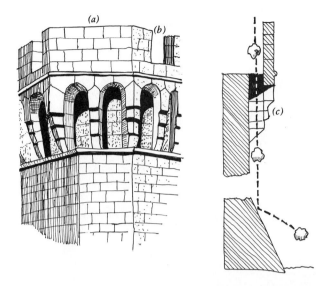

Figure 5.15 Battlements (as shown in perspective and section): (a) merlons; (b) crenellations; (c) brattices. (Adapted from *Funk & Wagnall's New College Standard Dictionary,* edited by Charles Earle Funk, 1947.)

palace walls in Assyria. During the troubled history of Byzantium this type of fortification was perfected and brought home, lock, stock, and barrel, to Europe by the crusaders. The Normans owed their suzerainty in part to their administrative ability, in part to their combined skill in masonry construction and knowledge of military defenses.

Battlements is the inclusive name for the low, notched wall that surmounts a building (Figure 5.15). The open spaces left in a parapet from which to shoot are called *crenellations. Merlons* are the solid part of the battlements. When besiegers began tunneling near the base of a fortification, it became expedient to build out a temporary breastwork which served not only for purposes of observation but also as a platform from which to hurl destruction on the forces below. These *brattices* soon became a permanent fixture and the battlements were extended to accommodate them. The openings in the floors of these platforms, useful for pouring hot oil or dropping stones on the heads of invaders, are the *machicolations*. Sometimes this name was assigned to the complete parapet. Long after they had served their military purpose bratticed battlements were used as decorative cornices. Be-

cause a license to crenellate was the prerogative of nobility, the implications are clear.

Following the comparatively peaceful era of Charlemagne's reign, fortified castles became the order of the day north of the Alps. The aristocracy were constantly engaged in defense against Norsemen, Hungarians, and Slavs. Along the lower Loire River the great round towers of Losches, Langeais, and Chinon, in part still standing, help us to understand the era of the early counts of Anjou, such as the violent Fulk Nerra (987–1040) from whom the dynasty of the French kings is descended. Farther upstream the thirteenth-century hall of the Counts of Blois is built two stories high on a double row of vaulted arches separated by a line of columns.

Although castles are as ubiquitous as donkeys in Spain, the most formidable are located near the present cities of Seville, Trujillo, and Segovia. They remain convincing proof that the ownership of a castle in Spain should be no idle boast. In Germany the number of schloss ultimately rose to an estimated 10,000.

In England, except for a pre-Norman fortification ascribed to Edward the Confessor, castles date from the time of the Norman invasions. William the Conqueror had come from the province of Normandy, north of the Seine, which had been ceded to his ancestor, Rudolph or Robert, the leader of a band of raiding Norsemen. William controlled England by assigning land to his vassals on condition that they build fortified castles and answer to him as liegelord or king.

English castles were built until the fifteenth century when actual warfare gave way to tourneys. The nobility, who had been the military arm of feudalism, found their social usefulness usurped by the protection provided by paid mercenaries, hired with the coin of the realm.

The first English castles, known as *mote and bailey castles (mote,* mound), were erected of wood on hastily dug earthworks, the earth thrown up from the excavation of a surrounding ditch. A wooden hall, in plan and construction like the Anglo-Saxon *heall* (see p. 156), was erected on top of the mound. A palisading was constructed around the mound which enclosed the *bailey* (the English *ward*), a space which contained the livestock. The *barbican* was a further extension

153

with its own palisades and ditch to protect the entrance.

In the *Domesday Book,* the 1086 census of his island possessions ordered by William, forty-nine castles were recorded. Documentary evidence lists eighty-six at the end of the century.[7] As fortified dwellings mushroomed, the Norman kings wisely restricted the placing of battlements on buildings except by license to crenellate granted by the crown. The first were issued during the reign of the first Plantagenet, Henry II, and the last by Henry VI. In all 335 licenses had been granted in the three intervening centuries.

During the first half of the twelfth century stone towers surrounded by stone walls and known as *shell keeps* rose to replace the early earthworks. The outstanding example is the Tower of London. William imported a Norman monk, Gundulf, who supervised construction and many of the subsequent forms were of French derivation. The keep or actual building might be either of two types. The *hall keep,* from the Anglo-Saxon *heall,* had wooden walls raised high enough to conceal its gabled roof. The thickness of the walls provided space for a walk. The *tower keep* might have as many as four stories, a basement floor, an entrance floor, a hall or main floor, and a *chamber* or upper floor. The name *keep*—meaning to protect from danger—was of comparatively late derivation. The French word was *tower,* from *tur* or *tor,* meaning a high place. Keeps are often known as *donjons* in France, a term that became associated with the underground prisons found in French castles. A French dungeon with an opening only in the top was known as an *oubliette*—from *oublier,* to forget—from which there was no return. Sometimes today when we question progress, it might be well to recall the times when a man of power could enjoy life above a cellar in which his victims languished in a living death.

By the last of the twelfth century and the early thirteenth, the *rectangular keep* had succeeded the shell variety. This was the most common English plan, which was essentially a walled court with a great keep appended to a rear corner (Figure 5.16). When, in the course of time, new and superior instruments were developed for

Figure 5.16 Guy's Tower at Warwick Castle, Warwickshire. Finished in 1394. Height, 128 ft. This is a superb example of military architecture of a comparatively late date. (G. C. Ball.)

siege warfare—such as the *trebuchet,* a military engine for hurling stone—high stone walls (often rising 45 ft as at Warwick) and deep moats were required. These rendered high towers ineffectual, although gate towers and portcullises were part of the new scheme. In consequence of the comparative security castle buildings began to spread along the inner face of the enclosure, perhaps the origin of the Tudor courtyard house.

In thirteenth- through fifteenth-century England, when the central monarchy was growing stronger, the lightly fortified manor made its appearance (Figures 5.17, 5.18, and 5.19).

Are the churches, monasteries, palaces, and fortified dwellings all that we know of pre-Gothic work in Europe? This is largely true. Yet a literary tradition of Germanic-Celtic accomplishment survives and a few remains substantiate it. The Roman writer Tacitus has this to say:

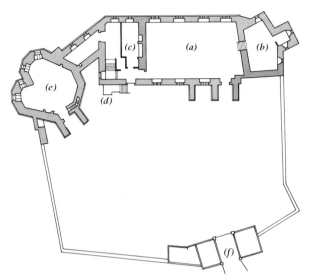

Figure 5.17 (above) Plan of Stokesay Castle, a fortified manor house. Shropshire, thirteenth century: (a) hall; (b) north tower; (c) undercroft of solar; (d) stairs to solar; (e) south tower; (f) Elizabethan gatehouse. Originally the only entrance to the solar was by exterior stairs off the inner court. (Adapted from Sir Banister Fletcher, *A History of Architecture*, eighteenth edition, New York: Scribner's; London: Athlone Press, 1975.)

Figure 5.18 (right) Great Hall at Stokesay Castle, showing stairs that lead to the Solar. Craven Arms, Shropshire, thirteenth century. (G. C. Ball.)

Figure 5.19 (below) Stokesay Castle. A fortified manor house. Shropshire. Parts date to the twelfth century. Great Hall, thirteenth century. (G. C. Ball.)

. . . none of the German tribes live in cities, that even individually they do not permit houses to touch each other: they live separated and scattered according as spring water, meadow, or grove appeals to each man; whether it be precaution against chances of fire, or just ignorance of building.[8]

English tradition is based on these Germanic (Anglo-Saxon) tribal dwellings. The fortified community was called a *burg* (borough, bury). The buildings of each family were grouped around a central home or *ham*. The largest was the *heall* or hall. The smaller huts, called *burs* or *bowers*, were the sleeping quarters for the women and children.

The Germanic hall has remained the central feature of the English home. From present buildings of a lower social level and from Icelandic and Germanic sagas[9] we can guess its nature. The early hall had a very low door and a high threshold which made entry hazardous for an enemy to attempt. An opening in the center of the roof admitted some light and air (a window or wind's eye) and likewise allowed smoke from the central fire to escape. Two long rows of stationary seats built along the sides constituted the furniture. Such were the principal halls of England before the coming of the Normans.

The hall for communal living and the bower for private were ultimately incorporated under one roof for the purpose of protection. The Norman word *chamber* was gradually substituted for the Anglo-Saxon *bower,* and the hall and chamber together became the nucleus of later houses (A.-S., *hus*).

As we consider the typically English house, we first visualize those of the flowering English countryside, called by the gentry their country *seats* or *places*. Their antecedents may be found in the early years of this millennium when, in addition to the castles of the major nobility, the manor house, or home of the lord of the manor, developed. As previously defined, a manor was a self-sufficient estate, somewhat analogous to the early *villes* in France and villas in Italy. It could be a parcel held in trust for a feudal lord or it might be the property of some member of lesser caste, possibly a knight (who owed military allegiance up the line). Although the manor was a nonmili-

tary subdivision, the manor house might in special necessity be fortified. Stokesay, in Cheshire, was of this order (Figures 5.18, 5.19). Boothby Pagnell had no defenses.

Although the manor house stood somewhat isolated in a manorial park, the homes of the villeins, serfs, or peasants were clustered near a communal village green, adjacent to the church. A village was thus in origin an agricultural community, distinct from a town or trade center.

A few houses date from the centuries now under discussion. Not significantly different from those of later medieval times, we defer a comprehensive description until later.

Gothic Church Architecture, 1200–1550

The last few pages have taken us chronologically well down into the territory of Gothic architecture, which copied much from its predecessors, yet synthesized its borrowed details into a unique expression. Well under way by 1200, before the Romanesque had expired, it was characterized by rib vaults, pointed arches, flying buttresses, all used to attain such a carefully planned system of counter thrusts that equipoise seemed the function of the linear skeleton, to which a membrane was affixed.

Semicircular vaults, whether groin or rib, had always posed a problem, for obviously the diagonal arches would be higher than the transverse. This discrepancy in height could be remedied only by raising the lower arches on stilting (literally on stilts made with flat stones) or conversely modifying the shape of some or all of the arches. Both expedients were used by the Romanesque builder. The result, however, was never entirely satisfactory: the former course often produced awkward-appearing proportions and the latter resulted in clumsy and unsafe curves. This problem became even more complicated when ribs were placed over rectangular sections, for example, in the bays of a one-aisle church, which were longer than broad.

The answer came in the use of the pointed arch and vault, which, being designed on two centers, could be raised to any desired height (Figure 5.20). Thus two arches could rise from unequal spans to the same altitude. With the two

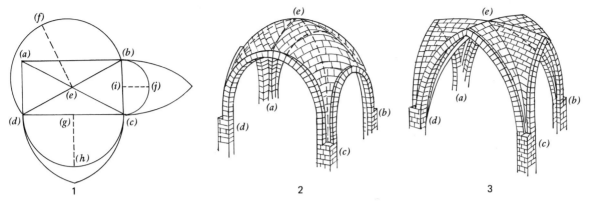

Figure 5.20 Manner of solving problem of creating transverse and diagonal vaults of the same height: (1) ABCD, oblong bay; GH, IJ, EF, varying heights of circular arches raised on transverse and diagonal. (2) The resulting domical vault obtained by use of circular arches. (3) The result obtained by the use of pointed arches with differing centers and radii; ribs can reach the same height. (Reproduced by permission of the publisher from Helen Gardner's *Art Through the Ages*, Fourth Edition edited by Sumner McK. Crosby, © 1959 by Harcourt Brace Jovanovich, Inc.)

vaults leveled to the same elevation, one advantage lay in the possibility of using a flat rather than a domical roof, a substantial saving in material. The pointed arch and vault, being taller in relation to span, were more vertical in thrust, hence more stable. It is claimed that pointed arches originated in Syria as early as the reign of Justinian. Their first major use in western architecture was in the third church at Cluny (ca. 1088–1130).

The pointed arch and vault then began it. It was soon clear that if the ribs of the longitudinal axis were stilted the combined thrusts of longitudinal, transverse, and diagonal arcs could be carried through a conoidal section and be met at the impost by a comparatively narrow abutment. By erecting an external buttress, starting from a detached pier and placed to take the vaulting thrust at its two most vulnerable points, the spring and haunch (the chief curvature between the spring and crown), the support could be made light and linear. These are the *flying buttresses* (so called because their arcs leap over space) which so clearly indicate part of the dynamic machinery that sustains the building. It is important to note that because the buttresses meet the vaults at a point a new inside-out connection is created. Here the externals not only

disclose the internals, as in the Romanesque, but they actually seem to be an extension of them (Figure 5.21).

The walls, no longer loadbearing, were opened to large translucent windows and thus the magic of medieval stained glass, the glory of Chartres Cathedral (1194; Figure 5.22) and the seemingly total glass enclosure of Sainte-Chapelle (1248) in Paris, was invited.

The complete synthesis into a new whole called Gothic architecture matured in France in the cathedrals of Chartres, Reims (1210–), Amiens (1218; Figure 5.23), and Beauvais (1247–). This period is often called "High Gothic." By the middle of the thirteenth century its structural logic was fully understood. It possessed what Nikolaus Pevsner described as a "balance of high tensions."[10]

After resolving the technical problems, these daring builders adventured with the aesthetic potential. First came breathtaking heights, emphasized by tall narrow shafts reaching up to where the quadripartite vaults began. The wide and open gallery tended to disappear and was replaced by low triforia which scarcely seemed to divide the upper thrust of tall piers and pointed clerestory windows. With two centered arches the bays could be longer than broad, again emphasizing height but at the same time quickening the eastward horizontal rhythm. On the exterior, whenever the mature Gothic churches received their planned quotas of towers and spires, their vertical versus horizontal forces were somewhat equally balanced. In addition, not only the diagonal direction of the oblique ribs in the interior but also the inclined direction of the fly-

157

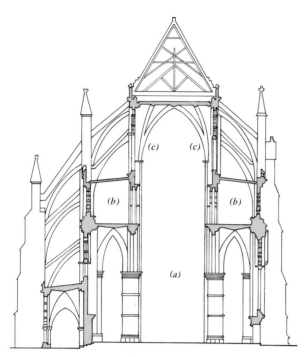

Figure 5.21 Gothic structural system. Transverse section through the nave of Westminster Abbey, London: (a) nave; (b) triforium; (c) clerestory. (Adapted from Sir Banister Fletcher, *A History of Architecture*, eighteenth edition, New York: Scribner's; London: Athlone Press, 1975.)

ing buttresses on the exterior drew attention and made a strong empathetic appeal.

The years spanning the crystallization of the Gothic style in architecture are considered to have been comparatively open ones for European

Figure 5.22 Chartres Cathedral, 1194–1260. (Lauros-Giraudon.)

intercourse. The first part of the fourteenth century is sometimes known as the era of *international style* in European art. In its development influences crossed and recrossed the Channel, the Alps, the Pyrenees, and the Baltic rivers, aided by the mobility of such architects as the Frenchman known as William of Sens who designed the choir of Canterbury cathedral (ca. 1174–). Nevertheless, there were noticeable regional developments within the total Gothic orb.

English churches did not exploit the full-fledged Gothic structural system so completely as the French. Generally longer and lower than those of the continent, their cathedrals are inclined toward a rectilinearity of plan with a squared east end. Transepts are prominent and, as at Salisbury (1220–1258), frequently doubled. Towers appear over the central crossing (Figure 5.24) and as at Wells (1186–) were strengthened by strainer arches (1338). The west portals, which in France retained stone sculpture, were relatively plain. Few are the examples of fully developed flying buttresses. With these characteristics the English Gothic is more horizontal in emphasis than its French counterpart and is less easily seen as a whole comprised of parts that fuse in extended lines and spatial measures (Figure 5.25).

This is not to say that it is less Gothic. Every country that came within the influence of Gothic structural development created magnificent churches which used the new capabilities and synthesized from them forms in which the Gothic demonstration of advanced interior-

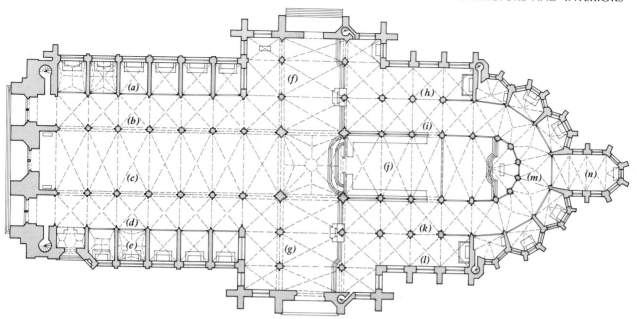

Figure 5.23 (above) Plan of the French Gothic Cathedral at Amiens, begun in 1210: (a) chapels; (b) north aisle; (c) nave; (d) south aisle; (e) chapels; (f-g) transept; (h-l) chapel; (k-i) aisles; (j) choir; (m) ambulatory; (n) chapel. (Adapted from Sir Banister Fletcher, *A History of Architecture,* eighteenth edition, New York: Scribner's; London: Athlone Press, 1975.)

exterior fusing is remarkably evident. But the manner and even the degree is varied.

Within this Gothic norm, southern France, Italy, and Spain placed emphasis on a sense of space. This was accomplished in part by minimizing the separation of aisles from nave. The *Hall church,* which originated in Germany, was popular in the south of Europe. Here the side aisles, as tall as the nave, made possible a structure in which the thinnest of internal piers emphasized the expression of space rather than mass.

Like most styles, the Gothic progressed toward a late phase which is generally associated with more elaborate decoration. However, there has seldom been architecture in which decoration was so merged with its skeleton that at times it became indistinguishable from it. These decorative-structural qualities, exploited especially in the development of the vault (Figure 5.26), re-

Figure 5.24 (right) Salisbury Cathedral, Wiltshire, 1220–1258. (British Tourist Authority.)

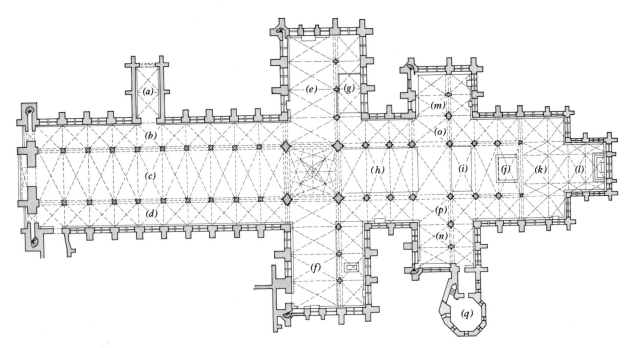

Figure 5.25 (above) Plan of Salisbury Cathedral, an example of English Gothic, 1220–1258; (a) north porch; (b) (d) aisles; (c) nave (e) north transept; (f) south transept; (g) organ; (h) choir; (i) presbytery; (j) high altar; (k) processional path; (l) lady chapel; (m) northeast transept; (n) southeast transept; (o) north choir aisle; (p) south choir aisle; (q) sacristy. (Adapted from Sir Banister Fletcher, A History of Architecture, eighteenth edition, New York: Scribner's; London: Athlone Press, 1975.)

Figure 5.26 (below) Types of Gothic ribbed vault: (a) quadripartite vault; (b) plan of Gothic complex ribbed vault with (1) lengthwise transverse rib; (2) crosswise transverse rib; (3) diagonal rib; (4) crosswise transverse ridge, (5) transverse ridge; (6) tiercerons; (7) liernes. (Perspective, redrawn from a University print; plan, after Fletcher.)

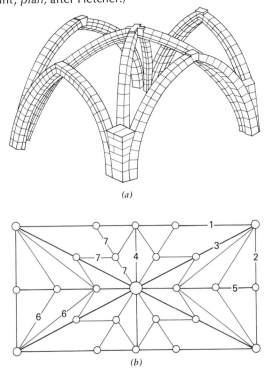

sulted in those phenomenal star and fan vaults (Figure 5.27) most seen in England and Eastern Europe. These gossamer structures were accomplished by adding a ridge rib to the vocabulary of transverse and diagonal. Then came the ribs that lead from the capitals of the columns to points along the ridge, in England called *tiercerons*. Tertiary ribs which do not spring from impost or ridge but serve to connect the various main ribs are known as *liernes*. Constructional geometrics may be hard for the layman to follow, but it is not difficult to see the figures that result or to comprehend the undulating linear flow from bay to bay. At the same time it can be appreciated that the entire intricate network begins to assume the character of a decorative web rather than a structural necessity.

Elaborate vaulting was to be found on the continent as well as in England. On the other hand,

Figure 5.27 Nave of King's College Chapel, Cambridge, 1446–1515. Fan vaulting, 1512. (Pitkin Pictorials Limited, Publishers.)

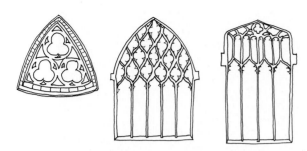

Figure 5.28 English Gothic windows: (a) with geometric tracery; (b) with curvilinear tracery; (c) with rectilinear tracery. (Adapted from Sir Banister Fletcher, *A History of Architecture*, eighteenth edition, New York: Scribner's; London: Athlone Press, 1975.)

the development of *curvilinear* and *rectilinear* decoration refers specifically to English styles. The words apply largely to patterns in tracery rather than to design aspects of the entire building. The earliest form of tracery is known as *plate* tracery, obtained by piercing a solid wall. It does, however, convey an impression of solidity. By contrast the later *bar* tracery is made by piecing together shafts of stone, wood, or metal to form the shapes. Bar tracery lends itself to linear patterns. In elaborate curvilinear form it is to be seen at Exeter (1280), Lincoln (1290), and Ely (1321).

From an initial profusion of curvilinear designing English architecture reacted with an aspect known as *rectilinear*. Gloucester's south transept (1337) remains its most consistent example. Rectilinear is characterized by the absence of the vagaries of the curvilinear. Walls are logically composed, glass is in rectilinear framing, and vaults, although often intricate, assume more straightline webbing. Rectilinear and curvilinear were frequently concurrent phenomena (Figure 5.28).

The elegant attenuated vertical expression of the Gothic in France is sometimes referred to as the *rayonnant* phase, which evolved from the High Gothic of the great churches of Notre Dame and Chartres. Rayonnant actually means "emitting rays" like the calyx of a flower, which rayonnant interiors suggest. The late decorative phase of French Gothic is, on the other hand, known as *flamboyant* because its ogival curves suggest the flickerings of a flame. In French work from 1300 to 1500 many constructional features are elaborated with these flamelike lines.

Ogivals are of course drawn with the use of reverse curves of varying centers. The potential of several centers was used by the English to create their four-centered arch which is first seen in the south transept at Gloucester. Commonly known as the Tudor arch, it has a low and comparatively broad point. The royal house of Tudor, however, postdated its initial use by more than a century.

In reviewing the scope of Gothic ecclesiastic building, one point of reference may well be its structural logic and the manner in which it is made evident to the viewer. Another may be the decorative features and their relation to the structure (Figure 5.28). Perhaps the most important relevance is in its spatial organization and, most particularly, its directionally dictated visual movement.

Although the Gothic opened up an entirely new field of inside-outside relations, created awe-inspiring space and, by its chromatic embellishments, transcendent experience, nevertheless its directional thrusts were always somewhat ambiguous and as time went on became more so. Soaring vertical members were prominent; the horizontal and even the diagonal could become equally insistent.

Sculpture in the round, a pronounced and glorious part of many continental churches, may be used as an illustration of the effectiveness of the many decorative adjuncts that accentuated this directional equivocality. Columns of many shafts are oriented toward the rib thrusts. Sculpture likewise sways and bends with a multiplicity of stations (Figure 5.29). There is, indeed, in the pliancy of the lovely French madonnas, an underlying connection with the Virgin cult and the feminine psyche of the chivalric codes, so pronounced in thirteenth- and fourteenth-century ideology.

With this higher relief we are less able to recognize a surface as belonging to a wall, which seems to dissolve as a vertical unit. No longer do we see a solid bounded box as in the Romanesque but rather a textural net that encloses tremendous pulsing space. It is a lattice in which all of the separate parts are meshed to provide unity with interpenetration of exterior and interior in an unprecedented manner.

Gothic, in its static balance and its progression

toward some climaxes (e.g., the rose window on the east front), forecasts the Renaissance and the Baroque; its emotional sweep toward the heavens suggests the Middle Ages; its directional uncertainty indicates the swan song of the Medieval religious drive. And its structure predicts twentieth-century skeletal framing.

Secular Architecture, 1200–1550

By the thirteenth century secular architecture in the form of civic buildings—town and guild halls, hospitals, inns, and colleges, as well as domiciles—had become sufficiently important to take to itself some of the structural means and decorative enrichment of the churches. To the extent that this is so such architecture deserves to be called Gothic. The plan type for much civic architecture, however, derived from the private dwelling rather than the house of worship (Figure 5.30). Civic functions were still comparatively uncomplicated and there was no call for vast law courts, theaters, or public baths.

Plans of houses and their derivative architectural types were basically two. The first descended from the classical court enclosure. The central court, known as a *cortile* in Italy, a *patio* in Spain, a *cour* in France, a *court* or *close* in England, and a *cloister* when attached to a religious chapter, suggests enclosure within walls. It therefore bore an analogy to all fortifications in which the dwellings were incorporated into the enceinte. The court-type building remained the favorite of the southern countries. The second house type was the descendent of the Germanic hall and bower, generally favored in the north. There it frequently teamed with a walled enclosure because of its earlier history in centuries of warfare. Now walls could mean social rather than military seclusion.

Italy. We look to Italian urban architecture for that awakening of civility which we equate with the later Renaissance palazzo. Although Rome suffered many misfortunes during the Middle Ages, the presence of the papal see (except for a period of exile at Avignon, 1305–1378) guaranteed a degree of law and opulence that accounts for important dwellings such as the P. Venezia (1455). This was built for Cardinal Pietro Barbo,

Figure 5.29 Statues on the central portal of the west facade of Reims Cathedral, ca. 1225–1290. (Bildarchiv Foto Marburg.)

later Pope Paul II. Although provided with battlements, its horizontal string course and overall bisymmetry proclaim it one of the earliest palaces of the Renaissance. The P. Orsini, on the other hand, had been a theater under Augustus, was altered over the centuries, and is the sole survivor of a building that has been inhabited since the days of classical Rome.

The Davanzati Palace in Florence may serve as an example of Italian civil architecture of the fourteenth century (Figure 5.31). It is one of the few left almost intact, although its roof loggia is a replacement for original battlements. At a time when rustication (i.e., masonry of rough surfaces but straight edges) was common the Davanzati was built of ashlar stone (i.e., flat surfaces with straight-cut joints). It rose four stories, again significant of the scarcity of land in enclosed towns.

The palazzo is located on the Via Rossa, the street of the wool merchants. It was registered in the name of its sixteenth-century owners, the Davissi family, as the "palace of the three wool shops," and whereas the ground-story windows of feudal strongholds were small and grilled and the large portal was strongly barred, the three

Figure 5.30 (above) Palazzo Vecchio, Florence, 1298–1314. Built as Palazzo dei Priori for the Signoria, in 1569 it became the residence of the Medicis. (Alinari-Giraudon.)

Figure 5.31 (below) Palazzo Davanzati, Florence, fourteenth century. (Alinari/Editorial Photocolor Archives.)

wide-arched openings of the Davanzati suggest its mercantile nature and take us straight back to the Rome of the insulae.

One enters by the central door (note bisymmetry) into a space that extends across the front. This is groin vaulted in three sections to bear the heavy weight of the upper tile floors. When vaulting was absent, upper floors were necessarily of broad wooden boards. The faintly frescoed coat of arms of the Davissi, never erased by the later owners, the Davanzati, can be seen on the walls. This *l'ingresso* substitutes for the smaller passage which is customary in a building not associated with business and off which would be the warden's rooms.

From the vestibule a door leads to the vertically developed cortile. Its surrounding colonnade supports groin vaulting which rests directly on the octagonal pillars. Off this court narrow winding stone stairs mount between walls by a number of flights to the top story. This arrangement is customary for medieval staircases, although later ones are open and straight. In the Davanzati eery shafts of light filter through the narrowest of slits to dramatize the ascent.

The *piano nobile* is one flight up—the principal floor or floor of the nobles (*piano* means either soft or level). Here are the living quarters of the family, with the most important room, *la sala,* across the front. Other rooms lead from it, one opening into the next. In the Davanzati planning is advanced and, although rooms are interconnected, a loggia surrounds the cortile, giving access to adjoining spaces.

The second floor (Figure 5.32) above the ground has smaller compartments, or *cameras,* generally used for bedrooms. Both sanitary and culinary facilities are located on this level. The Davanzati has the great luxury of possessing a walled-in dumbwaiter reaching from the ground elevation to the top story, where the servants were lodged. The sala likewise has three trapdoors or machicolations in its floor—handy for defense.

The *piano nobile* contains a small chapel with its *prie-dieu,* or prayer stand, ubiquitous in this land. The Davanzati family passed into oblivion with the death of its scion, who as a comparatively young man hurled himself from the parapet into the street. One wonders what failed him in his little sanctuary.

Figure 5.32 Palazzo Davanzati. A second-floor room. Florence, fourteenth century. (Alinari/Editorial Photocolor Archives.)

The principal room in the Davanzati has a combination of rough plaster and stone walls, a heavily beamed ceiling, a tile floor, and a large hooded chimney place. Although many fourteenth-century palaces still retain their small Gothic two-light fenestration, five large heavily shuttered windows in the Davanzati allowed plenty of illumination. One likewise notices that stories as well as windows grow smaller on the upper floors. The progression, which was probably dictated by practical reasons, suggests some innate reverence for classical Vitruvian growth proportions.

The sense of space in this ancient home is magnificent. The long sala, which occupies the width of the building, is now sparsely furnished in suitable scale. The appointments are arranged with studied formality. Bare walls predispose toward certain types of embellishment. Hangings are germane and certainly were used throughout the continent as tapestries, leathers, and embroideries testify. In the Davanzati hooks are to be seen wherever the fabric is now absent.

In lesser rooms, more cubicle in proportions but still large by today's standards, geometric and small-figured frescoes cover many partitions. In one of the four second-story cameras these are painted to represent curtains, a medieval exam-

Figure 5.33 Ca d'Oro, Venice, ca. 1430. (G. C. Ball.)

ple of *trompe l'oeil* and perhaps of intentional faking. One room has a charming colored frieze of parrots, another of prideful peacocks. In their domestic way they are more intimately comprehensible than the important Renaissance frescoes of later buildings. Note also that the placement of these embellishments breaks the high camera into smaller horizontal divisions. Several rooms incorporate built-in cupboards, a refinement many years delayed in the north. All principal bedrooms have sanitary closets let into the walls.

Returning to the street, which now resounds with Alpha Romeos, we observe the iron rings for tethering horses, sconces for torches, and projecting hooks for horizontal poles to carry decorative banners and tapestries for gala days. On workdays these rods were useful for drying wool.

In the sixteenth century the first Davanzati owner, Bernardo (1529–1606), fitted a room as his study. A famous historian and man of letters, he translated Tacitus for the purpose of testing the conciseness of the Italian language. How typical of Italian culture that the tradesman, the capitalist, and the *man of universal learning* were not too far apart.

Medieval Venice, even as the modern city, presented its own version of everything. The thirteenth to the fifteenth centuries were its most prosperous. The Ducal Palace owes its present Gothic form largely to a reconstruction in the fourteenth century. The scheme of short round columns which carry arcades of pointed arches with their trefoil and quatrefoil cusping in the lower stories and the superimposed sheer marble wall patterned to resemble latticed brickwork (this was in the sixteenth century, following a disastrous fire), presents a hybrid of East-West that could only spell Venetian-Gothic.

Other examples, with their delightfully decorative Gothic gingerbread, were built from the twelfth to the fifteenth centuries. The Ca d'Oro (Figure 5.33) was one of the earliest of the typically Venetian arrangements in which the facade was broken by a central passage extending from canal to street and by a line of windows that lightened this route and the large principal salon (the *portego*) of the first floor. This arrangement later became bisymmetrical. With danger of invasion minimized, ornamental balconies overlooking the waterways became popular.

France. Medieval French chateaux, because they frequently added pavilions with the centuries, cannot be easily pegged to any one time or style. Blois, for instance, on the banks of the Loire in old Touraine, was begun in the thirteenth century, extended under Louis XII in the fifteenth, given its Renaissance countenance under Francis I in the sixteenth, and finished in the seventeenth with a wing by Gaston d'Orleans, designed by the greatest of French architects, François (not Jules, his grandnephew) Mansard.

To find a chateau that is predominantly Gothic we leave the lower Loire valley, Angers, Chinon, Langeais, and Losches, and follow history upstream to the point at which Amboise rises high above the river, here divided by the *Ile d'Or*. An island in a stream makes bridge-building easier. Certainly a stone bridge was here in Roman days. Bridges likewise facilitate enemy approach. King Charles VII appropriated the towers of Amboise from the Counts of Anjou and strengthened them. His son, the crafty Louis XI, used the buildings for his domestic ménage.

Although subsequent life at Amboise relates it to the Renaissance, its architecture is almost entirely Gothic. Amboise, then, may stand as an example of a French Gothic chateau, significant as a royal dwelling and a building that unites the era of untenable fortresses to that of habitable homes. We must seek the Gothic character of Amboise in the embellishments of the exterior, for much of the interior has gone. Looking at its *Logis du Roi*, or royal suite, we note the battery of tall, slender windows alternately spaced with shallow Gothic piers, the whole resting on a flow of round-arched vaults. The dormer (*lucarne*) windows of the facade are closely articulated with the fenestration below in true French Gothic fashion. They are also arrayed with pinnacles and topped by ogival pediments. Similar Gothic facades can be seen in other chateaux. Probably the loveliest is Josselin in Brittany and the most famous, Mehun-sur-Yèvre, which is illustrated in the horary of Jean, Duc de Berri, brother of Philip the Bold of Burgundy.

The flamboyant hood moldings over the two courtyard doors at Langeais (Figure 5.34) illustrate full well how Gothic embellishments served as window dressing for its domestic architecture. The doors beneath are low, flat-headed, and primitive. Similar moldings are to be seen over the gateway to the Paris home of the Cluniacs, l'Hôtel de Cluny, now the Cluny Museum, treasury of the domestic arts of France.

Certain Gothic details are structural. Spiral stairs wrapping themselves around a newel post, a well-known Gothic detail, are features of the

Figure 5.34 Gothic door on a turret at Langeais, one of the chateaus of the Loire valley. (G. C. Ball.)

Figure 5.35 Hôtel de Jacques Cœur, Bourges, 1443. (Lauros-Giraudon.)

two Charles VIII towers at Amboise. They are seen again at Chaumont, and in the Louis XII wing at Blois where they may have served as prototypes for the famous Francis I staircase at Blois and at Chambord.

Gothic structure is to be expected in St. Hubert's chapel in the gardens at Amboise. Much of its decoration is the most exquisite of Gothic tracery. But just as a Renaissance rondel sneaks in among Gothic trefoils of the facade at the home of Agnes Sorel, mistress of Charles VII, so here the famous lintel carving which depicts the saint's conversion, with its trend toward naturalism and its sculpture in higher relief, is more Renaissance than Gothic. Charles VIII built the chapel and Francis I, who in his insouciant manner professed such love for all Italian art, allowed

Leonardo to be buried in an unmarked grave barely one mile distant. His tomb is now in St. Hubert's. Thus one of the great men of the Italian Renaissance lies in a Gothic chapel in southwestern France.

Pretentious town houses of this era in France were built as court houses. Only the smaller homes faced directly on the street. An example of the former is the House of Jacques Coeur, minister of finance to Charles VII, in Bourges (Figure 5.35). This large structure is built around a court that abutted on the city wall, as at Khorsabad. The *corps de logis,* or family living quarters, were placed around this *cour.* The family chapel, with its large Gothic pointed window (of the type *lancet,* with the arch center outside the window span) and with its balcony filled with Gothic tracery, was located over the gateway. Windows, though not so narrow, are arranged in tiers over the end gables. The house has seven turret stairs.

France is said to be the home of stone architecture. In the north it uses the fine-grained white limestone known as Caen; in the south a native coarse and light volcanic material. The limestone traveled to England with the Conqueror and can be seen in the Tower trim.

The indigenous small homes of France (Figure 5.36) some of which remain from the twelfth century, have either loadbearing stone walls or half-timber construction. Except that French roofs are steeper and their stout oak members are carved with the most exuberant Gothic imagery, a small Gothic French house is similar to many to be found in the north.

England. England affords the most extensive picture of the middle-class country home of the Gothic period. Following the War of the Roses, which decimated the ranks of the old nobility, and with the boom in the wool trade in the eastern counties, a strong middle-class gentry appeared. The present-day amenities of living have descended from their homes. Whether we realize it or not, we owe much to the English squire.

When armed castles spread their living quarters along the rear wall of a fortified enclosure, the hall and chamber were retained as the nucleus of the dwelling (Figures 5.37, 5.38). The hall was a large and tall, gable-roofed structure. At Penshurst (Plate 8) it is 62 ft long, 39 wide, and 48 high. With its private apartment it measures 120 ft. Many ecclesiastic and royal halls are more extensive.

This complex had a typical plan. The public entrance, known as the lower end, is opposite the chamber end. It is often shielded by a fore-building known as a *porch,* which leads to a passage from which the buttery (French: *bouteiller,* cup-bearer) and the pantry (French: *pantier,* one in charge of bread) could be entered. An inner screen on the hall side was pierced by two entrances, placed to obscure the view of the service doors from the inner room. Another short spur screen protects these openings from the wind. Above the screen is a gallery, conjecturally referred to as the space occupied by the minstrels.

With the replacement of feudal cadres by mer-

Figure 5.36 Small half-timbered house, Chartres, fifteenth century. (G. C. Ball.)

cenaries, camaraderie likewise tended to vanish and the need was felt for a separation of owner from retainer. This led to the creation of a raised platform or *dais* at the upper end of the hall from which doors led to the chamber.

Because this room was a comparatively intimate area, it was smaller than the communal hall. It was soon given a ceiling (French: *ciel,* roof), and a second story known as the *solar* floor (possibly from the French *solive,* joist). Gradually the

169

Figure 5.37 (above) Penshurst Place, Kent, 1340. (G. C. Ball.)

Figure 5.38 (below) Plan of Penshurst Place, Kent, fourteenth century: (a) entrance; (b) court; (c) great hall; (d) dais; (e) hearth; (f) screens; (g) pantry; (h) buttery. (Adapted from Banister Fletcher, *A History of Architecture*, eighteenth edition, New York: Scribner's; London: Athlone Press, 1975.

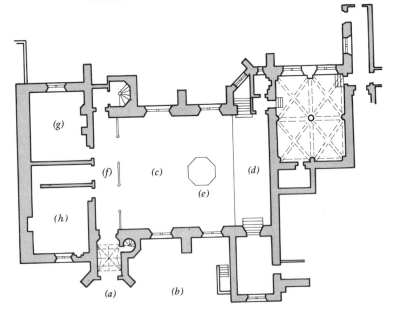

upper room usurped some of the functions of the ground-floor chamber, which was then reserved as a special audience or reception room. It became variously known as the parlor (French: *parler*, to speak), or withdrawing (drawing) room.

Small Norman manors, such as Boothby Pagnell, raised their halls one story above ground. Their smaller size made possible the elevation of a wooden floor supported by internal pillars or vaults. The only entrance to this structure was by an external flight of stairs which ran parallel to the wall. The ground story was used primarily for storage and service, and a small private depot at the upper end could be reached only by an interior connection from the chamber above. This arrangement of a two-story building descended as the pattern of the smaller English house that might have belonged to a yeoman's family.

The fifteenth century marked the transitional period in which castles were no longer necessary to nor attainable by an impoverished nobility and in which the gentry, ever-increasing in affluence, emulated the building forms the aristocracy had favored. It was at this time that the normative late medieval manor house emerged. It consisted of a large hall, used for assembly, private quarters

170

Figure 5.39 Little Moreton Hall, Cheshire, 1559–1580.
(G. C. Ball.)

on two levels at the upper end, and service quarters at the lower, above which might be a guest chamber. With the affluence of the owners accommodations proliferated. They were spread along the inner sides of a rectangular court, the vestigial relic of the walled enclosure of castle days. Thus the hall type of house met the European court house, and the union remained for a long time the prototype of the English Great House, an important and pretentious dwelling of both country and city.

The smaller town house developed on lines derived from its country cousin adapted to its needs. Because of land limitations, common party walls were essential. An asymmetrically placed opening that conserved space led through a passage to a rear service court. A trade area, a parlor, or both were located on the ground level. The story above ground constituted the general living quarters. The loft under the steep gabled roof was for servants and children or served for the storage of produce, or for drying clothes. In port towns, as in Holland, it was frequently a warehouse, reached, as can be seen by external pulleys and large doors, from the outside.

England offers a diversity of building materials and for this reason English architecture, especially domestic architecture, reveals a strong regional character. In Cornwall, in the southwest, in which hard granite abounds, there were such formidable fortresses as St. Michael's Mount on the Cornish coast. The famous Cotswald houses, in an area that cuts diagonally across the country from southwest to northeast, are built of an indigenous, softer sedimentary limestone. Shropshire, Lancastershire, and Cheshire, in the northwest, boasted fine stands of trees which account for their unique black and white half-timbered buildings like Little Moreton Hall (Figure 5.39). Southeast England used the clay of the river beds and, nearest to the sea traffic with Flanders from which some claim that ballast brick was imported, had built with brick since Roman times. However, even here, as long as forests remained, wood was the usual material. Only when its supply was depleted did masonry return. Little Wenham Hall, built in Suffolk during the thirteenth century, remains the first Medieval example.

English timber work has always been notable and as such became the guide for much construction in the English colonies of the New World. One type of Anglo-Saxon wood construction, known as *cruck*, contains the germ of all half-timber work. Trees were boughed from ground to ridge, and were braced by branches designed to make the frame rigid. Their forked ends formed decorative finials which were imitated later in stone *crockets*. When the ridge crockets were in position, it was an indication that the ridge pole had been reached, a general cause for jubilation. This ceremony is repeated today in the flag raising over the highest member of a new building.

In cruck work the spaces between timbers were wadded with branches laid with clay, known as *wattle and daub*. Thus the framework was separated from the filling and a form of structural decorative patterning resulted.

Post and beam structure is merely a variant of cruck. It was common to the Continent, to England, and to America. Except for a lower rubble story, it is similar to the timber building of northern Asia Minor. Stout posts are tenoned into a *sleeper* or *sill*, a large square timber placed on the ground or on top of a low masonry base. These vertical supports rose to the second story where *girts* or framework beams were mortised into position. The girts, in turn, held the smaller beams or *joists* which spanned the floor. A similar frame upheld the roof, the structure of which is detailed later. The front and rear girts which support the roof are known as *plates*. Additional exposed cross bracing of the frame again formed pleasing patterns.

The intervening spaces were filled in a variety of ways, perhaps with wattle and daub, narrowly spaced *studding* (small vertical laths) chinked with clay, or crude brick *nogging*. Throughout southeast England nogging is quite handsome and distinctive in pattern. Another type of early

filling, known as *brattice*, was made from vertically placed boards which had outer edges rounded from the tree.

The upper stories of post-and-beam buildings frequently projected beyond, or "jetted" out from the lower. It is easy to suggest functional reasons for such planning; however, one structural explanation lies in the fact that this practice equalized the load placed on the first-floor posts. Carved bosses were integral with the projecting second-story posts and are a forceful decorative feature of this architecture.

The framework roof on many English buildings is oak or chestnut. Its outer covering is thatch, tile, shingles, or lead—a native commodity. So skilled was the English wright that he could build a watertight roof which was almost flat like the roof at Little Wenham Hall which is probably a sixteenth-century copy of the original. Some roofs were cradle shaped, approaching the round arch. The customary form, however, was the gable, which rises to a central ridge and may or may not possess a ridge pole. When this framework is exposed to the interior it is known as an *open roof*. It might also be concealed behind a flat ceiling of beams and joists.

The gable is strengthened by pairs of rafters that meet at the ridge and by pairs of *purlins* placed horizontally. A *tie beam* is the simplest manner of stiffening a gable (Figure 5.40). Sometimes the tie is braced by a *king post* or two *queen posts*. In a *trussed* roof each pair of principal rafters is additionally buttressed by diagonal cross beams.

The most elaborate of English roofs is the *hammer beam*. In the trussed roof the rafters rest on the outer edges of thick walls. Vertical supports are raised near the inner edges to close in the awkward space. The triangles formed proved to be an additional prop and perhaps suggested the idea that a multiple of these structures would serve to translate the weight lower in the building. When this system was highly developed and embellished with carving or paint, elaborate decorative formations known as *hammer beam roofs* were the result.

Wood paneling of interior wall surfaces became customary in the later middle ages, but even in the northern countries it was scarcely used before the fifteenth century except in screens and stalls. Called *wainscot* in England, it was little known in domestic work before the sixteenth century and then might cover only the lower portion of the wall.

The character of this work is a pretty good indication of its age. As early as the thirteenth century, before elaborate panels were introduced, vertical boarding, which was exceptionally well done by the English wrights, was tongue and grooved to a flat face on one side and overlapped as *clapboarding* on the other. The flush face presented an excellent surface for painting which was a frequent finish. The King's Chamber at Compton Wynyates is an interesting example.

Enclosure with small panels as distinct from boards is later in origin. It is similar in structural principle to wood furniture framing (see p. 177). Both depend on conjoined right-angle supports into which a wood panel is fitted. The method of joining is some variant of the idea of inserting one piece into or against another with the application of cohesion by expert fitting, pressure locking, or possibly applied dowels. Grooving, rabetting, and mortise and tenoning suggest well-accepted methods. Medieval panels are characterized by carved designs which increased in intricacy over the years. Names like *linen fold* or *parchment* have been given because of the fancied resemblance to folds of cloth or paper, but they are of recent origin; the patterns were designated simply as *wavy wood* in their day. It probably occurred in this manner. A narrow wooden panel was grooved into the uprights (known as *stiles*) and horizontal supports (known as *rails*). In thinning the edges of the panel to fit into these framing members, the center would obviously remain as a ridge, from which several decorative splines might be planned that could be developed as fancy led. Ogivals and trailing grapevines were other representations.

Fine medieval woodwork was of quartered oak and on the Continent likewise of chestnut. Most often it was pit sawn. In this method the saw was maneuvered with one man standing in a pit and the other above. Timber for paneling, as for exterior framing, was customarily riven because riven or split lumber best withstands the weather.

The men who created fine woodwork were the

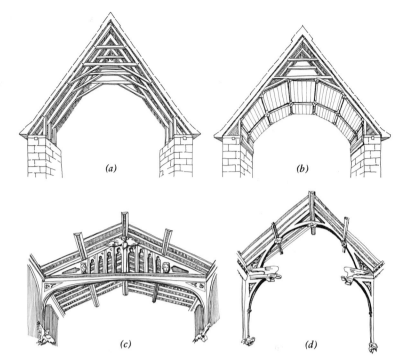

Figure 5.40 English timbered roofs: (a) trussed rafter; (b) barrel; (c) tie beam; (d) hammer beam. (Adapted from Sir Banister Fletcher, *A History of Architecture*, eighteenth edition, New York: Scribner's; London: Athlone Press, 1975.)

same as those engaged in cabinetry. Coming under the jurisdiction of the guilds, their organization was similar throughout the western world. The man who in England was the *carpenter* or *joiner* was the *menuisier* in France and the *falegname* in Italy. More intricate carving was done by the *carver*, the *ymager*, and the wood *scultore*, respectively. An apprentice served a long tutelage under a *master*, *maître*, or *mastro* and was required to pass a rigorous examination before being allowed to become first a *journeyman* (permission to travel) and finally a master (permission to practice independently).

Because the art of glassmaking was all but lost to the west and openings were vulnerable spots in the architectural armor, early medieval windows made do with small apertures pierced through wall or roof. Oiled cloth or boards restricted the elements and the intruder. When walls were thick, the loophole was canted both internally and externally to allow maximum penetration of light.

173

SOME MEDIEVAL HOUSES

ITALY

Abbey of Monte Cassino (Benedictine)	Near Rome	529
Palace of the Doge	Venice	Ninth century
P. Orsini	Rome	Eleventh to fifteenth centuries
Castel dell'Ovo	Naples	Twelfth century
P. Loredan	Venice	Twelfth century
La Zisa	Palermo	1154–1166
Castel Spini-Ferroni	Florence	Thirteenth century
Monastery of S. Francis	Assisi	1228
P. del Podestà (Bargello)	Florence	1255
Castel Nuovo	Naples	1279
P. Pubblico	Siena	1289
P. Vecchio (Figure 5.30)	Florence	1298
P. Davanzati (Figures 5.31, 5.32)	Florence	Fourteenth century
Castel S. Elmo	Naples	Fourteenth Century
Monastery S. Martino	Naples	1325
C. Volterra	Volterra	1345
C. Visconti and Sforza	Milan	1368–1450
Ca d'Oro (Figure 5.33)	Venice	1430
P. Venezia	Rome	1455

SPAIN

The Alhambra (Figure 5.14)	Granada	1309
The Alcazar	Seville	1350
The Alcazar	Segovia	1352

GERMANY

Schloss Marienburg	Marienburg	1280
Schloss Meissen	Meissen	1471
Rothenburg, Medieval fortified town		

FRANCE

Monastery of Cluny (Benedictine)	Burgundy	910
C. Chinon	Old Touraine	Tenth century
C. de Langeais (Figure 5.34)	Old Touraine	Twelfth century
C. de Losches	Old Touraine	Twelfth century
C. Gaillard	Les Andelys	Twelfth century
Monastery of Fontevrault	Old Touraine	1115
Mont S. Michel	Off Normandy	Thirteenth century
C. de Blois	Old Touraine	Thirteenth century
Carcassone, Medieval fortified town	S. France	Thirteenth century walls
Aigues-Mortes, Medieval fortified town	S. France	1240
Palace of the Popes	Avignon	1334–1352

FRANCE (continued)

C. de Pierrefonds (restored nineteenth century)	Oise	1392
c. d'Amboise	Old Touraine	Fifteenth century
House of Jacques Cœur (Figure 5.35)	Bourges	1443
Hôtel de Cluny	Paris	1485
C. de Josselin	Brittany	ca. 1500 rebuilt

ENGLAND

C. Dover	Kent	pre-Norman
Tower of London	London	1078
Warwick Castle (Figure 5.16)	Warwick	Eleventh century
Windsor Castle	Windsor	Eleventh century
Boothby Pagnell Manor	Lincolnshire	Twelfth century
Jew's House	Lincoln	Twelfth century
Fountain's Abbey (Cistercian)	Yorkshire	1135–1150
Alnick Castle	Northumberland	1150
Stokesay (Figures 5.17, 5.18, and 5.19)	Shropshire	Thirteenth century
Little Wenham Hall	Suffolk	Thirteenth century
Penshurst Place (Plate 8; Figures 5.37 and 5.38)	Kent	1340
Kenilworth Castle	Warwick	1346
Fish House	Meare, Somerset	1350
Bodiam Castle	Sussex	ca. 1386
Hurstmonceaux	Sussex	Fifteenth century
Hever Castle	Kent	1462 rebuilt
Compton Wynyates (Figures 8.1 and 8.2)	Warwick	1528
Little Moreton Hall (Figure 5.39)	Cheshire	1559

When glass became more readily available, the small panes, often lozenge shaped, were fastened together by leaded strips known as *calms* and affixed to an iron frame. This frame, in turn, was mounted in the center of the wall. The *jamb* is the straight side of the wall into which the window is inserted. The *reveal* is the part of the jamb that lies between the glass and the wall surface. These names are equally applicable to similar parts of doors. A *splay* refers to a reveal that is cut diagonally from a wall. Framed windows were later finished with a suitable molding. Where this is found, splaying is eliminated.

Throughout their long history windows assumed various forms. Byzantine architecture commonly used the *bifora* (Italian: double opening), which descended to the Romanesque. It consisted of a double arched recess separated into two vertical parts by a stone shaft or column.

The heads of Romanesque windows were round-arched. Even in English domestic architecture the bifora or similar form was used in the chamber end by the twelfth century.

In the Gothic the spaces between supports were opened to still larger glass areas. As they increased in size, the frames were unable to sustain the added leaded panes. Extra rigidity was provided by stone stanchions or *mullions*—the vertical members—and horizontal *transoms*. A window *light* is the window space included between them.

When window shapes and moldings followed the various pointed arch styles, increasing difficulty was experienced in fitting window to opening. This is one reason given for the invention of the elaborate mullion tracery found in Gothic windows.

The number and size of windows increased

with wealth and more peaceful times. In both church and civic architecture most of the space between buttresses was opened to glass.

An important placement of windows in English domestic architecture was on the court side of the dais where the large bay projected into the yard, balancing the entrance porch on the lower end. A *bay* or *bow* window extends to the ground. An *oriel* is elevated and frequently found in the solar.

Vulnerable windows were protected by internal shutters made of thick wood laminations braced with iron bands and secured with iron nails (hand forged and extensively used in medieval carpentry since the thirteenth century). These shutters were barred like doors with shafts that slid back into the walls of the reveals. Enormous and attractive wrought hinges are also of this period.

The interior space between window and wall surface in domestic work provided a pleasant place for a seat, sometimes reached by steps, from which the courtyard activities could be viewed. A refinement came with the separate framing of the lower section of the window light and pivoting it to provide ventilation.

Doors and their framing were impressive decorative features. The wooden door itself, constructed like the wooden shutter, often occupied only a small part of the space. It closed against stone jambs. The tops of doors were straight or, like the windows, followed the prevailing architectural style.

Two forms of stairs remain—the Gothic spiral which clung to the newel post around which it twined and the straight flight which was supported by the wall. The newel stairways were often enclosed in their own turret. Treads were stone or solid timbers.

Fireplaces, common only in the north, were for centuries merely a raised hearth in the center of the hall. Later, wall fireplaces vented through the surround, and chimneys with flues appeared in the thirteenth century.

Early coverings for the hearth were hooded, a form that prevailed long on the Continent and existed parallel to the vertical breast that extended into the room. In England the fifteenth-century Tudor fireplace was flush with the wall and the stone opening was a four-centered arch.

Dimensions were generous, an Italian outlet being easily 8 ft high, the Tudor somewhat lower and broader. Obviously sizes differed with circumstances.

FURNITURE

Sources

Comparatively few pieces of medieval furniture antedating the fourteenth century are extant, yet they merit study as representing the basis of the tradition of European furniture. Additional information regarding the Romanesque and Gothic periods comes from designs in stone sculpture and from medieval manuscripts. Pictorial evidence must, however, be greeted with a degree of skepticism because popular imagination and the copying of ancient sources led to inaccuracies. Contemporary inventories and histories, on the other hand, are fairly reliable. Conjecture may be the firmest ground in presuming that men who made the elaborate woodwork of church and guildhall were not inept at framing furniture. Such proficiency must be sought first among the craftsmen who worked for the church and then among those who supplied nobility rather than those who served the needs of the common man.

Materials and Techniques

Wood was at hand. Climbing the hills of Umbria and Tuscany, one reaches the province of the nut trees, which, as one goes still farther north, are abundant on lower terrain. Italian furniture was early and persistently made of chestnut and walnut, though oak is not absent. Beech and elm, commonly used in European furniture, have not withstood the ravages of time so well, and pieces made from these woods exist only from later centuries. As the hardwood forests retreated, the Italians turned to their softer timber, the pine and the poplar. This accounts in part for their later artistry with painted furniture.

The earliest French furniture is predominantly of oak, as the provincial work of Normandy and north central France is today. It is only in the late fifteenth century and the ascendency of the Burgundian-Flemish school of craftsmen that light-colored and fine-grained French walnut occurs. Medieval English furniture is invariably of oak because walnut did not make its appearance until the seventeenth century. One of the definitive books on the subject of English furniture[11] dubbed the period before 1660 *The Age of Oak.*

As early as the thirteenth century a class of workmen became detached from the guild of masters, although still under its jurisdiction with respect to the cutting and curing of wood. These men were defined in England as the *arkwrights* (those who fashioned *arks* or chests) and in France as the *huchiers* (the *hutch* was a chest for storage of provisions). It is not clear that the Italians sponsored a similar organization. These workmen specialized in making small movable pieces of furniture for average uses. They may also have taken over the construction of doors, window moldings, and various nonstructural building parts.

Movable furniture was scarce during the Middle Ages, for most pieces were built into the walls. It is an indication of social change when a group of men undertakes the manufacture of furniture. The French word for furniture, *les meubles,* and the German, *die möbel,* suggests a mobility of household effects which had previously existed largely with respect to the coffer and chest and later referred to innumerable articles that could be transported from one location to another.

The earliest type of movable furniture construction was in fact no construction at all, being merely a plank laid on trestles. If trestles were large enough, the very weight of the top anchored them in place. A smaller piece, however, had to be stabilized. Pegging or wedging the legs into the top to form a triangular shape was one solution common to provincial furniture from the milking stool to the *Windsor chair.*

Another early and very crude manufacture consists of butt ending solid supports to tops or seats. Adhesion of the pieces was made with dowel pegs known as *trenails* or, in cruder work, with metal nails. This boxlike construction, like the fourteenth-century oak coffer now at the Louvre, was often reinforced by bands of iron.

Fine structure was that of framing in which a rectilinear support was made by light members placed at right angles to one another and *mortised and tenoned* into position. In a mortise and tenon joint, similar to one that is *dovetail* or *grooved,* an extension of one piece fits into a socket in another. As in wainscoting, the panels that were usual to framed furniture were often carved toward the edges for better fitting. Parchment and linenfolds were the result.

The use of lathe turning at an early date is disputed. It has been suggested[12] that medieval sculpture that illustrated turned pieces was in reality the result of carving in imitation of the lathe turning of late Roman examples. An ample chair with turned members dating around 1200 is in Hereford cathedral.[13] In England turned pieces which were especially fashionable at the beginning of the sixteenth century may indicate the reintroduction at that time of the principle of the lathe.

Types and Forms

The *trestle table* represents the earliest extant table type. It has been popularly imagined as standing in the center of the hall, although paintings more often indicate its use along the side. Because diners were generally seated on one side only to facilitate service this placement would be more expedient for both utility and safety.

A cloth was placed over the top and free side of the table. This was originally called a *tablier* or *apron.* In the thirteenth century linen cloths designated as *nappes* were used in France.[14] Properly speaking, long trestle tables are the only true *refectory tables,* customarily seen in the dining hall or refectory of an ecclesiastic house (Figure 5.41).

Two old English trestle tables are at Penshurst, each 27 ft long and 3 ft wide. They were made in the late fifteenth century some 150 years after the erection of the hall.[15] These tables, however, were more often contemporary with the building and were included in its price.

Renaissance paintings frequently indicate three tables placed in "U" formation around the sides of a room, not unlike the Roman triclinium arrangement, although designed for a larger number of guests. Manuscript illustrations also show tables arranged in circular form, which may have been inspired by Roman customs (Figure 5.42).

Figure 5.41 Medieval refectory table used in the refectory (dining hall) of a religious house. Wall painting at Monte Oliveto Monastery near Siena: *St. Benedict and His Monks,* by Giovanni Antonio Bazzi, il Sodoma, 1477–1549. (Alinari/Editorial Photocolor Archives.)

Symbolism cannot be ruled out—the Christian significance of the perfection of the circle—the persistence of the chivalric tales of the *round table.*

Smaller tables for specialized purposes were introduced at a remote date, although few remain. Used for writing, for intimate dining, and for games, they are mentioned in inventories and shown in Medieval manuscripts. One small table was known as the *credence* (Latin: *credere,* to believe). High personages feared to eat or drink until the food had been tested by a servitor in their presence, thus guarding against poison. Supposedly this testing was done from a portable table; hence the credence. In later years when its former significance was forgotten, a small octagonal table reserved this name until well into the sixteenth century.

One framed table was placed in the English hall between the two openings in the lower end screen (Figure 5.43). To increase its length an

ingenious *drawtop* was invented in the late fifteenth century.[16] Where the framed table extended beyond the supports two leaves were added which swung from under these ends to form an enlarged top. The capacity furnished was so useful that many dining tables not originally so equipped were later altered to include drawtops.

Seating furniture, in medieval inventories, was frequently ambivalent and served several functions. A chest, for instance, was not only a receptacle for storage, it also served as a table, a bed, and a seat. Often the tops of long benches were hinged to provide access to storage space within. An English piece of this design is commonly referred to as a *settle.* The Italian *cassapanca,* a Renaissance piece, combines the Italian name for chest, *cassone,* with what may be a corruption for *banco* or bench.

The ordinary seat was a stool or bench. Chairs with arms and backs belonged to VIPs. The small stool (French: *escabeau;* Italian: *sgabello*) or the long bench (French: *banc;* Italian: *banco*) was the counterpart in design to the dining table it accompanied. On the Continent the stool was

Figure 5.42 *Round Table of King Artus of Brittany,* fourteenth-century miniature. This miniature shows a Medieval circular table. Bibliothèque Nationale, Paris. (Phot. Bibl. nat. Paris.)

Figure 5.43 (above) Long table from St. Donat's Castle, Glamorganshire, Wales, first half of the sixteenth century. Length, 3.6 m, width, 80 cm, height, 80 cm. Oak. Metropolitan Museum of Art, New York. (The Metropolitan Museum of Art, Fletcher Fund, 1949.)

Figure 5.44 (below) Panelback chair (derived from a choir stall). French, fifteenth–sixteenth centuries. Metropolitan Museum of Art, New York. (The Metropolitan Museum of Art, Rogers Fund, 1907.)

frequently graced with a back and later graduated to a class of seating furniture with arms, but was never an important piece.

Writers do not always make a distinction between a bench and a *form* (French: *forme)*. Because the French *forme* designated a choir stall, that name has frequently been assigned to the long seat which has a low back and dividing arm rests.[17]

The reference to choir stalls suggests the fact that seats were often built into position. In many Italian paintings of the Last Supper we see a room with seats built along a wall, they frequently had paneled backs and dividing arms, and, according to legend were found in the Germanic hall. Recall that in the Anglo-Saxon epic *Beowulf* there is a description of the monster Grendel tearing loose the seats in the mead-hall. Such fixed seats have survived in the bishop's throne and the abbot's stall. (Note the connotation in the word *installation*—to place in the honored seat.) Indeed these church stalls, on which more care was expended than on any similar household artifact, were the prototypes of the first important English chair known as the *choir stall chair* (Figure 5.44).

We have a precedent for the individual movable straight-backed chair in the famous one that belonged to Maximianus, the sixth-century bishop of Ravenna, which is now assembled in the Cathedral in that city. This episcopal throne made of carved ivory plaques set into a wood frame is important to art historians because its representational design indicates a fusion of antique realistic figure modeling and the stylized flat patterning of the eastern tradition.

Another famous historical piece is the bronze throne chair[18] of the Merovingian king Dagobert, now in the Bibliothèque Nationale in Paris (Figure 5.45). Its design, derived from the Roman curule, has animal legs and a back that incorporates circular patterning. This type became known as a *falstool, une chaise pliante,* or a *folding stool.* Its later Renaissance counterpart is known as a *Dante* or *Savanarola chair* because of its association with the personal belongings of these famous men (see Figures 6.42 and 6.43).

Figure 5.45 Bronze throne of the Merovingian King Dagobert, 623–638. Bibliothèque Nationale, Paris. (Giraudon.)

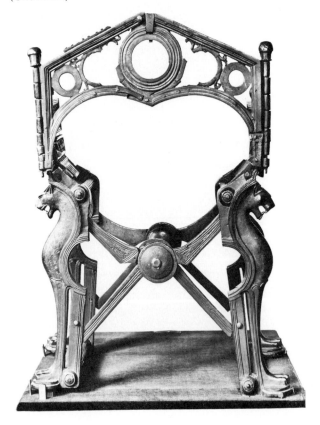

The most famous seat in English history is the framed model known as the *Chair of St. Edward,* or the English coronation chair, which stands in Westminster Abbey.[19] It was named in honor of King Edward the Confessor (1042–1066), of the line of Alfred, because of the veneration accorded to him and because most of the coronation regalia was by tradition assigned to him. The chair, however, was made later (ca. 1300) on order of King Edward I's builder, Master Walter. It is built of oak carved and decorated with paintings and mosaics. Under its seat rests the famous *Stone of Scone* or *Stone of Destiny,* which is associated with Scottish coronations and which Edward I brought back from Scone in 1296.

The *bed* (French: *lit;* Italian: *letto*) was an essential article, although in medieval households it had not yet attained to the importance that accrued later, when it was often a prime legacy mentioned in wills. Originally and commonly, the bed was the top of a chest or a *pallet,* a narrow stand covered with straw. The important part of the piece was the canopy overhead and its surrounding walls of curtains. This constituted what we might call a bedroom or room for a bed. Like seats, the bed was frequently built-in, stationary room equipment. Many Gothic paintings show beds as wall recesses or cupboards with an affixed shelf on which the bedding was placed. Provincial Europe still features this type of alcove. As night air was considered harmful, tightly closed wooden doors or curtains served to keep it out. The bed was sometimes raised on a wooden platform to protect it further from cold drafts.

When a bed stood in the center of a room, the *canopy* or *tester,* from which the curtains hung, was sometimes suspended from the ceiling beams (Figure 4.46). The curtains were looped up during the day. The next step was a bedstead with four corner posts to support the surround. The actual pallet was often separated from the foot, although the headboard was usually attached. In these early beds the rails were laced with ropes on which the bedding was placed.

In Italy the earliest beds date from the fifteenth century. There is no complete English bed dated earlier than Elizabeth's reign, although several posts of the late fifteenth century remain.[20]

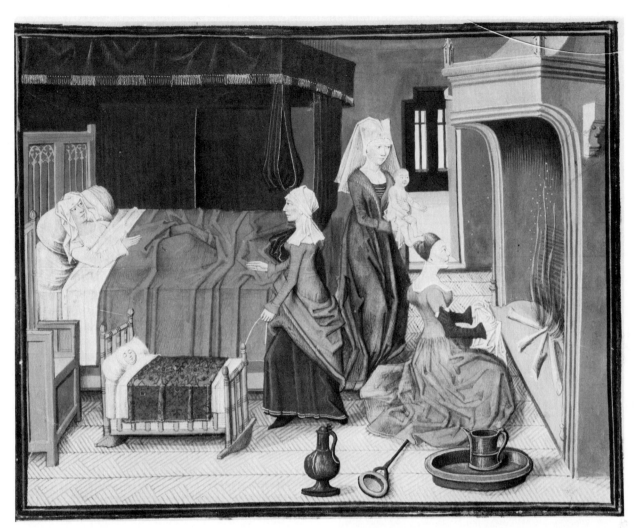

Figure 5.46 *The Birth of St. John.* Miniature by Loyset Lidet. (Manuscript, Ms 9967, fol 47 verso.) Died in 1478. Bibliothèque royale Albert Ier, Brussels. (Copyright Bibliothèque royale Albert Ier, Bruxelles.)

The most ubiquitous type of medieval furniture was the *chest* (Italian: *cassa* or *cassone;* French: *coffre;* Dutch: *kas*). Chests were valuable not only for storage but also for travel. Odom[21] suggests that in Italy at this time princes sometimes traveled with a train of 100 chests. Some form of slanting top developed from the need to shed rain and snow when exposed to bad weather. Gothic Italian chests are low, generally with flat tops and straight-framed sides. Some rested directly on the floor and had strongly molded bases. Early chests open on pin hinges. By the fourteenth century in England and earlier on the Continent iron clamp hinges were substituted.[22]

As the number of pieces proliferated, names flooded the vocabulary. Nothing, however, can be more frustrating than the inconsistency with which labels are sometimes handled, even in museum parlance. But titles are useful and a few are tenacious. A *hutch* (French: *huche*), for instance, which now implies any bin or chest, originally meant a chest with doors. Doors are rarely found on English pieces before the fifteenth century, and a central one precedes an era of two.

Hutches were intended for the storage of provisions. Thus they were pierced for better ventilation. A smaller cabinet was called the *livery cupboard* because food was delivered to retainers from this source.

The etymology of the word *cupboard* and of the specialized pieces of dining room furniture that descend from it is both interesting and instructive. A cupboard was originally a side table or chest on which the silver cups were laid; a lower compartment was provided later for their safekeeping. From this origin the name has been generalized to designate any cabinet with doors. In Italy many storage compartments were let into the thick walls, which accounts for the scarcity of movable ones in that country.

A *sideboard*, a simple shelf on which to place viands, assumed the function of a cupboard. An article that looks like two tables mounted one above the other is called a *two-tiered sideboard* by some writers; by others a *buffet*.[23] The word *buffet* (French) is a general term for a cabinet for table ware, just as the word *cabinet* is generic for a small case or cupboard.

The French credence table loaned its name to the Italian *credenza*, a cabinet with doors. One is mentioned as early as 1466 at the time of the Medici-Rucellai wedding feast, although the era of its popularity came later in the Renaissance. Another borrowed name is the *credence*, mentioned in French and English inventories. It is a unique object that resembles a low cupboard surmounted by a tall back and eventually a canopy. It usually carries smaller storage cabinets in step-back arrangement.

The *dresser* (French: *dressoir*, from *dresser*—to arrange or lay out) was still another species of dining-hall furniture—a cupboard with open shelves in the superstructure (Figure 5.47). In France the number of permissible shelves is said to have been dictated by rank, royalty being allowed four or more. These demountable pieces are frequently spoken of as *meubles à deux parts*. Many tall chests were constructed so that the upper portion could be disjointed from the lower —the eighteenth-century highboy being one of the best known.

All of these elaborate types of dining furniture made their initial appearance in the late Gothic, when living again became sumptuous. Georges Chastelain, the chronicler of Philip, the reigning Duke of Burgundy in the fifteenth century, describes a court banquet:

> The Duke had made in the great hall a dressoir constructed in the form of a round castle, ten steps in height, filled with gold plate in pots and flagons of various kinds, amounting to 6000 marks not counting those on top which were fine gold set with rich gems of marvelous price.[24]

This may be press-agent advertising, but nevertheless—!

One of the largest cupboards or cabinets with doors was the *armoire*, designed to store clothes or armorial equipment. This cabinet was often built into a wall and as such it took the place of a small room known as the *garde-robe* or ward-

Figure 5.47 French dresser, late fifteenth or early sixteenth century. Trimmed with Gothic tracery and finial figures of a monk and two lay persons. Crowned royal arms of France on central panel of cupboard. Linen-fold panels in lower recessed area. Iron locks and bolts. Height 94 cm. Wallace Collection, London. (Crown Copyright, reproduced by permission of the Trustees, The Wallace Collection, London.)

robe. The fact that it was the medieval counterpart of our dressing room led to the confusion or substitution of this name for the space containing the sanitary outlet of Medieval fortresses —the *garde-robe*.

A small piece, a combination of table and box or chest, was the French *prie-dieu*, and the Italian *inginocchiatoio* or prayer stand, placed in the bed chamber or oratory.

Another small chest, with slanting top, was the reading stand, which did not appear as an article of domestic furniture until the late fifteenth century, although seen earlier in connection with the work of scribes. In the study of Duke Federico di Montefeltro of Urbino—that little gem of a room now at the Metropolitan Museum of Art (taken from the Ducal Palace at Gubbio and a counterpart of the one at Urbino)—part of the paneling could be pulled from the wall to reveal a seat and reading desk, added evidence of the growing literacy in Tuscan court circles in the fifteenth century. This library, which is more suitably discussed under the Italian Renaissance, was, however, as unusual as the ability to read or the availability of reading matter, despite the invention of the movable type printing press.

Types of Furniture Decoration

Medieval furniture of importance was often lavishly decorated. Carving, known as *chip carving* because the chips were cut out with a carver's gouge, was the customary method of wood ornamentation north of the Alps. Except in Venice and the most northerly provinces, Medieval carved pieces were rare in Italy.

The Gothic French were the carvers par excellence, especially of chests. Many were sold to England during the fifteenth century, proof of the repute of the French craftsman and carver. This work may be divided into two artistic classes. That done in the cosmopolitan *Ile-de-France* possesses the clarity, delicacy, and preciseness that one associates with that nation's art. The work done in Burgundy, sponsored by its immensely wealthy and powerful dukes, is far more robust, imaginative in its invention, and less constrained to follow scholarly models. Because of the close ties at this time between Burgundy

and Flanders, Flemish artists were often the creators of the Burgundian pieces. Flemish work, even when it invaded England, is characterized by generous high-relief carving. English carving, on the other hand, is distinguished by sturdiness and tighter composition.

One seeks to develop by close observation an ability to appreciate regional differences. These distinctions are not so much a matter of tracing this or that motif. Sometimes a wandering craftsman (and there were many, despite legal attempts to curb their movement) or a foreign import would introduce new patterns. But the manner of the hand is the matter of the heart. This cannot change so easily.

In addition to stylistic differences, progress in skill is to be noted in Gothic furniture carving. Early work is relatively flat because the carvers merely chipped away the background and were content with a flat design in low relief. As experience was gained, the patterns were deeply undercut and the surfaces were likewise modulated, until finally the composition stood out as delicately modeled lacework. Some of the finest Gothic-inspired pieces, spoken of as Rhenish, were done in what is now Germany during the fifteenth and sixteenth centuries.

Inlay, known in Italy as *intarsia*, was the typical Italian form of embellishment that reached its zenith of perfection during the last quarter of the *quatrocento* and the first of the *cinquecento* (the 1400s and 1500s, respectively) in what is considered the years of the Italian Renaissance. The impulse toward this type of ornamentation may be anticipated by the craft of the *Cosmati* in Rome. This guild took its name from the Cosmati family, whose skill was directed toward inlaying white marble with small bits of colored stone, gold, and glass in geometric patterns, an enterprise that flourished from 1100 to 1300.

In Venice during the *trecento* the Embracchi family was famed for a particular type of inlay done with bone, ivory, and light-stained wood. It is, in turn, the prototype for *certosina* (Figure 5.48) done almost a century later in the neighborhood of Pavia, the old Lombard capital and early university town. This type of intarsia derives its name from the nearby Certosa charterhouse of the famous Carthusian monastery.

Figure 5.48 Italian chest with certosina work, fifteenth century. Walnut and ivory. Length, 124.5 cm, width, 52 cm, height, 59 cm. Nelson Gallery of Art, Kansas City, Missouri. (Nelson Gallery-Atkins Museum, Kansas City, Missouri, Nelson Fund.)

Pastiglia, or plastic composition, is a type of gesso in low relief long favored by Italians for the enrichment of their furniture. Pastiglia was essentially the work of the painter, much as texture painting is today, but is not the same as the later gypsum gesso which is applied in much higher modeling. A wood surface was prepared with a layer of gesso or plaster of Paris and then built up with more colored gesso applied with a brush. Cennino d'Andrea Cennini[25] wrote a students' guide to methods of painting in fifteenth-century Florence. In this he emphasizes the difference between the two techniques.

Although the Italians expanded their fondness for pictorial expression in color through intarsia and pastiglia, they never abandoned the use of tempera and later of oil as traditional media. Vasari (1511–1574), the Italian painter, architect, and writer, says:

> At that time [meaning the Gothic] it was the custom of people to have in their chambers great wooden chests of various forms, and everyone used to have them painted with the stories from the myths of Ovid [the Renaissance is dawning]

or other poets, or hunting scenes or jousts, or tales of love according to the taste of each one. And at the same time were painted the beds and chairs and other furniture of the rooms.[26]

The Cleveland Museum of Art has a panel, taken from such a chest (Figure 5.49), which represents a horse race in the streets of Florence, painted around 1417. We note the bareback riders crossing the finish line in front of the grandstand and marvel, as one does at the Palio in Siena today, that the host of spectators—men, women, and children—escape from being trodden to death by the avalanche of horseflesh descending on them. The festivities were gala for the wedding of Tommaso di Giovanni de Berto Fini and Giacoma de Filippo Aldobrandini. What could the bride have thought had she known that a scene from her marriage coffer would repose five centuries later in a museum in a land then unknown?

The *finish* on medieval furniture is disputed. Most was probably left without a preservative coating. Although Macquoid[27] says that varnish did not appear on English furniture until the middle of the sixteenth century, Cescinsky suggests a century earlier.[28] The contradiction is probably due to confusion of definition. Certainly an oil base varnish was not commonly used until the mideighteenth century.

TEXTILES

General Development

Penelope, according to Homer, supervised the production of her household textiles within the precincts of her own home, a precedent followed by most matrons in an agrarian society. Under prosperous urban conditions large-quantity specialization was required to provide the requisite cloth.

During the Middle Ages the maw of demand extended to such articles as rugs, household furnishings, and clothing. In addition to textiles made from the usual fibers, Europe bought the leathers of the Levant and of Cordoba in Spain, where the industry had attained an outstanding level of expertise. Cordoban leathers were stamped with patterns in high relief, gilded, and painted. Gilded leathers were known as *cuirs d'or* in the Medieval trade. Furs, too, served many uses and were fashionable even in the warmer climates.[29] Russian pelts, the sable and the otter, became a chief source of revenue in Tsarist Russia.

Wool and linen constituted the chief staples of European cloth. Flanders (so named since the seventh century, now part of Belgium, Holland, and France) supplied superior woolen goods known as "Frisian" yardage to every corner of Europe. The wealth of such cities as Ghent, Ypres, and Bruges was originally based on the textile industry.

Textile development played an important role in the political history of the later Middle Ages. It was, for instance, the reliance of the Flemish on English wool that caused them to align with that country against France in the Hundred Years War (1338–1453). Almost a century later, when England had begun to process her own wool, the towns of the Lowlands took sides with France against the Hapsburg emperor, largely because his policy allowed an open door to English woolens.

During the fourteenth century there was a major transfer of the quality woolen goods industry away from Flanders, much of it going to Florence. This was due not only to the rigid trade barriers that the Flemish themselves had erected but likewise was caused by the vision of the Italian merchants who sensed an advantage in importing cloth in the gray (unfinished) and then refining it by dyeing, fulling, shearing, and tailoring so that it might be sold at a greater profit. In the textile economy of Florence cloth refining antedated spinning and weaving and wool preceded silk.

It is, however, in relation to fabrics largely silk that textile styles must be defined.[30] Despite the enormous prices that silks commanded, the princes of church and court kept a traffic in the precious material alive at all times. The China silk industry, which had suffered during the unsettled years of the post-Han Dynasty, was revived by the house of T'ang (618–907). By then the opportunist western market had successfully introduced

Figure 5.49 *Horse Race in Florence.* Painted panel from an Italian chest. Florence, ca. 1417–1418. Poplar. Cleveland Museum of Art. (The Cleveland Museum of Art, The Holden Collection.)

Figure 5.50 Byzantine textile, *Castor and Pollux,* probably a reproduction of an ancient piece. The Textile Museum, Washington, D.C. (Textile Museum, Washington, D.C.)

sericulture into Syria, the Greek islands, and the plains south of the Balkans. The story of Nestorian monks importing the eggs of the silkworm and the seeds of the mulberry tree from China in the heads of their staffs—a feat considered to have been underwritten by the Emperor Justinian (527–565)—is at least within the realm of historical probability.

Beginning with the wealthy Sassanian rulers of the native Persian dynasty (226–642) who established and revitalized textile centers in Susa and Shuster, Iranian patterns were carried to the Orient as well as to the Occident. The Byzantine rulers at Constantinople encouraged a more systematic knowledge of silk production and weaving, which in time spread through the Mediterranean region. Prominent manufactories were located at Byzantium, Antioch, Alexandria, and Antinoë. Coming under the domination of Islam

in the seventh century, Syrian and Egyptian weavers brought the silk industry to Spain under the patronage of the western caliphate at Cordoba. All of Andalusia teemed with silk workshops and important centers of Islamic weaving were established in Sicily and southern Italy.

Thus we see how events joined to locate the centers from which came the luxury fabrics of Europe during the Middle Ages and which, in turn, provided the bases for later developments in the silk industry in Italy and France.

Early Medieval textiles in general, although certainly not exclusively, were designed with a circle or rondel as a basic motif (Figure 5.50). Within this chain repeat the representational design was derived from Classical, Near Eastern, Christian, or Islamic imagery. Classical subject matter is seen in a silk (fifth to seventh centuries) woven in Egypt or Asia Minor (Figure 5.50). Here the Dioscuri, the twin brothers Castor and Pollux, accompanied by winged genii, are pouring a libation at the sacrifice of two steers. Eastern motifs are seen in the textiles of the Sassanian Persians, in which rosettes may be combined with small fauna such as ducks, roosters, or pheasants. Mounted hunters as well as facing horses frequently occur.

Later Byzantine iconography is present in the silks produced during the reign of the Emperor Justinian and in the period between the end of iconoclasm (843) until the conquest of Constantinople after the fourth crusade. This time is often referred to as the golden age of Byzantine art, when the Macedonian and Comnene rulers were its great patrons. One of the most glorious textiles that came from the Byzantium court looms is now in the Church of St. Eusèbe in Auxerre (Figure 5.51). It consists of a repeat of stylized eagles 81.3 cm high by 54.4 cm wide, each holding a jeweled ring in its beak and standing on a base ornamented with a row of pearls. The ground is imperial purple, the design in yellow and a soft blue-purple tone. Talons and other details are in a deep blue green. The eagle was the standard of the Roman legion but the symbolism of the great bird is much more complex and may reach as far back in time as the storm bird worshiped in ancient Mesopotamia.

Such magnificent textiles were often the property of the Christian church. The Vatican pos-

Figure 5.51 Byzantine textile. Silk. According to tradition, this is part of a textile that was placed by the Empress Galla Placidia as a shroud on St. Germain. Church of St. Eusèbe, Auxerre. (Giraudon.)

sesses an outstanding silk of the eighth century that displays scenes from the Annunciation and the Nativity in its rondels. Its provenance was conjecturally Alexandria or the imperial looms at Constantinople. The interlace and rosette motifs, however, are tinged with the stylization of the Middle East.

Persia, a most important silk-weaving center during the Middle Ages, influenced Byzantium and the Orient by transporting designs and techniques. Because of the sensational finds in such ancient necropolises as Raiy, near Teheran, we now have a better insight into the importance of Persia as a font of textile expertise. Raiy was a capital during the rule (under Seljuk Turkish overlords) of the native house of Buyid (945–1055). These Raiy silks indicate a reconciliation between the Persian aesthetic genius and the proscriptions imposed by Islam. The Moslem forbade the depiction of living things; the Persian circumvented this edict by resorting to his talent for formalizing and made beautiful decorative designs from such patterns as the *simurgh* (half-beast, half-bird) and scenes from the celestial banquet and the hunt.

With the spread of Islamic workshops to the west, Spain and later Sicily produced silks that took their rightful places among the superb Medieval textiles. Here, too, realistic depiction was harnessed to stylized form. Mythological figures are seen, such as the harpy—half-beast, half-human—dragons, and sphinxes. Flora along with inanimate objects such as ropes of pearls are most often present, and beautiful cufic script, either informative or purely decorative in nature, frequently appears. The Spanish cities of Cordoba, Almeria, Malaga, and Seville were principal silk-weaving centers, and Syracuse flourished in this capacity in Norman Sicily.

Over the six centuries or more from the fall of Rome to the beginning of the Gothic period in northern Europe the looms of the Near East, southern Egypt, Spain, and Sicily developed textiles that were worthy of hanging in the palaces of the Sassanian and Byzantine rulers and formed church and mosque adornments and grave goods for potentates all over the most civilized areas of the western world. As if the rondel could create a bond between disparate ideologies, many designs differing in origin will combine in that alli-

ance to which art is prone. Even so plodding a beast as the Indian elephant does not escape. A famous cloth found in Charlemagne's tomb shows a caparisoned pachyderm enclosed in a rondel. Of later date than the emperor's death (it was added as burial homage on the occasion of a formal tomb opening), this piece is a Byzantine silk woven in the eastern capital in the tenth/eleventh century. It is but another example of the rich design produced on the Medieval looms that exemplified the indigenous genius for handling woven pattern shown by the several peoples and cultures involved.

This elephant textile is possibly a representation of Abu-al-Abbas, the favored pet who lumbered beside the Frankish monarch on his journeys, a gift of the Arabian potentate Harun-al-Rashid. Charlemagne's beast—at once so dainty, yet so unwieldy, is alone in his confinement. Many contemporary creatures were duplicated *affronté* (facing each other) or *adossé* (back to back), thus forming a doublet and preserving classic bisymmetry. At other times the same or equivalent patterns were arranged in rows. Always, stylization was preserved.

Weaving expertise was also transmitted from these Medieval centers to the Far East and ultimately to the weavers of Italy and northern Europe. A weave previously alluded to called *compound* (in modern historical contexts) was most often used. This is a complex technique that involved two sets of warp threads and one of weft. One set of warp threads bound down the wefts; the second set simultaneously controlled the pattern wefts by alternating them on the face or back of the fabric, as required by the design. The finished appeared as one web and as a variant of the tabby (plain) or twill (a diagonal weave produced by progressions of overshots from one to four in a prescribed order). Unlike the damask weave, it did not produce a reversible cloth.

The technique of the compound weave was elaborated about the tenth century to include the *diasper weave*. *Lampas* and the type of cloth known today as *brocatelle* are examples of the diasper weave of museum terminology. Here there are two sets of warps and two wefts. The looms were normally equipped with a ground harness that controlled a ground binding system and a figure harness in charge of patterning. It then became possible to have a ground in one texture and a relief in another. Although the textile was still one web, a distinct separation of parts, which gave a three-dimensional impression, is clearly discernible.

It is possible to produce these intricately woven fabrics by hand-manipulation of a simple loom (it is thought, for instance, that the Peruvians may have worked in this manner), but progress was facilitated by the invention of the *draw loom,* in which the threading and manipulation was rendered easier by group organization of the warp threads. Separate groups were attached to cords drawn to the top of the loom which enabled a *drawboy,* sitting above the apparatus, to handle the bundles as dictated by the graphs. The principle of this loom had long been known and it appeared in Egypt during the third and fourth centuries. Persian and Byzantine weavers (e.g., in Syria) had full command of the draw loom between the fourth and the sixth centuries, and it was certainly fully developed in Byzantium and Antioch by the eighth, in Spain by the tenth, and probably in Italy and northern Europe by the thirteenth. It was not known in China before the T'ang Dynasty (618–907).[31]

Chinese Silks

The first Chinese silks of importance to the West were those of the later years of the T'ang Dynasty. Influence was at that time a two-way traffic over the silk trade routes, which inaugurated an exchange of artistry that had elements of international character. Chinese silk designs became more complex as well as more controlled (Figure 5.52). The rondel motif, which might consist of several conventional cloud bands or be cleverly designed in such detail as the flight of birds or intertwining of vines, begins to take on the character of the late Medieval and Renaissance ogival. Row designs are frequent and the imposition of various bands of color over other patterns occurs. Again the central rosette was developed without reference to an enclosure. The phoenix, or bird of happy augury, assumes a spirited stance with upraised leg and bristling wings. Animals are prone to gyrate in and around the enclosure in

Figure 5.52 Chinese textile, Yüan Dynasty, 1278–1368. Lampas weave. Silk with gold thread. Height, 44 cm, width, 33 cm. Cleveland Museum of Art. (The Cleveland Museum of Art, Purchase from the J. H. Wade Fund.)

lively fashion. We remember the advice of the Chinese painter and art critic Hsieh Ho (fl. 500) that painting should preserve the vitality of the spirit and conform to representation of the natural world. To combine these two admonitions, which seem so antithetical but are so interwoven, has been the very soul of Chinese art. The T'ang textiles are known by virtue of central Asian excavations.

The Sung Dynasty, although famed for its patronage of the arts, had because of diminished land holdings lost extensive western commerce. Little is known about the textiles of the Sung Dynasty largely because they are so rare. Their exact character must be surmised in the pieces that belong to later times. The progression is toward freedom of pattern and to a sophisticated concealment of regimenting factors. Simultaneously, contrapuntal sequences of shape, color, and even texture are followed. These affected Gothic Italian textiles both in imagery and arrangement of design.

The eruption of Mongols from central Asia in the thirteenth century, which localized in China in the Yüan Dynasty, brought modifying influences in the manner of greater vigor and more somber coloring. Native styles were never completely displaced, the late Medieval silks leaning heavily on floral motifs accompanied by inexhaustible Sino imagery and symbolism.

Gothic Textiles

With the twelfth/thirteenth centuries the era of late medieval or Gothic textiles emerges. Spain, although producing sumptuous textiles that required skill, artistry, and money, was slow to throw off the Saracenic influence. This lingered in the peninsula long after the expulsion of the Moors in 1492.

In eastern Europe the ascendency in textile manufacture now passes to northern Italy. Byzantium, harassed by Turkish invasions and by the crusades, lost its supremacy. Saracenic Sicily, under the competent administration of the Norman counts, had produced some of the finest of the late Byzantine designs. In 1266 the island came under the rule of the French Angevin Count Charles. This event was preceded by many years of unsettled conditions in which the cold war between the papacy and the emperors was concentrated in the south. Many textile workers, seeing the handwriting on the wall, moved to welcoming towns in northern Italy.

Thus began what was to become the glorious era of Lucchese[32] (Lucca in Tuscany) weaving of the thirteenth and early fourteenth centuries (Figure 5.53). The internecine wars of this city, particularly with Pisa, created the opportunity for the later supremacy of Florentine, Venetian, and Genoese ateliers. Across Alpine passes, along the Rhine, German cities carried on a flourishing business in printed goods by attempting to copy the more expensive silks in cheaper ways.

With this era we move out of the orb of direct Moslem influence and into the Christian. The princes of the church as well as the realm had been buyers throughout the Medieval period of altar cloths, hangings, and vestments. Now, however, all manner of ecclesiastic needs were provided for in increasing volume. Many museums today display the *cope*, resembling a circular cape, or the chausuble of some Medieval prelate.

Orphreys (a Latin word signifying Cyprean gold) were narrow bands affixed to vestments. They were specialties of Cologne weaving, hence sometimes called Cologne bands, although many of equal worth were woven in Lucca. Gold thread was often added to the basic silk. This was thread with a linen core on which was twined a narrow strip of animal membrane covered with gold leaf. Pure gold wire, gilded silver wound around silk, was sometimes used for embroidery and brocaded fabrics, but it was not strong enough for use as warp on a loom.

The diasper or lampas continued to be used as the weave in many of these silks. The Lucchese are credited with having been the first weavers in Europe to make any extensive use of the velvet weave, and indeed it could have been their invention. This is a pile weave which requires the insertion of wires parallel to the weft over which an additional warp pile can be passed to create a three-dimensional texture. Additional warp frames must be added to carry this pile thread. Although Lucca wove all manner of velvets, it was Florence, Genoa, and Venice that were associated with the height of fashion in elaborate velvets during the fourteenth and fifteenth centuries.

Patterns from the Gothic north, from Islam, the Near East, and China joined to make the Lucchese textiles a wonderful medley—perhaps the first truly European, and at the same time worldwide, art forms. Christian stories are skilfully woven to the accompaniment of Chinese cloud bands, waves, and mountains, and chivalric tales sport castles, knights, falcons, woodland animals, and walled gardens. One earmark of the patterning is the jagged points of such details as wings, sun rays, halos, and animal claws. Undoubtedly associated with the light motif of Christian symbolism and owing something to the dictates of the loom on which weft pattern threads are more securely

Figure 5.53   Textile. Part of the back of a chasuble. Italy, fourteenth century. Height, 42 in., width, 27 in. Orpherys (embroidered bands) from fourteenth-century Cologne. Cleveland Museum of Art. (The Cleveland Museum of Art, Purchase from the J. H. Wade Fund.)

Figure 5.54 *Bayeux Tapestry,* detail: Harold is told of the comet, eleventh century. Bayeux, Musée de l'Évêché (Giraudon. Avec autorisation spéciale de la ville de Bayeux.)

anchored when ending on the diagonal, these flamelike embellishments could present a fascinating study. They appear on textiles from China and are seen in many Indian and Persian prints; they are the joy of Russian-Caucasian rugs and remain the insignia of France's Sun King, Louis XIV.

The chief delight of Lucchese silks and those made by Lucchese workmen who emigrated to other textile centers is their fantasy coupled with realism and possible symbolism. Who but a Medieval Lucchese would allow a lion to shake a tree in which was entrapped a helpless doe or a graceful swan? Or place a falcon as oarsman to a canine passenger whose boat calmly rides a tree-bound lake on which turbulent waves support a bevy of paddle ducks? Needless to say, these representations were seldom regimented bisymmet-

rically but were of row or step-up repeat skilfully concealed by intermediate breakups or connecting florals.

With the advent of velvets and more significantly pretentious fabrics the era of realism tended to pass. Its demise introduced a quite different aspect of tradition, dominated by the abstract ogival or pomegranate design. Conjecturally, the ogival is traced to the Indian pine cone, the oriental poppy, the Persian palmette, and the doubled cloud band. Before it settled down to the rigorous confines of its Renaissance existence, it had a fling when a sinuous curved band, a descendent of the vine and arabesque, threw off ogival flora alternately to the right and left as it swung warpwise along the textile. This version was prevalent in fifteenth-century Venetian velvets.

With the ogival and pomegranate one is confronted with when and how to introduce the Renaissance, which are perplexing questions, for the late fifteenth century in Italy as surely belongs to that style movement as the pomegranate growing south of Naples belongs to the native countryside. We are here witnessing the time drag in styles caused by the Alps. When in the eighteenth century the style pendulum swings from north to south, we shall know that the trans-Alpine kingdoms have, artistically speaking, finally arrived.

No account of medieval textiles could exclude mention of a famous medieval embroidery, somewhat erroneously called the *Bayeux Tapestry* (Figure 5.54), for it is not a tapestry at all, but stitchery done with two kinds of woolen thread on linen, worked partly in outline stitch, with solid portions in laid-in technique. About eight colors in various tones of green, blue, red, yellow, and gray were used arbitrarily for design emphasis rather than pictorial reality. The hanging is 231 ft long and only a little more than 19 in. wide. It is composed of six smaller pieces of varying lengths.

The work has been customarily attributed to Matilda, William the Conqueror's queen, but certainly not proved, although noblewomen, with time on their hands, embroidered as a form of diversion. Upward of three dozen embroiderers are said to have been employed at the court of Philip of Burgundy.[33] The Bayeux Tapestry was a work that undoubtedly called for the talents of an excellent designer and a man of learning who supplied the titles as well as the arrangement. Made probably shortly after the Norman conquest of England, it is of incalculable value in describing the warfare, customs, and buildings of the time. It now reposes in the cathedral at Bayeux, France, although a good set of photographs can be seen at the Victoria and Albert Museum in London.

Museums collect the sumptuous textiles of a period. Most materials from the Middle Ages, despite the extensive metropolitan ateliers, were local products, either from household looms or small manufactories. Wool and linen were the local fibers and weaves were simple. Printing and embroidery furnished the embellishment.

Medieval buildings relied on fabric to provide the comfort that the building and lack of furniture denied. Cloth was used for portable walls and, as a token of a family's importance, meticulously reported in inventories.

A quantity of stuff was required to make a bed.

Softness was first achieved with a straw mattress. Sheets were not used in the manner to which we are accustomed but rather as an individual wrapping for the sleeper.[34] Warmth was secured with fur coverlets or *featherbeds*, which were coverlets stuffed with feathers. Warm woolens functioned likewise. The bed curtains provided warmth and privacy.

Many loose cushions added softness to bed, palette, and chair, and *bolsters* are still common in Europe. *Hassocks* were mentioned in the inventory of Duke Philip in 1420. A cushion shape seen in many Dutch genre paintings is a square one with knotted ends.

Linens were needed as covers for sideboards as well as dining tables, and valuable oriental rugs were used as table runners. Again reference must be made to paintings and inventories lest we fall into the error of thinking that textiles of bygone ages were handled as they are today.

TAPESTRY

The most important textiles to come from northern looms during the late Middle Ages were the woolen tapestries of Paris, Arras (lending its name to tapestries in general), Tournai, and Brussels. These high warp workshops were established in the first half of the fourteenth century and came into prominence during the fourteenth, fifteenth, and early sixteenth centuries. Under the patronage of the Dukes of Burgundy the Flemish looms of Tournai and Brussels eventually became the most distinguished.

Tapestry weaving is an old art and by no means exclusively European. The ancient tombs of Egypt have yielded tapestries. The Greeks and Romans knew them and remnants of Greek tapestries from tombs on the border of Russian land around the Black Sea are on view at the Hermitage in Leningrad. Late Hellenistic and Roman weavings came from the looms of Alexandria and from Syria during the centuries of occupation of these territories by the Greeks and Romans.

Coptic tapestries, as distinct from late classical, relate to Egyptian art associated with the expansion of Christianity in Egypt. However, they were likewise made for Moslems and continued to be long after the Islamic conquest. In a sense, Coptic art is the art of the people of Egypt as distinct from the court art of the Ptolemies, the Romans, and the Islamic rulers. The generally known Coptic tapestries are often small rondels woven into decorative inserts on garments.

Less familiar and much more important to our study are the many beautiful wall hangings from Egypt (Plate 9). These are the earliest tapestries in the Western sense. Because of the favorable climate, a significant number have been preserved in Egypt, but they must represent more that were in use around the Mediterranean at that time. Dating from about 1060 is a renowned silk tapestry in Bamberg Cathedral which measures more than two meters in each direction. Its subject is the Byzantine Emperor. In the symbolism of many of the early Egyptian pieces the interesting fact is that, although they were made in Christian centuries, the subjects, with rare exceptions, are pagan—Dionysian themes concerned with fertility, a mixture of antique characters that included, for instance, Nereids, and eastern motifs such as the horse and the tree. A floral surround, arranged naturally in a garden, appears to be a forerunner of *millefleur* backgrounds in later northern work.

The American Indians, particularly in Peruvian civilizations, understood the tapestry technique. In the Far East the Chinese also used it, calling it the K'ossu weave.

Tapestry weaving is in reality a simple process understood by most primitive peoples. Basically it consists in threading a warp of heavy yarns, which in the tapestries of Europe are usually cotton or linen. Wool also makes a fine tapestry warp but is more difficult to keep dimensionally stable. Across these warps a finer weft is interlaced in a plain weave. This weft is characteristically wool. Silk, gold, and silver threads are used but actually contribute little to the tapestry effect. The weft is colored and the various tones are dictated by the pattern. The color is then drawn to the back of the cloth and the next one is taken up.

Use of the plain weave with heavier warps created a ribbed or *rep* fabric which of itself is an uninteresting cloth. Skilled designers learned to use the inherent character of the weave to create pictorial contrasts of tone and texture. Three interconnected textural qualities may be exploited, the first of which makes artistic use of the raised *ribs*. In the best tapestry designs they were placed horizontally as the tapestry hangs. Therefore the cloth is turned at an angle of ninety degrees from the direction in which it was woven. The ribs constitute a foil against which are played *hatchings* and *slits*. The second textural quality inherent in good tapestries is related to *hatching*. Because the colored weft threads must terminate on different warps if a cleavage of the cloth is to be avoided, a diagonal movement of the colors results. These shafts are known as hatchings and are planned to effect transitions from tone to tone, hence constitute the half-tones.

The third quality to be noted is the exact reverse of the second. All fine tapestries may have *slits* made by ending the colored yarns on the same warp. These are consciously used to create deep shadows by reflective absorption of light rather than by dyed yarn tone, a more effective means. These slits, if they are long, are loosely sewed together on the wrong side after the work is finished, but this must be done with skill to maintain the intaglio effect.

In the best tapestries the pictorial interest should be manipulated to provide textural interest. One should observe raised lines in horizontal ribs, contrasted with vertical shafts of flat color and deep shadows for modeling. The combination of these resources in a two-dimensional cloth calls for the skills of the weaver and artist. Silk tapestries, because of the equality of weight between warp and weft, cannot achieve the same textural effect, although the finer thread makes representation more easily accomplished. They must be considered as textiles that use the tapestry technique to obtain comparatively flat contrapuntal patterns in brilliant color.

European Gothic tapestries were woven on *high warp* (haute lisse) or *low warp* (basse lisse) looms. The high warp has its warp strung in vertical position, the low warp, in horizontal. On the high warps the sheds are formed in primitive fashion by the leash stick and individually controlled heddles. On low warp looms the shed is made in a manner similar to that of all two-harness looms. Leashes are used on all warp threads; the harness is connected to foot treadles. This process is much faster in operation.

Weaving on both looms is done with the wrong side of the cloth next to the weaver. The *cartoon* or pattern followed is behind or above the weaver on the high warp loom, under the warp on the low warp. An outline of the pattern on the cloth is used in the high warp; in the low warp a reversal image is required if the design is to duplicate the artist's rendering. As this is not always supplied, some low warp weavings turn out as mirror images of their cartoons. On certain looms, notably at Beauvais, the tracing of the underlying pattern onto a transparency obviated this necessity.[35]

High warp weaving is best for large pictorial tapestries not only because of the width limitations of the horizontal loom but because the weaver has the opportunity of going to the front to judge his work while in progress. Artistic creation cannot be planned entirely from a cartoon as every colorist knows. The nineteenth-century Gobelin director Chevreul wrote a treatise on this aspect of the subject in which he demonstrated how flat color on a cartoon differed from color obtained with yarn.[36] Therefore the weaver, like the musician, must be conceded the position of artist. He recreates and interprets. This fact is obvious when several tapestries woven from one cartoon are compared.

Among the four periods into which European tapestry is grouped, namely, Gothic, Renaissance, Baroque, and eighteenth century, the first is top ranked, judged for suitability of design to medium. Gothic tapestries, which are superficially recognizable because they have narrow borders or none at all, have little traffic with three-dimensional effects. Like Gothic painting, their patterns are two-dimensional, enriched with a third magnitude of texture. Thus Gothic tapestries are preeminently suitable for wall hangings because they do not distort the plane of the wall. By a happy coincidence the vertical shafts of light that enhance good tapestry design harmonize with the pointed verticality of Gothic shapes. Like the tall hennins (i.e., one-pointed head coverings), the slightly later escoffiers (i.e., two-horned headdresses) worn by fifteenth-century women, and the pointed arches of Gothic buildings, it all seems of a piece.

Although accounts of northern European tapestries exist throughout much of the Middle Ages and small ones are extant from the twelfth century, the most famous Gothic tapestries belong to the fourteenth and fifteenth. The earliest are religious in character, often narrating a biblical story or illustrating a medieval religious concept. We may take the *Apocalypse* set preserved in the cathedral at Angers as an example. Actually it is the only complete fourteenth-century group to have been preserved. It was woven during the reign of the French King Charles V, Charles the Wise (1364–1380), he who for a short time held the central French throne against the combined forces of the English to the west and the Burgundian-Flemish to the east, and—what is more important to our story—acted as a medieval Maecenas to encourage the arts at his court.

The Apocalypse tapestries (Figure 5.55) were created to the order of the Duke of Anjou, Charles's brother. Several of them bear symbolism that would assign them to him, and one bears the monogram LM, that of Duke Louis and Marie de Bretagne, his wife. The counts of Anjou who figure importantly in medieval English and southern Italian history, and whose stronghold was the lower Loire, were a forceful lot, endowed with "brilliant and varied natural powers crossed by a strange vein of spasmodic and unreasonable piety or superstition."[37] Certainly Louis was no exception, and if he acted somewhat less than the saint in his alleged treatment of his charge, his young nephew Charles VI, he may be assumed to have atoned with the sums he donated for the creation of such works as the tapestries in question. These were not completed until 1453.

The Apocalypse bears the name of the first-known tapestry craftsman, Nicolas Bataille, *tapissier-marchand* (weaver and merchant), whose Paris atelier created goods of the highest merit. The design was executed by Jean de Bruges, court painter to Charles V, from an illumined copy of the Apocalypse which the king owned and loaned for the purpose. When completed, the set contained ninety separate scenes divided among seven tapestries and measured 18 ft high by 472 long. Because of almost criminal neglect, they were worn to a smaller size (14 by 328 ft), when they were again recognized during the nineteenth century for their historical and aesthetic worth.

Figure 5.55 *The Apocalypse Tapestry,* detail. France, fourteenth century. Cathedral at Angers. (Lauros-Giraudon.)

Another religious tapestry with which the Apocalypse set may be profitably compared is the *Seven Sacraments,* which consists of five fragments containing seven scenes and which may have been woven at Arras (Figure 5.56). With the exception of one section, which is the property of the Victoria and Albert, they belong to the Metropolitan. The remaining tapestries, only a part of the original fourteen scenes, illustrate the seven sacraments of the church both in respect to their origin and to their fifteenth-century celebration. The probable dating is bracketed by 1440 and 1480, almost a century later than the Angers group.

A stylistic comparison of the two sets is therefore meaningful. The greater finesse of the weaving, accentuation of ribs, increased size of the human figures in relation to the background, bolder delineation of the vertical folds of the garments, and use of hatchment shadings to accentuate the three-dimensional effect can be noticed as time passes. The Sacrament tapestries possess one of the first complete Gothic borders, in this case a remarkable semblance of a brick wall and surrounding foliage. The events in the later work

are compartmentalized by rounded pillars, a strategy that renders sequels easier to read.

In the fourteenth-century pieces the convention of showing exterior and interior views simultaneously, derived from Tuscan painting via Avignon, is noted. In the Sacraments the spectator is outside the building viewing an interior scene. In the earlier work the landscape is important. The starlit sky, the craggy earth, and the feathered foliage present lyric views.

Although most of the characters in both sets are involved with in-group action and take no account of the spectator's concern, we find the most tightly knit organization of participants in the Apocalypse set. Here groups at the left are most carefully isolated from those at the right and are involved in some centralized action, whereas in the Sacraments interest is dissipated in the composition.

Continuing the tradition of the Metropolitan Sacraments is the *Credo* series in the Boston Museum of Fine Arts, bracketed between 1475 and 1510, and, from stylistic analysis, possibly woven at Tournai (Figure 5.57). In 1477, during the events that surrounded the defeat of Charles the Bold of Burgundy by Louis XI of France, the then Burgundian town of Arras was sacked by the French. This ended its supremacy as a weaving center and

196

its downfall was for a period the gain of the Burgundian-held town of Tournai.

The illustration of the Apostles' Creed, known as the *Credo,* offered much opportunity for portraiture and human involvement because the medieval church made the prophets of the Old Testament the ideological partners of the apostles of the New, while associating the pairs with articles from the Christian code of belief. Although the figures in the Boston Museum tapestry are not so large as those in the Sacraments, other stylistic characteristics like fine weaving, pronounced ribs, noticeable drapery folds, and increasing three-dimensional effect are similar.

As secular life became more luxurious, the court and the designer turned to it for subject matter. The past, with its dubiously authenticated tales that glorified a motley assortment of heroes such as the Trojan war lords, Alexander, Caesar, Charlemagne, and Arthur, was pictured. The stories in medieval form are found in the *Chanson de Geste,* the French epics that flourished from the eleventh century to the sixteenth. A speaking acquaintance with the complex allegories and symbolism of the chivalric conventions is necessary to interpret correctly the scenes in the *Rose Garden* pieces, the *Unicorn* sets, and the *Fountain of Life* series, all frequently grouped under the heading of Gothic *Country Life* tapestries because they perpetuate a highly romantic way of

Figure 5.56 (above) *The Seven Sacraments Tapestry,* detail—Baptism. Franco-Flemish. Tournai, workshop of Pasquier Grenier, fifteenth century. Wool and silk. Height, 152.5 cm, length, 141 cm. Metropolitan Museum of Art, New York. (The Metropolitan Museum of Art, Gift of J. Pierpont Morgan, 1907.)

Figure 5.57 (below) *Credo Tapestry.* In four scenes: Creation, Baptism, Nativity, and Crucifixion. Tournai: Franco-Flemish, late fifteenth century. Museum of Fine Arts, Boston. (Courtesy, Museum of Fine Arts, Boston, gift of Robert Treat Paine II in memory of his son.)

197

living and code of existence within an out-of-doors framework quite opposed to the indoor happenings of the Tournai religious-oriented work. Theirs is the world of the allegorical poem *Roman de la Rose* with its double meanings, with one side turned toward the ecclesiastic orientation of the medieval and its actual story facing the secular and often erotic life of the fading court of chivalry. Play-acting in an age of transition.

The Metropolitan Museum owns the three large tapestries known as the *Rose Garden,* which were woven at Tournai or by Tournai weavers in France. It has been pointed out that the background stripes of red, white, and green were the emblematic colors of Charles VII of France (1422–1461). Although the tapestries show no perspective, it will be noticed that the verdure springs full leafed from its roots and that it sometimes overlaps and is again half hidden by the figures, the lords and ladies enjoying the flowers, the men with their short *houppelands* and enormous draped *chaperones,* the women in their long-waisted *surcoats* and often with cauled hair surmounted by a turban (notice that even the lines of the costumes are coming down). The strong folds of the garments are skilfully designed in colors to create a superimposed rhythm on the basic patterns, altogether a remarkable creation as complex and diverse as the web of late Gothic architecture.

The famous unicorn series (Figure 5.58), of which one set of six tapestries is in the Cloisters of the Metropolitan Museum and probably the most famous group is at the Cluny Museum in Paris, indirectly celebrate the virtues of a noble lady who is shown with the lion as a symbol of strength and the fabled unicorn, of virginity. The Cluny set designates the heroine as the central figure in all of the groupings. The Metropolitan ensemble immortalizes the hunt of the unicorn and in the last number shows it in captivity underneath a pomegranate tree, the fruit of which is synonymous with life. This set was presumably a marriage presentation, which possibly celebrated the nuptials of Louis XII and Anne of Brittany in 1499.

One should notice the superior handling of color in the Metropolitan weaving. The shading over the arms, for instance, is planned from a light yellow red in the highlights to a deeper bluish red in the folds, in the manner in which natural sunlight alters hues.

The Rose Garden and the Unicorn tapestries hold our interest as illustrating transitional styling from late Gothic to nascent Renaissance. Even when there are many figures they are grouped around a central motif which is somewhat isolated by foliage. Although deep space is not indicated and perspective is accomplished only by overlapping and tilting of the foreground plane, nevertheless a foreground, middle ground, and background is attempted. Architectural features are reserved for the last.

It is now thought that the Rockefeller (Metropolitan) unicorn tapestries were woven at Tournai. They were designed by a superior artist known only as the "Master of the Lady of the Unicorn," who is credited with work ranging from about 1480 to the early sixteenth century. The Cluny set was probably woven in France during the same years.

The Tournai tapestries can be allied to a more provincial assemblage of similar stylistic character, which is designated as the Loire group and must have come from some stationary or itinerant workshop in the Loire basin where royal patronage at that time was not wanting. The workmen may have been those who were dispossessed at Arras or French weavers returning from Tournai. Some of these tapestries are known as the Chaumont group because of resemblances of architectural motifs in the cloths (e.g., the flaming mountain motif) to those in the chateau of Chaumont. This castle was being rebuilt at that time by Charles d'Amboise, Maréchal de France and brother of the famous Georges of early Renaissance fame.

One of the Loire *Country Life* tapestries called the *Concert* is now in the *Musée des Gobelins.* Here we find the customary flora studding a dark blue ground with figures grouped clearly around a fountain. No attempt to show perspective has been made, and an odd reduction in scale occurs in some of the lesser personages, such as the lady riding a hobby horse, another playing a viol, and the youth with a falcon. Even the major characters gesture rather awkwardly. Clearly this was no

Figure 5.58 *The Hunt of the Unicorn: The Unicorn in Captivity*. Tapestry. Franco-Flemish. From the Château de Verteuil, late fifteenth century. Metropolitan Museum of Art, New York. (The Metropolitan Museum of Art, New York, The Cloisters Collection, Gift of John D. Rockefeller, Jr., 1937.)

Figure 5.59 *The Story of Perseus and Andromeda.* Tapestry. Flanders, early sixteenth century. Wool. Height, 3.21 m, width, 4.47 m. Cleveland Museum of Art. (The Cleveland Museum of Art, Gift of the John Huntington Art and Polytechnic Trust.)

consummate artist designer such as the unicorn series could boast.

The Cleveland Museum of Art owns a *Perseus and Andromeda* tapestry (Figure 5.59) manufactured at Tournai about 1480, which illustrates the best and the weakest traits of this late Gothic era. It can be read in reverse: at the right Cepheus and Cassiopeia, parents of the maiden; in fore center the brave hero slaying his foe as a nude and chained Andromeda (early Gothic figures are well draped) looks on in amazement; left, Perseus taking his vows before the altar; and finally, far left, the happy ending in marriage—all in a framework of Gothic castellation and many flowers (*millefleur*). Scenery is indoors and out; figures are large and small; separation of groups is partly realized by columned spaces. The superb rhythm, seen, for instance, in the scrolling of Perseus's cloak as played against the dragon's tail, is all Gothic, whereas the somewhat confused tension between the vertical and horizontal emphasis—as exemplified, respectively, in the garment folds and horizontal bands of ornament—indicates an age that is no longer decisive. Perseus, in truth, is slaying the dragon of an imaginative medieval world for all time.

MEDIEVAL CARPETS AND FLOOR COVERINGS

Today a new home as well as varieties of civic buildings may be advertised as "fully carpeted." Such a statement would have been unintelligible to good Queen Elizabeth (1558–1603), who is

200

said to have had rushes as floor covering in the antechamber of her apartments at Greenwich.

Carpets or rugs, whichever terminology you choose, originated in the Middle East, in the countries of Afghanistan, Persia, the Caucasus, to name a few. Sheep raising in the high uplands advanced a technique that required only the simplest of vertical looms and that, by combining plain weave with hand knotting created pile textures in many faceted designs. Since the Pazyryk find it has been recognized that pile fabrics were made during the Persian Achaemenid dynasty (ca. 550–330 B.C.), and doubtless the art was continuous before and after.

The carpets that were made did not, however, find their way into Europe until the twelfth century. Their manufacture followed in the footsteps of the Saracens into Syria, Egypt, and Spain, but no extant Spanish carpets antedate the fifteenth century, although literary sources tell of pile carpets woven in Moorish Spain.[38] Spanish carpets are lovely weavings of geometric design and deep, dark colors. The Cleveland Museum possesses one that measures the unusually large size of 13 ft, 9 in. in length and 7 ft, 9 in. in width. It is composed of octagons enclosed in large-scale rectangles, a favorite Asian motif.

Spanish rugs are woven with a knot tied over one warp thread. Other Orientals (i.e., rugs made in the east) used the *Sehna knot,* where the pile is twisted under one warp, then up and over the next, to be brought to the surface adjacent to each, or the *Ghiordes knot,* where the pile is crossed over two adjacent warps to be surfaced between them (Figure 5.60).

Islamic weavers reputedly set up looms in Paris in 1295. Nevertheless, carpets at this time were so foreign to European custom that when Eleanor of Castile (she for whom Edward I of England—1272–1307—set up the Eleanor Crosses at each stop of her funeral cortège) came to England as a bride the carpeting of her suite "in the Spanish fashion" is said to have surprised and somewhat shocked the English, who had considered carpets appropriate to a church but not a dwelling.

It was truly a case of "she came to conquer," for small carpets of oriental source appear in Europe close on the heels of the Crusades. In paintings by the fourteenth-century Dutch "little mas-

ters" an oriental-type rug is frequently seen at the foot of the Virgin. French miniatures of the fifteenth century show similar small carpets in the chamber of a noble or below a king. For other than royalty they were too precious to tread on, although they were often used as banners, table covers, and wall decorations.

The first imported rugs were the work of the Ottoman Turks, marketed and possibly made in the *tiraz* or imperial workshops at Brusa and later at Constantinople. Some think that Turkey was also acting as port of call for carpets traveling from farther east. *Turkey carpets* was the general European name for any and all rug importations.

In recent descriptions writers have looked to medieval painting in which artists used these costly fabrics as props, much as a family heirloom would be painted with each sitter. Thus one rug, recognized by its pattern of diamonds and hexagons with a sprinkling of Chinese symbolism and surrounded by bold Saracenic interlace, has come to be known as the *Holbein* type, taking its name from the artist Hans Holbein, the Younger (1497–1540).

Gradually an acquaintance with floor coverings, as a badge of status and as handsome ornaments, won them favor. In retrospect we know that the East kept for its own regal use the truly magnificent carpets they had woven since the late Middle Ages. These now constitute the most

Figure 5.60 Oriental rug knots: (a) Ghiordes; (b) left-hand Sehna; (c) right-hand Sehna.

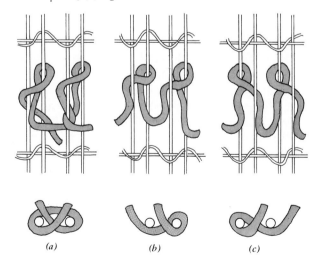

(a) (b) (c)

famous museum collections. A discussion of their character is deferred until the section that deals with the sixteenth century.

CERAMICS

Oriental Ceramics

On the other hand, the story of the finest ceramics is one for a chapter covering the medieval. In China this includes the production of the T'ang (618–907; see burial statue, Figure 4.23), Sung (960–1279), Yüan (1260–1368), and the early years of the Ming (1368–1644) dynasties. In Persia another source of good ceramic design, it is comprised of three peak developments—that of the second Moslem caliphate, the Abbasid (750–ca.1100), especially as it centered around the capital at Baghdad during the ninth century; the years dominated by the Seljuk Turks (particularly the twelfth century), and finally the Mongol suzerainty (in the thirteenth century). It is not always appreciated that the east carried the torch for ceramic development during a millennium when Europe was making none but the crudest of products.

Chinese Ceramics. The advances made in terms of materials and technique were one reason for the preeminence of Chinese ceramics. By consistently improving their kaolin and feldspathic formulas the Chinese added the discovery of feldspathic glaze to their achievement of success. This is the only glaze that will withstand the high fire of the china kiln. Kaolin, or china clay, which the Chinese found at hand and which gave a ware stonelike quality under fire, has a preponderance of alumina or feldspar in its composition. Petuntse, or china stone, which paradoxically gives flux to the kaolin, is also a combination of feldspar and sand or silicon. A glaze that is feldspathic becomes integral with the body in high firing and enhances its qualities of translucency, hardness, and tonal resonance. The Chinese prized a characteristic of unctuousness to the touch, a quality similar to the sensation of handling cool jade. Whereas a lead glaze tends to lie on the surface because it is given a lower firing, a feldspathic glaze seems to come from deep within. The two were often used on the same piece in later works, thereby introducing several layers of light refraction. This technique of multiple glazing was highly exploited in Ming ceramics.

Dr. Lee,[39] in his account of Sung ceramics, suggests a geographical basis for consideration. The kilns of northern China were coal-fueled and conical, a shape that could not tolerate the higher temperatures of the wood-burning, elongated *dragon* kilns, which were built along the hillsides of southern China. Northern wares, therefore, are more likely to be cream-white stoneware, whereas the southern are porcelaneous with bodies slightly tinged with blue or green. In any case, imperial production at the kilns at Ching-Te-Chên, which became the greatest in the world during the Ming Dynasty, are outside this statement. In 1127, when the Sung court was forced to flee south of the Yangtze, the northern royal kilns grew cold. Certain northern characteristics appear in southern wares following this exodus.

The ceramics of the Sung Dynasty represent the classics of the orient in the sense that in material and aesthetic perfection they are both the norm toward which earlier types advanced and from which later ones developed in more specialized fashion. The word *elegance* is much abused in descriptive parlance. In the case of Sung ceramics its use would certainly be justified as suggesting the most skillful and artistic fashioning of a medium. Moreover, Sung ceramics, elegant in a uniquely Chinese manner, suggest such assured completeness of perfection that they seem almost to be aloof from the world and to exist in one of their own making. This is true despite a hard-to-resist desire to touch these pieces of tactile charm.

Tz'u Chou ware comes closest to folk art in the Sung inventory (Figure 5.61). The Chinese word *chou* (pronounced as *jō*) means place. *Tz'u Chou* was named for a kiln site in the north. The typical northern stoneware body is covered with a white or brown slip on which the design is customarily painted in brown or white. *Sgraffito* and *intaglio* as well as inlay variations of this simple decoration also appear.

A second northern type, which has plebeian overtones in that it is neither pretentious in body nor in glaze, is *Chün Chou*. It is a grayish stoneware burned brown in exposed parts. Its glaze is opaque blue to purple, colors caused by muffling the kiln with ashes. Consequent burning without sufficient oxygen creates the desired hues from the copper oxides and minute amounts of iron filings present. Chün Chou is much imitated today, but a trip to a museum for a critical appraisal of the softness of the changeable colors of the Chinese Chün will be rewarding as a lesson in discrimination.

Climbing up the ladder of expense we reach the celadons, whose light yellow-green coloring is said to have given them the name of a shepherd character who wore a gown of similar hue in a French seventeenth-century play, Astrée, by d'Urfé. Another explanation of the name connects celadon with Saladin, an Egyptian sultan who was fond of giving pieces of the ware as gifts. Both stories bear witness to the continuing popularity of these quietly unobtrusive porcelaneous masterpieces.

The celadons were the successors to the southern Yüeh of the Han Dynasty. Made in the south and north during the Sung Dynasty, they are a gray-bodied porcelain covered with a glaze colored by ferrous oxide combined with minute amounts of cobalt. The southern celadons, made at Lung-Ch'üan and frequently called by that name, developed a stronger green to bluish color and a jadelike touch in the kiln. They are considered precious and deserving of inclusion among the six classics of the Sung. All celadons are sparingly and integrally decorated; in the north they emulate Tz'u-carved and incised ornament, done in the body before glazing; in the south the Lung-Ch'üan, often without pattern, relies on the undulating curves of the vessel to reflect the depth of glaze.

White Ting ware (pronounced ding), the true porcelain of north China, has a developed feldspathic glaze. Its name is that of a town in the northern province of Chinli near Peking. Its glaze was of fine quality known as Pai (i.e., white) Ting. Very rare indeed are a few pieces glazed in black or purple and known as Black Ting. The lip ring of Ting bowls is frequently left unglazed and is bound with copper or silver. The thin fine glaze may run down the body, collecting in tiny droplets. Decoration is chaste and is either low relief modeling or shallow incising. After the Sung court fled south, the manufacture of this ware was continued, now known as Southern Ting.

Several imperial Sung chinas are of supreme quality. One is Kuan Yao (ao pronounced ow as in how). Yao is the Chinese word for ware and Kuan means imperial. Therefore, although the name Kuan is specific for one highly esteemed product of the imperial kilns, it could likewise serve to separate imperial from nonimperial manufacture. Kuan Yao was made in an imperial factory near the capital of Honan province and was continued in the south under royal patronage. Kuan is a grayish or brownish porcelain with a feldspathic glaze often of soft, almost robin's egg blue. The unusual factor in Kuan is the introduction of crackle. Crackle that resulted from

Figure 5.61 Chinese ceramics. (Left), high-footed bowl, Tz'u-chou glazed stoneware, thirteenth–fourteenth centuries; height, 12 cm. (Center), tea bowl, northern black ware, ca. twelfth century, diameter, 12.5 cm. (Right), spouted ewer with handle, Tz'u-chou buff stoneware with carved underglaze slip decoration, tenth–fourteenth centuries; height, 17.5 cm. Cleveland Museum of Art. (The Cleveland Museum of Art, Purchase from the J. H. Wade Fund.)

tensions set up between body and glaze in the kiln was probably at first fortuitous but later fully controlled. It was much prized by the Chinese, who considered that it added textural interest.

Ko Yao is another southern porcelain scarcely distinguishable from the southern Kuan (and by some not considered imperial Sung) except that quite perceptible bubbles may occur by the potter's intention. Ko ware has a major crackle accompanied by a minor one that becomes, as it were, the second theme. *Ko* means *elder brother*, presumably of two Changs who, by somewhat dubious tradition, made this china.

Among all Sung porcelains the rarest type is the *Ju* (pronounced *ru*); possibly only twenty-odd pieces remain (Figure 5.62). Ju is very thinly potted, high-fired white ware, with a feldspar glaze that has the slightest blue tinge, probably caused by traces of cobalt. Ju Chou is in Honan, south of the Yellow River and west of Nanking. The story is told that the Ju potters were commanded to move to the capital of Honan and to work at the kilns at Ching-Te-Chên because of the superiority of their work. Ju was first made there in 1108 and the fires went out in 1127, a fact that accounts for the small number of recognizable pieces. To know and appreciate them, the simplicity of their forms, the quality of their faint crackle, the ice chill of their bluish tint softened by refraction from their deep unctuous

Figure 5.62 Circular brush washer. Ju ware. China. Northern Sung Dynasty, late eleventh–early twelfth centuries. Diameter, 12.8 cm. Cleveland Museum of Art. (The Cleveland Museum of Art, Purchase, John L. Severance Fund.)

glaze, one must visit them again and again. It is unfortunate that not everyone can touch them for they possess inviting tactile qualities. To my taste they are ceramic perfection.

From the utmost in refinement to qualities no less sought after both then and now, we turn to the heavy stoneware bowls covered with a dark brown glaze that were exported in large quantities to Japan. They were used for tea waste and are called *Temmoku* in Japanese or *Chien* in Chinese. The tea ceremony which entered Japanese culture as a Chinese Buddhist rite grew to full significance about the beginning of the fifteenth century. The Japanese, probably because their Shinto religion extols the virtue of control over the elements by craft, have always entertained a fondness for materials left in their natural state and an interest in the objects that contribute to daily living. These qualities added to their enjoyment of Temmoku bowls. The Japanese made stoneware with feldspathic glaze that possessed similar attributes.

The foregoing types suggest some of the outstanding ceramics manufactured under the Sung emperors. Their distinction lies in the perfection of means to ends and in the quietness with which they manage to conquer one's sensibilities. Under the Yüans the porcelain body was again improved at the reopened royal kilns at Ching-Te-Chên. With true barbarian love of color, deep tones of many hues rather than monochromes were used in the glazing. Enamel painting with overglazes was initiated. These innovations resulted in the remarkable finesse of the Ming and Ch'ing china, which is more fully discussed in that context.

Persian and Other Mideastern Ceramics

Medieval Mideastern ceramics require attention because they inaugurated the techniques followed for centuries in Europe. Moreover, they are exceptionally beautiful. Persian pottery, to use it as an example, does not win because of its ground, which is often sandy, coarse, and friable. Not only were porcelain materials not at hand, the Persian potter was not primarily interested in fineness of body or appeal to touch. He invites the eye through depth of color and applied pattern. If Chinese wares are as restful as the calm of the sea, the Persian suggest the rhythm of the waves—sometimes clean cut and definite, again breaking with the foam of myriad secondary ripples carried in their train.

During the Sassanian dynasty the chief emphasis was on the elaborate gold and silver vessels prized by the display-minded court.

In the seventh and eighth centuries events put Mideastern work back in its own channel. In 642 the followers of Mohammed conquered Iran in the name of the prophet, and, chronologically speaking, began the *Early Islamic Period* in eastern art. In 750 the second or Abbasid Moslem caliphate (the first—the Omayyad, 661–750) transferred the political capital from Damascus to Baghdad. This movement not only brought Islamic influence closer, it also based Mideastern art more firmly in its own traditions.

The fourth Abbasid caliph, Haroun al-Rashid (786–809), he of *Arabian Nights* fame and the friend of Charlemagne, received a gift of 2000 pieces of T'ang ceramics from the governor of the eastern province of Khorasan. Recent excavations near Samarra, up river from Baghdad and a short-lived ninth century capital (836–892), have disclosed shards of oriental origin which may have been part of that treasure. Much of it was Yüeh (forerunner of celadon) and a small number of pieces came from the imperial Chinese kilns. This exposure to fine eastern ceramics must have boosted the value of earthenware in the coinage of art and prodded the potter to emulate his oriental brother.

The earliest of the Mideastern wares of the eighth and ninth centuries uses the *engobe* technique. *Engobe* is the French name for clay slip. In engobe the vessel was covered with a white slip. The linear design was sgraffito and the whole was dipped in a lead glaze that (in imitation of T'ang mottled pieces) was then splashed with the old tried and faithful metallic oxides—copper for green, manganese for purple, and iron for brown. However, the colors could not be well controlled under the firing of the fluid glaze and the clearcut pattern often seems incongruous with the murky hues.

This ware was made largely in the western part

of the empire. A different approach was taken simultaneously in the far eastern portion of Islam. Independent Persian dynasties, chief among which was the Samanid (874–999), had been allowed to emerge under the watchful eye of the caliphate at Baghdad. Samarkand, their principal city, and Nishapur were among the ceramic centers. A tendency of the easterners was to mix their pigments with clay slip before application over a white engobe covering. Greater clarity resulted. Moreover, the Persian struck his stride in many designs that were a skilful combination of Iranian and Islamic patterns. One of the strongest statements made by the Samarkand potters was done with a black kufic script as sole embellishment over a white slip.

We must revert to Mesopotamia to follow the development in Mideastern ceramics known as lusterware which involved the addition of tin to the by-now-common lead glaze. The new formula may have been used years earlier both in Egypt and Mesopotamia. A stanniferous oxide glaze is opaque and white and thus can function as glaze and ground. Because its fusing temperature was not too critical, patterns done with metallic oxides could be quickly painted on the glaze and then fired. The result was a hard, lustrous layer that adhered tightly to the clay foundation. This method preserved for the gifted potters their native ability to bring freshness and surety to their designs. With modifications and improvements, often with the addition of added metallic luster coats, some variant of this technique thereafter became the norm for Mideastern ceramics.

The luster technique traveled from lower Mesopotamia to Egypt, where at Fustat, outside Cairo, it flourished during the Fatamid dynasty (969–1171). It is believed that the Egyptian potters may have come from Rakka, near Samarra, when that area was experiencing pressure from the Seljuk Turks. It was certainly from Northern Africa that the stanniferous luster arrived in Spain as majolica.

Once the Asiatic tribes called Seljuk (from an ancestral leader) had successfully intruded into the mideast, they adopted the Moslem faith and settled down to an expediently permissive rule. From the mid-eleventh until the early thirteenth

Figure 5.63   Pottery bowl. Lakabi ware. Iran, eleventh-twelfth centuries. Diameter, 40 cm. Cleveland Museum of Art. (The Cleveland Museum of Art, Purchase from the J. H. Wade Fund.)

century, when overcome by the invading Mongols, the country and its industries prospered. The ceramics of this era are frequently called Seljuk-Persian.

One advancement made at this time was the reintroduction of an artificial paste for a white ceramic body, doubtless much like the original Egyptian frit on which alkaline glaze had been used. It was white and translucent but did not have the hardness of porcelain. Again the famous Chinese white wares probably triggered this innovation. The Seljuk pieces were at first carved and pierced in obvious imitation of the Chinese Ting. Later a number of Mideastern polychrome designs of people, animals, and birds, Arabic vines, half palmettes, and meanders, appeared with luster glazes on the new body. The higher firing which was now possible caused some unanticipated changes in the old glaze colors. The exquisite turquoise glaze was perfected. Raiy (Rhages) and Rakka were important centers.

Still the Persian sought to increase his range of colors. Some hard-to-control pigments were found to be workable when placed in cloisons or ridges of clay. This is the distinguishing feature of *lakabi* (Figure 5.63). Cloisoned pattern was a skill brought to perfection by the Chinese Ming potters. It has always seemed that, whatever the gain, this technique lost the freshness of approach which is the Eastern artist's supreme contribution.

Both raised and flat patterns occur in the lustered ceramic tiles that are the glory of Moslem wall decoration. Tile work developed to a stage in which the curves of mosque domes and smaller interior niches or *mihrabs* (before which the devout, facing toward the sacred city of Mecca, kneel in prayer) could be covered with ceramic mosaics so perfectly executed that they obliterated all but the finest plaster joints (Figure 5.64). Kashan in Persia was noted for its tiles. Pattern was abstract and made much use of texts from the Koran done both in Cufic and the more cursive Neskhi scripts.

One last time the mideasterner inaugurated a multicolor process. This was painting with enamel or low-fire colors—pigments placed on top of the fired glaze and given a low *feu*. The Persian name for this process is *minai* (enamel). Much finer pattern delineation could be done in this manner. With this potential the minai painters copied the stories that were incorporated in illuminated manuscripts of the time: episodes from the tenth-century epic by Firdausi, the *Shah-nameh,* with its tales of Persian heroes, such as Bahram Gur, or Rustam, are illustrated on one plate. Their enjoyment requires close inspection and the use of the mind as well as the emotions. It is indeed a compliment to the Persian aesthetic genius that the empathetic appeal is not completely sacrificed in the jewellike rendering.

In 1225 the last and most devastating invasion of the Middle East took place, that of the Mongols under Genghis Khan. Although it is astounding how soon art recovered from the scorched-earth policy of these attackers, nevertheless the sobering effect of the Asiatic was felt. Somber colors predominated—a darker blue, a blackish yellow. Designs, frequently placed in radiating panels, picked up the tribesman's predilection for stripes. Chinese motifs proliferated. Gradually

Figure 5.64 Tiled *mihrab* and frieze. Isfahan. Safavid Period, sixteenth century. Porcelain. *Mihrab:* Height, 2.91 m, width, 2.46 m. Frieze: Height, 69.75 cm, length, 15.66 m. Cleveland Museum of Art. (The Cleveland Museum of Art, Gift of Katharine Holden Thayer.)

an amalgam was effected. The western patterns become less stylized. The blue-and-white wares of the orient, which Persian cobalt had originally made possible, were copied. The unique quality of Persian work departed, but a fusion, predominantly and unmistakenly Iranian, remained throughout the ensuing centuries.

Spanish Ceramics

The arrival of Islamic people in Spain during the eighth century heralded a reawakening of ceramic production. Lusterware became an important export commodity. The name *majolica* was assigned by the Italians because it was shipped from the island of Majorca off the east coast of Spain. Its later production centered in the province of Valencia in southern Spain and in the lit-

tle town of Paterna. The work done there was similar in spirit to the finest Persian and Egyptian. Until the end of the fourteenth century the Spanish colors were limited to the well-known purple and green with a glaze of yellowish cast. Forms were often utilitarian, such as the *albarello* drug jars.

This is probably an opportune time to remark that in the entire scope of art terminology no name seems to be so loosely interpreted as that of majolica. The classic definition restricted the term to tin-glazed pottery, usually painted with metallic oxides and certainly possessing a well-defined luster. The word *faience* (from the town of Faenza, near Florence) was reserved for stanniferous glazed wares but did not necessarily entail luster treatment. Faience, so defined, will be found in French ceramics and certainly in those of Delft, Holland. Recall that alkaline-glazed early Egyptian was, or rather is, frequently called faience, and the name is often applied to any lead-glazed ware. Standardization of terms would certainly not be amiss!

207

Figure 5.65 Majolica, two-handled oak-leaf jar. Florence, second quarter of the fifteenth century. Cleveland Museum of Art. (The Cleveland Museum of Art, Purchase from the J. H. Wade Fund.)

Italian Ceramics

Italy, where lustered majolica may have been made before the fifteenth century, stepped up production at this time in competition with the Spanish imports. Only the earliest Italian designs belong to the Hispanic-Moresque stylistic tradition. Later, although both body and luster were improved, the patterning turned from the vigorous mideastern manner toward the newly revived realism that marked the return to classicism known as the Renaissance. The center for early work was near Florence, where in the Castel Fiorentino fragments have been found. Surrounding Tuscan towns, notably Montelupo and Pisanello during the first part of the fifteenth century and Faenza during the last, produced lusterware.

These potteries favored a rich blue glaze with a pattern outlined in purple with only minute amounts of green, colors to be seen on the oak leaf jars (Figure 5.65). These large, two-handled jars were ornamented with a bold oak leaf (the insignia of the Rovere family, contemporary lords of Urbino) used alone or combined with other patterns such as the *fleur-de-lis* and animal and human heads.

In the second half of the fifteenth century the majolica palette was extended to include a dark blue, an orange, and more emphasis on the green. Gothic foliage and bird motifs such as the peacock feather are common. Often the decoration includes panels with medieval stylized fauna, painted with the utmost skill. Following these fifteenth-century schools, Italian majolica responded to the Renaissance tradition and is therefore discussed in Chapter 6.

The Della Robbias should be numbered among the most renowned producers of stanniferous glazed pottery (see Figure 6.54). Luca Della Robbia (1400–1482) was the founder of the dynasty. His followers were his nephew Andrea (1435–1525) and Andrea's sons. From a technical viewpoint their success was due to the great delicacy with which they modeled their work because tin glaze was then capable of covering the basic and finer clay but did not clog the detail. From a stylistic point of view the Della Robbias stand with a foot in the door of the Renaissance and are another art form to be considered in that context.

Ceramics of Northern Europe

Glazed pottery was common in Europe during the Middle Ages. It was generally of a utilitarian order because the abundance of metals and the skill of the metal worker had crowded clay as an art medium. Medieval pottery of France was crude and at first unglazed. When later it was lead-glazed, the color was brown from the iron that was locally and unavoidably present. Gray-green glazes, again due to iron, were often used over a white slip. Wares were both sgraffito and modeled. Towns in the south of France, notably Avignon, Beauvais, Savigny, and La-Chapelle-des-Pots, were pottery centers.

In England Roman kilns were known to have

existed, but ceramic production apparently died as an art and little of note is recorded until the seventeenth century.

The German tradition was for modeled pottery and stoneware. Not much of historical importance appears so early, however.

GLASS

Eastern Glass

Because of the unsettled conditions in western Europe from the fourth to the ninth centuries, the production of fine glass was concentrated in the east, principally in Syria in territory where by legend the craft had been born, and because the transparent medium was as precious as gold it was only natural that its manufacture should remain close to wealthy patronage. In a manner somewhat paralleled by ceramics, we may name this output Syrian, Byzantine, Sassanian, Persian, Iraqian, Islamic, or Egyptian, according to the place and time in which it was made. Centers were Antioch, Damascus, Aleppo, Alexandria, and Rakka—all names we have met before. Given a common background in character of molten metal, differentiation is by means of basic design and ornamentation.

Grouped as Near Eastern glass, its technique was both blown from the blowpipe alone (called *off hand*) or shaped with the blowpipe and using the assistance of the mold—processes perfected since Roman manufacture. Shapes were numerous—mostly utilitarian articles such as amphoras, jugs, drinking vessels, plates, and various bottles including those for perfume. The metal was of sodium lime composition. The Syrian and Eastern were lighter in weight than the Egyptian and tended to be yellowish to green in color.

The earliest pieces, those antedating the Islamic conquest, are largely decorated with trailing stringers or prunting. Much of this embellishment shows a second color—purple, blue, or green—although a few pieces are monochrome. The effect here is three-dimensional, the design, meritorious. Many small articles, however, especially among the unguentaria, are largely *tour de force* objects of the blower's skill and are frequently elaborately reticulated.

Cutting or engraving returned to favor after the fourth century. After the Islamic conquests the glass world of the East was in closer contact with Persia, where a tradition for cutting and casting had survived. The Persians made a conscious attempt to emulate the clarity of rock crystal. During the Baghdad Abbasid caliphate the country produced glass of fine quality which again indicated the Iranian elegance in handling simple form and supporting decoration.

The most famous eastern glass is the richly enameled and gilded product of the twelfth to fourteenth centuries, the technique of which was perfected in Syria.[40] Other centers, as far east as Rakka, were also in production. Enamels for glass adherence must fuse sooner than the metal to which they are applied; otherwise the vessel would collapse under the enamel firing. Appropriate enamels anneal to the glass surface to create a semiopaque pattern that yields a luminous transparency when held up to the light.

Many of these beautiful enameled glasses were designed as lamps to be hung in mosques (Figure 5.66). Quite naturally their decorative patterns were inscriptions from the Koran and Islamic arabesques. Turkish designers favored flowers like the tulip and carnation. With the inroads made by the Mongols some Chinese motifs appear.

Western Glass

Stained Glass Windows. A mosque so illuminated would be the emotional counterpart of European Gothic churches lighted by their stained glass—a twilight world played on by colored light. Stained glass was the supreme contribution of the Middle Ages to the art of glass making. Its preeminence was in part due to an attempt by its creators to imitate precious gems, in part to a desire to tell biblical stories in symbolic language, in part to create a masterful work of art, and to exploit the potentials of medieval glass technique.

One method of producing a sheet of glass was by cutting and flattening a small cylinder from the blowpipe. This was a method later perfected by the Venetians in making what was known as *broad glass* for mirrors. Another technique twirled the puntil and used centrifugal force to broaden

Figure 5.66   Mosque lamp. Damascus, ca. 1355. Enameled glass. Height 30.5 cm. Corning Museum of Glass, Corning, New York. (Corning Museum of Glass.)

and a roller to flatten a globular gather to make what was known as *crown glass*.[41] In the process of extricating the puntil its mark might remain, a badge of distinction in old windows. Rondels that bore these impressions, called *bull's eyes,* were reserved for important locations.

Neither method of sheet glass manufacture produced large pieces; to cover larger openings necessitated the joining of the sections by the calms previously mentioned. These heavy lead strips help to create the visual power of the twelfth- and early thirteenth-century windows. True, the glass itself is colored throughout in the old pieces rather than coated with a thin gather of color as in the more recent.[42] This permits deep refraction, a process by which intensification results from multiple return of light on itself.

But the great artistry of medieval cathedral windows, like those of Chartres and Notre Dame, lies in the uncanny knowledge that the designer seems to have possessed in juxtaposing the hues.

Although the central portal window in the west wall of the Chartres nave impressed me most in this respect, it was a glass panel (Plate 10) on exhibit from the Paris *Dépôt des Monuments Historiques* that provided the neatest and best explanation of the optical laws involved. This portion of what was presumably a choir window from the Cathedral of Lyon represents the head of the Prophet Jeremiah.[43]

The style is that of the Byzantine frontal image with an upward glance which removes the viewer from close communion and which aligns the prophet with the celestial world. The eyes of the seer and his pointed beard are among the lightest notes, tinted with a pale azure blue. They accentuate the heartlike shape of the face, the flesh of which is a correspondingly light warm tone. Bold strokes of dark pigment and calms outline the principal features and echo the arrangement of the glass. This contrast of tone accentuates the luminosity of the face.

The intense reds and blues of halo and background, respectively, are made richer and deeper by the dark outlines. When seen from a distance these would probably combine to a shimmering purple, thus causing pulsations of translucency to emanate. This is undoubtedly one reason for the purplish light that seems to pervade Chartres and Notre Dame. Last of all, the rim of pearls in the halo, the lightest notes in the image, defines the head and gives the illusion of self-luminosity.[44] Thus they became the richest of backdrops for the image of the prophet.

Much has been written about the glory of medieval stained glass, but further appraisal is better left to whoever becomes enmeshed in the wizardry of early cathedral glass. The men who made these windows were, as Henry Adams has suggested, not professional colorists but amateurs. "Primitive man seems to have had a natural colour-sense, instinctive like the scent of a dog."[45]

Utilitarian Glass. Northern Europe, which made all varieties of Roman glass until late in the classical era, went into a production slump from about A.D. 400 to 800. Nevertheless, it is known that glass houses existed in Spain, Normandy, and the Rhineland, and some Merovingian and German pieces are of considerable merit.

Window glass was an early commodity, although possibly not an extensive one. The Anglo-Saxon chronicler Bede[46] reports that in 674 an abbot of Wearmouth sent abroad for craftsmen to glaze the church windows. This was exceptional, for many cathedral windows remained unglazed at a later date. We read of Lawrence (Laurence Vitrearius) who, coming from Normandy in the early thirteenth century, established himself in the "Surrey-Sussex weald, near the present town of Chiddingford. He supplied both clear and colored glass for the windows at Westminster."[47] This area south of London, rich in wood for fires and bracken for alkali, became the first home of the English glass industry.

With the Carolingian renaissance business picked up. Accounts tell of a group of Syrian Semitic men in Picardy and the continuation of centers along the western side of the Rhine, such as Aix-la-Chapelle, Cologne, and Liége—all important ecclesiastic towns.

Frankish glass from the low-lying land of Normandy and Picardy is known as verre de fougère (glass of the fern), so called because of the source of its principal alkali, a form of potassium rather than the soda familiar in southern glass. This results in a harder metal. Little is known about these Frankish enterprises, although contemporary inventories list glassware and some was presumably manufactured locally. In fourteenth-century French drinking vessels are referred to as glasses, which would indicate a general acceptance of the material.

The contemporary Rhine glass is known as waldgläs, whose alkali derived from the forests of beech and similar woods. Actually its properties differed little from the verre de fougère. This medieval German glass, now often called Lorraine glass, took its name from the districts of Alsace-Lorraine east of the upper river. This designation leaves out of consideration a producing district east of the Rhine and north of Italy. Of little significance during the period under discussion, it became the native soil of a large category of glass

now known as German. We shall see that German glass, which became prominent during the seventeenth century, differs considerably in composition, hence in stylistic character, from either Lorraine or Frankish glass.

Lorraine glass of this date is simple Gothic glass, manufactured in the shape of utilitarian bottles, jugs, and beakers. It owes its green coloring to impurities in the sand. One type of small cup had prunts or knops, small excrescences on the exterior that resembled blobs of meringue on a pudding. These pieces are known as warzengläsen or nuppen. Blown into a mold, it was easy to make them taller and thus to evolve that capacious northern drinking vessel known as the beaker. From this type many specialized forms developed. A base and stem appeared. When the top was curved inward the roemer was born. The Dutch verb roemer means to praise, and this was the ceremonial glass for toasts.

Leaving the northern glass of the potash tradition, we turn to Italy and the south. Two centers of importance emerge. The first is Altare near Genoa whose glassmen are known as Altarists. Their ultimate origin and history is conjectural but it is surmised that the Syrian glassmen of Picardy migrated to this region at the time of the Norman raids in the tenth century. The Altarists may have emigrated from Syria at the time of the crusades.

Their work, both in metal and in style, resembled that of the Venetians who rose to ascendency in the southern glass market almost contemporaneously. The great centuries of Venetian supremacy are the three following the mid-fifteenth. From the Gothic no authenticated piece of Venetian or Altarist glass remains. However, it must have been precisely these years that served to incubate the northern Italian glass tradition by whatever name it is to be called.

STONES, METALS, IVORIES

Byzantine and Sassanian Silver

During recent years the gaps in our knowledge of metal work from the fourth to the seventh centuries have been to large extent closed. Impor-

211

tant post-Roman pieces, both of liturgic and domestic character, now reside in our foremost museums. Lacking nothing in finesse or technique as inheritors of the skill of Near Eastern and Roman metal workers, they are often the most interesting evidence with respect to style borrowed from both sources. Early Byzantine and Sassanian silver embraces the eastern tradition that relies largely on graceful shape for its emphasis and adds the Roman with its repoussé encrustations of realistic figures.

One area on which this silver throws some light is that related to table usage. One museum collection of Byzantine silver contains two bowls, sweetmeat and sauce dishes, a pitcher, ewer, ladle, two spoons, a magnificent silver candlestick, and a tall silver vase (Figure 5.67). Another boasts a spoon and a fourth-century fork. Any testimony to the use of forks was extremely rare in Europe before the late Middle Ages. Several two-tined forks are illustrated in early Christian manuscripts, but there is little material proof of their existence. Luxury standards in the wealthy Byzantine court are thus apparent. The Byzantine wife of an eleventh-century doge of Venice brought forks with her from her homeland and was accustomed to carry food to her mouth with

"fascinuli aurei atque bidentes" (gold, two-toothed sticks).[48]

The vase in this treasure quite clearly descends stylistically from the Roman tradition. Around the principal band a repoussé technique delineates bacchanalian revels, and the segregating border is a lovely version of the egg and dart, treated as an acanthus leaf. Above is a zone of cavorting animals and below are sinuous water forms that relate to Egypt and the south. The rabbit or hare on the vase is the long-eared variety native to Egypt and sometimes called the Syrian hare.

The striking thing about many of the other pieces is their un-Roman appearance. Simple, beautiful shapes, quietly adorned with fluting, engraving, and enameling, they indicate a lineage from the East where patterning is absent or concentrated in surface or edging devices.

During the sixth century Byzantine pieces, especially those from imperial workshops, had identification marks on the reverse which are helpful in locating their source of manufacture.

Sassanian silver, which would match in date the early Byzantine, is represented by several centuries of Russian finds now largely at the Hermitage. The imagery in gilt relief on Sassanian silver would indicate an influence from the plastic style of the Hellenistic Mediterranean. Iconography is an interesting mixture of royal hunting scenes scrambled with Bacchic subject matter. Lions are oriental and the vine is prevalent. Royalty is caparisoned with proper insignia, but the fertility goddess is in many cases nude, as she would have been represented in the classical West.

In technique many of these Sassanian vessels are superb. The figures were separately cast and then attached to a previously prepared and grooved ground by metal flanges. Further engraving and chasing (as well as gilding to enrich the whole) are so skillfully done that they make a common royal workshop almost a necessary assumption.

Later Medieval Metal Work

In the Gothic era of northern Europe silver work came under guild supervision and much was produced for state and church. The term *hallmark* is

Figure 5.67 Byzantine silver with *pearled border* decoration. Syria(?), fourth century. Bowl: diameter, 28 cm. Lamp and stand: height, 49 cm (lamp is detachable from the stand). Cleveland Museum of Art. (The Cleveland Museum of Art, Purchase from the J. H. Wade Fund.)

used to describe the mark of the Guild Hall or official headquarters of the English silversmith's guild, a factor since 1327 when the London office controlling the quality of silversmithing was granted its charter. Provincial guilds were not authorized until the sixteenth century.

As an example of silver standardization and an indication of legality, the silversmith guild regulated the percentage of silver to alloy that was permissible to use in silver offered for sale. With the exception of several short interludes to be considered later, this standard has remained official in Great Britain ever since.

The word *sterling*, another first for England, refers to the coinage standard. London silver was never marked with the word sterling, although *sterl* does appear from time to time as a standard mark on silver from certain provincial towns. It became the legal designation for all silver of coinage standard in America after 1865.

Liturgic silver—the *chalice* or drinking vessel used to hold the consecrated wine during the celebration of Holy Communion in the Christian church, the *paten* or plate used for the sacred bread or host, reliquaries, ornate covers to the Codexes or Books of the Gospels, portable altars, crosses, and shrines—all became quite plain in design during the iconoclast era of the eighth century in the eastern empire. After restrictions were lifted in 787 by the Council of Nicaea, there followed, not only in Byzantium but in all of Christendom, an almost barbaric return to sumptuous splendor. Late medieval work with silver and gold, known as *orfèverie* in France, combined rich enamels, precious stones, and carved ivory with costly metals to create such liturgic treasures as the chalice of the famous Abbot Suger of Saint-Denis (Plate 11) now at the National Gallery of Art in Washington. Needless to say, royalty was not far behind in ordering regal pieces to supply its needs.

Much of the medieval gilt work was done by the mercury process in which gold was mixed as an amalgam with mercury and applied in the liquid state. Subsequent heating volatilized the mercury and left the thin layer of gold adhered to the plate. Because the mercury fumes were exceedingly poisonous, the process was finally abandoned in favor of the gold-mixed-with-honey process or more often working with gold leaf overlay. Sassanian silver was gilded by the mercury process.

Islamic influence in the East introduced a new type of metal work in brass which reached its zenith from the twelfth to the fourteenth centuries (Figure 5.68). The process was that of in-

Figure 5.68 Ewer. Iran, Seljuk period, ca. 1250. Brass engraved and inlaid with silver. Metropolitan Museum of Art, New York. (The Metropolitan Museum of Art, Rogers Fund, 1944.)

laying brass with a precious metal such as silver. This must be distinguished from *niello* work, another ancient eastern technique in which engraved lines on a silver or enameled plate are filled in with an amalgam of silver, sulfur, and lead. In the process of fusing niello turns black—hence the name. In the silver-on-brass vessels the precut silver was placed into undercut grooves in the brass and the engraving tool was further used to trace delicate designs onto the metal. These lovely articles, made in centers as dispersed as Persia, Mosul in Mesopotamia, and Syria, were a principal commodity of trade from the Near East to Europe. Unfortunately many of these ancient trays and ewers have lost much of their original inlay. Superficially, the Persian pieces can be identified by their faceted, fluted contours, whereas those of Mesopotamia have a more angular shape often called the Mosul design.

Medieval work in brass, copper, and bronze was exceedingly popular in Europe. It is known as *Dinanderie,* named for one center of the craft, Dinant in Flanders. In addition to utilitarian objects such as candlesticks and andirons, these European centers made many small decorative figures for domestic and ecclesiastic use. *Aquamanilia* or water pourers in such forms as lions, falcons, griffins, and horses with riders were all represented in the species. Dinanderie waned in Europe after the fourteenth century because of the need for metals in artillery warfare.

Limoges in France and Hildesheim in lower Saxony were famous for their ateliers in enameled metals. When inlaid in grooved metal plates, they are known as *champlevé* enamels. In *cloisonné* the enamels are inserted between metal ridges or cloisons protruding from the piece rather than grooved into it.

The production of enameled articles was widespread and continued long enough to develop consecutive styles. It began with a period when the enameling filled in engraved lines on a plate (known as *vollemail,* full enamel) to a time when the major portion of the design was reserved (i.e., left in the base metal) and only the background was filled with the enamels, to the stage in which the entire pattern was worked in base relief enamel and riveted to the plate as a plaque.

Figure 5.69 *Châsse* (front and back views). Champlevé enameled. France. Limoges, thirteenth century. Height, 24.5 cm, width, 23 cm, diameter, 10 cm. Cleveland Museum of Art. (The Cleveland Museum of Art, Gift of S. Livingston Mather, Philip R. Mather, Constance Mather Bishop, Katherine Hoyt Cross, and Katherine Mather McLean, in accordance with the wishes of Samuel Mather.)

Figure 5.70

In style, these enamels illustrate the progression from compartmentalized Romanesque design to the unified Gothic (Figures 5.69 and 5.70). In the French champlevé châsse illustrated the front is architecturally divided by straight horizontal bands of ornament. The contained little figures carry out the vertical emphasis. The small rosettes are kept tightly within their frames. On the rear face of the chest the rosettes connect the framework circles and the curved diagonal lines created by the angel wings cause a second interpenetration of one area by another. The dates of the little casket are given as the decades between 1200 and 1230. The artist who created the front was stylistically retarded, whereas the man who did the back suggests an advanced point of view.

The name *Limoges enamel* is sometimes restricted to painting done on a previously fired enamel surface with finely ground low-firing enamel colors. Frequently the pattern is found on both sides of a plate (see Chapter 7).

Wrought iron as an art medium developed an aesthetically high standard during the Middle Ages. Ornamental railings, grilles, lighting fixtures, mounts, locks, hinges, *lavabos* (washbasins), and even furniture were made from this ductile material.

Andirons, which came into use when the fire was removed to a wall hearth, were first made of wrought iron. The earliest used in England were slender tripods that supported horizontal bars. Casting of iron was first done in Sussex in England in the fourteenth century, following which, andirons became heavier and more ornamental. Early ones were likewise made of brass or bronze. Frequently crouching animals decorated their bases; hence *fire dogs*.

Candlesticks present as many materials and forms. Most brass pieces are French or Flemish. The French seem to have preferred the pricket variety, whereas the round, open-socket top is common in England. Many of the stems of Gothic candlesticks were lenticular, resembling thin, sharp-edged spools set on top one another, although other varieties of molding appear early. Multiple-socket pieces are extremely rare. Bronze pieces occasionally are figural and as such expressive of their time.

Household Articles—the Little Things

It is well to remind ourselves as we contemplate the commonplace objects of the northern Middle Ages that the use of these articles often differed from today's.

In tableware, for instance, individual dinner plates were unknown. Silver dinner plates, in sets of twelve, were not used in England before the Tudors, and were not common before the eighteenth century in France.[49] The name *plate* is derived from a thin sheet of metal from which plates or platters were made. Pewter and even wood were the usual materials.

Margaret Paston, of a middle-class English family of the fifteenth century, wrote to her husband during one of his frequent business trips to London:

> Also if ye be at home this Christmas, it were wele do ye should do purvey a garnyssh or tweyn of powter vesshell, ij basanes, and ij hewers, and xij candlestikes, for ye have to few of any of these to serve this place.[50]

Guests, using only three fingers, helped themselves from a common dish shared by at least two persons. Note Chaucer's description of the prioress in the *Canterbury Tales*:

> At mete wel-y-taught was she withalle,
> She let no morsel from her lippes falle,
> No wette her fingers in her sauces depe.

Servants offered meat on a long skewer or pointed stick, which the diners placed for cutting on a large slice of bread known as a *trencher*. The French word is *trenchoir*, coming from *trencher*, to cut. Wooden platters on which to carve food later became associated with the word.

Porringers were first known as *porridgers*. Their form was that of a bowl from which semi-liquid food could be taken. The two handles on English porringers did not appear until the seventeenth century. Porringers were shared by two guests.

Spoons and knives were in general use but, as previously mentioned, forks were not. In England their common acceptance dates from the Res-

215

toration (1660) and the introduction of certain French amenities.

The large platter on which a joint of meat was carried to the table was the *charger*. The carved food was placed on the *voyder* for distribution.

The vessel for holding wine was the *flagon* (French, *flaçon*), frequently mentioned in medieval inventories. The flagon had a long neck and flat ovoid body, a shape derived from the old leather pilgrim bottles. The ceremonial vessel for wine drinking was the *mazer* (Figure 5.71). It was customarily made from figured maple wood and later had metal mounts. The name is thought to have derived from that of the wood. Some conjecture that it comes from the German *masa,* meaning spots, as on the bird's eye-maple. However, the winecup was often made of silver like the English *Studley bowl* of the fourteenth century which is engraved with a Gothic script alphabet. This historic and handsome piece is one of the treasures of the Victoria and Albert Museum in London.

When a mazer was raised on a stem during the fifteenth century, it became a *standing cup.* Strangely enough, cups were frequently made of exceptional materials such as coconut shells or ostrich eggs, silver mounted. Standing cups were likewise communal in use. The *beaker* was another shared vessel, rated farther down the social ladder in drinking etiquette. A beaker resembles a tall table glass. The individual receptacle for wine was the *tumbler* or *bolle.* No early ones are extant but the stubby rounded shape is frequently seen in manuscripts.

The *tankard* has a curious history. It was first a large wooden pitcher bound with metal which derived its name from wooden water containers so bound. The name descended to mugs of the same character. In medieval England they were called *cans;* the word *tankard* is of Elizabethan origin.

The container for salt, an expensive commodity, was a prestigious article in the medieval household. The *standing salt,* or tall shaker, was placed in the center of the high or dais table in medieval England. Smaller open *cellars* arranged along the other tables came to be known as *trencher salts.* The name is said to have originated from the name of the cutting knife used to lift the salt to the food.

Figure 5.71   Double mazer. Germany, ca. 1530. Maple with silver-gilt mounts. Height, 24.8 cm. Cleveland Museum of Art. (Cleveland Museum of Art, Purchase from the J. H. Wade Fund.)

The *ewer* (French, *aiguière)* or tall pitcher and the basin or *salver* were among table appointments. Servants offered a basin to guests both before and after each meal. The hands were placed in the bowl and water was poured over the fingers; they were then dried with a towel.

French literature of the period mentions the *drageoir* or sweetmeat dish. It held those tasty morsels that completed the feast.

DESCRIPTIVE SUMMARY

The thousand years that spanned the Middle Ages was an uneasy period of transition—a pause in time that introduced variant cultures to the inheritance of Rome, Greece, and the Near East. The result was a fusion and a new creation rather than an assimilation.

The greatest artifact of the period—the cathedral—demonstrated a new means of bringing measured movement into space, of opening phenomenal space oriented both in and out, and of filling space with an ambience of color, light, and texture.

The unsettled nature of the times and the open communal condition of its living account for the fact that valued belongings were portable, placed for storage and cartage in iron-bound chests that were thereby easily guarded. They were the cloths, the precious plate, glass, and gems that were displayed only on special occasions. They were made doubly significant because sumptuary laws and symbolic codification allowed their use only by princes of the cloth and of the blood.

Furniture, which was vulnerable and not easily transportable, showed little of the finesse that was manifest in the other arts. It is not that the craftsmen were lacking in skill; it was that sturdiness and solidarity were requisite to utilitarian needs. With the waning of the Middle Ages and in such courts as the wealthy Burgundian magnificent stationary furnishings began to appear.

At the end of the Medieval period stands the gate to the modern world. Its blueprint had already been made; indeed, the blueprint for the future may have been in preparation. This period saw the broadening of cultural territories, the mobility of society, faith in a new ideology, viability in the symbols of prestige, and the lessening of permanency in the accouterments of living. Yet it is important to note how hearth, cloistered bed, and sanctuary were provided—warmth, privacy, and spiritual asylum were part of life. With somewhat similar conditions today, can we provide an answer so suitable?

217

CHAPTER SIX

The Italian
Renaissance

1400 TO 1600

The most beautiful and proportionable manners of rooms . . . are seven, because they are either made round . . . or square, or their length will be the diagonal of the square, or of the square and a third, or of one square and a half, or of one square and two thirds, or of two squares.

Palladio, Book 1, Chapter 21

Italy of the Renaissance (1400–1600) in many respects provides an introduction to the modern western world. The present lay five hundred years ahead. Looking back by half millennia we could travel from 1500 B.C., the time of early contacts between Asia and Europe, to the beginning of Greece and then its prime (our font), the development of the sibling culture in Rome, the enlargement of the family of nations during the Middle Ages, to our emerging image with the rising generations of the fourteen hundreds.

Time is always in arrears to art. Certain fourteenth-century painters, such as the Sienese Simone Martini (ca. 1285–1344) and the even more innovative Florentine Giotto di Bondone (ca. 1266–1337), indicate even at so early a date how painting had turned from the religious symbolic icons of former years to a representation which, although essentially pious in intent, was imbued with an emotional and very human content (Figures 6.1 and 6.2).

The formal elements were altered also. Some of the flat gold backdrop, the *orfèvrerie* favored by the all-powerful Medieval church, remained and some of the heavenly hosts and dainty star-dewed flowers were slow to leave the stage. But they were pushed by a new way of handling space, first as shallow enclosure and finally, with an awakening knowledge of perspective, as three-dimensional volume. With Tommaso Masaccio (1401–1428), in his *Trinity* fresco at Santa Maria Novella, Florence, deep space is not only shown, it is given a simulated framework of the classical Roman *arch order* (i.e., a central arch flanked by two columns). Concern for mankind, with horizons stretched in space and time was relevant to the 1400s, an era customarily called the Renaissance, or rebirth. It was a time characterized by a new alignment of values and interests that evoked a surge of intellectual and artistic creativity. In art the Renaissance has been described as having early, high, and late phases; the dates for each are understandably somewhat flexible.

Florence was the leading Italian city during the first period. At the beginning of our story it had emerged from an era when the feudal aristocracy and then the craft guilds held the reins of government within a nominal republic to one in which moneyed banking interests were powerful. A

Figure 6.1 *The Annunciation*. Simone Martini. Painted for an altar in Siena Cathedral, 1333. Tempera on wood panel. Uffizi Gallery, Florence. (Alinari/Editorial Photocolor Archives.)

likely transition could be made in the persons of the family of wealthy wool merchants turned international bankers—the Medici. Undoubtedly as wise and at times as ruthless as the writer Machiavelli indicates by his concealed portraits in *The Prince,* they were, like other Renaissance princes, anxious to augment their prestige by sumptuous donations to the church and to the building of grandiose palaces.

ARCHITECTURE

Early Renaissance Architecture

During the thirties Cosimo de' Medici, then head of the family, decided to add a cloister to his favorite church of San Marco in the northern part of town. He was a man genuinely scholarly as well as religious, and this addition would serve him both as a sanctuary and as a retreat from civic cares, for he had recently been elected *Gonfaloniere,* or head, of the *Signoria,* the ruling political body.

Cosimo was also interested in providing a suitable location for his extensive library of precious manuscripts from the classical writings of Greece and Rome. This collection antedated the placement of 10,000 in the later Medici library, the Laurentian, at the Medici parish church of S. Lorenzo—actually the first corpus open to all scholars and thus the first public library on the continent. A few years hence and Pope Nicholas V, the former librarian for Cosimo, founded the Vatican library. Thus the scholastic phase of the Renaissance may be said to have been officially nurtured.

Cosimo selected his favorite architect, Michelozzo diBartolommeo (1396–1472), to design the additions to San Marco and later commissioned him to rebuild the new Medici palace on the Via Cavour. The latter is now known as the Medici-Riccardi palace, having been bought from the state by the Riccardi during the seventeenth century. The Medici palace (Figure 6.3) was all that a fifteenth-century palazzo should be. It was built of large blocks of local stone, with a ground story of *rusticated* masonry. This rough cutting of massive rocks, separated from one another by deep

Figure 6.2 (above) *Lamentation.* Giotto, ca. 1305. Fresco. Arena Chapel, Padua. (Alinari/Editorial Photocolor Archives.)

Figure 6.3 (below) Palazzo Medici-Riccardi. Michelozzo, architect. Florence, 1430, with later additions. (Martin Linsey.)

Figure 6.4 Palazzo Rucellai. Leon Battista Alberti, architect. Florence, 1446–1451. (Marburg/Prothmann.)

joints, provides the perfect feel for "wall" architecture, in which partitions must be adequate load-bearing members. Notice, however, the gradual transition in coarseness of treatment and in the proportional lowering of the three stories. We do not find this calculated change in the fourteenth-century Davanzati palace. Some formal organization has been introduced. Although the most important treatise on the "new" art principles was a decade in the future, the idea of commensuration in architecture was evident.

The Medici palace needs basic rustication to control its size, ultimately 225 ft in length by 190 in width. One of the noticeable differences between fourteenth- and fifteenth-century town dwellings is this immensity for which the Medici-

Riccardi set the standard. Indeed its pretentions cost the Medici their first banishment from Florence (1433–1434)—the party of the nobles used it as a pretense: too big for a republic. Obviously this is aristocratic architecture—the aristocracy of money. Moderate-sized homes were built, but expense is usually required for a pacesetter. The Medici palace, painfully regular although not yet bisymmetrical in the classical fashion and boasting little to relieve its severity, was saved from triviality by the size of its stones. Homes of importance were still fortresses and in Italy turned their formidable aspects toward the street.

The demarcation of the floor levels of the Medici palace is accentuated by a *string course*, a marked horizontal banding of stone, which provided lateral emphasis not found in such Medieval buildings as the Florentine Palazzo Vecchio (Figure 5.30). The crowning 10-ft projection of the cornice at the Medici fosters the earthbound illusion. How different this is from the skyward thrust of the preceding Gothic style; yet the upper windows are still the earlier *bifora* or *two-light* windows, introduced into round Renaissance arches.

The Rucellai palace is another Florentine Renaissance landmark (Figure 6.4). It was built for Giovanni Rucellai, whose son Bernardo married Lorenzo de' Medici's sister Lucrezia (Nannina). The Medici-Rucellai combined coats of arms may be seen on the facade.

It is this front, designed by Leon Battista Alberti (1404–1472), that we must now consider. The Roman disposition of pilaster strips, Doric style on the ground story, Ionic on the first, and Corinthian on the second, is used to articulate the long face of smooth stone (i.e., *ashlar*) in a manner consistent with new classic academic principles. The palace comes off rather lamely, however, in comparison with such strong characters as the Medici-Riccardi or other Florentine palazzos like the Strozzi. The pilasters appear to be linear bands that have little connection with the underlying structure. Alberti unified a composition through measure and used an ancient language as a scholar, but he did not show himself to be a master of tectonics. His ornaments seem "hung on" rather than integral.

In this respect he became a true disciple of

222

Figure 6.5 Dome of Florence Cathedral. Filippo Brunelleschi, architect, 1420–1436. Campanile (bell tower) by Giotto, begun 1334–1337. (G. C. Ball.)

Renaissance architecture, which placed its first emphasis on visual effects. Only in a secondary manner was it concerned with structural matters. It boasted no innovations (except for the dome on a drum) to building morphology, and, although it used the trabeated (post and lintel beam) construction of the Greek and the arched of the Roman, it never worshiped building anatomy for its own sake. The Renaissance architect did not hesitate to cover joints with stucco or indeed to create false ones (e.g., as in the Strozzi) when visually requisite; and he shamelessly and without disguise used tie rods and chains to strengthen arches, vaults, and domes. He painted an architectural grid of classical orders on facades when it suited his purpose. This "outrageous" behavior was not the result of ignorance on his part; it was in deference to a principle that seemed more important in his eyes—the visual formalizing principle. How a thing looked was of more consequence than any disclosure of the logic of its construction.

If the twentieth century does not feel in complete rapport with this doctrine, it must be admitted that it brought some lovely benefits. Look at the work of Filippo Brunelleschi (1377–1446), an older architect, often called the father of the Italian architectural Renaissance. He designed the Foundling Hospital at San Marco and the dome of the Florentine cathedral (Figure 6.5), Sta. Maria del Fiore. The latter is a curious mixture of build-

223

Figure 6.6 Florence cityscape, (G. C. Ball.)

ing on a ribbed foundation in the Gothic manner and of elevation on a drum, customary in the later Renaissance. The roof line, best observed over the housetops of Florence rather than from the ground as conjoined with the nave, dominates the skyline and pins down the town with its compelling, subtle, unadorned shape (Figure 6.6). Alberti says, ". . . ample to cover with its shadow all the Tuscan people." The *Duomo* (i.e., cathedral) was later crowned with a small, classically inspired cupola known as a *lantern,* a custom that was followed for every subsequent dome down to the local ones on state capitols.

Brunelleschi, as a young man and following his failure to win the contract for the bronze doors of the Florentine baptistry, had left his home city to study in Rome. On his return he demonstrated

Figure 6.7 Pazzi Chapel of the Church of Santa Croce. Filippo Brunelleschi. Florence, begun 1430–1433. (Alinari/Editorial Photocolor Archives.)

Figure 6.8   (above) Pazzi Chapel, interior. Filippo Brunelleschi. Florence. (Alinari/Editorial Photocolor Archives.)

Figure 6.9   (below) Plan of the Pazzi Chapel, Florence,
ca. 1430. (After Geymüller.)

that he was quite capable of using the classic
vocabulary of column, arch, and entablature (i.e.,
the superload—specifically architrave, frieze, and
cornice) and the classic formal syntax in a manner
consistent with Greece and Rome. One master-
piece is the Pazzi Chapel (ca. 1430; Figure 6.7)
done for the family who were the political arch
enemies and rivals of the Medici. This little gem
is to be seen in the cloister of the Holy Cross
(di S. Croce). Free-standing Corinthianlike columns support an entablature above which half-
columns and a central arch demark the wall of
an upper story. The round arches of porch and
interior rise from similar supporting members,
made more visually emphatic by contrast of
tones, dark against white (Figure 6.8).

The real importance of this building lies not
so much in its antiquarian verbiage but rather in
its clarity of form (Figure 6.9). Anyone who is
sensitive to spatial organization can appreciate
and enjoy the rational arrangement of the Pazzi
architecture. Viewed across the level lawn of the

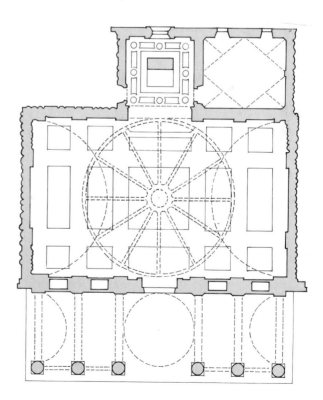

cloister, it consists of an open porch, the regular module of which is the square. The inner building repeats this meter, doubling its depth, centering it with a dome, and extending it by a central projection for the altar. Interior and exterior, plan and elevation have shared proportions that clarify the whole.

Here we meet the essence of the architecture that historians have called the Renaissance. It presents a rational, lucid, and mathematical point of view, quite opposed to a predominantly mystical Medieval expression. It was a point of view that sought to unite the matter of this world with the world of the mind. It was the point of view from which modern science, hence the modern era, was born.

Renaissance Doctrine

Alberti may with some justice be called the first Renaissance *universal man,* by which we mean a man versed in all aspects of noteworthy human endeavor—the humanist: architect and painter, scion of a noble family which had been permanently banished from Florence, and a student of law, philosophy, and natural science at the University of Bologna. In 1431 he was attached to the Curia in Rome.

Alberti wrote three principal books, which were popularized by the invention of the printing press. Their subjects were the "new" approach to painting, sculpture, and architecture. *De Re Aedificatoria,* the one on architecture, contained the first Italian definition of the five classical orders (i.e., the classical columns with their superstructures) since the time of the Roman author and architect, Vitruvius.[1]

Alberti's treatise was followed by those written by others who preached much the same gospel: Filarete, Giorgi, Leonardo da Vinci, Vignola, Serlio, and Palladio are among the number. All of their texts advocated a conscious conformity to the canons of antiquity. To accomplish this they returned to prescriptions that had descended from the writings of the Greeks—Pythagoras and Plato—and the Roman architect Vitruvius. The architecture of the high Renaissance, in particular, is marked by an attempt at strict adherence to these newly publicized classic rules.

A review thus tells what the Renaissance architect thought when he planned a building. The need to order a design by means of mathematical ratios was fundamental. This doctrine advanced from coordination by means of commensurate arithmetical numbers to that obtained by a series of incommensurate geometric figures, each related to the one that followed by its diagonal. A progression of these spatial measurements, if used in a restricted manner, can undoubtedly cause regulated eye movement. The Italians may have been trying this systematic approach to proportional divisions of space in some of the buildings already cited.

The Vitruvian proportional system which influenced Renaissance writers likewise stressed the relation of this mathematical order to the measures of the human body. This seemed rational to a culture that was beginning to focus on the human aspects of the religious world. The Renaissance proportional system had come full circle—integrating numbers, the geometry of abstract space, humanity and religious beliefs—a neat little philosophical bundle.

From such thinking came three suppositions: first, a reaffirmation of faith in ideal architectural canons exemplified in classical architecture; second, the idea that good art required the application of reason to sensuous matter; and, third, the importance of the architect as the initiated and learned man who understood all this.

Such uniform logic inevitably led to creations with similar visual attributes. Based on the human figure, buildings were bisymmetrical, articulated largely by a repetitive module. Because of their relation to earthbound humanity, buildings had horizontal emphasis. The whole, as representing perfection, favored a square or circular form with its inherent egocentricity. Such at least is the shape of things in the Early Renaissance.

In addition to formal considerations, the Renaissance architect gave lip service to what is perhaps the most important heritage handed down by Vitruvius. This relates to the overall important purposes of architecture. They are described as *convenience, durability,* and *beauty.* In other words, a building must suit its overt purpose, must be durable in structure, and fulfill an aesthetic need. It is not easy to run this troika in harness. If the Renaissance made beauty the lead horse, who is to blame?

High Renaissance Architecture

As the Early Renaissance is considered in terms of Florentine building, so the High Renaissance belongs to Rome and essentially to the sixteenth century. Venice, too, may be considered ancillary. The hotbed of family and city rivalries which plagued the fifteenth century was aggravated in the sixteenth by international complications. Both the French and the Spanish laid claims, based on marriage and inheritance, to territory in Italy. Factions in Italy, in turn, made alliances with foreign powers in order to maintain equity at home.

Despite the fact that Rome had been mercilessly sacked in 1527 by Spanish mercenaries, the Papacy, returned from its exile in Avignon, was anxious to create its own pomp. Drawing into its orbit the greatest talents of the time, the Sistine Chapel was glorified, the Vatican Palace and Library were built, and St. Peter's was completed. Members of new and wealthy Roman families, such as the Borgia and Farnese, not only entered the Holy See but likewise bedecked the Eternal City with a rash of residences that remain the epitome of the Renaissance palace and villa.

When the architect Donato d'Agnolo Bramante (1444–1514) came to Rome in 1499 from his birthplace in Urbino, after some twenty years of practice in Milan, the power of the papacy was in the hands of the infamous Alexander VI (Rodrigo Borgia). Donato at first acquired only the opportunity to be on the architectural staff of the Vatican and to paint the armorial bearings over the holy door of S. John Lateran for that pontiff. When in 1503 the great Julius II of the Rovere family of Urbino became pope, Bramante was sought by him for more important work. Two buildings will forever sing his praises.

Under Alexander he began a memorial in the cloister of S. Pietro in Montorio to the memory of the famous saint who was martyred there. The *Tempietto*, or little temple, is undoubtedly the gem of High Italian Renaissance architecture (Figure 6.10). An outer colonnade of unadorned Tuscan columns (i.e., the Italian column, which

Figure 6.10 The Tempietto (S. Pietro in Montorio). Donato Bramante. Rome, ca. 1502. (Alinari/Editorial Photocolor Archives.)

is derived from the Greek Doric but is without shafts and with a base) is combined with a pilastered wall of an inner cella, with preservation of the structural identity of each. The building is elevated on a plinth, as Alberti advised for a church—a Tuscan characteristic. It is round in shape, again bowing to antiquity and giving religious meaning in the perfection of the circle.

The dome is raised on a low drum and mounts from the wall of the inner structure, piercing

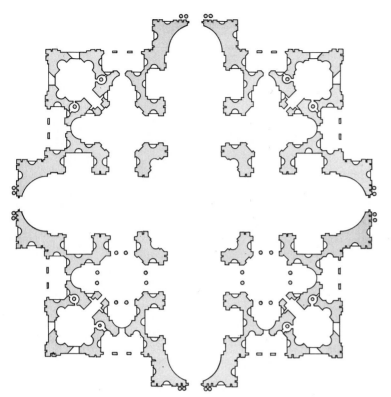

Figure 6.11 Original plan for St. Peter's, Rome. Donato Bramante, 1506. (After Geymüller.)

through the balcony floor to crown the whole. One point about the architectural proportions is particularly important. The spacing between the columns is what Vitruvius called a *diastyle* (i.e., the diameter of three columns used for the spacing between any two). This creates a statement more powerful than words or symbols because it is based on bodily empathy, on serene reflection on the final sacrifice of the apostle. Thus the building is not only a satisfactory assertion of its structural framework and a unified documentation of the classical heritage, it is an emotional expression of its reason for being. At this point the High Renaissance had arrived.

The Tempietto was a comparatively small building from which the Italian Renaissance moved to a phenomenal scale. In 1505 Pope Julius II commissioned Bramante to rebuild St. Peter's, the central church of Roman Catholicism.

The architect planned the present concept of a Greek cross that is enclosed, except for terminal domed apses, within a square (Figure 6.11). This

was in accordance with the Renaissance advocacy of a centralized church expressed in idealized form and the cross for its Christian symbolism. The interior space, majestic and complex, featured interlocked crosses as extensions from the major axes. A hemispherical dome was to have covered the central space. When Michelangelo (as we shall see) was called on to finish the mother church, he somewhat altered the original concept in the interest of greater forcefulness and unity in the design, thereby sacrificing some of the complexity. The original development, however, was the work of Bramante, and his church—with its classical centralized regularity, its grandeur, yet humanly comprehensible form because of the spatially broken units—proves that its creator deserves his accolade as the master of the Italian High Renaissance.

In 1546 Michelangelo Buonarotti (1475–1564) took charge of the building on the death of Antonio da Sangallo the Younger (1483–1546), the last of a succession of architects who had succeeded Bramante. In Michelangelo's plan we are aware not only of great magnitude but also of that same interpenetration of space that Bramante had initiated (Figure 6.12). We note the square, the cross, and the circle, as they unite and depart from one another—an organization that provides great vitality because the mind can align spaces at will. At the same time Michelangelo strengthened the interior square in Bramante's plan, enlarged the piers of the dome, and altered its shape to that of an ellipsoid on a drum (Figures 6.13, 6.14, and 6.15). These changes created a more highly integrated and dynamic hierarchic statement in which ultimately all interior visual forces merged and mounted in the center. In 1606 Carlo Maderno lengthened the nave to form a Latin cross, ostensibly to provide requisite congregational space, but thereby destroying some of the centralized orientation of the composition.

It is often nothing short of uncanny to watch the forces that create art change quickly with the tenor of the times and by the agency of some genius who seems tuned to the shifting winds like an Aeolian harp. Michelangelo was precisely that. By the second quarter of the sixteenth century the protestant reformation had shattered the

228

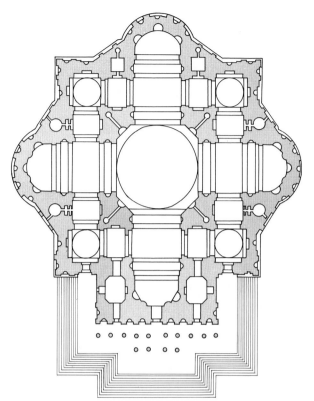

Figure 6.12 Plan for St. Peter's, Rome. Michelangelo. ca. 1520. (After Letarouilly.)

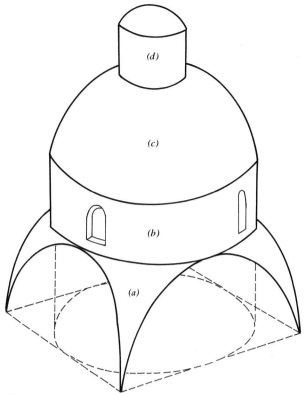

Figure 6.13 Diagram of a Renaissance dome on a drum: (a) pendentive; (b) drum; (c) dome; (d) cupola or lantern.

invincible image of the orthodox church. In his lifework Michelangelo shows the result of this religious struggle on the vision of an extremely sensitive and powerful artist. On the Italian stage art could never again, no matter how it wished to conform to the past, be strictly the child of rule.

This new freedom begins to show even in Roman palaces. The Palazzo Farnese (Figure 6.16), completed in 1548 for the family of Pope Paul III, Alessandro Farnese, is our example. It was probably begun with its large rectangular mass by Bramante. Its continuation is credited to the younger Sangallo, with additions to the second story and entrance by Michelangelo. The Farnese is bisymmetrical and regular but *astylar* (i.e., without use of the orders) except for the upper-story *aediculae* (i.e., the architectural framing of doors or windows, usually by two columns, entablature, and pediment). The window surrounds of the Farnese *piano nobile,* or main floor, with alternate triangular and segmental pediments sup-

ported by columnettes, and those of the second floor, with pediments pierced by arches, are referred to as *tabernacle* windows. Seen on the drum of St. Peter's, they became synonymous with the Roman High Renaissance. Michelangelo is credited with having added the ground-story windows to the Medici-Riccardi palace, which are of this order, having filled in the earlier and more usual arched openings (see Figure 6.3).

Roman travertine stone is softer than that of the north. Therefore the character of architectural dressing is finer, surfaces are smoother, and joints are less conspicuous. In the Farnese the wall masonry is largely covered with stucco, again accentuating a growing Renaissance tendency to unify a building rather than to subdivide it. This wall surface in the Farnese provides a dramatic contrast with the rustication of the central doorway and the corner quoins (i.e., dressed stones laid at the corners of a building so that they make an irregular pattern). Over the rusticated doorway Michelangelo placed an immense cartouche

229

Figure 6.14   St. Peter's Rome, exterior, 1506–1626. (Anderson-Giraudon.)

Figure 6.15   St. Peter's Rome. Interior view looking from the canopy (or *baldacchino*) by Bernini, 1624–1633, toward the apse, with the Cathedra of St. Peter, by Bernini, 1656–1665. (Photo Researchers.)

Figure 6.16 Palazzo Farnese. Bramante, Antonio Sangallo the Younger, and Michelangelo. Rome, 1534–1546. (Lauros-Giraudon.)

in which the Farnese coat-of-arms was incorporated. Attention is thus called to the door. Accentuation of the central axis in this manner becomes a prominent mark of the late Renaissance and oncoming Baroque idiom. Where the architecture of Bramante was restfully static, movement began to intrude. Despite these forward-looking innovations, the Farnese illustrates the High Renaissance in its great size, its easily comprehended regularity and bisymmetry, its inward look, and its use of the classical language.

The inner courtyard of the Farnese offers an unusual opportunity to note the changes that occurred in the style of the Renaissance in the years intervening between Bramante and Michelangelo. The first two stories present the usual picture of the Roman arch order with rounded columns in stylistic tiers supporting an entablature and apparently functioning as quasi-load-bearing members. On the third story Michelangelo substituted overlapping pilasters which, although they resumed the Renaissance tendency to use classical members as ornament, nevertheless better preserve the sense of wall architecture pierced by windows. Although actually becoming more intricate and original in the use of his forms, Michelangelo became more logical in his expres-

sion of structure. The passage from the central vestibule goes straight through to the garden entrance and the 81-ft cortile has its major stairs enclosed within the palazzo walls, thus preserving the squared cortile intact; the whole is a splendid example of the majestic inner court in the home of a powerful Renaissance family. Pope Paul III (1534–1549), whose portrait by Titian hangs in the Capodimonte Museum in Naples, was Alessandro Farnese.

In the same era as Michelangelo we must consider briefly the younger man, Raphael da Sanzi (1483–1520), who like Mozart was a genius who died far too soon. Best known as a painter, especially of the frescoes of the *Vatican Stanze*—the series of rooms begun for Pope Julius—he handled architecture in a painterly way. By this we mean that he was interested in contrasts of tone, texture, and shape, the total organized in a complex manner, as though he were orchestrating the surface of a canvas. This concern for thematic development through the use of visual components increased as the Renaissance progressed.

Raphael's residence (no longer standing) known as the Palazzo Vidoni Caffarelli (ca. 1515–1530) but more often called The House of Raphael, may be used as an illustration. The facade arrangement of details fits into the Renaissance pattern of organization, but we note more manifest planar contrasts. A highly rusti-

232

cated ground story is set against an upper level of smooth masonry. The *piano nobile* and second story are grouped and united by tall, highly modeled and paired Doric columns supporting a bold architrave. This division of the facade into but two horizontals simplifies and unifies the total composition. At the same time the rhythm of the individual details is more complicated; for example, the columns with window aediculae form a pronounced a-a-b, a-a-b pattern.

Raphael, in his short and successful life, is important to our story in several ways. As superintendent of Roman antiquities under the Medici Pope Leo X (a post indicative of the new veneration for the classic past) he examined the ancient palaces that were being excavated beneath the Palatine Hill, especially the Golden House of the Roman Emperor Nero. The decorative masques, fanciful arabesques, and other embellishments that were found on the walls of these underground buildings became very popular as sources of design for current use. They were called *grottesques* because of their discovery in buried grottoes, and because many had been made in stucco a vogue for the use of this material in Renaissance building decoration resulted. The Palazzo Spada may be cited as an example.

Late Renaissance or Mannerist Architecture

Within the last few academic generations it has become customary to call the final seventy-five years of the sixteenth century in Italian art the period of Mannerism. Although this cognomen is perhaps more applicable to painting than to architecture, we use it to imply characteristics that, on the one hand, refer to a unique way of handling the classical heritage and, on the other, may exemplify a tendency toward self-conscious eccentricity for the sake of pleasing a moneyed clientele. The architecture of Bramante and his followers was, like that of classical Greece, almost too regular, simple, and circumscribed for continued interest to any save the highly sensitive eye.

Michelangelo in some of his works certainly led the way, though no one would accuse him of playing to a gallery. What he did, as indicated

by his writings, was prompted by deep personal conviction about the necessities of the particular situation. It was Michelangelo who wrote to Pope Clement VII: "I beg of you that none may be set in authority over me in matters touching my art."[2] His genius was simply in tune with the times.

Michelangelo was by temperament a sculptor. In every structure he touched space organization became plastic, complex, and intricately integrated, as noted in S. Peter's. Movement and vitality emanated from his fingertips. In the buildings and redesigned concourse he planned as the Campidoglio—the civic center of the Capitoline Hill (1540–1644)—he made a prime factor of trapezoidal space, aligning his three buildings on it to draw one toward the axial Senate House or toward the Roman statue of the emperor Marcus Aurelius mounted in the center of the square.

At the same time his unification of the building facades by means of tall pilasters, hereafter known as the *colossal order,* indicated that ability of the greatest High Renaissance designers to organize into a whole while preserving the integrity of multiple parts. The balustrade which is worn as a diadem creates a less earthbound building than a heavy cornice would have done. It becomes a significant feature of Late Renaissance architecture.

In the Medici parish church of S. Lorenzo in Florence Michelangelo designed the Laurentian Library and anteroom (1524–1557) and the family's mausoleum (1523–1529; Figure 6.17), both of which exhibit unprecedented ways of handling the classic medium. In the library vestibule giant pillars of unorthodox height are recessed in pairs in the wall. Are they upheld by the corbeled brackets below or do they lift the piers above? Turning to the mausoleum, the pilaster architrave is broken by the inner frame, the ears of which rest on the lintel. Only the inner molding of the segmental pediment seems precariously poised on any beam. The syncopated cadence of the advancing and receding wall planes is made more dramatic because of the light and dark contrasts.

What these details have achieved as a sequence of individual notes the giant balustrade of the library stairs has done with a sinuous line. Its swelling curve seems to spill the library space out into the vestibule. Movement of a sweeping nature has been introduced. Thus boldly Michelangelo used the details of Renaissance architecture with a greater sense of unity, with greater contrast, movement, and drama than any of his contemporaries. His dates belong to the Renaissance, but he led the way both to Mannerism and the Baroque.

One of the architectural types most instrumental—possibly because less urban and important—in representing new architectural forms was the country and suburban villa. This, of course, was a conceit from late Roman days, and for the wealthy it served the purpose of escape from the city.

Late Renaissance villas are noteworthy for their handling of inner and outer space. In this respect one of the Medici villas, *Poggio a Cajano* (1480 Figures 6.18 and 6.19); is an antecedent. The Medici built, in all, three villas near Florence. The first two were done by Michelozzo; the last, the *Poggio,* was the work of Giuliano da Sangallo (1445–1516), the uncle of the younger Antonio. The *Poggio* owner was Giovanni, Lorenzo's son and the future Pope Leo X.

The smooth-textured exterior of the villa and the astylar treatment of its facade, contrasted with its classic pedimented front (known as the *temple front*), forecast a format that had its influence on the later architect, Palladio. Incidentally, the temple pediment at *Poggio* is ornamented with the six balls and ribbon of the Medici coat-of-arms, which brings to mind Palladio's injunction that this was a suitable place to display symbols of family status.

Originally, the flight of stairs at the entrance to this villa was planned at right angles to its present location. Then, and even now, it is an invitation to enter a central space that pulls the eye toward the doorway. Here a large hall extends to the limits of the building square. As seen in the plan, this becomes the basis for the intersection of inner spaces, a far cry from room opening into room around a *cortile,* as in contemporary city palaces derived from the Florentine bastions.

Two Roman villas, of 1516 and 1550, respectively, are among the earliest to present a horseshoe plan opening on the gardens. The first is the *Madama,* associated with Margaret of Austria (Parma) who came to live there following the death of her husband Alessandro de' Medici. A fatality of the siege of Rome in 1527, it was never completely restored. The original design was Raphael's.

Figure 6.17   New Sacristy, San Lorenzo, Florence. Michelangelo, 1524–1534. (Alinari/Editorial Photocolor Archives.)

Giacomo da Vignola (1507–1573) was the principal architect for the villa of Pope Julius III in Rome. Known as the *Villa Giulio* and now housing the Etruscan Museum, its U shape opens to its grounds. Such villas as this one were not intended as permanent residences, for often they contained no sleeping accommodations. Rather they were pleasant pavilions where one might entertain guests or spend an evening away from the metropolis.

In the Italian villa the garden, ever since Sangallo's day, is such an auxiliary to the house and such an extension of its space that it is hard to say which is more important. Indeed Vignola owes most of his renown to his being a master of this phase of planning. Villas and even city palaces began to acquire short rear wings and open loggias for a better view of expensive landscaping (e.g., the Palazzo Pitti). With Bramante at the Vatican, an already existing villa, the *Belvedere,* was connected with the palace by a series of courts and terraces, all carefully planned in the Italian manner.

The Italian garden is a formal one that incorporates verdure, sculpture, terraces, and architectural backstops. When most elaborate, it is divided into compartments that act as so many rooms and often constitute spaces that seem to

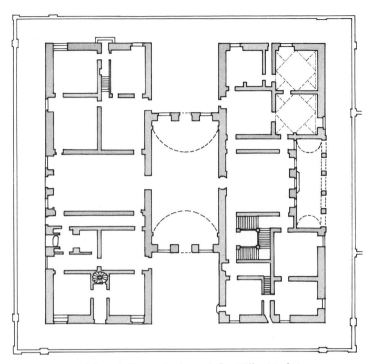

Figure 6.18 (above) Ground plan of the Villa Medici, Poggio a Cajano. Near Florence. Giuliano da Sangallo, ca. 1480. (After Geymüller.)

Figure 6.19 (below) Villa Medici, Poggio a Cajano, near Florence, 1480–1485. Giuliano da Sangallo, architect. (Alinari/Editorial Photocolor Archives.)

Figure 6.20 Palazzo del Te, the garden facade. Mantua, 1525–1535. Giulio Romano, architect. Note the unclassical varieties of spacing and supports. (Marburg/Prothmann.)

expand and contract with a pulsating beat. When this occurs on several levels, a natural habitat for grottoes, watercourses, and winding stairs is provided. As a terminus, an *exedra* is frequently planned. This is a semicircular colonnade fitted to act as a delimitation and at the same time to provide a view beyond. Here we realize the promise expressed in the great Roman antecedents (see Chapter 4).

On occasion a building might better be called a summer palace than a suburban villa, particularly when the intention was to build an extensive menage as an auxiliary home. Such was the Palazzo del Te (1525–1535; Figure 6.20) near Mantua, designed for the first Gonzaga Duke, Federigo II, and said to have been planned as a honeymoon retreat. Giulio Romano (ca. 1492–1546) was the architect. The palace consists of a main one-story building disposed around a courtyard, with an extensive court at right angles to it. The latter is open only on one side; the others contain buildings used as quarters for the famous Gonzaga stud horses. The open court was the scene for fetes and "diversions" popular with the court.

Not only is this placement of open court and main building at variance with the Renaissance bisymmetrical tradition but much about the ar-

chitecture is also unorthodox: variations in the widths of bays, pronounced rustication contrasted with severe flatness, irregular entablatures, odd placement of windows. In a court that Romano added to the Gonzaga palace in Mantua columns are strangely contorted. It is all irrational, distorted, and romantic, and at times seems to have been created out of sheer exhibitionism. We remember that Michelangelo took liberties with strict classicism when it seemed that the situation demanded it. Michelangelo, however, was never capricious, and when his architecture is examined closely it is evident that he always preserved a sense of integrity and unity, which such men as Romano appear to have abandoned. The Palazzo del Te is one outstanding example of that individualism which invades art during the latter part of the sixteenth century and which we call Mannerism.

The Venetian Renaissance and Palladio

Venice was another imposing center of Renaissance art. It had its High Renaissance landmarks as well as those of the later Mannerist era. Looking both to the classical East of Byzantium and to the West of central Italy, its architecture has recognizable components from each. The Palazzo Vendramin (Figure 6.21) on the Grand Canal is one of the most impressive Renaissance houses on the waterfront. It was completed in the Quattrocento (fifteenth century) by Pietro of the Lombardos, who had emigrated from their native Lombardy in the early years of the century and made many contributions to the architecture of their adopted city.

Jacobo Sansovino (1486–1579), who was called from Rome to build the library on the Piazza of San Marco, was likewise the architect of several High Renaissance palaces, including the *Palazzo Corner Ca' Grande* and the *Palazzo Manin,* all of which possess the typical Venetian plan of central hall with rooms off either side. Above is located the grand salon (the *portego*) which leads to a balcony overlooking the canal. As the Renaissance progresses the decoration becomes more centered on this axis. A boldness of forms on its facade accompanied by plain flanks is characteristic.

The courtyard of the Ducal Palace was restored after the fire of 1483 but the interiors were not finished until the middle of the sixteenth century. We note in the cortile the *Scala dei Giganti* or Giant's Staircase (so named because of the gargantuan statues of Mars and Neptune at its head—Sansovino), which, erected at right angles to the wall, creates that sort of grand entrance much used by Palladio and in many later mansions inspired by his work.

The Library finished by Sansovino in 1536 demonstrates the Roman arch order in fairly orthodox fashion. However, it manages to create, in its rich decor, its counterplay of large and small columns on its principal story, the open colonnade on the ground, the tall proportions of the openings, and the lacy balustrade of the crown— the synthesis of boldness and filigree of light and dark patterning, of solid and void, that unites the East and West in classic fusion.

If it was the contribution of Sansovino to speak for Byzantium as well as for Rome, it was the mission of Palladio to codify the Renaissance in an attractive and eminently usable form not only for his time and place but also for the future. Andrea di Pietro della Gondola (1508–1580) was born in Padua and was intended by his parents for a career in stone carving. Fortunately his talent came to the notice of the wealthy patrician humanist, Count Giangiorgio Trissino of Vicenza, a small city northwest of Padua and Venice. The

Figure 6.21 Palazzo Vendramin. Venice, 1481–1515. Pietro Lombardo, (G. C. Ball.)

youth was taken into his household as a member of a group of young aristocrats who were studying the humanities. Andrea concentrated his attention on architecture and developed an impresssive scholarship in the works of the classicists and especially of Vitruvius. It was Trissino who gave the young man his *nom de plume,* Palladio, an angel of deliverance in the epic poem *Italia Liberata dai Goti* (the Liberation of Italy from the Goths), which Trissino had written.

In 1570, just ten years before Palladio's death, his *I Quattro Libri dell' Architettura,* the first four

237

of a projected series of architectural books, were published. Although Palladio's architecture merits study quite independent of his writing, one can readily understand the former after studying the latter. Moreover, texts, because of their reprints, became an accessible source for promoting the Palladian style.

In his writings Palladio subscribes to the Vitruvian code of utility or convenience, durability, and beauty as basic standards. Under the functional, he implies all of those psychological factors that we would include under the heading "suitability to purpose." Thus a temple should be designed ". . . in the best and most noble form our condition will permit."[3] It did not seem incongruous to Palladio, steeped in ancient classicism, to refer to Christian churches as temples.

Something of aesthetics he weaves through every consideration; for example, "a building, which should be of one piece,"[4] should not have parts done in a rusticated manner if it is small in size and intended to appear "neat" and "delicate."

Both from the standpoint of structural necessity and from that of beauty he gives his version of the architectural orders and suggests where each should be used. He advocates not only colonnades but also arcades with application of the Roman arch order.

Palladio's most significant contribution relates to his system of proportioning room spaces. Based ultimately on Vitruvius and before him on Pythagoras-Plato, Palladio proceeds by visual demonstration to show how an entire building should be integrated by certain ratios of numbers. He limits his approval to seven shapes (the title of this chapter), only one of which—the square and its diagonal—represents an incommensurable ratio. He explains how a builder might choose a module of 2 ft. The plan of a hall might be 16 x 24 ft, or a ratio of 2 : 3, one of the recommended room shapes. The adjoining room is then allowable at 24 × 36 ft. He, as did Pythagoras, justified his ideas by relating them to musical consonances. But an understanding of his thoughts on this matter requires concentrated mental involvement which in today's values is usually not considered worth the price. However, they were taken very seriously during the seventeenth and eighteenth centuries and, at least in principle, are certainly not trivial.

Actually they are a lot of fun as an intellectual game. Could they have any precise validity in design? In his completed buildings Palladio shows himself to be something of a Tartuffe when he deviates from rigid adherence to his own doctrine. He suggests that, personally, he might regard the eye as the final decisive instrument. It is not canonical proportions but proportions as they appear visually that are important. Here, of course, he is echoing the basic belief of those Renaissance men who subscribed to Neoplatonism. This was a late Platonic theory as it descended from the third-century philosopher Plotinus. It sets forth the idea that man ascends to God through an awareness of beauty. It gradually influenced Renaissance culture to an appreciation of the role of imagination as an adjutant to rule in the creation of art.

Palladio's buildings can speak for themselves. He was a great architect, certainly not so original, but neither so iconoclastic, as Michelangelo—great rather in his ability to weave convenience, durability, and beauty into a fabric that was well contrived for its times and for future centuries whenever similar conditions prevailed. In this sense Palladianism became classic.

The two Venetian churches of his later years, S. Giorgio Maggiore (Figures 6.26 and 6.27) and Il Redentore, his Vicenza palaces and Basilica (town hall to which he gave a face-lifting), and the Teatro Olimpico—all illustrate in one manner or another his individual solutions to the problems presented. All incorporate fundamental principles that can be illustrated in part by a series of nineteen villas built in the Veneto. We know them either by the extant buildings or in Palladio's renderings.

They were intended for a special kind of patron—Venetian noblemen who were living on their land and were trying to make a living from it. Men of astuteness as well as of learning, they sought the most scientific agricultural methods to reclaim what was unpromising territory for farming. Reverses in Venetian commerce during the fifteenth and sixteenth centuries had forced them to this way of life and they were anxious to make it pleasant and prestigious as well as remunerative.

Figure 6.22 (above) Villa Rotonda (Villa Capra). Vicenza, begun in 1550. Andrea Palladio. Statues on stairs by Lorenzo Rubini. Pediment statues added in 1606. (Phyllis Dearborn Massar.)

Figure 6.23 (below) Villa Rotonda, interior. Vicenza, begun in 1550. Andrea Palladio. Painting in two rooms by Alessandro Maganza, 1599–1606. (Phyllis Dearborn Massar.)

Palladio's villas before mid-century show an indebtedness to many a Renaissance architect and to old villas of earlier centuries. When he approached his mature years, his designing became unique, although not stereotyped. These later dwellings fall into approximately the following chronological order: Villa Capra, known as the Rotonda because of its form (Figures 6.22 and 6.23); the Villa Pisani; Villa Badoer; Villa Foscari; Villa Barbaro (Figure 6.24); and the Villa Emo. In each we can observe a clear tripartite division of the facade with its hierarchal bisymmetrical order. In each the central axis is marked with the pedimented entrance that merits its name, the *temple front*. Other villas done before 1550 are of the *stripped style* and substitute central arches for the classic pediment.

Often the central building is connected by low-lying arcaded passageways to two end structures (Figure 6.25). Palladio believed that in the working complex he was creating one should be able to move from part to part under cover. He also considered these arcades as places for the storage of farm implements; the actual facilities, however, were located behind and below the walkway and out of view. In the Villa Badoer, as in other plans, the lateral passageways stretch out their arms in

Figure 6.24   (above) Villa Barbaro. Maser, 1555–1559. Andrea Palladio. (Copyright, J. B. Vincent.)

Figure 6.25   (below) Plan of Villa Badoer. Near Rovigo, 1554–1563. Andrea Palladio. (Adapted from Palladio, *Quattro Libri II,* Dover, 1964.)

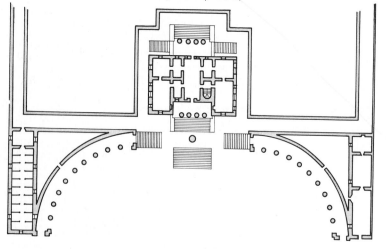

circular arcs to embrace the landscape. Thus a linear connection of building and environment became at once centripetal and open-ended.

Although Palladio's town buildings take much from Mannerist architecture in presenting syncopation of mass and void accented with columns and entablatures, his villas move toward a flat and almost barren facade. Brick is covered with stucco to make a plane of one texture and to save on expense. Marking the corners with quoins is omitted in the interest of greater merging of parts. String courses are neither usual nor emphasized. Windows are plain and frequently without classical aediculae. Attic windows are small and tucked inconspicuously close to the eaves. The Villa Rotonda (Figure 6.22), which crowns a hill and was intended as a *belvedere* or occasional entertainment house rather than a working villa, has this sort of facade treatment on all four sides so

Plate 1 Fragment of wall painting from the palace at Mari. Northern Mesopotamia (now Syria), eighteenth century B.C. Dry wall painting. Louvre, Paris. (Clichés Musées Nationaux Paris)

Plate 2 Bull from the Ishtar Gate, Babylon, ca. 570 B.C. Sculptured enameled brick. Vorderasiatisches Museum, Berlin. (Vorderasiatisches Museum, Berlin/DDR)

Plate 3   Detail of fresco from the island of Thera (Santorini), Greece, 2000–1500 B.C.
National Museum, Athens. (Hirmer Verlag München)

Plate 4   The Acropolis, Athens, seen from the northwest. Greece. Date of building of
the Parthenon, 448–432 B.C. (Hirmer Verlag München)

Plate 5 (*Opposite*)   *The Interior of the Pantheon*. Rome, A.D. 118–126. Painting by Giovanni Paolo Panini, ca. 1750. National Gallery of Art, Washington, D.C. (National Gallery, Washington, Samuel H. Kress Collection)

Plate 6   Episode from *The Odyssey*. Wall painting from a house on the Esquiline Hill, Rome, first century B.C. Vatican Museums. (Photograph by the Vatican Museums)

Plate 8   The Baron's Hall, Penshurst Place. England, 1340. (By permission of Viscount De L'Isle, V.C., K.G., from his collection at Penshurst Place, Kent, England)

Plate 10 *Head of the Prophet Jeremiah*. Stained glass, probably from a choir window of the Cathedral of Lyon, ca. 1225. 26³⁄₈ x 32¹⁄₄ in. Paris, Dépôt des Monuments historiques. From *Treasures from Medieval France*, William D. Wixom, exhibition catalog, The Cleveland Museum of Art. (Photo courtesy Cleveland Museum of Art; Raymond Laniepce, Paris, photographer)

Plate 11   Chalice of Abbot Suger of Saint-Denis. St. Denis, France, ca 1140. Sard-onyx, gold, silver-gilt, gems, and pearls. Height 7 7/32 in. The National Gallery of Art, Washington, D.C. (National Gallery, Washington, Widener Collection)

Plate 12 The central compartment from an Egyptian geometric medallion carpet. Mamluk, sixteenth century. Wool, sehna-knot. The Metropolitan Museum of Art, New York. (Metropolitan Museum, Fletcher Fund)

Plate 13 (*Left*) Lustered majolica plate. Maestro Gubbio. Signed, 1526. Italy. Depth, 10⁵/₈ in. The Cleveland Museum of Art. (Cleveland Museum of Art, Purchase from the J. H. Wade Fund)

Plate 14 (*Left*) Group of Ch'ing Dynasty overglaze porcelains. Reign of K'ang-hsi (1662-1722). China. (*a*) Jar, *apple-green* glaze; (*b*) and (*c*) two water pots, *peach-bloom* glaze; (*d*) Pilgrim bottle, Lang-yao, *oxblood* glaze. Heights, 2⁷/₈ in. to 8⁷/₈ in. The Cleveland Museum of Art. (Cleveland Museum of Art, Bequest of John L. Severance)

Plate 15 *The Triumph of Fame* goblet. Ascribed to the workshop of Angelo Barovier. Murano, Italy, ca. 1475. Height 7¹/₂ in., depth 7⁷/₈ in., including the restored foot. The Toledo Museum of Art, Toledo, Ohio. (Toledo Museum, Gift of Edward Drummond Libbey)

Plate 16 *Cour de Marbre*, Versailles. Louis Le Vau. France, ca. 1661–1670. (Clichés Musées Nationaux Paris)

Plate 17   *Galerie des glaces*, Versailles. Charles Le Brun and Jules Hardouin Mansard. France, ca. 1680. (Clichés Musées Nationaux Paris)

Plate 18   The Tryconnel Room, Belton House, Lincolnshire. England, ca. 1689. (Courtesy of the Trustees, Belton Trust Estate)

Figure 6.26 S. Giorgio Maggiore. Venice, 1565. Andrea Palladio. (Photo James S. Ackerman.)

that a quadruple view can be presented. The center is raised to a low-lying dome on drum, which makes the building itself a climax to the land on which it is placed.

Within the general patterns of Palladian architecture two town buildings present unique though relatively secondary features. In the Basilica, in order to plan for a symmetrical front over an existing Medieval building characterized by irregular disposition of openings, Palladio devised an arch order supported on paired columnettes. This became the prototype of the *Palladian window*, with a central higher arched opening and two lower flanking rectilinear ones. Likewise the municipal theater of Vicenza has become noteworthy because by using the newly learned laws of perspective Palladio created a permanent stage that presented an illusion of deep space.

Palladio's churches, like the designs for his villas, were destined to affect ecclesiastic buildings down through the centuries (Figures 6.26 and 6.27). Here he had the problem of placing a temple front on a three-divisioned interior to make clear the distinctions between main nave and side aisles. This is skillfully solved by double or triple triangulation, so well distributed that the broken pediments on the exterior seem more like an echoing rhythm than like fractionated portions of a whole.

Palladio's buildings command a centralized and frontal attention at the same time that they disperse their energies laterally. They project into space as they present recessed planes and voids. They belong to the ground as they preserve a certain aloofness of height. They are not grand and unapproachable as palaces, but they are dignified by an imposing portico. They possess that first style that can be made smaller and still preserve its dignity.

They definitely belong to the lucid world of the Renaissance aristocratic humanist but also to a new order of men where moving up the ladder is

Figure 6.27 S. Giorgio Maggiore, interior. Venice, 1565. Andrea Palladio. (Phyllis Dearborn Massar.)

possible and where wealth need not be colossal. In some way perhaps because their creator was a genius, their rational form appeals visually whether or not we are conscious of underlying ratios. Palladio's buildings, even today, become the handle that we of the twentieth century grasp most easily when looking to the past for our social sanctions.

SOME ITALIAN RENAISSANCE HOUSES

P. Medici-Riccardi (Figure 6.3)	Florence	1430 (with later additions), for Cosimo il Vecchio; architect, Michelozzo; Gozzoli frescoes
P. Pitti	Florence	1435 (with later alterations), for Lucca Pitti; possible first architect, Brunelleschi, then Ammanati for Duke Cosimo de'Medici in 1549
P. Rucellai (Figure 6.4)	Florence	1446, for Giovanni Rucellai; architect, Alberti
Ducal Palace	Urbino	1447, for Federico Montefeltro; architect, Laurana
P. Tornabuoni	Florence	1450
P. Venezia	Rome	1455, for Cardinal Pietro Barbo, Pope Paul II
P. Spinelli	Florence	1457; for Tommaso de Lionardo Spinelli
V. Medici	Fiesole	1458; architect, Michelozzo
V. Medici Poggio a Cajano (Figures 6.18 and 6.19)	Near Florence	1480, for Giovanni de'Medici; architect, Giuliano da Sangallo
P. Vendramin (Figure 6.21)	Venice	1481–1515; for Calergi; architect, Pietro Lombardo
P. Gonzaga	Mantua	Built since fourteenth century; one of the architects, Giulio Romano; Mantegna frescoes; Titian, portraits of the Emperors
P. Strozzi	Florence	1487, for Filippo Strozzi; architects, da Maiana, Cronaca
P. della Cancelleria	Rome	1495–1505, for Cardinal Riario; possession of the popes; architect, Bramante
V. Farnesina	Rome	1506, for Agostino Chigi; architects, Peruzzi, Raphael
P. dei Tribunali	Rome	ca. 1512; architect, Bramante
Vatican Palace	Rome	Begun in fifteenth century, continued in sixteenth; architect for several courts, Bramante
V. Madama	Rome	1516–1527, for Giulio de'Medici, cousin of Pope Leo X and later Pope Clement VII; architect, Raphael
P. del Te (Figure 6.20)	Mantua	1525–1535, for Federigo Gonzaga II; architect, Giulio Romano
P. Massimi	Rome	1529; architect, Peruzzi
P. Corner della Ca' Grande	Venice	1532; architect, Sansovino
P. Spada	Rome	1534, for Cardinal Capodiferro; architect, unknown, stuchi by Mazzoni
P. Farnese (Figure 6.16)	Rome	1534–1546, for Cardinal Alessandro Farnese, Pope Paul III; architects, Bramante, Antonio Sangallo, the Younger, Michelangelo
V. Pisani	Bagnola	1540–1560; architect, Palladio
P. Thiene	Vicenza	1545–1550, for Marc Antonio Thiene; architect, Palladio
V. Farnese	Caprarola	1547, for Alessandro Farnese, nephew of Pope Paul III; architect, Vignola

V. d'Este	Tivoli	1549, for Cardinal Ippolito d'Este; architect, Piero Ligorio
P. Grimani	Venice	1549; architect, San-Michele
V. di Papa Giulio	Rome	1550–1555, for Pope Julius III; architects, Vasari, Ammannati, Vignola
V. Capra or Rotonda (Figures 6.22 and 6.23)	Vicenza	1550, for Monsignor Almerico; architect, Palladio
V. Badoer (Figure 6.25)	Near Padua	1554–1563; architect, Palladio
P. Chiericati	Vicenza	1554–1557, for Girolamo Chiericati; architect, Palladio
V. Emo	Fanzolo	1550s; architect, Palladio
V. Barbaro (Figure 6.24)	Maser	1555–1559, for Fratelli Barbari, architect, Palladio
P. Uffizi	Florence	1560–1580; architect, Vasari
V. Foscari	Near Venice	1560; architect, Palladio
P. del Quirinale	Rome	1574; architect, Fontana

INTERIOR DESIGN

Space Organization

Architecture has customarily been defined as space art, meaning that its development occurs in three-dimensional space. In its production historical epochs differed in the relative importance they placed on exterior versus interior space. With the Medieval an ambivalent plateau is reached where exterior and interior space seem to merge. Unlike the Greek, where interior space is negated, and the Roman, where the interior and the exterior possess individual character without necessarily coming to terms, the Middle Ages created an aura of ambient space somewhat ill-defined in shape.

With the Renaissance interior space is not only important it also gradually becomes the vortex for architectural organization. Every successive era will have to reckon with an interrelated interior-exterior spatial form. Because this interaction will involve the disposition of interior furnishings, a discussion of its character is appropriate to any proper consideration of interior design.

Renaissance space, at first regular, bisymmetrical, relatively static, and horizontally oriented, gradually began to be organized vertically as well as horizontally, and the eye is moved toward a central focus. The means is found first in the character and placement of positive details such as windows, doors, classical pilasters, columns, and pediments and finally in proportional arrangements between the spaces themselves.

The shape of Renaissance space is generally rectangular, although circular apses, exedrae, and domes appeared with time. After the acme was reached in such High Renaissance work as St. Peter's in Rome (the area of which is almost twice that of the Gothic Milan cathedral) and the Farnese Palace (whose main hall is approximately 50 by 75 by 30 ft high), size, type for type, became smaller. S. Giorgio is only one-fourth the horizontal dimensions of the Roman apostolic church. The fortunes of the Vatican and the Farnese, however, were not those of the Venetians nor of the Foscari and the Barbaros of Vicenza. It was an added credit to the Renaissance that the churches and the dwellings of the gentry could be reduced in size in the interest of greater human significance, practicality, and cost without sacrificing an aura of distinction. The central hall at the Villa Elmo is a 27-ft cube. Compensation was, of course, made by extended and more interesting vistas.

Except in the work of architectural geniuses, the Italian Renaissance introduced little that was new in practical planning. Many churches were involved in the problem of combining the centralized plan with the elongated nave, and most private buildings were still opening room onto room around a central court.

With the late Renaissance domestic circulation improved. Palladio's villas often introduced a lateral passage that frequently terminated in a subsidiary hall or first-floor chamber. A clear passage sometimes extended through the building in both directions, thus providing an extended view and allowing for cross ventilation.

Small suites of rooms were occasionally designed. Isabella d'Este at Mantua possessed such an apartment, the famous *Paradiso,* the personal haven that she spent her married lifetime adorning with her fabulous collection of art objects, books, and musical instruments. In later years of widowhood we have her *Grotta* in which she could live divorced from the generation that had taken command after the death of her husband (Francesco Gonzaga)—one of the first recorded mother-in-law suites.

Stairs had graduated to greater importance, although they were still found off the cortile. Palladio asserts that stairs should be ample and accessible but, as we have seen, except for the grand exterior flight, he does not give them much attention and they are never allowed to intrude on the major spaces. Because in his buildings the connections between stories are service stairs, they need not be imposing. The Renaissance magnified only those stairs that belonged to the nobility—for example, the *Scala d'Oro* in the Venetian Ducal Palace or the stairs in the vestibule of the Laurentian Library on which a railing separated the social castes, as we shall see later in Bernini's *Scala Regia* in the Vatican. Occasionally oval flights occur, as in the Villa Caprarola and the Palazzo Quirinale.

Architectural Detail

Such architectural detail as windows and doors rightfully belong to the exterior and interior, a fact that once again emphasizes the futility of separation. We note, however, that the Renaissance architect did make some distinction between the two in the matter of architectural trim.

Windows in Renaissance buildings show a progression from the Gothic *bifora* of many Florentine palaces to the larger cross-mullioned Guelph window (Guelph refers to the papal party as opposed to the Ghibelines, the party favoring the Holy Roman Emperors, which was vested in the German house of Hohenstaufen). During the fifteenth century the Renaissance round-arched window became popular in Rome. It, in turn, was superseded during the early sixteenth century by the rectangular window that often had pedimented aediculae. Here we see our first differentiation between exterior and interior. The aedicule with a pediment is rarely seen on the interior of residential structures, although it may be found as important framing in religious ones. (Recall that it was first used in Christian symbolism, in which it is known as a tabernacle for enclosing religious art.) Interior trim, as in all countries when the Renaissance intruded, advanced slowly in a progression from simple stone or plaster to the use of architectural dressing which incorporated moldings, pilasters, and entablatures. Michelangelo, who used scrolls, architraves, and flat projections on the windows of the Laurentian Library, was somewhat of an innovator in this respect.

It is interesting as well that in the tallest of rooms, a small square or oval window might be used as an extension of the major opening. This in time is seen as the only window in the second story, placed inconspicuously high under the eaves, thus minimizing the cleavage of a building into two horizontal parts. Palladio engineered what he called a thermal window, a large one with southern exposure, placed to regulate the heat flow into the building, perhaps our first solar opening.

Needless to say, the window panes, for which the glass was made in northern Italy, were not large and were joined by leaded *calms* or frames. Paneled interior as well as exterior shutters on the first-floor windows and exterior grilles in the ground story existed until late in the Renaissance. In the Villa Farnese at Caprarola the use of blue canvas awnings on the exterior of the loggia overlooking the garden is documented. There seems to be no evidence of interior curtains, and with thick wall and deep reveals they would have been superfluous. One must remember, too, that large light sources provide relatively glareless light. Small windows, even within the larger, might be casement. These characteristics can be seen in the painting by the Venetian Vittore Carpaccio (ca. 1450 to ca. 1522), *The Dream of Saint Ursula* (Figure 6.28).

In speaking of doors we shall have to exclude

Figure 6.28 *The Dream of Saint Ursula*. Vittore Carpaccio (1486–1525). Galleria Dell'Accademia, Venice. (Osvaldo Böhm.)

the supreme examples of bronze castings such as those on the Florentine baptistry done by Lorenzo Ghiberti (1381–1455). Most doors were paneled and given architectural treatment on the exterior similar to that of windows. At times, the actual doors were handsomely carved. They were embellished on the interior sooner than the exterior with an architectural enframement like the marble surround of the doors in the *Sala dei Gigli* (lilies) in the Palazzo Vecchio (carved by the da Maianos, Benedetto, 1442–1497, and Giuliano, 1432–1490), and the cedar doors of the *Sala del Collegio* in

the Ducal Palace at Venice by da Ponte (Jacopo Bassano, 1510–1592).

Fireplaces, like other openings, conformed to the large scale of rooms, often with an aperture 8 ft high embellished by the use of classical ornament. Frequently they were surmounted by a flat entablature and receded to the wall as a hooded chimney piece. One of the loveliest is in the Room of the Angels (*Sala degli Angeli*) at the Urbino palace (Figure 6.29) with its sculpture by Domenico Rosselli, who likewise carved the room's stone door frames. The intarsia in the doors was designed by Sandro Botticelli (1444–1510).

Niches as architectural wall embellishment

245

Figure 6.29   Fireplace of the Sala degli Angeli, Palazzo Ducale, Urbino. (Alinari/Editorial Photocolor Archives.)

which reappeared with the late Italian Renaissance echoed those in the classical Pantheon in Rome. Their aesthetic purpose was undoubtedly to provide sculptural relief for the flat walls between the massive piers that support vaults and domes. They finally became decoration that created counter rhythms of their own, as seen, for instance, on the exterior of the Palazzo Spada in Rome. They were usually framed with aediculae that became more purely ornamental than classical in inspiration as time went on. They might also incorporate over-scaled statuary (more frequently found in loggias, as in the Palazzo del Te) or be used as receptacles for patterns of inlaid marble (Villa Madama) or for frescoes (Villa Imperiale, Pesaro).

Interior Surface Treatment

In addition to these architectural details of Renaissance buildings—windows, doors, fireplace, and niches—we note an ever-increasing tendency to enrich interior surfaces with permanent surface decoration rather than with movable hangings.

Parqueted stone remains the usual finish for important floors whenever the structural underpinning would support its weight. This often formed the most elaborate mosaic patterning and sometimes it was a simpler dark/light checkerboarding. Upper floors were wide-planked wood and, if paintings are to be trusted, left bare. In Venice the use of terrazzo made from marble chips, as in the *Sala del Collegio* in the Ducal Palace, was common. It was highly recommended by Palladio.

Ceilings, even in domestic buildings, were no longer exclusively flat, beamed, or coffered, for many were vaulted or coved. In all cases, as wealth permitted, they were likely to bear decoration—carving at articulation joints, painting and gilding on structural members, and plaster and fresco on coves and vaults as well as on walls.

Wood wainscoting was scarcely necessary for comfort in Italy and, when it did appear during the Renaissance it had advanced to the stylistic stage in which the panels were large and architecturally conceived, as in the Doge's Palace in Venice. Often these panels were decorated with intarsia (i.e., mosaic woodwork).

As the Renaissance developed the orders become usual to important interiors. Intervening spaces are filled with frescoes by some of the world's most famous painters, a prime reason for visiting Italy. It is thought that much Renaissance painting was true fresco in the sense that discreet sections of the wall were maintained as wet plaster. However, the fresco mixture probably contained some agglutinate, possibly a saponified oil, to make it cohere to the surface. When finished, ironing with a hot instrument provided a smoother and less chalky surface.[5]

Looking into the Palazzo Medici-Riccardi and into the private chapel on the first floor, we see one of the most charming story-telling frescoes. It was painted in 1459 by Benozzo Gozzoli (1420–1497) and its topic is *The Journey of the Magi* (Figure 6.30). Gozzoli drew on his youthful recollections of the brilliant pageantry that accompanied the religious Council of Ferrara-Florence, held in the latter city in 1438–1445. Two of the eastern potentates attending this august body were prototypes of two of the magi in the fresco. The third was Lorenzo, grandson of Cosimo. Various other members of the family are seen in the retinue. Many of the costumes, such as the floppy turban worn by the riders in the middle distance, were those introduced to fashion by the eastern visitors.

Note how this painting looks back to Medievalism and forward to the Renaissance. As the procession, mounted on its gold-caparisoned steeds, winds over the flower-studded path with eerie lights and dark hill forests as a backdrop, one is not far removed from the Middle Ages and the fairyland side of the Early Renaissance. On the other hand, the angels on either side of the altar are flesh and blood, three-dimensional images far removed from the flat-patterned icons of earlier years.

At a slightly later time (1474), in the Ducal Palace at Mantua, Andrea Mantegna (1431–1506) finished murals on the walls in one of the tower rooms (the *Camera degli sposi* or bridal chamber) with scenes of importance to the reigning Gonzagas (Figure 6.31). We see episodes concerned with the arrival of a papal messenger who announced the election of Francesco Gonzaga to the College of Cardinals. This position was equivalent to social elevation for any Italian family,

Figure 6.30 *The Journey of the Magi,* detail. Benozzo Gozzoli. Palazzo Medici-Riccardi, Florence, 1459. Fresco. (Alinari/Editorial Photocolor Archives.)

especially one that had won its place by military prowess.

This fresco is a distinct advance in style over that of Gozzoli. The piece is compartmentalized by simulated architecture, and the principal action occurs on a horizontal beam that corresponds to a dado. All is against a backdrop of the rolling hills of Lombardy—but not of the plains around Mantua. Despite its theatrical scenery, the composition is more classical than the Medici murals. The simulated architecture, the figures with their organized confrontations and statuesque character, speak of classical balance, poise, and reason. The narrative fulfills the advice that Alberti gave

to painters to idealize their subjects as complete "happenings" (i.e., *istoria*) that involve a small number of persons, in which the action is clear, possibly pointed out by a narrator who stands on the sideline and describes the important scenes. The whole must possess classic formality. In conforming to these injunctions, the Gonzaga frescoes illustrate High Renaissance dictates. Raphael da Sanzi (1483–1520) in his "School of Athens" fresco at the Vatican, which symbolizes the history of human knowledge and wisdom, provides a more monumental example of this mural art.

The late Renaissance as it verges on Mannerism can best be known through Michelangelo Buonarroti's (1475–1564) ceiling in the Sistine Chapel (Figure 6.32). What subject could have greater enormity than that of the creation of man? In his

Figure 6.31 Episode in the history of the Gonzaga family. Fresco by Andrea Mantegna. Ducal Palace at Mantua, Camera degli sposi, 1474. (Alinari/Editorial Photocolor Archives.)

idealization of the human form Michelangelo shows himself the true child of the Renaissance and of the neoplatonism that worshiped beauty personified. Michelangelo was a devoutly religious man, and, in his first work at the Sistine (1508–1512), done when he was only thirty-three, he paints an omnipotent and compassionate God. Note that on the ceiling Adam is stretching his finger horizontally to his creator.

In handling the material on the ceiling, Michelangelo created an architectural framework that does not contradict the actual vaulting but gives it added clarity and significance and provides for a completely new, complex, and coordinated unity. The light that shines on these scenes is now clear, the forms are modeled in full round, the arrangements are both compartmental, yet

Figure 6.32 (right) Sistine Chapel, interior. The Vatican, Rome. Ceiling (1508–1512) and *The Last Judgment* (on the altar wall, 1534–1541) painted by Michelangelo. (The Vatican Museums)

extended beyond their boundaries. Above all, the figures move and exist in the world of dynamic human forces, the vitality of God's creation in an earthly world of problems. Classicism as a dead and calm conception is bowing out to a vigor that uses it with the originality of a genius of a new era. Here are the strongest moral sermons ever preached portrayed by realistic human figures and clamped into man-made architecture—the zenith of humanism.

The period in which Mannerist art flourished—the last three quarters of the sixteenth century—was marked by the antiphonal voices of a severe counterreformation on one side and a worldly aristocratic existence on the other. Much of Mannerist interior fresco painting falls within the latter category. In this respect its artists attempted to portray a sensuous happy existence, to titillate the craving for the new, and to serve both factors by using classical mythology to veil the ambitions and desires of wealthy clients.

Figure 6.33 (right) Fresco on wall of Villa Barbaro at Maser, 1528–1588. (Alinari/Editorial Photocolor Archives.)

First a look at those Xanaduish retreats, the Italian villas. The Villa Farnesina (across the Tiber from the Palazzo Farnese) illustrates several phases of the movement. No less a hand than Raphael was the director and principal painter, although Baldassare Peruzzi (1481–1536) painted the first-floor salon. Raphael in his mural, which pictures the voyage of the sea nymph Galatea, exhibited a new and moving sequence of counterthrusts that broke narrowly conceived compartments and thus was truly prophetic of styles of the future.

Peruzzi has vaunted his knowledge of perspective to enormous success in painting *trompe l'oeil* to give us a convincing scene between large rounded pillars of contemporary Rome and Janiculum Hill. This use of what might be termed faking was prevalent during the latter Renaissance, and one purpose in the conceit was to merge the indoors with the out, a kind of transitional indoor-outdoor device.

Trompe l'oeil has had a long history in wall decoration, and Paolo Cagliari, known as Veronese (1528–1588), is possibly king of the craft; his work in the Villa Barbaro is a paradigm not only for the type but for its use within the Mannerist tradition (Figure 6.33). Here we find an illusion of reality that is convincing enough to tempt one to open a painted door or to climb a frescoed stair. Complete architectural settings, with statues in niches and stucco enrichment, are simulated. For this sort of production it was usual to employ two designers. The painter of the background was the *quadraturista* or *architetturista*. He was a more highly esteemed and remunerated person (because of his knowledge of canons and the orders and of perspective) than the *figurista,* who was concerned only with the figures. Veronese's brother, Benedetto, may have been the *quadraturista* at Villa Barbaro.

Whereas the murals of Veronese simulated reality with paint, the private cabinet of Duke Federico at Urbino earlier created illusion by intarsia. It appears in a small room lined with cupboards and shelves, some open and some closed. Everything is casual, as though the Duke had just departed, leaving his massive folios and metronomic instruments exposed. In reality there is only one functioning cabinet. The overall de-

Figure 6.34 The study of Duke Federico de Monte-feltro of Urbino at Gubbio. Designer: Francesco di Giorgio of Siena (1439–1502). Probable maker: Baccio Pontelli of Florence (ca. 1450–1492). Fifteenth century. Intarsia. Metropolitan Museum of Art, New York. (The Metropolitan Museum of Art, Roger Fund, 1939.)

sign is credited to Sandro Botticelli (1444–1510), although Francesco di Giorgio (1439–1502) was the *architetturista*. A similar small study from the Duke's apartments at Gubbio can be seen at the Metropolitan Museum of Art (Figure 6.34).

Palladio prescribed white for the interiors of his villas, although many of his patrons augmented this background with colorful frescoes, no doubt considered as status symbols. Most Renaissance writers, following Vitruvius, had specified white for church interiors because of its symbolism of

purity. Other intuitive reasons may have played a part. It must have seemed pleasant to clear away the dusky interiors of the Middle Ages and to introduce the brightness of light colors. Moreover, when white was used on bare walls against the geometry of architectural props, as in the Pazzi Chapel (Florence, by Brunelleschi), *Sant' Eligio degli Orifici* (Rome, by Raphael), and San Giorgio Maggiore (Venice, by Palladio), late Medieval texture is traded for sharp, clear architectural form. Many Renaissance buildings, even when ceilings are elaborately painted, preserve white walls for statues, *stucchi* (i.e., stucco work), and tapestries. Venice with Palladio and Veronese is unique in uniting the two worlds of architect and muralist to form a delightful ambience of shelter, *plein air*, and color.

251

Figure 6.35 Gallery in the Palazzo Farnese: ceiling painted by Annibale Carracci with scenes from Ovid's *Metamorphoses*. Rome, 1597–1604. Fresco. (Alinari/ Editorial Photocolor Archives.)

From 1597 to 1609, Cardinal Odoardo Farnese commissioned Annibale Carracci (1560–1609) from Bologna to paint the series of frescoes that covers the ceiling of the Gallery in the Farnese palace (Figure 6.35). The large room was to be decorated with mythological scenes from Ovid's *Metamorphoses*. Although the concept was that of an all-conquering power of love ennobled by reference to the gods of antiquity with spiritual rather than carnal connotations, nevertheless Annibale and his older brother Agostino (1557–1602) presented the scenes with such narrative drama that they might readily be enjoyed for their sensuous character. His enticing palette bor-

rowed much from Venetian coloration. When the tale is of the pagan gods there is plenty of room for eroticism. Profane, voluptuous treatment is characteristic of the manner of the Late Renaissance muralists. In the wake of the Counter Reformation and its cruel treatment of heresy the mundane princes of the time seemed to prefer amoral scenes on their palace walls.

Stylistically, the work of the Carracci is typical of *fin-de-siècle* form. Because the hall had a coved, vaulted ceiling, Annibale compartmentalized his scenes and surrounded them with *trompe l'oeil* frames to give the illusion that they were easel pictures—a technique known as *quadri riportati*. He foreshortened the enclosed image, however, to make it appear to be viewed naturally from below. The vault corners were filled with illusionistic statues of giants and youths who supported a heavy cornice done in the same manner. The Carracci organized the individual scenes along classical formal lines, controlled from the center and using color as chiaroscuro (i.e., natural shading) to emphasize form.

Thus it can be seen that these fashionable painters of the turn of the century were of their own era in their handling of subject matter, somewhat retrogressive in their tight classical form, and of the future in their illusionism. The world of the late Renaissance Mannerists was above all else an eclectic rather than a highly original one. It was in a sense an imbalanced culture that had been defied by rationalism, Protestantism, and the armies of the north and would wait until the next century before making a successful reassertion.

Furnishings and Their Arrangement

As we walk into Renaissance buildings and study their movable contents, we realize that in those years interior design was not an isolated art. Interiors and their belongings were of a piece. Articles were few, functional, and precious. Arrangement conformed to room shapes but was not conspicuously bisymmetrical.

FURNITURE

Renaissance furniture is grand; it is aristocratic without ostentation. This expression is created by scale, by the proper balance between flamboyance and austerity of form, and by consummate skill used in fabricating beautiful ingredients.

Materials

Italian furniture of the quattrocento and cinquecento added little to the media of the late Middle Ages—walnut was still the important wood, mortise and tenon still the usual construction. Embellishment by carving was centered in Lombardy and Venice, where it came under the master hand of Formagini of Bologna. Florence and Rome became prominent in this art in later years. *Intarsia* remained in fashion, often in the nature of *certosina*. *Pastiglia* was also continued.

Figure 6.36 *Cassone.* Venice, sixteenth century. Walnut. Height, 68.5 cm. Cleveland Museum of Art. (The Cleveland Museum of Art, The Coralie Walker Hanna Memorial Collection.)

Types

Types built on the late Medieval stock of necessities proliferated. In northern Italy the chest (*cassone*) developed a molded body ornamented with carved geometrics, frequently in the form of strapwork (Figure 6.36). In the next stage it was elevated on short feet, often of animal shape, and the panels were embellished with some Renaissance motif such as the *guilloche* or the *arcade*. With typical Tuscan restraint this carving was refined and formalized. Early Roman design reflects this northern influence.

During the late Florentine Renaissance Duke Cosimo I imported many Flemish craftsmen for his tapestry factory. From this time Flemish ornament appears on northern Italian furniture. We see vigorous turning, pendant drops, and raised pilasters. The chaste character of the carving was diminished.

High and Late Renaissance Roman chests show bolder modeling in their decoration (Figure 6.37). Some Roman cassone resemble antique sarcophagi with carved sides and top and heavy lion feet. In a class-conscious society they display the family's coat of arms. Figures from classical mythology, free-standing caryatids (supports in human form), and *grottesques* are frequent.

Cabinets with doors (the *credenza*) and with drawers appear (Figure 6.38). In Genoa, in northwest Italy, a high cupboard in two parts evolved.

Figure 6.37 (above) *Cassone*. Italy, ca. 1560–1570. Walnut with partial gilding. Length, 167.5 cm, width, 57 cm, height, 65 cm. Nelson Gallery of Art, Kansas City. (William Rockhill Nelson Gallery of Art, Kansas City, Missouri, Nelson Fund.)

Figure 6.38 (below) *Credenza*. Brescia, mid-sixteenth century. Walnut. Height, 127.6 cm. Cleveland Museum of Art. (The Cleveland Museum of Art, The Coralie Walker Hanna Memorial Collection.)

Each part had two doors and one of the halves contained drawers. With the spread of learning the writing cabinet loomed important. In Spain, hence in Spanish-held Italy, a particular form of high desk on a stand which had spiral-turned legs (undoubtedly an Indian import) is known as a *vargueno*. Their interiors, as well as those of many cabinets, were elaborately inlaid and gilded.

The long *table* was elaborated (Figure 6.39). End supports with pillars were added and the horizontal stretcher carried an arched balustrade. The central pedestal table, for use in smaller rooms, entered the picture. One that dates from the second half of the sixteenth century stands on lion's feet, its base a voluminous vase flanked by three S scrolls quite separate from the pedestal. Its top uses one immense walnut plank. Wall tables and various smaller framed pieces were made.

Although the Medieval platform *bed* remained, the pillared substitute that carried a classical entablature became common. One is seen in *The Dream of Saint Ursula* by Vittore Carpaccio (Figure 6.28). Venetian documents describe the canopied bed as being "in the French fashion."

The *sgabello* or narrow stool chair remained the common seat (Figure 6.40). Chairs of the order of the *sedia* were infrequently used before the fifteen hundreds. This variety had a tall, straight back and arms that progressed to a shapely curve with vigorously molded hand grips. Finials ending in elongated leaves projected above the back. Sled runners extended in front. The *sedia* (Figure 6.41) was frequently upholstered in leather or cloth, sometimes ornamented with a fringe.

The folding chair was more usual to the sixteenth century. It could be transported easily and might be taken outdoors on a hot evening. The Dante form is the simpler (Figure 6.42), whereas

Figure 6.39 Table known as the Farnese. Giacomo Barozzi da Vignola. Italy, ca. 1565–1537. Marble. Height 11.3 m, length, 3.8 m, width, 1.69 m. Metropolitan Museum of Art, New York. (The Metropolitan Museum of Art, Harris Brisbane Dick Fund, 1958.)

Figure 6.40 (left) *Sgabello*. From the Palazzo Strozzi, Florence, ca. 1490. Walnut, carved and inlaid. Metropolitan Museum of Art, New York. (The Metropolitan Museum of Art, Fletcher Fund, 1930.)

Figure 6.41 (right) Italian arm-chair (*sedia*). From the Borghese Palace, Rome, sixteenth century. Walnut with leather upholstery. Metropolitan Museum of Art, New York. (The Metropolitan Museum of Art, Gift of Miss Annie May Hegeman ,1932.)

255

Figure 6.42 Folding chair (Dante chair). Lombardy, sixteenth century. Walnut with certosina inlay. Metropolitan Museum of Art, New York. (The Metropolitan Museum of Art, Fletcher Fund, 1945.)

Figure 6.43 Folding chair (Savonarola chair). Lombardy, ca 1500. Walnut with inlaid certosina work of ivory and metal. Metropolitan Museum of Art, New York. (The Metropolitan Museum of Art, Gift of William H. Riggs, 1913.)

the Savonarola had multiple spokes attached to armpieces and runners (Figure 6.43). Loose cushions were provided.

The *cassapanca* (Figure 6.44) or long chest with arms, back, and lid in the seat, preserved from earlier centuries, took on embellishment suited to the Renaissance.

ADDENDA

Easel Pictures in Frames

With the exploitation (or discovery?) of oil technique by painters of the Lowlands, such as the Flemish *Master of Flemalle* and the Dutch Van Eycks (Hubert, 1370–1426, and Jan, ca. 1390–1441), paintings were less perishable and popular demand produced pictures detached from the wall. Understandably, portraits became fashionable, and to this we owe some of the most in-

gratiating works of the Renaissance—handsome scions of noble families, regal women adorned with the family jewels (Figure 6.45), revealing likenesses of the ecclesiastic potentates and sober, austere puritanical men of the Counter Reformation establishment. It would be far better to sit to a camera than to expose oneself to the merciless and incisive brush of the Renaissance masters.

Moreover, the invention of printing facilitated the production of graphic copies. It is difficult for us to assess what an important happening this was. Hence visual images could belong to the many rather than the few.

Easel pictures were done by graphic processes and began to be as popular as painting and drawing. The oldest form of impression, the woodblock, had been used during the Middle Ages for patterning cloth. Relief cutting of graphics on metal—at first on copper, later on steel—began in

Figure 6.44 (above) Bench (*cassa panca*). Florence, mid-sixteenth century. Carved walnut. Metropolitan Museum of Art, New York. (The Metropolitan Museum of Art, Rogers Fund, 1912.)

Figure 6.45 (below) *Portrait of a Young Lady*. Agnolo Bronzino (1503–1572). Original frame. Italy. Height, 60 cm, width, 48 cm. Cleveland Museum of Art. (The Cleveland Museum of Art, Leonard C. Hanna, Jr., Bequest.)

the 1400s. One form, engraving, is done with a burin and punch to cut away areas, first so that the incised patterns held the ink (i.e., *intaglio*) and later moving to *relief,* where the remaining line made the pattern. Engraving was especially popular during the seventeenth century, and the Italian school, represented by the early work of Marcantonio Raimondi (1488–1527), illustrates the preference felt by southern artists for volumetric design.

Etchings are made by a corrosion process in which a plate is blackened and the design is traced; it is then cut with acid. Etched lines, which can be made with little muscular effort, tend to represent the individual calligraphic style of the artist most sensitively. Although etchings on copper were made during the Renaissance, their popularity is of later date and reached one of its peaks during the eighteenth century.

The various printing processes include the still-later drypoint (instrument pulled toward the worker, thus creating a soft, velvety black burred edge) and nineteenth-century developments (e.g., lithograph). Several may be included in one print. If tones are desired, the respective counterparts for the engraving and etching are the mezzotint and the aquatint. Color was added with a hand-done wash or by superimposing several plates.

Small pictures required frames. Renaissance frames follow classical formal traditions of which there are several stylistic varieties. The earlier models consisted of a flat panel bordered by moldings. Then the tabernacle type, which derived its name from the tabernacle motif used in much early Christian art. The *tondo,* a round frame frequently embellished with high-relief carving, was occasionally given added gesso treatment with a final coating of gold leaf. These frames were usually commissioned at the same time as the painting. Thus the two were mated from the start. In themselves the frames added a decorative accent to the dimmer recesses of church and palace.

Where were these pictures hung? Most are now found in galleries, even local ones like the Pitti Palace in Florence where they are arranged to cover the walls, which are painted plaster or stretched silk. This, of course, often places them in awkward positions for viewing, especially when dadoes are high. By analogy with interiors in paintings from the Lowlands, where rooms have high wooden paneling, pictures were hung directly on it as well as on the bare plaster above. Illustrations of interiors of the Italian Renaissance are few and the individually framed picture is not indicated.

Musical Instruments

With the advent of the Renaissance the old Medieval instruments, such as the psaltery and the fiddle, were discarded or altered in favor of those that could better render the new polyphony—the organ, other keyboard instruments, and the lute. The first two of these classes were large enough to occupy a permanent position in any interior.

The lute, a graceful contrivance with pear-shaped contours and dulcet tones made by plucking the strings, was the instrument of the Renaissance. Introduced into Spain by the Moors, its most perfect embodiment was provided by the German and Italian *luthiers* of the fifteenth and sixteenth centuries. A *luthier* was a maker of stringed instruments.

The three principal viols (successor to the fiddle), namely the treble, tenor, and bass, were kept in a chest made to house them. This cabinet then became an added piece of interior furniture. The oldest true violins date from the late sixteenth century.

Keyboard instruments, a development from the orient, were known in the Middle Ages but became increasingly popular in the Renaissance. The *clavichord* is a percussion device; the *harpsichord* is one in which the strings are plucked with quills. The clavichord and the organ became prominent during the later Renaissance and the Baroque. The *virginal* and the subsequent *spinet* are also plucked instruments. In the virginal the strings are parallel to the keyboard; in the spinet, at right angles. The virginal, so popular in Renaissance England, was designed to be placed on the table or lap.

In Veronese's painting of *The Marriage at Cana,* now at the Louvre, you will see his representation of the Venetian painter Titian (1487–1576) playing a bass, Tintoretto (1518–1594) with the viola, Jacob Bassano (1510–1592) with the flute, and Veronese himself with a violincello. What a happy conceit for a first-century marriage feast.

TEXTILES

General Development

Textiles were possibly the most important exports of the Italian Renaissance. The weaving centers at Genoa, Milan, Ferrara, Bologna, and especially Florence and Venice, supplanted Lucca and earlier Palermo. During the fifteenth century Italian craftsmen began to emigrate to France, to Lyon and Tours, to Flanders, and to Switzerland. By the sixteenth century silk weaving was well established north of the Alps but was not yet sufficiently developed to compete commercially with the south.

The chief competition experienced by Italian industry during the Renaissance came from the looms of Turkey in such cities as Brusa. It was the merchants of Venice who profited by trading eastern wares to the north European potentates. Following the Battle of Lepanto (1571), when the

Figure 6.46 Velvet. Ogival pattern. Italy, sixteenth century. Silk and metal thread. Length, 40.5 cm, width, 25.5 cm. Metropolitan Museum of Art, New York. (The Metropolitan Museum of Art, Rogers Fund, 1909.)

Venetians failed to follow up their initial victory, the glory of the queen city of the Adriatic faded, never again to dominate the Mediterranean.

The finest of Renaissance silks were pile weave velvets frequently woven on a satin ground. The complicated diasper weave which controlled double warps and wefts was used for elaborate brocatelles. Multicolored designs, brocading with gold wire wound around a silk core, piles of different heights and cut and uncut piles in the same cloth —all of these elaborations endowed the fabrics with a three-dimensional character as well as design potential.

Patterns that were larger and more formalized showed compactness and bisymmetry. The enclosing motif was an ogival, derived ultimately from Islamic textiles (Figure 6.46). One type of contained ornament—often called the Italian artichoke or pomegranate and possibly a derivation from the pine cone—frequently formed the network for an intricate pattern enclosed in an ogival framework. These subsidiary forms passed through several stages of development from the fifteenth to the seventeenth centuries. At first merely sprouting from an ogival grid, they later dominated the enclosure and may be said to have metamorphosed into a vase and floral shape which confines itself to the ogival—the *jardinière* velvets so popular during the sixteenth century. Again a fruit or flower may swing from a broad, wavy, decorative band.

Certain *ciselé* or cut velvets resembled iron grilles in pattern and in linear character. These have been called *ferroneries* (Figure 6.47) and were a particular product of Venice. Genoa, with its *velours de Gênes*, featured many smaller patterns on an undulating base. The Turkish looms produced new floral forms, especially the indigenous carnation and tulip, frequently done in bright colors on a white satin ground. The Turkish

Figure 6.47 Brocaded velvet. Venice, second half of the fifteenth century. Cleveland Museum of Art. (The Cleveland Museum of Art, Purchase from the J. H. Wade Fund.)

Figure 6.48 Chinese tapestry. Section of a screen panel. Ming Dynasty, 1368–1644. Silk and gold. Cleveland Museum of Art. (The Cleveland Museum of Art, Gift of Mr. & Mrs. J. H. Wade.)

floral generally appears in an ogival frame, which was smaller and more precise than its Italian counterpart.

Oriental and Persian Textiles at the Time of the Renaissance

Foreign influence in art occurs whenever men or goods travel and when the quality of foreign

artifacts is intriguing. The Chinese Ming dynasty (1368–1644) successfully pursued a policy of opening southern sea routes to trade and of tempting the West with beautiful silks as one of their commodities. Few masterpieces from this era are intact, however. Those that remain indicate an advanced mastery of complex design and of outstanding workmanship. The Cleveland Museum of Art shows a silk and gold tapestry (Chinese *k'o-ssu* weave) of unusual expertise (Figure 6.48). Silk tapestry fabrics with an equalization of warp and weft thread sizes cannot be judged by precisely the same standards as the western tapestries in which contrasts in texture between warp and weft play an important role. Within their métier, that of painting with silk, the Ming tapestry represents excellence. Here is shown the greatest freedom of patterning with curved line development, enlivened and enriched by combinations of abstractions and stylized renditions of rocks, flowers, and birds underneath a canopy of clouds. Done in vivid hues, there is design competence in gradations of size and color intricately interwoven like a symphonic poem.

The Persians under the Safavids (1492–1736), the first national dynasty in several centuries, maintained a court of great magnificence. It was in the day of the famous Shah Abbas (1587–1628) that the weavers produced the finest silk velvets and other complex fabrics. Abbas' grandfather, Shah Tahmasp I (1524–1576), had sent an expedition to China to seek a cooperative transfer of instruction and inspiration. From this source and at the time of the Mongol invasion of Timur (1369–1405) were introduced such eastern motifs, as the phoenix, to which the Persians added many of their own—the mounted hunter, the animals, and the hyacinth, iris, and tulip.

Quite apart from their use of this enlarged vocabulary, the Persians developed what might be called the *theme with variations* organization of textile design (Figure 6.49). It was not new to them and can be found also in the Chinese tapestry just described. The Persians, however, formalized the concept and thus made it at once clearer and more complex. There was often organization against a contrasting background, frequently the Mongol-inspired row designs against blank space. On this is woven the tale of variation. The patterns may be stepped up diagonally, reversed, or overlapped. But, above all, in a color advance seldom equaled in textile design except in the tapestries of Peru, the Persian weaver imposed different color sequences on the same basic pattern. This sort of development of one design component (e.g., shape) in terms of another (e.g., color) the West never really learned until the twentieth century.

Italian Tapestries

To speak of Italian tapestries before those of France and the Netherlands is certainly putting the caboose at the wrong end of the train. However, the former did play a role in the development of the latter, which is justification enough.

Tapestries, it will be recalled, rose to high excellence in northern Europe during the late Middle Ages. This was largely because the northern designers understood how to exploit the textural advantages of the weave to create pictorial wall hangings in which pictures and cloth supported one another.

During the Renaissance the Estes of Ferrara (1436–1559), the Gonzagas of Mantua (1419–   ) and the Medici of Florence (1547–1737) founded tapestry factories, seeing in these hangings another means of decorating the large plaster-covered walls of their palaces and a source of aggrandizement of their noble families. They commandeered the services of the best Renaissance painters to make their designs: Cosimo Tura as well as Dosso and Battista Dossi, court artists of Ferrara, Andrea Mantegna of Mantua, and Francesco Salviati and Vicenzo de' Rossi for the Medici. Even Leonardo da Vinci painted for tapestry. Bronzini, Titian, and Veronese followed during the High Renaissance. The most famous of the teams of designers was that of Raphael and his sometime assistant Giulio Romano (see Figure 7.15); because their work was done in Brussels it is considered in the Franco-Flemish section. It serves to introduce the odd paradox with which tapestry weaving at this time found itself confronted.

Because of the preference of the Italians for painting, tapestries had not found equivalent favor as wall decoration. When the tapestry factories were opened in the fifteenth century, Italian painting had left the world of Gothic flat pattern-

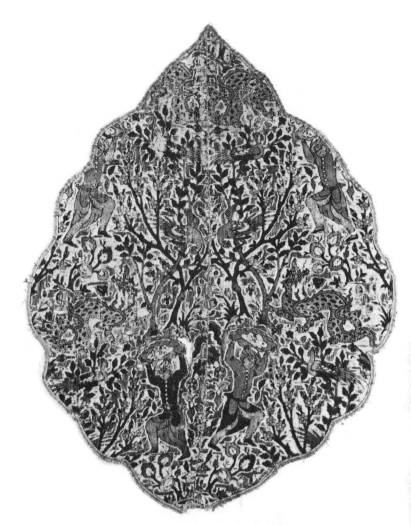

Figure 6.49 Velvet-weave panel. Iran. Shah Tahmasp period, 1524–1576. Silk originally covered with strips of silver gilt. Designs of Alexander the Great (Iskander). Cleveland Museum of Art. (The Cleveland Museum of Art, Purchase from the J. H. Wade Fund.)

ing for that of modeling in deep space. Steeped in this Renaissance idiom, those artists who began to design tapestries borrowed from the painterly style. Not adept at the technique of converting tempera paintings into working cartoons, the Italians had to import Flemish weavers to render the Italian paintings workable or to send Italian designs north for weaving. Neither process was entirely satisfactory. It was this dichotomy of skills, however, that eventually introduced the realistic picture rather than the Gothic flat-stylized idiom so suited to tapestry texture as the norm for Renaissance tapestry design.

261

Carpets

The carpets that graced honored places in late Medieval and Renaissance Europe were imports from Turkey to Venice known as Turkey carpets. Actually they were for the most part products of Turkish looms. They were comparatively small, hand-knotted, tufted fabrics of the types often called Holbein, Lotto, or Bordone, designs associated with the paintings of these artists who used them somewhat as props, displayed them as table coverings, and occasionally as hangings. Characterized by geometric arabesques or medallions in vivid tones of green, blue, red, and gold, and by a thick coarse pile, they provided just the accents needed. They were important because they fostered a desire on the part of those who saw them for wool-pile floor coverings.

Although the first European imports were commercial commodities, the royal looms of Persia, Egypt, and Turkey were at that time weaving magnificent palace carpets for private royal consumption. These fabulous pieces were scarcely known in Europe until later centuries, when some were presented as gifts to western courts. Their story must be told if only because of their influence on French production of the seventeenth century and later imports from the Near East to Europe.

Egypt had produced hand-knotted rugs since the time of the Fatimid Dynasty (968–1171), when the country on the Nile had developed into a brilliant center of Islamic culture. From small beginnings the craft was enlarged in the ateliers of Cairo under successive dynasties. Under the Mamluk rulers (1252–1517) rugs of mosaic-pavement design (Plate 12) combined colored threads into patterns that are masterpieces in the juxtaposition of color to produce changeable effects.

In 1514 the Ottoman Turk, Selim the Grim, conquered the Persian capital of Tabriz and took large numbers of weavers back to Constantinople (specifically to Brusa) to produce oriental carpets to his order. He then proceeded to subject the Mamluk rulers of Egypt and usurped their industries. The years bracketing the European Renaissance were those of the finest rug production across the Bosphorus and Dardanelles, but their factories looked back to Persia for the artistic vision and craftsman's skill that were exemplified.

The story of Persian rugs can now be traced to the Achaemenid Persian Empire (600–330 B.C.) in the design of the Pazyryk carpet, a small rug found in 1947 in a nomad chieftain's grave in northern Siberia (see Figure 2.27). To the native dynasty of the Safavids (1502–1736) we credit our first treasures. The most famed ruler of this house was Shah Abbas (1558–1629), although in respect to rug manufacture we must also acknowledge his grandfather Shah Tahmasp.

The most significant Persian designs in carpets feature multiple borders, which may have derived from the ancient fire-altar symbolism. These borders enclose central medallions that probably came from the cross symbol of the fire altar of Zoroaster.

The oldest medallion carpets are clearly defined and angular; later ones have softened contours in the manner of Persian rugs in general. They progress from one large central motif to the inclusion of several subsidiary ones. On this meager framework stylized flowers and animals and many additional frills were added. Many were Chinese-inspired. Indeed, one persistent pattern, known as the *Herati*, originally associated with carpets woven in the Mongol capital of Herat in eastern Persia, can best be described as two lanceolate leaves surrounding a rosette or small medallion, which took the form of an oriental poppy or an Indian pine cone.

Certainly the most famous of the medallion carpets is the *Ardebil Carpet* (Figure 6.50), now in the Victoria and Albert Museum. In 1539, the year it was woven, it was placed in the royal ossuary at Ardebil, high in the Karadagh mountains to the east of the capital of Tabriz. Its exact duplicate, dated 1536, was likewise located in the tomb and is now in a private collection in the United States. What a tangled web is made by the tracks of art objects! The artist of the Ardebils was Maksoud, a not unworthy contemporary of Michelangelo and Titian.

The complex design he created consists of a central light cream medallion on a deep Persian blue ground. In general the Persian is a blue-dominated scheme, for even the reds have a bluish overcast. To these two base colors the

Figure 6.50 The Ardebil carpet. Iran, 1539. Victoria and Albert Museum, London. (Crown Copyright, Victoria and Albert Museum.)

Persian added a natural wool ivory and certain blue greens. Green was featured in strongly Islamic rugs. Around the central motif of the Ardebil there are sixteen smaller ogival patterns that resemble a star or snow crystal with its external radiations. Many medallion patterns have longitudinal appendages often called *pole medallions*. They are frequently seen in Hamadan or Shiraz carpets of the nineteenth century. In the Ardebil these poles represent red mosque lamps from which numerous light rays again emanate.

The ground made from the finest Sehna knots

(i.e., under one warp, over and under the next) is covered with blossoms and is surrounded by three intricate borders. The whole is a magnificent example of that ability of the Persian to maintain the harsh mountain tops of order while descending to the intimacies of beloved naturalistic detail. The tomb carpet bears the inscription:

I have no refuge in the world other than thy threshold. My head has no protection other than thy porchway.

From the central medallion carpet springs a variety of offshoots. One is known as the Herat, or Herat-Ispahan (Figure 6.51). Herat, always a prominent rug-weaving center, was reputedly the source of this design, later found on carpets

Figure 6.51 Carpet. Herat-Ispahan type. Indo-Persian, 1570–1600. Wool. Length, 2.64 m, width, 1.43 m. Winterthur Museum, Winterthur, Delaware. (Courtesy, The Henry Francis du Pont Winterthur Museum.)

made in the central plateau capital of Ispahan. In these carpets the outline of the large medallion is lightly traced, appearing as though it were *ciselé,* like the Venetian velvets. The pattern is composed of a fourfold reversal that consists of medallions or palmettes interspersed with oriental cloud bands and intertwined with arabesques.

Animal and hunting rugs constitute another major type of museum carpet. The Persian manufactories were at Tabriz and Kashan. Old Kashan carpets with silk pile are priceless today. Animal and hunting rugs were favorites with the Indian Mughal emperors: Akbar (1556–1605), Jahangir (1605–1627), and Shah Jahan (1628–1658) who

Figure 6.52 Hunting carpet, detail. Iran. Mid-sixteenth century. Silk and silver. Field of salmon pink. The segment includes part of the large central green medallion and a wide crimson border of stylized genii. An outer border with palmettes is not shown. Österreiches Museum für angewandte Kunst, Vienna. (Österreisches Museum für angewandte Kunst, Wien.)

built the Taj Mahal in memory of his wife Mumtaz Mahal. The Mughals came from Ferghana and Samarkand and were descended from Timur (i.e., Tamerlane). Weaving of wool floor coverings had not been a notable achievement of the native Indians because climate and the beauty of the tiled backgrounds of their palaces did not foster a need for this art. The Mughals, however, opened state looms at Agra, Fatpur, and Lahore in the north of the peninsula. Many of the workers were imported, often forcibly, from Persia. This may account for certain resemblances between the rugs of the two countries.

Differences are also to be noted, never more so than in hunting and animal rugs. The most famous of these is a Persian weaving, now at the Austrian Museum for Applied Art in Vienna (Figure 6.52). The Boston Museum of Fine Arts possesses an outstanding animal rug from India (Figure 6.53). Persian rugs are likely to have the deep blue and ruby red suffusion already alluded to. Their Indian counterparts verge on a clear, bright, but lighter palette.

Sometimes Indian characteristics of pattern will be found in conjunction with the Persian palette. The Cleveland Museum of Art has a rug in the floral design known as *millefleur,* or thousand flowers, which frequently appears in later rugs woven in the adjacent Persian province of Kerman. It is a very fine weaving with 400 knots to the square inch. The flowers are dainty sprigs shown with roots and all—an Indian characteristic. The border is narrow and delicate, more Indian than Persian. The ruby ground would shame the velvets of the cardinals.

Persian animal rugs often differ from the Indian in the bisymmetrical formality of their arrangement of detail. In addition, their stories are less happy. In the Boston carpet we see the Indian potentate observing, from his canopied vantage point, a wilderness of delightfully depicted animals—the doe, the water buffalo, the leopard and cheetah, and the lion, the griffin, and the antelope, pursued, pursuing, and captive. Monkeys and birds laugh down from the trees, and viands are being prepared for the delectation of the party. Persian genius was often more callous. In the Vienna carpet, for instance, one palfreyed rider is shown severing a gory animal. Horses, in-

Figure 6.53   Hunting carpet. India, seventeenth century. Museum of Fine Arts, Boston. (Courtesy Museum of Fine Arts, Boston, gift of Mrs. Frederick L. Ames, in name of Frederick L. Ames.)

cidentally, are not shown in the Indian designs.

The Indian arrangement is quite asymmetrical and follows a loose S pathway held together by the finest of line tracery. In some rugs this line forms an ogival network. In the Boston carpet, animal tails and plumed foliage become thin tracts that serve to connect various elements in the pattern. The griffin's appendage becomes enmeshed with that of a fine-feathered phoenix, ties itself into a knot, and eventually serves to ensnare a baby elephant. The whole emerges to disclose what we would interpret as a sense of humor. A national flavor is again seen in border palmettes, where a masque, sometimes human, sometimes animal, is displayed. These motifs, flanked by lanceolate leaves, are the Indian version of the Persian *Herati*. Sharp points on foliage, characteristic of Indian rendering, lend a certain etched quality to the design, which contrasts with the more painterly fashion of Persia.

The fourth classification of the museum-caliber carpets of the period are the garden carpets. This type may be the most ancient, for the Persian, in an arid land, looks to his small irrigated garden as to a spiritual oasis. Flora are of principal importance to oriental weavings and, no matter whether realistic or highly stylized, they are never totally absent. In a garden rug, then, only the framework is unique. It consists of crossed paths with what purports to be a pool of water in the center. Sometimes the flowers and trees, drawn in elevation view, sprout from the runways and are reflected in the waters.

As an offshoot of the garden carpets we find the vase or *Joshagan* examples, named for a town again on the border of the great desert, where these rugs were woven. In place of the corner medallions of the Herat-Ispahan rugs we find large vases, evidently inspired by patterns on Ming-dynasty Chinese porcelain. These carpets are rare and for the most part exist only in fragmentary form.

The last class of great Persian carpets consists of a few superlatively designed Mohammedan prayer rugs, marked by a prayer niche (i.e., *mihrab*) at one or both ends, which the faithful turn toward Mecca. The exquisite prayer rugs of this particular period are also frequently characterized by a mosque lamp hanging in a pillared niche. Turkey was the real home of prayer rugs because in that country religious zeal was most orthodox. It has been said that Turkish patterns are nothing but frozen Persian ones. In these outstanding religious carpets, however, the Turk yields nothing to any other nation in the suavity of his design or in the finesse of his craft. The James Ballard collection at the Metropolitan Museum of Art shows a sixteenth-century example which, in soft yellow reds, light blues, and a niche panel of dark green, is pure color wizardry.

Although these old Turkish carpets used subtle tones, the Turkish artist was generally bolder with his paint brush and successful in combinations of opposites, such as red and green. Green is the sacred color of Islam, as yellow is of Buddhism. Green was supposedly restricted to use in prayer mats.

The Caucasian oriental carpet, always the work of the nomad, is represented by some ancient dragon rugs dating as far back as the fifteenth century. Here we see creatures from the deep recesses of primitive imagination created with typical nomad angular stylization and with the boldest strokes of color. The Caucasian, who dwelt in the mountainous regions between the Black and the Caspian Seas, often finished his designs with jagged edges that resemble bursts of flame. These easily turn into geometric swastikas and latch hooks, which spell trans-Eurasia. Mt. Ararat in the high Caucasus mountains could well have prompted the Noah's Ark carpets that display humans and animals in pairs. The legend is clear. Never great court weavings, the bold angularity and color of the Caucasian carpets, whether judged by the relatively few that have descended from the fifteenth and sixteenth centuries or by the many that became articles of commerce in the nineteenth, speak of the strength of a people who sought refuge in the heights and who had the stamina to endure there.

Although we learn in the literature that they are old and, from fragments of the Shoso-in Imperial Treasure of Japan, that they date from the T'ang Dynasty, not much can be said with authority about early Chinese rugs. Because none reached the West before the late nineteenth century, little of their history is known, but with recent scholarly research, some of the finest have now been allocated to the seventeenth century in which context we have described them.

Turkoman rugs, from the vast territory across southern Asia east of the Caspian and west of the Himalayas, are fairly rigid in their use of tribal *guls* or octagonal patterns. Some of the heritage rugs, which came from around Samarkand and Kashgar, with mixed patterns of the Turkoman, Chinese, and Persian, show indication of being very old. Like the Chinese, they came from the hinterland at a late date and until recently little opportunity has been provided for systematic historical research.

CERAMICS

Majolica and Tin-Glazed Wares

A study of Italian Renaissance ceramics should properly begin with the production of majolica that took place in many prominent ateliers soon after the midfifteenth century. Located at Faenza, Caffaggiolo, Castel Durante, Urbino, Derute, and Gubbio, these centers flourished in approximately that order. The characteristics of each school were sufficiently unusual to provide continued interest to the student and collector.

A classical description of majolica states that it is tin-glazed pottery that has been given an extra luster with metallic oxides.[6] This definition applies to the museum majolica of the fifteenth and sixteenth centuries (see Chapter 5). The Italian technical achievement was ultimately to acquire a thinner potting and to perfect a stanniferous glaze that provided a harder and less porous surface and thus permitted more detailed painting.

The range of available colors was no greater. It may be said to have progressed from earlier work, largely done in cobalt blue, to manganese aubergine and copper green and various tones of ochre yellow. However, the Italian, ever facile with the brush, learned to combine pigments to obtain many coloristic effects.

Although the earliest Italian pieces preserved some of the vigor of the Iberian stylized decoration and coupled with it a degree of realism in the portrayal of foliage, animals, and humans, the later developments along the line of story-telling

(*istoria*) technique are best known. These pieces were frequently intended as gifts or "show" items, in the form of large plates or bowls and decorative two-handled vases. Famous paintings or engravings were copied as in the majolica cistern from Urbino, on which *The Judgment of Paris* is rendered from an engraving by Marcantonio Raimondi after a painting by Raphael. Free borrowing of ornament from Renaissance documents was usual. Family coats of arms were often used. The Castel Durante shops, located near Urbino, favored oak-leaf foliage, the predominant motif in the arms of the Rovere family which succeeded the Montefeltro. *Rovere* means oak tree. Venice with its eastern bias showed flowers, foliage, and fruit, and even turbaned gentlemen of oriental background.

Near the middle of the sixteenth century it became customary for the majolica artist to sign and date his work. Thus we have come to know Francesco Xanto Avelli and Nicola da Urbino, Baldassare Manara of Faenza, and Maestro Georgio Andreoli of Gubbio. The small town of Gubbio on the eastern slope of the Apennines had long been a center of the potter's industry. Here a sculptor, exiled from his native Pavia, came in 1498. Gubbio was then owned by Urbino, whose reigning duke was sufficiently astute to welcome such foreign talent. Maestro Georgio's early work was in sculptured and glazed terra cotta, but at some time he transferred to majolica and became one of the great masters of lusterware (Plate 13). It requires no laboratory diagnosis to appreciate the exquisite soft faun-colored glow that was one of his specialties. His ruby red represents the pinnacle in sensuous luster coatings. Pieces done in other factories were often sent to Gubbio for an added luster coating by this master craftsman.

Admittedly there is considerable question about the aesthetic propriety of painting an approximation of an easel picture on such utilitarian clay objects. Yet the representation was so skillfully done by these Renaissance men that the work merits appreciation for what it is—pictorial essays on a unique ground. It is an added fillip when that base has the charm of what the Italians call *madre-perle*.

Faience was also developed in Italy. This was

Figure 6.54 *Madonna and Child with Scroll.* Luca della Robbia. Florence, fifteenth century. Glazed terracotta. Height, 79 cm. Metropolitan Museum of Art, New York. (The Metropolitan Museum of Art, bequest of Benjamin Altman.)

the medium for most of the ceramic sculpture that came from the Italian kilns. Because of improvements in the stanniferous formula, it could cover the basic clay without clogging the detail. Justly famous practitioners were the Della Robbias, first Luca (1400–1482; Figure 6.54), and then his nephew Andrea, followed by the latter's sons.

Luca sculptured the marble reliefs that grace the *Cantoria,* or singers' pulpit, in the cathedral at Florence (ca. 1435). This appears to have been his only major work in this medium before he turned to ceramic modeling. Andrea created the series of cartouches enclosing the *bambinos* (infants) that appear on the facade of Brunelleschi's Foundling Hospital in Florence. Girolamo (1488–1566), one of Andrea's sons, returned to France in the train of Francis I and subsequently made the tiles for the facade of the Chateau de Madrid, a famous building, now destroyed, on the banks of the Seine.

The art of Della Robbia ceramics must have struck an oddly foreign note in that distant location and in such a setting. It is an art profoundly Tuscan Renaissance in character because it embodies a simplicity, sweetness, and forthrightness, along with a certain reserve or aloofness, that is distinctive of Tuscan culture. It could take the mystic faith of the Middle Ages, put it into Renaissance garb, and place it gracefully and seriously into its architectural decoration.

In the beginning the Della Robbias worked in statuesque white, then added pale blue, and finally the potter's complete range of tones. When Luca's guiding hand was removed, there was a tendency to cheapen the product in the direction of over sentimentality. At its best, never was a simple household icon better suited to its material and to its people.

Oriental Ceramics at the Time of the Renaissance

In 1368 the Chinese house of Ming seized control from the weakening Mongol or Yüan Dynasty. Their capital, first at Nanking in central China and then at Peking (1421) in the north, remained the capital of the Chinese emperors of the Ming and the later Ch'ing or Manchu (1644–1912) Dynasties.

The Ming Dynasty inaugurated a policy of subsidy and control of native products which, if it could not combine the subtle refinement with strength of the Sung Dynasty ceramics or the vigor of the Yüan, did lead to the epitome of excellence in body and glaze. The development under the Ming Dynasty was continued under

268

the Manchus. For our purpose the latter will require only brief mention. The products became more precious on the one side and more commercial on the other.

The most significant outgrowth in Ming ceramics lay in the perfection of the Chinese glazes, chief among which was the underglaze blue first initiated during the Yüan Dynasty. China or porcelain is that ceramic which, because of its kaolin (i.e., china clay) and petuntse (i.e., china stone, largely feldspar, used for kiln flux), can be high fired to a very hard and usually translucent body. In underglaze decoration the design was placed on the biscuit (unfired ware) before immersion in a feldspathic glaze. Glaze, decoration, and body were then fired at one time to create a union that produced three-dimensional depth. The glaze showed no evidence of overlay, as a low-fired lead glaze sometimes does. Because the biscuit was dry but absorbent, the design needed to be swift and sure, as in majolica. In the Ming Dynasty ware it acquired the magic that the oriental artist has with the brush. The finest blue-and-white porcelain was made during the reign of Hsüan Tê (1426–1435), although production continued through the eighteenth century. This may have been the china that Rupert Brooke, in his poem, "The Great Lover," written before his tragic death in World War I, had in mind:

> These have I loved:
> White plates and cups, clean-gleaming,
> Ringed with blue lines

Persia and Turkey (at Isnik, the ancient Nicaea) imitated the Chinese blue and white using an artificial paste body.

An underglaze red known as *sacrificial red* formulated in the reign of Hsüan Tê repeated a much earlier Chinese product, the secret of which had been lost. This color was made by reducing copper oxide to pure metal in a reduction kiln. A stem cup in the Metropolitan Museum shows a red underglaze fish beneath a greenish white transparent layer.

In addition to this underglaze painting on porcelain, the Ming period is famous for its monochrome glazes. Two varieties of the famous white ware should be mentioned. One, made at the imperial kilns at Ching-Te-Chên, exemplified the utmost refinement of the porcelaneous body and feldspathic glaze. Known as *Pai Ting*, it is both incised and modeled.

In the south of China, at Tê-hua in the province of Fukien (across from Taiwan), a less regal white china made its appearance. Much of it was subsequently exported and the Europeans dubbed it *blanc de Chine*, a highly logical name. It was similar in body to the imperial wares, but heavier, creamier, and with a higher, waxier gloss. Much of it was formed into figurines, of which those of *Kuan-yin*, the Buddhist Goddess of Mercy, are well known.

This white ware constituted one of the popular Ming monochrome glazes. In addition, the blue and red underglaze colors were sometimes applied without pattern. The remainder of the Ming monotones were overglaze colors, which were added after the porcelain with its feldspathic glaze had been fired and were incorporated in a second firing with a lead glaze dip. These overglazes (meaning over feldspathic glaze as the term is applied to china) were subject only to low firing and are often known as enamels.

During the late Ming Dynasty and fulfilling their promise during the Ch'ing we see many variations of these monochrome glazes (Plate 14). The famous yellow enamel glaze was made with antimony. The reds appeared as the *Lang* or oxblood (*sang de boeuf*), an underglaze copper. *Peachbloom* was a later, more delicate version of the copper red. The deep cobalt underglaze of the Ming Dynasty evolved into the lighter *claire-de-lune*. In overglaze colors the Ch'ings produced an apple green from copper and an olive green with an addition of iron. Complex combinations of glazes with both underglaze and enamel patterning were devised.

The three-colored ware of *san-ts'ai* and the five-colored or *wu ts'ai* are almost too well known in the western market to need description. The technique used cloisons of pottery slip, as did the Medieval *lakabi* pieces of Persia. In China these cloisons were frequently colored with aubergine violet, made with manganese. The enamel colors then painted on the glaze within these armatures were iron red, copper green, and an iron yellow. To these three the *wu*

Figure 6.55 Plate from Medici factory, Florence, ca. 1580. Soft-paste porcelain. Diameter, 28 cm. Cleveland Museum of Art. (The Cleveland Museum of Art, Purchase, John L. Severance Fund.)

ts'ai added a turquoise green, likewise made from copper and a cobalt underglaze.

The final development of this type of production, which occurred during the seventeenth and eighteenth centuries, included the *famille* porcelains. The French assigned these names according to the predominant hue in the composition. They are *famille verte* (green), *famille rose* (a light soft red), *famille jaune* (yellow), and *famille noire* (black). Sometimes reserved panels of one family (e.g., a rose, done on a white background, would appear on a jar, the main body of which was another color (e.g., black).

Italian Ceramics as Influenced by China

Our interest has led us far afield from the Italy of the sixteenth century both in location and time. Porcelain, especially the blue and white and the white wares that were being imported into Renaissance Italy, proved to be overwhelmingly popular. The beauty of the new products and their smooth white surfaces led to a late vogue for leaving majolica white, sometimes with a

blue pattern. This was made into relatively thinly potted table services.

The objective, however, was to learn the secret of the delicate, vitreous, hard *china*. The Italians called it *porcelain* because of its resemblance to the porcellana, a cowrie shell. Thinking, quite naturally, that the secret must lie in the addition of glass frit to the pottery clay, the Italians tried this method and manufactured a translucent cream-bodied ware known as *soft paste* china. But the kiln temperature proved critical, the pieces were brittle and not very durable, and the cost of production ran high.

Experiments in creating soft paste china, presumably successful, were made in several Italian cities during the sixteenth century but only the product of one factory remains. This establishment, called the Medici factory, was located at Florence under the patronage of the Grand Duke Francesco Maria de Medici (1541–1587) and flourished from 1570 to 1603 (Figure 6.55). Marks may consist of the dome of the cathedral at Florence, coupled with an F, or the Medici coat of arms which consisted of a crown and six balls or *palle*. The pieces, of which less than forty are extant, were coated with a stanniferous glaze and then generally decorated with blue oriental-inspired designs. Francesco devoted much of his time to science and it is thought that he may have perfected the soft paste formula used at his factory. He had a very able artist, Bernardo Buontalenti, working with him and for him in this enterprise.

GLASS

Although glass was produced in several centers in northern Italy, it was Venice and its glass houses that ultimately took the lead. The workshop of the Barovier (Beroviero) family is associated with the early progress of the art (Plate 15). In the fourteenth century Bartholomeo Barovier skillfully prepared formulas for coloring glass and for the enamels with which it was decorated. Angelo Barovier, who died in 1460, is mentioned as having perfected a formula for crystal-clear glass. The Murano production, made on the off-shore island where their glass house was located, forged to the front in the industry with these carefully guarded secrets.

In the Museo Vetrario, or Glass Museum, on the island the famous *marriage goblet* made by the Barovier family in the late fifteenth century illustrates the character of early Renaissance glass. On a background of intense dark blue or green, the decorative enamel pictures presented rather stiffly stylized versions of classical themes, symbolic *romans,* or popular genre tales. The characters frequently form a procession between borders of serrated and dotted decoration reminiscent of metallic prototypes. Even the forms of early goblets, with their knobs and ribbed stems, are similar to those of Medieval chalices.

In the sixteenth century the shaping became less dependent on metal work and better suited to glassblowing, being more rounded and flowing. A greater freedom in decoration accompanied this change. Characters often became playful, as in the *putti* on the tazza in the Cleveland Museum of Art (Figure 6.56). The background colors also developed clarity and, with this advance, the enamels grew thinner and the entire depiction more painterly. The tazza shape itself became broader and shallower in keeping with the horizontality of much Renaissance work.

The clearness of *cristallo,* although never comparable to modern glass, was likewise improved. Seaweed was used in Venetian glass for the major alkaline element in the batch. This automatically makes a soft glass and one ideally suited to blowing. Though not as clear or as hard as modern Venetian glass, nevertheless Renaissance *cristallo* was such an improvement over earlier glass that new uses and new types of ornamentation evolved.

One use for clear glass is for mirrors. Glass mirrors were almost entirely unknown in Europe before the sixteenth century and even then, of course, were very small. Mirror backing at that time was made of thin coatings of tin or lead. Hanging mirrors were so precious that they were protected by silken draw curtains. *Églomisé* plaques, in which the painting is done on the reverse side of clear glass and then backed with gold leaf, were treasured.

Another form of decoration done on *cristallo* was engraving made with a sharp-pointed dia-

Figure 6.56 *Tazza* with putti frieze. Venice, ca 1490. Height, 19 cm, diameter, 23 cm. Cleveland Museum of Art. (The Cleveland Museum of Art, Purchase, John L. Severance Fund.)

mond instrument. This *diamond point engraving* was carried to an inartistic conclusion by the glassmakers of the Netherlands, who produced stilted pictorial scenes on glass. Worse—commemorative portraits were made, for which there was, of course, a thriving market.

Clear and colored glass were at times combined to make fanciful blown sculptural images of sea creatures for handles on tazzas, ewers, goblets, and bowls (Figure 6.57). Colored and opaque white milk-glass rods were inserted in stems, and patterns resembling the amphoristas of ancient Egypt were attained. The most attenuated patterns were known as *lacy glass* or *latticinio.* This should not be confused with glass of American manufacture known by the same name. Again, colored glass tubes, fused together, created many-hued nosegays, known as *millefiore* glass.

271

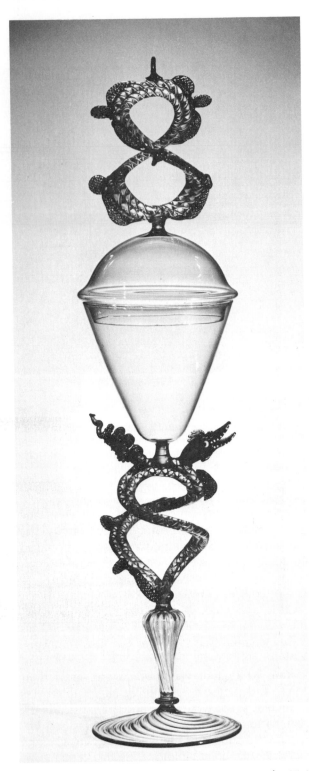

Figure 6.57   Dragon-stem goblet. Venice. Height 35.6 cm. Corning Museum of Glass, Corning, New York. (The Corning Museum of Glass, Corning, New York.)

Despite the most drastic legal measures taken by the Republic of Venice to prevent piracy, inroads were made on its manpower by the inducements of foreign courts. Coupled with the lowered economic status of the Venetian state, the glass industry of Venice suffered a decline. The expert craftsmanship and poetic fantasy of the Renaissance was all but lost for several centuries until revived after World War I.

STONES, METALS, IVORIES

Skillful handling of precious metals and stones, which (with a pardonable mixture of languages) came under the guilds of the goldsmith, the fondeur, and the lapidary, has always been expensive. Princes acquired treasures in these materials during the Renaissance.

In Italy the Florentine sculptor and goldsmith Benvenuto Cellini (1500–1571) combined several artistic abilities in one person. A tempestuous character but a most talented virtuoso, his statue on the Ponte Vecchio possibly brings to mind tales from his autobiography rather than recognition of the man as creator of the bronze Perseus in the *Loggia dei Lanzi* in his native city or as the author of a treatise on the goldsmith's craft.

One of his most remarkable pieces is the large salt cellar (made for Francis I of France and presented to Archduke Ferdinand of Austria by Francis's grandson, Charles IX), now at the Kunsthistorisches Museum, Vienna. A similar article by a contemporary Florentine craftsman is the celebrated Rospigliosi Cup (Figure 6.58) formerly the property of Prince Rospigliosi of Tuscany, now at the Metropolitan Museum. Both objects illustrate an extravagance which, although constructed around some utilitarian vessel such as ewer, tazza, salt or sweetmeat dish, was primarily concerned with displaying wealth.

The Rospigliosi Cup is a delightful combination of Medieval fantasy and Renaissance realism and purpose. It introduces that soupçon of playfulness for which we are eternally in debt to Italy. The plodding tortoise, who rides a chimerical dragon on his back, which in turn flips its tail and wings to uphold the graceful golden cup the handles of which consist of a creature half sphinx,

Figure 6.58 *The Rospigliosi Cup*. Attributed to Jacopo Bilivert. Netherlandish artist, active in Florence. Last quarter of the sixteenth century. Gold, enamel, and pearls. Height, 19.5 cm, length, 23 cm, width, 21.5 cm. Metropolitan Museum of Art, New York. (The Metropolitan Museum of Art, bequest of Benjamin Altman, 1913.)

half mermaid, is Renaissance in its design. Each part is distinct as a conceptual image and in its function. It is quite unlike some Mannerist pieces that involved *istoria* (i.e., stories) in scenes and overlapping detail.

The salt cellar (Figure 6.59) is more classical in its symbolism. Above a molded base that bears cartouches representing the seasons and the di-

visions of the day sit two opposed figures cast in the round, one of Neptune guarding the salt—that costly product of the sea—and the other the earth goddess, from whom the pepper is acquired. The cellar is made of solid gold and measures nearly a foot in width. It was completed in 1544, just one year before Cellini returned from France to his native Florence.

Renaissance goldsmiths frequently traveled from the court of one prince to that of another. Thus their work gained something of an international character. In Italy Antonio Pollaiuolo (he who drew *The Battle of the Nudes*, one of the first studies of human anatomy seen in violent

273

Figure 6.59 *Salt cellar*. Benvenuto Cellini. France, ca. 1544. Kunsthistorisches Museum, Vienna. (Kunsthistorisches Museum, Wien.)

action) and Francesco Salviati had trained as goldsmiths and later became painters. But some men, like Giulio Romano, whom we have met as an architect, or Perin del Vaga, Raphael's pupil, did not understand metalworking although they furnished the goldsmiths with designs. In such a system, in whatever field it is found, there comes a time when structural necessity parts company with ornament.

Small statues from the hand of the fondeur were also prized by the Renaissance. They indeed became some of the first of the knickknacks with which persons of substance sometimes embellished their homes as a declaration of their taste. Padua, where the great Florentine sculptor Donatello (1386–1466) had worked and where his equestrian statue of the Gattemelata, the condot-

tiere, still stands, was an important center for the production of small as well as large bronzes. Andrea Briosco, called Riccio (1470–1532), and the French immigrant known as Giovanni da Bologna (1529–1628; Figure 6.60) were creators of models that often measured no more than 6 in. in height.

Their subjects were classical personages, animals, or fanciful creatures from an antique world. Sometimes, as in the products of the goldsmiths, the representational was combined with the useful in such objects as inkwells, candlesticks, and mirror handles.

It is to the purely decorative metal statuettes, however, that we look for unique skill in the modeling hand of the Italian. The best of the Renaissance examples possess a strength and sculpturesque character that belie their small size. As demonstrated in large sculptures, bronze was a fitting medium for muscular mass and, at the other extreme, linear emotionalism.

Figure 6.60 Bronze falcon. School of Giovanni da Balogna. Italy, sixteenth century. Height, 34 cm. Fogg Art Museum, Cambridge, Mass. (Courtesy of the Fogg Art Museum, Harvard University, Bequest—Grenville L. Winthrop.)

Stemming from utilitarian needs were the objects made in Venice of bronze inlaid with the precious metals. Obviously this craft was learned from the Levant, where similar objects in brass were made throughout the Middle Ages. Practitioners of bronze work in Renaissance Italy were known as *azzimini*.

One should observe closely the wrought iron details that are part of Renaissance Italian architecture—the torch and standard brackets, the tether rings, and even the bars from which to flaunt hangings. There were few that were not works of art. The beautiful lantern at the corner of the Strozzi was done by the famous ironsmith Caparro. Lorenzo de Medici is said to have favored an old craftsman, Niccolo Grosso, who amused his patron by perversely refusing to take anyone out of turn, be he ever so wealthy.[7]

DESCRIPTIVE SUMMARY

Italy in the fifteenth and sixteenth centuries began the art world's trek into today. Society turned its back on the feudal political system and on the solely religious philosophy of the Middle Ages. It turned toward capitalism and toward a rationally organized mode of thought. Stimulated by broadened horizons, artistic creativity burgeoned. The initial result in architecture and the decorative arts we have followed in this chapter. Meanwhile, cultures across the Alps were not static and their contributions must be considered next.

CHAPTER SEVEN

The French Renaissance

1450 TO 1600

All men desire to know.

Rabelais

Que scais-je? What do I know?

Montaigne

CULTURE SPAN

The middle of the fifteenth century marked the consolidation of France as a nation-state. With the withdrawal of the English at the close of the Hundred Years War, with the victory over the powerful Dukes of Burgundy, the marriage of the French crown to the domain of Brittany, and finally with the military entrenched in royal hands, France emerged a unified kingdom. Her rulers, from Charles VIII to Francis I, were free to press their claims to the inheritance of certain Italian cities. Because similar demands were being made by the Spanish monarchs, the scene was laid for a three-sided war which ultimately involved the Papal See and Spain's dependency, the Netherlands.

The French kings, who led their armies in person, had ample opportunity to observe the advanced standard of living and the intellectual milieu of Renaissance Italy. Returning to France, each in turn brought in his retinue distinguished artists: Leonardo da Vinci, Benvenuto Cellini, and Sebastiano Serlio, along with lesser luminaries.

The struggle for political power during the sixteenth century was a bitter one because of the frequent accompaniment of religious strife. Many craftsmen, like the Huguenots in France, Moslems in Spain, and Catholics in England, were executed, exiled, or forced to relinquish their means of livelihood because of the senseless bigotry that impoverishes states. A temporary setback in artistic progress usually resulted from the dearth of skilled workmen.

When the Bourbon King of France, Henry IV, issued the Edict of Nantes, which granted a degree of religious freedom to the Huguenots, a number of Frenchmen who had fled to the Netherlands in the wake of the persecutions returned to their homeland. This accounts in part for the northern influence on the French decorative arts throughout the seventeenth century. Many, however, never went back, and we pick up the thread of their story in England and again in America.

Despite the rampant dogmatism and intolerance of the late Valois reigns, the French genius for liberality and disposition for penetrating scrutiny appears in much of the Renaissance literature. Subtle raillery and sharp wit began that early to take deadly aim at cocksure authority.

ARCHITECTURE AND INTERIORS

French Renaissance architecture is best understood in the light of its regal building. Here the exteriors and interiors are so historically associated with their habitats that the unified approach seems advisable.

Charles VIII and Louis XII

French royalty, ever the *bon vivants,* began to glorify its domestic architecture during the Renaissance. With comparative peace, the chateaux gradually abandoned their old fortifications and in place of crennelated towers substituted classical adornments long before they assumed the rigor of classical style.

Our story might well begin with the Chateau d'Amboise. In 1492, when but twenty-two years of age and free from the guardianship of his sister, Anne de Beaujeu, Charles VIII undertook the reconstruction of this castle which had originally been the property of the Counts of Amboise and which they had found convenient to donate to the crown. It was here that the young monarch on his return from the Italian campaigns brought a band of foreign workmen, among whom were Dominique de Cortonne, known in French annals as Il Boccador, and Guido Mazzoni, often called Paganino, with the avowed intent of introducing qualities of Italian style. Paganino built the tomb for Charles at St. Denis, the royal pantheon in Paris.

This was in 1498. The king while riding had been the victim of an unusual and fatal accident, having struck his head on a low arch along a garden walk. This tragic incident reminds us of the lowness of Medieval doorways.

Charles had no direct male descendent, his son having preceded him in death and having been immortalized along with his little sister in the Cathedral at Tours. Their lovely sarcophagus in marble, thought to be the work of one of the family of Italian sculptors by the name of Juste, is an eternal message of passing styles. Recumbent infants, guarded by Medieval angels, lie on their cold bed, and fat little Renaissance amorini and foliage run rampant around the base. It should be visited by all who wish to understand.

Louis XII of the Orleans branch of the Valois

came next to the throne. More interested in military exploits than in building, he left the aggrandizement of his reign, by coincidence, in the competent hands of another member of the powerful Amboise family—Georges, Cardinal Archbishop of Rouen. Between 1500 and 1515 this efficient servant of church and state rebuilt his chateau at Gaillon southeast of the Normandy capital. Part of its facade has been removed to the court of *l'Ecole des Beaux Arts* in Paris. In the gate house at Gaillon we see flanking turrets, octagonal rather than round. The conical roof has descended in height toward a Renaissance horizontal. Delicate classical pilasters flank door and window in mounting tiers in a manner destined to become typical of French expression in the new style. The windows are no longer mere slits in the wall and in the tower sections are capped with segmental pediments. String courses provide leveling emphasis. It is not known which builders were responsible for this hybrid architecture built at this early date on the banks of the Seine, but it is thought that some of Charles's Italian protégés were included.

It can be understood, however, why the initial group of immigrants working in the court of Charles and the domain of Georges should be known as the *School of Amboise,* a title somewhat doubly earned. They were not the great artists of the Italian Renaissance, for whom plenty of work existed at home. As lesser talents, they were merely the splash zone of cultural waves and were destined to be engulfed by the firmly entrenched native craftsmen on the one hand and a second surge of their countrymen on the other.

Francis I

Francis I, that indomitable Italianophile and magnificent spendthrift, brought back some of the Renaissance cream in his train. Leonardo da Vinci came in 1516, living near Amboise until his death. Benvenuto Cellini has been accounted for. Il Rosso (later gallicized to Maitre Roux de Roux), a native of Florence, arrived at Fontainebleau in 1530 at the age of thirty and seems to have remained in charge of a band of Italians, working in this favorite chateau of the later Valois until his death eleven years later. This group is known as the *School of Fontainebleau.*

Whereas the Amboise men were predominantly ornamentalists, the later contingent might be called interior designers, but they had not yet achieved an architectural sense. That they enriched the cold halls of the royal domain cannot be denied. This, however, was not enough. There was still no real understanding between native builder and the invading foreign artist. Compare, for instance, the strength of Michelangelo's figures as they articulate his created canopy on the Sistine ceiling with the feebleness of Francesco Primaticcio's elongated ladies as they languidly drape themselves over the architectural forms in the Fontainebleau galleries. Francesque Primadicis (Primaticcio) was the Bolognese sculptor who came to the chateau in 1531. He worked there under succeeding leaders, namely Il Rosso, Serlio, and the Frenchman Philibert de l'Orme (Henri II's reign), and finally, with the advent of Catherine de Medici to control as Queen Mother, was put in command of the Fontainebleau workshops.

Sebastiano Serlio, another native of Bologna, apparently was in charge from 1541 until the death of Francis. As Serlio was sixty-five when he left Italy, it is scarcely surprising that the chief evidence of his work at the French court was the completion of his eight volumes on architecture, three of which were published posthumously and all of which acted as guides to northern architects. He codified the five orders and served to advertise the style of the High Renaissance through his drawings.

King Francis, a son of the south of France, spent untold sums in building and remodeling his chateaux along the pleasant valley of the Loire. They exhibit what may be dubbed a proto-Renaissance style, "the New Fashion," as it was known in France.

Blois had been the Medieval residence of the early Counts of Blois along the upper river. Its main hall, now designated as the *Salle d'États* because it served from 1576 to 1588 as the seat of the States-General, still occupies its northeast corner. The entrance facade was completed by Louis XII. Built in the native idiom of brick walls with stone quoins, it has a wealth of Italianate as well as Gothic detail. The crown and porcupine of Louis combine with classic vases and arabesques. Above the gate is the famous equestrian statue of the king; not the original, however, which was destroyed during the French revolution. The windows rise in an unbroken flank, heralding the new manner.

The adjacent Francis I wing (Figure 7.1) at Blois goes slightly farther in breaking with the old and crying the new. Its facade is the white stone that characterizes the region; its horizontality is securely lined with string courses; its escalade of windows is flanked by pilasters, each pair rising from high pedestals, and topped by a classically inspired architrave. A welter of classical detail forms the cornice. Windows assume four sections, the stone mullions and transoms form a cross; the lucarnes or dormers rise flush with the outer walls; and a balustrade is in classical fashion. In addition we find a great deal of Renaissance decoration: statues on pedestals and in niches, low relief carvings interspersed with the royal insignia of the salamander. The spiral outside staircase has always elicited much comment, although it is really nothing but a Medieval newel in classical dress. It is not known for certain who designed this wing. Knowing the character of the King, it probably evolved from the ideas of Francis himself.

Chambord (Figure 7.2), with its tremendous bulk and its significant formal approach, indicates in its plan (Figure 7.3) certain fundamental changes for which the French must be given full credit. The central, crossed hallways which lead to the centrally placed stairs open onto corner apartments, off which, in turn, are chambers no longer completely intercommunicating. Women, always of great account in the annals of France, may have been responsible for the niceties of French layouts. Chambord also typifies the French adjustment to the inner court plan, which features a front wall that is little more than a screen (after centuries in which it was needed for defense), flanked by lower wings and backed by the family residence or *corps de logis*.

The central spiral staircase at Chambord is enclosed and surmounted by a veritable Disneyland lantern. It must be seen from the roof to appreciate its classical pillarettes and scrolls, which combine with Medieval lozenges of insert slates and Gothic dreamworld fantasies. Chambord is said to have been built for the Duchess d'Etampes. Certainly this would lend substance to the remark of the French writer of the eighteenth century, Chateaubriand, who described the parapets of Chambord (Figure 7.4) as the

Figure 7.1   Chateau Blois, the François I wing. France, 1515–1524. (Giraudon.)

Figure 7.2 (above) Chateau Chambord. France, ca. 1526. (G. C. Ball.)

Figure 7.3 (below) Plan of Chateau Chambord. Loire-et-Cher, ca. 1526. (a) moat; (b) terrace; (c) central double spiral staircase. (Adapted from Sir Banister Fletcher, *A History of Architecture,* eighteenth edition, New York: Scribner's; London: Athlone Press, 1975.)

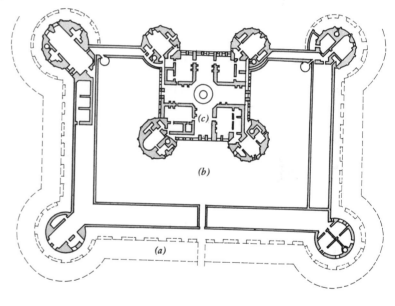

Figure 7.4 (left) The rooftop at Chambord. (G. C. Ball.)

Figure 7.5 Chateau Azay-le-Rideau. France, 1518–1529. (G. C. Ball.)

head of a cavalier in lace frills rising from the strong joints of a Medieval knight in armor.

At the time that Francis was busy with his Loire chateaux (and others such as the Chateau Madrid, St. Germain-en-laye, and Villers Cotterets—the first destroyed, the second restored, and the third now turned to other uses—Francis built prodigally and like the true artist was seldom interested in a creation once it was completed), his men of finance were erecting homes nearby. Azay-le-Rideau (Figure 7.5) and Chenonceaux (built over the River Cher) were originally constructed for Gilles Berthelot and Thomas Bohier, respectively. Both edifices finally reverted to royal hands, for Francis possessed that regal habit of being generous and unquestioning with men of power so long as they traveled his way. When his purse was not filled, the belongings of his servants were forfeit.

Azay-le-Rideau is a gem of early French Renaissance architecture, and it would serve any student well to take a hard look at the building in order to note how amazingly a style can take on a national flavor and still remain essentially within the mode. Rigidly bisymmetrical, stories marked by courses, large windows in unified composition, flat pilaster treatment of the facade, it nevertheless preserves the picturesque quality of the high roof and conical tower, together with the typical lucarnes, which France was not to surrender until the period of the Grand Monarch.

Where Azay features the *appartement* plan, Chenonceaux, a-building for another century, returns to rooms opening off a long internal corridor. Connected with court domestic troubles of the latter part of the century, it is more interesting as history than as architecture.

In the latter role Fontainebleau (Figure 7.6) is probably the most important of the French chateaux of this period. Taking its name from the fountain of Bliaud, located in the geographical center of the surrounding forest, Francis's interest in extending an old hunting lodge on the location prompted almost continuous building. At his death in 1547 the structures surrounding the oval courtyard had been restored. This is often called the *Cour d'Honneur*, with its *Golden Doorway* and St. Saturnin's Chapel. He enlarged the courtyard to the west, known as the *Cour du Cheval Blanc*, named for the equestrian statue of Marcus Aurelius which it once contained. To connect his two enterprises the Gallery of Fran-

Figure 7.6 Chateau Fontainebleau, *Cour du Cheval-Blanc*. France, 1528. The present staircase was built in 1634 by Jean Decereau. (© Arch. Phot. Paris / S. P. A. D. E. M., 1979.)

cis I was built. This is the one whose interior decoration became famous as the work of the Fontainebleau School.

One cannot gain a true picture of these elaborate rooms at Fontainebleau without relating them to other French interiors of the period. In the native interior, rooms were, like Rabelais's fictional king, gargantuan. Floors were still of stone or patterned tile and windows were four-light in the manner of the Latin cross. Six divisions were more usual in the second half of the century. Flanking pilasters and entablature gradually appear. Doors may have had classic ornamentation in their surround but in general were let into deep stone reveals.

Above a high dado walls were of stone with or without plaster. Tapestries were the usual coverings but occasionally a wall would be painted or frescoed. Early Renaissance ceilings were heavily beamed and painted. Coffering to be seen in the Gallery of Henry II at Fontainebleau was later introduced. Here, however, the newer fashion of vaulted ceilings had been requested but denied because of the necessity of providing more wall space for fresco decoration.

Frequently two fireplaces served important rooms but their openings were at first plain and flush with the wall. In the second half of the fifteenth century chimney breasts projected into the room and were generally treated with classic columns and entablatures but without regard for classic proportions (Figure 7.7).

On this kind of background came the work of the Fontainebleau School. As seen in the Francis I Gallery, the floor is parqueted wood in herringbone pattern. The large panels of the high dado are filled with carvings of classic motifs, often with a cartouche (an ovoid decoration surrounded by scrolls or set into scrolls) in their center.

Above this paneling Primaticcio placed stucco decoration that frequently enframes pictures and uses female figures as quasi-supports (Figure 7.8).

283

Figure 7.7 Chateau Blois, interior. Beamed ceiling. Fireplace with salamander, the emblem of Francis I, and ermine, the emblem of Queen Claude. France. (G. C. Ball.)

These lithesome women of delicately chiseled beauty were embraced by the French as prototypes of a typical style of pulchritude. We shall see counterparts in Goujon's statues at the Louvre and in much work thereafter. The decoration in this long gallery has often been criticized as unarchitectonic, but given such a protracted space, quite unclassical in its proportions, interest has been maintained by the sculptural decoration, each panel of which is different from its neighbor in detail, making a trip down the gallery's length a provocative experience.

In Henri II's gallery at Fontainebleau, which was actually intended as a ballroom, the mantel is a unified composition that reaches to the ceiling and is made to resemble two stories of architecture, with round columns on the first and flat pilasters flanking the second, the whole enclosed in an arched design. Wall construction here is of massive piers with round-arch openings into deep-set windows, the two having been planned to carry the load of the intended vaulted ceiling. The name of Niccolo dell'Abbate should find a place, even in this limited list of the many who "decorated" the chateau. As Primaticcio's good man Friday, it was he who actually executed much of the stucco work and painting for which his master is credited. A local mason, Gilles le Breton, was charged with building the chateau, and it was a good seven years before operations were sufficiently organized for any interior treatment. It is small wonder that the purposes of builder and interior designer ran in opposite directions.

Any account of French architecture must acknowledge the importance of the Louvre, the building which has been the home of kings, a royal manufactory, a refuge for pensioners of the crown, and the most all-inclusive of art museums. In the southwest corner of the old Cour Carré stood a Gothic chateau which appears in the illustration for October (Figure 7.9) in *Les Tres Riches Heures du Duc de Berry* (1413–1416), done by the Limbourg brothers. In 1546 Francis commissioned Pierre Lescot (ca. 1515–1578) to build a more expansive palace around the old chateau. Lescot came of a French family of the legal profession, and although opinions differ as to his training and competence he was the first Frenchman to whom the name of architect with all that the term implied in Renaissance nomenclature could be applied. Associated with Lescot was the sculptor and architect Jean Goujon (1510–1572), possibly the more talented man of the two.

The interest of Francis in the Louvre, as indeed in Fontainebleau, was in part political. Following his defeat at the Battle of Pavia in 1525, he recognized the advisability of making Paris his working capital and of building and promoting building by his courtiers in this centralized location.

Lescot and Goujon—who like Siamese twins seem always to appear with interlocked names, possibly expressing the truth of what Reginald Blomfield asserts that "Lescot never undertook a building unless Goujon were associated with him"[1]—worked on the west facade of the old

284

Figure 7.8 Chateau Fontainebleau. The King's Staircase. France, first half of the six-teenth century. Work of the Fontainebleau School under the direction and influence of Primaticcio. (© Arch. Phot. Paris / S. P. A. D. E. M., 1979.)

285

Figure 7.9 *Octobre* from the *Très Riches Heures du Duc de Berry*. France, 1413–1416. Musée Condé, Chantilly. (Giraudon.)

chateau. Under Louis XIII the north and east sides of the Medieval building were demolished and the west wing of the present court, which is four times as large as the former, was extended from the Lescot and Goujon portion (Figure 7.10). The entire new west front, of which the Clock Pavilion (Pavillon de l'Horloge) is the center, deserves

study as a Renaissance document, for Lemercier, its architect under Louis XIII, continued the style of an earlier age (Figure 7.11).

The design of the Lescot "square court" facade, which pivots on the center of three pavilions, is a two-storied structure plus attic. This emphasis on a central motif and the rhythmic punctuation of the facade by salients (pavilions, projecting subdivisions of a large unit) indicate the dawning comprehension of Renaissance principles of bisymmetry and centralization. We note that ground floor windows are enclosed in round arches and that upper ones are pedimented. The French vocabulary which at first favored flat pilaster treatments has now given place to paired semiattached columns. Heavy string courses emphasize horizontality. The niche statues not only show the influence of the Fontainebleau school but also indicate Goujon's grasp of the relation of sculpture to architecture, which the Fontainebleau work does not. The steep slate roof that uses lead cresting remains the defiant French gesture. Whether because of national temperament or because of the timely influence of the Italian school, French architecture both exterior and interior during the early sixteenth century never quite assumed the rigor and discipline of the Italian High Renaissance style but, even in adopting Renaissance prescriptions, showed addiction to the tenets of Mannerism.

Second Half of the Sixteenth Century

By the second half of the sixteenth century native Frenchmen had increased in stature and were able to take over the architectural helm and guide it in the ways of the new style. Henri II did not possess the artistic temperament of his father and was content to leave the architectural affairs of the realm in the hands of Philibert de l'Orme (ca. 1515–1570), a native of Lyon who had studied architecture and gained prestige by visiting Rome. In all probability he came from a family of masons and his work indicates the hand of a zealous, honest builder who followed as closely as possible the letter rather than the spirit of the classical doctrine. For Diane de Poitiers, the king's mistress, he built the bridge over the Cher at Chenonceaux, that she might enjoy her fa-

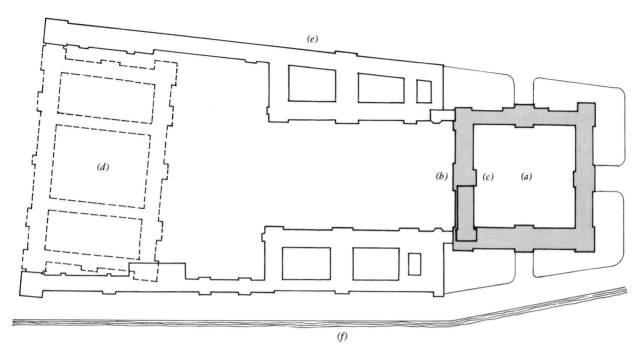

Figure 7.10 (above) Plan of the Louvre, Paris: (a) court of the Old Louvre (P. Lescot, 1546–1549); the old chateau occupied the southwest quadrant of the present Court Carré; (b) Pavillon Sully); (c) Pavillon de l'Horloge; (d) position of the destroyed Tuileries Palace as originally designed; (e) the north facade along the Rue de Rivoli; (f) the south facade and the Quai du Louvre along the River Seine. (Adapted from Sir Banister Fletcher, *A History of Architecture,* eighteenth edition, New York: Scribner's; London: Athlone Press, 1975.)

Figure 7.11 (below) The Louvre, *le Cour Carré* (the Square Court), west facade. Paris. *Left portion of building:* begun in 1546 by Pierre Lescot, with sculpture by Jean Goujon. *Central section* (under the elevated roof): the Pavillon d'Horloge, by Jacques Lemercier, built between 1642 and 1654. *Right portion of building:* built by Lemercier as a replica of Lescot's building on the left. (Lauros-Giraudon.)

vorite sport of hunting on the far side of the river. The galleries above the bridge were later completed by Jean Bullant. For Diane de l'Orme likewise designed the famous classical entrance to the chateau at Anet, with its thin attempt at veiling the identity of the royal favorite in the guise of Diana, goddess of the hunt.

When Henri died the stars of both paramour and architect were waning. The real source of power then, and until her death in 1589, was the Queen Mother, Catherine de Medici. Indeed so bitter and so disastrous were the religious dissensions she provoked that little of moment in the arts occurred during the last half of the century.

Catherine's name is indelibly associated with the building of the Tuileries (Figure 7.10), the palace she planned on the west axis of the enlarged Louvre. It was burned to the ground by the Commune revolutionaries in 1871. Its development is linked to several of the names prominent in the architecture of the period. Oddly, the former royal appointee remained in control until 1570 when Jean Bullant (ca. 1520–1578) succeeded him. Bullant was apparently a man of kindly and modest disposition, quite the opposite of his predecessor and undoubtedly more than willing to kow-tow to the royal presence. His rise had been gradual, forwarded by Anne de Montmorency, Constable, or ranking officer, of the royal household. Bullant and Montmorency came from Écouen. Although Bullant was one of the many writers who published treatises on the classical orders (almost as numerous and necessary to professional respectability as Ph.D. theses are today), his reputation may well rest on some of his small buildings, particularly the petit chateau at Chantilly known as the Chatelet, and the funerary chapel at Anet, dedicated to Diane. Here we see two qualities that represent the quintessence of the characteristics which we associate with the French genius. We can note experimentation with advancing and receding planes, with cornices that cast shadows, with extensions, columns, and niches that allow a play of light and shade—in short with essays in designing with light which is a keynote of the Baroque. Coupled with this is a restraint imposed

in the interest of architectural form, particularly as it emphasizes rhythmic proportions. An artist can almost be tempted to play the funerary chapel as a dance, a piece of music, or a cadenced poem, a bit of French Mannerism.

In the final years of the century mention must be made of the du Cerceau family of architects, several of whom appear to have gained prominence in each generation. The progenitor was Jacques Androuet (1515–1585), whom we must forever bless, not for his building—for no appreciable evidence of any exists—but rather for his writing and drawing, which is copious. His draftsmanship is exquisite—engravings of ornament, furniture, and many French buildings long since gone.

In his *Livre d'Architecture,* written in 1559, Jacques Androuet du Cerceau discussed the town house of the affluent merchant as well as that of nobleman. This is the first public recognition of the economic importance and needs of a growing middle-class clientele.

The more compact form of these dwellings is significant. They were not mansions enclosed in curtain walls. They were generally of the block type, often with pavilion extensions. Planning was in apartments, often containing two suites linked by a living room or *salle*. The grouped spaces consisted of a *chambre*, a *cabinet*, and a *garde-robe*. Making allowances for looseness of terminology, this meant a room for family living adjoined by two small private areas. The *salle* functioned for more public intercourse.

SOME FRENCH RENAISSANCE HOUSES

Martinville	Seine Inferiure	1483
Chaumont	Loire-et-Cher	1472–1511, for Duc Charles I, II
Gaillon	Eure	1501–1509, for Georges d'Amboise, Cardinal Archbishop of Rouen
Amboise, Francis I wing	Indre-et-Loire	ca. 1515
Blois, Francis I wing (Figures 7.1 and 7.7)	Loire-et-Cher	1515–1524
Chenonceaux	Indre-et-Loire	1515, for Thomas Bohier; later architect for bridge—de l'Orme
Fontainebleau (Figures 7.6 and 7.8)	Saone-et-Loire	For Francis I, Henri II *et al.;* complicated succession of architects

Azay-le-Rideau (Figure 7.5)	Indre-et-Loire	1518–1529, for Gilles Berthelot
Chambord (Figures 7.2, 7.3, and 7.4)	Loire-et-Cher	1526, for Frances I
Beauregard	Loire-et-Cher	1543–1553, for Jean du Thier; architect—Serlio
Ancy-le-France	Yonne	1546, for Count de Clermont; attributed to Serlio
Anet	Eure-et-Loire	1548, for Diane de Poitiers; architect—de l'Orme
Louvre (Figures 7.9, 7.10, and 7.11)	Paris	1546 and after, for Kings of France; architects—Lescot and Goujon, de l'Orme, Jacques du Cerceau
Vallery	Yonne	1548, for Maréchal Saint-Andre; architect—attributed to Lescot
Écouen	Seine-et-Oise	1550–1560, for Anne de Montmorency; architect—Jean Bullant
Fleury	Seine-et-Marne	1558, for Nicolas Clausse; architect—attribued to Lescot
Petit Chateau Chantilly	Seine-et-Oise	1560, for Anne de Montmorency; architect—Jean Bullant
Tuileries	Paris	1566 and after, for Catherine de Medici; architect—de l'Orme, Bullant et al.

FURNITURE

General Development

During the fourteenth and fifteenth centuries the court of Burgundy attracted the skilled craftsmen. Most early French Renaissance furniture came from this source. As the woodworkers were often imported from the Netherlands, we note the influence of this country on the Burgundian style. Pieces are heavy, frequently with the large, round *Dutch bun foot*. Many of them are elaborately carved, with representational ornament of deep undercutting. Gothic motifs find favor. Despite the repeated use of embellishment at the expense of form, the work is all so expertly done in the fine native honey-colored walnut that its imaginative effulgence seems a virtue.

No better exponent of these distinctions is to be found than Hughes Sambin (ca. 1520–1602). Born somewhere near Dijon, the capital of Burgundy, the son of a cabinetmaker, he became a *menuisier* (a cabinetmaker), an *ymager* (a carver), and a designer-illustrator of ornament. His major work is to be seen in Dijon integral with the woodwork of buildings rather than as a maker of *meubles*. It is customary to refer to objects as fashioned on the designs of Hughes Sambin, although reference to the Burgundian school (Figure 7.12) would be more nearly correct, for no

piece of furniture can be credited to him with certainty.

It was inevitable that the most advanced pieces made in Burgundy or in France would eventually be influenced by Renaissance taste and that adornment with pilasters and classic entablatures would replace Medieval fantasy. There is often no more interesting hybrid in the whole world of furniture design than those pieces that are neither of the past nor of the future as they come from Burgundy in the early sixteenth century.

In some instances the furniture that graced the new chateaux of royal France came directly from Italy or was designed by Italian immigrants. It was undoubtedly from this source that the fondness for inlays invaded the north. An early example appears in the second half of the sixteenth century. This date is given to a cupboard (armoire) in the Wallace Collection, which is inlaid with plaques of marble (Figure 7.13). This famous assemblage of French furniture is now housed at Hertford House in London. It was the collecting sense of the Marquess of Hertford (1800–1870) and his son, Sir Richard Wallace (1818–1890), that is responsible for its outstanding caliber and the generosity of Lady Wallace in presenting it to the English nation that made it available.

The cataloguing instinct has led to the classification of the furniture of the reigns of Charles VIII, Louis XII, and especially Francis as early Renaissance. The middle Renaissance styles then

Figure 7.12   Walnut cabinet. School of Burgundy, style of Hugues Sambin, mid-sixteenth century. Height, 1.5 m. Cleveland Museum of Art. (The Cleveland Museum of Art, Bequest of John L. Severance.)

belong to the courts of Henri II and his sons. The late Renaissance of Henri IV and Louis XIII we leave to the proto-Baroque.

Types

Chests were ubiquitous during all of the sixteenth century, as the French courts seemed forever on the go. A step in the direction of greater stability is seen in the large cabinets or *bahuts*, usually constructed as *meubles à deux parts*. Again the Wallace collection shows an early Renaissance dresser of about 1500 with linenfold paneling and exquisite Gothic tracery of the fine linear quality

290

that is typical of work in the Ile-de-France rather than Burgundy.

Characteristic of the work of the middle Renaissance is a similar cupboard decorated with herms and panels that display relief carvings of water gods and sea nymphs, certainly of the Burgundian school. The rustic *gaine* (i.e., tapered post) on the upper portion is based on "an engraving, dated 1536, by Agostino dei Musi, called Veneziano (ca. 1490–after 1536)."[2] This indicates

Figure 7.13   Cupboard (*armoire*) in two parts. France, second half of the sixteenth century. Walnut inlaid with plaques of marble. Height, 2.21 m. width, 1.04 m, depth, 45.5 cm. Wallace Collection, London. (Reproduced by permission of the Trustees, The Wallace Collection, London.)

the swiftness of the revolution that ushered in the Renaissance.

Chairs, of which few antedating the midcentury have survived, become more common with the reign of Henri II. The style was simple—actually little more than a framed box with a low back (to allow for the starched ruff). They were high in the seat, with stretchers designed to keep the feet off the cold floor. The earlier high-back chair, known as the *caquetoire,* persists, but in a lighter version. Its back, like that of the *escabelle* or stool chair, is narrower than the front and its turned members are braced by floor runners.

Tables fit neatly into the usual Gothic to Renaissance progression. The framed and pedestaled table came early to France and smaller sizes for specialized uses are indicated. In the Cleveland Museum of Art one sees a square table (Figure 7.14) rich in carving and marquetry, which reputedly belonged to Francis II. I have often imagined the feet of Mary Queen of Scots, as the child bride of Francis II, propped up on its rungs.

Much attention was lavished on the *bed.* Next to the chest it became the symbol of family con-

sequence. No longer placed in an alcove, it was brought out into the room and became forthwith another bit of Renaissance architecture—pillars, entablature, and all. The framework was exposed and from it the richest of hangings were suspended. Of great size, it was a pivot of social life from which calls were received. This custom, which seems so odd to us, must be viewed in light of the times, when rooms were drafty and cold and when the nobility were accustomed to very little of the privacy that is our privilege today.

TEXTILES

Anyone who has walked the stone halls of the Loire chateaux can appreciate how welcome the warmth and color of the woolen hangings could be. This need became less urgent with the advent of paneled and frescoed walls and parqueted floors, which arrived with the end of the sixteenth century.

Tournai, unlike Arras which Louis XI had appropriated to France, remained in the domain of Flanders and continued as a weaving center of importance. It passed into the possession of the German Prince Maximilian I (1493–1515) by virtue of a hastily arranged marriage with Mary,

Figure 7.14 Table. Burgundy, second half of the sixteenth century. Walnut with marquetry top. Height, 88.3 cm. Cleveland Museum of Art. (The Cleveland Museum of Art, Bequest of John L. Severance.)

daughter of Charles the Bold of Burgundy, suzerain of the Lowlands. Under Maximilian's grandson, Charles V (1519–1556), the city of Brussels became the recipient of the royal favor, a transfer said to have been caused by pro-French spirit at Tournai. Brussels soon became the most important tapestry atelier of the sixteenth century.

Before turning northward to the Hapsburg sphere of influence, we pause to note that the kings of Renaissance France were beginning to think in economic terms with an eye to the textile profits of Italy and the Netherlands. By the sixteenth century silk weaving was well established in Lyon but could not yet compete with its neighbors to the south. Francis I opened a tapestry workshop at Fontainebleau into which he lured whatever Flemish weavers there were in France. This factory existed for only thirty years. Its tapestries are distinctive in design and show clearly the influence of the Italians then in residence at the chateau. With borders of Etruscan wall decoration (Renaissance borders grow wider) and with birds and animals scattered over the body and linked with graceful arabesques, they appear more as wall spacers than as organized murals, the counterpart of Primaticcio's plaster decoration. Henri II subsidized a Paris factory, but the industry awaited the vision of Henri IV and his ministers to establish in 1603 the royal atelier at the Louvre.

The Brussels tapestry factories flourished as the French failed. Bernard van Orley, court painter to Margaret of Austria (daughter of Maximilian and Regent of the Netherlands), designed such important pieces of the early fifteen hundreds, as the *Hunts of Maximilian* tapestries which are now at the Louvre. The scenes, supposedly near Brussels, are so realistic that many of the local buildings can be identified. The subject matter for this series likewise showed the tendency to perpetuate the histories of the royal families, a direction that reached its climax in the seventeenth century in the murals that celebrated the apotheosis (deification) of many of the crowned heads of church and state.

The emperor Charles V (Charles I of Spain) succeeded his grandfather Maximilian. For him the painter Lucas van Leyden designed the Brussels tapestry sets called the *Months of Lucas* into which were woven scenes of typical activities of the month that give us, as was true of many of the earlier illuminated manuscripts of the *Hours,* intimate glimpses of contemporary life. Many of these well-loved tapestries were copied in later years, sometimes without change and sometimes in the current fashion.

The influence of Renaissance Italy can be observed in such works. Figures are larger and well grouped in compositional units. Interiors, natural scenery, perspective, and the indication of shallow space begin to intrude. Borders increase in scale and are filled with the bounty of nature or with mythological figures. Not yet completely pictorial in the Renaissance manner, this early group from Brussels combines some of the standards of Gothic with the best compositional talent of the Renaissance.

Moreover, they were woven with the skill that only money and large organizations can produce. The original cartoons needed the hand of an expert weaver. Pierre van Pannamaker executed the van Orley tapestries. In 1528 it was ruled that Netherland tapestries be marked with the name of the city and manufactory. (Note that medieval anonymity had departed.) The mark of Brussels was a red shield that contained two Bs, one for Brussels, one for Brabant. A monogram of the maker was used during the sixteenth century in Brussels; that of Pannamaker was a left-handed *P* growing from a *W.*

In 1515 Pope Leo X (whose portrait by Raphael hangs in the Uffizi) paid the first commission to this artist for painting the famous cartoons for the *Acts of the Apostles,* which were to hang on the walls of the Sistine Chapel to complement the forceful ceiling finished by Michelangelo in 1512. The tapestries (Figure 7.15) were woven at Brussels under the direction of Pierre van Aelst, a leading Brussels manufacturer and tapestry chamberlain to Philip the Handsome of Burgundy, son of Maximilian.

The Raphael cartoons were presumably ten in number, and in the incredibly short time of four years at least seven were completed as weavings. They were first displayed in the Sistine on December 26, 1519. At the time of the 1527 sack of Rome all ten hangings were taken as loot. After disgraceful treatment they were finally returned to their rightful home but were again commandeered and sold at the time of Napoleon's occupation of the capital. Since 1808 they have resided on the walls of a gallery in the Vatican, let us hope never more to leave.

The original cartoons were the inspiration for many complete and partial sets of weavings. In 1630 Charles I of England bought them to use as models in the English Mortlake tapestry factory.

Seven of the cartoons hang on the walls of a special room in the Victoria and Albert. Accurate copies which were given by Charles I to Edward Sackville, fourth Earl of Dorset, may be seen in the cartoon gallery at Knole House in Kent.

Figure 7.15 *The Miraculous Draught of Fishes,* 1515–1521. Tapestry. Designer, Raphael Sanzio; weaver, Pieter van Aelst. Sistine Chapel, the Vatican. (The Vatican Museums.)

Figure 7.16 St. Porchaire Pedestal Cup. France, sixteenth century. Faience. Cleveland Museum of Art. (The Cleveland Museum of Art, Purchase from the J.H. Wade Fund.)

Among the auxiliary sets of tapestries woven during the sixteenth century the best can be seen in the Berlin Museum, in the National Collection in Austria, and in the Royal Spanish collections.

As important as the Raphael tapestries are as individual works of art, their significance becomes apparent only when they are considered in terms of their intended location in the Sistine. In the first place their candalabralike borders projected upward the architectural painted pilasters which then existed on wall frescoes below. Pictorially they illustrate episodes in the lives of Saint Peter and Saint Paul and were hung around the room to the right and the left of the altar in a logical progression.

The tapestries were planned so that in internal design in both form and lighting they strengthened their several positions in the chapel and indeed carried design elements consecutively from one hanging to another, as though they were an oriental scroll painting. This is the sort of continuous movement we first saw in Raphael's *Galatea* in the Farnesina.

In these tapestries, then, we see interior embellishment that uses portable elements designed to fit into a spatial complex, functionally, expressively, and aesthetically. They may be said to mark the high point in the union of architectural and decorative design demonstrated in the Renaissance tradition. This is indeed true of the entire interior of the Sistine.

The Raphael tapestries were so favored in Italy and the north that the teaming of Flemish weavers and Italian cartoonists (such as Giulio Romano) was given an impetus. Hence we find increasing use of late Renaissance stylistic traits in Brussels work—the lower horizon, the attention paid to sky and atmospheric effects, the use of deep space vistas, the prominence given to horizontals—all painterly devices that weakened the strength of tapestry ribs and hatchings. This unsuitable marriage of Flemish and Italian traditions, coupled with the troubled years of the Netherlands' political history, spelled the beginning of the end of Flemish leadership in the tapestry industry.

WALLPAPERS

It would be expected that, following the innovations in paper manufacture and printing, the idea of using these processes to create less expensive wallcoverings would occur.

The first wallpapers were possibly created in France by a guild known as the *dominotiers* (manufacturers of *domino* or marbleized papers, playing cards, and comic pictures). These papers were small, 14 by 18 in., and were used for lining cabinets and the flyleaves of books. Considerable improvement in technique and design awaited the developments of the next centuries.

CERAMICS

Progress in the potter's art in northern Europe is a saga of the seventeenth century. In France and the Netherlands, however, interesting *faience* was manufactured during the sixteenth. This term is used here to describe tin- or lead-glazed earthenware. In France centers at Rouen, Moustiers, Nantes, Nimes, Quimper, Sceaux, and Nevers operated continuously from the late fourteenth century.

During the reign of Henri II a unique pottery was made at St. Porchaire in southwest France (Figure 7.16). It is variously known as Henri II, Oiron (because it was thought to have been made at the Chateau d'Oiron), and St. Porchaire. It was intended for utilitarian table use by the nobility, and if it scarcely warrants a high place in artistic excellence it is nevertheless important as an indication that table use was demanding such articles as bowls, cups, ewers, salt cellars, and candlesticks made of pottery. St. Porchaire body was white clay with a cream glaze. Designs were stamped on it while the clay was still damp,

Figure 7.17 Ceramic platter in the manner of Bernard Palissy. France, ca. 1510–1590. Lead-glazed earthenware. Length, 52 cm, width, 39.5 cm. Metropolitan Museum of Art, New York. (The Metropolitan Museum of Art, Gift of Julia A. Berwind, 1953.)

much as a stamp is tooled into leather. Then various colored slips were rubbed into the depressions. It was then given a lead glaze and fired. Early patterning is neat and conventional. Later development was toward sculptured and highly ornate forms. About eighty pieces of St. Porchaire are known to exist.

The name of Bernard Palissy (1510–1590) has become famous in ceramic history (Figure 7.17). Palissy was one of those human documents whose personal story makes news. He had been by trade a glass painter and by avocation a naturalist and amateur chemist. One day a friend showed him a white porcelain cup. The beauty of the object intrigued him and he was off on the rainbow quest.

To this end his story is one of failure because Palissy became impoverished by his search for

the elusive secrets of chinaware. However, he was able to demonstrate his aesthetic aptitude for plastic form through the medium of enameled pottery characterized by pieces done in fanciful shapes—lizards, snakes, turtles, cabbages, and all other living creatures with the exception of kings.

He nevertheless had traffic with royalty, for his pottery was brought to the attention of the French court, where (one wonders whether with a Don Quixote twist) he was given what certainly must remain one of the strangest titles on record—"Inventor of realistic pottery to the King and Queen Mother." A protestant, Palissy was thrown into the Bastille after the St. Bartholomew carnage. This was undoubtedly due to the intercession of Catherine de Medici and it saved his life. He remained in the Bastille until his death in 1590. Pieces ascribed to him are now to be seen in many museums, testimony to the persistent devotion of an amateur craftsman to the creative ideal and to the doctrine that such talent is best when kept closest to the soil.

In 1548 Guido di Savino, an Italian, set up shop at Antwerp. In the *Vleesch Huis Museum* one can see a treasured faience tile—a memorial to Savino and his sons. From Antwerp protestant refugees carried the art to Holland. Rotterdam and Haarlem became pottery centers dating from the end of the sixteenth century.

Historic ceramics know no borderlines. Although some faience was made in Germany, it was not a characteristic medium. With a local clay that would high fire the Germans made stoneware (i.e., ceramics of refined clay, high fired, between pottery and porcelain in hardness of body) as well as pottery. With a natural bent for the plastic arts they created modeled and incised pieces, jugs, plaques, and stove tiles.

STONES, METALS, IVORIES

Painting with enamels on metal gained in France the important place accorded to majolica in Italy. The southern city of Limoges became the outstanding center of the industry. Enamels are painted onto a fired flux coat and fixed in the kiln. Often as many as five coverings are used. In *grisaille* the first enamel is black and shadings are added in opaque white of varying intensities.

Designs for this work are typically Renaissance and pieces were signed with the artist's name. These signatures should be interpreted as representing the seal of a specific atelier rather than of a particular painter. The tendency toward mass production during the late Renaissance weakened Limoges artistically. Thereafter the output was undistinguished and of little importance in the overall of French industries.

On the other hand, French silver, and especially French domestic silver, has always maintained a high standard of excellence, but because of the need to melt family plate in times of national crisis, of forced disgorging when silver was needed for coinage, and later, of fusing pieces to create a more fashionable style—articles from the sixteenth and seventeenth centuries are rare.

The French have marked their silver since the fourteenth century, when a master was required to identify all articles from his establishment. This stamping usually combined his initials with some unique rubric, and, in general, the guild warden's marks and tax payment credentials.

Until the middle of the sixteenth century French articles conformed to the Medieval tradition. In its later years Mannerist styles were in evidence in pieces that came largely from workshops at Fontainebleau and followed designs by the French engravers Jacques Androuet du Cerceau, René Boyvin (ca. 1530–1598), and Étienne Delaune (1518–1583). As in Cellini's work, the rendering of handles and supports in human form is a recurring theme. In the Mannerist designs these are well-stylized classical caryatids. On silver plates the figures of Tritons and sea gods are reminiscent of Italian patterns. When figures were made plastic by embossing and chasing, relatively flat strapwork often serves to frame the repoussé. Such interlacing, and the occasional use of squat bun feet on caskets, indicates Dutch origins.

Although French silversmiths usually veered toward formal restraint in their interpretations, one master of the Fontainebleau school who practiced in Lyon and signed his initials C.C. is noted for the production of writhing shapes which look almost like precursors of the Art Nouveau of the nineteenth century. Such taste has been dubbed by some writers *Neo-Gothicism*, a tendency that seems to erupt at intervals on the European scene. Perhaps it may call to our attention the fact that Gallic taste which was longest exposed to Roman classicism presents at its best a supreme example of contrast in art— refined formal austerity enhanced by and enhancing the most subtle playfulness and moving asymmetry.

Mannerist Goldsmiths of Germany

The strong schools of Renaissance goldsmiths which practiced at Nürnberg and later at Augsburg are important to our story because they represent the peak of romantic handling of classical subject matter; in other words, the epitome of Mannerism in this medium. Strict control over guild standards was exacted. The most renowned leader of these ateliers was Nürnberg's Wenzel Jamnitzer (died in 1585), whose work is stamped with the Renaissance spirit; it bears such details as triglyph friezes, bucaria, lion masques, and highly embossed acanthus foliage, all inlaid with shells, jewels, and mother-of-pearl. In opposite

character he made casts from natural forms, almost Palissy-like. The classic and the barbaric are strangely interwoven in the creations of these forgemen who seem at once to have descended from Vulcan and Thor.

DESCRIPTIVE SUMMARY

The almost two hundred years in which Italy formulated her Renaissance were, in France, telescoped into the sixteenth century. This northern country annexed the outward rationale and classical trappings of Renaissance architectural art and endowed it with an unmistakably Gallic grace, even though she belatedly arrived at strict architectonic logic.

Undoubtedly her outstanding contribution lay in space planning, especially in dwellings. Her prophetic functionalism might have become a pattern as early as the next century had not the most autocratic regime known to western civilization exercised control for so long.

CHAPTER EIGHT

Sixteenth-Century England

God Almighty first planted a garden. And indeed it is the purest of human pleasures. It is the greatest refreshment to the spirits of man, without which buildings and palaces are but gross handiworks; and a man shall ever see that when ages grow to civility and elegance, men come to build stately sooner than to garden finely, as if gardening were the greater perfection.

Francis Bacon, Essay XLVI, *Of Gardens*

CULTURE SPAN

From the late fifteenth century until the seventeenth England responded to economic, political, and religious forces similar to those that had affected the continent. Henry VII, by his marriage to Elizabeth, daughter of Edward IV, united the rival factions of the nobility represented in the *War of the Roses* by the red rose of Lancaster (Henry's lineage) and the white rose of York (Elizabeth's). The Tudors thereafter showed the double rose as their emblem. Finding himself in a situation somewhat akin to the insecure command that Louis XI of France had earlier inherited, he ruled the nation with a firm hand in an era not notable for fostering the arts.

The story of his son, Henry VIII, is too well known to need recounting. His differences with the church at Rome, occasioned by his insistence on a divorce from Catharine of Aragon, eventually led to the enacting of the Act of Supremacy, by which the king and his successors were appointed head of the Church and clergy of England. This had one important consequence for the history of English art. The suppression of the monasteries and the confiscation of their property under Henry's orders robbed the country of many treasures and deprived it of the services of the most expert craftsmen—those who had been trained by and who had served the ecclesiastic communities.

As in France during the second half of the sixteenth century, religious problems were complicated by political issues. Elizabeth's alliance with the Protestant Netherlands and war with Catholic Spain led in the first instance to the introduction of Renaissance-style influences from the Lowlands and in the second to that ultimate victory of the English on the high seas which founded her worldwide empire and gave her indirect dominance over the styles of the New World.

At the time of the first Tudors the pattern of living on the manorial estate still persisted. Most men had been free of serfdom since the fourteenth century. The small homeowner held his land as a *copyholder* (cottager)—a tenant with his rent fixed for life, a *freeholder* (yeoman) who could buy his land, or a laborer on the land of another. The entire manor was still operated on the Medieval system of villeinage, in which the acreage was divided into a number of tillable strips and a common pasture used by all.

During the sixteenth century many owners of manors found it profitable to redistribute the land, consolidate the fields, and usurp the commons. This widespread practice, known as the enclosure movement, was accompanied by an increase in the rents of the cottagers. This hardship was one of the causes of the later exodus to the New World where land was known to be plentiful.

On the other end of the financial ladder men grew wealthy. The church properties were granted to favorites of the crown. Mercantile interests in the far eastern trade were lucrative and culminated in the organization of the English East India Company in 1600. The profits in wool of the Midlands were guaranteed by enlarged landholdings. These were the fortunes that built the great houses of sixteenth-century England.

ARCHITECTURE

Early Tudor

Tudor architecture, like Tudor England, came belatedly and never completely to the knowledge that the Continent was embracing an Italian culture. Throughout the century the manner of building was not greatly altered; planning indicated only minor changes and style trends were worn more as ornaments hung on a native fabric than as a mode thoroughly assimilated. Not for one hundred years, in the architecture of Christopher Wren, would the Renaissance seem thoroughly at home in England.

Tudor architecture must be described largely in terms of domestic building. This was in the country rather than in the city, for the Englishman at heart has always been an outdoors man and a lover of the land. His country seat brought him more prestige than his townhouse, and even when the former meant attentive administration it could also mean hunters and hounds, gardens, and urbane social gatherings. The gentle art of conversation, described by one who knew the

300

Figure 8.1 (above) Compton Wynyates. Warwickshire, ca. 1528. (G. C. Ball.)

Figure 8.2 (below) Plan of Compton Wynyates. Warwickshire, ca. 1528. (a) court; (b) chapel; (c) parlor or withdrawing room; (d) hall; (e) buttery; (f) kitchen; (g) stairs; (h) porter. (Adapted from Sir Banister Fletcher, *A History of Architecture*, eighteenth edition, New York: Scribner's; London: Athlone Press, 1975.)

life of the English gentry well, coursed "over all the happenings of life, skating gracefully from one subject to another, never dwelling ponderously on anything, but always touching delicately and briefly, in the true sense of humanism."[1] So V. Sackville-West tells of the England of Elizabeth, of the Sackvilles at Knole, and the Sidneys at Penshurst.

One wonders whether this was the normal manner of activity in such an early Tudor house as Compton Wynyates (Figure 8.1) in the Vale of Evesham in Warwickshire. Its very name, *cumbe* in Saxon, means "hamlet in the hollow," which suggests a pleasant home surrounded by vineyards ("wynyates").[2] The present house was begun in the late fifteenth century but is largely the product of the first part of the sixteenth, when Sir William Compton, favorite of Henry VIII, added many features to the hall and began the chapel.

The estate today, like so many in England, represents many years of building, with alterations and additions. England is a land that has little patience with the doctrine of obsolescence. Although this may at times exasperate visitors from the west, it has its compensations in the production of roots, memories, and loyalties for which newer cultures have not found a counterpart.

Despite some changes, Compton Wynyates is essentially early Tudor architecture. In plan it is a group of buildings around a square courtyard

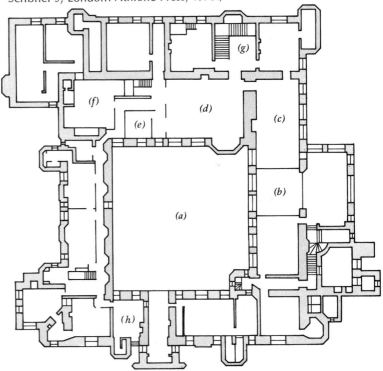

(Figure 8.2). Its materials are a weathered conglomerate—brick, stone, and half timber. It presents battlemented and gabled silhouettes with a multitude of chimneypots that break the sky. It is entered by a handsome stone, four-centered Tudor archway. The hall is on the far side of the court, which shows its Medieval origins. A double-door screen with linenfold paneling dates from the time of the Merry Monarch. The fire in the center of the hall remained until the eighteenth century. The upper end contains a handsome bay window imported from an earlier location and added to in its present. Access to the upper story was by turreted stairs, the remains of which are now concealed beneath the present floor. Compton Wynyates is the essence of English charm in its expression of gracious living on a more than meager but never ostentatious scale.

Tudor was an indigenous English style, common to the home of the prosperous yeoman, the squire, and the lord. It persisted occasionally until the present, although subject to minor changes in the interest of greater convenience and different uses of space. A broad staircase to replace the tower spiral rose from the upper end of the hall. The erstwhile chamber, again at the dais or private end, became the withdrawing and later the drawing room. The fireplace was located in the center of the long wall.

Elizabethan

Henry had built one palace that indicated an awareness of continental trends. *The Royal Palace of Nonsuch,* demolished about 1687 (excavated 1959), provides an example of the early invasion of bisymmetry onto the English scene. The facade on the garden side was flanked by two fantastic octagonal towers—the central mass terminated by opposing towers was an ubiquitous sign of monumental Tudor architecture thereafter.

Likewise matters of Renaissance detail date from the first half of the century. In a choir stall one sees a Renaissance rondel high up among the linenfold paneling. In Hampton Court Palace, which like Azay-le-Rideau and Chenonceaux paid the price of its grandeur by polite transferal to the crown, there are terra cotta medallions of Roman emperors on the great gate house, probably the work of the Italian Giovanni da Maiano. Both Cardinal Wolsey (the former owner of Hampton Court) and Henry VIII imported Italian craftsmen; the tomb of Henry VII by Pietro Torrigiano (1472–1528) was the most celebrated example of their skill. Following the separation of

the English church from Rome, these men were in alien territory and were neither productive of further artistry nor effective in training Englishmen. Probably most of them returned to Italy.

Queen Elizabeth, although she used all of her father's houses, did not make her reputation as a builder of palaces. Her courtiers, however, did. With her usual astuteness the queen inaugurated the custom of traveling with her large retinue on visits to the country seats of her most influential and wealthiest subjects. This travel was called a *Royal Progress.* When one pauses to consider the psychology of the situation—a woman and a queen to be entertained, one who could be favorably impressed by the nature of her surroundings—is it any wonder that these landowners spent lavishly on the rapid building of pretentious houses for display? All this cost the crown not a farthing while it enabled Her Majesty to appraise the loyalty of her court.

Culturally, England, despite the separation of the classes, was more unified than the Continent. Tudor architecture, as seen in palaces, manors, and ecclesiastic, scholastic, and civic buildings, is one manifestation of this fact. The new buildings of Elizabeth's reign made a show of grandeur and aped a foreign style which indicated that the social structure was changing. Thereafter architecture, at least, indicated a division of society's ranks.

Renaissance influence became fashionable. Not only was Serlio known in England but such men as John Shute, an Englishman in the service of the Duke of Northumberland, was sent by the duke to study in Italy. In 1563 Shute wrote the first English treatise on architecture. It included engravings of the orders. John Thorpe (ca. 1563–1655), an employee of the Royal Office of Works, compiled from existing buildings plans that are now preserved in Sir John Soane's Museum (which is devoted to architecture). Thorpe has been called the first English architect.

The basic attributes of Elizabethan architecture were similar. Grand size, of course, went with pretention. It was accompanied by relative compactness, regularity, and bisymmetry. Barrington Court, built by a friend of Henry and still extant, has a bisymmetrical plan and flanking wings rather than a closed court. The hall entrance is in the center of the building, the kitchen forced to the left wing in order to place the lower end of the hall at the center of the front.

An Italianate loggia was frequently built along the garden or rear wall of the dwelling, over which, and connecting the two wings, was added a low-ceilinged room called the *long gallery*. It became something of a family sitting room and the hall took on the aspect of a ceremonial entrance. The withdrawing (drawing) room was set aside for formal entertaining—today's separate areas of family room, hall, and living room had begun.

As on the Continent, the walls surrounding the court became lower or disappeared completely, although the formal court remained and frequently the gate house was retained as a status symbol. At a time when the Italian house opened only on its garden and the French were using the semblance of walls, the English Elizabethan country house, for instance, Kirby Hall, had large windowwalls for both front and garden facades. It possessed no enclosing court.

The Elizabethan mansion (for so this new edifice was called) grew proportionately tall in order to square off its compactness. Robert Smythson,

Figure 8.3 Hardwick Hall. Derbyshire, 1576–1597. Robert Smythson, architect. (Marburg/Prothmann.)

a freemason engaged in the building of Longleat, Wollaton, and Hardwick (Figure 8.3), acquired an amazing degree of coherence in his work by effective massing and the unifying principle introduced by repetition of the orders and hiding of untidy details behind balustrade. Central emphasis was gained in domed lanterns. Likewise the walls of the central hall were frequently raised to provide clerestory lighting. The effect of all this, as seen, for instance, at Wollaton, is to inaugurate the hierarchic design with central emphasis, associated with the late Italian Renaissance. This is a far cry from the indication of bisymmetry that the Nonsuch towers created, which, like the tower of the early Renaissance Italian palace of Venezia, called attention away from the central axis.

After the legitimate architectonics of these mansions is allowed, we note that the picturesque is never absent. Their real fun quality lies in their use of ornament. During Elizabeth's reign, with English amity toward the Netherlands, an immediate source of Renaissance inspiration came with the arrival of Huguenot craftsmen, refugees from Flanders. Direct impact was augmented by books of ornament from the same quarter. A century after Gutenberg's bible was printed in movable type in the Lowlands Antwerp was a flourishing center of publishing and the reproduction

of graphic prints. Among the books that found their way to England were H. Vredeman De Vries's (1527–1604) *Architectura* and *Compertimenta,* both published in the sixties, and Wendel Dietterlin's (ca. 1550–1599) books on the orders and architecture which came out in the nineties. To these publications the English designers turned for their decorative enrichment. To them we owe the strapwork, the grotesques, the arched gables, and the sculptural extravaganza that we associate with the homes of Elizabethan England. With the Stuarts of the next century these fantastic creations sobered down. In the meantime they remained superb monuments to a new, proud, confident, and boastful society.

Of other structures of the sixteenth century we need say little. Fine as they were, their tradition was Gothic. This was especially true of the academic buildings at Oxford and Cambridge, many of which are so engagingly Tudor Gothic that they set the tone for academic construction since then. Of churches, England was well supplied, and except for the introduction of a pulpit and lectern to bring the minister into the nave there was little need for change at that time.

The principal mercantile building of note was the Royal Exchange in London, founded by Sir Thomas Gresham in 1566. Opened by Queen Elizabeth in 1571, it was Flemish Renaissance in style, built around a loggia courtyard. With some market halls built in similar manner, it served to acquaint the English with the changing architectural scene. But they can scarcely be called classical except in a northern Mannerist sense.

SOME ENGLISH TUDOR HOUSES

Whitehall Palace	London	Medieval York Palace, London residence of the Archbishop of York; crown property after the downfall of Wolsey; enlarged and renamed by Henry VIII; Banquet Hall, architect Inigo Jones (1619–1621); all but this hall burned in 1698
Paycockes	Essex	ca. 1510, for Thomas Paycocke; National Trust property
Barrington Court	Somerset	1514–1520, for Lord Daubeny
Hampton Court Palace	Middlesex	1515–1530, for Cardinal Wolsey; additions for Henry VIII; eastern front redesigned for William and Mary by Sir Christopher Wren
Sutton Place	Surrey	ca. 1520–1530, for Sir Richard Weston; home of the Dukes of Sutherland
Compton Wynyates (Figures 8.1, 8.2)	Warwickshire	ca. 1528, for Sir William Compton
St. James's Palace	London	1531; rebuilt by Henry VIII on site of old leper hospital; later work by Inigo Jones for Charles I; by Sir Christopher Wren for Charles II; John Nash for George IV
Nonsuch Palace	Surrey	1538, begun by Henry VIII, finished by Earl of Arundel; returned to crown in 1591; demolished in 17th cent.
Lacock	Wiltshire	1540–1549, for Sir William Sharington; old abbey converted to house
Longleat	Wiltshire	1541–1580, for Sir John Thynne
Old Somerset House	London	1547–1552, for Protector Somerset; now destroyed
Charlecote Park	Warwickshire	1558, rebuilt for Sir Thomas Lucy
Little Moreton Hall (Figure 5.39)	Cheshire	1559–1580, for the Moreton family

Losely Park	Surrey	1561–1569, for Sir William More
Haddon Hall (the long gallery)	Derbyshire	1567–1584
Castle Ashby	Northamptonshire	1572, for Lord Compton; architect John Thorpe; entrance later by Inigo Jones
Kirby Hall	Northamptonshire	1572, for Sir Humphrey Stafford; architect, John Thorpe; later additions by Inigo Jones
Hardwick Hall (Figure 8.3)	Derbyshire	1576–1597, for "Bess of Hardwick," Countess of Shrewsbury; architect, Robert Smythson
Longford Castle	Wiltshire	1578; architect, John Thorpe
Burghley House	Northamptonshire	1577–1587, for Cecil, Lord Burghley; architect, John Thorpe
Wollaton Hall	Nottinghamshire	1580–1585, for Sir Francis Willoughby; architect, Robert Smythson
Montacute	Somerset	1595, for Sir Edward Phelips
Knole House	Kent	1603, hall rebuilt and staircase built for Sir Thomas Sackville, first Earl of Dorset

INTERIOR DESIGN

The space conceptions and planning of Tudor buildings were discussed with their architecture.

Architectural Details

Architectural details of the interior need further appraisal (Figure 8.4). Early wooden doors were customarily set into stone jambs. When walls were paneled, inner doors followed suit and their frames were also of wood. A fine door corresponded to the interior paneling in its design. Doors of less pretension were made of broad boards, battened crosswise and butt-jointed. Ornamental iron hinges and cross braces added to the sturdy effect. Door heads were flat or featured the Tudor four-centered arch.

The manufacture of glass of reputable quality began in England about 1500. Windowpanes, which had previously been small and frequently diamond shaped, were changed to larger rectangles. Although most windows were still in fixed position and stone-mullioned, the hinged casement did occur, often within a larger rigid enclosure. The slanted interior jamb began to give way to the rectangular. Oriel, bay, and flat windows appeared in their usual places. Armorial stained glass brought prestige.

Fireplaces were important adjuncts. Standards of comfort were raised and the wall fire was counted on to furnish the necessary heat, which at best was toast on one side and chill on the other. Drafts were inevitably produced by the air currents. The early Tudor fireplace was of ample size. Its breast was of stone, a four-centered arch surmounted by a mantel frieze of typical motifs, possibly *quatrefoils* bearing Gothic tracery of moldings and vines in the spandrels. The final rectangular surround would be composed of bold stone moldings. One fireplace opening at St. James's Palace is 7 ft broad with moldings approximately 1 ft wide. The entire surround is 7 ft high.

Toward the end of the Tudor period the centrally located fireplace and its superstructure had become the principal decorative feature in a room. The top of the opening was flat and the elaborate wood or stone mantel assumed a classical pattern that displayed flanking columns and a complete entablature. Above this was an elaborate chimney breast, often taking its tone from Flemish sources.

Stairs, which in less pretentious building remained the newel type, were supplanted during Elizabeth's reign by at least one imposing stairway mounting from the chamber end of the house. This was supported from the wall and as-

Figure 8.4 Tudor Room from Somersetshire, ca. 1490. A "turneyed" chair can be seen on the left and a panel-back chair on the right. Museum of Fine Arts, Boston. (Courtesy, Museum of Fine Arts, Boston, gift of Mrs. Edward Foote Dwight in memory of her father and mother.)

cended by easy flights and broad landings. The railings were molded and the balusters were turned. The newel posts were often elaborately carved with fanciful beasts for finials, altered, as the Renaissance pattern books emerged, to classical terms and figures.

Interior Surface Treatment

Floors were much as they had been: stone, terra cotta, or clay on the ground floor, wood in ran-dom width above. The Dutch humanist writer Erasmus, who visited England, complained of the filthy condition of the rushes strewn on the floor. Oriental carpets in the form of small rugs had not become the rule except in wealthy establishments.

The open timber roof, common to the Medieval hall, was less frequently found in the Elizabethan mansion. Henry's hall at Hampton Court and the halls at Trinity College, Cambridge (1604), as well as at Wollaton and Longleat, are all hammer beamed, but by 1536 the watching tower at Hampton had a plaster ceiling. (The *seeling* denoted the covering of the open roof structure and the paneling of walls.)

The patterns imposed on these plaster ceilings differed with circumstance, from plain to elaborate. They took their point of departure from Gothic ribbed vaulting and were designed with geometric patterns that formed ribs, from the intersections of which molded bosses hung. Flattened ribs and finally the Flemish-inspired strapwork then occurred. Such ornamental stucco decoration is known as *pargework* or, when elaborate, sometimes by the Italian name *stucco-duro*. The basic ceiling was flat, coved, or vaulted.

The first paneled rooms appeared toward the end of the fifteenth century, most frequently in the smaller drawing rooms where the expense would not be prohibitive. Oak and sometimes fir were used with patterned inserts occasionally done in dark or fumed oak, poplar, and fruit woods. Stands of walnut were allegedly planted in England, but the wood was not available for extensive use until the next century. The Earl of Pembroke is known to have set out deal trees (a form of pine) at Wilton Park in Wiltshire, reputedly in 1565. This extremely fine and lustrous wood warms to a deep honey color with age.

The size of the panels remained stationary throughout the century—approximately 3 ft high by almost 2 ft wide. Paycockes in Coggeshall, Essex, is a fine example of a small house with rooms entirely paneled in linenfold. Paycockes belonged to an affluent wool merchant of that name.

The panel with the rondel and head profile enframed is contemporary with linenfold. It may well have been Italian in origin; the same may be claimed for the arcaded panels of the latter part of the century. Some of the finest work of this nature is in ecclesiastic buildings. The screen and stalls at King's College Chapel, Cambridge, are Renaissance in feeling and were reputedly done on the order of Henry VIII between 1533 and 1535 by Italian carvers. These may have been the men who made the panels for Cardinal Wolsey's chamber at Hampton Court.

This paneling sometimes extended over the entire wall; often it was only on the lower section up to a high *dado*, which was separated from the upper wall by a molding strip. Another name for the paneled section was *wainscot*. The wall above the dado might be plastered and handled as a frieze, for which a great deal of freeform treatment was allowed. For this reason an examina-

tion of English Renaissance friezes can be a continuing source of interest. Designs taken from the Flemish books can be easily identified and are often spaced by classical motifs such as the pilaster and the *cartouche* (a conventionalized ornament in the form of an embossed shield or oval). The most delightful friezes resulted when the sculptor gave free rein to his imagination.

Occasionally walls or ceiling compartments were painted, but this was not customary in England until the late Baroque.

Toward the end of the century classical pilasters frequently appeared on panels to support a decorative architrave, frieze, and cornice. Rather than using them as room spacers, which suggested supporting members, the English workman frequently added pilasters to conceal the butt joining of a group of panels.

FURNITURE

General Development

As to furnishings in general, they were not yet so numerous and their placement could not have been planned in a formal manner. Objects in pairs, for instance, are not found.

It is customary to divide Tudor furniture history into two periods: the *Early Tudor* of the reigns of the two Henrys, Edward VI, and Mary and the *Elizabethan*, obviously named for Anne Boleyn's daughter. This separation is logical not only because of slight changes of style that occurred between the last of the fifteenth century and the beginning of the seventeenth but also because of the disparate finesse between the production of the early and late years. This was due to the absence of expert guild-trained woodworkers after the dissolution of the monastery schools.

In early Tudor furniture we occasionally see Italian Renaissance motifs, probably inspired by the handicraft of some immigrant artist. In similar manner the Flemish pattern books, as well as the chisel of a displaced Huguenot, introduced Flemish Renaissance design into Elizabethan furniture, but much of the embellishment consisted of sturdy English geometrics.

Figure 8.5 *Yorkshire* and *Derbyshire* chairs. England, sixteenth to seventeenth centuries. Oak. Height 81.5–113 cm, width, 45–48 cm. Victoria and Albert Museum, London. (Crown Copyright, Victoria and Albert Museum.)

Materials and Construction

Although framed construction was well known in fine work of the sixteenth century, many Tudor pieces returned to butt jointing and battened ends. Advanced and crude construction will often appear in the same piece—a certain indication that the carpenter or joiner knew well how it should be done but considered it not worth the labor, an unthinkable situation under previous rigid guild rule. Cosmopolitan Elizabethan furniture is framed.

Most Tudor pieces were of oak, the wood that seems to symbolize the sturdy qualities of England and is never without representation in English furniture. Lesser woods were used—beech, ash, elm, and deal. They have not survived so well and are rarely seen from this early date.

Finishes were negligible; when used they consisted of oil or wax. Painting, as embellishment or preservative, was not unusual.

Carving was the fundamental ornament, but *inlay* and *marquetry* were practiced. The last refers to a mosaic pattern of small pieces. *Parquetry* is its equivalent for use on floors. The *Nonsuch chests* are examples of marquetry, which had its heyday in the seventeenth century.[3]

Types and Descriptions

Very little Tudor furniture remains. Compared with today's production, very little ever existed. The box type, *chair,* derived from the choir stall, came earliest only to evolve into the more elaborate *panel back* or *wainscot* chair, the English equivalent of the Italian *sedia* or the French *caquetoire*. Turned legs were supported by stretchers. Arms, when present, gradually acquired graceful and comfortable curvature. The fairly high-framed back included a carved panel. Seats were high, at least 22 in., in order to clear drafty floors. Squab cushions were let into a recessed seat as the demand for comfort became important. The fashion for upholstery came in with the last years of Elizabeth's reign but it was not usual until fifty years later. It consisted of padding of horsehair or tow, covered with fabric.

A more colloquial style which put in a late appearance has been dubbed the *Yorkshire* or *Derbyshire* chair (Figure 8.5). It had an armless seat, and uprights that ended in carved finials of waterleaf derivation which resembled certain Italian pieces. Its back showed two or three carved and hooped bars with acorn pendants suspended and the center of the crosspiece was shaped like an oriental crescent. In some variations the rungs supported arcades of spindles. The southern and Spanish overtones in design, and the fact that these chairs were located in the northeast counties has fostered the idea that they may have been introduced as the cargo of some Spanish galleon wrecked or unloaded on a wild English shore.

Figure 8.6 *Nonsuch* chest. England, ca. 1560–1600. Inlay on wood. Victoria and Albert Museum, London. (Crown Copyright, Victoria and Albert Museum.)

The X or curule chair was likewise found in England, although more in Stuart than in Tudor years. Holbein painted a portrait of Queen Mary seated on one that was upholstered in red velvet and gold fringe, fastened to the frame with brass-headed tacks. This particular chair may have been a direct Spanish import brought in by her husband Philip of Spain. With a single flower held primly in her hand, she does not appear to be enjoying her splendid throne nor, for that matter, her very existence.

Near the end of the century the odd *turneyed* or *stick-back* chair appeared. It was made entirely by the wood turner on a pole lathe and its joinery was that of the pegged furniture of every subsequent age. Largely of fruit woods, it was obviously an item of less cost. Stools, with the character of chair types, were the usual seat at least until the eighteenth century.

Chests certainly continued to be made, their styles corresponding to other furniture types. One variety called *Nonsuch* (Figure 8.6), which appeared between 1560 and 1600, was unique. At this time Nonsuch Palace belonged to the Earl of Arundel but seems to have been favored by Queen Elizabeth and to have been virtually preempted by her. The famed meeting with Essex on his return from the Irish encounters took place there. The *Nonsuch* chests were inlaid with

a crude facsimile of the palace front, and it can readily be seen why they would be popular.

Cupboards were used for the storage of ceramic and metal dishes. During the late sixteenth and early seventeenth centuries a specific type known as the *court* or *short* cupboard was fashionable (Figure 8.7). This resembled a two-tiered buffet with a small cupboard occupying the central position on the second shelf. The bottom shelf was open or sometimes enclosed in another cupboard.

Another type common in Wales was known as a *deu-darn* or *tri-darn*. Its open shelves above the cupboard were typical of the piece known in France as the *dressoir* and in England as the *dresser*. Other varieties of cupboard such as the Medieval press (i.e., clothes), the livery, and the almery continued to be made.

Figure 8.7 Tudor *short cupboard* with bulbous turning, nulling, and strapwork. England, late sixteenth century. Victoria and Albert Museum, London. (Crown Copyright, Victoria and Albert Museum.)

The substantial board of Tudor days was the trestle *table*. Small tables such as the box table with a hinged top are occasionally found. The framed table, since the midsixteenth century, was supported by upright posts tenoned into the top and braced by low-placed stretchers. It was frequently equipped with a draw leaf (Figure 8.8).

Only a few headboards and some posts remain from early Tudor *beds*. The bed was always one of the most important household items. In Shakespeare's will he gives ". . . unto my wife my second best bed with the furniture."[4] All of his other possessions of value went to his daughters, his sister, and their offspring. The "furniture" of a bed is its bedclothes and hangings.

The Victoria and Albert Museum displays the *Great Bed of Ware,* which Shakespeare mentions in *Twelfth Night.* Actually these Tudor beds were of tremendous size—in fact like a small room (Figure 8.9). Some of them were 10 to 11 ft long and of almost square proportions. Only the headboard was attached to the bed frame; the foot posts were separate when they were tall enough to support the *canopies* or *testers* (the terms are interchangeable) from which hung the curtains.

Ornament on Tudor furniture takes on a character that is unmistakably English. Most obvious is the oversized development of the bulbous leg which made its appearance in the last years of Elizabeth's reign and so is often considered a Flemish importation. This design, however, is to be seen in a less highly matured state in tables belonging to the early Tudors. It may well be an English expression of an Italian Renaissance motif which is represented by a large vase pedestal. The earliest Elizabethan bulbs are the largest; later examples are smaller, more attenuated, and resort to turning for some of their ornamentation.

The carving on the upper portion of these knops is usually in a pattern known as *gadrooning* or *ruffling.* This is a repetitive type of radiating lobe which when placed spirally on an apron goes by the name of *nulling,* an effect similar to that of repoussé fluting on silver. The lower section of bulbous turnings incorporates foliage, said to be the stalked tulip and acanthus leaves.

On the aprons of tables and the friezes of bedsteads nulling was succeeded by flat strapwork. On the Tudor bedstead at the Metropolitan Mu-

Figure 8.8 Tudor framed *draw table*. England, sixteenth century. Victoria and Albert Museum, London. (Crown Copyright, Victoria and Albert Museum.)

seum of Art this strapwork in the form of reversed S's creates a lyre-shaped motif. As the seventeenth century approached, panels on headboards became more regular and geometric and contained rectangular bosses similar to those that appeared later on Stuart wall paneling.

Arcades and lunettes evolved from Gothic geometric forms such as the diamond and circle. The guilloche and the geometricized grapevine (figure S, again) were used. The enclosure of a medallion head in a circlet, known as *Romayne* work, is of Renaissance derivation, much of which came to England in the Flemish and German pattern books. It is not to be supposed that the English carvers entirely forsook their Gothic imagery in working on the finest of Tudor furniture. All forms of animal are represented as supports, and what Cellini was to metalry and Palissy was to ceramics the English woodcarver was to furniture. Stylized floral forms, always beloved by the English, appear as the tulip, the ball flower, and of course the Tudor rose. These are particularly applicable to the inlay designs that gained in popularity toward the end of the century.

TEXTILES

Although not notable for its textiles, the Tudor period can claim several firsts. In the village of Barcheston, in Warwickshire, a certain Squire Sheldon opened the first English tapestry factory during the reign of Queen Elizabeth. Wisely he made use of the help of Flemish weavers. At Compton Wynyates there is a Barcheston tapestry panel of Frederick, Elector of Palatine, who married Elizabeth, daughter of James I. The Hanoverian line of English royal descent came from this union.

Another example of a first, somewhat related to textiles, is the wallpaper found in 1911 on the ceiling beams of the Master's lodgings at Christ College, Cambridge. The design, attributed to

311

Figure 8.9 Tudor Elizabethan bed. Cumnor Place, Berkshire, late sixteenth century. Oak with inlay of walnut, ebony, and ash bole. Length, 2.66 m, width, 1.84 m, height, 2.63 m. Metropolitan Museum of Art, New York. (The Metropolitan Museum of Art, Gift of Irwin Untermyer, 1953.)

one Hugo Goes, is that of a highly conventionalized Renaissance pomegranate, no doubt an attempt to imitate a contemporary textile pattern. Printed by woodblock on the back of a news sheet which contained an account of the death of Henry VII and a proclamation by Henry VIII, the year 1509 when the master's lodgings were completed is assumed. In reconstructed form and in remnant, it is in the Victoria and Albert Museum.

English textiles have always been renowned for their embroidery, which was done by gentlewomen as well as by professional embroiderers. In the 1560s a Broderer's Guild was founded which guaranteed the quality of all embroidered cloth offered for sale. Crewel work was popular during the late Elizabethan and early Stuart regimes. Crewel patterns, which featured many of the Italian Renaissance motifs supported on sinuous trellises of grapevine curves, proved to be a suitable foil for the larger scale of rooms, win-

dows, and furniture. Crewel work was done with hand-dyed woolen yarn on crash linen. The most prominent stitch was the chain, although many others were used as fillings. The number and variety of embroidery stitches perfected by the English embroiderer was remarkable.

It should be mentioned that embroidery on silk with silk or gold thread was also much practiced in Elizabethan England. Indeed, in the homes of the wealthy during most of the Tudor reigns silk was the preferred material. Italian velvets and embroidery in raised patterns (sometimes appliqued on plain silk) were fashionable. The Elizabethan era was a period of triumphant display and belongings of silk were regarded as status symbols.

Although expensive foreign fabrics were certainly imported by the rich (Bess of Hardwick ordered Brussels tapestries that correlated with room dimensions for Hardwick Hall), the middle classes were emerging as potential customers. William Harrison writes in 1587:

. . . so in times past the costly furniture stayed there, whereas now it is descended yet lower, even into the inferior artificers, and many farmers, who . . . have, for the most part, learned also to garnish their cupboards with plate, their joined beds with tapestry and silk hangings, and their tables with carpets and fine napery, whereby the wealth of our country . . . doth infinitely appear.[5]

GLASS

Glass was one of England's early manufactures. We left the story of Medieval English glass with Laurence Vitrearius, who was established in the weald or wooden area of Sussex-Surrey in the early thirteenth century. Manufactories for making church window glass antedated Laurence by at least four centuries.

The exhaustion of the wood supply is thought to have caused the eventual decline of glass production in the area south of London. It was re-established in the coal-burning and now principal manufacturing area of Newcastle-on-Tyne.

During the sixteenth century a new impetus was given to the industry by the immigration into

England of Protestants from Lorraine (an early center of manufacture of northern European glass) and Venetians of the Altarist tradition (from Altare near Genoa, an early center of southern European glass). The leader of the Lorrainians was a man known as Carré of Antwerp; Giacomo Verzelini was the most important among the Venetians. Eventually both groups found it expedient to set up glass houses in London, where the demand for quality tableware was growing. Verzelini's proved the more profitable venture, and in December 1575 he obtained a licence that gave him a twenty-one year monopoly in the manufacture of Venetian glass in England. On his retirement in 1592 the work was underwritten by Sir Jerome Bowles who continued the operation until the early years of the next century.

Tradition attributes about eight extant glasses to Verzelini, four of which were shown in the exhibition of 1968 at the British Museum in honor of the International Congress on Glass held in London in that year. Illustrated is one owned by the Fitzwilliam Museum at Cambridge (Figure 8.10), probably diamond-point engraved by the French immigrant Anthony de Lysle and dated 1578.

CERAMICS

It was not until the seventeenth century that England began to develop prominence in the manufacture of ceramics. Pottery was undoubtedly made but no documented pieces have survived.

STONES, METALS, IVORIES

With gold and silver and other metals the story is different. New types indicated a turn toward more polite amenities. Individual plates, possibly the two-tined fork (Queen Elizabeth reputedly owned one), the silver candlestick, and the elevated *tazza* arrived. Knives were still the long, steel hunting variety but were given ivory handles.

The earliest silver spoons are preserved from Tudor silver. Similar to the Byzantine, they had fig-shaped bowls and round or hexagonal stems. Ball termini, now known as *knops,* were com-

Figure 8.10 Verzelini goblet. London, 1578. Fitzwilliam Museum, Cambridge, England. (Fitzwilliam Museum.)

mon. The handles were embellished with ornament in the form of an acorn, a bunch of grapes, or a bird. Continental spoons were frequently topped with small figures, whence the concept of the apostle spoons may have derived. These sets of thirteen included the figure of Christ and were intended as christening gifts. Few collections remain intact (Figure 8.11).

313

St. Simon Zelotes 1628 · St. Mathias 1628 · St. Thomas 1628 · THE MASTER 1658 · St. John 1628 · St. Andrew 1628 · St. Matthew 1628

St. Phillip 1574 · St. James the Greater 1604 · St. Peter 1621 · St. James the Less 1631 · St. Bartholomew 1634 · St. Jude 1640

Figure 8.11 Set of spoons—the Twelve Apostles and Christ. London. 1574–1658, assembled from various sets. Sterling and Francine Clark Art Institute, Williamstown, Mass. (Sterling and Francine Clark Art Institute, Williamstown, Massachusetts.)

By midcentury mazers were superseded by standing cups, which began with the squat Medieval font cup shape whose bowl is low and broad. Taller cups with bowls more attenuated took the form of V and U shapes; one was egg-shaped, another an inverted bell. Two-handled cups and smaller wine cups were in the Tudor inventory, some of which followed the trend of Germanic Mannerist design and were embellished with cast figures and incorporated foreign materials such as rock crystal, gems, and even the coconut in their makeup. Others were relatively simple and depended on engraving and chasing for flatter patterns.

Standing salts remain the most conspicuous articles of Tudor ware. These, too, were influenced by Mannerist trends. The English silversmith delighted in concealing the functional aspect of the salt container with an architectural framework or by disguising it in a clock or other mechanical piece. Although none of the latter has survived, one was described in the inventory of Queen Elizabeth's plate in 1574.[6]

During the reigns of Henry VIII, Edward, and Mary Tudor metal was thin because of the inflationary price that resulted from an effort by the state to allay some of Henry's vast debts. To make a mickle look a muckle, repoussé technique was often used. Frequently strengthening wires were soldered to the edges of vessels.

A silver collector is interested in dating silver by its marks. After 1300 silver that met the government sterling requirements was punched with

314

a leopard's head (actually a lion in front view wearing a crown). This was the royal guarantee of coinage content which by the Statute of 1367 the maker was required to fulfill. The third compulsory cipher was the date letter, which occurred after 1477, the letter A being used for 1478. Various kinds of alphabet denote successive cycles, and a table must be consulted to establish the exact year of fabrication. In 1545 a fourth mark seems to have been decreed by the Goldsmith's Company. A lion in profile, known as the *lion passant* or *passant guardant* was specified as assurance that the metal was the old sterling standard and not that of the debased coinage of the realm. This symbol, often alluded to as Her Majesty's Lion, refers to the fact that one of Queen Elizabeth's first acts was to restore coinage to its sterling value, a value that was maintained until the twentieth century.

POSTSCRIPT

Incidentally, Queen Elizabeth played the virginal. An instrument that belonged to her is in the Victoria and Albert Museum. Put this down as a postscript to a remarkable reign—hard headed, perceptive, and withal strangely impressionable—a monarchy prophetic of England's future.

DESCRIPTIVE SUMMARY

Did England ever have a Renaissance period in art? It has been argued pro and con, as, indeed, has the corresponding question—did England ever have a Baroque? Certainly the Renaissance had little liaison except with the years of Elizabeth's reign. And even then it was a difficult import onto native soil. England does supremely well what she does naturally. To the Renaissance she merely contributed some robust drama, but to the sixteenth century she gave the perfection of her native Tudor idiom, a gift without equal for the land. Not for another century, and with the architecture of Christopher Wren and the furnishings it annexed, would the formal Renaissance or the comely Baroque seem right for English soil. Then it would belong to the people.

CHAPTER NINE

Baroque Italy

1600 TO 1700

The people is a beast of muddy brain
That knows not its own force, and therefore stands
Loaded with wood and stone; the powerless hands
Of a mere child guide it with bit and rein.

From the sonnet on the *People*
by Fra Tomasso Campanella (1568–1639)
English translation by John Addington Symonds

CULTURE SPAN

One must believe, as one studies the political writings of Machiavelli in the sixteenth century and Campanella in the seventeenth, that both men wished for the good of Italy and the Italian people. In the means they advocated there was a world of difference. The earlier author was a pragmatist and felt that for his time an enlightened despotism was the only possible political answer. The later writer was an idealist and, much to his own grief, preached a doctrine that focused on awakening the populace to its potential. In this Campanella speaks to the future.

The most radical dissension of the sixteenth century was religious. The church responded with the Inquisition for its sword and a persuasive emotional art for its allure.

Baroque art, the art of the seventeenth century—whether or not we credit the origin of the name to that of a shell, *barocca*, of irregular shape—was one of many conflicts, opposites, and irregularities. Its content differed in the several countries of western Europe. Underneath these variances we sense a common strain. Where Medieval art was an art of spiritual revelation and Renaissance art, one of humanistic rediscovery, the Baroque was one of exemplification—*here I stand*. Its patrons, whether church, prince, or establishment, were fundamentally vaunting a way of life. The seventeenth century had the need to sell in the various European countries, in one case the religious experience, in another, the pride of state, and, again, bourgeois substance.

In Rome the Apostolic See was represented by the scions of wealthy families such as the Borghese (Pope Paul V, 1605–1620, Camillo Borghese), and Barberini (Urban VIII, 1623–1644, Mafeo Barberini), the Pamphili (Innocent X, 1644–1655, Giambattista Pamphili), and the Chigi (Alexander VII, 1655–1677, Fabio Chigi). It was the members of these houses who commissioned the numerous churches and the works of art they contained. The same men built the palaces and villas in and around seventeenth-century Rome for their own aggrandisement.

Beyond Rome Spain ruled the greater part of Italy. Much of the machinery of absolutism lies in its social panoply and that of Iberianized Italy

must have been inordinately grand and stuffy. In Florence, for instance, Cosimo, the first Duke of Tuscany, married to the immensely wealthy Eleanor of Toledo, had ordained a miniature replica of the Spanish court. Consider the rich stuffs and jewels that adorn the Duchess in her well-known portrait by the Mannerist painter Angelo Bronzino and the following description of Florentine life by the traveler Lassels will take on new meaning:

> It is the custom here in winter to invite the chief ladies of the town (married women only) to come and play at cards on winter evenings for three or four hours apace; and this night in one palace, another night in another palace. In every chamber the doors are set open and for the most part you will see eight or ten chambers on a floor, going on of one another, with a square table holding eight persons, as many chairs, two silver candlesticks with wax lights in them and a store of lights around the room. At the hour appointed, company being come, they sit down to play, a cavalier sitting between every lady and all the women looking as fine in cloths and jewels as if they were going to a ball. The doors of these rooms being open, the women glittering and all glorious, you would take these palaces to be the enchanted palaces of the old king of the mountain.[1]

In seventeenth-century Rome social life was considerably less circumscribed. Such men as Pope Paul V's nephew, Cardinal Scipione Borghese (whom the sculptor Bernini has immortalized), famed for his lavish entertaining and his expenditures for art, fostered a more informal and more worldly wise existence.

In the northwest in Savoy and Piedmont French influence grew by virtue of Bourbon successes in the continental wars and royal family alliances. French prestige, like that of Rome, fostered a more genial social atmosphere.

Meanwhile, in the far south of Italy, in such smaller towns as Lecce and Bari, a world of merchants and professional men lived quite removed from the high courts. Here the grand manner of the Spanish-inspired Baroque was distilled into the smaller homes with their enormous portals and gay heraldic devices which still enliven the quaint, sunny streets. Here was the counterpart of the bourgeois society that had built the flourishing ports of Flanders and the Netherlands and had created its version of the current style. Here was art by the people rather than art instigated to influence or impress people. Sometimes understandably gauche, the architecture of the south indicated how very close Baroque art had always been to the emotions of people.

ARCHITECTURE

As design, what is the meaning of the Baroque architectural style? Size is likely to be grandiose, although in Italy this was true of palaces rather than churches. Shapes veer away from the regular and rectangular and are often molded in three dimensions. In France this characteristic is less true. Coloristic patterns and the use of light as a design factor are notable, especially in Italy. Texture becomes an important design component.

In organization forms are more open, the diagonal direction more prominent, thematic development more complex. All of this is accomplished within skillfully dictated rhythms which set a unity over the whole. Indeed, even in structure the Baroque shows remarkable inventiveness in molding all of the past into one new entity.

The best-known architect of the early Baroque was Carlo Maderna (1556–1629). Pope Clement VIII (Ippolito Aldobrandini, 1592–1605) had appointed him architect of St. Peter's. Maderna was faced with the unenviable task of altering Bramante's and Michelangelo's church in order to annex a long nave of the basilican type for the purpose of accommodating the larger congregations appropriate to the principles of the counterreformation. His work as a designer was here somewhat circumscribed by the already existing building as well as by the new functional requirements. Nevertheless, Maderna preserved a classical order with a necessary majesty, wholly in keeping with the character of the building. As the first architect for the Palazzo Barberini, his work was left unfinished at his death, and the extent of his involvement is not clear.

We must turn to such designs as that of Sta. Susanna (Figure 9.1), the old church altered to its present form in 1603, to see Maderna at his most

Figure 9.1 Facade of Sta. Susanna, Rome. Reconstruction by Carlo Maderna. 1597–1603. (Alinari/Editorial Photocolor Archives.)

characteristic. Sta. Susanna is extended from the earlier church done principally by Vignola,[2] which became the pattern for many Jesuit (the Society of Jesus, an order organized in 1534 under papal control) churches of the seventeenth century. In Maderna's Sta. Susanna, although it is correct in its classical elevation, we observe a newly acquired ability to fuse a building into a visual whole with both horizontal and vertical

319

movement fully contained. Admittedly, the sumptuous scrolls which encase the upper story are effective agents of this result, but the proportional relationships that Maderna contrived are even more skillful means. Notice, for instance, that even the widths of the bays are increased toward the central portal.

The high Baroque in Italy is synonymous with the work of three men—Gianlorenzo Bernini (1598–1680), Francesco Borromini (1599–1667), and Baldassare Longhena (1598–1680). These three displayed group as well as individual characteristics that entitle a whole period to be set off from its predecessors.

As an illustration of the characteristics of Baroque building let us examine the Palazzo Barberini (Figures 9.2 and 9.3). The Barberini Pope, Urban VIII, commissioned first Maderna and, on his death, Bernini, and finally Borromini to complete and enlarge an old palace in the north central part of Rome. Although the original plan for the seventeenth-century palace is credited to Maderna, its execution was the work of the two younger architects, Borromini assisting Bernini. Undoubtedly this pair introduced some details of their own interpretation (e.g., the particular type and use of the orders on the facade are attributed to Bernini; the framing bands used on the

Figure 9.2 (above) Palazzo Barberini. Rome, 1625–1633. Carlo Maderna, Gialorenzo Bernini, Francesco Borromini, architects. (G. C. Ball.)

Figure 9.3 (below) Cartouche over central window of the facade of the Palazzo Barberini, Rome. Barberini insignia: three bees plus the keys of St. Peter and the papal crown; the keys and crown represent the Barberini Pope Urban VIII. (G. C. Ball.)

long wings, to Borromini).[3] Thus three of the leading architects of the seicento had their fingers in the pie. Maderna's first scheme, judging from a drawing now preserved at the Uffizi, corresponded to the usual Renaissance palace plan somewhat in the image of the Farnese. The present layout (Figure 9.4) resembles a truncated letter H. It has a shallow court in front and two wings.

The exterior facade, probably established in outline by Maderna, holds to the classic pattern of three stories of superimposed orders—the Doric, Ionic, and Corinthian—with heavy horizontal entablatures as separation, large arched windows in the seven frontal bays, and an open arcade on the ground. On close inspection we notice illusionistic devices intended to alter spaces visually; for instance, the windows on the second story, which are necessarily smaller than those of the *piano nobile,* are designed with a false perspective to give them the appearance of greater size. *Trompe l'oeil* is a common practice throughout the Baroque, having spread from its home in northern Italy. The undulating capping over the windows of the front recessed bays is undoubtedly the work of Borromini and illustrates that architect's tendency to mold his contours in three dimensions.

One enters by a central imposing vestibule which, with broad stairs that mount by easy rises along the walls, dominates the scene and conspicuously unites the ground and first floors. Because the enlarged stair area preempts space, the principal salons of the *piano nobile* are not in the usual Renaissance position of front center but are located at right angles to the vestibule in the wings. (The stairs and the placement of these rooms is attributed to Bernini.[4]) Display rather than functional planning often dictates the Baroque.

From the largest hall in the Barberini, the one for which Cartona painted his famous ceiling, doorways open from room to room along the window wall (Figure 9.5). This creates one of the first and grandest of those vistas that produce an illusion of immeasurable space, although with a limited amount of privacy. The idea of vistas opening along an axis is not new. It is found in Palladio's villas, and indeed it has been said that

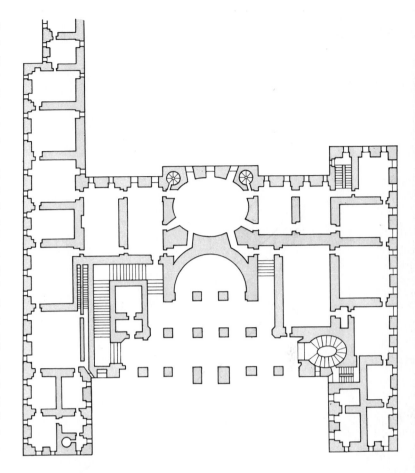

Figure 9.4 Plan of Palazzo Barberini, Rome, shows the palace before rebuilding ca. 1670. (After Letarouilly.)

a Venetian thinks in terms of "visual continuities," whereas a Tuscan thinks in terms of "blocky units."[5] Palladio, however, opens his enfilade through central doors; in the P. Barberini the doors are all at one side adjacent to the windows.[6] The effect of this on the beholder is one of a corridor upon which directional light plays into caverns beyond. This is Renaissance straight linear development, coupled with Baroque spatial extension, given an oblique emphasis by the agency of light.

Attention should also be called to the one oval staircase, to the oval room at the rear of the palace, and the apsaidal space before it (now haply occupied by an enormous elevator). The Baroque was addicted to molding space, squeezing it at one point, expanding it in another—space that constantly changes its form.

Figure 9.5 Passage opening on major rooms on the *piano nobile* of the Palazzo Barberini, Rome. (G. C. Ball.)

The Barberini palace, with its amplitude, its emphasis on the moving three dimensions, its open rather than closed form, all done with light as well as with mass, indicates that added characteristics have been imposed on a fundamentally classic framework by the dynamics of a new era. It is a return in new garb to the late Roman space extension of the Emperor Hadrian's villa rather than to the static space of the Greek Parthenon or the Roman Pantheon.

322

The second Barberini architect, Gianlorenzo Bernini, is known to all as the creator of the bronze *baldacchino,* the canopy that covers the altar at St. Peter's in Rome, and of the throne of St. Peter in the apse (see Figure 6-15). Art students also recognize his hand in the design of the Scala Regia in the Vatican Palace and the colonnade in St. Peter's piazza. It is typical of this sculptor, who, as the protégé of Scipione Borghese, was recommended to the Pope and became "architect of St. Peter's," that he regarded all space as his bailiwick and treated each sector as though it were to be modeled by his hands. And his hands were into most of the commitments of the Baroque, for, like Raphael, he was an amazing individual, seemingly capable of enlisting the services of many men, some of whom worked devotedly under his command.

In the church of S. Andrea al Quirinale (Figure 9.6), close by the Quirinal and Barberini palaces, Bernini created a small oval edifice preceded by an oval courtyard (Figure 9.7). The use of the oval rather than the round form is in itself an indication of more subtle power-packed geometry. Notice the manner in which the architect compels the vision to move toward the central portico to rest on the doorway and ultimately to be swept upward to the statue of Andrew over the portal of the sanctuary (Figure 9.8). Here sculptural realism takes over in the ascending figure of the saint, even as the symbolic dove epitomizes the apse decoration of St. Peter's. Bernini would have made a wonderful framer of pictures, for he could manipulate any aesthetic complex to emphasize and enhance a center of interest. And for Bernini this was often contrived to be the vortex of his transcendental vision.

S. Andrea repays the fullest study of the methods used to secure results. The moving lines, the crescendo scaling in size and sculptural qualities all indicate a feeling for a restless welling of energy with which everyone from the nomad who migrated from the Tigris and Euphrates aeons ago to the astronauts who sought the moon feels akin. Notice, however, that Bernini never abandoned the rational basis of classical architecture, even though he certainly distorted it.

Bernini also plays on the senses to cause pure delight, a practice fully condoned by the church.

Figure 9.6   S. Andrea al Quirinale, Rome, 1658–1678. Gianlorenzo Bernini. (Alinari/ Editorial Photocolor Archives.)

323

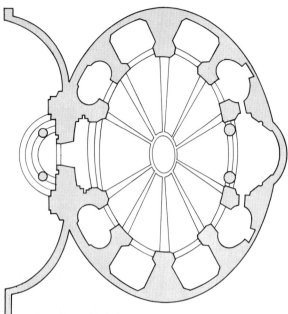

Figure 9.7 Plan of S. Andrea al Quirinale, Rome, 1658. Bernini. (After de' Rossi.)

The richest of textures are used. Colorful marbles are played against statuesque white for drama. The flood of light from the clerestory provides an immaterial component which focuses the attention and pervades the atmosphere. It was the genius of the seventeenth century to harness many aesthetic components into a whole, as opera did with music, drama, and the dance.

The artist who enlarged Bernini's scope was quite a different person—Francesco Borromini, a man more as Michelangelo, moved to art by in-

Figure 9.8 S. Andrea al Quirinale, Rome, interior, 1658–1670. Gianlorenzo Bernini. To the right is the pillared enframement that leads into the apse. Note the broken pediment at its top that provides a base for a dramatic statue (not visible here) of S. Andrea ascending heavenward. Alinari/Editorial Photocolor Archives.)

ner frustrations and maladjustments. One of his contributions to architecture, of which it stood in need, was the development of the encompassing shape that made it possible to walk around a building and view it from all angles with equal satisfaction. To this end Borromini eliminated corners and undulated walls, a ruse which in the hands of a lesser genius would have resulted in nervous gyration.

Borromini used fewer sensuous ingredients than his predecessor but developed them into complex rhythms and countermovements such as had their musical correspondence in elaborate fugues. Take the small church of S. Carlo alle Quattro Fontane (Figure 9.9) as an example

Figure 9.9 S. Carlo alle Quattro Fontane, Rome, the facade, 1665–1667. Francesco Borromini. The facade was completed much later than the rest of the church. (Alinari/Editorial Photocolor Archives.)

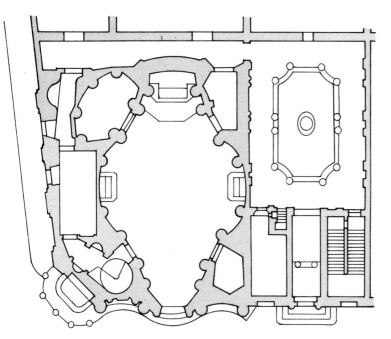

Figure 9.10 Plan of S. Carlo alle Quattro Fontane, Rome, 1638. Borromini. (After E. Hempel, *Francesco Borromini*, Vienna, 1924.)

(again on the Quirinal hill). S. Carlo was part of a Spanish Trinitarian monastery built on an irregular plot of land. Within a geometric form of two equilateral triangles with adjoining bases, Borromini designed the interior as a waving wall fortified with four large columns projecting from each longitudinal side (Figure 9.10). On the angles above the wall are mounted four pendentives after the Byzantine tradition and above them and resting on a continuous architrave is a tall oval dome and still farther up the cupola. All combine to provide a seemingly endless gesture that soars to great heights.

Borromini was the son of an architect and a nephew of Carlo Maderna. Thus it was natural that he should have accompanied his innovative planning with a tectonic and structural sense. His daring engineering was indeed the quality in his work most admired by contemporary architects. We have seen the serpentine wall in Hadrian's villa, the dome on pendentives in Byzantine work, and the dome over an oval in S. Andrea. Borromini synthesized the three systems into one (Figure 9.11).

The complexity of the visual qualities of the interior of S. Carlo may be further analyzed. The rhythms in the edifice are all architectonic. It is a moving building rather than one in which flat walls are broken by curved niches. Within this overall pattern minor themes exist that seem to answer one another in complex cadences and to possess that capability, without which no art comes alive, of offering the viewer choices of arrangements so that the route which his vision must take is never monotonously fixed. On the longitudinal axis, for instance, the eye could pick up the two groups of four columns with the broader resting point between, or minor arrays of the arched niches may be experienced.

We may likewise note the coloristic sequences and especially the unique use of light that Borromini introduced into architecture. Dark accents in the alternating niches carry the eye to the apse behind the altar. The lower part of the church is in comparative shadow compared with the light of the dome. Here low-placed windows force a flood of lateral light on the interesting geometric coffers of the ceiling, while from the cupola concentrated light pours down from above. The dome thus seems to be suspended in space, to lack corporality. Stone is given the illusion of weightlessness. This character has great appeal to us in the twentieth century.

The facade of S. Carlo, which has almost psychopathic movements, was executed years after the interior was completed, and it was one of Borromini's last works. In the meantime other churches had risen at his hand—S. Ivo della Sapienza and S. Agnese in Piazza Navona, among them.

We have spoken of S. Carlo as a moving building. To note this is important to any understanding of Baroque Italian art—and Italy was the fountain head of the Baroque. The climax in S. Carlo is not a picture, as in the Renaissance, nor is it a three-dimentional statue as in S. Andrea. It is a dome, and, more importantly, it is the light from the heavens shining through that dome. Such transcendental illumination is in reality the epiphany of Italian Baroque religion. It is, after the harsh cruelties of the Inquisition, the emotional answer, the emotional resurgence of catholic faith as sponsored by the church, as intrinsic to the people, and as created by the artists of the seventeenth century.

Melodrama will on occasion be likewise found

Figure 9.11   S. Carlo alle Quattro Fontane, Rome, interior of the dome, 1638–1641.
Borromini. (Alinari/Editorial Photocolor Archives.)

in illusionistic ceiling painting in such churches as the Gesu, Rome, where Giovanni Gaulli (1639–1709) painted *The Triumph in the Name of Jesus*. But this work seems almost too facile, too literal, and too illusionistic, with its blue sky and clouds, to be sincere. It no doubt appealed mightily to its audience; to us the hard and forthright architectural expression carries greater conviction, leaving the *trompe l'oeil* for palaces.

Baldassare Longhena we know as the winner in the Venetian contest to build Sta. Maria della Salute, without whose immense scrolled buttresses and golden dome Venice would never again be Venice. Its theatrical splendor seems so right in the city of shimmering light and color. Even the palace he built for Leone Pesaro, although conventionalized Venetian Renaissance somewhat in the manner of Vignola, does present relations of large rounded columns advancing from flat walls which are proportionately interesting and moving.

A younger architect from Modena in northern Italy, the priest Guarino Guarini (1624–1683) has commanded much attention of late for his outstanding structural innovations. As a learned teacher in the Theatine order Guarini studied in Rome and traveled extensively before settling in Turin in 1667, the year of Borromini's presumably self-inflicted death. It was during the last seventeen years of his life, while working for Carlo Emmanuele II of Savoy, that Guarini's significant architecture was completed. To choose between his churches, the Cappella della Sindone and S. Lorenzo at Turin, we may with profit regard the latter. In its octagonal plan, the segments, bridged by pillars and arches, create a convex intrusion toward the center in a manner that obscures the initial geometry. Further transformations as the building rises on pendentives to dome create a verticality that is typical of his work.

Guarini's chief contribution lies in the new character given the vault and dome, the pinnacle of the structure (Figure 9.12). Medieval vaults, especially those in Moresque Spain, rested on an intricate network of ribs. Guarini, who had worked in Spain, abandoned the cells between the ribs and erected his domes like floating orbs on support from the intersection of the rib network. Thus it may be said that he wedded the classic dome with its uninterrupted surface which rested on pendentives or drum to the Gothic ribbed construction. When flooded with lateral light this created the impression of an infinite dome rising behind a geometric web.

The Palazzo Carignano which Guarini built during the closing years of the century may be considered the paradigm of the Baroque palaces of the era. Its curved facade with its unique treatment of classical details surprisingly is built of brick. Its magnificent axial staircase returns the palace plan to Renaissance centrality and dominates the interior in a manner that forecast the eighteenth century. Again we note the light introduced from within the vaulting of the main salon.

In Guarini's architecture we see the creation of a mind that united clear rational thought (he wrote an admirable book on civil architecture which clearly derived from his teaching of mathematics) and an emotional artistic urge. There is here that conjoining of seventeenth-century French reason as exemplified by Descartes and the fertile genius of the Italian to translate abstract ideas into psychological experience through the medium of art. It is in a sense a reversal of the emphasis of Greek art and thought. Because Guarini was also a priest, he acted with the religious fervor of seicento Italy to objectify in architecture a reaching for ineffable space and, symbolically, the infinite.

SOME ITALIAN BAROQUE HOUSES

P. Podesta	Genoa	1563 and after, for the Lomellini family; architect, Castello
V. Mondragone	Frascati	1573–1614 and after, for Cardinal Altemps; architects, M. Longhi, Vasanzio
P. Pitti	Florence	Late sixteenth and early seventeenth centuries, with additions for the Grand Dukes of Tuscany; architect, Ammanati

Figure 9.12   S. Lorenzo, Turin, interior of the dome, begun in 1668. Guarino Guarini. (Alinari/Editorial Photocolor Archives.)

Some Italian Baroque Houses (continued)

P. Borghese	Rome	1590 and after, for Pope Paul V; architect, Flaminio Ponzio
P. Mattei	Rome	1598–1618; architect, Maderna
V. Pamphili	Rome	Seventeenth century, for Pamphili Pope Innocent X; architect, Algardi
P. Reale	Naples	1600, for Viceroy Count Limons; architect, Fontana
P. Rospigliosi-Pallavicini	Rome	1603, for Cardinal Scipione Borghese; architect, Vasanzio
V. Borghese	Rome	1605, with later additions, for Cardinal Scipione Borghese; architects, Giovanni Vasanzio (Johann van Santen), Asprucci (eighteenth century), Canina (nineteenth century)
P. del Quirinale	Rome	Additions 1605 and after, for Pope Paul V; architects, Flaminio Ponzio, Maderna
P. Barberini (Figures 9.2, 9.3, 9.4 and 9.5)	Rome	1628–1633, for Barberini Pope Urban VIII; architects, Maderna, Bernini, Borromini
V. Isola Bella	Stresa	1630–1671, for Count Carlo Borromeo; garden designer, Angelo Crivelli
P. Montecitorio (*Ludovisi*)	Rome	1650, for family of Pope Innocent X; architects, Bernini, Fontana
P. Chigi	Rome	1664, for Cardinal Flavio Chigi; architect, Bernini
P. Rezzonico	Venice	1679; architect Longhena
P. Pesaro	Venice	1679–1710, for Leone Pesaro; architect, Longhena
P. Carignano	Turin	1679–1692; architect, Guarini

INTERIOR DESIGN

Space Organization and Plans

In Dwellings. Although the Renaissance scale was retained, the closed plan for dwellings, inward-oriented around a central court, was often changed to the winged arrangement heretofore characteristic only of the *villa suburbana.* In the Pitti Palace in Florence only one side of the building, toward the rear gardens, is open, whereas in the Barberini there is also a forecourt. When built on a hillside, access to the gardens was often direct from the *piano nobile.*

The vestibule assumed central importance and the stairs were magnificently displayed to connect it visually with the first story.

Planning for apartment living was retarded. Rooms were stretched out in sequence but the arrangement of openings was at the side, thus inaugurating the Baroque tendency toward asymmetry but also creating rectangular rooms unbroken by passages. The large salon, often as much as 30 ft high and of commensurate size, was common. Some of these rooms were used as private art galleries even in their day. Oval rooms, were introduced.

In Churches. The Baroque tendency was toward the oval plan and a break with the one-angle, one-route viewpoint along the nave was apparent.

Architectural Details

How seldom art annals permit us to see the interiors of domestic buildings. In visualizing the doors and windows of Italian Baroque architecture, one must constantly remember that its garments were classical Roman—pilaster, pillar, entablature, and round arches. These were, however, arranged to introduce an entirely new concept of dynamic movement. The emotional energy of the creators revealed itself in individual architectural expression—pillars were frequently diagonally oriented, architraves broke into pediments, and scrolled cartouches crowned the whole. Arched windows sometimes occupied the complete space between exterior framing orders. Exterior balustrades and interior dados raised the actual window to a normal 30 in. above the floor. In height it reached to the architrave. Another type of window with a crowning entablature both exterior and interior acquired Baroque handling by means of broken surfaces and alignment in several planes. Interior aediculae made bold use of ears, and alternation between arched and triangular pediments created a drama of complexity.

Hearths which maintained the same tendency toward elaboration as other details possessed high relief and interrupted and often curvilinear contours. Bold cartouches and armorials played havoc with the orders and enormous brackets supported the mantels. Again adornment veered toward pompous classicism. Niches were filled with oversized statues that often projected beyond the plane of the wall. It was all of a piece.

Interior Surface Treatments

Floors, characteristically tiled, were introduced in wood parquetry in dwellings. Although beautiful paneling, partial or complete, persisted, the Italian, always a muralist at heart, favored plaster and paint. Mixed media—murals and ceiling frescoes often combined with three-dimensional stucco (e.g., Palazzo Pitti by Cartona)—become Baroque fashion.

The leading muralists of the early seventeenth century in Italy were Guido Reni (1575–1642), who did the Aurora ceiling in the Palazzo Rospigliosi, Domenichino Zampieri (1581–1641) of the Palazzo Mattei, Giovanni Lanfranco (1581–1675), who worked with Domenichino, and Francesco Albani (1578–1660) in the Palazzo Giustiniani (now Chigi-Odescalchi). These men indicate the course of official painting which followed in major ways the fashionable, sophisticated, but somewhat superficial eclecticism of the Carracci.

Compartmental frescoes were soon altered by Pietro da Cartona (1596–1669). In the ceiling of the principal hall of the Barberini Palace (1633–1639), in a gigantic work designed to glorify the Barberinis by showing their symbol, the three Bs, worthy of transportation to heaven, the painter preserves the all-encompassing architectural frame but breaks it at the slightest provocation with all manner of incidentals, such as dolphins and putti. We notice that figures intrude behind and in front of the feigned architecture. Although this handling was not new—it had been done by Mantegna and Veronese—Cartona enlarged its scope. This involved a more knowledgeable use of perspective and a greater extension of space. It is to the Baroque that we owe the swirling, upward orientation of the entire scene toward a fissure in the heavens.

Three-dimensional sculpture, often incorporated in fixed frames as well as niches, was likewise used to adorn interior walls. This can be seen as part of an art movement toward less permanent backgrounds. The mirror and the easel painting became more common and were frequently hung against wall coverings of damask or velvet.

Furnishings and Their Arrangement

Once more the statement can be made that although furnishings in magnificent settings were large and sumptuous they were not numerous nor was their placement necessarily bisymmetrical or formal. Salons were rooms of state; people at least had space in which to move. Not until the monarchy of France became absolute did furnishing *en suite* become fashionable.

FURNITURE

Character and General Development

Seventeenth-century Italian furniture—which was at first characterized by classical interpretations—gradually moved toward plastic forms. In the north where the princes of the Hapsburg Empire set the *bon ton* in their preference for ponderous grandeur, an international standard of less ostentatious French taste gradually intruded.

331

Materials and Construction

Walnut remained the principal furniture wood and many handsome carved pieces in this medium still exist. In the opulent pieces of northern derivation a composite of materials was more usual. Ebony, gilt bronze, intarsia in *pietra dura* (i.e., marble on a stone base), tortoise shell, and ivory—all produced the colorful effects desired. The Grand Duke Ferdinand established a factory in Florence for the manufacture of this variety of sumptuous furniture, which resembled Louis XIV designs.

Northern Italy likewise favored painted furniture. Brescia, near Milan, and Venice were the Italian centers of manufacture. Italian painted furniture, most commonly seen in commodes, is not made in the same manner as its French lacquer counterpart. The practice was to paint with watercolors over a gesso ground and to sustain with a coat of varnish. It is generally without gilding or competing elaborateness of form. The typically Venetian colors were cream, yellow, blue, and yellow red (Chinese red). Although the final product was not so enduring as a lacquer finish, the process was more quickly completed and resulted in a high degree of aesthetic excellence.

Types and Descriptions

Furniture types in Baroque Italy do not differ radically from those of the Renaissance. Some cassone remained in the provincial centers. The credenza held its own until the period was well advanced when its popularity gave way to that of the commode or large chest of drawers.

A cabinet designed for the storage and display of art objects grew popular as leisure to select and money to buy increased. These luxury cabinets are well represented by the Medici example which is now in the Uffizi and by another known to have been made by Philip Hainhofer (1578–1647) of Augsburg, which is now in the Pitti Museum. Both bear the Medici coat of arms of the six balls. The Hainhofer piece is made of ebony and resembles two tiers of architecture each using the triumphal arch motif and showing the more sober design of the early seicento. On the base enclosing the drawers the geometrical intarsia agrees with this somber spirit.

The floral motifs in the body, alternating on dark and light ground, are characteristic of Florentine pictorial effects. The statuettes at the corners represent Peace and Abundance and are executed in a restrained Florentine style. The angel above the coat of arms and the scrolls on the capital and pediment are Mannerist shapes often used by Borromini. A piece such as this, derived from several stylistic sources, can be called eclectic.

The Wallace collection in London exhibits a *sgabello* (Figure 9.13) from this century which indicates its Baroqueness merely in its shaped carved rails. The important chair of the period is the *sedia* or armchair (Figure 9.14). The example shown, from the Metropolitan, not only uses scrolling curves in the arms but extends the large scrolled feet in a diagonal direction in advanced seicento fashion. A scroll that breaks abruptly in its course is termed the Flemish scroll; it appears in England on Carolean chairs which were of Flemish design.

The seat and back of the sedia at the Metropolitan are upholstered. This variety of upholstery which is permanently attached to the frame is known as *slip-over* to distinguish it from the *slip-on* which covers the removable seat.

Although the principal *stanza* (i.e., room) was grandly but sparsely furnished in compliance with Italian tradition, the smaller more intimate *camera* was equipped with pieces designed to add to the comfort and convenience of everyday life. Bookcases, card tables, and consoles, with a growing emphasis on horizontality, if not yet on small size, were conspicuous.

Frames

Baroque picture framing may be characterized as exaggerated extension of Renaissance traits. The carved foliage frame was made with deeper cutting and more vigorous movement. The profile of the molded Gothic frame became broader and bolder and often incorporated the ovolo. It was frequently lacquered or painted and gilded.

The finest of the carved frames were made in France. During the Louis XIV period gilding on

Figure 9.13 Italian chair (*sgabello*), seventeenth century. Carved walnut. Height overall, 106.5 cm, height of seat, 47 cm, width 45 cm, width at front of seat, 32 cm. Wallace Collection, London. (Crown Copyright, reproduced by permission of the Trustees, The Wallace Collection, London.)

Figure 9.14 Italian armchair (*sedia*), late seventeenth century. Walnut. Height, 116 cm, width, 63.5 cm, depth, 67.7 cm. Metropolitan Museum of Art, New York. (The Metropolitan Museum of Art, Gift of Mrs. Russell Sage, 1909.)

333

gesso became as important on picture frames as in wall decoration. The plainer ovolo frame was favored in the Lowlands, where its somber rich tone was an excellent complement to genre painting.

Musical Instruments

In the manner that Protestant litany made full use of the sonorous organ, chamber music, which served the courtly scene, chose the spinet. Spinets, on stands with legs, joined the ranks of stationary furniture.

The finest spinets of late sixteenth and early seventeenth centuries were made in Belgium by several generations of the Ruckers family. These instruments had much decoration lavished on their cases. Rubens is known to have painted some of the Ruckers spinets.

Harpsichords, similar to the spinet but further developed in keyboard potential, had been made since the Renaissance. Their fashion, however, was late Baroque and eighteenth century. The nephew of Hans Ruckers, Joannes Couchet, enlarged the manuals so that two tiers might be used simultaneously, thus making the instrument peculiarly suited to Baroque polyphonic style. Because the casing for Italian harpsichords was usually separated from the instrument, it furnished opportunity for the most lavish three-dimensional sculptural forms. That the Italians were capable of exploiting this potential can be illustrated by a seventeenth-century Roman harpsichord, now in the possession of the Metropolitan Museum of Art (Figure 9.15).

Timepieces

European timepieces from the fourteenth century are still in use, as represented by the town clock of Rouen and the striking clocks of Salisbury and Wells cathedrals in England. These clocks are weight-driven mechanisms. After the invention of the coiled spring by the Italians in the fifteenth century timers could be smaller. During the Baroque they became fashionable in private houses. The finest of the seventeenth-century clocks were made in France and England and are described in that context.

TEXTILES

In Italy the cities of Genoa, Florence, and Venice retained their ascendency as producers of magnificent textiles throughout the first part of the seventeeth century. Following art trends, design organization became more complex; for instance, three-dimensional velvets, enriched with varicolor, different heights and types of pile, and with more complicated background weaves were abundant. Elaborate brocatelles fulfilled the requirement for sculptural effects.

Patterns were no longer the neat, bisymmetrical ogivals of the Renaissance. Like painting, nothing could be restrained within bounds. Contrasts of tone, say crimson on white, not only contributed a dramatic effect but also suggested the spirited tension that underlay the Baroque.

Baroque Italian Tapestries

The Medici factory in Florence operated during the entire seicento, although it, too, felt French competition. The master tapestry weaver during the early part of the century at this atelier was Bernadine van Asselt, who designed the tapestry *Moses Striking the Rock,* now at the Metropolitan. Later the most prominent designer was the Frenchman Pierre Lefevre. The combination of his skill and Medici resources turned out such outstanding products that the covetousness of Mazarin, the French statesman, was aroused. Lefevre was recalled to his homeland to reorganize the royal factory at the Louvre. Although he later returned to Florence, his son Jean was the first of the line of famous Lefevres at the French Gobelins.

In 1633 Cardinal Francesco Barberini, nephew of Pope Urban VIII, opened a factory at the Barberini palace. The Barberini tapestries all bear the famous crest of the family, which includes the golden bees. The Cleveland Museum of Art owns a set of *Dido and Aeneas* tapestries designed by Giovanni Francesco Romanelli (1610–1662), who was placed in charge of designing tapestries for the Barberini factory (Figure 9.16). One of each set of the Dido weavings was signed "M/Wavter" by the master weaver Michel Wavter. The Cleveland museum set is thought to have been made at his workshop in Antwerp. Other sets from the cartoons may have been woven by Wavter on the Barberini looms.[7]

Baroque tapestries are large and have exceedingly wide borders that incoporate many theatrical devices and architectural enframements.

CERAMICS

There was no conspicuous development of ceramics in Italy during the seventeenth century. Native faience continued to be made in a tradition which reaches to the present.

Figure 9.15 Harpsichord supported by Tritons, with gilded gesso relief, shows the procession of Galatea. Rome, seventeenth century. Metropolitan Museum of Art, New York. (The Metropolitan Museum of Art, The Crosby Brown Collection of Musical Instruments, 1889.)

GLASS

Italian Glass

Except for the production of large mirrors and crystal chandeliers, glassmaking in northern Italy had reached its zenith. The wars of Venice against the Turks and the heightening of commercial interests in the north caused a decline in the Venetian glass industry which lasted until this century.

Despite legal restrictions, Venetian glassmen, lured by promises of rich awards, emigrated in large numbers. Nor is it recorded that the government seemed unduly concerned about the exodus. Hence the historian has greater difficulty distinguishing glasses made in such countries as the Netherlands, which was invaded by the Ital-

Figure 9.16 *Cupid in the Guise of Ascanius Presenting Aeneas to Dido.* Second in a series of eight Dido and Aeneas tapestries, midseventeenth century. Designed by Giovanni Francesco Romanelli and woven by M. Wavters. Silk and wool. Height, 4.19 m, width, 6.35 m. Cleveland Museum of Art. (The Cleveland Museum of Art, Gift of Mrs. Francis F. Prentiss in memory of Dr. Dudley P. Allen.)

ian craftsmen, from the native Venetian product. Glasses from several sources are often classified as Venetian type, or *façon de Venise,* to distinguish them from German glass, which is of entirely different nature. Venetian glass of the seventeenth century no longer seems to have the exuberance that it once possessed. *Tour de force* becomes common and basic shapes more complex.

One outstanding accomplishment which furthered the art of glassmaking can be credited to Italy. In 1612 Antonio Neri, a Florentine who was apparently engaged in some sort of glass production in Pisa, wrote *L'Arte Vetraria* (The Art of Glassmaking). It is perhaps indicative of Venice's loss of control of the glass industry that a non-Venetian could have written this guidebook. It is likewise a token of the international interest in the manufacture of glass that in 1662 the work was translated and published in English.

German Glass

At this point in time the logic of separating German glass into east and west divisions becomes evident. German glass, as the term is used here, refers to the product of the German states east of the Rhine and north of Italy. As the southern section of this territory encompassed erstwhile Bohemia and Silesia, this glass is often referred to under those names. During the early seventeenth century the northern cities of eastern Germany—Hanover, Brunswick, Brandenburg, and Potsdam—opened glass houses.

Although this district was on an eastern route from Venice, the Germans never favored the delicate glass from the south. Theirs was a harder, clearer glass built around potassium and chalk (lime) as the metal, which acted as an anticorrosive, thus deflecting the "glass disease" that had destroyed many pieces by decomposition. For a time after the British success with the addition of lead the Germans followed suit, thereby improving the bell-like tonality at the expense of hardness and clarity.

From this base the Germans made their colored glasses—"Bohemian" green, strong blue, and ruby. For the last gold and tin were added to the batch to produce, under proper firing, the sort of refraction that flashed red or blue with variations in thickness.

Enameling is an embellishing technique associated with much German glass. This might be the true enamel, which was fused to the glass, or, on occasion, *cold painting* or pigmentation adhered to the surface by an adhesive such as varnish. Although the roemer (a ceremonial glass with flared top and base) was rarely enameled, the beaker (a capacious drinking vessel), the *humpen* (a similar tall drinking vessel with an in-turned rim—presented to honored guests), and the *stangengläser* (a narrow, cylindrical, footed glass) were the types favored for such decoration. Lending themselves equally well to inscriptions, armorial crests, religious scenes, narrative sequences—and customarily dated—these enameled vessels provide a fascinating record of the princely houses of the Baroque in Middle Europe.

Wheel and diamond point engraving, as well as deeper wheel cutting, was a decorative technique to which the German glassmen turned. Caspar Lehman, an engraver of metal, who worked for the Hapsburg emperor Rudolph II (1576–1612), adapted his technique to glass and produced the earliest known piece in the German tradition, a beaker dated 1605. Four years later he was granted the exclusive right to engrave glass. The Schwanhardts of Nuremberg were the next noteworthy men in this line. Their work represents the zenith of the *Nuremberg school* which practiced the art in that city during the late seventeenth and early eighteenth centuries (Figure 9.17). Bohemia and Silesia again entered the market after the finish of the Thirty Years War (1618–1648) and did wheel engraving on fine glass bodies with a skill that has never been surpassed.

Deep cutting, which seems more in keeping with Baroque shapes, is a technique that has been practiced by the Germans since the seventeenth century.

Netherlandish Glass

West Germany and the Netherlands is territory considered in the Lorraine tradition. Indeed, any designation of *Lorraine* or *Lotharingian* is pointless after the midseventeenth century, for the Rhenish men who orginated the type were thereafter comparatively inactive and production passed to the Netherlands.

Belgium imitated the soft glass of the Venetians, largely because they had access to Spanish coastal *barilla*, or soda. Liége and Antwerp became the centers of glassmaking. Because not only the metal but also the blown shapes imitated

Figure 9.17 Covered engraved goblet. Nürnberg, ca. 1660–1680. Height, 37.3 cm. Corning Museum of Glass, Corning, New York. (The Corning Museum of Glass, Corning, New York.)

the fanciful Adriatic production, this output has been rightly dubbed *façon de Venise*. The work excelled in technique but could not duplicate the freedom of design inherent in the southern examples.

STONES, METALS, IVORIES

Throughout this chapter the bonds of Baroque Italian art have been extended to include some of the art of middle and northern Europe. This has been rationalized because of the ties the Hapsburgs had with Spain and Italy at that time.

Figure 9.18   Silver platter, *Diana and Actaeon*, 1613. Paul van Vianen. The Netherlands. Length, 52 cm, width, 41 cm. The Rijksmuseum, Amsterdam. (Rijksmuseum, Amsterdam.)

Northern silversmiths who made table and display plate were called on for much of the European court silver. The van Vianens—Paul and brother Adam—a family of silversmiths, served the royal households during the first part of the seventeenth century, and Adam van Vianen's son Christian and Johannes Lutma were leaders during the last part of the Baroque era. The styling was essentially that of Netherlandish Mannerism. We illustrate with a dish made in 1613 by Paul van Vianen, now in the Rijksmuseum in Amsterdam (Figure 9.18). Although more Mannerist than Baroque in its symmetry around a central motif, it is essentially in the latter style in its emphasis on the climactic moment of a dramatic episode—where Actaeon was turned into a stag for interrupting the goddess Diana in her bath.

Figure 9.19 The Trevi Fountain. Probably inspired by designs of Bernini. Erected by Nicola Salvi in 1762 against the end of the Palazzo Poli. The central figure represents Neptune. The niche figures represent health and fertility. Rome. (G. C. Ball.)

The event of changing, the dramatic moment, was the one chosen by the Baroque sculptor.

Repoussé, the technique most seen in these large vessels, enabled the smith to obtain a sculptural effect and to stretch even the vast amount of metal available from the New World to meet the demands of a fast-growing clientele.

Combinations of Materials

Combinations of materials have already been mentioned in connection with much Baroque work. This is nowhere more strikingly illustrated than in Bernini's Cathedra of St. Peter, which is a composite of gilt bronze, marble, and stucco. Adding still another ingredient—flowing water—the Italian obtained some of the loveliest embellishments in the entire decorative orb. Baroque fountains favor not so much the single figure as the underwater world of some fabled sea god with weeds dripping from the Tritons, shells, and dolphins of natural rock grottoes. Notice that the water is cascading and splashing (Figure 9.19), never gushing—so much more rhythmic and soothing, although perhaps not so suited to today's tastes. An example is the seventeenth-century fountain on the stone terrace of the Pitti Palace in Florence. Done by Antonio Susini and Francesco Ferrucci, it makes use of bronze and stone.

DESCRIPTIVE SUMMARY

Baroque Italian architecture and its accompanying enterprises is a typically regional adaptation between the necessity for form in art and the inherently human need for excursion beyond. At this particular position in time-space, the most eloquent answer had to be ecclesiastic, and thus it was organized in three-dimensional extension, with the heavens its vortex. A new direction was given to architecture which, however, seemingly untectonic, was nevertheless prophetic.

The fact that light played an important new role is also prescient. That chromatic color reasserts its potential is by way of predicting that its omission could contribute to emotional sterility.

In all of this development the decorative arts (the term is used to signify those additions, both functional and aesthetic, that are useful to architecture) made a not inconsequential donation.

339

CHAPTER TEN

Baroque France

1600 TO 1700

La parfaite raison fuit toute extrémité,
Et veut qu l'on soit sage avec sobriété

Le Misanthrope, Molière

(Perfect reason shuns all extremes,
And desires that one be good with moderation.)

CULTURE SPAN

On July 31, 1589, the last of the sons of Catherine de Medici was murdered at Saint Cloud, the victim of religious political intrigue. Thus ended the line of the French House of Valois. The new king, Henry IV, known as Henry of Navarre, descendant of a cadet branch of the royal family, ascended the throne as the first monarch of the House of Bourbon. A protestant, he had officially abjured his religion at the Royal Abbey of St. Denis. However, he wisely issued the Edict of Nantes in 1598, which granted the French Huguenots (i.e., the French protestants) equal political rights with Catholics. The civil religious wars were, at least in their most bloody manifestations, at an end. Many émigrés returned, and France was enriched by an influx of skilled craftsmen, the class largely representative of the Huguenot faith.

Henry's reign was much concerned with recouping the state finances and reestablishing royal power. When it was tragically terminated, again at the hand of a fanatic, a nine-year-old boy ascended the throne as Louis XIII, but with the help of his minister Richelieu (1585–1642) the control of France was effected and foreign policies were inaugurated to strengthen French position abroad.

Accordingly, when Louis XIV was crowned king at the age of five (an achievement that was duplicated seventy-two years later by his great-grandson), he inherited power and prestige that was soon to be made almost absolute by the skillful manipulations of his ministers Mazarin and Colbert.

This power had not been obtained without considerable opposition. Episodic war was waged throughout the century. Hostilities developed from intramural factions and from alignments undertaken to establish a balance in European power. The position of France, which would be strengthened after the Thirty Years War, was weakened during the latter part of Louis's reign by attempts made to establish the claims of the Bourbon family to territories in the Lowlands, the Palatinate, and Spain. Only in the last did the king achieve any measure of success when his grandson ascended the Spanish throne as its first Bourbon monarch.

Foolishly Louis made another tactical error when in 1685 he revoked the Edict of Nantes. Again the Huguenots fled their homeland, some to the Lowlands, many to England, and this time to America. Less vigorous in wealth, power, and citizenry, France descended to the young Louis XV in 1715.

The seventeenth century has become known as the *grand siècle* of French culture, comparable to the cinquecento in Italy and the age of Elizabeth in England. This was the age in which French art reached its most glamorous pinnacle and most significant form. That its distinctive expression took place in the arts of environment is likewise of historical importance. The particular stamp that the French placed on art, and for the moment on Baroque art, was based on three factors, namely, classical antiquity, the rule of reason, and the precepts of political-social form. Although these determinants were influenced by the mold of post-Reformation Italy, nevertheless France "did its own thing" in an unforgettable way.

Antiquity was prescribed much as it had been elsewhere by Renaissance interpretations. In France Serlio and de l'Orme had published versions of the orders, Francis I had subsidized the publication of Greek texts, and translations from Greek literature into French had appeared contemporaneously with the Italian translations of Petrarch (e.g., those of Pierre Bercuire).

Reason, however, bore a slightly different shade of meaning north of the Alps. Emanating from the thinking of Descartes, it conceived the logical mind as the only source of right thinking, hence as the font of all good—political and aesthetic as well as moral. *Reason* in the French sense is that rigorous training of the mind that frees it for sensitivity.

Onto this background the temperament of the court of Louis XIV, and indeed of the king himself, impinged. Louis was a man who combined considerable charm and effective administrative ability with a willingness to assume the imperious role into which he had been cast. He managed his court as though it were one large family, living in one vast salon, in which he sat at the center of the head table. Rigidly prescribed social forms were the only possible means of making such close and intimate relationships feasible.

That such amenities had ultimately descended from Spain and Italy into the salons of such women as the Marquise de Rambouillet, herself Italian bred, is beside the point. In the feminine-dominated gatherings of Paris the encounters of aristocracy and belles-lettres that took place provided an intellectual atmosphere and an easy grace that was less characteristic of their court prototypes.

The social code of the court at Versailles, on the other hand, was mandatory and unquestioned. One of the paradoxical results of the philosophy of such men as Descartes is that expedience and necessity were accepted as a dictate of reason and so absolutism and a strict caste system was upheld as right. Louis supported this belief with a curious array of talents and became for his age the supreme arbiter of social, artistic, and political power.

French seventeenth-century art thus was Baroque much circumscribed by the rational and bent toward living gracefully with an absolute government through the agency of social form.

ARCHITECTURE

Style Henry IV, Louis XIII

Until the governmental reins were firmly in his grip, Henry IV could not be unduly concerned with the arts. " 'France and I' he wrote in 1598, 'have need of a breathing space.' "[1] This hiatus, however, was not to last long. It was Henry's foresight that first envisaged the arts as an instrument of statesmanship. He established ateliers for artists in the Louvre and, when trouble developed with the established guilds because of royal privileges, he divorced the members of the palace workshops from guild restrictions. In this manner a talented class was created, one that was backed by wealth and consecrated to providing superb products in the art of furnishings.

Henry likewise subsidized French artists for study in Italy and for practice in France. This principle, which culminated in the establishment of the *French Academy at Rome* in 1666, guaranteed an increasingly classical orientation for France, even while Italy was at the height of the Baroque.

The first Bourbon centered his court in Paris much as his grandson would do later at Versailles. To make the Medieval city attractive to a nobility that had been enjoying life in chateaux scattered throughout the countryside Henry inaugurated a metropolitan scheme of demolition, renovation, and city planning. The territory involved lay east and south of the Louvre on the banks along the Seine. He carried to completion the third bridge over the river, the Pont Neuf. He bought a large tract of land nearby in the *Quartier Antoine* in what came to be known as the *Place Royale* (since the Revolution, the *Place des Vosges*) and another in the *Place Dauphine* on the *Ile de la Cité*. For these areas squares flanked with residences were planned and the initial units were completed at royal expense. The nobility was encouraged to build according to approved architectural planning and for quite nominal prices.

The long blocks of buildings that rose on this site were rescued from monotony by interspersed pavilions. The ground stories were fronted by structural arcades supported by Doric pilasters integral with the piers. The old Medieval city had been built of wood with only a few stone churches and palaces. Henry's additions were in the provincial brick with stone quoins and towering slate roofs. Much of this old brick has since been covered with plaster, but whatever remains has mellowed with age. These buildings form a counterpart to the brownstones of New York, which seem rather friendly in comparison with the fronts of the mansions on Fifth Avenue. Paris, too, would soon become a grand city of white limestone, but that was not in Henry's day.

If one likes one's art history by association, the Place Royale is inhabited by many a ghost of the seventeenth century, including Mme. de Sévigné, one of the greatest of letter writers, who was born in 1616, at number eleven. Her correspondence is a discerning and indispensable as well as delightfully entertaining report on the current *tableau vivant*. How like France that it should have been written by a woman!

Because this style of the first Bourbons possessed grass roots, so its loveliest manifestations were in the countryside. We may take as an example a chateau like *Rosny* (Figure 10.1), not far from Versailles, designed for Henry's friend and minister, the duc de Sully (1560–1641). Built of muted brick and stone, it consists of one solid block with two bisymmetrically arranged end pavilions. Horizontal courses are prominently marked and windows, in the French manner, are tiered to lucarnes (i.e., dormer windows). The front entrance has pretentions to classical ordonnance. Dignified, indigenous, and of manageable size, it is a charming country home not unlike its counterpart in England at the time of the Restoration. It suggests the presence of a real country gentry, and, if any one thing can be held against Louis XIV, it is that by his policy of eviscerating the lesser nobility he robbed the nation of the vigorous element that might have needed these dwellings.

Figure 10.1   Château Rosny. Paris, 1594 and following. Some later alterations were made during its ownership by the Duchesse de Berry. (© Arch. Phot. Paris / S. P. A. D. E. M., 1979.)

The palace enterprises of Henry and his son involved the extension of the Louvre galleries along the Seine, the demolition (Henry seemed to believe in the dictum that to create one must destroy) of the two remaining sides of the old palace which surrounded a small court, and the completion of the western wing. Henry likewise advanced the work at the Tuileries and Fontainebleau. His most important palace remains the Luxembourg, which he intended as a residence for himself and his second queen Marie de Medici.

Engaged in these enterprises was a new and younger group of architects, Jacques Androuet du Cerceau, II (ca. 1550–1614), Jacques Lemercier (1583–1654), and Pierre LeMuet (1591–?1669). Salomon de Brosse (1565–1626) was the architect of the Luxembourg, which in its pronounced rustication resembled the Pitti Palace in Florence, which had been Marie's home. Except for scale and materials, the French classical picture of Rosny is again evoked.

Many churches were built in Paris and the

Figure 10.2 Château de Maisons-Laffite, 1642–1650.
François Mansard. Near Paris. (Lauros-Giraudon.)

provinces after the turn of the century, for most of which the Jesuits with their program of educational missionary work were responsible. Lemercier contributed two of the most outstanding and representative models, the Church of the Oratory and that of the Sorbonne. The style is known as the manner of the Jesuits, the prototypes of which are Vignola and della Porta's Church of the Gesù and Maderna's Sta. Susanna in Rome. Plans consist of a central nave without side aisles, the place of the latter taken by shallow recesses or chapels. Transepts are minimal. The exterior facade customarily features three sets of pillars on each side of center. These are arranged in two tiers, the end pillars on the second tier usurped by a Baroque cyma scroll. This form of church architecture became fairly standardized probably because it was simple, functional, and repeatable, and in a manner it represented a classically correct appearance with a bow to the new principle of continuity.

Onto the stage that displayed this academic competence there intruded a genius in the person of François Mansard (1598–1666). This man (a great-uncle of Jules Hardouin Mansard, the architect of Versailles) created the model of what may be regarded as early French classicism, in which all the ingredients are molded into one organic whole by a skill in subordinating lovely ornament and correct ordonnance to the building proportions and scale. His creations epitomize the French instinct for ordered relation and for finesse in detail without being dryly academic.

Born in Paris and orphaned very young, Mansard probably received little formal architectural training. After completing several minor commissions François became the favorite architect of Gaston de France, Duc d'Orléans, brother of Louis XIII. For him he designed the block that constitutes the west side of the Chateau de Blois. Although incomplete in many of its details, it still remains a masterpiece. Perhaps more famous is the building known as the Chateau de Maisons (Figure 10.2) or often as Maisons-Laffitte, the name of its last owner, who had the unenviable reputation of having mutilated the grounds. The Chateau, done on order for René de Longueil, President of the Parliament, is a stone block with short extended wings. It is possessed of a masculine vigor and simplicity, without shunning beautiful detail, yet with no show of parade.

At the height of his career Mansard built several Paris *hôtels,* the chief of which was the transformation of the Hôtel Carnavalet, home of Mme. de Sévigné from which much of her gossip of Paris was penned. It is now a Museum of the History of Paris.

Author of several Paris churches, he was never permitted to complete the finest, the Val de Grâce, southwest of the Luxembourg. The church was planned by Anne of Austria, wife of Louis XIII, as a thank offering for the birth of her son, the future Louis XIV. Mansard, its architect, was deposed of his command on charges of having exceeded his budget (not, may we say, an unusual occurrence today). He died shortly thereafter.

Style Louis XIV

The work of François Mansard constitutes a bridge to the architecture of the reign of Louis XIV. The first important architect of this era was Louis Le Vau (1612–1670), designer of the chateau near Melun known as Vaux-le-Vicomte (the vales of the viscount) for Nicolas Fouquet, Louis's Minister of Finance (Figures 10.3 and 10.4). Here the soon-to-be-famous trio, Le Vau, André Le Nôtre, and Charles Le Brun, as architect, landscape architect, and interior designer, respectively, collaborated for the first time. Vaux-le-Vicomte exemplified in its circular entrance and in its oval rooms the Baroque approach to space planning for which its author was noted.

As a well-known aside—the estate of Vaux incited the jealousy of the king and Jean Baptiste Colbert (1619–1683), a courtier then rising to power. Foquet, an independently wealthy man, was arraigned on charges of mishandling state funds. A very personal account of the trial is to be found in the letters of Mme. de Sévigné, who felt that the charges were false. Fouquet was imprisoned for life in a castle on the border of Piedmont.

Le Vau came nearer to court preferment in his work for Cardinal Mazarin, who was the first of Louis' prime ministers. The architect was commissioned to complete the buildings on the north, east, and south sides of the Louvre and to design as well certain rooms of the interior, including the rotunda of Mars and the gallery of Apollo.

It was in the history of Versailles that Le Vau looms most important. And indeed this architectural phenomenon is the story of French taste during Louis' reign. Versailles, situated on a low rise of land some fifteen miles southwest of Paris, had been a small hunting lodge built by De Brosse for Louis XIII. This building (often known as Versailles I) was used by the young Louis XIV more as a pleasure pavilion where he entertained his youthful favorite, Mlle. Louise de la Vallière, the first of several notable women—Mme. Montespan and Mme. Maintenon—who exercised power over the throne.

In 1661, on the death of Mazarin, the king, then twenty-three years of age, assumed his personal rule. His plans for Versailles grew with his power. Le Vau, then superintendent of royal buildings, was called to make Versailles a palace for the king. One restriction, always insisted on by Louis, was that the facade of his father's country seat should not be disturbed. Le Vau consequently enclosed and extended the old chateau with three structures centered on the west or garden side (known as Versailles II or the Chateau Neuf—the new chateau). When Le Vau died in 1670, his son-in-law François Dorbay continued the work to its completion in 1672. The Chateau Neuf bears the seed, but not the full flower, of the Palace of Versailles.

It is still in the eyes of many the most charming section of the establishment. This is true if one prefers one's nobility clad in provincial but substantial brick and stone, in buildings with wrought iron balustrades and leaded roofs, all gleaming in a fairyland covering of gold, just the right combination of corporality and dreams to justify its existence. Le Vau placed the royal escutcheon over the central doorway which supplied a touch of hierarchy without which a Baroque building would not be complete. There is nothing in all history quite like Versailles II (Plate 16) and all the lovelier by comparison with

Figure 10.3   Château Vaux-le-Vicomte, 1557–1661, Louis le Vau. Near Paris. (© Arch. Phot. Paris / S. P. A. D. E. M., 1979.)

Figure 10.4   Plan of ground floor of the Château Vaux-le-Vicomte, 1657 Le Vau. (After Jean Marot.)

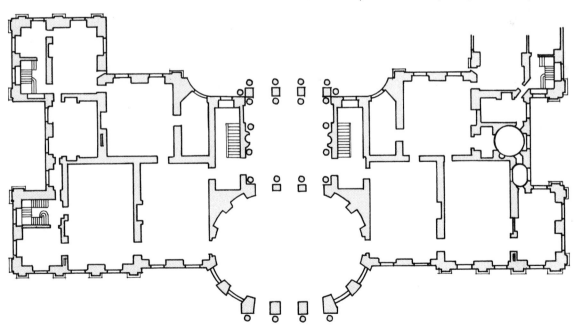

its later treatment. Its claim to fame lies not in any architectural ability to project grandeur so much as in an elegant theatricality that accords well with its character as a royal homestead for an ingenuous court. Praise Louis, a childishly sentimental patriarch, as well as a canny and privileged autocrat, for his stubborn protection.

The early palace consists of a classically bi-symmetrical two-story facade capped with a tall Mansard roof. (This type of roof whose lower slope is the only visible one was not invented by either of the men whose name it bears, having been used as early as Jacques Lemercier.) On the garden front the stone ground story was arcaded, the tall principal floor with central setback possessed pilasters and columns, and the second or attic floor presented a flat silhouette against the sky. Crowned with a balustrade, it introduced an Italianate touch to France, the land of towering roofs. From this west viewpoint the Chateau Neuf provided a modeling of planar space (which the Hall of Mirrors later destroyed) that might be seen in Mannerist work in Italy.

One fancies that Louis must have been a horti-culturist at heart, for at no time did he neglect his gardens. In working out his plans he was not slow to recognize the genius of Fouquet's land-scapist and secured André Le Nôtre (1613–1700), son and grandson of royal master gardeners, for his own ends. Le Nôtre had studied painting and architecture in his youth, and it is understandable that he should have united the practical knowl-edge of gardening with the designer's instinct for planning. He was the first man to make land-scaping a profession. Le Nôtre's plans were based on geometric lines and commanding vistas, ar-ranged in bisymmetrical order and subdivided by foliage into regular compartments like a Renais-sance ceiling. His style of landscape, which was copied all over Europe, came to be known as Le Jardin Français. He himself is said to have planned many famous gardens in this style, in-cluding those of the Quirinal, the Vatican, and St. James's Palace in England.

In 1661, on the death of Mazarin, Colbert be-came first minister and controller-general of finances. He lost no time in reorganizing the na-tional economy to the advantage of the state rather than of the private purse. Part of his plan lay in subsidizing and controlling the decorative arts to the end that France reigned supreme in their production. His personal taste leaned toward a rigid classicism, which in serving an absolute monarchy became oriented toward the pompous and the grand. Inasmuch as the prefer-ence of the architect Le Vau had been for the liberties of the nascent Baroque, the two men did not make an easy team.

In Colbert's program the Academies played their part. An Academy, which takes its name from the ancient academy of Plato, which was held in a garden in suburban Athens near the sanctuary of the hero Academus (387 B.C.), was at first merely a group of men who during the Italian Renaissance met regularly to discuss mat-ters of aesthetic importance.

From such discussions, given the proper sanc-tions, a cult of authoritative taste easily grew. In France during the seventeenth century it was given government warranty by the establishment of royal academies. The statements of these august bodies amounted to a code of rules to which the artist must comply or lose royal prefer-ment. Such loss in an absolute monarchy was serious indeed. The system amounted to an iron vise into which art was clamped in order to sub-serve the state.

In 1635 Cardinal Richelieu had given official recognition to an informal group which met to discuss the arts. This was the Académie Française, dedicated to improving the French language and to treating matters pertaining to the arts and sciences. In 1648 Colbert inaugurated the Aca-démie Royale de Peinture et de Sculpture to handle the fine arts more adequately. The Aca-démie d'Architecture followed in 1671. François Blondel (1618–1686) was its first professor and author of Cours d'Architecture, which attempted once more to delineate architectural standards.

The efforts of the architectural academy should not be entirely deplored. In place of a laissez faire policy it sincerely tried to search for an ideal. The classic art it fostered seemed in tune with the French rationale. The schooling of the Academy provided the world with some of the best architecture within this norm.

The tyranny of the Academy was the whip of correctness. It was probably for this reason more than any other that Bernini, who was invited to come to Paris in 1665 by Colbert and the king to submit renderings for the east front of the Louvre, suffered the humiliation of having them ultimately rejected. His plans had carried a curved front, which simply could not fit into the French conception of classical architectural thinking.

The design of Claude Perrault (1613–1688), with whom Le Vau and Le Brun collaborated, was used for this enterprise (Figure 10.5). It was a stroke of French genius to enclose the old facade with a colonnade of coupled columns centered on one and flanked by two bold pavilions—to lift the principal story above a ground floor which acts as a stylobate to set off its grandeur—and to cap the central motif with a tabernacle front that pierced a flat balustraded roof. The proportions, except as one might prefer slightly more accent on the axis, are excellent, which is to say that they are not monotonous and that they do support a balanced vertical and horizontal movement within a restful unity. This was as great a work in the French classical idiom, with its Baroque overtones of eminence, as the Tempietto was of the Italian classical or S. Carlo of the Italian Baroque.

Figure 10.5   East facade of the Louvre. Claude Perrault, Louis Le Vau, and Charles Le Brun. Paris, ca. 1667–1670. (© Arch. Phot. Paris / S. P. A. D. E. M., 1979.)

In 1678 after some eight years of changing architects Colbert, who had annexed the position of *Surintendant* of royal building, gave Jules Hardouin Mansard (or Mansart, 1646–1708) full charge of the work at Versailles. Jules is said to have taken his great-uncle's name in order to incur royal favor. His own family, the Hardouins, were artists. With Mansard began the third stage in the building of Versailles (Versailles III), the one that contained all the mature symbolism of the sun king's reign.

Louis's decision to move the court to Versailles is one of the few he made against the advice of his minister. Throughout the construction of the palace Mansard and even Colbert acted as agents of the king's wishes. Louis had the wisdom to place the economy and technical proficiency of his project into competent hands, but he never entirely relinquished the aesthetic reins. On the exterior the result is a curious combination of the new French orthodox classicism and a preservation of the provincial character of Versailles I, combined with Le Vau's Baroque decoration in the facades facing the front or marble court (Plate 16). This gives Versailles a strange dichotomy: the quality of being one of the grandest palaces in the world, yet remaining a cheerful, friendly backdrop for the royal family—the two faces of the French seventeenth-century absolutism.

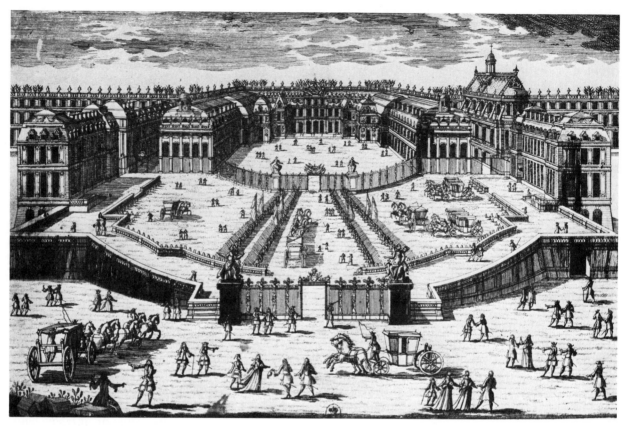

Figure 10.6   East front of the Palace of Versailles (from an old print). France, 1661–1715. Louis Le Vau and, later, Jules Hardouin Mansard, architects. (Marburg/Prothmann.)

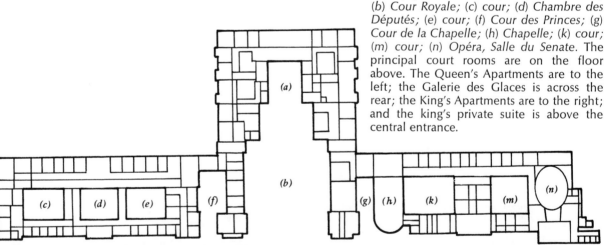

Figure 10.7   Plan of the Palace of Versailles, ground floor. (a) *Cour de Marbre;* (b) *Cour Royale;* (c) *cour;* (d) *Chambre des Députés;* (e) *cour;* (f) *Cour des Princes;* (g) *Cour de la Chapelle;* (h) *Chapelle;* (k) *cour;* (m) *cour;* (n) *Opéra, Salle du Senate.* The principal court rooms are on the floor above. The Queen's Apartments are to the left; the Galerie des Glaces is across the rear; the King's Apartments are to the right; and the king's private suite is above the central entrance.

This enormous architectural mass continued to expand from this time until Mansard's death in 1708 and that of the king in 1715 (Figures 10.6 and 10.7). This amounted to extending the palace arms to provide halls of state and new lodgings for the minister, to building a new gallery—*le Galerie des Glaces* (Plate 17)—with accompanying salons for state entertaining, the constructing of two immense lateral wings for the court and offices, the enclosure of the royal chapel in the north arm, the building of the stables and the second or Grand Trianon.

350

Mansard was likewise the architect for the chapel of *St. Louis des Invalides,* which now houses the tomb of Napoleon. He was responsible for the Place Vendôme, the Place des Victoires, and the Maison de St. Cyr, all in Paris. The royal residence of Marly near Versailles, destroyed during the revolution, was also his creation.

However history may rate him as an architect, it is certain that he was a practical and ingratiating administrator for the enterprises of the king. At his death he was Chevalier de l'Orde de St. Michel, Comte de Sagonne, Superintendant of the King's Buildings and Gardens, and Director of the Royal Arts and Manufacture and of the Academies of Painting, Sculpture, and Architecture—in almost absolute control of the arts of France.

Because France under the Sun King has bequeathed us some of history's rare architectural complexes on which collaborative teams had labored, we postpone a stylistic summary of their exteriors until after an appraisal of the interiors.

SOME SEVENTEENTH-CENTURY FRENCH HOUSES

PERIOD OF HENRY IV, LOUIS XIII

P. Louvre (Figures 7.9, 7.10 and 7.11)	Paris	Gallery of the court facing the Seine (remodeled under Napoleon III); one wing of Tuileries, under Henry IV; architect, Jacques du Cerceau
		North and east sides of the old chateau were demolished; northwest section and Pavillon de l'Horloge were built under Louis XIII; architect, Lemercier
P. de Fontainebleau	Fontainebleau	Cour Henry IV; Chapel La Trinité; architect, Lemercier; Galerie des Cerfs (Pavillon de la Bibliothèque); architect, de Brosse(?)
P. de Luxembourg	Paris	1615–1624, for Henry IV and Marie de Medici; architect, de Brosse; now home of the French senate
P. de Richelieu	Paris	ca. 1629–1636, for Cardinal Richelieu; architect, Lemercier; called P. de Cardinal, now P. Royale
C. de Selles	Loire-et-Cher	1585 and 1640, for Philippe de Béthune, Comte de Selles, brother of Sully
C. de Rosny (Figure 10.1)	Near Paris	1595, for Duc de Sully
C. de Richelieu	Richelieu	ca. 1620, for Cardinal Richelieu; architect, Lemercier; now destroyed
H. de Sully	Paris	1624–1630, for Sully; architect, Jean du Cerceau
C. de Versailles	Versailles	1624–1626, hunting box for Louis XIII; architect, de Brosse
C. de Balleroy	Near Bayeux	ca. 1626; architect, François Mansard
P. Mazarin	Paris	ca. 1633, for Mazarin; architect, Le Muet; now incorporated with the Bibliothèque Nationale
C. d'Effiat	Near Vichy	ca. 1632, for the Marquis d'Effiat, Maréchal de France; architect unknown
C. de Cheverny	Loire-et-Cher	ca. 1634, for the son of Henry IV's chancellor, Philippe Hurault; architect unknown; still in the family; interiors are well preserved
C. de Blois	Near Tours	Southwest side, 1635, for Gaston de'Orléans; architect, F. Mansard
C. de Tanlay	Burgundy	ca. 1642, for financier, Michel Particelli; architect, Le Muet

Some Seventeenth-century French Houses (continued)

EARLY PERIOD OF LOUIS XIV, 1643–1678:
PREDOMINANTLY BAROQUE

C. de Maisons (Figure 10.2)	Paris	1642–1650, for René Longueil; architect, F. Mansard
C. Oiron	Near Chinon	1645–1667, bought by Mme. Montespan and furnished for her son, the Marquis d'Antin
H. de Beauvais	Paris	1656; architect, Lepautre
Vaux-le-Vicomte (Figures 10.3 and 10.4)	Near Melun	1657–1661, for Fouquet; architect, Le Vau; landscape architect, Le Nôtre; interior designer, Le Brun
C. Neuf de Versailles (Versailles II) (Plate 16; Figures 10.6 and 10.7)	Versailles	1661–1678; architect, Le Vau et al.
P. Saint Cloud	Near Paris	For Monsieur, brother of Louis XIV; architect of later wings, 1677, Antoine Lepautre; demolished
C. de Clagny		1674–1680, for Mme. Montespan; architect, J. H. Mansard

CENTRAL PERIOD OF LOUIS XIV, 1678–1699:
PREDOMINANTLY CLASSICAL

P. Louvre (Figure 10.5)	Paris	East front, 1667–1670, architects, Perrault, Le Brun, Le Vau
P. Versailles (Versailles III) (Plate 17, Figures 10.7 and 10.8)	Versailles	1678 on; architect, J. H. Mansard
H. Lambert	Paris	Before 1642, for Lambert de Thorigny; architect, Le Vau; first of the ceilings by Le Brun
H. Carnavalet	Paris	1544, enlarged 1660, first architects, Lescot, Bullant, du Cerceau; second architect, F. Mansard
C. de Maintenon	Eure-et-Loire	1676–1685; reconstruction by J. H. Mansard
C. de Marly		1679–1683; architect, J. H. Mansard; destroyed during the Revolution
Le Grand Trianon	Versailles	1688; architect, J. H. Mansard; given to Mme. de Pompadour by Louis XV

INTERIOR DESIGN

Space Organization

The French have always laid the restraint of reason on their arts, which means that within the compass of any style trend they have taken the moderate course and have given a unified form to its expression. This statement proves true even in the range of the architectural works of the seventeenth century, in which the exteriors move inexorably toward strong classical statements (e.g., the East Front of the Louvre) and through-out the era the interiors maintain Baroque overtones.

This coalescing principle derives from the unity of purpose found in the building. The aim was clear—to glorify an earthly despotism. The classical rules dictated by the academies decreed orthogonal rooms of similar heights arranged enfilade, a vista that opened tremendous space on a horizontal axis.

Madame Maintenon, who was married morganatically to Louis late in his life, complained in her memoirs of the lack of seclusion and of the tiring routine of public surveillance given to private lives. The king, however, is said to have enjoyed such attendance and to have valued it as a means by which he kept his courtiers attached to his person. His formally arranged bedchamber over the central entrance had a direct line of sight that led down the small marble court through the larger Cour Royale to the Place d'Armes and out to the *Avenue de Paris,* which led straight to the capital. What more symbolic vortex could one wish for personalized political power?

Louis was God's emissary—the Divine Right of Kings had its apotheosis in the Sun Monarch. Therefore even church architecture (e.g., Mansard's chapel at the Invalides), although it may open an interior dome to tremendous height and its outer shell to unusual verticality, does so in a simplistic and uncomplicated way. There is no elaborate geometry or torsional ascension. Logic rather than the emotions is solicited—the logic of rule by divine sanction.

Unfortunately authority by its very nature is often strangely unaware of advanced thought. Although in townhouses of the early century the *corps de logis* was customarily but one room in depth and the planning long remained bisymmetrical and enfilade, in Vaux-le-Vicomte Louis le Vau created a double breadth and a planned apartment grouping (*en suite*). He added more stairs for convenience and extended an oval salon to the garden.

In Paris he (as well as the architect Pierre Le Muet who published a manual of townhouse architecture in 1623) divided the court in front of the dwelling into two—a *cour d'honneur* approached through the main gateway and a service court lateral to it—again a separation in the interest of nicety. On the far or garden side the house proper extended the width of both courts and it possessed advanced planning. Toward the end of the century Mansard himself as well as his contemporary Pierre Bullet (1639–1716) introduced asymmetrical planning and oval spaces in some drawings.

France took the lead in advanced planning for sanitation. Seventeenth-century Versailles possessed such luxuries as a *cabinet des bains.* Outdoor closets existed in much of the country and, contrary to accepted legend, were part of the equipment at the royal palace. Despite its fusty aspects, the world of Louis XIV was more civilized than that of François I.

The Designers and Their Organization

Before the reign of the Sun King interior design in France came under the direction of the architect. In isolated instances, like that of the group of designers under Primaticcio at Fontainebleau, the interior work was quite separate from the architecture and as a consequence turned out to be Mannerist Italian Renaissance. The structure was provincial French with early Renaissance detailing.

In the midseventeenth century the situation changed. Organization of the environmental arts became at once more complex and at the same time more closely integrated. Architect, landscape planner, and interior designer coordinated their efforts in a large building organization. In the domain of royalty this is known as the *Bâtiments* and inclusion on its roster marked success for an artist in whatsoever capacity.

Here the hierarchy of legitimate control descended from the king to his minister of state, and then to the chief administrative officer of the organization, who carried the title of *Surintendant.* Colbert at times kept the prerogatives of this last office in his own name. J. H. Mansard, appointed *Surintendant* in 1699 toward the end of his career, was one of the few professional men ever to hold this important position.

The architectural stewards ranged from the *Premier Architecte* to subordinates whose relative positions can be gauged by their recompense. Lemercier was chief architect until his death in 1654, Le Vau until his in 1670. Then, following some obscure appointments, Mansard assumed the title officially in 1683.

The position of Charles Le Brun (1619–1690) is less clear. He had worked with Le Vau, originally at Vaux-le-Vicomte, then soon at the royal palaces, and had been called to the Bâtiments shortly after the plans for Versailles began to take form. He had also carried out some independent architectural commissions.

Le Brun's rise was seemingly ordained. As a Parisian youth of eleven, he had come to the attention of Chancellor Séguier and was placed by him in the studio of the painter Simon Vouet. In 1642 at twenty-three he was in Rome in company with the famous French painter Nicolas Poussin. Returning to Paris in 1646, he was soon employed by Fouquet at Vaux. Thereafter his rise in court circles was rapid and in 1662 he was ennobled.

Possessing the ingratiating gifts of a diplomat, it is rumored that not all his actions were exemplary. He is said, for instance, to have incited Colbert against his former employer Fouquet and to have carefully planned his campaign by which he found favor first with Mazarin and then with Colbert.

In 1663 Le Brun was awarded a post that made him virtual dictator of the decorative arts of France. Colbert appointed him *Director de la Manufacture Royale des Meubles de la Couronne,* when inaugurating the policy that brought these arts under state control and housed them in the ateliers of the Louvre.

In 1664 he was designated *Premier Peintre* of the realm, a title he held for his lifetime. It was in this capacity that he directed the ornamentation of Versailles by working in close affiliation with Le Vau and then with Mansard.

Under Colbert he was instrumental in founding the French Academy of Painting and Sculpture and subsequently the French Academy at Rome. By commanding the industrial arts through the Louvre office and the artistic world through the Academy while he worked at Versailles at a time when there was no firm architect, Le Brun imprinted his artistic character on the aesthetics of France.

Le Brun and Mansard accomplished as an official team what neither could have done so well alone. Le Brun was an astonishing virtuoso, a painter of great facility who possessed powers of execution (although not of artistry) that rivaled Michelangelo's. Like Mansard he understood group organization. His principal painting, done by himself or by his pupils working from his designs, is in the Gallery of Apollo at the Louvre and in the state salons of Versailles.

Other competent designers were employed and at times favored for royal work. The painter Pierre Mignard (1610–1697) was preferred by the prime minister Louvois, who followed Colbert. He had decorated the Chateau of St. Cloud for the king's brother. Pierre Cailleteau, called Lassurance (?–1724), is credited with designing the king's apartment which was renovated toward the end of the century. His title was *Dessinateur.*

One unique office was that of *Menus-Plaisirs.* It was a private appointment by the king and did not come under the Bâtiments. Given the specific charge of planning royal festivals, the encumbent frequently assisted at personal designing jobs for the royal household. Jean Berain (1640–1711), probably in that capacity, did some of the late work at Versailles which showed Rococo tendencies.

Chronology

Interior design in France during the seventeenth century, like architecture, had three phases. The first division encompassed the reigns of the first two Bourbons; the second began with the reign of Louis XIV and extended to 1678 when J. H. Mansard took nominal charge of the vast enlargement of Versailles (officially in 1783); the third ends only with the close of the seventeenth century. During the last fifteen years of the Sun King's life (1700–1715) building enterprises were not so numerous, although certain projects were completed.

Period I: 1594–1643. This was a period of transition when both academic classicism and Italian Baroque tendencies made inroads.

Doors remained comparatively low and single-valved (i.e., swinging from one side).

Windows were still tall and narrow and, although they reached higher in the rooms, which also had Medieval verticality, they extended down only to the dado. Mullions and transoms were stone. Chimney breasts projected into the room and were often embellished with a superstructure of Baroque character.

Stairs rose by easy grades and were placed against the wall. Compared with their later prominence, they were relatively unimportant design elements.

Floors in important rooms were customarily patterned, often in stone, occasionally in wood.

Walls in domestic buildings were covered with *boiserie* (wood paneling) except for major halls (e.g., at Maisons) in which immense size and classical prototypes militated against such treatment. As noted in Italy and later in England, panels were larger in sizes that related to the proportions of the space. The fields projected from the level of the stiles and rails and are finished with a bold bolection molding (i.e., one that bridges two surface levels and incorporates torus or semicircular profiles). Classical ordonnance is not unusual, as noted in the Louis XIII galleries and in the St. Trinité Chapel at Fontainebleau. Often the woodwork extended only to a high dado. Permanent murals in architectural frames, tapestries, and occasional easel portraits adorned the upper wall.

Ceilings remained heavily beamed until a surprisingly late date in the simplest installations. In more fashionable circumstances the Italian coffered variety is found.

Period II: 1643–1678. This was the time of high Baroque influence when Le Vau was the preferred architect at Versailles. Little of Le Vau's Versailles has remained untouched except for the spaces in the *Salon de Diane* and the *Salon de Venus,* which have been preserved almost in entirety. Therefore we must study his style and that of mid seventeenth-century France from his other buildings, especially Vaux-le-Vicomte, the Hôtel Lambert, and his work at the Louvre.

Le Brun used the double-valve door at Vaux and he favored it thereafter. Frequently the door and the overdoor paneling were unified by enclosure within a heavy molding which reaches to the cornice.

Windows assume greater importance. At Vaux-le-Vicomte they rise in three tiers up to the room entablature and down "presque jusque à terre" (almost to the ground). Tall windows may contain as many as eighteen panes in height and four across (two panes wider than those of the first part of the century).

It then became customary to separate the mantel from the chimney breast, which thus stepped back to the wall plane. This innovation coincides with the use of marble for the sumptuous fireplace surrounds, which were particularly handsome when finished with a heavy convex molding. A painting with a carved or stucco garland enframement often enriched the chimney breast.

Although François Mansard's hall at Maisons gave promise of elaboration in the treatment of stairs, we must wait until Versailles II and the now extinct *Stairway of the Ambassadors* (1671) to reach planning comparable to the Italian. This was a central flight to a landing which then divided into two separate flights along the wall to the next story.

Except for an increasing use of marble, floor treatment remained about the same.

Certain changes in wall treatments became evident. Verticality was accentuated and the horizontality of the dado less stressed. The latter was of greater height. Panel dimensions varied within a space to accord more with room proportioning. Ordonnance, although not usual, did occur. Both pilasters and entablature are introduced in the *Galerie d'Apollon* at the Louvre. In the *Cabinet des Bains* Le Brun, working with Le Vau, inserted consoles in the frieze. This treatment, derived from the same done by Pietro da Cartona at the Pitti Palace in Florence, became a favorite of the period. Sometimes a bold convex molding was substituted for the frieze. Thus Baroque curvilinear details were made prominent even while wall embellishment apparently adhered to classical doctrine.

The Royal monopoly of such marble factories as those of Campan left little supply for others. Although the walls in much of Le Vau's work at Versailles were in marbles of contrasting tones—a brilliant stroke of Baroque drama—most French rooms were still paneled in wood. These might be decorated with painted arabesques or stucco reliefs.

Entries for the purchase of Venetian glass occur in the first royal accounts of 1664, the date when the main series of financial records begins. Small rooms, or cabinets, lined with mirrors became the fashion—one which prompted Colbert to subsidize a royal glass factory. Later the method of pouring large sheets of glass was inaugurated there; hence the potential for lining such spaces as the *Galerie des Glaces* was made economically feasible.

Ceilings were increasingly vaulted and plastered. Domed vaults (known in America as cloister vaults) rose directly from a square or polygonal base by the use of ribs. They were well adapted to compartment painting. However, it was the painter and architect Giovanni Francesco Romanelli (1610–1662), Cartona's pupil, who, working in Paris, introduced breaking zonal boundaries by peripheral figures.

Simpler plaster ceilings were characteristic of smaller halls. On the ground floor they were flat; on higher floors they were coved, a form that became almost a French idiom.

Period III: 1678–1699. In 1678 Louis began his stupendous building operation. In the end Versailles would be a combination of the White House, the Supreme Court Building, the Pentagon, and the Capitol. In addition it housed the courtiers, the king's chapel, and years later a center for the performing arts.

It was in the interior that Mansard and Le Brun (with younger designers toward the end of the century) created a distinct and mature Louis XIV style. Its essence was that of a classically oriented framework within which Baroque liberties executed with French finesse prevailed.

Space Organization

Dimensions remained regal. The *Galerie des Glaces* (Plate 17), which in many respects represents the apotheosis of the style, is 240 ft long, 35 wide, and 42 high. Nevertheless, despite vaulted ceilings, rooms remain rectangular and space experience is not complex. Except for special galleries, rooms of approximately equal cubic content open into one another to create vistas of uniform, imposing, boxlike space.

Architectural Details and Surface Treatment

When Mansard created the marble stairway (1680), he followed Le Vau's use of contrastingly toned colored marbles to make it correspond (in decoration but not in plan) to the then existing *Escalier des Ambassadeurs.* Elsewhere he introduced the muted marbles of the late Versailles

walls. With his general use of wood floors, the separate parts of the spaces were fused into a new atmospheric unity. Floors are parqueted in a pattern that has come to be known as the *Versailles.*

Floors like those in the main galleries of the Louvre were marble frequently inlaid with metal—pewter and latten. We must remember that the chief reason for subsidizing the Savonerrie factory was to produce carpets for the royal needs and that the many halls, now bare, were then, by record, covered with the richest pile rugs. Because of Le Brun's office, the same embellishments of design and the same high standards of craftsmanship were evident throughout the building.

Fusion of color was also accomplished by illumination. The Gallery at Versailles is lighted by seventeen window bays that face the same number of mirrors. Three hundred and six beveled mirrors mounted in copper frames were used in Mansard's great hall. Reflected light spills onto the floor and into the surround as in an Impressionist painting. At times this light echoes the linearity of the space and the diagonal parqueting of the floor.

Between each grouping of windows and mirrors the spaces are broken by niches occupied by sculpture or by panels that display gilt metal trophies. Pilasters that rise from a low pedestal support typical Le Brun entablatures in which the frieze is punctuated by paired consoles. The pilaster capitals are the variety he made famous, in which the French *fleur-de-lis* and palms substitute for the Corinthian acanthus, and a small sun for the rose of the abacus.

The wall materials, as far up as the frieze, are marble and metal. Both frieze and sculptural surround of the oval ceiling tablets are gilt stucco, once more in the Mannerist form of mixed media organized here into a single effect.

The windows of which we have been speaking are arch headed and reach from floor to cornice. They are double-valve, truly French windows, used here for the first time. Some French arched windows are designed without imposts and with a continuous architrave in Italianate style.

Double-valve doors are now universal. They are carved and gilded wood, like those of the

356

staircase entrances, and occasionally glass. Within a typical wood panel the rails are arched to fit into a concavity in the principal panel ground, and a second decorative breakdown creates a field of circular medallions. Although the door framing is flatheaded, it can be fitted into an archway enriched by an overdoor treatment to make one composition.

Fireplace mantels are marble, low, and horizontal in proportion. The rectangular opening was surrounded with the customary bolection molding, which sometimes receded to a narrow shelf, as in the *Salon de la Paix* (Figure 10.8), and sometimes to the plane of the wall, as in the *Salon de la Guerre*. The overmantel or chimney

Figure 10.8 Palace of Versailles, *Salon de la Paix.* France. 1678–1686. Charles Le Brun and Jules Hardouin Mansard. (Cliché des Musées Nationaux—Paris.)

breast contained some large pictorial work—in the former salon a later picture of Louis XV with his family, in the latter a mounted equestrian statue of Louis XIV in stucco but intended to be replaced with marble. Unfortunately Louis's luck did not last long enough for this to be done. Some smaller cabinets have chimney breasts of mirrors, a treatment that forecast the next century.

One characteristic of Versailles is the fact that even as early as the *Galerie des Glaces* a unified wall treatment to the great height of the frieze was accomplished. The attic story, which often separates the classical ordonnance of the wall and the area of the ceiling, has been omitted. This unified verticality is a French contribution.

The painted decoration of the ceilings in the west flank of rooms was the personal work of Le Brun and his pupils and glorified the successes

of the first part of Louis's reign. The overscaled painting in each division follows the older Renaissance style of compartmentalization whereby each episode is kept within its stucco or painted frame.

Decoration

Because French decorative ornament plays so important a role in the next centuries, a descriptive account is here given.

The Italian Baroque *cartouche* was used in France as early as the reign of Henry IV. It can be seen at Fontainebleau in the overdoor treatment of the Trinité Chapel and was commonplace in Rubens's tapestries. Although Le Brun used it as an ornament, his forte was the flatter *medallion* or *tablet,* noted in his "Story of the King" weavings. The *winged cartouche* is observable at top center of the "Triumphal Entry." The *trophy* likewise appears frequently in the work of this master designer.

The Roman *grotesque* changes its name to the French *arabesque.* When Simon Vouet (1590–1649) decorated the queen mother's apartment in 1643, he began a new vogue for painted arabesques. The French idiom consists of a central medallion supported by pairs of figures with acanthus and other foliage as adjuncts.

Le Brun favored the Vouet type arabesque. He often added the decorative motif known as the *lambrequin,* a fold or canopy of drapery. His arabesques are also distinguished by the use of decorative connecting flat *bands,* transferred from Italian marble floor intarsia and pattern books. Such bandwork can be seen in the carved and gilded wooden doors (1678) at the Palace of Versailles, executed by Philippe Caffieri from designs by Le Brun. The design is replete with rigidly bisymmetrically arranged foliage, intertwined L's, chimeras, cornucopias, the sun disk emblem of the King, the shield, the lyre, and the crown. These are only a few of the ideas in Le Brun's immense repertoire.

Furnishings and Their Arrangement

French furniture and furnishings as we know them in our museums today were first made in the seventeenth century in the ateliers of the Louvre and attained their distinctive decorative character only with the reign of Louis XIV. As the Bourbon court remained settled in one location and *meubles* belied the necessity for their name, more fragile decorative techniques such as marquetry and metal mounting could be applied to furniture without danger of destruction in transit. Sumptuous hangings and floor coverings could be made for location, and exquisite china and large pieces of silver had a permanent place.

Foreign monarchs such as Marie de Medici (wife of Henri IV) and great collectors such as Mazarin introduced the first pieces of marquetried furniture from Italy and the Lowlands. To copy this new elegance skilled craftsmen had to be imported, and we find that Mazarin, himself an Italian, brought to Paris the celebrated Dutch cabinetmaker Pierre Golle and the Italian *fondeur* (worker in metal) Philippe Caffieri (1634–1716), founder of a large family of fondeurs prominent in the French furniture arts, chief of whom were his son Jacques (1678–1755) and grandson Philip (1714–1774).

Laurent Stabre (?–1624) is the first recorded holder of a royal patent which exempted him from the restrictions of the French furniture guilds. Little is known about him except for this distinction. A royal patent holder was given lodging and work space in the Louvre and thus became a pensioner of the crown. In return he was obligated to work for the king. Another of the early Louvre pensioners was a Swiss émigré, Pierre Boulle, probably the uncle of the famous craftsman of Louis XIV's reign, André Charles Boulle (1642–1732).

Gradually, as shown by the two examples cited, the families of the immigrants adopted their new country and, by the royal policy of preferment to children of crown patent holders, should they prove able, became important to the French furniture industry by teaching native craftsmen the foreign techniques.

Fouquet, in building Vaux, had gathered his helpers together in a center at the town of Maincy. When he fell, Louis virtually transferred this enterprise to the small village of Gobelins, then on the outskirts of Paris. There in 1662 Colbert established the *Manufacture Royale des*

Meubles de la Couronne and placed Le Brun from Vaux in command. This date may then be taken as the beginning of French ascendency in the decorative arts, which attainment was exactly Colbert's purpose. Because of the training programs incorporated in the enterprise, the unparalleled resources available, and by reason of central control of quality and style, an industry developed that set a standard of excellence for at least a century and a half. Articles were numerous, paired pieces were frequent, and formal foreordained bisymmetry of placement had begun.

FURNITURE

Materials and Processes

French furniture had been made largely from native woods—oak in Normandy and Brittany (recall Theodore Thoreau's oaks of Barbizon), walnut in the central and southern portions of the country, some chestnut near the Italian border, and always the fruit woods—cherry, plum, and pear—for the smaller pieces. The more exotic woods began to appear, chief among which was ebony, the hard black variety from Ceylon or the more variegated type, now known as antimacassar, but then called Coromandel wood from the islands east of India's Coromandel coast.

It remained for André Charles Boulle to gather the materials and processes already at hand and to create from them a style of furniture embellishment so distinctive that its generic name thenceforth was his (Figure 10.9). Theretofore, and especially in Italy, where marquetry and intarsia were favored techniques, the woods were varied and the inlay had been that of a variety of materials—marble, tortoise shell, and ivory being among the most prominent. Boulle concentrated on brass and tortoise shell, augmented by gold and silver. His patterned inlays were made by gluing together two or more layers of brass and shell and cutting out the decoration from the sandwich. When separated, it made two designs, one of brass on a ground of shell, known as the *première-partie* (first part), and the second of shell on a ground of brass, known as the *contre-partie* (counterpart). Either or both were then applied as a veneer. Customarily, twin cabinets would be made, one of *première-partie* and the other of *contre-partie*, to be used in the same room. Often gold leaf or other suitable foil was placed under the translucent shell and the brass was frequently engraved. A red foil was much admired in later work in the reign of Louis Philippe in the nineteenth century, when Louis XIV style had a return to fashion. A recent advertisement, for instance, told of "one of a pair of red Boulle and contre-Boulle commodes." The great precision seen in the inlaid patterns in these advertised cabinets marked them to the cognati as more recent than any work done by Charles André. Old boulle is consequently known as "old black boulle." Old boulle cabinets are generally of oak body and the parts that are not inlaid are veneered with ebony.

Boulle also made pieces of wood marquetry on tortoise shell, a technique he later abandoned for his metal work. When this wood and shell patterning appears (e.g., on a Cleveland Museum of Art cabinet), it can be used to identify a piece as seventeenth century.

Something of the history of this famous cabinetmaker: André Charles Boulle, the second generation of the same name in France, was admitted to the Louvre to fill the place vacated by the death of Jean Massé, *ébéniste du roi*, a celebrated cabinet maker of the early seventeenth century. Boulle was recommended for the position by that indefatigable talent scout, Colbert. ". . . le plus habile ébéniste de Paris," said the prime minister to Louis.

One wonders what motivated the passion of this expert craftsman for collecting. Usually artists are not addicted to it, for the urge to create seems to take precedence over that of acquisition. Boulle, on the contrary, almost went bankrupt to buy old masters' drawings as well as prints and paintings by Baroque artists. In 1720, twelve years before his death at ninety, a fire utterly destroyed Boulle's workshop in the Louvre. Thereafter he quite understandably relegated more of his work to his four sons who had followed his calling. Because he devoted most of his time and money to his possessions, he died a poor man.

Figure 10.9   Wardrobe (*armoire*) attributed to André Charles Boulle. Paris, seventeenth century. Height, 2.54 m, width, 1.63 m, depth, 33 cm. Veneered on oak with ebony and boulle marquetry of brass, partly engraved, and tortoise shell. Bronze mounts, chased and gilt. The large vertical door panels are veneered in première-partie and the horizontal panels are in contre-partie. Wallace Collection, London. (Crown Copyright, reproduced by permission of the Trustees, The Wallace Collection, London.)

Boulle had made much furniture for Versailles; the series of cabinets for the *Galerie des Glaces* and a large part of the furniture and embellishments for the apartments of the Dauphin, where inlay was installed in the floors and occasionally in the wall paneling.

Gilt bronze mounts, *known as ormolu*, much used by Boulle, were first added to furniture to protect the corners made vulnerable by marquetry. For these mounts a wood or wax model would be supplied by the sculptor, from which a bronze casting was made that would subsequently be tooled or chiselled by the *chiseleur* to the desired sharpness and depth. It would then be gilded, at that time probably by the old and dangerous mercury process which burnished to a richer tone than any used subsequently.

Boulle as a protégé of the king was permitted his own staff of specialized assistants. Ordinarily the craft guilds organized in the seventeenth century were highly exclusive, much as trade unions are today. The *menuisier* might work only in solid wood. To recognize the new specialist who veneered the carcass in ebony, the term *ébéniste* was officially added in 1743. Ironically, the use of ebony was going out of fashion at that time, not to return to the popular scene until the rebirth of the classical style toward the last of the eighteenth century.

In addition, a piece of furniture might pass through the hands of a *fondeur*, a member of the metal worker's guild; a *doreur*, a member of the gilder's association; the *tapissier*, for its upholstery, and the *peintre* for its painting. Only the crown, the titular head of all of the guilds, could cut across the manufacturing lines thus drawn.

Another basic material used in this extravagant royal furniture was silver—sometimes wooden furniture to which silver was attached, sometimes solid or *massie* silver. Mr. Watson in preparing the catalog for one of the most famous collections of French furniture says:

> The finest furniture produced at the Gobelins during the first two decades of the factory's existence, is not represented in the Wallace collection at all and is scarcely to be found elsewhere.[2]

He refers to the silver furniture of the state rooms at Versailles. Almost all of this was melted down to allay the national debt incurred in the pursuance of Louis's late and unsuccessful military campaigns. A tapestry made at the Gobelins illustrates a royal visit made by the king to the Gobelins and shows the workmen exhibiting some of this furniture.

Marble became as popular for table tops as for room revetments. In addition to solid slabs of colored stones—white from Carrara in Italy; black marbles from the Lowlands; blue green from Egypt, *Antin* streaked with violet; *Portor*, white and grey with veins of orange and black; *Levanto Rosso*, a dark red and black with green—there was *Breccia*, marble fragments that the earth recements into whole stone.

Another new look was that of Oriental lacquer, which continued in popularity throughout the Louis XV period. Oriental lacquer is a technique as old as the Chou Dynasty (?–256 B.C.) in China and the Nara regime (A.D. ?–645) in Japan. Unlike the synthetic resins in contemporary lacquers, eastern lacquer came from the exudate of a tree, somewhat akin to a sumac. In skilled oriental work a number of thin coatings, well rubbed to a satiny finish, were applied. Sometimes they were placed upon a bed of gauze to give the necessary body. The result was not unlike that of the many thin coats of paint customarily applied to a top-grade interior paint job.

The Oriental lacquer set up such a hard finish that it was possible to paint on it: to engrave, to inlay, and to deep carve. This Eastern decoration introduced the occident to the oriental manner of illustration and gave impetus to the somewhat later vogue for *chinoiserie*.

Types and General Description

Because the Louis XIV period was the first in which French furniture pieces became numerous, it is only then that many furniture types subdivided into the myriad genre associated with their manufacture.[3]

Storage furniture was still the chest and cabinet until well into the seventeenth century. These pieces came in many varieties which descended the social ladder to emerge as French Provincial when made at a distance from *cour et ville*. Some valuable and interesting examples in this category which date from the seventeenth century are still obtainable, although the finest are museum pieces.

The function of the chest was often usurped by a standing cabinet with drawers behind doors or an *armoire* (wardrobe) that boasted shelves. *Armoires* were made by Boulle (Figure 10.9). Cabinet is a safe generic term for any of these pieces. The word also describes a small room or closet, a form often in use at that time when even royalty sometimes wished for privacy. The *cabinet à conseil* (a room for private discussions), the *cabinet aux medailles* (a room for the collection of curios)—these are written across the pages of history.

The French provincial cabinet was made of local woods, with an occasional bow to the exotic when ebony or even mahogany for a cornice or a molding could be procured from a ship moored at a nearby seaport. The proportions of the cabinets in the early part of the century were lower and broader than the attenuated forms that came later. Their carved decoration was likewise bolder and more geometric in its resemblance to the English Jacobean. Whereas early pieces had round turnings, later ones, with their large Dutch bun feet, sported spiral adjuncts and panels divided into ogivals.

The French writer Colette (1873–1954), in "My Mother's House," describes the old family cupboard (cabinet) which her mother in her older days tried to move, an act that nearly cost her life:

> The cupboard was a massive object of old walnut, almost as broad as it was high, with no carving save the circular hole made by a Prussian bullet that had entered by a right hand door and passed out through the back panel.

Colette makes of this article a symbol, brought with the bride to her new home, polished with zeal until it acquired the inimitable bloom of the antique, and passed on to her children, a memory of a home kept stable by the tenacious will power and courage of just such stock as the French novelist describes.

Although the armoire was the largest of the pieces of storage furniture, the French craftsmen lavished their skill on innumerable small *coffres* which were intended for the keeping of precious possessions. The *coffre de mariage* was a small arched chest coupled with a stand with a recessed top to keep the chest in place. The stand usually had one drawer. These little chests were given on the occasion of a wedding and were considered important additions to a room. A few have survived.

In the latter part of the seventeenth century a low cabinet with drawers—the *commode*—became fashionable for storage. The sense of the word is clear. It was more commodious and convenient for laying out articles of clothing. The piece was known in northern Italy as early as the sixteenth century.

Seating furniture at the time of Henry IV and Louis XIII did not differ radically from that used by the late Valois. It was hard-bottomed and low-backed, possibly in deference to the padded skirts and breeches and wide ruffs. Short-legged chairs were placed by the fire. Those with longer legs and stretchers were used at the high tables, also designed with low supports so that the feet could be propped off the ground. Legs were turned either in round or spiral form. Outlines were square and uncompromising. Many seats were armless. The narrow *caquetoire* and *caqueteuse* continued in use as a variety of high stool with a back. All are frequently seen in a series of engravings by the French artist Abraham de Bosse (1602–1676) which deals with interior scenes of middle-class life.

At the court of Versailles there was a need for seats of various heights—now, however, for reasons of etiquette. Louis, Duc de Saint-Simon, describes in detail the mandates relating to priorities. The top level rank, the upholstered armchair, was *le fauteil à bras*. Next came the high-backed chair without arms, *la chaise à dos* (to back). The *tabouret,* a low, upholstered stool, was permitted only to the highest order of nobility as a seat when in the presence of the king. *Banquettes* were longer editions of tabourets and the folding stool, a *pliant* or *ployant,* was the lowest grade of seat at court.

At one time it was recorded that the Duchess of Mantua arrived at the palace of Vincennes: ". . . she called, and was so dumbfounded to find herself offered only a *ployant* that she sat down, but when her senses returned somewhat later, she left and never again set foot inside the door."[4]

On the occasion of the marriage of Saint-Simon and of the reception of his duchess at court, he writes:

That same evening the King desired the bride to be presented to him in Mme. de Maintenon's room, which my mother and hers accordingly did. . . . Thence they went to supper where the new duchess was given her *tabouret*. The King said as he sat down to table, 'Pray, Madame, be seated.' He looked up as his napkin was being unfolded, and seeing all the duchesses and princesses still standing, half rose from his chair and addressing Mme. de Saint-Simon said, 'Madame, I have already desired you to sit,' whereupon all those who had the privilege sat down, Mme. de Saint-Simon between my mother and hers, who came after her in the order of precedence. Next day the entire court visited her in bed in the apartments of the Duchesse d'Arpagon, which were more convenient being on the ground floor. The maréchale de Lorges and I were present only for the visit of the royal family.[5]

All of this stiff ceremony seems to us the more incomprehensible when we are told that the public (if properly attired!) was permitted to walk

Figure 10.10 Sofa and two armchairs. Savonnerie wool pile fabric upholstery. The low stretchers suggest that the chair legs may have been shortened. France, ca. 1717. Cleveland Museum of Art. (The Cleveland Museum of Art, Purchase, John L. Severance Fund.)

along the window side of the dining parlors to observe the formalities, although separated from the table by a row of Swiss guards.

Carving on the seating furniture succeeded turning as embellishment. The curvature of the supports was Baroque in character and Baroque C scrolls appeared between the front legs. As styles moved toward classicism during the latter part of the century legs became squared and tapered, united with saltire (X-shape), recessed (H-shape), or serpentine flat stretchers. These numerous forms are to be found in various combinations which often do not seem to be consistently grouped.

One set of French chairs, presented as a royal wedding gift during the early years of the eighteenth century, are seventeenth century (Figure 10.10) in style. This set has rectilinear legs—a form best suited to carving and inlay—which obviously were cut short at some later date to make the pieces more compatible with eighteenth-century scale.

With this group we see a *sopha*, or sofa—a name in use since the early seventeenth century. The class name for seats capable of serving several persons was *canapé*. Its earliest version was the *chaise longue* (long chair) or *lit de repos* (bed for reclining, day bed). This was originally a refinement on the narrow pallet on which a retainer might sleep. Upholstery on a *chaise longue* was not usually affixed, whereas the sofa had a back and was fully upholstered or caned.

Tables were suited to chairs. The large rectangular table took precedence, and, fitted with a

marble top, boasting an apron of encrusted metal decoration, and with legs of any of the corresponding forms, it occupied the place of honor in any sizable room.

Although Henry IV articles were simply turned and had stretchers, several advanced forms came into use with the new century. The *console* was oriented to the wall and was designed to be placed below a mirror. The *bureau* or writing table followed the need in an age studded with letter writers and keepers of memoires: the Cardinal de Ritz at the time of Louis XIII; Mme. de Sévigné, Mme. Maintenon, and Saint-Simon, somewhat later; Pepys and Evelyn in England. The period is well documented with informal asides. Hence the bureau. It first consisted of a table on which a superstructure fitted with drawers was mounted. Then, when an addition was placed below the table, it was described as *bureau plat,* a large table with a single row of drawers, the center one slightly recessed. Examples that remain date largely from the eighteenth century.

Tables de jeu or *à jouer* there certainly were, for many games were played. A large billiard table stood in the Versailles Hall of Diana. The Hall of Mars featured small tables with fold-up flaps for customary evening pastimes. The court is said to have enjoyed the many games of chance played there.

The most important *bed* had its canopy supported by four posts. It was known as the *lit à colonnes.* The *lit à la duchesse,* which supported its tester and curtaining from the wall at the head of the bed, was introduced in the late seventeenth century. The older form of support from the ceiling remained in continuous fashion and was given elaborate treatment at that time. A balustrade surrounded the royal bed and entrance was forbidden all but the *valet de chambre—* hence that coveted position. Molière, of all people, served for a time as *valet-de-chambre tapissier* to Louis XIV, a sinecure inherited from his father.

In addition to these basic pieces, innumerable furnishings began to spell a well-equipped interior. At Versailles they were designed for location. The *bronzes d'ameublement,* which consisted of many small articles such as lighting fixtures, fireplace accouterments, and bases for sculpture, *écrans* or small screens for a number of uses but more often for protection against fireside heat, and clocks, barometers, astrolabes, musical instruments, all are mentioned in the contemporary literature and, following the fashion, were lavishly decorated.

Timepieces

Lewis Mumford may claim that town clocks were the drill sergeants that broke in the modern era. If so, the seventeenth century, when household timepieces became more readily available, certainly scurried us into today. Because England assumed leadership in horology, a discussion of its development is deferred until later chapters.

Nevertheless, French clockmakers were highly skilled. There the clock became an essential part of room decoration, following it closely in style. In France the maker of the clock case loomed as important as the maker of the works.

The earliest pendulum-regulated French clocks appeared near midcentury. They were designed either as mantel or as wall pieces, were quite severely architectural in style, and perhaps because of their somber cast were known as *religieuses.* The ornateness of ormolu and boulle soon altered any pious demeanor they possessed. When bronze mounts took the form of realistic statues at pinnacle and base, an arched, somewhat triangular undulating form resulted. The actual dial plates were covered with a black fabric, often velvet, the chapter ring was metal usually gilt, and the hour plaques were typically enamel—the whole very rich and ornate. Early French clocks bear only niched five-minute marks.

Mantel clocks are frequently inventoried as *horloges de cheminée,* and appear with the advent of the separate mantel and shelf. As wall clocks they are often designed in one piece with their brackets and are then known as *cartels.* Sometimes they stood on their own floor pedestals (Figure 10.11). Long and narrow, they made excellent embellishment for paneled interiors.

The long case clocks, known as *regulateurs,* were never very popular in France. With weights and pendulums fitted into a comparatively narrow tall frame, they were given extra width at the bob level to accommodate the swing. This often resulted in an awkward design.

TEXTILES

During the seventeenth century the ascendency of France in the silk industry and in the making of carpets was well established. In Normandy a start was made in the culture of flax and the spinning and weaving of linen. The foresight of Henry IV, implemented later by Colbert and linked to French designing talent, gave France top rank in luxury fabric creation.

Silk weaving had been fostered at Lyon and Tours ever since Charles VII in 1450 and Louis XI in 1466 granted special privileges—in both cases scarcely kept—to weavers settled in these towns. Though additional progress was made under the early Bourbons, the cost of raw materials still limited production and luxury fabrics were largely imported.

The work remained a cottage and family industry until 1600, when Claude Dangon, an Italian in France, invented an improvement on a loom for pattern weaving which made possible the creation of the large intricate designs then so fashionable.[6] In addition to this stimulus, Henry IV issued a decree forbidding the importation of elaborate silks—another edict more broken than kept. Henry also subsidized the planting of 60,000 young mulberry trees and established new looms.

It remained for Colbert to inaugurate the system that regulated the output in every respect. He gained the services (often by questionable means) of some of the most talented of Italian artists and technicians and turned over to Le Brun the task of guaranteeing both quality and quantity.

Early French seventeenth-century designs imitated the effulgent ogivals of Baroque Italy. Soon, however, the pattern field began to loosen and unity was destroyed as details separated from the whole (Figure 10.12). If Baroque art in its most emotional, exuberant, and plastic stage was not to find a congenial home in France, no more explicit proof of this could be advanced than is to be seen in the disintegration of pattern in these French fabrics before they were set on their own unique course.

Figure 10.11 Pedestal clock. France, early eighteenth century. Boulle workshop(?). Oak veneered with boulle marquetry of engraved brass on tortoise shell. Figures and mounts: chased ormolu. Height of clock, 1.25 m; of pedestal, 1.63 m. Wallace Collection, London. (Crown Copyright, reproduced by permission of the Trustees, The Wallace Collection.)

Figure 10.12 Silk lampas textile. France, early seventeenth century. Musée Historique des Tissus, Lyon. (Musée Historique des Tissus.)

In 1650 the industry hit its stride. The French translated the ogival into the large *jardinière* or floral vase design and there the classicising and refining influence took over (Figure 10.13). In this design a very important aesthetic principle is demonstrated, namely that largeness in total scale of framework pattern is not the only criterion for judging size similarities in art. The French preserved magnitude in Louis XIV textiles as they had in their furniture, but the attention to fineness of detail, to precise linear definition, well-modulated shading, carefully juxtaposed hues—rich reds, greens, and blues against a white satin background—and to a tightly knit organization of parts to whole bespeaks a discernment that would

gather momentum until it reached the unity seen in the textiles of the late century. It is this unity of elegance—attention to all details to the perfection of the whole—that is the predominant lesson we can learn from the art of seventeenth-century France. Anyone who knows Duchesse lace understands how the fine detail gathers strength until it becomes the enveloping swirl. Lace representations as background play an important part in the textiles of the *fin de siècle*.

Brocatelles and lampases and brocaded satins became more prominent toward the end of the century and were favored over velvets for upholstery. They combined depth of body with fine silk thread which in large scale and fine detail were characteristics that distinguished the classical period of Louis XIV's reign.

Tapestry weaving was by no means a forgotten art in the northern Lowlands during the seventeenth century. In general, however, Flemish designers and techniques were inferior to the French. Among the principal *oeuvres* were copies of Renaissance sets reproduced with wider borders. The work of Rubens, who designed for both France and Flanders, calls for special attention.

It is necessary first to introduce the French looms on which some of his pieces were woven. In 1603 Henry established a factory for tapestry weaving at the Louvre and gave special privileges to two Flemish weavers, François de la Planche (van der Planken) and Marc Coomans, which established them in royal service. The small factory they supervised was quite close to the house of a family of wool dyers named Gobelin, on the left bank of the Seine at the end of what is now the Avenue des Gobelins.

As previously mentioned, this factory, with other small establishments, was consolidated in 1667 under the name of the *Manufacture Royale des Meubles de la Couronne,* later to become known simply as the Gobelins. Here also were gathered artists and artisans in many other lines whose skills thereafter were to be employed in the decoration of the royal palaces. Colbert was its administrator and Le Brun, its supervisor. Today not only the Gobelin tapestry works but the Beauvais and the Aubusson, whose stories are to come, are congregated in this quiet spot in the middle of noisy Paris. It is a bit of the past,

366

the old courtyard with its statue of Colbert, the founder.

Contemporary with the state acquisition of the Paris factories and their consolidation as one establishment, another factory was encouraged by the government. This was at Beauvais, 50 miles north of Paris where several small concerns were struggling to keep alive. A Paris tapestry dealer by the name of Louis Hinart, a native of Beauvais and owner of tapestry looms, was given considerable financial aid by the government for the purpose of making the Beauvais industries successful. Thus in 1664 the Beauvais tapestry works were begun. This undertaking was promoted by Colbert because he foresaw financial benefit to France if a factory could be organized to conduct a business in less expensive wares for a less restricted clientele. Customers might be the nobility, the wealthy, and the foreign market, whereas the output of the Gobelins was royal property.

Another French district in southern Auvergne was the home of several small tapestry ateliers, one in the town of Felletin and another at Aubusson. Some small support was given these establishments by sending Gobelin cartoons to the weavers. It was later in the eighteenth century that the government took forceful and meaningful steps to improve the quality of Aubusson output and to place the factory on a sound financial base. Aubusson, among its types of production, specialized in smaller pieces used for screens, upholstery, and carpets.

These three, Gobelins, Beauvais, and Aubusson, each with a different operating policy, are accountable for the supremacy of French Baroque and Rococo tapestries.

The seventeenth-century tapestries resembled the Baroque hangings of Italy in size and in having wide framelike borders, which held many motifs of a theatrical nature as well as the cartouches, tablets, and trophies of French stock. With the exception of certain Beauvais verdure tapestries, the scenes were pictorial, done more in imitation of painting design than with a recognition of tapestry potential. The setting was frequently drawn from a low or unusual viewpoint and so included a large area of sky that was difficult to render interestingly in tapestry technique. Figures on Baroque tapestries are large and theatrically placed.

Figure 10.13 *Jardinière* lampas silk. France, seventeenth to eighteenth centuries. Height, 68.5 cm, width, 49.5 cm. Metropolitan Museum of Art, New York. (The Metropolitan Museum of Art, Rogers Fund, 1909.)

The dominant line is curved, sweeping diagonally into space.

The Rubens tapestries, done in this Baroque idiom, are the most famous of the early seventeenth century. Peter Paul Rubens (1577–1640) was born in Antwerp but lived and painted in Italy, Holland, Spain, and England, in each of which he received his commissions from court and church.

He created four tapestry series, among which the *Story of Constantine* was woven both at the early Gobelins and Brussels (Figure 10.14). The narrative was a favorite hero story used since the Renaissance and represented by versions from the brush of such famous painters as Raphael and Romano. Louis XIII ordered the French set of twelve tapestries, seven of which now hang in the colossal entrance of the Philadelphia Museum of Art. The originally intended location for

367

Figure 10.14 *The Battle of the Milvian Bridge.* Tapestry. Designed by Peter Paul Rubens, early seventeenth century. Philadelphia Museum of Art. (Philadelphia Museum of Art: Given by the Samuel H. Kress Foundation.)

the twelve tapestries, each 16 ft high, is not positively known. Certainly they could have been used only in one of the long galleries of a large French chateau or palace, possibly the Louvre.[7]

When designing for a Renaissance corridor, the artist's intention might be to display the pictures sequentially in balanced arrangements. During the seventeenth century, with the grand gallery flanking a tier of rooms, it was the inner wall that gained first attention. It would be seen in an asymmetrical line of sight by a person entering a door adjacent to the windows. In the Constantine set of tapestries Rubens anticipated this change in French architectural planning. Not only is the internal organization of each of the Constantine hangings more agitated and directional in its thrust than that of any Renaissance piece

but it is evident because of the directionally ordered light that he intended them to be hung asymmetrically and in order. His great painting series concerned with the life of Marie de Medici, designed for the Luxembourg and now at the Louvre, suggests a similar concept. Thus furnishings were conceived for a particular location, and the artist resolved many factors in planning his ensemble. When the individual items are mobile, as in the case of framed pictures or tapestries, this fact is likely to be forgotten. It is important, however, to stress it in considering interior design as an art that qualifies architecture.

The next chapter in the history of seventeenth-century French tapestries belongs to the Louis XIV Gobelins and to Charles Le Brun. It has been aptly said that Le Brun was not just one man—he was a syndicate. At the Gobelins he was assisted by many other painters: Vandermeulen, Bonnemer, Sain-Andre, Ivart, Ballin, and De Melun—names seldom heard except in this association.

368

Le Brun designed more than eighty tapestries and more than four hundred paintings—a prodigious output however accomplished.

The fourteen pieces known as the *Story of the King,* which glorifies the first twenty-five years of Louis' reign (Figure 10.15), are possibly Le Brun's most famous tapestries. Four sets were made, although only the first was executed on high warp looms. Some of the pieces were designated for the Halls of Apollo and of Mercury at Versailles and happily are being replaced there, taken from the National Collection for that purpose. This first set of high warp and the first of the low warps were begun in 1665 and took fifteen years to weave.

The fifth member of the *Story of the King,* and certainly the best known, represents the triumphal entry of Louis into Dunkirk. The *Entrance to Dunkirk* should be contrasted with the *Flight over the Milvian Bridge* of Rubens' Constantine tapestries (Figure 10.14). The wide frames of the borders are almost their only points of similarity. Even here the cartouche figures more prominently in the earlier tapestries, whereas the tablet or medallion that encloses the Chi, Rho (X, P—the first two letters of the Greek word for Christ) and the royal *fleur-de-lis* is seen in the top frame of the Le Brun set. Le Brun has refined his details, which, still fitting into the Baroque pattern, give greater prominence to figural motifs designed in more natural and attenuated style. Even the acanthus is less vigorously plastic and more Renaissance in feeling as befits the classical work of the later Louis reign.

The major scenes are also in contrast. The swirling pattern of Rubens covers most of the panel, whereas Le Brun features the placid Dutch landscape. Here Louis' horse, standing on a hillock, certainly possesses the stance that Bernini made famous in his equestrian statue of the king. Louis seems more concerned with his portrait

Figure 10.15   *The Entrance of Louis XIV into Dunkirk.* Tapestry. Charles Le Brun, the Gobelins. France, ca. 1665. Mobilier National. (Collection du Mobilier National, Paris. Cliché des Musées Nationaux—Paris.)

image than with the perilous Baroque descent into which he is about to be plunged. The chaotic picture in the Rubens Philadelphia Museum tapestry interlocks many planes and leaves us somewhat concerned about which heads belong to which hoofs and feet. Thus the difference which fifty years and the forces of the academy could make on French art even within a stylistic phase.

Le Brun died in 1690. It has been said that had he lived longer he would have run out of triumphs of Louis to celebrate pictorially. The late wars of state were not successful and the state treasury was almost bankrupted by its efforts in trying to finance them. Many of the Gobelin weavers remained unpaid for long periods. Finally in 1693 the Royal Manufactory closed its doors, not to reopen until the next century.

For one last moment at the closing of the century we turn to the Beauvais factory, which despite the generosity of the crown had experienced severe financial difficulties. In 1684 the works were taken over by Philip Behagle, who is said to have curried favor with Louis' mistress Madame Montespan. Behagle was singularly successful, and at the time of the shutdown at the Gobelins he secured the services of some of their foremost designers, including Jean Berain. The Berain-designed tapestries—for instance The Charlatan set made for the Comte de Toulouse—although bisymmetrical in arrangement, contain much fanciful imagery: domed central pavilions supported by pillars with opposed scrolls, bandwork, and swirling foliage, and drapery accompanied by living forms of delicate contour.

Beauvais tapestries at this time were signed by the proprietors, Hinart and Behagle. Early Gobelins exhibit a P for Paris in combination with the fleurs-de-lis, followed by the name of the particular proprietor of a specific shop. After 1662 the Gobelins used G or Gob for Gobelins, followed by the insignia of the proprietor. Many Gobelins remained unsigned.

WALLPAPERS

The chief innovation in the manufacture of wallpapers during the seventeenth century was in papiers veloutés or flock papers, which were made and used in France and England. A textile pattern was hand blocked in varnish on paper. Powdered wool which was then sprinkled over the paper adhered to the varnish to create a raised pattern. Le François of Rouen is credited with this invention, although it is unlikely that it had not been done before his time because flocking on cloth was well known.

The use of wallpaper was still restricted. It awaited the manufacture of paper in rolls, the fashion impetus that arrived with the painted papers of the orient, and the economic forces that coincided with the predominance of middle-class culture in the eighteenth century to popularize this type of wall covering.

SEVENTEENTH-CENTURY FRENCH AND ORIENTAL FLOOR COVERINGS

In addition to the flat-woven tapestries of the Gobelins, Beauvais, and Aubusson, France produced a woolen floor and upholstery fabric—hautelaine (high wool)—which was a pile fabric. This was the Savonnerie, made in an offshoot of Henry IV's ateliers at the Louvre. The Savonnerie factory was at Chaillot, then a suburb of Paris. Its story is the following:

In 1604 Pierre Dupont, an illustrator of sacred books, made copies of popular Turkey carpets and showed them to the King. This led to the opening of the Louvre atelier, the output of which was again restricted to royal consumption. Then, as in the parallel Beauvais instance, a second workshop was opened—to offset English and Spanish competition—in the buildings of a former soap factory (Savonnerie) with fewer restrictions on sale. The director was Simon Lourdet, a former pupil of Dupont. In 1672, under royal edict, the two factories combined to effect a consolidation similar to that of the Louvre tapestry factories and the Gobelins.

The distinctive contribution of the Savonneries (the name was continued) lay in their designs. Instead of copying the oriental patterns and colors, the French turned to their architectural ceiling borders as frames for flowered carpet fields. Naturally this close analogy between architecture and carpet design was more pronounced under the aegis of Charles Le Brun and is accurately shown in the large Savonnerie (Figure 10.16) at the Metropolitan, one of ninety-three ordered for the *Grande Galerie* of the Louvre. The frequently black background on which the Savonnerie patterns were projected thus accentuated the strong, lighter tones of the design.

Needlepoint (embroidered cross stitch on canvas) rugs were manufactured in certain convents, notably that of St. Cyr subsidized by the King and Madame Maintenon.

Rugs called *Polonaise* were actually woven in Persia during the seventeenth century, as investigations have disclosed. They were intended as gifts from the Persian Shahs to the courts of Europe. Their patterns are those of the Persian Herat but their color schemes were dictated by European taste and are lighter than the usual Persian range. Moreover, many are silk and gold weavings. The fact that they have been called Polish rugs is due to another of those misunderstandings of history. Many of them found their way to Poland, then a rising power. There they lay incognito until brought to the Paris exposition held at the Trocadero in the last century. Erroneously supposed to have been Polish weavings, they were given this misleading name. The Living Hall of the Frick Museum of New York contains a very rare seventeenth-century Herat rug of the variety often called Polonaise.

Chinese Orientals may be described in a seventeenth-century context because it is difficult to assign any earlier date with certainty to any complete Chinese carpet, although Chinese rug weaving undoubtedly is ancient.

Chinese rugs are woven with a Sehna knot and thus can be fine weavings. One of the earliest of the great Chinese carpets is owned by the Metropolitan Museum of Art, the gift of J. Pierpont Morgan. It illustrates admirably the character of the national product. In the first place the colors are simple, being predominantly blue and gold. Yellow because of its manifold symbolism was basic.

Chronology and description of the finest antique Chinese rugs defy tabulation. The oldest carpets used simple borders, and it is almost a certain indication of a later date to find the mul-

tiple bands common to Persian carpets. The mark of veneration is some example of the fret border without corner designs. Early examples are likely to show a single medallion center, which is often round and has a characteristic open center taken from the coin or "cash" symbol. Several medallions may be arranged around a central field in symmetrical order. The background may be plain or show the Chinese lattice pattern. The exterior border is commonly blue, although some of the Ming rugs are brown.

During the late seventeenth and early eighteenth centuries European influence on China is represented in their rugs by a border of floral forms and by a proliferation of narrow bands. The body of the field only then acquired many of the sacred symbols of the Taoist and Buddhist religions, such as the bat, the lotus, and the cloud band. In the carpets contemporary with the period we are studying the motifs tend toward a classical bisymmetrical arrangement. Later weavings lose this symmetry.

Temple carpets, which are rare and superlative seventeenth-century pieces, show a base border of the sacred waves and the sacred mountain and a beneficent five-toed dragon is likely to be present. In all, the character is unmistakably Chinese, and even when many items are included an uncluttered effect is miraculously maintained.

Figure 10.16 Savonnerie carpet with the arms of France. France, seventeenth century. Wool. Length, 9 m, width, 4.88 m. Metropolitan Museum of Art, New York. (The Metropolitan Museum of Art, Rogert Fund, 1952.)

NORTHERN EUROPEAN CERAMICS AND A SHORT ACCOUNT OF CONTEMPORARY ORIENTAL CERAMICS

In the north the Lowlands antedated France as a flourishing commercial center of the ceramics industry. Pottery had been made and sold in the vicinity of Delft since the second half of the sixteenth century. About 1650 the industry received a real impetus when the beer business, a local goldmine, became so competitive that many of the brewers failed. It occurred to some of the thrifty burghers to try their hands at making pottery in the vacated beer emporiums. The enterprise proved successful despite the fact that much of the raw material had to be imported.

Possibly the attempt made by the new wares to imitate the very popular underglaze blue and white porcelain of China created a demand. Although certain borrowed decorative motifs might have been used, the Delft patterns were in the main pictorial. Many of the best Netherlandish painters did the Delft scenes. Among them were Frederick van Frijtom, Abraham de Cooge, Aelbracht Cornelis de Keizer, and the families of Pijnackers, Wouters van Eenhoorn, and Louwijs Fictoor.

The process of making Delft pottery was similar to that of making majolica with the omission of the luster metals. The plate, having acquired a preliminary low firing, was dipped in tin enamel. When partly dry, a design was painted on in blue and filled in with green, yellow, red, and violet. It was then covered with a thin lead glaze and given a second firing. Sometimes red and gold were added at later firings.

Manufactories existed in France throughout the seventeenth century, although none obtained the Delft reputation. Some of these old French kilns are staging a revival today. The wares are customarily lead-glazed and have quaint provincial patterning.

The Germans never took kindly to making pottery. Although faience was produced at such places as Hamburg and Frankfort, it was for stoneware that the country was noted. Much was unglazed or salt glazed (i.e., by use of salt thrown over pieces during firing).

Oriental porcelain of the seventeenth century, during the late Ming Dynasty (which ended in 1644, almost contemporary with the beginning of the reign of Louis XIV, had developed the perfected glazes of *ox blood, peach bloom,* and *claire de lune.* Three- and five-color famille porcelains became the epitome of multiglaze work (see pp. 269–270).

Japanese and Korean ceramics first came to the attention of the West during the seventeenth century. The prominence accorded to the tea ceremony at this time called for ceremonial attention to naturalness in all forms of artistic expression. This led to the production of rough-appearing bowls and pots in which the colors were so muted and of the earth that they seemed appropriate to the rustic teahouse and its surroundings. The imported Chinese Temmoku (tea) bowls had a wide market among tea fanciers.

Meanwhile, Japan was making porcelain for the European market. A family named Kakiemon from the Arita region produced a type of hard paste china which is overglaze painted. Its design had great influence on later European work and on the subsequent Imari porcelain of Japan.

STONES, METALS, IVORIES

Extant silver from the seventeenth century is still a rarity. Like the architectural styles the existing pieces range from the elaborate to the chaste and simple.

In 1938 the Metropolitan Museum in New York held the first comprehensive exhibition of French silver in this country. For many old enough to remember it was an introduction to what has seemed to be the finest domestic silver ever produced. There is no denying the beauty of English and American silver, especially of the eighteenth century. Its glory lies in the formality of some of its classic designs. The French touch, in addition to possessing unsurpassed technical skill, combined simplicity with more ornate decoration done with outstanding clarity and economy.

Numerous pieces were produced, each of which could be correlated with corresponding English types. The *écuelle,* for instance, was an individual two-handled dish that corresponded to the American porringer. The two-tined fork appeared before the middle of the century, and a set of table utensils containing a knife, four-pronged fork, and spoon dates from 1677. Although French silver does not carry a date mark as does English, the chronology can be deduced from the warden's mark and from the tax discharge. The pieces just referred to bore no maker's mark, although customarily French silver did. Incidentally, Louis, according to his sister-in-law, Charlotte Elizabeth of Bavaria, did not approve of knife and fork—fingers were more direct.

Styles in silver as in all decorative media traveled from France as a vortex, losing only a short time in the process. In silver pierced and cut-card work are characteristic of the late seventeenth century. Pierced work is clearly described by its name, for piercing often appeared on the flat handles of objects. The name *cut-card* is given to elements that appear to have been cut from thin cardboard patterns and then adhered to the silver body.

DESCRIPTIVE SUMMARY

The seventeenth century was the time for France to make its own advancements in architecture and the accompanying arts. The seventeenth century stands at the pinnacle of that development in which absolute power (represented by Versailles) had little in common with the people's way of life.

In this development the reigns of the first two Bourbons were merely a tune-up. Classical maturity arrived only with the work of François Mansard, which shows a sense of proportioning that is the pure essence of ordered beauty.

With the beginning of the Sun King's reign the Baroque of Italy introduced the drama of tonal contrasts, pompous scale, sumptuous materials, and license in the use of ornament. Freedom was even responsible for some liaison with oval spaces and with the typical French tendency toward planar syncopation, although such deviation was not acceptable to the royal mind. Nor was the French demonstration of practicality demonstrated in apartment planning welcomed by a monarch who thrived on parade.

When Jules Mansard and his orchestra played their variations on the theme, an essentially French syndrome of Baroque qualities—the fusing of contours by light and muted tones, the scale achieved in conjunction with linear fineness, and the sumptuousness with elegant refinement—came into being. In France forever after excessive license would be castigated by formal unity, characterized in architecture by ordonnance, regularity of meter, a nicety of execution, and a precision of detailing.

On first sight Versailles appeared to be a symphony of contrasts—the endlessly classically regimented facade pitted against the prominent scrolls of decoration and furniture. Yet, as we learn to know Louis and his court and the palace in which they lived, is it so contradictory or isolated a phenomenon? The French nation is a unity at heart and its art is not various. The king was no uncommon man and what he succeeded in giving France has a colloquial touch. It was sensuous Gallic as well as regimented Frankish to the core and it was ruled by a hard-headed practicality, essentially feminine.

The interior of Versailles touches on its luxurious urbanity. The East Front of the Louvre stands for its bow to formal rationality. The wing buildings of Versailles are its academicism. Its planning skills speak for its pragmatic outlook. The Marble Court is its opening trills; the *Galerie des Glaces* is its late sonorous harmony, its rich oboe tones which would never again be heard with such authority and opulence. In a sense the art of the French seventeenth-century architectonics forecasts its counterparts in the music of Cesar Franck and Claude Debussy rolled into one.

JAPANESE SCREEN ARTISTS

It may seem odd to include Japanese decorative art under the aegis of France. Yet both countries show a predisposition toward the ornamental that makes such placement seem not only legitimate but also the only possible one to use.

Although trade with China had opened a vista to the orient during the Middle Ages, there was little awareness of the islands of Japan. Moreover, commerce with the archipelago was discontinued by Japanese edict from the early seventeenth century until the midnineteenth (1853), when Commodore Perry succeeded in negotiating an open-door trade policy.

373

Figure 10.17 *The Pass through the Mountains.* Sixfold screen by Roshu. Japan, seventeenth century. Ink and color on gold-ground paper. Height, 1.52 m, width, 2.68 m. Cleveland Museum of Art. (The Cleveland Museum of Art, Purchase, John L. Severance Fund.)

Japan in the meantime had developed from a country of small feudal divisions to a nation welded into a unified whole by military (samurai) shoguns. A people with a strong tradition of native crafts, which possibly resulted from the need to sustain an existence from meager natural resources, had developed an aesthetic sensitivity to nature and natural forms that became an important element in their religion (Shintoism). This had gained an elegant nicety sharpened by contact with the polished courts of China.

When the results of this island life were seen by western eyes, a building art was revealed of temples and castles, the dark wooden interiors of which were enriched by some of the world's most fabulous decoration. Although lacquers and ceramics and textiles were a part of this tradition, it is the wall decoration, which consisted of folding screens, that remains architectural decoration of the first order.

The earliest examples of this art date to the Fujiwara court (897–1185, also called Late Heian); others to the Ashikaga or Muromachi period (1392–1573). The screens were undoubtedly inspired by Chinese examples of hanging and hand scrolls, particularly of the late Sung Dynasty

monochrome style. The famous triad of Ashikaga painters—Shubun (ca. 1390–1464), his pupil Sesshu (1420–1506), and Sesson (1504–ca. 1589)—illustrate this assertion in such sixfold pieces as the *Winter and Spring Landscape* in the Cleveland Museum of Art, *Flowers and Cranes* in the Tokyo Kosaka Collection, and the Cleveland *Tiger and Dragon,* respectively. Considering that they measure in excess of 12 ft in length and between 5 and 6 in height, the visual carrying power imparted to ink and paper by the agency of tonal values is astounding. Each artist is unique in his genius. Nevertheless, each used the traditional flowing rhythms to carry the eye from right to left to the borders of the picture where a subtle balance would be established. All is accomplished by the placement of shapes and by the agency of *notan* (schematic arrangement of lights and darks).

With the later Momoyama period (1573–1615) Japanese families, growing affluent, again sought their status symbols in an art that looked to China. This time, however, the patrons, being Japanese warlords, favored more forceful compositions. This stylistic trend reached its zenith during the early Edo or Tokugawa period (1615–

374

1868) in which shades of powdered lapis blue, malachite emerald, crimson, and purple effected broad sweeps of color on backgrounds of gold and silver leaf. One must look long and feel strongly the qualities shown in the work of the individual painters of the Momoyama—Kanō Eitoku (1543–1590), Hasegawa Tōhaku (1539–1610), Kanō Sanraku (1559–1635), and Kanō Tannyu (1602–1674). Such works as the *Cypress Tree* in the Tokyo National Museum, the famous *Pine Wood* screen in the same location, *Trees, Flowers, and Rocks* on a screen of sliding rather than folding panels in the Daikaku-ji in Kyoto, and the sliding panels of the *Tigers and Bamboo* in Nanzen-ji in Kyoto show, respectively, each man at his best.

With the seventeenth century and the military dictatorship of the Tokugawas Japanese movable wall decoration reached its apogee in the work of Sōtatsu (1576–1643), Kōrin (1658–1716), Roshū (1699–1776), and the already more refined work of Kenzan (1663–1743), Kōrin's brother. The first two had indeed given their names to this Tokugawa school as the Sōtatsu-Kōrin style, in which greater realism, figure interest, and a combination of decorative painting in color on a subdued level seemed to revert to the more delicate taste of the painters of the Ashikaga period. We may regard the *Thunder God and Wind God,* a twofold screen in the Kennin-ji in Kyoto, the *White Prunus in the Spring* in the Tokyo National Museum, the *Pass through the Mountains* in the Cleveland Museum of Art (Figure 10.17), and the hanging scroll *Baskets of Flowers and Weeds* in the Matsunaga collection in Tokyo as representative.

One can easily realize the impact that these masterpieces had on the occident when they were first brought to popular attention during the last century. This was wall decoration of fervent movement, yet restful, of decorative flat pattern rather than perspective, of color, and again of tone, organized in complex harmonies. This was a surge away from classical bisymmetry and Baroque plasticity, which remained within the compass of architectonic planes.

CHAPTER ELEVEN

Seventeenth-Century England

Believe it, Lords and Commons, they who counsel ye to such suppressing do as good as bid ye suppress yourselves; and I will soon show how. If it be desired to know the immediate cause of all this free writing and free speaking, there cannot be assigned a truer than your own mild and free humane government; it is the liberty, Lords and Commons, which your own valorous and happy counsels have purchased us, liberty which is the nurse of all great wits. . . . Give me the liberty to know, to utter, and to argue freely according to conscience above all liberties.

John Milton, *Areopagitica*

CULTURE SPAN

On Elizabeth's death in 1603 the House of Tudor became extinct. James VI of Scotland, who inherited the throne by direct descent from Henry VII, assumed the title of James I of England, the first monarch of the Stuart line. He united England and Scotland in his person, but parliamentary unification of these neighboring countries was not effected until the reign of Queen Anne, the last ruler of the Stuart dynasty.

The autocratic policies of the early Stuart kings led ultimately to civil war. Having blood ties with France, they emulated its absolutism. But France was not England, where a strong tradition of civil rights supported by both aristocracy and upper class and now descending to the middle class upheld constitutional prerogatives. The Stuarts lost one king to the executioner's block and another by forced abdication before they learned this fact.

The decade of the interregnum does not present a pleasant picture. Many of the leaders of the Cromwellian rebellion were religious dissenters who because of their antiritualistic beliefs were frequently destructive of art treasures. In their military encounters they wantonly demolished furnishings of many royalist homes. During Cromwell's reign a goodly number of royal sympathizers came to America, among them the ancestors of George Washington and Thomas Jefferson.

Charles II had lived at the court of his cousin Louis XIV during much of his exile. It is small wonder that on his return to England to accept the throne (the Restoration), although he was not foolish enough to duplicate the mistakes that had cost the life of his father, he was inclined to live in the manner to which sojourn at the French court had accustomed him. A reactionary period of luxury and profligacy followed the tight puritanical Commonwealth.

Throughout the seventeenth century in all of Europe the involvement of religious issues in politics and the economy created confusion. This was nowhere more evident than in the relations between France, England, and Holland. At times the English were allied with the French in disputes with Dutch shipping interests; at others England was a partner of the Dutch against France in religious differences. Because the English church, which since Elizabeth's time had been Protestant, felt itself threatened by the supposed Catholic sympathies of the Restoration Stuarts, a return to a firm Protestant succession was invited in the persons of James II's daughter Mary and her husband King William of Orange. From then on protestantism prevailed in England.

The seventeenth century was not the *grand siècle* of English art or, for that matter, of English political prestige. In the arts with which we are concerned it looked toward the Italy of the Renaissance and often toward the Baroque of the Lowlands. It created no great palaces but rather built homes and churches which reached out to the people.

ARCHITECTURE

Jacobean

English seventeenth-century architecture embraces three styles and two men. The first chronological division called *Jacobean* (for James) includes much of the building in the reigns of the first two Stuarts—principally the great houses for those whose fortunes were assured by the new regime.

James I had retained Robert Cecil, a prominent minister of Elizabeth's reign. Cecil, created Earl of Salisbury, built Hatfield House (Figure 11.1), which, with Audley End and Charlton, embraced the past and bowed to the future.

These houses were of a size that aligned them with the palatial Hardwick and Wollaton. Materials in many Jacobean examples are local brick with stone quoins. Even though flatter roofs may have elaborate balustrades, countless ill-assorted chimney pots crowned them. Facades of bays and pavilions with their immense windows wove in and out. Double-curved and crow-stepped gables looked toward Holland for inspiration (Figure 11.2), and ornament often came from the Flemish school, either directly from the texts that inspired Elizabethan extravagance or more likely from the actual presence of foreign craftsmen. The English had not yet developed the confidence that would

Figure 11.1 Hatfield House. Hertfordshire, 1607–1611. Robert Lyminge, architect. (British Tourist Authority.)

allow the handling of their decorative art by native talent.

Aside from casual nods to the Renaissance tradition in the use of the orders, the chief innovation seen in these mansions lies in a planning technique that placed progressively greater emphasis on formality and function. Bysymmetry became a conscious aim. The hall, which began at Hatfield to run at right angles to the facade, was entered through a central porch and door. Its purpose changed from that of a living room with directional movement from the lower end toward the dais to one that provided equal access to both wings of the house. In other words the central hall was emerging. To facilitate articula-

tion a long gallery ran along the front or rear of the first story.

Inner rooms were grouped bisymmetrically about the hall—possibly parlors on one side balanced service areas and suites of private rooms on the other.

Quite progressive are the open H and U plans of the majority of buildings. Some, even of the preceding century such as Wollaton, subscribe to the block principle and thus have fenestration on all four sides. The exterior conforms with planting formally done in four discrete sections, each oriented toward a face of the dwelling. The time had not arrived when the entire landscape would be welded into a whole.

In London the nobility continued to build the court type of house (e.g., erstwhile Clarendon

Figure 11.2   Broome Park, the garden facade. Denton, Kent, ca. 1635. (G. C. Ball.)

House in Piccadilly, built by Pratt for Charles II's Lord Chancellor; like Fouquet, his aspirations cost him dearly). Crowded conditions in urban situations, however, denied the average citizen so much land. Therefore the Medieval houses with their multigables facing the street perpetuate the quaint appearance of such towns as Chester and Shrewsbury. Larger cities could not withstand the later growth patterns and in them it would be difficult to locate relics of the Elizabethan or Jacobean past.

Inigo Jones (1573–1653) was the first architect to make radical changes in the aspects of old England. There were other men—some provincials, like Robert Lyminge and the Smithsons, father Robert and son John. Allusion has been made to John Thorpe who was a member of the King's Works, the English counterpart of the French Bâtiments. Thorpe wrote about classic principles but built in the Elizabethan manner.

In April 1613 Inigo Jones was given the highest post in the Royal Works, that of Surveyor, the equivalent of the French *Surintendant*. He was then forty years of age, with about as many to go. Jones was one of those men of genius about whom little was known until he had already risen well above his contemporaries. A native Londoner, the son of a clothmaker, he seemed born to uneventful living. Our first knowledge of the man was as a skilled draftsman, one who could encompass an entire composition in a unified conception with his vocabulary of line and command of tonal values. He may indeed have trained in Italy, as his skill would suggest.

His first commissions, like those of Berain in France, were court masques, a form of entertainment usually based on some mythological theme, in which the dialogue was subordinated to lavish visual trappings. All the Stuarts were friendly toward art and spent more for this purpose than the Tudors. Because Jones collaborated with playwright Ben Jonson in dramatic ventures, it was probably in this partnership that he was recommended to Prince Henry, the young heir-apparent, and became his principal architect.

Although the social circle of the young prince was a brilliant one, it perished with his untimely death in 1612. Inigo Jones's next patron was Thomas Howard, created Earl of Suffolk by King James. The Earl's father, Lord Arundel, who met his fate in the Tower, paid the price for his alliance with the cause of Mary Queen of Scots. When Mary's son James became King of England, he naturally attempted to make atonement to the second Howard. He must have succeeded, as the rebuilding of Audley End, the ancestral Howard home, would suggest.

From the stepping stone of Suffolk's influence, Jones moved into the King's Works, and soon after went to Italy in the company of the Princess Elizabeth and her new husband, heir to the throne of Bohemia (probably Jones's second visit). It was in Venice that he procured a copy of Palladio's *Quattro Libri dell'Architettura,* which is to be seen at Oxford University. Its influence on Jones and English architecture was tremendous. Thus armed, Jones returned to England as an authority, possibly the only man in the country who could claim to be conversant with Italian Renaissance architecture and Palladio. In his notes we read:

> . . . so in achitecture ye outward ornaments oft [ought] to be solid, proporsionable according to the rulles, masculine and unaffected.[1]

With these convictions he proceeded to give En-gland an interpretation of Roman architecture filtered through the lens of Palladio, such as the Continent had never really received and England did not use again in such pure form for another century. This purist architecture may be called the second style of the English seventeenth century.

Fortunately his major works, the Palace at Greenwich, the Banqueting Hall at Whitehall, the Royal Chapel at St. James's and St. Paul's, Covent Garden, were in or near the metropolis, for his dedication was to the strict classicism that has always seemed foreign to the informal life of the English countryside. His name is connected with country seats at Wilton and at Stoke Bruerne Park, but as so often happens when a man becomes famous and much in demand these houses were executed by intermediaries and, at least on the exteriors, are something of a compromise.

In the Queen's House at Greenwich (Figure 11.3), which Jones designed for the first Stuart queen, he suddenly turned his back on all that was rambling, asymmetrical, whimsical, and prodigal in preceding styles of English homes and substituted a type that was compact, bisymmetrical, canonical, and singularly modest for its purpose. It had been a somewhat capricious indulgence on

Figure 11.3 The Queen's House, seen from the south. Greenwich. Inigo Jones. 1616–1635. Colonnades now mark where a road once ran. The dome of the chapel of the Royal Naval College is seen beyond the house toward the Thames. (British Tourist Authority)

the part of James I to select this site as a gift for his wife, Anne of Denmark. Because of the circumstances of history, a "right of way" existed through the royal domain at Greenwich, downstream from London. This road, which stretched from Deptford to Woolwich, separated the garden of Elizabeth I from the royal park. Over this highway was a gatehouse, the function of which was to stop traffic whenever the court chose to cross. It was this gatehouse that James ordered destroyed and in its place a permanent bridge, incorporating a house, was to be built (Chenonceaux without the river Cher!). Although altered at later times, the Queen's House, as it came to be known, stands today, much as it was built, astride the former highway. In 1697 the course of the old road was changed and only the portion in the arcaded approaches to the building is still visible. The house is now a central feature of the National Maritime Museum, to which the property was converted in 1928.

Viewed in its first stage of completion in 1635, the building was a hollowed bisymmetrical block, astylar on its north or Thames side. Its flat roof is

balustraded. The lofty entrance hall is a Palladian cube in proportions, 40 ft in each dimension. This became a place of assembly and intercommunication, functions that the central hall was to fill throughout the next two centuries of English building.

Its most astounding feature is the balcony with which it is surrounded, cantilevered from the wall by huge brackets but otherwise nonsupported. In a room at the side of the hall, in the manner of Palladio, stairs led to the first floor (Figure 11.4).

Jones reveals his artistic capabilities to the full at Whitehall. On January 12, 1619, the old Banqueting Hall, the building used for state entertaining, was burned. Jones was charged with rebuilding it, and in this connection projected plans for a vast new palace complex which, because of the tragic course of events, was never completed. The Banqueting Hall (Figure 11.5) stands today, a monument to the genius of its architect.

It is a rectangular block, three stories high, its exterior rigidly bisymmetrical. Although the Queen's House has orders only on its south front, Whitehall bears its proper contingent of Ionic and Corinthian columns, pilasters, and entablatures. First-story windows are alternately triangularly and segmentally pedimented. Above them the dentiled cornice accentuates the building's

Figure 11.4 The Tulip Staircase in the Queen's House at Greenwich. Inigo Jones, architect and designer. Handwrought iron balustrade. (British Tourist Authority.)

Figure 11.5 Banqueting Hall, Whitehall, London, 1619–1621. Inigo Jones, architect. (G. C. Ball.)

horizontality, as does the balustrade around the flat roof. Whitehall, as originally planned, was to have been built entirely of fine white limestone from the Isle of Portland. In its altered form, however, the ground floor is darker stone from Oxfordshire and the upper stories are stone from Northamptonshire with only details in Portland limestone. Thus color helps to accentuate horizontal story differences.

Jones's porportional sense was excellent. The building is emphasized vertically by the columniation and by the horizontal divisions that carry the eye upward by virtue of their commensuration. Central emphasis is obtained by the greater projection of the four columns placed there. The overall proportions, lower and broader than those of Italian Renaissance buildings, provide an air of English substantiality. It should be noted that Whitehall gives little clue to the placement of the double cube hall within, once again an in-

dication that the concept of interior and exterior was not yet fully integrated.

In 1618 a Commission on Buildings was set up in London. Its duties were a mixture of those of a planning commission and a board of control. Inigo Jones as the King's Surveyor was the executive. In this capacity he was connected with the fringe land development of Covent Garden, north of the Strand on the property of the Earl of Bedford. In the planned square of this project, Inigo designed the church on the west side. It was burned in 1795 but rebuilt as a replica of the original. An Etruscan type structure, it is phenomenal in London. Its style may have been prompted by the fact that it was the earliest of protestant churches and so might be cloaked appropriately in the earliest and most austere of the Roman styles (according to Vitruvius and Palladio). Jones likewise designed the classical chapel opposite St. James's Palace for the Catholic queen of Charles I, Henrietta Maria (Figure 11.6).

Of the two country houses connected with Jones, Wilton, the Wiltshire home of the Earl of

Figure 11.6 Chapel for Henrietta Maria, Queen of Charles I. St. James's Palace, London. Second quarter of the seventeenth century. (G. C. Ball.)

Pembroke, was intended to have been but a wing of a larger dwelling. Like Whitehall it is lovely in iself. It has a flat balustraded roof, slightly raised end pavilions, and a prominent central arched and pillared door. Here is a simpler, more vernacular example of classicism than was seen in England before the Restoration. We shall later be concerned with its famous double-cubed room (Figure 11.10). Stoke Bruerne Park in Northamptonshire is the first English example of curved colonnades and forward pavilions—a plan favored by Palladio in his villas.

This Italianate architecture, both of pure form and with English proclivities, does not look so strange to us after the Georgian and the ultra-Palladian periods of the eighteenth century. It must have appeared startling in its day, for it was

well ahead even of French building of the early seventeenth century.

Interregnum

During the interregnum little was built in England. It was evident, however, that Englishmen with pretentions to architectural status would build differently once they had seen the Queen's House, Whitehall, and Covent. One such was Roger Pratt (1620–1684), a man almost fifty years the junior of the great architect. In the late fifties he helped to build Coleshill in Berkshire for his cousin Sir George Pratt. It was an architectural tragedy that this house burned in 1952, for it was one of the first classical buildings to look undeniably at home on English soil and to be the prototype of the work of the next hundred years of domestic building.

Coleshill (Figure 11.7), with its tall chimneys, its dormers, and its emphatic Baroque doorway, was certainly not Palladian classical, but because of its central block plan, low hipped roof, roof balustrade, quiet masonry, quoined corners, and flat facade, its first story elevated above an *English basement* (i.e., the service area partly below ground level), and above all its centralized bisymmetry, it was a far cry from a Jacobean mansion like Hatfield.

Pratt, a well-to-do Englishman, properly educated at Oxford and the Inner Temple, and widely traveled on the Continent (living for a time in Rome with John Evelyn, the English diplomat and diarist), had just the requisite equipment to appreciate the niceties and forward-looking qualities of Jones's buildings and at the same time sufficiently cultured to make of them an architecture that England could wear unaffectedly. Pratt was associated with only a few houses; he came into his inheritance as Sir Roger Pratt and retired to the pleasant life of the English squire.

Late Stuart

The Restoration was neither an era of large fortunes nor of settled conditions. No great palaces were built, although there were some grand

Figure 11.7　Coleshill House, Berkshire, 1650–1664. Sir Roger Pratt, architect. (Marburg/ Prothmann.)

houses, such as Chatsworth for the Duke of Derbyshire, known today for its sumptuous interiors and art collection.

It was a period of middle-class prosperity and many commodious homes were built, the general character of which represented a composite of classicism seen through the eyes of Palladio and Jones, of Jacobean as it preserved English and Flemish Baroque, and finally of Holland, as revealed in a certain propriety and trimness. It is on view at Groombridge Place, at Honington, at Belton, and Eltham Lodge. It was the forerunner of the Georgian.

The designer of Eltham Lodge was Sir Hugh May (1622–1684), second in command to Sir Christopher Wren, England's next famous architect, as Comptroller of the Royal Works. May had spent considerable time in Holland where many English royalists lived in exile. Even before the arrival of the Dutch William and his English wife

Mary the stage was set for an English house like Eltham.

Eltham was the home of Sir John Shaw, about which in 1664 Sir John Evelyn wrote that he went "to Eltham to see Sir John's new house now building." A description sums up the type. It is free from any trace of Medievalism—a block rectangular building characteristically of red brick with stone corner quoins. The quoins were omitted at Eltham and stone was frequently used throughout the late Stuart period in lieu of brick (e.g., Mompesson in Salisbury, 1701). The stone or wood trim was generally but not invariably white. Windows at first were properly mullioned and transomed and proportionately tall; later the sash window of broader and lower dimensions took over. The doorway, centered on the bisymmetrical composition, was accented by some form of classically inspired surround. Pretentious houses might have a pronounced central projecting pavilion, marked by the Palladian temple front and some form of ordonnance. The doorway pediment was often of Baroque inspiration, a broken segmental design crowned, for example, with a cabochon or urn.

Horizontality was increasingly preserved by a string course that separated the stories. The hipped roof, a Holland importation, was pierced with dormers and, when truncated, mounted with a balustrade and capped with bisymmetrically arranged tall chimneys. In materials, proportions, and a tidy classicism it was English, and later American, and one of our most endearing forms.

The name of Sir Christopher Wren looms most important in late Stuart architecture, the third style of the seventeenth century. It was he who set it firmly on the path of disciplined thought and on the straight middle course between tradition, need, and fashion.

Wren was the scion of an ecclesiastic family of the highest order; his father was rector of a Wiltshire village when Christopher was born in 1632 and Dean of Windsor at the time of the civil disturbances.

To understand the nature of Wren's architectural career and the quality of his contribution to English design, it would be helpful to consider the intellectual climate in Europe during the seventeenth century and the important part that England played in it. It is not too much to claim this age as the meridian from which one can look backward toward the classical belief that the sun revolved around Greece and Rome—belief in a fixed earth-centered and man-related universe—to a forward glimpse of a cosmos in which motion is nature's first law, in which matter interacts with matter, and in which physical laws can be tested by measurement. It is the story of the birth of modern science, and to prove that a man can have several facets to his personality, the politically unscrupulous Sir Francis Bacon in 1620 published his thesis in defense of experimental science. Galileo died and Newton was born in 1642.

The thinking that turned away from the deductive method of reasoning to that of inductive learning from observed facts to general laws soon spawned many practical advances—the proof of the circulation of the blood, the laws relating to the volume and pressures of gases, the mathematics of objects in motion, and the understanding of the properties of light—to name but a few.

In a secondary manner the revolution that overturned the traditional conception of the physical world inevitably tumbled the pillars of the philosophical—the belief in the divine rights of kings, in the inflexibility of social castes, and even in many of the dogmatic convictions of religion. Wren was close to the vortex of these concerns. His role, however, was that of an eminent transitional figure, neither prophet nor iconoclast, but one who, in several fields, synthesized the best of the past with the future.

Oxford University became an important center of the experimental sciences, and Wren, as a student, was totally absorbed in this work, in mathematics, in particular, the route that led him to architecture. When only twenty-five he was professor of astronomy at Gresham College, London, and later at his Alma Mater. The informal meeting of learned men who gathered at Gresham led to the formation of a society to discuss scientific problems. This evolved into the Royal Society of Science (1660) in which Charles II took much interest. Thus he came to know Christopher Wren.

Another influential friend was Gilbert Sheldon, a Warden of All Souls College at Oxford and later Bishop of London. Not only did Sheldon call on Wren for his first architectural work—the design of the theater that Sheldon gave to Oxford—but it was Sheldon who brought Wren into the discussion of the renovation of St. Paul's Cathedral, the old Gothic structure to which Inigo Jones had given a new west front. In this connection Wren felt the need for travel and study on the Continent. Although he never went to Italy, he visited France and was on the scene at the opportune moment to meet Bernini and to have the merest glimpse of the latter's plans for the east front of the Louvre.

Returning to London, he was catapulted by the king into the office of Surveyor of the Royal Works over the heads of two more experienced men, Hugh May and John Webb (1611–1674), a pupil of Jones. As Surveyor his job was to supervise the king's building needs, and his direct concern with ecclesiastic work in the inner city was negligible. After the London Fire he nevertheless proposed plans for rebuilding central London, predicated on a standard type of brick architecture and a regular grid of city streets. These plans were never carried out, for they would have required time and money to execute and there was neither at hand.

In these years, however, he was by circumstance drawn into the problem of the complete rebuilding of St. Paul's Cathedral and the inner city churches (of which about eighty-seven of an existing 126 were burned). Because the funds for the latter were to come from a royal tax levied on coal embargoes, Wren was consulted and actually did design most of the fifty-one that were built.

It was his fate to plan the first English churches in large enough number to set a type for protestant worship. Ever since the time of Henry VIII existing buildings had been used for the new liturgy. However, this was an adequate solution only for the smallest parish churches. The new religion required more space for the laity and less separation between them and the clergy. The great fire provided the immediate opportunity for the construction of buildings in direct answer to this need.

The interiors of Wren's churches present a variety of space plans. It is evident that he was experimenting in the design of an appropriate structure for the service, site, and available financial resources. The most traditional, hence Gothic, restoration was at St. Bride's, Fleet Street, which contains a vaulted nave, aisles, a towered west end, and an untraditionally small eastern chancel. In St. Mary-at-Hill, Wren used a domed covering on a square plan, and in St. Mary-le-Bow a similar central emphasis is laid out. This was quite in agreement with bringing the congregation together in one place. One of the most prophetic solutions is to be found in St. James's, Piccadilly, which is a galleried, two-storied structure with a vaulted nave and aisles—a form often followed in English churches of the eighteenth century.

On the exterior Wren created the steeple, a compromise between the Renaissance dome on a drum, embellished with classical drama, and the old Gothic spires of the lost Medieval London churches. In function the new steeples held the bells and so allied themselves with the campanile or bell tower. In St. Mary-le-bow, in the old Bow tower (named for the Gothic buttresses or bows which had been its major support) Wren surmounted the bell stage with small classic temples and then capped the whole with an obelisk or tapering shaft of stone. Between the two classical tempiettos he placed a ring of volute buttresses, which gave the parishioners some reminiscent tie with their old beloved *bows*. So began the classic church with a spire, one of the really original English contributions to architecture. It was later to be handled with greater architectural unity by Sir James Gibbs (see Volume 2, Chapter 4).

St. Paul's, the cathedral that towers over London, may be viewed as another compromise of Gothic buttressing, classical forms, and concealed structural necessity (Figures 11.8 and 11.9). Many who criticize the church from an aesthetic point of view feel that the twin western towers detract from classical clarity (although St. Peter's was originally designed for two western towers). The principal ring of pillars around the drum is held to be less effective than the grouping on St. Peter's. Again the coupled columns on the raised portico are said to create a weaker statement than the repetitive rhythm of the Roman cathedral. The side facade is not symmetrical with the front and the ornament is over lavish, *ad infinitum*.

It must be remembered that Wren, like Bramante, did not have a free hand, for the Board of Commissioners forced several changes of plans. His first model had a strength and simplicity that the executed work may have lacked. St. Paul's, however, possesses great virtues. Its scale secures the London scape in a manner equaled only by the Duomo in Florence (true before the advent of the high rise!). The interior light reveals a strong interplay of structural shapes ascending at the crossing toward the oculus of the inner dome. Even without the benefit of Bernini's central altar and flash of gold in the chancel, it is an outstanding Baroque architectural achievement and solidly English.

Sir Christopher did many other buildings. His name is associated with several houses—Belton, Honington, and Groombridge Place. He was also the architect for the William and Mary enterprises at Hampton Court and Kensington, and in the next century for Marlborough House in London for the Duchess Sarah. None of these dif-

Figure 11.8 St. Paul's Cathedral, London, seen from the south, 1675–1711. Sir Christopher Wren, architect. (British Tourist Authority.)

fered greatly from the late Stuart type. Almost in a domestic vein were the Greenwich and Chelsea Hospitals and the London Customs House. Tom Tower, the ceremonial entrance to Christ Church, Oxford, showed Wren's sympathy with the forms of the Gothic past, whereas his Cambridge buildings, particularly his Trinity College Library, were in sparse classical form. In all we see the same mind at work, the pragmatic builder and scientist, interested in structural manners and suiting a learned classical background to present needs and often respectful of old stylistic solutions which he was not the man to cast aside brashly.

388

Figure 11.9 St. Paul's Cathedral, London, interior looking toward the chancel, 1675–1711. Sir Christopher Wren, architect. (Courtesy of A. H. Benade.)

In closing the career of Sir Christopher Wren, it must be told how, after the turn of the century, impatient factions levied charges against him of ineptness and even of mishandling funds. The latter allegation was utterly false. But the architect was growing old. St. Paul's had been years in the building and possibly Wren was no longer so vigorous in overseeing the work. In a quite unprecedented action he was relieved of his office as Surveyor of the King's Works. It is noteworthy that he was defended in the Spectator Papers by Sir Richard Steele on August 9, 1709. Always a modest and unassuming man, he accepted his dismissal with dignity. He lived fourteen more years and died at the age of ninety-one when George I was on the throne and few could remember the bloody days of the civil wars or of pre-fire London. How little could they appreciate that to the very number and importance of Wren's buildings England owed the fact that it had finally taken the classic to its heart.

SOME SEVENTEENTH-CENTURY ENGLISH HOUSES

Audley End	Essex	1603–1616, for the Earl of Suffolk; architect, John Thorpe
Charlton House	Greenwich	1607–1612, for Sir Adam Newton
Hatfield House (Figure 11.1)	Hertfordshire	1607–1611; for the first Earl of Salisbury, Robert Cecil; architect, Robert Lyminge
Holland House	Kensington	1607, for Sir Walter Cope; architect, John Thorpe
Knole House, remodeling	Kent	1610, for Thomas Sackville, first Earl of Dorset
Ham House	Surrey	1610, for Sir Thomas Vavasor; additions later in the century
Blickling Hall	Norfolk	1616–1628, for Sir Henry Hobart; architect, Robert Lyminge
Queen's House (Figures 11.3 and 11.4)	Greenwich	1616–1635, for Queen Anne of Denmark and Queen Henrietta Maria; architect, Inigo Jones
Banqueting Hall, Whitehall (Figures 11.5 and 11.12)	London	1619–1625, for King James I; architect, Inigo Jones
Castle Ashby	Northamptonshire	ca. 1624, for Henry Compton, first Earl of Northampton; Inigo Jones, facade
Stoke Bruerne Park	Northamptonshire	1629–1635, for Sir Francis Crane; assistant to Crane, Inigo Jones
Broome Park (Figure 11-2)	Kent	1635 (later home of Lord Kitchener)
Kew Palace	London	1631, for Samuel Fortrey, a Flemish mechant
Wilton (Figure 11.10)	Wiltshire	Rebuilt after fire, 1648–1653, for 4th Earl of Pembroke; architects, Inigo Jones and John Webb
Coleshill (Figure 11.7)	Berkshire	1650–1664, for Sir George Pratt; architect, Roger Pratt
Thorpe House	Northamptonshire	1656; architect, John Webb
Ashburnham House	London	1662, for Mr. Ashburnham; architect, Christopher Wren (?)
Eltham Lodge	London	1664, for Sir John Shaw; architect, Hugh May
Honington Hall	Warwick	1680; architect, Christopher Wren (?)
Chatsworth House	Derbyshire	1681; for the Dukes of Devonshire; architect, William Talman
Chelsea Hospital	London	1682–1692, for the crown; architect, Christopher Wren
Belton	Grantham	1689, for Lord Brownlow; architect, Christopher Wren (?), (Plate 18)

Hampton Court	Middlesex	(remodeled east wing, 1689, 1702), for the crown; architect, Christopher Wren
Kensington Palace	London	Remodeled, 1690–1704, for the crown; architect, Christopher Wren
Greenwich Hospital	Greenwich	1696–1705, for the crown; architect, Christopher Wren
Groombridge Place	Kent	For Mr. Packer; architect, Christopher Wren

INTERIOR DESIGN

Before delving into the particulars of seventeenth-century English interior design we note the similarities in development between it and the French. France progressed from a colloquial version of classicism to an assay at Baroque flourish to exhibit her own constrained and quite indigenous combination of the two. Except for the Cromwellian interlude, England did the same. But the styles that emerged on either side of the channel, made abundantly clear in the next century, were tinged with national character. During the eighteenth century they were worn so naturally that they appeared to be creations from their home soil.

Space Organization and Planning

As detailed under architecture, interior space, although still colossal in exceptional buildings, grows more compact (and incidentally more practical). Classical cubic proportions become more favorably viewed (the principal room at Belton is 35 by 30 by 19 ft). Few deviations from tectangular space were tried except where curved arms embrace the countryside, circular form encloses a Sheldonian theater, or the vaulted and domed ceilings of churches open upward.

Architectural Details

Inigo Jones still used stone-mullioned and transomed windows. Wherever another variety is found in his buildings it was a later edition (e.g., the Queen's House, 1708). The next step taken, after the Restoration, gave the casement a frame, mullion, and transom of wood. Double-hung sashes were the favorite of Wren.

The origin of the sash window is unknown.[2]

The word *sash* is a corruption of the French *chassis*, and its earliest application denoted a frame of wood distinguished from a leaded light. Despite the French origin of the word, the actual artifact traveled from England to France. The earliest record of an installation of sash windows with lines and pulleys is at Whitehall (1685) and Windsor (1686). However, double-hung windows had already been in use in other forms. Apparently only the lower sash was lifted, and often the upper sash was the larger so that the frame might not break at eye level.

Windows of the first half of the century were taller and slimmer, the tendency to greater width increasing with time. This, of course, is outside any consideration of the large Jacobean windows which are in a class by themselves and belong in the pattern of Elizabethan Renaissance.

At Coleshill and Belton the principal windows have eighteen panes of six rows of three. The glass is slightly beveled. Individual lights increased in size after the Restoration and may have been about 12 in. broad by 15 high. The window extended from the dado to the architrave.

Unusual shapes were not uncommon. Arch tops and bull's-eye openings are seen at Hampton Court.

Window and door treatments have much in common and, if certain allowances can be made for deviations, may be treated together. Door paneling corresponded with that of the architectural interior. The *fin de siècle* door, which continued into the eighteenth century, had six to eight paneled fields.

Any surrounds on Jacobean openings were simple. As the period progressed, moldings became bolder and full ovolos found favor. Some were mitered near the top to include projecting ears. Although window aediculae customarily lag

391

Figure 11.10 The Double-Cube Room at Wilton, Wiltshire, 1648–1653. Designed by Inigo Jones and John Webb with Vitruvian proportions of the double cube. Planned to accommodate the Van Dyck and Rubens paintings owned by the Pembroke family. Gilt furniture designed by William Kent, 1730. (British Tourist Authority.)

behind doors in style, in the Carolean era both often had an ovolo frieze, some variety of cornice, and a Baroque pediment (i.e., broken in contour or scrolled). Side brackets were constantly in evidence. When window frames were located near the wall exterior, as was usual, any decorative treatment had to be made an adjunct of the inner wall surface with related panels on the jambs. This kind of finishing made it necessary to simplify any cloth treatment of curtains and to use them within the window recess (if at all).

From such indigenous wall treatment it is a bit of a shock to be transported to Wilton to its double-cube room (Figure 11.10), which is a composite of Versailles and Fontainebleau with overtones of Palladio. Recall that Jones used a Palladian window on his facade. On the interior doors to the double-cube a full and heavy classical aedicule encloses the simple frames, which are broken by Le Brun panels. Classical wreathed garlands and heads fill the flat architrave and frieze. A broken pediment supports Michelangeloesque reclining figures and embraces a Baroque cartouche. Plaster ornaments adorn the walls.

There is nowhere to go from there but to the simpler combination of the classical with the stately woodwork of the Restoration. This we see in many budding Georgian interiors like the one illustrated (Plate 18).

The fireplace is now the central decorative feature. The progression in England was similar to that in France. The Jacobean fireplace, like that of the first Bourbons, projected into the room and had a huge, floor-to-ceiling superstructure. The Restoration fireplaces were less elaborate and clung closer to the wall. The detached mantel occurred more frequently during the reign of William and Mary.

In the building of Jacobean mansions skilled foreign craftsmen were imported to create the elaborate marble chimney breasts which had many classical features but could likewise be loaded with decoration of the German and Netherlands schools. Much use was made of the superstructure for a display of coats of arms and family ciphers.

One of the loveliest fireplaces ever to have been devised was the Restoration type to be seen at Belton (Plate 18). The fielded overmantel panel is graced with swags of Grinling Gibbons carving. This chimney breast sometimes displayed an oil painting or remained unadorned, its rich patina offering sufficient attraction. The fire opening was surrounded by a heavy bolection molding, usually of beautiful colored marble. Wren also favored the corner fireplace.

One popular treatment in vogue after 1688 was the *trumeau* above a smaller mantel. This consisted of a mirror supermounted by a painting framed with the wall in a unified composition. Although the glass works at Lambeth rendered mirrors more accessible, the English never used this form of decoration to the degree practiced by the French. The Duchess of Portsmouth is said to have possessed a glass-lined room and a door of mirrors is mentioned at Chatsworth. Firedogs and a metal fireback were the usual fireside accouterments.

As stairways became more important (but still generally occupied their isolated spaces), the Jacobean builders substituted carved panels in place of balusters, as seen at Ham House. The idea for solid sides is a Dutch feature (Figure 11.11). In line with the love of carved woodwork which the century expressed we note that many examples

Figure 11.11 Staircase from Cassiobury Park, Watford, Hertfordshire, ca. 1677–1680. Grinling Gibbons. Pine, ash, and oak. Also note the small table with inverted cup legs and saltire stretcher, two Carolean chairs, knee-hole desk, and embroidered mirror frame. Metropolitan Museum of Art, New York. (The Metropolitan Museum of Art, Rogers Fund, 1932.)

lack string courses and that carved and scrolled spandrels were substituted.

Handrails are generally wide and flat. When balusters returned to fashion they were turned and twisted (a favorite Carolean manner) or the squared French type. The classic vase form became fashionable toward the end of the century.

Wrought-iron handrails were used by Jones (e.g., Greenwich, the *tulip stairs;* Figure 11.4) and Wren. The most celebrated designer of ironwork was Jean Tijou, who planned the fine stairs at Hampton Court. Tijou was a Frenchman and is best known for the altar rails and choir grilles at St. Paul's. He came to England in 1688 with William III and stayed until 1712.

Interior Surface Treatment

Little need be added to any former description of floors. Great spaces still had their marble surfaces, as seen in the Queen's House where Nicholas Stone (1586–1647) and Gabriel Stacey repeated the pattern of the compartmented ceiling in black and white. Nicholas Stone, apprenticed in London, went to Amsterdam and trained under that city's official master mason and sculptor. Returning to England, he executed many royal commissions, eventually becoming master mason to the King in 1632. The line between a sculptor mason and a structural mason was not very tightly drawn in the seventeenth century.

In addition to these marble parquets, the usual floor was wood with wide boards. Important Stuart rooms were wall paneled, whereas subordinate spaces may have had wainscoting only to the dado, with plaster above. Palatial interiors contained murals done by the foremost artists of the day, as in the drawing room of the Queen's House painted by Peter Paul Rubens and Jacob Jordaens and the hallway in Hampton Court King's Stair Hall by Antonio Verrio.

Early woodwork was still predominantly oak but changed to walnut with the Restoration. Pine (English deal) is frequently seen in more informal settings. The size of the individual panels, at first small and nearly square, later ordered in accordance with the room size and bisymmetrically arranged, increased with the years. Jacobean panels were often filled with round-arched arcades or interlaced with strapwork (bands) in bold relief. An embossed cabochon (a convex-shaped ornament) frequently occupied the panel field.

Sometimes the Jacobean designers got out of hand and delighted in elaborate carving or stucco work in the Flemish Wendel Dietterlin fashion— a bit of carry-over from the Elizabethan. The hall screen at Audley End is a good example. Ham House carries the manner to a high Baroque pitch.

The frieze seen above early Jacobean panels was a first introduction to classicism. Soon pilasters were used to space panels, often in company with a superimposed entablature.

The large panels of the Carolean period projected beyond the stiles and rails (often referred to as *fielded panels*) and the whole is surrounded with a handsome bolection molding. As the century drew to a close, smaller more delicate surrounds appeared.

English woodwork—although it seems a sacrilege—was frequently painted, often in the interest of pictorial representation or simply to introduce color. Tones grew lighter toward the end of the century. Quite often woodwork was grained to resemble oak or walnut.

The seventeen hundreds represent the pinnacle of English woodcarving. Many of the craftsmen are known, such as John and Matthias Christmas who carved the beams in the Queen's boudoir at Greenwich. There is no second to the work of Grinling Gibbons. The nature of his work is realistic, although with its close affiliation with nature it preserves the stylism that saves it from mawkishness. This is related to Gibbons's observation of the organic growth pattern of each species. Horace Walpole, writing in the next century, says the following:

> There is no instance of a man before Gibbons who gave to wood the loose and airy lightness of flowers, and chained together the various productions of the elements in a free disorder natural to each species.[3]

Grinling Gibbons was born in Holland in 1648 and died in England in 1720. Certainly he is most famous for the stalls of St. Paul's Cathedral, London, although equally fine examples of his work may be seen at Trinity College Chapel and the library at Cambridge University, Windsor Castle, Whitehall, and on the archbishop's throne at Canterbury. It is reputed that he carved the fireplace garlands at Belton, the ceiling at Petsworth, and much ornamental work at Chatsworth.

We might have known little about Gibbons, the man, were it not that two who knew him were diarists, John Evelyn and Samuel Pepys. Evelyn speaks of discovering him in his cottage carving a copy of a figure from Tintoretto's *Crucifixion*. This was in 1671 when the demolition of St. Paul's was in progress. Evelyn secured him the patronage of Sir Christopher Wren. He was also introduced to the King, who again must be credited with that discernment in the arts that led to Gibbons's preferment and eventually to his appointment as Master Wood Carver to King George I in 1714.

At the Earl of Essex's house in Cassiobury Gibbons produced a lavish scheme of interior design in carving. The staircase from this mansion is at the Metropolitan Museum of Art in New York (Figure 11.11). Although it is certain that Gibbons in his busiest years employed other men and had what amounted to a factory of woodcarving, this in no way disparages the genius who controlled the output.

One essential difference between Tudor architecture and late Elizabethan or Stuart was the loss of the exposed structural ceiling and its replacement by a covering of plaster. When stucco ornament in imitation of fan vaulting or of geometric strapwork was used, these ceilings became very busy affairs, far too much for visual comfort in a low room like the long gallery.

Gradually plaster compositions took on the room dimensions. Large central ovals were included in coffered enclosures or projected from plain backgrounds. The actual patterns seem limitless. As the period became more classically oriented they assumed the form of wreathed motifs or of the foliation found in Gibbons's woodcarving.

In company with ceiling extravaganzas much license was demonstrated in plaster friezes. Many of their ornaments were lifted from a book published in 1633 by the Frenchman Jean Barbet,

entitled *Livre d'Architecture*. The frieze might have been flat like the one at Coleshill, which was ornamented with high relief cartouches and wreaths. The French coved ceiling likewise became a vehicle for plaster ornamentation, both on the cove and on the central area thus reserved.

Important ceilings were grist for the painter's brush. Certainly the most famous is in the Banqueting Hall at Whitehall, where in 1635 Rubens painted the scene symbolic of the apotheosis of James I and the birth of Charles (Figure 11.12). The latter admired it so much that he forbade masques to be performed in the hall for fear of fire. It is ironic that Charles stepped from a window at the Banqueting Hall onto the platform on which the executioner's block was placed.

The ceiling compartments from the central hall at Greenwich's Queen's House (now at Marlborough House where they were taken by the Duchess) are by Orazio and Artemisia Gentileschi of Pisa, whereas Giulio Romano painted the large rectangular panel in the Queen's bedroom, which was sold by the enemies of Charles I. The painting at Windsor and later at Hampton Court was the work of Antonio Verrio, later joined by the French painter Louis Laguerre. This later work indicates the same stylistic change that occurred on the continent—from painting in the confined architectural setting to frescoes that covered the entire space.

The double-cube room at Wilton was the work of Edward Pearce the Elder and Thomas de Critz. This pretentious hall was actually designed as a setting for ten of Van Dyck's large canvases of the royal family. One word of caution about all historic rooms—the restorer's hand is sometimes overly zealous; theatricalism and expediency sometimes replace simplicity and authenticity.

Sir James Thornhill (1675–1734), who painted the dome of St. Paul's and the Great Hall in the Wren Royal Naval Hospital buildings at Greenwich, was easily the most distinguished English muralist. We recall that Wren questioned the aesthetic propriety of altering the architectural concept of the cathedral with the eight scenes that depict the life of St. Paul which Thornhill placed there. Each of them is framed in its own painted surround. Alexander Pope, too, had something to say about mural painting:

Figure 11.12 The Banqueting Hall, Whitehall, London, compartmented ceiling, 1635. Paintings by Peter Paul Rubens: *The Apotheosis of James I* (central oval) plus other flatteries of England and her ruler. Hall in double-cube proportion designed by Inigo Jones, 1619–1622. Length, 111 ft, width and height, 55½ ft. (British Tourist Authority.)

> At painted ceilings we devoutly stare
> Where sprawl the saints of Verrio and Laguerre.

That such decoration seems more suited to the gilded and plastered rooms of the Continent than to the simple elegance of superb English woodwork is conceded by many.

Furnishings and Their Arrangement

If one is endowed with unusually clairvoyant eyesight, one may see on the river side of one of the busiest squares—London's Trafalgar—the ghost of Northumberland House, the town residence of the wealthy Percy family during the Stuart reigns. We may agree with its description:

> The rooms were hung with beautiful tapestries, and rich damask, with large glasses and frames of exquisite workmanship, and richly gilt. There were some fine pictures . . . by Titian and other masters. In some of the rooms may be seen large chests embellished with old genuine Japan, which being great rareties are almost invaluable.[4]

Obviously these were fine articles commanded by wealth, but no accounts have been found to yield any record of planned design. England during the seventeenth century could not command the resources of France.

FURNITURE

Chronology: Period Names

Although extant pieces of seventeenth-century English furniture are limited in number, the names of the furniture styles, as if to atone for the deficiency, are proliferated. Jacobean (1603–1649), Cromwellian (1649–1660), Carolean or Restoration (1660–1688), William and Mary (1688–1702), and later Queen Anne 1702–1714) are names encompassed in the broader categories—Early Stuart, Protectorate, and Late Stuart. There may be some justification for this abundant nomenclature in Baroque England because England during this century experienced what might be considered three major revolutions, each successful in introducing power elements that could be associated with completely different tastes. The first in 1649 introduced puritanical principles; the second in 1660 brought a French flavor, whereas the Dutch William and his Queen Mary arrived on the crest of influence from Holland. And we should not forget that the first Stuart, James I, came from Scotland.

Materials and Processes

Quality pre-Restoration English furniture remained of oak because the country possessed

396

insufficient walnut for extensive use. Indeed, England maintained a strong oak tradition even into the eighteenth century. With the Restoration, however, enough fine furniture was made of walnut to dub late Stuart "the age of walnut."

Reports are confirmed that stands of walnut planted during Elizabeth's reign had come to maturity by 1660. Early Restoration furniture was made of solid walnut, whereas later good English walnut became scarcer. At this time wood was imported from France and from the American colonies.[5] The French variety is a considerably lighter wood, and the imports from Virginia were the *black walnut,* a darker wood with still more shaded striations.

Carving and turning remained the fundamental English means of ornamenting furniture, although the beautiful grain of English walnut was often relied on for sufficient interest. On the return of Charles II both processes became exceedingly fashionable. With skilled native carvers at hand, the cutting became deep and full and strong, exhibiting less of the crisp linear character of its contemporary Bourbon counterpart.

Marquetry remained in favor on case goods throughout the changing fashions. The Jacobean work often continued the manner of Elizabethan inlay, with preference for such materials as mother-of-pearl and colored marbles. Carolean and later craftsmen used the various wood grains to effect their patterns, often crossbanding one figure with another. The preference for marquetry wanes after 1700, although it was used in ornamental pieces such as clock cases and large cabinet bodies.

Ormolu never became popular in England, but marble and silver were continental extravagances that found favor. Evelyn describes a suite of silver furniture seen in the apartments of the Duchess of Portsmouth, the favorite of Charles II. Windsor Castle also has a collection of silver furniture, a phenomenon not equaled in France because of their war losses. Documentation of the Windsor pieces is indefinite, but among those listed in the 1725 inventory two tables, three mirrors, a pair of stands, and two andirons are probably seventeenth century.

Lacquered furniture was popular, both of the eastern variety which the English called *Indian*

and the English-crafted, called *Japan.* The latter was on pine with a build-up of whitened size, which was then colored and polished. Recall that Evelyn alludes to expense when he says of his portrait painted by Kneller:

> . . . in a lakered frame . . . in consideration of its first luster being nothing inferior to gold . . . and the twentieth part of the charge.

Queen Elizabeth had chartered the East India Company for trading with the orient, but only with the arrival of Charles II's Queen Catherine of Braganza and her fashionable southern court were the exotic cargoes of the three-masted carracks much sought by the English. (It is recalled that Catherine also brought the Port of Bombay as part of her dowry. It was ceded by Portugal to England and became a useful port of call to the East India Company.) One of the chief imports was the tropical cane called *rattan.* Unlike the English basket materials—reed and willow—it was a trailing palm about 500 ft long which when stripped of its leaves was flat rather than round in contour.

Although less fashionable chair seats clung to the old "rush" weaving, the popularity of cane grew. This related to the Portuguese fashions and likewise to the need for quick furniture production after the London fire. The caners, it is said, all had shops clustered near the churchyard of old St. Paul's, convenient to the East India docks. When a large cargo came in, there was a great rush to transfer the cane into a salable product. The man who lagged behind might find his goods a drug on the market.

Finishes on wood were still rare and many pieces had none or depended on a coat of wax for protection.

Organization of Craft

The multiplication of furniture types was in large measure due to a subdivision of the crafts at the time of the Restoration, a development similar to that which occurred in France. The following chart indicates the changes which took place in England:

Guild	Responsibility
Before the Restoration:	
Carpenter and carver	All fine furniture
Arkwright	Mill variety of furniture
Joiner	"Joined" or simple furniture; following the dissolution of the monasteries, scope was enlarged
After the Restoration (especially in London):	
Cabinetmaker	Cupboards, tables, drawers
Chairmaker	Seats, beds
Turner	Inexpensive turned pieces
Joiner	Likewise inexpensive wares, picture frames, etc.
Japanners, upholsterers, etc.	

Types and Description

Large scale characterized all the furniture that was made in the period under consideration. Jonathan Swift (1667–1745) may have been looking back to his childhood for memories of the land of Brobdingnag. Certainly somewhere around 1700 the scale of furniture descended toward an approximation of what we should consider normal today. The years circling 1700 may be considered as the parting of two furniture worlds, the first facing back toward grandeur, the second predicated on grace and comfort. In England we may make a further division: the grandeur preceding the middle of the century was pompous and heavyset; only with the Carolean court did ease and attenuation develop.

Storage furniture remains fundamental. The Jacobean chest resembled its paneled-room backdrop. The linen fold and "nonsuch" scenes of the Tudor pieces changed into arcaded panels with heavy geometric strapwork or Renaissance carving. During the second quarter of the century fielded geometric panels often occurred and the flat stiles by which they were separated were frequently embellished with split spindles. For their manufacture a piece of wood was sawed in two, glued together again, turned on a spindle, reseparated, and finally applied as ornament with its flat side down.

The earliest English examples of chests of drawers date from the midseventeenth century. From this time on the derivations of the chest are many —the tall chest on a stand (Figure 11.13), the chest with drawers above a cabinet, the dresser with shelves above a chest, the china cabinet with a glass-doored cupboard resting on a chest of drawers. The names assigned to these pieces often differ from writer to writer, from country to country, and from century to century. This is particularly true of the two-tiered chest better known as the *highboy*, a nineteenth-century name applied in America. In the seventeenth century, the era of its English popularity, it was referred to by many contemporary English writers as a *tallboy* and by eighteenth-century Americans as a chest of drawers. Present-day English writers often refer to it as a *chest of drawers on a stand*. In any case, the piece of furniture so designated is a chest consisting of a separate upper portion of five flush drawers, each surrounded by a molding strip. The uppermost two drawers may be subdivided into threes and twos, respectively. The lower portion or *lowboy*, often used as a dressing table, generally consists of a tier of three drawers, the two outer ones being the deepest. The William and Mary highboys (said to have been introduced from Holland at that time) have flat tops surmounting the heavy ovolo molding. The lower section is skirted with an ogival apron. They stand on five or six legs tied together with a stretcher (see section on chairs for leg characteristics). A pronounced cornice molding caps the lowboy, separating it from the top section, which can be independently lifted by its side handles. Although these handles may be *bail* shaped, the drawer pulls of William and Mary pieces are in the contour known as *inverted pear*. Some Dutch-inspired chests of this period have squat *Dutch bun* feet and their engraved brass escutcheon plates are large and handsome. Jacobean furniture by contrast had wooden knobs and no ornamental brass, the appearance of which is largely a Restoration phenomenon.

The development of English desks during the latter part of the seventeenth century deserves comment. The small slant-top lid box on a stand had been an early form and remained in general use. Newer forms include the fall-front desk on a stand and the desk with slant lid and bookcase superstructure, known today as a secretary. French names were often given to writing desks—the *bureau* and the *scrutoire* (i.e., *escritoire*)—although some of their characteristics, such as the arched, hooded tops and the large bun feet, were probably Dutch importations.

Seating furniture in the first of the seventeenth century was unmarked by change in design. The panel back remained the norm, although bulbous turning on the legs and carving on the backs, which had been quite vigorous, gradually became more subdued.

The Cromwellian interlude managed to wipe out even that amount of contrived grandeur. Typical chairs were as little vainglorious as their "roundhead" masters—lower back, broader seat, cubelike proportions, and perhaps some simple bobbin or spiral turning, the latter conceit originally an import from the Indies. Often without arms, the chairs were designed to accommodate the voluminous garments of the period and for this reason they were dubbed the *farthingale*. Midcentury chairs possessed the refinement of upholstery which often covered the back as well as the slip-on seat. Cowhide, *turkey work* (see section on textiles), or some other variety of stout material was applied with oversized, brass-headed tacks.

Restoration chair backs, influenced by the French etiquette of the tabouret, soon became higher and their proportions more attenuated. It is this courtly custom of class distinction in seating that accounts for the large number of stools that have been preserved. These small seats possessed all the characteristics of chairs, for they accompanied them in sets. Notice that they were not designed with plain rear legs and so were not intended merely as an ornamental appendage to be placed against a wall.

In the Carolean (Figure 11.14) and William and Mary chairs a progression of stylistic details was evident, not all of which followed one another in clearly defined order. The evolution, however, did change somewhat in this fashion. After the spiral supports came a return to elaborate carving. The designs were composed of C and S scrolls, particularly in the form of that sharply fractionated pattern known as the *Flemish scroll*. This was made in many ways to form legs, stretchers, central splats, and crests. During the reign of

Figure 11.13 Chest of drawers on a stand. England, ca. 1688–1703. Style of William and Mary. Victoria and Albert Museum, London. (Crown Copyright, Victoria and Albert Museum.)

Charles II carving might well have been combined with the newly popular caning and baluster supports remained not unusual throughout the period. The cresting rail was at first tenoned between the uprights but progressed to a doweled crest that covered them, a noticeably weaker construction. The most elaborate chairs were upholstered, usually with rich velvets often finished with braiding or fringe held in place by large, brass-headed tacks.

Arms, slanting downward as in Cromwellian seats, became horizontal and more graceful in

399

their curving sweep. Stretchers, which at first were baluster-turned, soon assumed a vertical position; these were placed between the two front legs and adopted the vogue for carving. In

Figure 11.14 Carolean-style chair, England, 1680–1685. French walnut. Note the Spanish club feet, the scroll supports, the caning, and the spiral turning. Metropolitan Museum of Art, New York. (The Metropolitan Museum of Art, Kennedy Fund, 1918.)

the reign of William and Mary stretchers assumed the Flemish saltire, in a horizontal position, capped with a finial. The French serpentine stretcher was also seen at that time.

In the William and Mary period a tendency to use plainer and turned forms of legs appeared in all furniture types, a change in taste largely due to the immigrant craftsmen—the French Huguenots who fled their country after the revocation of the Edict of Nantes and the Dutch cabinetmakers who came with William. It would be wise to take a memory-recording look at these changes because they will appear in America on similar pieces. They have frequently been assigned specific designations, such as *inverted cup, trumpet, vase, spindle, Flemish scroll, quadrangular* (derived from the French and thus often called Marot; see Daniel Marot under The Craftsmen later in this chapter), and others easily recognizable by shape resemblance.

Chair feet also had many molds. The *Spanish* or *Portuguese scroll,* which has vertical grooves, is a backward-turned scroll flattened in shape. The *Dutch bun* was likewise used, and various turned feet appeared.

Looking across the channel to the Dutch paintings of such men as Vermeer, we see a provincial chair with a tall spindle or a split baluster back which had its counterpart in England and America.

After the day bed, which declined in fashion toward the end of the century, came the settee, a piece that resembled a double chair. From William's day—when these chairs were upholstered—they possessed a high double S or *cyma*-curved back. It is strange that during the reign of Queen Anne, the time of cabriole or S-curved legs, the upholstered settee back was not scrolled but was usually straight in contour.

Beds became increasingly important. As in France, women of rank were accustomed to entertain visitors while in bed. The English diarist Samuel Pepys records for July 12, 1665:

> After doing what business I could in the morning, it being a solumn fast day for the plague growing upon us, I took a boat and down to Deptford, where I stood with great pleasure an hour or two by my Lady Sandwich's bedside talking to her (she lying prettily in bed).

The bed with footposts of oversize bulbous turning reached its apogee during Jacobean days. Made of oak, it was most lavishly carved, with headboards that frequently showed pilastered and arcaded panels or strapwork geometrics. In the higher rooms of the last half of the century bedsteads grew to impressive heights. Two of these, which are in the Victoria and Albert Museum, tower to 14 and 17 ft. The testers were raised on tall slender posts which supported elaborate cornices, the only exposed woodwork. The remainder was covered with "strained stuff," cloth glued to the body so tightly that it revealed all of its contours. The bed was then elaborately curtained. The top was frequently capped at the corners with plumes as though it were a palfrey decked with its master's pennon. In place of such ornaments, vase-shaped finials were also found.

Tables continued long and narrow for the early Stuarts. Some were 30 ft in length and of draw construction. Tops were less heavy and were banded at the ends with narrow boards to prevent warpage. Carving took on Jacobean character, the straight-edged apron being carved with lunettes.

The round gate-legged table appeared before the time of the rebellion. At first of considerable size, it was well adapted to dining in one of the smaller parlors which were common in large homes. Drop leaves belong in the same category, and then as now provided flexible table space for diminishing room sizes.

The number of types of small table increased. Card playing was the favorite drawing room pastime. One popular table had multiple tops and so could be adapted to chess and backgammon as well as cards. When goods arrived from the orient, tea drinking and china collecting necessitated tea tables. On September 25, 1660, Pepys wrote:

> And afterwards I did send for a cup of tea (a China drink of which I had never drank before), and went away . . . all the afternoon [I was] among my workmen til ten or eleven at night and did give them drink and merry with them . . . to bed.

Timepieces

Clocks are among the objects for which English craftsmen of the late seventeenth and eighteenth centuries were justly famous. The initial cause of this supremacy lay in the invention of refinements which improved the accuracy of timepieces.

Clocks must possess some form of energy to turn a calibrated wheel and some system of accurately regulating that energy in discrete intervals. The earliest source of the first had been falling weights and of the second, some form of escapement which kept the wheels and pinions (collectively known as the *train*) periodic.[6]

Whereas weight-driven mechanisms had been in operation since the fourteenth century, the next origin of driving power, the coiled spring, invented in Italy, was in use by the last quarter of the fifteenth. It allowed the manufacture of smaller, lighter, hence more portable timepieces.

Jacobean weight-driven clocks assumed the shape known as lantern clocks—a rectangular box surmounted by a domical bell of lantern outline. Spring-driven Jacobean clocks might be drum-shaped or tower-shaped and were small enough to be placed on a table.

These, however, were not the precision instruments to which we are accustomed. This accuracy was made possible by the application of the pendulum (and its counterpart, the balance spring in watches). The principle of the pendulum, discovered by Galileo and requiring only minor modifications to make it effective, was simply the fact that a swinging body is nearly isochronous (performing each vibration in the same time, regardless of the amplitude of the arc). Obviously a pendulum, once set in motion and properly adjusted, would serve to regulate wheels geared to definite intervals. Credit for the inventions that implemented the use of the pendulum to the regulation of clocks has been claimed for the English scientist Robert Hooke (1635–1703), friend of Christopher Wren, and the Hollander Christian Huygens (1629–1695).

The English Clockmakers Company was chartered in 1631 to protect home manufacture. Important early members were those of the Dutch Fromanteel family (with Ahaseurus as patriarch) and Thomas Tompion (1639–1713; Figure 11.15), who assisted Hooke in making the first balance spring watch which was presented to the King in 1675.

The new precision delicacy of clock works made it desirable to encase them. Moreover, as the train of the new mechanisms was improved

Figure 11.15 Long-case clock, England, late seventeenth century. Thomas Tompion. Victoria and Albert Museum, London. (Crown Copyright, Victoria and Albert Museum.)

masterpieces were produced when both ranked high.

The two types of clock which resulted are known as the *long-case clock* and the *bracket clock,* one for the floor and one for the stand. In America these terms are roughly synonymous with the *grandfather's clock* and the *shelf clock,* respectively. In the evolution of these timepieces the seventeenth century was one of individual experimentation with respect to mechanism and to case. Seventeenth-century clocks are thus much sought after by collectors.

Long-case clocks, none of which may be said to antedate 1659, were at first equipped with short pendulums and the cases were seldom more than 6.5 ft high. These short long-case clocks should not be confused with the later dwarf long-case clocks which were perfect miniatures of the mature long-case clock in every respect and stood 5 ft high. In America they are called grandmother's clocks. As the century progressed and mechanisms improved, both clocks and pendulums were protracted, the overall height of the former increasing to 7 and eventually to nearer 9 ft. This is the measure to the top of the arched head of the oak clock that Tompion made and gave to the city of Bath and now resides in its pump room.

As a clock always contributed to family prestige, the best possible housing was provided. Early cases were of ebony or laburnum over oak. Veneering of tortoise shell and inlay with metal, as well as marquetry, were customary. Firms such as Fromanteel and Clarke added much ornate metal work to the exterior of their frames. Late Stuart pieces, which were walnut, relied most on elaborate figured wood and crossbanding for their appeal.

The cases of long-case clocks were divided into three parts, of which the lowest was the plinth on which the works rested. In seventeenth-century models these were plain and unpaneled and were separated from the trunk by an ogival molding.

The trunk or thin central portion of the case had three panels contained within a flush door. When cases grew elaborate, the paneling was discarded because of its interference with the ornamentation. An oval window later allowed a view of the pendulum.

The trunk joined the hood or upper portion of

to run for eight days without rewinding, the ballast in a weight-driven instrument became unduly heavy and clocks could not be hung from the wall. Support from the floor was required. Spring-driven clocks might rest on a table but the pendulum regulator forecast taller proportions. To lessen the overall weight the cases were now of wood. At this point, about the middle of the seventeenth century, two separate craftsmen became involved in turning out a clock—the maker of the works and the maker of the case. In various periods one or the other might excel and the clock in a convex molding. The shape of the first hoods was architectural—columns, entablature, and pediment. The columns, at first the Corinthian, later assumed the spiral twist. Variations of both occur. The portico top disappeared after 1685, and moldings of infinite variety were piled on the cornice. Soon a shallow and then a more complete dome was added, which again had its variations.

The clock face possessed its own changing characteristics, usually caused by alterations in the mechanism. The earliest pieces had narrow *chapter rings*—that part of the dial on which the hours are marked. The quarter-hour divisions were found inside this chapter ring, the minute marks, outside. The hour hand, which had been an arrow on sixteenth-century clocks, became a simple pierced ornament approximating that shape. The minute hand was plain.

As additional features, such as striking mechanisms, calendars, and phases of the moon, appeared, the hood was made larger. The chapter rings grew broader and incorporated quarter hour and minute symbols. The face likewise was forced into an oblong shape to accommodate the new contrivances. Thomas Tompion devised a semicircular opening known as the *break arch* at the top of the face to hold certain of the indicators. This in turn led to the arched top of the hood, which form became fairly general during the next century. Early clocks usually struck the hour but not the quarter hour. In order to conserve power, one maker, Joseph Knibb (1640–1712), devised a system of striking known as Roman striking because it was correlated with the Roman numerals on the dial. This involved two bells with different tones to interpret the figures related to the Roman numerals V and I.

As in early French clocks, the dial plate was first covered with black velvet with a plain silvered or gilt chapter ring. Engraving, chasing, and repoussé appeared regularly on clock faces. Spandrels of metal were customary—the earlier ones often incorporating cherubs' heads which changed later to devious ornamentation and often to women's heads. The maker's name was in various locations on the face. Gradually metal chapter rings gave way to enamel.

Virtually all that has been said about long-case clocks applies to bracket clocks of the period.

These, of course, were spring-driven and regulated by a pendulum. From about 1685 the architectural top of these clocks gave way to the domed and later to a bell shape. A metal-domed top may be known as a basket top. Bracket clocks were soon supplied with a handle to facilitate moving.

Nothing in contemporary design can take the place of the mechanical clock which has been household property since the seventeenth century. Sensuously sonorous and visually ornate, it occupied a psychological position more like that of another human than did any other artifact, as it spelled out the time difference between being and nonbeing. An interior with a clock, the proper kind of clock, an intoning clock, and a long-possessed one, is never lonely.

Mirrors

Mirrors, on the contrary, respond to light and to people. Their popular arrival with the later seventeenth century corresponds to English home manufacture and, as on the Continent, to the Baroque interest in the pyrotechnics of light.

Before the reign of Charles I there were no English mirror or plate glass factories. By 1664 sufficient production warranted the organization of the Worshipful Company of Glass-Sellers and Looking-glass Makers. The most famous firm was that begun by the Duke of Buckingham at Vauxhall in 1673. Competition soon sprang up. First heard from during the 1690s, John Gumley opened a fashionable gallery shop in the Strand, of which Richard Steele says:

> I shall now give an account of my passing yesterday morning . . . in a Place where People may go and be very well entertained, whether they have, or have not, a good Taste. They will certainly be well pleased for they will have unavoidable Opportunities of seeing what they most like . . . I mean their dear selves. The Place . . . is Mr. Gumley's Glass-Gallery over the New Exchange . . . when a Man walks in that Illustrious Room, and reflects what incredible Improvement our Artificers of England have made in the Manufacture of Glass in Thirty Years time.[7]

Sizable mirrors were fashionable in the Restoration. These larger glasses, of which one in the

Victoria and Albert Museum is nearly 4 by 6 ft, were *pier mirrors,* to be hung on the wall (i.e., *pier*) between two windows. A table was customarily placed underneath. Frequently pier mirrors came in pairs because of the triple windows on some facades. Contemporaneous nomenclature called mirrors *looking-glasses* and those intended for placement over a mantel, *mantel-glasses.* Some smaller mirrors were hung over tables or stood on low chests in dressing rooms.

Figure 11.16   Carolean mirror and table, England, latter part of the seventeenth century. Note the serpentine stretcher, spiral and vase-shaped legs, and the floral marquetry. Victoria and Albert Museum, London. (Crown Copyright, Victoria and Albert Museum.)

The earliest mirrors, other than pier, approximated square proportions (Figure 11.16), and became taller with time. The first were single-paned, later ones, double, the break occurring at the arch at the top. The glass was then beveled. The mantel glass was long in proportion to height and was composed of three plates, the center one, the largest.

Frames varied. Carving of Restoration genre created some of the most endearing examples. Later specimens were broad, either ovolo or flat and often had scrolled hoods. Silvered wood, cut glass, lacquer, floral marquetry, and even embroidered cloth over wood were used as frame material.

Musical Instruments

These instruments were not extensively manufactured in England at that time but were nevertheless prominent accouterments in social surroundings. After the proscriptions of the Puritanical midcentury, we read of the fiddle, the lute (Pepys: "Up and very angry with my boy for lying long a bed and forgetting his lute."), violins, theorbos (an instrument similar to the lute but with increased sonority), virginals, espinettes (which Pepys bought in place of a harpsichord because it "takes up less room"). Purcell and Haydn could not have created in a climate cold to music.

Fireside Fixtures

With the increasing use of coal in place of wood, the cast-iron grate appeared. Improvising on old equipment, the andirons or firedogs were first used to hold the basket grates. The fireback, a reflective metal screen, was placed to the rear of the fire opening and was frequently quite handsomely cast, using current imagery as design inspiration.

The Craftsmen

Who were the craftsmen who first made this furniture for what John Evelyn chose to call a "politer way of living"?

Gerrit Jensen or Johnson is really the first English furniture designer of whom we have knowledge, but nearly all of the particulars of his life are lost. His name, often found Anglicized in contemporary records, suggests that he was born abroad and was either Danish or Dutch. The chief period of his activity began about 1680 when his first bill in the Royal Household is dated. It is certified that he belonged to the Joiners' Company in 1685 and that he held a royal warrant as cabinetmaker to all of the later Stuarts. In 1693 he had a workshop in St. Martin's Lane. This is an interesting corroboration of the fact that, in the decades after the London fire, the furniture makers who had formerly occupied premises in the City were now moving around the bend in the Thames to occupy quarters that were nearer the more fashionable sections of town around Whitehall—"the Court End." Jensen is referred to as "cabinet maker and glasse-seeler" in one of the royal documents, and much of his time seems to have been occupied in installing mirrors in the crown properties.

In the collection of furniture at Windsor are three pieces that invoices connect with Jensen. One is a marquetry writing table, another a marquetry cabinet with glass doors, and the third, a writing desk inlaid with silver and brass. Although he lived into the reign of Queen Anne, his style is characteristically of the seventeenth century and very much in tune with contemporary French design. He was one of the few English craftsmen to work metal into furniture inlays somewhat in the manner of Boulle.

A Frenchman who greatly influenced the English cabinet trade was Daniel Marot (1663–1752), the celebrated French decorative artist. As a Protestant entering the service of William of Orange at the time of the Revocation of the Edict of Nantes he is thought to have been in England from 1694 to 1698. If he was not, it is nevertheless certain that his engraved designs were well known there and must have influenced the highly exuberant scroll patterns of William's reign.

Jean Berain also worked for a time in England.

TEXTILES

Expensive textiles, such as silk weaving, had never been a principal manufacture of England. This was true despite the fact that Bethnal Green and Spitalsfield, in the eastern part of London, were centers of sericulture in which Anglican silk embroideries had been produced since the Middle Ages. In 1562 the guild for silk throwers was founded there and Elizabeth did all in her power to foster silk production. James I sponsored an incorporation of silk weavers. During William's reign a group of French Huguenot refugees settled at Spitalsfield, the only district allowed to these foreigners. There they wove silks that were simplified versions of French fabrics. The quality of these late Stuart silks, both those of the English weavers and those of the French, was very good. The silk enterprise in this area, however, was almost entirely discontinued during the nineteenth century.

With wool, which is the basis for tapestry weaving, England has been more fortunate. Henry I had long ago imported sheep raisers from Flanders, and Cistercian monks in due time had developed production until England became virtually the world's center of wool production. With the dissolution of the monasteries the control of the industry passed into the hands of midland capitalists such as Walter Jones, owner of Chastleton House, Oxfordshire.

As previously mentioned, tapestry weaving had been practiced sporadically in England on a limited scale. Because one of the purposes of the tapestry works at Barcheston (founded in Tudor times, see Chapter 8) was to give employment to the local population, only Englishmen were hired, a factor that accounts for the predominantly provincial character of the product. One of the finest sets of tapestries produced by the factory consisted of a series of topographical maps of the various English counties, made into cartoons by Richard Hyckes and his son, the former of whom was in charge of the shops. Because Hycks had studied in Holland, many of the elements in this series and in an earlier seventeenth-century group called the Seasons showed foreign influence.

James I had no interest in the Barcheston and companion factory at Bordesley (director Thomas Chaunce) and they closed during his reign. The first Stuart monarch wished to emulate the court of France and rather than subsidize a provincial enterprise he founded the tapestry studio of Mortlake near London in 1629. In its heyday, from then until about 1636, its output rivaled in quality that of the early Gobelins and is said to have surpassed that of Brussels. The inability of Charles I to continue subsidies resulted in quick deterioration of the standards. Mortlake, however, struggled on until closing in 1703.

The Marquis of Buckingham (duke after 1623), a friend of the Prince of Wales, was the guiding spirit behind the Mortlake. Its proprietor was Sir Francis Crane, whose death in 1636 marked the end of the finest output. Charles I, as prince, was responsible for the procurement of the Raphael cartoons for the *Acts of the Apostles* set, from which the Mortlake wove copies of seven. The cartoons now hang in a special room in the Victoria and Albert, and one set, woven at Mortlake, hangs in the State Drawing Room at Chatsworth. The borders on these English tapestries are ascribed to Van Dyck and to Francis Cleyn, a German artist in England. The Mortlake mark is the red cross of St. George on a white shield.

Pepys in his diary for September 5, 1663, says, "Bought my wife a chint, that is a printed Indian cotton for to line her study." This indicates the early fashion for cotton and printed fabrics, a vogue generally associated with the eighteenth century. Actually, the British printing industry was well established in the east of London by 1700. Both the silk men of Spitalsfield and the wool textile manufacturers entered a bill in Parliament to prohibit the importation of Indian prints and to curtail British "callicoe printing," with, of course, no success. With printing on cotton and linen, we enter a field in which England was preeminent. In the seventeenth century the Indian imports actually dominated the market because of the glamour that accrues to a foreign product. In some instances the English actually sent patterns to India for the cotton printers to follow.

One might with some justice consider embroidery to be the tapestries of England. Crewel work continued to be fashionable in Jacobean times and witnessed a considerable revival in fashion at the end of the seventeenth century and the beginning of the eighteenth, when large-scaled patterns with waving and branching stems and leaves were so popular for hangings.

Stump work likewise appears on many Jacobean and Carolean frames and precious boxes. In stump embroidery a large repertory of stitches was used to produce a three-dimensional effect over a padding of wool or hair. The flame design, which was popular, is said to have been a transplant from Hungarian embroidery. It is made in vertical rows but the pattern becomes one of large zig-zags.

Needlepoint was the principal means of simulating the effect of tapestry. This is a small stitch taken with wool across the square of an open-meshed canvas. Queen Mary is said to have favored this genre and indeed to have set the tone for the practice of homely crafts by the court ladies. A small cross stitch taken diagonally across half a canvas square is known as *petit point* (small stitch), whereas the usual stitch is called *gros point. Turkey work* was a hand-knotted technique done on canvas and was probably considered the equivalent of the Savonnerie pile hand-knotted fabrics that the French frequently used for upholstery. The name, of course, derives from knotted Turkish rugs.

The latter part of the Stuart period was a Roman holiday for the upholsterer's art. Upholsterers were known as *upholders,* a company of whom is said to have been founded in the fifteenth century. They were originally second-hand dealers and therefore dealers in old clothes. Their vocational elevation occurred during the seventeenth century.

Whereas the tall ornate French chairs were customarily upholstered with Italian and later with French velvets, brocatelles, and hand-knotted Savonneries, plain velvets, needlepoints, and damasks were the stuffs used in England during the William and Mary period. Heavy leather and embroidery of the heavier sort seems to be more characteristic of Cromwellian coverings.

Gimps, galons, braids, cords, and tassels adorned much of the furniture. The upholstery became more important than the piece itself. Every age since can show some indication of this love of stuffs, for which the Victorian should not be forced to assume all of the blame.

CERAMICS

English kilns had produced folk pottery for local trade as far back as the records go. Few names have survived and we pay our respects to Ralph and Thomas Toft (probably brothers) of Staffordshire because they signed some of their work and thus provided a peg for nailing down the English tradition at the point to which it had arrived by the end of the seventeenth century. No apologies for its quality need be extended. On well-potted utilitarian pieces and on occasional marriage and ceremonial plates the style of animal and floral depiction was fresh and vigorous. It was done both with colored slip and in intaglio.

A second seventeenth-century potter, John Dwight (ca. 1637–1703), who had a factory at Fulham near London, typifies another approach. He attempted to create and to merchandise a product on a larger scale and to a wealthier clientele. John Dwight was an independent experimental craftsman in the hire of the London Glass Sellers Company, a large jobbing concern that included ceramics on its inventory. The enlarged market for ceramics was due not only to an increased leveling of wealth but also to the notion that tea and other newly imported commodities were best served in china. The elaborate silver of earlier days was suddenly less in demand. Dwight's medium was a high-fired stoneware for which he claimed an untenable identity with porcelain.

Dwight's production did not have the ingenuous artistry of good folk tradition, nor did it possess that ease with the classical idiom to which he aspired. Among other pieces Dwight made figurines with a covering of salt glaze.

The London ceramic industry drew foreign craftsmen. Shortly after 1688 two brothers, John and Joseph Elers, emigrated from Holland. Settling at Fulham, they produced a comparable fine stoneware. Despite many such skilled potters it was the Staffordshire district that was destined to be the ceramic capital of England. That story is told in Volume 2.

GLASS

Following Verzelini other attempts had been made during the Jacobean period to capture the national product by monopolistic licensing. One firm, that of Sir Robert Mansell, built a big business by this means. Mansell represented the new capitalistic trend in industry by which one could grow wealthy by managing those who knew production and by gaining monopolies that drove competition off the market.

Such large-scale endeavors were destroyed in the fifties. With the Restoration it was the Glass-Sellers Company, a group of merchandisers, who undertook to fill the demand for fashionable glasses. They were well aware that the English glass of the Verzelini formula was too fragile to satisfy the utilitarian market. What they needed was a glass that had clarity and strength. It was George Ravenscroft (1618–1681), a man possessed of a good scientifically oriented education, who came to their assistance (Figure 11.17). He

Figure 11.17 Decanter of English lead glass, perhaps by George Ravenscroft. England, third quarter of the seventeenth century. Smithsonian Institution, Washington, D.C. (National Museum of History & Technology, Smithsonian Institution, Photo No. 45185-C.)

had been a prosperous London shipowner engaged in the Venice-Turkey trade and had doubtless become aware of glass problems in his contacts at Murano. With a knowledge of chemistry as a selling point, he offered his services to the Glass-Sellers and became what we should call a researcher in the field of glass production. He opened first one and then two glass houses for carrying on experimentation and hired experienced glass men to attend to the practical aspects of the operation.

Even so, Ravenscroft's course was not smooth. His early glass was subject to what is known as "crizzling," a form of progressive decomposition. It may have been the English translation of the Italian Neri's "Art of Glass" that suggested the potential of lead oxide placed in a batch. After numerous experiments the glasses were of sufficiently good quality to warrant their marketing in 1676. Ravenscroft died in 1681 almost at the same time that his contract with the company expired. A man by the name of Hawly Bishopp took over the largest of the Ravenscroft houses and is thought to be the one who in reality standardized the recipe for lead glass to a point at which future production was of predictably high quality.

The first Ravenscroft glasses were marked with a seal that consisted of a plain glass disk. In May 1677 the famous raven's head was substituted and remained in use until his death. About fourteen pieces marked with this seal are known.

Lead glass is heavier than the Venetian but not so heavy as the German. Being softer than the latter, it is more easily and deeply carved and engraved. Although it fused at a lower temperature than the Venetian, it was not so tractable for blowing into fanciful shapes. It has great clarity and light dispersing quality, although its light seems to possess a velvet softness in comparison with the brilliance of German glass. English lead glass is often known as flint glass, a cognomen that relates to its hardness and quartzlike clearness rather than to its composition, although it is probable that English flints became the usual source of the silical ingredient.[8]

Engraving was used to personalize glass by the addition of insignia. Jacobite glasses made for those who favored King James II or his descen-

dents are a collector's item. Soda metal continued to be manufactured in Britain for ordinary wares.

STONES, METALS, IVORIES

The reigns of the first two Stuarts became progressively more difficult and less prosperous for the goldsmiths of England. The extravagances of the court and the civil wars, both of which cost money, created a drain on the supplies of the precious metal. Charles was notoriously skilled in usurping, even under politer terms, private stores. In such unstable times merchants who had customarily placed their capital in the royal mint found it safer to place it in the goldsmiths' vaults to be lent for usury. The opening of the Bank of England in 1694 did much to alleviate monetary problems.

Although fewer silver objects were made during Jacobean years, nevertheless the number of types multiplied, thus indicating the practice of greater amenities. This tendency accelerated after the Restoration.

The style of the seventeenth century is difficult to tabulate. The influence of France, the Netherlands, and of native tradition can be traced during any decade. Likewise political and economic factors united with the social to modify the scene. Jacobean and Cromwellian pieces are sturdy and may be quite plain with engraving as the only embellishment, or they may have shallowly reserved patterning of typical geometrics thrown into relief on a chased background.

With the return of the Stuarts design becomes more florid. Two types of decoration are prominent. One, and the simpler, is a cut-card technique by which a design with the appearance of a cardboard cutout is applied to a simple metal form. The other resorts to high relief embossing in broad lobes in an attempt to make thin metal look heavier. This practice continued in William and Mary silver as classical fluting, variously known as *gadrooning*.

From 1697 until 1719 the Brittania Standard of higher silver purity for goldsmiths' work was enforced. This was the legal means of stopping the conversion of coinage into silver objects so favored by the growing numbers of an affluent clientele. The effect of this law was to cause another return to quieter surfaces and heavier pieces, for the softer metal would not stand up so well under hammering. Fluting was another means of securing the desired rigidity. During the enforced high standard period the figure of a woman (Brittania) was added to the London assay marks.

Types of silver make an interesting social study. The elaborate salts of Elizabeth's reign begin to bow out. They were first replaced by relatively simple bell shapes, still, however, about 10 in. high. These in turn gave way to the open trencher salt or salt cellar. Some bells came apart in sections, one of which was reserved for the precious spices of the orient. Later the castor with large openings (sometimes called the *muffineer*) was used for condiments.

Communal drinking vessels were exchanged for smaller goblets, two-handled cups, and wine cups (i.e., tumblers). During the reign of James I tall steeple cups, 13 to 26 in. high, sang the swan song of the standing cups. Their tops were surmounted with the tall steeple or obelisk-shaped ornament seen in an example from the Wallace collection. Notice here that the scrolled brackets are cast, a technique that came into favor with thinner hollow ware.

Beakers assumed a simple flaring shape often seen in Dutch examples and were frequently engraved with stylized floral designs of a somewhat provincial nature. Their flared bases are embellished with acanthus of low embossing. This style finds echo in the flagons. The ample tankards, however, are more substantial and severe in pattern, as befits trenchermen accustomed to stout and ale. Their shape changes from the straight-sided, flat-topped variety of the Jacobean to the Commonwealth type with a molded base and flattened, stepped-up cover. A later form stood on small ball feet and had a flat cover with rounded edges.

Table service from the time of the Restoration was not unlike table service today. Forks grew more common and were even sold in sets. The English fork was two-tined. The egg-shaped bowl of the spoon (the *Puritan spoon*) was introduced at the time of Charles I. Now at one with the handle, the latter being flat, it was reinforced on the rear by a long flange called the *rat tail*. The trifid-shaped handle terminus was an innovation of about 1660.

Early candlesticks were short, straight pillars with broad circular grease pans and plain flanged stands—a wonderfully functional design. Later both squared and rounded baluster-knopped pedestals supported short columnar candleholders.

Silver coffee-, tea-, and chocolate pots arrived with the seventies and at first were all similar in shape, that of a tall tapering cylinder with straight sides, straight spout, and dome cover. They were small because the imported beans and leaves were luxury items. Coffeepots preserved something of their original form throughout their existence, always being larger than teapots and vertical in extension. Teapots, less than 6 in. high, assumed a round shape with curving spout.

A final word about sconces, candelabra, and chandeliers: although glass and silver were favored for those in private use, churches and public buildings from the time of the Stuarts were equipped with some of our handsomest brass heirlooms. A few may have been of Holland manufacture but many were undoubtedly English. They merit the most careful attention and even an unpretentious English church may hold a fine example.

DESCRIPTIVE SUMMARY

The seventeenth century in England was one in which the architectural arts tried to adopt classicism in both a purist and Baroque manner, but, like Gaul, the phenomenon broke into three parts: the first, the Jacobean, was a style grafted onto British stalks; the second—by the inspiration of one man, Inigo Jones—was a purist and never native episode; the third, in rather direct contact with the budding world of empirical science and quantitative measurement, began that merging of sturdy individualism, classical regularity, and Baroque charm that we find in the work of Wren.

Furnishings followed architecture in these respects, although they were never so elegant nor so unattainable as their French counterparts. Only when fashion rather than indigenous style was given the upper hand did tasteless grafts appear.

During the eighteenth century, developing from the seventeenth, Britain created her own amalgam, expressive of the English gentry rather than of a wealthy aristocracy. England tried but missed absolutism and an absolutist art.

General References

There is no surer way for a writer to cut himself down to size than by attempting a bibliography. The lacunae in his own reading glare from every card index compendium. The basis for the inclusion of any book must be a combination of readability, availability, and quality—all neatly balanced by a particular purpose. Neither date of publication nor of reprint can be certain guides. This list is offered with the modest hope that it will answer a variety of needs. As the text is intended to be no more than an introductory survey, so its bibliography should lead from there. This is a process of finding an interest and then going on to ever-widening horizons and deeper knowledge.

This bibliography takes us only into the first round. Many of the books can be bought on today's market without breaking a bank roll. Those with high prices or early publication dates may be sought in libraries. Some of the best sources for up-to-date information are magazines dedicated to the history of the arts which we are studying. The latest findings and viewpoints will naturally appear there before they can find their way into more expensive books. In the decorative arts, the catalogs of the noteworthy museum collections should be consulted and owned whenever possible. Specialized bulletins of the leading museums are rich sources of erudite material. These entice one to travel in order to visit treasures at first hand. Such personal experience will give the serious student a lifetime of pleasure and can add a dimension that even the finest reproductions in books cannot convey.

Archaeology

ARTAMANOF, M., Ed. *The Dawn of Art: Paleolithic, Neolithic, Bronze Age and Iron Age Remains Found in the Territory of the Soviet Union.* The Hermitage Collection. Leningrad: Aurora Art Publishers, 1974.

BIBBY, GEOFFREY. *The Testimony of the Spade.* New York: Knopf, 1956.

CERAM, C. W. *Gods, Graves, and Scholars.* Translated by E. B. Garside. New York: Knopf, 1951.

CHILDE, V. GORDON. *The Dawn of European Civilization.* 6th ed. rev. New York: Knopf, 1958.

———. *New Light on the Most Ancient East.* New York: Grove, 1957.

CLARK, GRAHAME. *Prehistoric England.* Rev. ed. London: Batsford, 1962.

EVANS, ARTHUR JOHN. *The Palace of Minos.* 4 vols. New York: Macmillan, 1921–1935.

LUCAS, A. *Ancient Egyptian Materials and Industries.* 2nd ed. rev. London: Edward Arnold, 1934.

MAIURI, AMEDEO. *Herculaneum.* Novara: Instituto Geografico de Agostini, 1963.

———. *Pompeii.* Translated by V. Priestley. 4th ed. Rome: Libreria dello Stato, 1949.

MARINATOS, S. *Crete and Mycenae.* New York: Abrams, 1906.

MYLONAS, GEORGE EMMANUEL. *Ancient Mycenae:*

The Capital City of Agamemnon. Princeton: Princeton University Press, 1957.

PARROT, ANDRE. *Sumer.* Translated by Stuart Gilbert and James Emmons. 2 vols. London: Thames & Hudson, 1960.

RICE, DAVID TALBOT, Ed. *The Great Palace of the Byzantine Emperors.* Edinburgh: University Press, 1958.

ROBINSON, DAVID M., and J. WALTER GRAHAM. *The Hellenic House.* Excavations at Olynthus. Johns Hopkins University Studies in Archaeology, No. 25-VIII. Baltimore: Johns Hopkins University Press, 1938.

WEINBERG, SAUL S. *Stone Age in the Aegean.* Cambridge: Cambridge University Press, 1965.

WOOLEY, LEONARD. *A Forgotten Kingdom.* Baltimore: Penguin, 1953.

———. *Ur of the Chaldees.* New York: Norton, 1965.

Architecture

ACKERMAN, JAMES S. *Palladio's Villas.* Institute of Fine Arts, New York University. Locust Valley, New York: Augustin, 1967.

ADAMS, HENRY. *Mont-Saint-Michel and Chartres.* New York: Doubleday, Anchor Books, 1959.

BLOMFIELD, REGINALD THEODORE. *A History of French Architecture from the Reign of Charles VIII till the Death of Mazarin.* 2 vols. London: G. Bell, 1911.

BLUNT, ANTHONY. *Art and Architecture in France: 1500–1700.* Rev. ed. Harmondsworth: Penguin, 1973.

BOETHIUS, AXEL. *The Golden House of Nero.* Ann Arbor: University of Michigan Press, 1960.

BRAUN, HUGH. *An Introduction to English Medieval Architecture.* London: Faber & Faber, 1951.

———. *Old English Houses.* London: Faber & Faber, 1962.

BURCHARD, JOHN E., and ALBERT BUSH-BROWN. *Architecture in America.* Boston: Little, Brown, 1961.

CANTACUZINO, SHERBAN. *European Domestic Architecture: Its Development from Early Times.* Great Britain: Dutton, Studio Vista, 1969.

COLVIN, H. M. *A Biographical Dictionary of English Architects, 1660–1840.* Cambridge: Harvard University Press, 1954.

CONANT, KENNETH JOHN. *Carolingian and Romanesque Architecture: 800–1200.* Baltimore: Penguin, 1959.

CONNOLLY, CYRIL, and JEROME ZERBE. *Les Pavillons.* New York: Macmillan, 1962.

DE NOLHAC, PIERRE. *Versailles and the Trianons.* New York: Dodd, Mead, 1907.

DREXLER, ARTHUR. *The Architecture of Japan.* New York: Museum of Modern Art, 1955.

DUTTON, RALPH. *The Chateaux of France.* London: Batsford, 1957.

EBERLEIN, HAROLD DONALDSON, and CORTLANDT VAN DYKE HUBBARD. *Historic Houses of George Town and Washington City.* Richmond: Dietz, 1958.

FLEMING, JOHN, HUGH HONOUR, and NIKOLAUS PEVSNER. *The Penguin Dictionary of Architecture.* Harmondsworth: Penguin, 1966.

FLETCHER, BANISTER FLIGHT. *A History of Architecture by the Comparative Method.* 18th ed. New York: Scribner's, 1975.

FRANKL, PAUL. *Gothic Architecture.* Translated by Dieter Pevsner. Baltimore: Penguin 1962.

GARVIN, AMELIA BEERS (WARNOCK). *Historic Houses of Canada.* Toronto: Ryerson, 1952.

GIEDION, SIGFRIED. *The Eternal Present: The Beginnings of Architecture.* 2 vols. Princeton: Princeton University Press, 1962 and 1964.

GROPIUS, WALTER. *Architecture in Japan.* New Haven: Yale University Press, 1960.

GUINNESS, DESMOND, and WILLIAM BRYAN. *Great Irish Houses and Castles.* New York: Viking, 1978.

HAMLIN, TALBOT. *Architecture, an Art for all Men.* New York: Columbia University Press, 1961.

HUSSEY, CHRISTOPHER, and JOHN CORNFORTH. *English Country Houses.* 3 vols. New York: Oxford University Press, 1955–1958.

———. *English Country Houses Open to the Public.* 4th ed. London: Country Life, 1964.

INN, HENRY. *Chinese Houses and Gardens.* S. C. Lee, Ed. New York: Hastings House, 1950.

KISHEDA, HIDETO. *Japanese Architecture.* Tokyo: Japan Travel Bureau, 1960.

KRAUTHEIMER, RICHARD. *Early Christian and Byzantine Architecture.* Baltimore: Penguin, 1965.

LAVEDAN, PIERRE. *French Architecture.* Harmondsworth: Penguin, 1956.

LAWRENCE, A. W. *Greek Architecture.* Baltimore: Penguin, 1967.

LEES, MILNE JAMES. *The Age of Inigo Jones.* London: Batsford, 1953.

LLOYD, NATHANIEL. *A History of the English House from Primitive Times to the Victorian Period.* New ed. London: Architectural Press, 1951.

LOWRY, BATES. *Renaissance Architecture.* New York: Braziller, 1967.

MACKENZIE, WILLIAM MACKAY. *The Medieval Castle in Scotland.* New York: Bloom, 1972.

MASSON, GEORGINA. *Italian Villas and Palaces.* New York: Abrams, 1959.

MAZZOTTI, GIUSEPPE. *Venetian Villas.* Rome: Carlo Bestetti-Edizioni d'Arte, 1957.

MILLON, HENRY A. *Baroque and Rococo Architecture.* New York: Braziller, 1961.

MORSE, EDWARD S. *Japanese Homes and Their Surroundings.* Magnolia, Mass.: Peter Smith, 1961.

PAULSSON, THOMAS. *Scandinavian Architecture.* London: L. Hill, 1958.

PEVSNER, NIKOLAUS. *An Outline of European Architecture.* Baltimore: Penguin, 1960.

RIDER, BERTHA CARR. *Ancient Greek Houses.* Chicago: Argonaut, 1964.

SITWELL, SACHEVERELL. *Great Houses of Europe.* 2nd ed. New York: Putnam, 1964.

SMITH, EARL BALDWIN. *Egyptian Architecture as Cultural Expression.* New York: Appleton-Century, 1938.

SMITH, WILLIAM STEVENSON. *The Art and Architecture of Ancient Egypt.* Baltimore: Penguin, 1958.

STODDARD, WHITNEY. *Art and Architecture in Medieval France.* New York: Harper & Row, 1966.

SUMMERSON, JOHN. *Architecture in Britain: 1530 to 1830.* 4th rev. and enl. ed. Harmondsworth: Penguin, 1963.

————. *The Classical Language of Architecture.* Cambridge: M.I.T. Press, 1963.

————. *Sir Christopher Wren.* Hamden, Connecticut: Archon, 1965.

TANGE, KENZO. *Katsura: Tradition and Creation in Japanese Architecture.* New Haven: Yale University Press, 1960.

TANZER, HELEN H. *The Villas of Pliny the Younger.* New York: Columbia University Press, 1924.

TORROJA, EDUARDO. *Philosophy of Structures.* Translated by J. J. & Milos Polivka. Berkeley: University of California Press, 1958.

VASARI, GIORGIO. *The Lives of the Artists.* A selection. Translated by George Ball. New York: Viking, n.d.

VIGHI, ROBERTO. *Villa Hadriana.* Translated by J. B. Ward Perkins. Rome: Tipografia Artistica—Editrice, 1961.

WHEELER, MORTIMER. *Roman Art and Architecture.* New York: Praeger, 1964.

WHITE, JOHN. *Art and Architecture in Italy: 1250-1400.* New York: Viking, Pelican, 1967.

WITTKOWER, RUDOLPH. *Art and Architecture in Italy: 1600-1750.* Baltimore: Penguin, 1965.

YOSHIDA, TETSURO. *The Japanese House and Garden.* New York: Praeger, 1955.

Art History

ALDRED, CYRIL. *Akhenaten and Nefertiti.* New York: Viking, 1973.

BECKWITH, JOHN. *Early Medieval Art.* New York: Praeger, 1964.

CARTER, DAGNY. *The Symbol of the Beast.* New York: Ronald, 1957.

FRANKFORT, HENRI. *The Art and Architecture of the Ancient Orient.* Baltimore: Penguin, 1959.

GARDNER, HELEN. *Gardner's Art through the Ages.* 6th ed. Revised by Horst de la Croix and Richard G. Tansey. New York: Harcourt Brace Jovanovich, 1975.

HARVEY, JOHN. *The Gothic World, 1100–1600: A Survey of Architecture and Art.* New York: Harper & Row, 1969.

HINKS, ROGER. *Carolingian Art: A Study of Early Medieval Painting and Sculpture in Western Europe.* Ann Arbor: University of Michigan Press, 1962.

HOLT, ELIZABETH G., Ed. *A Documentary History of Art.* 2 vols. Garden City, New York: Doubleday, 1958.

HUTCHINSON, R. W. *Prehistoric Crete.* Harmondsworth: Penguin, 1962.

JANSON, H. W. *History of Art.* Rev. and enl. ed. Englewood Cliffs: Prentice-Hall, 1969.

LEE, SHERMAN E. *A History of Far Eastern Art.* Englewood Cliffs: Prentice-Hall; New York: Abrams, 1964.

————. *Japanese Decorative Style.* New York: Prentice-Hall, 1961.

LEES-MILNE, JAMES. *Baroque in Italy.* London: Batsford, 1959.

LLOYD, SETON. *The Art of the Ancient Near East.* New York: Praeger, 1963.

MacKENDRICK, PAUL. *The Greek Stones Speak.* 2nd ed. New York: St. Martin's Press, 1962.

————. *The Mute Stones Speak.* 2nd ed. New York: St. Martin's Press, 1961.

MOREY, C. R. *Christian Art.* New York: Norton, 1958.

PAINE, ROBERT TREAT, and ALEXANDER COBURN SOPER. *The Art and Architecture of Japan.* Baltimore: Penguin, 1955.

PARROT, ANDRE. *The Arts of Assyria.* New York: Golden Press, 1962.

POPE, ARTHUR U. *An Introduction to Persian Art since the Seventh Century A.D.* Reprint of 1931 ed. Westport, Connecticut: Greenwood, 1972.

RICE, DAVID TALBOT. *Byzantine Art.* Rev. ed. Baltimore: Penguin, 1954.

RICHTER, GISELLA M.A. *Ancient Italy: A Study of the Interrelations of Its Peoples as Shown in Their Arts.* Jerome Lectures, 4th series. Ann Arbor: University of Michigan Press, 1955.

————. *A Handbook of Greek Art.* 4th ed. Greenwich, Connecticut: Phaidon, 1965.

————. *Metropolitan Museum of Art: Handbook of the Classical Collection.* Cambridge: Harvard University Press, 1953.

SICKMAN, LAURENCE C., and ALEXANDER COBURN SOPER. *The Art and Architecture of China.* 2nd ed. Baltimore: Penguin, 1960.

SMITH, WILLIAM STEVENSON. *Ancient Egypt as Represented in the Museum of Fine Arts, Boston.* Boston: Museum of Fine Arts, 1960.

WARNER, LANGDON. *The Enduring Art of Japan.* New York: Grove, 1958.

WHEELER, MORTIMER. *Roman Art and Architecture.* New York: Praeger, 1964.

WITTKOWER, RUDOLPH. *Art and Architecture in Italy: 1600–1750.* 2nd rev. ed. Baltimore: Penguin, 1965.

WIXOM, WILLIAM D. *Treasures from Medieval France.* Exhibition catalog. Cleveland: The Cleveland Museum of Art, 1967.

WOLFFLIN, HEINRICH. Translated by Kathrin Simon. *Renaissance and Baroque*. Ithaca: Cornell University Press, 1964.

WOOLEY, LEONARD. *The Art of the Middle East*. New York: Crown, 1961.

Carpets

BODE, WILHELM von, and KUHNEL. Translated by Charles Grant Ellis. *Antique Rugs from the Near East*. 4th rev. ed. Braunschweig: Klinkhardt and Biermann, 1958.

DILLEY, ARTHUR URBANE. *Oriental Rugs and Carpets*. Revised by Maurice B. Dimond. Philadelphia: Lippincott, 1959.

DIMAND, M. S. *Oriental Rugs in the Metropolitan Museum of Art*. With a catalog of rugs of China and Chinese Turkestan by Jean Mailey. New York: Metropolitan Museum of Art, 1973.

ERDMANN, KURT. *Oriental Carpets*. New York: Universe Books, 1962.

HACKMACK, ADOLF. *Chinese Carpets and Rugs*. New York: Dover, 1973.

HAWLEY, WALTER AUGUSTUS. *Oriental Rugs, Antique and Modern*. New York: Tudor, 1937.

JARRY, MADELAINE. *The Carpets of the Manufacture de la Savonnerie*. Leigh-on-Sea: F. Lewis, 1966.

LEWIS, GEORGE GRIFFIN. *The Practical Book of Oriental Rugs*. New rev. ed. Philadelphia: Lippincott, 1945.

MUMFORD, JOHN KIMBERLY. *Oriental Rugs*. New York: Scribner's, 1929.

REED, CHRISTOPHER DUNHAM. *Turkoman Rugs*. Cambridge: Fogg Art Museum, Harvard University, 1966.

Ceramics

BARRET, F. A. *Worcester Porcelain*. London: Faber & Faber, 1952.

BEAZLEY, J. D. *The Development of Attic Black-Figure Vase-Painters*. Oxford: Clarendon Press, 1956.

BOGER, LOUISE A. *Dictionary of World Pottery and Porcelain*. New York: Wittenborn, 1971.

BURTON, WILLIAM. *A General History of Porcelain*. 2 vols. London and New York: Cassell, 1921.

———. *History and Description of English Porcelain*. Elmsford, New York: British Book Center, reprint of 1924 ed.

CHAFFERS, WILLIAM. *Marks and Monograms on European and Oriental Pottery and Porcelain*. London: Reeves, 1954.

COOK, ROBERT MANUEL. *Greek Painted Pottery*. Chicago: Quadrangle Books, 1960.

COX, W. E. *The Book of Pottery and Porcelain*. London: Batsford, 1947.

EBERLEIN, HAROLD DONALDSON, and ROGER WEARNE RAMSDELL. *The Practical Book of Chinaware*. New ed. enl. and rev. Philadelphia: Lippincott, 1948.

FRANKFORT, HENRI. *Studies in Early Pottery of the Near East*. 2 vols. Royal Anthropological Institute of Great Britain and Ireland, Occasional Papers, No. 8. London: Royal Anthropological Institute, 1927.

HANNOVER, EMIL. *Pottery and Porcelain*. Bernard Rackham, Ed. 3 vols. London: E. Benn, 1925.

HONEY, WILLIAM BOWYER. *English Pottery and Porcelain*. 5th ed. rev. London: A. C. Black, 1964.

KOVEL, RALPH M., and TERRY H. KOVEL. *Dictionary of Marks: Pottery and Porcelain*. New York: Crown, 1953.

LANE, ARTHUR. *Early Islamic Pottery*. London: Faber & Faber, 1947.

———. *French Faience*. London: Faber & Faber, 1948.

———. *Greek Pottery*. London: Faber & Faber, 1948.

———. *Later Islamic Pottery: Persia, Syria, Egypt, Turkey*. London: Faber & Faber, 1957.

LITCHFIELD, FREDERICK. *Pottery and Porcelain*, Revised and edited by Frank Tilly. New York: Barrows, 1963.

LIVERANI, G. *Five Centuries of Italian Majolica*. New York: McGraw-Hill, 1960.

MILLER, ROY ANDREW. *Japanese Ceramics*. After the text by Seiichi Okuda and others. Tokyo: Toto Shippan, 1960.

ORMSBEE, THOMAS H. *English China and Its Marks*. Great Neck, New York: Deerfield, 1959.

OSGOOD, C. *Blue and White Chinese Porcelain*. New York: Ronald, 1956.

RACKHAM, BERNARD. *Italian Majolica*. London: Faber & Faber, 1952.

RAPHAEL, MAX. *Prehistoric Pottery and Civilization in Egypt*. New York: Pantheon, 1947.

RICHTER, GISELA. *Attic Red Figured Vases*. New Haven: Yale University Press, 1946.

———. *The Craft of the Athenian Potter*. New Haven: Yale University Press, 1941.

———. *Shapes and Names of Athenian Vases*. Wilmington, North Carolina: McGrath, 1973.

SAVAGE, GEORGE. *Porcelain through the Ages*. Baltimore: Penguin, 1954.

———. *Pottery through the Ages*. New York: Barnes & Noble, 1964.

THOMPSON, DOROTHY BURR. *Troy: The Terracotta Figurines of the Hellenistic Period*. University of Cincinnati. Princeton: Princeton University Press, 1963.

VYDROVA, JIRIKA. *Italian Majolica*. London: Spring House, 1960.

Clocks

BRITTEN, F. J. *Old Clocks and Watches and Their Makers.* 7th ed. G. H. Baillie, C. Clutton, and C. A. Ilbert, Eds. New York: Bonanza, 1956.

BRUTON, ERIC. *Clocks and Watches, 1400–1900.* New York: Praeger, 1967.

LOOMIS, BRIAN. *The White Dial Clock.* New York: Drake, 1975.

SYMONDS, ROBERT WEMYSS. *Thomas Tompion, His Life and Work.* London and New York: Batsford, 1951.

Design Theory

BERENSON, BERNARD. *Aesthetics and History.* Garden City, New York: Doubleday, Anchor Books, 1948.

BLUNT, ANTHONY. *Artistic Theory in Italy: 1450–1600.* Oxford: Oxford University Press, 1962.

BORISSAVLIEVITCH, M. *The Golden Number and the Scientific Aesthetics of Architecture.* New York: Philosophical Library, 1958.

BRUMBAUGH, ROBERT SHERRIL. *Plato's Mathematical Imagination; the Mathematical Passages in the Dialogues and Their Interpretation.* Bloomington: Indiana University Press, 1954.

GIEDION, SIGFRIED. *Space, Time, and Architecture.* 4th ed. enl. Cambridge: Harvard University Press, 1962.

GILBERT, KATHERINE EVERETT, and HELMUT KUHN. *A History of Aesthetics.* Rev. and enl. Bloomington: Indiana University Press, 1954.

HAMBIDGE, JAY. *The Parthenon and other Greek Temples: Their Dynamic Symmetry.* New Haven: Yale University Press, 1924.

KAUFMAN, EMILE. *Architecture in the Age of Reason.* Cambridge: Harvard University Press, 1933.

LEFF, GORDON. *Medieval Thought, St. Augustine to Ockham.* Baltimore: Penguin, 1958.

MUNRO, THOMAS. *The Arts and Their Interrelations.* New York: Liberal Arts, 1949.

SCOTT, GEOFFREY. *The Architecture of Humanism.* Garden City, New York: Doubleday, Anchor Books, 1954.

WHITE, JOHN. *The Birth and Rebirth of Pictorial Space.* New York: Yoseloff, 1958.

WITTKOWER, RUDOLF. *Architectural Principles in the Age of Humanism.* Columbia University Studies in Art History and Archaeology. New York: Random House, 1965.

WOLFFLIN, HEINRICH. Translated by Kathrin Simon. *Renaissance and Baroque.* Ithaca: Cornell University Press, 1965.

Furniture

BAKER, HOLLIS S. *Furniture in the Ancient World.* New York: Macmillan, 1966.

BRUNHAMMER, YVONNE. *Meubles et ensembles epoques Louis XIII et Louis XIV.* Paris: C. Massin, 1966.

———. *Meubles et ensembles epoques Moyen et Renaissance.* Paris: C. Massin: 1966.

BURR, GRACE HARDENDORFF. *Hispanic Furniture.* 2nd. ed. rev. and enl. New York: Archive, 1964.

CAMPKIN, MARIE. *Introducing Marquetry.* London: Batsford, 1969.

DE BELLAIQUE, G. *Furniture, Clocks and Gilt Bronzes.* 2 vols. James A. de Rothchild Collection at Waddesdon Manor. London: National Trust, 1974.

DOMENECH, RAFAEL (Galissa), and LUIS PEREZ BUENO. *Antique Spanish Furniture.* New York: Archive, 1965.

EBERLEIN, H. D., and A. McCLURE. *The Practical Book of Period Furniture.* Philadelphia and London: Lippincott, 1914.

EDWARDS, RALPH. *The Shorter Dictionary of English Furniture.* London: Country Life, 1964.

ELLSWORTH, ROBERT HATFIELD. *Chinese Furniture.* New York: Random House, 1971.

FASTNEDGE, RALPH. *English Furniture Styles from 1500 to 1830.* New York: Barnes & Noble, 1964.

GLOAG, JOHN. *The Englishman's Chair.* London: Allen and Unwin, 1964.

———. *A Short Dictionary of English Furniture.* Rev. and enl. London: Allen and Unwin, 1969.

GONZALES-PALACIOS, ALVAR. *Il Mobile nei secoli: I-III Italia.* Milan: Fratelli Fabbri, 1969.

HACKENBROCH, YVONNE. *English Furniture with some Furniture of other Countries in the Irwin Untermyer Collection.* Cambridge: Harvard University Press, 1958.

HAYWARD, CHARLES H. *Antique or Fake? The Making of Old Furniture.* London: Evans, 1970.

———. *English Period Furniture.* Rev. ed. London: Evans, 1971.

HAYWARD, HELENA, Ed. *World Furniture: A Pictorial History.* New York: McGraw-Hill, 1965.

HEAL, AMBROSE. *The London Furniture Makers, from the Restoration to the Victorian Era, 1660–1840.* New York: Dover, 1972.

HUTH, HANS. *Lacquer of the West: The History of the Craft and an Industry 1550–1950.* Chicago and London: University of Chicago Press, 1971.

JERVIS, SIMON. *Printed Furniture Designs before 1650.* Furniture History Society. Leeds, England: Maney, 1974.

KATES, GEORGE N. *Chinese Household Furniture.* New York: Dover, 1962.

LIZZANI, GOFFREDO. *Il Mobile Romano.* Introduction by Alvar Gonzalez Palacios. Milan: Görlich Editore, 1970.

MACQUOID, PERCY. *A History of English Furniture.* 4 vols. London: Lawrence and Bullen, 1938.

MARGON, LESTER. *Masterpieces of European Furniture, 1380–1840.* New York: Architectural Book, 1967.

———. *World Furniture Treasures; Yesterday, Today, and Tomorrow.* New York, Reinhold, 1954.

ODOM, WILLIAM M. *A History of Italian Furniture from the Fourteenth to the Early Nineteenth Centuries.* 2 vols. Reprint of 1918–1919 ed. New York: Archive, 1966.

OLIVER, J. L. *The Development and Structure of the Furniture Industry.* London: Pergamon, 1966.

ORMSBEE, T. H. *The Windsor Chair.* London: W. H. Allen, 1962.

PEDRINI, A. *Italian Furniture, Interiors, and Decorations of the 15th and 16th Centuries.* Rev. ed. London: Tiranti, 1949.

RICHTER, GISELA M.A. *The Furniture of the Greeks, Etruscans, and Romans.* London: Phaidon, 1966.

ROE, FREDERICK G. *English Cottage Furniture.* London: Phoenix House, 1961.

SPARKES, IVAN G. *The Windsor Chair: An Illustrated History of a Classic English Chair.* Levittown, New York: Transatlantic, 1975.

VERLET, PIERRE. *French Royal Furniture.* New York: Towse, 1963.

———. *Le Mobilier Royal Français.* 3 vols. Paris: Editions d'art et d'histoire, 1945.

WATSON, F. J. B. *Furniture. Wallace Collection Catalogues.* London: Clowes, 1956.

Glass

ARMITAGE, EDWARD LIDDALL. *Stained Glass.* Newton, Massachusetts: Branford, 1959.

ARNOLD, HUGH. *Stained Glass of Middle Ages in England and France.* New York: Macmillan, 1956.

AUBERT, MARCEL. *Le Vitrail Francais.* Musée des Arts Décoratifs. Paris: Editions 2 Mondes, 1958.

THE BROOKLYN MUSEUM. *Glass and Glazes from Ancient Egypt.* New York: Brooklyn Museum, 1948.

CORNING MUSEUM OF GLASS. *Three Centuries of Venetian Glass. Special Exhibition, 1958.* Corning, New York: The Corning Museum of Glass, 1958.

HAYNES, E. BARRINGTON. *Glass through the Ages.* Baltimore: Penguin, 1964.

HONEY, W. B. *English Glass.* London: Collins, 1946.

SALDERN, AXEL VON. *German Enameled Glass.* Corning, New York: Corning Museum, 1965.

SCHRIJVER, ELKA. *Glass and Crystal.* 2 vols. New York: New York: Universe Books, 1964.

SMITH, RAY WINFIELD. *Glass from the Ancient World.* Ray Winfield Smith Collection. Corning, New York: Corning Museum of Glass, 1957.

THORPE, W. A. *English and Irish Glass.* 3rd ed. New York: Barnes & Noble, 1961.

Interior Design

DUTTON, RALPH. *The English Interior, 1500–1900.* London: Batsford, 1948.

EDWARDS, R., and L. G. G. RAMSEY, Eds. *Connoisseur Period Guides: Tudor, Stuart, Early Georgian, Late Georgian, Regency, Early Victorian.* New York: Reynal, 1958.

FRANKFORT, HENRI, Ed. *The Mural Painting of El' Amarneh.* London: The Egypt Exploration Society, 1929.

GABRIEL, M. M. *Livia's Garden Room at Prima Porta.* New York: University Press, 1957.

JOURDAIN, MARGARET. *English Decorative Plasterwork of the Renaissance.* New York: Scribner's, 1926.

———. *English Interior Decoration, 1500–1830.* London: Batsford, 1950.

LEHMANN, PHYLLIS WILLIAMS. *Roman Wall Paintings from Boscoreale in the Metropolitan Museum of Art.* Monographs on Archaeology and Fine Arts, No. 5. Cambridge: Archaeological Institute of America, 1953.

MAIURI, AMEDEO. *Pompeian Wall Paintings.* New York: Taplinger, 1960.

———. *Roman Painting.* New York: Skira, 1953.

MARTIN, JOHN R. *The Farnese Gallery.* Princeton: Princeton University Press, 1965.

OGLESBY, C. *French Provincial Decorative Art.* New York: Scribner's, 1951.

PRAZ, MARIO. Translated by William Weaver. *An Illustrated History of Furnishing from the Renaissance to the Twentieth Century.* New York: Braziller, 1964.

RIEDER, WILLIAM P., et al. *Highlights of the Untermyer Collection of English and Continental Decorative Arts.* Exhibition Catalog. New York: Metropolitan Museum of Art, 1977.

THORNTON, PETER. *Seventeenth Century Interior Decoration in England, France, and Holland.* New Haven: Yale University Press, 1978.

YARWOOD, DOREEN. *The English Home: A Thousand Years of Furnishing and Decoration.* New York: Scribner's, 1956.

Metals

BOUQUET, A. C. *European Brasses.* New York: Whittenborn, 1967.

CARDUCCI, CARLO. *Gold and Silver Treasures of Ancient Italy.* New York: Graphic, 1964.

DAVIS, FRANK. *French Silver 1450–1825.* New York: Praeger, 1970.

DENNIS. FAITH. *Three Centuries of French Domestic Silver.* 2 vols. New York: Metropolitan Museum of Art, 1960.

FRANK, EDWARD B. *Old French Ironwork.* Cambridge: Harvard University Press, 1950.

FREDERICKS, J. W. *Dutch Silver, Renaissance through*

Eighteenth Century. 4 vols. New York: Heineman, 1953–1961.

GARDNER, JOHN STARKIE. *English Ironwork of the XVII and XVIII Centuries.* New York: B. Blom, 1972.

HAYWARD, J. F. *Huguenot Silver in England: 1688–1727.* London: Faber & Faber, 1959.

STRONG, D. E. *Greek and Roman Gold and Silver Plate.* Ithaca: Cornell University Press, 1966.

TAYLOR, GERALD. *Art in Silver and Gold.* London: Dutton, Studio Vista, 1964.

WENHAM, EDWARD. *Domestic Silver of Great Britain and Ireland.* London: Oxford University Press, 1931.

Miscellaneous

THE CONNOISSEUR. *The Concise Encyclopedia of Antiques.* New York: Hawthorne, 1955.

COSTANTINO, RUTH T. *How to Know French Antiques.* New York: Potter, 1961; London: P. Owen, 1963.

HEYDENRYK, H. *The Art and History of Frames.* New York: Heineman, 1969.

IVINS, WILLIAM M., JR. *How Prints Look.* Boston: Beacon, 1958.

KOVEL, RALPH, and TERRY KOVEL. *Know Your Antiques.* New York: Crown, 1967.

MAYER, RALPH. *The Artist's Handbook of Materials and Techniques.* New York: Viking, 1953.

THORNE, J. O., Ed. *Chamber's Biographical Dictionary.* New York: St. Martin's Press, n.d.

THWING, LEROY. *Flickering Flames: A History of Domestic Lighting through the Ages.* Rutland, Vermont: Tuttle, 1957.

WATSON, F. J. B. *The Wrightsman Collection.* 2 vols. New York: The Metropolitan Museum of Art. Greenwich, Connecticut: New York Graphic Society, 1966.

WATSON, F. J. B., and C. C. DAUTERMAN. *The Wrightsman Collection.* Vol. 3. New York: Metropolitan Museum of Art, 1971.

WILLS, G. *English Looking-Glasses (1670–1820).* Foreword by John Hayward. Cranbury, New Jersey: A. S. Barnes, 1965.

WINTERNITZ, EMANUEL. *Keyboard Instruments in the Metropolitan Museum of Art.* New York: Metropolitan Museum of Art, 1961.

Periodicals

Abitare. Italy.

Antiques. New York.

Architectural Design. England.

Architectural Digest. Los Angeles.

Architectural Record. New York.

Architectural Review. England.

Bulletin de Liaison du Centre International d'Etude des Textiles Anciens. France.

Connaissance des Arts. France.

The Connoisseur. England.

Craft Horizons. New York.

Decorative Arts. Winterthur, Delaware.

Domus. Italy.

Furniture History. England.

Interior Design. New York.

Interiors. New York.

Journal of the Society of Architectural Historians. Philadelphia.

Studio International. England.

Social History

CARCOPINO, JEROME. *Daily Life in Ancient Rome.* Translated by E. O. Lorimer. New Haven: Yale University Press, 1963.

COULBORN, R. *The Origin of Civilized Societies.* Princeton: Princeton University Press, 1959.

FRANKFORT, HENRI. *The Birth of Civilization in the Near East.* Garden City, New York: Anchor, n.d.

GHIRSHMAN, R. *Iran.* Baltimore: Penguin, 1954.

GROENEWEGEN-FRANKFORT, H. A., and BERNARD ASHMOLE. *The Ancient World.* New York: New American Library, Mentor, 1967.

HAMILTON, EDITH. *The Greek Way to Western Civilization.* New York: Avon, 1973.

———. *The Roman Way to Western Civilization.* New York: Avon, 1973.

HARREL-COURTEZ, HENRY. *Etruscan Italy.* Translated by J. Hogarth. New York: Orion, 1964.

HARRISON, JANE ELLEN. *Themis, A Study of the Social Origins of Greek Religion.* London: Merlin Press, 1963.

HASKINS, CHARLES HOMER. *The Renaissance of the 12th Century.* Cleveland and New York: World, Meridian, 1957.

HEER, FRIEDRICH. *The Medieval World: Europe 1100–1350.* Translated by Janet Sondheimer. New York and Toronto: New English Library, Mentor, 1961.

HUIZINGA, J. *The Waning of the Middle Ages: A Study of the Forms of Life, Thought, and Art in France and the Netherlands in the XIVth and XVth Centuries.* Garden City, New York: Doubleday, Anchor, 1956.

LANGER, WILLIAM L., Ed. *Encyclopedia of World History.* Rev. ed. Boston: Houghton Mifflin, 1962.

LLOYD, SETON. *Early Anatolia.* Harmondsworth, Penguin, 1956.

———. *Twin Rivers, a Brief History of Iraq.* London: G. Cumberlege, Oxford University Press, 1947.

McGOVERN, W. M. *The Early Empires of Central Asia: A Study of the Scythians and the Huns and the Part*

They Played in World History. Chapel Hill: University of North Carolina Press, 1939.

MILLER, HELEN DAY (HILL). *Bridge to Asia: The Greeks in the Eastern Mediterranean.* New York: Scribner's 1967.

MUMFORD, LEWIS. *Technics and Civilization.* New York: Harcourt, Brace & World, 1963.

OLMSTED, ALBERT TEN EYCK. *History of the Persian Empire.* Chicago: University of Chicago Press, 1948.

PARROT, ANDRE. *Mari.* Neuchatel and Paris: Ides & Calendes, 1953.

PRITCHARD, JAMES BENNETT, Ed. *The Ancient Near East: An Anthology of Texts and Pictures.* Translated and annotated by W. F. Albright and others. Princeton: Princeton University Press, 1958.

RICE, TAMARA T. *The Scythians.* New York: Praeger, 1957.

RICHMOND, I. A. *Roman Britain.* 2nd ed. Baltimore: Penguin, 1963.

STEPHENSON, CARL. *Medieval History.* Edited and revised by Bryce Lyon. New York: Harper & Row, 1962.

WEBSTER, THOMAS BERTRAM. *From Mycenae to Homer.* New York: Norton, 1954.

YOUNG, G. F. *The Medici.* New York: Random House, 1930.

Source Books

ALBERTI, LEONE BATTISTA. *Ten Books of Architecture.* Translated by James Leoni. Joseph Rykwert, Ed. London: Tiranti, 1965.

HONNECOURT, VILLARD DE. *Sketchbook.* Edited by T. Bowie. Bloomington: Indiana University Press, 1959.

PALLADIO, ANDRE. *The Four Books of Architecture.* Reprint of 1738 Ware English ed. Introduction by A. Placzek. New York: Dover, 1965.

VASARI, GIORGIO. *The Lives of the Artists.* A selection. Translated by George Ball. Harmondsworth: Penguin, 1965.

VITRUVIUS, POLLIO MARCUS. *The Ten Books on Architecture.* Translated by Morris Hicky Morgan. New York: Dover, 1960.

Textiles

AMERICAN FABRICS MAGAZINE. *Encyclopedia of Textiles.* New York: Prentice-Hall, 1960.

BUNT, CYRIL G. E. *Byzantine Fabrics.* New York: Wittenborn, 1967.

DIGBY, GEORGE W. *French Tapestries.* London: Batsford, 1951.

FALKE, OTTO von. *Decorative Silks.* 3rd ed. London: Zwemmer, 1936.

HUNTER, GEORGE LELAND. *Decorative Textiles.* Philadelphia: Lippincott, 1918.

————. *The Practical Book of Tapestry.* Philadelphia: Lippincott, 1925.

JARRY, MADELEINE. *World Tapestry: From Its Origins to the Present.* New York: Putnam, 1969.

LEWIS, ETHEL. *The Romance of Textiles.* New York: Macmillan, 1953.

LURÇAT, JEAN. *Designing Tapestry.* London: Rohcliff, 1950.

MACLAGAN, ERIC. *The Bayeux Tapestry.* Rev. ed. Harmondsworth: Penguin, 1949.

MAYER, CHRISTA. *Masterpieces of Western Textiles.* Chicago: Art Institute of Chicago, 1969.

RODIER, PAUL. *The Romance of French Weaving.* New York: Stokes, 1931.

SANTANGELO, ANTONIO. *A Treasury of Great Italian Textiles.* New York: Abrams, 1964.

STENTON, FRANK. *The Bayeux Tapestry.* 2nd ed. rev. and enl. New York: Phaidon, 1965.

TAYLOR, LUCY D. *Know Your Fabrics.* New York: Wiley, 1951.

THOMSON, WILLIAM GEORGE. *A History of Tapestry from the Earliest Times until the Present Day.* London: Hodder and Houghton, 1960.

THORNTON, PETER. *Baroque and Rococo Silks.* New York: Taplinger, 1965.

WEIBEL, ADELE C. *Two Thousand Years of Textiles.* New York: Pantheon, 1952.

WEIGERT, ROGER-ARMAND. *La Tapisserie Française.* Paris: Larousse, 1956.

Notes

Introduction

1. Anne Morrow Lindbergh, *Locked Rooms and Open Doors* (New York and London: Harcourt Brace Jovanovich, 1974), p. 331.

Chapter 2

1. As quoted by R. Ghirschman in *Iran* (Baltimore: Penguin, 1954), pp. 165–166.
2. Alfred Lucas, *Ancient Egyptian Material and Industries*, 2nd ed. (London: Edward Arnold, 1934), p. 298.
3. *The Odyssey of Homer*, translated by S. H. Butcher and A. Lang (New York: Random House, Modern Library, n.d.), p. 209.
4. Hollis S. Baker, *Furniture in the Ancient World* (New York: Macmillan, 1966), p. 94.
5. V. Gordon Childe, *The Dawn of European Civilization*, 6th ed. (New York: Knopf, 1958), p. 17.
6. James Bennett Pritchard, Ed., *Ancient Near Eastern Texts Relating to the Old Testament*, 2nd ed. (Princeton, New Jersey: Princeton University Press, 1955), p. 286.
7. Leonard Wooley, *The Art of the Middle East* (New York: Crown, 1961), p. 157.

Chapter 3

1. Edith Hamilton, *The Greek Way to Western Civilization* (New York: New American Library, Mentor, 1954), p. 25.
2. Pollio Marcus Vitruvius, *The Ten Books on Architecture*, translated by Morris Hicky Morgan (Cambridge: Harvard University Press; London: Oxford University Press, 1926), Book 1, Chapter 3.
3. Vitruvius, *The Ten Books on Architecture*, Books 3 and 4.
4. John Summerson, *The Classical Language of Architecture* (Cambridge, Massachusetts: M.I.T. Press, 1963), p. 18.
5. Bertha Carr Rider, *Ancient Greek Houses* (Chicago: Argonaut, 1964), p. 237.
6. As quoted by Rider in *Ancient Greek Houses*, p. 228.
7. As quoted by Rider in *Ancient Greek Houses*, p. 228.
8. As quoted by Rider in *Ancient Greek Houses*, p. 222.
9. The following eight short quotations are from *The Odyssey of Homer*, translated by S. H. Butcher and A. Lang (New York: Random House, Modern Library, n.d.).
10. As quoted by M. A. Richter in *The Furniture of the Greeks, Etruscans and Romans* (London: Phaidon, 1966), p. 54.
11. *The Odyssey of Homer.*
12. *The Iliad of Homer*, translated by Andrew Lang, Walter Leaf, and Ernest Myers (New York: Random House, Modern Library, n.d.), p. 48.
13. As quoted by Brian A. Sparkes and Lucy Talcott in *Pots and Pans of Classical Athens*, American School of Classical Studies at Athens (Princeton, New Jersey: Institute for Advanced Study).
14. Jay Hambidge, *Dynamic Symmetry, the Greek Vase* (New Haven, Connecticut: Yale University Press, 1920).
15. Gisela M. A. Richter, *A Handbook of Greek Art*, 4th ed., newly revised (Greenwich, Connecticut: Phaidon, 1965), p. 305.
16. Taken from Xenophon's *Revenues of Athens*, as recounted in Truesdell W. Brown, Ed., *Ancient*

Greece (New York: Free Press; London: Collier-Macmillan, 1965), p. 14.

17. D. E. Strong, *Greek and Roman Gold and Silver Plate* (Ithaca, New York: Cornell University Press, 1966), p. 10.

18. Strong, *Greek and Roman Gold and Silver Plate,* p. 8.

Chapter 4

1. See Paul Frankl, *Gothic Architecture* (Baltimore: Penguin, 1962), p. 9, for a discussion of various vaulted structures and their stresses.

2. Axel Boëthius, *The Golden House of Nero* (Ann Arbor: University of Michigan Press, 1960), p. 56.

3. Boëthius, *The Golden House of Nero,* pp. 9 and 12.

4. Jérôme Carcopino, *Daily Life in Ancient Rome,* Henry T. Rowell, Ed., translated by E. O. Lorimer (New Haven: Yale University Press, 1940); see Chapter 2, "Houses and Streets."

5. Livy, *History of Rome.*

6. Helen H. Tanzer, *The Villas of Pliny the Younger* (New York: Columbia University Press, 1924), p. 13.

7. Karl Lehmann, "The Dome of Heaven," *Art Bulletin,* 27 (1945), 19 ff.

8. Tanzer, *The Villas of Pliny the Younger,* pp. 7–8.

9. Carcopino, *Daily Life in Ancient Rome,* pp. 67 and 70.

10. Tanzer, *The Villas of Pliny the Younger,* pp 7–8.

11. Tanzer, *The Villas of Pliny the Younger,* p. 10.

12. Tanzer, *The Villas of Pliny the Younger,* p. 18.

13. Tanzer, *The Villas of Pliny the Younger,* p. 18.

14. Tanzer, *The Villas of Pliny the Younger,* p. 10.

15. Vitruvius, *The Ten Books on Architecture,* translated by Morris Hicky Morgan (Cambridge: Harvard University Press, 1926), pp. 205–208.

16. Gisela M. A. Richter, *A Handbook of Greek Art,* 4th ed. (Greenwich, Connecticut: Phaidon, 1965), p. 275.

17. Helen Gardner, *Art Through the Ages,* 5th ed., revised by Horst de la Croix and Richard G. Tansey (New York: Harcourt Brace & World, 1970), pp. 194–196.

18. Vitruvius, *The Ten Books on Architecture,* Book 7, Chapter 5.

19. August Mau, *Pompeii: its Life and Art,* trans F. W. Kelsey (New York: Macmillan, 1904), p. 280.

20. As quoted by Norbert Guterman, compiler, in *Book of Latin Quotations* (Garden City, New York: Doubleday, Anchor, 1966), p. 55.

21. Jean Pierre Waltzing, *Corporations Professionnelles,* 4:1–49, as quoted by Carcopino, *Daily Life in Ancient Rome,* p. 179.

22. Warren E. Cox, *The Book of Pottery and Porcelain,* 2 vols. (New York: Crown, 1944), p. 392.

23. As quoted by Frances Rogers and Alice Beard, *5000 Years of Glass,* new revised edition (Philadelphia and New York: Lippincott, 1948), p. 26.

24. As quoted by G. M. A. Richter, *Ancient Italy* (Ann Arbor: University of Michigan Press, 1955), p. 57.

25. The reader is referred to D. E. Strong, *Greek and Roman Gold and Silver Plate* (Ithaca, New York: Cornell University Press, 1966), for a more complete listing of the objects.

26. John D. Cooney, "The Vicarello Goblet," *Bulletin of the Cleveland Museum of Art,* February 1967, pp. 35–41.

27. Sherman E. Lee, *A History of Far Eastern Art* (New York: Abrams, 1964), p. 48.

Chapter 5

1. Inclusive dates are those given in Helen Gardner, *Art Through the Ages,* 4th ed. (New York: Harcourt, Brace, 1959.)

2. David Talbot Rice, *Byzantine Art,* revised 1962 (Baltimore: Penguin, 1935), p. 56.

3. Axel Boëthius, *The Golden House of Nero* (Ann Arbor: University of Michigan Press, 1960), p. 178.

4. A copious body of literature deals with Medieval theories of proportion. Based ultimately on the notebooks of the thirteenth-century architect Villard de Honnecourt, and now preserved in the Bibliothèque Nationale in Paris, two articles bear directly on the statements made: Kenneth J. Conant, "The After-Life of Vitruvius in the Middle Ages," *Journal of the Society of Architectural Historians, 27,* No. 1, 33–38 (1968); and Elizabeth R. Sunderland, "Symbolic Numbers and the Romanesque Church Plan," *Journal of the Society of Architectural Historians, 18,* No. 3, 94–103 (1959).

5. Sir Banister Fletcher, *A History of Architecture on the Comparative Method,* 10th ed. (New York: Scribner's, 1961), p. 975.

6. Washington Irving, *The Alhambra* (New York: Macmillan, 1961), p. 13.

7. Edmund Basil Francis D'Auvergne, *The English Castle* (New York: Dodd, Mead, 1925), p. 4.

8. Tacitus, *Germania,* translated by Sir William Peterson (London: Putnam's, 1920), p. 287.

9. For example, the descriptions of the gatherings at Heorot in *Beowulf,* the oldest Anglo-Saxon tale.

10. Nikolaus Pevsner, *An Outline of European Architecture,* 7th ed. (Baltimore: Penguin, 1963), p. 112.

11. Percy Macquoid, *A History of English Furniture,* 4 vols. (London: Lawrence & Bullen, 1938).

12. Adolf Feulner, *Kunstgeschichte des Möbels seit dem Altertum* (Berlin: Im Propyläen-Verlage, 1927), p. 12.

13. Penelope Eames, "Furniture in England, France and the Netherlands from the Twelfth to the Fifteenth Century," *The Journal of the Furniture History Society, 13,* 192 (1977).

14. Edmond Haraucourt, *Medieval Manners Illustrated at the Cluny Museum* (Paris: Librairie Larousse, n.d.), p. 81.

15. Eames, "Furniture in England, France and the Netherlands," p. 221.

16. Macquoid, *A History of English Furniture,* I, 5.
17. Esther Singleton, *Dutch and Flemish Furniture* (New York: McClure, Phillips, 1907), p. 49.
18. Feulner, *Kunstgeschichte des Möbels seit dem Altertum,* p. 17.
19. L. B. Coventry, "English Coronations Chairs," *The Connoisseur,* May 1937, pp. 280–284.
20. Macquoid, *A History of English Furniture,* I, 13.
21. William M. Odom, *A History of Italian Furniture,* 2 vols. (Garden City, New York, 1918), 1:24.
22. Herbert Cescinsky and Ernest R. Gribble, *Early English Furniture and Woodwork,* 2 vols. (London: Routledge, 1922), 2, 2.
23. Macquoid, *A History of English Furniture,* I, 113.
24. Quoted by Esther Singleton in *Dutch and Flemish Furniture* (New York: McClure, Phillips, 1907), p. 38.
25. Cennino d'Andrea Cennini, *Il Libro dell'Arte,* translated by Daniel V. Thompson, Jr. (New York: Dover, 1933), pp. 72–74.
26. Quoted by William M. Odom in *A History of Italian Furniture,* 1, 8.
27. Macquoid, *A History of English Furniture,* I, 5.
28. Cescinsky and Gribble, *Early English Furniture,* 2, 164.
29. *Ciba Review, 114,* 25 (April 1956).
30. See the Introduction by Adèle Coulin Weible to *2000 Years of Silk Weaving,* exhibition catalog, Los Angeles County Museum, Cleveland Museum of Art, and Detroit Institute of Art (New York: E. Weyhe, 1944).
31. For these statements I am indebted to Dorothy Shepherd, Curator of Textiles at the Cleveland Museum of Art, by whose generosity permission was given to use the weave definitions from the provisional C.I.E.T.A. manuscript. The International Center for the Study of Ancient Textiles (C.I.-E.T.A.) with headquarters in Lyon, France, is an organization that is working for the standardization of museum textile terminology. The descriptions given are my interpretation of the C.I.E.T.A. terminology.
32. *Ciba Review,* "Lucchese Silks," p. 80.
33. Eric MacLagen, *The Bayeux Tapestry* (Harmondsworth, England: Penguin, 1943).
34. Haraucourt, *Medieval Manners,* p. 145.
35. *Ciba Review,* "Tapestry," 157 (January 1938).
36. M. E. Chevreul, *The Principles of Harmony and Contrast of Colours, and their Application to the Arts,* translated by Charles Martel (London: Bell, 1890).
37. Theodore Andrea Cook, *Old Touraine,* 2 vols. (London: Percival, 1892), 1, 18.
38. Dorothy G. Shepherd, "A Fifteenth Century Spanish Carpet," *The Bulletin of the Cleveland Museum of Art,* October 1954.
39. Sherman E. Lee, *Far Eastern Art* (Englewood Cliffs, New Jersey: Prentice-Hall, n.d.), pp. 359–379.
40. *Glass from the Corning Museum of Glass* (Corning, New York: Corning Glass Center, 1965).

41. This term is used in a different sense today to refer to a glass that possesses specific refractive properties.
42. James Rosser Johnson, *The Radiance of Chartres* (New York: Random House, 1965).
43. See William D. Wixom, *Treasures from Medieval France* (Cleveland Museum of Art, 1967), p. 10.
44. The optical laws that regulate these phenomena may be studied in many texts. We suggest Robert W. Burnham *et al., Color: A Guide to Basic Facts and Concepts* (New York: Wiley, 1963), Chapter 3.
45. Henry Adams, *Mont-Saint-Michel and Chartres* (Garden City, New York: Doubleday, Anchor, 1933), p. 151.
46. Pearce Davis, *The Development of the American Glass Industry* (Cambridge: Harvard University Press, 1949), p. 12.
47. Harry James Powell, *Glassmaking in England* (Cambridge: Cambridge University Press, 1923), pp. 10, 11.
48. As quoted by William M. Milliken in "Early Christian Fork and Spoon," *The Bulletin of the Cleveland Museum of Art,* October 1957.
49. Edward Wenham, *Domestic Silver of Great Britain and Ireland* (London: Oxford University Press, 1935), p. 73, and Haraucourt, *Medieval Manners.*
50. James Gairdner, Ed., *The Paston Letters,* 2 vols. (London: Camden Square, 1874), 2, 75. A garnyssh or garniture, is an ornament. In England the term is frequently used to refer to a set of three or five decorative pieces to be placed on a mantel.

Chapter 6

1. References for the successive steps in the codification of the orders: (a) Plato, *The Treatise of Timaeus,* on the theory of the relations of numbers to perfection; (b) Vitruvius, *The Ten Books of Architecture,* translated by Morris Hicky Morgan (Cambridge: Harvard University Press, 1926), pp. 78–86 and 102–113, on the canons of the three Greek orders, on the module as a unit of measurement, and on a description of a fourth or Tuscan order; (c) Leon Battista Alberti, *The Ten Books on Architecture* (New York: Transatlantic, 1966), on the correctness of Pythagorean proportions, on the column as essentially extraneous to the wall and as decoration on it, and on a description of the Vitruvian orders plus a fifth—the Composite; (d) Sebastiano Serlio, *The Orders,* 6 vols.— book 4 is the first publication that sets forth a canonical presentation of the five orders.
2. As quoted by Elizabeth G. Holt, Ed., *A Documentary History of Art,* 4 vol. (Garden City, New York: Doubleday, Anchor, 1957), 2, 11.
3. Andrea Palladio, *The Four Books of Architecture* (New York: Dover Publications, 1964), preface to Book 4.

4. Palladio, *The Four Books of Architecture,* Book 1, Chap. 10.
5. Leonetto Tintori and Millard Meiss, "Additional Observations on Italian Mural Technique," *The Art Bulletin, 16,* No. 3, 377–379 (September 1964).
6. William M. Milliken, "A Lustred Gubbio Majolica Dish," *The Bulletin of the Cleveland Museum of Art,* January 1942, pp. 7–8. This reference defines for the purist the nature of the ware labeled *majolica* in the major museums. Definitions change with time and many writers make no distinction between majolica and faience. See Chapter 5.
7. E. V. Lucas, *A Wanderer in Florence* (London: Methuen, 1923), p. 53.

Chapter 7

1. Reginald Blomfield, *A History of French Architecture,* 2 vols. London: Bell, 1911), I, 117.
2. F. J. B. Watson, *Wallace Collection Catalogue: Furniture* (London: Clowes, 1956), p. 6.

Chapter 8

1. V. Sackville-West, *English Country Houses* (London: Collins, 1932), p. 24.
2. Excerpt from official brochures of Compton Wynyates.
3. Herbert Cescinsky and Ernest R. Gribble, *Early English Furniture and Woodwork,* 2 vols. (London: Routledge, 1912), 2:249.
4. Brooke Tucker, Ed., *Shakespeare of Stratford* (New Haven: Yale University Press, 1926), p. 86.
5. William Harrison, "A Description of England," in *Holinshed's Chronicles,* L. Withington, Ed., 1889, p. 118. Quoted by Ralph Fastnedge, *English Furniture Styles 1500–1830* (Baltimore: Penguin, 1955), p. 18.
6. John F. Hayward, "The Mannerist Goldsmiths: 4, England, Part 3," *The Connoisseur, 164* (January 1966), 19–25.

Chapter 9

1. William M. Odom, *A History of Italian Furniture from the Fourteenth to the Early Nineteenth Centuries,* 2 vols. (Garden City, New York: Doubleday, 1918/1919), II, 20.
2. For Vignola and Jesuit churches, see Chapter 10.
3. Rudolph Wittkower, *Art and Architecture in Italy 1600–1750* (Baltimore: Penguin, 1958), p. 72.
4. Wittkower, *Art and Architecture in Italy,* p. 72.

5. James S. Ackerman, *Palladio's Villas* (Locust Valley, New York: Augustin, 1967), pp. 11, 12.
6. A type of planning found earlier but to less dramatic effect at Fontainebleau in France.
7. Ruth Rubinstein, "Giovanni Francesco Romanelli's Dido and Aeneas Tapestry Cartoons," in *Art at Auction: The Year at Sotheby's and Parke-Bernet, 1968–69* (London: 1969), pp. 106–119.

Chapter 10

1. Mariejol, *Hist. de France,* Lavisse, Ed., vi, 2, I, as quoted in Reginald Blomfield, *History of French Architecture, from 1494–1661* (2 vols., London: Bell, 1911), II, 31.
2. F. J. B. Watson, *Wallace Collection, Catalogue, Furniture* (London: Clowes, 1956), p. xxv.
3. We have used the definitive glossary in F. B. J. Watson's catalog of the Wrightsman Collection of the Metropolitan Museum of Art. Other famous collections of French furniture are in the Frick Collection in New York, the collection of the late James de Rothschild at Waddesdon Manor in Buckinghamshire, and at the Musée Jacquemart-André in Paris.
4. Duc de Saint-Simon, *Historical Memoirs,* Lucy Norton, Ed., 3 vols. (New York: McGraw-Hill, 1967), 1:471.
5. Saint-Simon, *Historical Memoirs,* pp. 63, 64.
6. A. Varron, "Technical Details of Silk Weaving and Dyeing at Lyons," *Ciba Review,* No. 6, p. 194.
7. John Coolidge, "Rubens and the Decoration of French Royal Galleries," *The Art Bulletin,* Vol. 48, No. 1 (March 1966), 67–69.

Chapter 11

1. John Summerson, *Architecture in Britain 1530–1830* (Baltimore: Penguin, 1963), p. 67.
2. Nathaniel Lloyd, *A History of the English House* (London: Architectural Press, 1931), p. 117.
3. Horace Walpole, *Anecdotes of Painting in England* (2 vols., London: Chatto and Windus, 1876), II, 168.
4. *Martha, Lady Giffard, Her Life and Letters,* Julia G. Longe, Ed. (London: Allen, 1911), p. 318.
5. Ralph Fastnedge, *English Furniture Styles* (Baltimore: Penguin 1955), p. 43.
6. Cf. F. J. Britten, *Old Clocks and Watches and Their Makers,* 7th ed. (New York: Bonanza, 1956).
7. Richard Steele, *The Lover,* May 13, 1714 (No. 34).
8. W. A. Thorpe, *A History of English and Irish Glass* (Boston: Hale, Cushman and Flint, 1929), pp. 125, 126.

Index

Pages in *italics* indicate illustrations.

INDEX